WITHDRAWN
HARVARD LIBRARY
WITHDRAWN

Realism, Tolerance, and Liberalism in the Czech National Awakening

Realism, Tolerance, and Liberalism in the Czech National Awakening
Legacies of the Bohemian Reformation

Zdeněk V. David

Woodrow Wilson Center Press
Washington, D.C.

The Johns Hopkins University Press
Baltimore

EDITORIAL OFFICES

Woodrow Wilson Center Press
One Woodrow Wilson Plaza
1300 Pennsylvania Avenue, N.W.
Washington, D.C. 20004-3027
Telephone: 202-691-4029
www.wilsoncenter.org

ORDER FROM

The Johns Hopkins University Press
Hampden Station
P.O. Box 50370
Baltimore, Maryland 21211
Telephone: 1-800-537-5487
www.press.jhu.edu/books/

© 2010 by Zdeněk David
All rights reserved
Printed in the United States of America on acid-free paper ∞
2 4 6 8 9 7 5 3 1

Library of Congress Cataloging-in-Publication Data

David, Zdeněk V.
  Realism, tolerance, and liberalism in the Czech National awakening : legacies of the Bohemian reformation / Zdeněk V. David.
    p. cm.
  Includes bibliographical references and index.
  ISBN 978-0-8018-9546-3 (hardcover)
  1. Bohemia (Czech Republic)—History—1618–1848. 2. Bohemia (Czech Republic)—History—1848–1918. 3. Bohemia (Czech Republic)—Church history—18th century. 4. Bohemia (Czech Republic)—Church history—19th century. 5. Reformation—Czech Republic—Bohemia. 6. Nationalism—Czech Republic—Bohemia—History. 7. Utraquists. I. Title.
  DB2176.D38   2010
  943.71′023—dc22
                                                                     2009054219

Woodrow Wilson Center Press
Washington, D.C.

The Woodrow Wilson International Center for Scholars is the national, living U.S. memorial honoring President Woodrow Wilson. In providing an essential link between the worlds of ideas and public policy, the Center addresses current and emerging challenges confronting the United States and the world. The Center promotes policy-relevant research and dialogue to increase understanding and enhance the capabilities and knowledge of leaders, citizens, and institutions worldwide. Created by an Act of Congress in 1968, the Center is a non-partisan institution headquartered in Washington, D.C. and supported by both public and private funds.

Conclusions or opinions expressed in Center publications and programs are those of the authors and speakers and do not necessarily reflect the views of the Center's staff, fellows, trustees, or advisory groups, or any individuals or organizations that provide financial support to the Center.

The Center is the publisher of *The Wilson Quarterly* and home of Woodrow Wilson Center Press and *dialogue* television and radio. For more information about the Center's activities and publications, including the monthly newsletter *Centerpoint,* please visit us on the web at www.wilsoncenter.org.

Lee H. Hamilton, President and Director

Board of Trustees
Joseph B. Gildenhorn, Chair
Sander R. Gerber, Vice Chair

Public members: James H. Billington, Librarian of Congress; Hillary R. Clinton, Secretary of State; G. Wayne Clough, Secretary of the Smithsonian Institution; Arne Duncan, Secretary of Education; David Ferriero, Archivist of the United States; James Leach, Chairman of the National Endowment for the Humanities; Kathleen Sebelius, Secretary of Health and Human Services

Private citizen members: Charles E. Cobb Jr., Robin Cook, Charles L. Glazer, Carlos M. Gutierrez, Susan Hutchison, Barry S. Jackson, Ignacio E. Sanchez

To James H. Billington

Contents

Preface xiii
Acknowledgments xix

1. The Czech National Awakening and the
   Bohemian Reformation in Recent Historiography 1

   Marxist-Leninist Interlude 2
   Schamschula, Macura, and Hroch 5
   Fin de Siècle Epitome: Hugh Agnew 10
   The Twenty-First Century 12
   A Neglect of "Golden Age" Liberalism 16

2. Tolerance, Universalism, and Plebeianism as
   Legacies of the Sixteenth Century 18

   The *Via Media* of Utraquism 18
   Tolerance and Liberalism 23
   Universalism 30
   Plebeianism 37
   The Ascendancy of the Towns in Culture 40
   The Plebeian Legacy of Utraquism 45

3. The Counter-Reformation and the Catholic Enlightenment:
   An Acute Antithesis 47

   The Cultural Revolution 49
   Leapfrogging the Counter-Reformation 53
   Catholic Enlightenment 58

4. Catholic Enlightenment and Utraquism:
   A Liberal Symbiosis   64

   Admiration for the Utraquist Century: Secular Aspects   65
   Reform Catholicism and Utraquism: Theological Aspects   73
   Lingering Religious Symbiosis   80

5. The Czech National Awakening as a Renaissance   83

   The Infrastructure of Restoration   83
   Reprinting the Classics   90
   Transmission in Textbooks   94
   Exalting the Bohemian Reformation in History and Literature   98
   Historical Rights of the Bohemian State   101
   A Reincarnation of *Das schöne oder goldene Zeitalter*   104

6. The Bohemian Fate of Johann Gottfried Herder   106

   Herder's Proto-Romanticism and Idealism   107
   Illusion of Herder's Influence   109
   The Slovaks' Romantic Idealism   117
   Limitation of Herder's Influence in Bohemia   120

7. The Roots of Resistance to German Idealism   134

   Existence over Essence   135
   The Protestant Lutheran Factor   141
   Seibt, Catholic Enlightenment, and Anti-Idealism   144
   Seibt's Contemporaries and Followers   148

8. Bolzano: Against Kant, Fichte, and Schelling   155

   Bolzano's Influence   155
   Bolzano's Liberal Catholicism   158
   Bolzano and Metaphysical Idealists   161
   Bolzano and Empirical Realists   168
   Seibt and Bolzano versus Herder and Kant   173

9. Hegel's Collision with the Catholic Enlightenment
   in Bohemia   174

   The Issue of Hegel's Influence   175
   Early Encounters with Hegel   181
   Bolzano and Hegel   183
   Final Assessment of Hegel   192

Contents

10. Bohemian Anti-Hegelianism: Slovak Contrast
    and Polish Paradox ... 194

    The Demise of Hegelianism in Bohemia 194
    Slovak Contrast 198
    The Divisive Hegel 207
    A Polish Paradox? 208
    The German Issue 212

11. Liberal Thought and the Authoritarian Church ... 215

    A New Counter-Reformation? 216
    Exner and Liberal Catholicism's Triumph in Philosophy 217
    Exner and German Idealism 220
    Bolzano and Exner 222
    Bolzano and Herbart 224
    Liberal Catholicism's Demise in Ecclesiology 227
    Religious Void in Bohemia 229

Epilogue: The Global Legacy of Bohemian Anti-Hegelianism ... 231

    The Austrian School and Analytical Philosophy 232
    The Prague Connection 237
    Local Legacy of Anti-Hegelianism: Bohemia's Political Culture 242

Appendix: Philosophy Professors at the Charles University
(Universitas Carolina) of Prague ... 245

Notes ... 247

Chronology of Events from the Bohemian Reformation
and the National Awakening ... 383

Glossary ... 389

Bibliography ... 393

Index ... 455

Preface

"Every Czech is to a great extent a child of the Enlightenment."

Thomas G. Masaryk, *Světová revoluce za války a ve válce, 1914–18*

This book attempts to shed new light on the character and formation of modern national consciousness and political culture in Central and Eastern Europe.[1] Against the usual view that national ideologies were simply constructs, if not inventions, from the early nineteenth century, the book explores how certain crucial ideas were transferred from premodern times. And instead of the usual emphasis on the role played by ontologically based cultural and national pluralism, derived from the milieu of a secularized Lutheran eschatology (reflected in German romanticism and idealism), the book stresses the role of the linguistically neutral Catholic Enlightenment, showing that the linguistic element was much less important. I argue that guiding social and political ideas mattered more than linguistics or folklore. The book focuses on the example of Bohemia, with references to neighboring countries: Austria, Lutheran Germany (Prussia and Saxony), Slovakia, Hungary, Poland, and Russia. The analysis may help illuminate the often noted exceptional tenacity of liberal democracy in Czechoslovakia, which retained a democratic form of government in 1918–38, while its neighbors adopted authoritarianism, if not totalitarianism.[2]

The main theme of this volume, however, transcends the issue of liberal political culture in Czechoslovakia (which figures more as the proverbial tip of an iceberg). It traces the much wider development of Austrian philosophy and highlights the crucial role of Bernard Bolzano, who epitomized the realistic and empirical tradition of Catholic Austria and of southern Germany, which also involved philosophers such as Johann F. Herbart, Christoph Bardili, Friedrich E. Beneke, William T. Krug, and Karl L. Reinhold. Much of this development had, in fact, occurred on Bohemian soil (favored by the happy marriage between the Catholic Enlightenment and the Utraquist legacy). Even in Bohemia, however, the rise of the realistic and empirical tradition was primarily the work of German-speaking thinkers, including— besides Bolzano— Karl H. Seibt, August G. Meissner, Michael J. Fesl, Franz Exner, and Robert Zimmermann. It had very little, if anything, to do with Czech ethnicity.

The derivation of national ideology from intellectual sources of the remote past is demonstrated by the link between the era of the Bohemian Reformation of the sixteenth century, known as the Golden Age, and that of the Austro-Bohemian Catholic Enlightenment of the late eighteenth century. Two perennial problems in Czech historiography have been the relationship between the Bohemian Reformation of the fifteenth and sixteenth centuries and modern Czech political culture, which emerged in the nineteenth century, and how to deal with the 1622–1781 intermezzo of the Counter-Reformation, an awkward issue for many. Traditionally, the two divergent viewpoints on this relationship were defined by Tomáš G. Masaryk, who postulated a disruption in Czech intellectual life between the sixteenth century and the Enlightenment, and by Josef Pekař, who sought to integrate the Counter-Reformation into a seamless web of a continuous cultural development. Masaryk viewed the ideological content of the awakening as cosmopolitan and universal, Pekař as ethnic and national.[3]

The dispute between Masaryk and Pekař that stretched over the twenty years from 1895 to 1914, therefore, concerned the impact of the Bohemian Reformation on the national awakening and on the subsequent "political culture" of Bohemia. Masaryk (1850–1937) saw a profound influence of the Reformation stemming from the theology and religious practice of the Unity of Brethren (a particular faction within the Reformation) that was transmitted to Bohemia in the late eighteenth century, thanks to the influence of the exiled Brethren on European, especially German, thought. Masaryk focused on Johann Gottfried Herder as the main transmitter of the Brethren's ideal of humanity and claimed that the German philosopher was the principal inspirer of the Bohemian awakeners. Pekař (1870–1937), the leading historian at the University of Prague, insisted in his polemics aimed at Masaryk that the hiatus between the Reformation and the awakening was too long and drastic to be bridged in any way. Instead, he suggested that the roots of the awakening should be sought in certain patriotic trends during the Counter-Reformation (without trying to rehabilitate the Counter-Reformation as such). Most subsequent historians accepted Pekař's judgment that Masaryk's interpretation was too abstract and theoretical and lacked sufficient empirical evidence.

In this study, I agree with Masaryk that there was a transfer of ideas from the Bohemian Reformation to the national awakening. I differ, however, in locating the source of the influential ideas not in the rigorous, puritanical sect of the Unity of Brethren but in the liberal, mellow mainstream of the Bohemian Reformation—the Utraquists.

The national awakeners of the Enlightenment era rediscovered, rehabilitated, and revitalized the literary heritage of the Reformation after a century and a half (1622–1781) of suppression by the intervening Counter-Reformation. The awakeners in the era of the Enlightenment were attracted by this legacy's liberal, tolerant, and plebeian (nonaristocratic) character (chapter 2), while they were repelled by the authoritarian, intolerant, and aristocratic tenor of the baroque culture of the Counter-Reformation (chapters 3, 4). The process of the recovering past thought is treated not as a resumption of identity, based on an essentialist concept of the nation, but as an empirically verifiable process through rereading and republication of the centuries-old records (chapter 5).

The subordinate position of language in the formation of political culture is demonstrated by the dominance of the intellectual and philosophical outlook derived from the Catholic Enlightenment, which continued in Bohemia during the first half of the nineteenth century. The Austro-Bohemian Josephist Enlightenment served as a connecting link between the irenic Utraquist culture of the remote past and the liberal political culture of the immediate future. The ideas stemming from this Enlightenment were diffused under the successive intellectual leadership of Karl H. Seibt, Bernard Bolzano, and Franz Exner, who in their teaching and writing promoted the concept of one universal culture and opposed the idea of multiple national idiosyncrasies, each animated by a distinctive language. The intellectual climate of Bohemia, therefore, remained unreceptive, if not hostile, to the views characteristic of Johann G. Herder and Georg W. Hegel, who in their national and cultural essentialism assigned crucial roles in the social and historical development to ethno-linguistic communities (chapters 6, 9, 10).

The rejection of metaphysically based cultural pluralism under the influence of the Catholic Enlightenment had further consequences for the formation of the Bohemian political culture. Freeing the individual from the subordination to the process of history or even nature (as Herder and Hegel taught) liberated him not only as a human being but also as a citizen, making him ontologically superior to the group, nation, or state (as Seibt, Bolzano, and Exner also taught). From a wider European perspective, the Bohemian intellectual pacesetters' embrace of the realistic, empirical, and individualistic orientation, as well as ontic pluralism, linked them philosophically to the "Austrian tradition," while their rejection of the idealist and collectivist outlook of ontological monism distanced them from the so-called German philosophical tradition.[4]

While the former tradition was initially conditioned by the Austro-Bohemian Catholic Enlightenment, the latter stemmed largely from Christian Wolff's metaphysics at eighteenth-century Lutheran universities (chapter 7)—hence the juxtaposition of the Catholic Enlightenment and Lutheran idealism in this book. In time or in history, these choices related both backward to the legacy of the Bohemian Reformation and forward to the anti-Hegelian tenor of the subsequent political culture of Bohemia. In space or in geography, these philosophical choices separated Bohemia from the domain of idealism in Central and Eastern Europe and annexed the country to the Western Euro-Atlantic realm, where eventually positivism and analytical philosophy prevailed.[5]

Beyond the chronological scope of the book, I point out how the realistic and empirical tradition continued to flourish at both the German and the Czech universities of Prague, as well as in other universities of the Habsburg Empire. In the early twentieth century, the tradition came to center on the Vienna Circle and on the Society for Empirical Research in Berlin. The rise of the Nazi regime forced its adepts to seek refuge outside Central Europe, especially in Britain and the United States, and the migration eventually led to a flourishing of analytical philosophy on a global scale beyond the Western world, particularly in Japan but also in Russia, China, India, Latin America, and Africa.

Three aids are supplied for the reader's guidance. An appendix lists the names of the professors of philosophy at the Charles University in Prague from 1753 to 1939. A chronology of events covers the periods of the Bohemian Reformation, 1415–1627, and of the National Awakening, 1740–1855. Finally, a glossary defines the less familiar terms.

Notes

1. The issue of modern nationalism has occupied the attention of many historians in the concluding decades of the past century. A recent survey by Hans-Ulrich Wehler lists the work of Benedict Anderson, John Breuilly, Rogers Brubaker, Ernest Gellner, Eric J. Hobsbawm, Miroslav Hroch, Hans Kohn, M. Rainer Lepsius, Wolfgang Schieder, and Anthony Smith; see Hans-Ulrich Wehler, *Nationalismus: Geschichte, Formen, Folgen* (Munich: Beck, 2001), especially 116–20. John Coakley, Walker Connor, Liah Greenfeld, Michael Hechter, Anthony Marx, and Tom Nairn should be added to the list. Political culture has been defined as "the set of predominant beliefs, sentiments and evaluations regarding the political system in which a group of people live and the role of the individual in that system." See Gabriel A. Almond and Sidney Verba, *The Civic Culture: Political Attitudes and Democracy in Five Nations* (Newbury Park, Calif.: Sage Publications, 1989), 12.

2. See R. J. W. Evans: "For years Czechoslovakia, by contrast with the surrounding states, conducted its affairs in a broadly orderly and stable way. It sustained real parliamentary procedures and an open and multinational cultural life." In "Introduction," *Czechoslovakia in a Nationalist and Fascist Europe, 1918–1948*, ed. Mark Cornwall and Evans (New York: Oxford University Press, 2007), 1. See also Sharon L. Wolchik, "Czech Republic," *Encyclopedia of U. S. Foreign Relations* (New York: Oxford University Press, 1997), 1:401; Stefan Auer, *Liberal Nationalism in Central Europe* (London; New York: Routledge Curzon, 2004), 107–13; Věra Olivová, "Idea československého státu, 1918–1938," in Stanislava Kučerová and others, *Bilance a výhledy středu Evropy na prahu 21. století: úvahy, svědectví a [fakta . . . k] 150 výročí narození T. G. Masaryka, 1850–2000* (Brno: Konvoj, 2000), 55–60; and the articles by Robert Kvaček, Josef Harna, [L'ubomír] Lipták, Milan Hauner, and Jaroslav Valenta in *Československo, 1918–1938: osudy demokracie ve střední Evropě*, ed. Jaroslav Valenta and others (Prague: Historický ústav Akademie věd České republiky, 1999), 1: 30–52, 73–81, 223–32. On the Czech side, Eva Broklová has advanced the claim for an even broader framework for modern Czech political culture, asserting that it represented a variant of the American and West European tradition, in contrast to the political cultures prevalent in Central and Eastern Europe, including Germany; see Eva Broklová, *Politická kultura německých aktivistických stran v Československu, 1918–1938* (Prague: Karolinum, 1999); see also reviews by Jan Rataj in *Český časopis historický* 100 (2002): 142–46; and Eagle Glassheim in *Kosmas* 16/1 (Fall 2002): 110–11.

3. Concerning the development of this controversy, see Milan Hauner, "The Meaning of Czech History: Masaryk versus Pekař," in *T. G. Masaryk, 1850–1937*, vol. 3: *Statesman and Cultural Force*, ed. Harry Hanak (London: Macmillan, 1989),

24–42; Miloš Havelka, ed., *Spor o smysl českých dějin, 1895–1938* (Prague: Torst, 1995), especially, 125–63; Eva Broklová, ed., *Sto let Masarykovy České otázky* (Prague: Ústav T. G. Masaryka, 1997), 47–65.

4. Barry Smith, *Austrian Philosophy: The Legacy of Brentano* (Chicago: Open Court, 1994), 1. See also Karl D. Bracher, *Die deutsche Diktatur: Entstehung, Struktur, Folgen des Nationalsozialismus*, 6th rev. ed. (Frankfurt/M: Ullstein, 1979), 9–10.

5. Milan Machovec, "Problematika dějin české filosofie," in *Filosofie v dějinách českého národa*, (Prague: Nakladatelství ČSAV, 1958), 26.

Acknowledgments

My interest in exploring the relationship between the Bohemian Reformation and the Czech National Awakening proceeded in two stages. First, during the work on my book, *Finding the Middle Way: The Utraquists' Liberal Challenge to Rome and Luther* (2003), a striking bibliographic phenomenon attracted my attention. A large number of sixteenth-century publications, which I used as primary sources, had been republished in the late eighteenth century. In the meantime, this literature had been suppressed during the period of the Counter Reformation in Bohemia (1622–1781). This reappearance led me, in the current project, to seek and delineate an intellectual symbiosis—on the basis of realism, tolerance, and liberalism—between the thinking of the Catholic Enlightenment and the Utraquist literature. At the second stage, I sought to examine the continuity between this symbiotic relationship (of the Enlightenment with Utraquism) and the emergence of a political culture in Bohemia during the first half of the nineteenth century. Ultimately, I concluded that the realist and anti-idealist thought of this latter era—epitomized by the writings of Bernard Bolzano—would be at the core of a subsequent global intellectual trend. Branded the Austrian philosophical tradition, it would eventually come to fruition via the Vienna Circle and the Berlin Society for Empirical Philosophy, in the worldwide flourishing of analytical philosophy.

Two colleagues made major contributions to the original development of my basic ideas on the Bohemian Reformation, Robert J. W. Evans, Regius Professor of Modern History at Oxford, and David R. Holeton, professor of liturgics at the University of Prague. Subsequently, John Coakley, professor in the School of Politics at the University

College of Dublin, and Josette Baer, senior lecturer in the Department of Philosophy at the University of Zurich, gave me valuable advice on substantial parts of the book manuscript. Robert Landers, Acacia Reed, and Maria-Stella Gatzoulis of the Woodrow Wilson Center staff, and, particularly, John W. Brennan, professor of history emeritus of Long Island University in New York City, together read the majority of the chapters for coherence and style, and made a number of helpful suggestions.

My senior colleagues at the Wilson Center, particularly President and Director Lee Hamilton and Executive Vice President, Michael Van Dusen, created an environment conducive to rigorous and broad scholarship. The Center's East European Program, under the leadership of Martin Sletzinger and Nida Gelazis, as well as the Kennan Institute, directed by Blair Ruble and William Pomeranz, offered intellectual stimulation through continuous contact with the current scholarship on Central and Eastern Europe. My office mates and fellow senior scholars, David Birenbaum, Dennis Kux, William Krist, William Milam, and John Sewell, provided helpful and congenial work conditions. I am grateful to those on the other side of the Atlantic, mainly in my native Czech Republic, who oversaw the publication of my articles in scholarly journals, including Vilém Herold, Josef Zumr, Petr Horák, Jaroslav Pánek, and František Šmahel.

Several institutions and organizations were particularly helpful in providing platforms for the development and dissemination of my scholarly work. The study of the Bohemian Reformation was encouraged by the Institute of Philosophy of the Czech Academy of Sciences, as well as the Institute's Collegium Europaeum–Research Group for the Study of European Ideas. Under the leadership of Vilém Herold, Pavel Baran, and Petr Hlaváček, the continuation (since 1994) of the biennial symposia on "The Bohemian Reformation and Religious Practice" has been ensured. The Czechoslovak Society of Arts and Sciences, under two successive presidents, Miloslav Rechcígl and Karel Raška Jr., has offered opportunities for presenting my research papers in its congresses and conferences, and the society's journal, *Kosmas,* edited by Clinton Machann, has been a venue for their publication. I am indebted to the librarians and archivists of the National Library, the National Museum, and the Central National Archive in Prague, as well as the Library of Congress in Washington, D.C., for their services and advice. My research work was facilitated by the assistance of successive interns between 2003 and 2008, Erin Stevanus, Evelyn Lin, Daniel Karl, Jonathan Sicotte, John Grossi, Katarina Csomova, and Petro A. Nungovitch. I also benefited from their youthful enthusiasm and eagerness to learn. My former coworkers in the Woodrow Wilson Center Library, Janet Spikes, Dagne Gizaw, and Michelle Kamalich, helped and encouraged me in current research. I am grateful to Joseph Brinley and Yamile Kahn of Woodrow Wilson Center Press for their long-term interest in my writing and research, and for seeing the book through to publication.

Some material in the book is adapted from my articles: "Národni obrození jako převtělení Zlatého věku" [The National Awakening as a Reincarnation of the Golden Age], *Český časopis historický* 99 (2001), 486–518; "Hegelova srážka s katolickým osvícenstvím v Čechách a zrod novodobého národního uvědoměni" [Hegel's Collision with the Catholic Enlightenment in Bohemia: The Genesis of Modern National Consciousness], *Filosofický časopis* (Prague) 54 (2006), 809–33; "Johann G. Herder and the Czech National Revival: A Reassessment," *Carl Beck Papers in Russian and East European Studies,* no. 1807, September 2007; "The Czech National Awakening and the Bohemian Reformation in Recent Historiography," *Kosmas: Czechoslovak and Central European Journal* 21/1 (2007), 1–20; "John Bowring and British Liberalism in the Czech National Awakening," *Slavonic and East European Review* 86 (2008), 634–64; "Masaryk a rakouská filozofická tradice: Bolzano a Brentano" [Masaryk and the Austrian Philosophical Tradition: Bolzano and Brentano], *Filosofický časopis* (Prague) 56 (2008), 345–61.

My academically inclined sons and daughters, Julie, Ann, Katja, Meg, Michael, and Stephen, each contributed directly or indirectly to the realization of this book. Above all, however, I wish to express my enduring gratitude to James H. Billington, the current Librarian of Congress, whose help and support have continuously accompanied me from the time of my dissertation research at Harvard in the late 1950s throughout the subsequent half-century of intellectual peregrination in Ann Arbor, Princeton, and Washington, D.C. To Jim, this book is dedicated.

Needless to say, I myself bear the responsibility for the interpretations and other contents of this book.

Washington, D.C.
October 2009

Realism, Tolerance, and Liberalism
in the Czech National Awakening

1

The Czech National Awakening and the Bohemian Reformation in Recent Historiography

The purpose of this bibliographic survey is to situate my interpretation of the Czech national awakening as a revival of the liberal ideas of the Utraquist literature within the historiography of the period from 1945 to the present. The analysis of the views of the historians within this time frame seeks answers to two questions: first, whether they perceive a significant relationship between the period of the Reformation (1415–1622) and the awakening (1773–1848); and, second, if so, in what ways they see that influence as effective. Hence, this chapter is concerned with recent literature on the Czech national awakening and the light it sheds on the awakening's connection with the Bohemian Reformation and, in particular, with the literary heritage of the sixteenth-century Utraquist period, also known as the Golden Age.[1] More specifically, the aim is to determine the extent to which historical literature has covered the awakeners' concern with reviving the intellectual legacy of the Bohemian Reformation in their own times. The survey notes the historians' attention to several such indexes of that concern: (1) the awakeners' efforts to recover the record of the sixteenth-century publications; (2) their efforts to reintroduce the ideas (both secular and religious) and language norms of this literature into the current intellectual ambiance; and (3) their attempts to rehabilitate the personages and the character of the Bohemian Reformation.

This chapter therefore surveys the representative literature on the Bohemian awakening in Czech, English, Russian, and German. The Marxist-Leninist literature of 1945–90, as might be expected, tends to be rather stereotypical. It is treated here not simply to beat a historiographically dead horse but because at least some historians, albeit starting before 1989, have managed to avoid following rigorously the Party line and attained Bohemian (and European) respectability after the Velvet Revolution.[2] The survey then proceeds from the Marxist-Leninist interpretations to major works on the Czech national awakening that were published outside the official doctrinaire framework, either abroad or, if in Bohemia, after the Velvet Revolution. Finally, the most recent views on the awakening and the Bohemian Reformation from the start of the present century are briefly examined.

Marxist-Leninist Interlude

Let us first turn to the treatment of the relationship between the Bohemian Reformation and the national awakening within the paradoxical tenets of Marxist-Leninist historiography. On the one hand, the "revolutionary" character of the Bohemian Reformation's radical strands was held in high esteem.[3] On the other hand, the Marxist metaphysics of historical materialism militated against a transfer of ideas over a lengthy hiatus. First, according to Marxism, the culture of a period, its intellectual superstructure, was to be a reflection of the economic and social base; hence, ideas played a derivative role in a particular historical era. Second, the economic and social base of the fifteenth and sixteenth centuries was feudal and therefore qualitatively different from the capitalist base of the late eighteenth and early nineteenth centuries. The intellectual superstructures of the two eras thus by definition had to differ fundamentally. Third, Marxist historiography had little incentive to emphasize the liberal features of either the Bohemian Reformation or the Enlightenment or to dwell on the parallel between the two. The intellectual outlook of the Utraquist sixteenth century was permissive, individualistic, and open-ended and was thus akin to the Enlightenment spirit that nurtured the national awakening. At either end, this outlook was at odds with the authoritarian, collectivist, and closed weltanschauung of Marxism-Leninism.

The major works typifying the Marxist-Leninist approach include the following: Josef Kočí, *České národní obrození* (1978), based on his earlier *Naše národní obrození* (1960); Antonín Robek, *Lidové zdroje národního obrození* (1974), and his *Městské lidové zdroje národního obrození* (1977); Josef Haubelt, *České osvícenství* (1986); and Josef Petráň and others, *Počátky českého národního obrození: Společnost a kultura v 70. až 90. letech 18. století* (1990).[4] Kočí's book, while factually informative, embraces the standard blend of orthodox Marxist interpretation with the simplistic nationalist beliefs à la Zdeněk Nejedlý.[5] The awakening, he says, was "a necessary and lawful process, sparked by the revolutionary changes of a transition from the feudal order to the capitalist one."[6] Robek likewise applied a rigid class interpretation to the awakening and saw it as a process driven by the force of economic and social laws that found expression in the desiderata of the manorial peasantry. According to him, "the National Awakening was a process, which ran its course objectively, not a process initiated or directed by the intellectuals, but as an objective and lawful process, which had, above all, objective economic and social foundations."[7] He specifically rejected the view that echoes of the Bohemian Reformation could have played a "progressive" role in the awakening.[8] His belief in the progressive role of the peasantry led him to attribute "antidemocratic tendencies" to the inhabitants of Bohemia's towns and to an understanding of the awakening as a "socialization" of the ideas of the manorial village.[9]

Since Haubelt's *České osvícenství* was published in a second edition in 2004, it will be noted along with the literature of the post-Communist period. The volume edited by Petráň, and prefaced by Kočí, still bears (presumably belated) marks of the Marxist-Leninist approach in its emphasis on the key role of the rise of the lower classes within the context of a transition from feudalism to capitalism.[10] In view of this economic and sociological causation, Petráň—like Robek before him—argues against the possibility that the Bohemian Reformation influenced the process of the national awakening. On the contrary, he views the late phase of the Bohemian Reformation as a period of particular cultural isolation that caused a developmental retardation in Bohemia's intellectual standards.[11]

Within the Marxist-Leninist historiography, two authors occupy a more distinctive and strangely contradictory place. Because of their departure from the conventional norms, they merit a fuller discussion. One is Bedřich Slavík, whose monograph, *Od Dobnera k Dobrovskému* (1975), ironically for a work published in the Communist era (or perhaps as an illustration of the saying *"les extrêmes se touchent"*), exudes the harshness of a conservative spirit of the Council of Trent (1543–63) in its negative attitude toward the Reform Catholicism of the Josephist Enlightenment. The other is Aleksandr S. Myl'nikov, whose Russian-language treatment of the topic, *Epokha Prosveshcheniia v cheshskikh zemliakh: Ideologiia, natsional'noe samosoznanie, kul'tura* (1977), was preceded by a longer Czech version, *Vznik národně osvícenské ideologie v českých zemích: Prameny národního obrození* (1974).[12] Surprisingly for one representing the school of Soviet historiography, Myl'nikov celebrates the tolerant attitude and advocacy of intellectual freedom in the Bohemian Enlightenment.

As for the first of these mavericks, Slavík departs from the focus on sociological causation according to the Marxist formula and turns more to literary and intellectual history. In the analysis of the revival, his complex taxonomy draws a distinction between the Viennese Enlightenment and Viennese Josephism, in addition to distinguishing between two Bohemian variants of combined Enlightenment and Josephism—an all-Bohemian territorial (*zemský*) and an ethnically Czech one. Tantalizingly, he suggests that the roots of the Bohemian Enlightenment may be sought as far back as the Renaissance, humanism, and Bohemian Reformation. Disappointingly, however, his subsequent treatment focuses only on the immediate eighteenth-century origins of the Enlightenment, and even those are limited to a Bohemian variant of the anti-Jesuit Jansenism and to an adaptation of Austrian Febronianism, advocating tight state control over church affairs.[13]

Nevertheless, Slavík dwells on the interest of the awakeners of the Enlightenment period in the Bohemian Reformation. In analyzing Mikuláš A. Voigt's *Acta litteraria Bohemiae et Moraviae* (1774–83), Slavík stresses several key points: (1) Voigt's efforts to defend Jan Hus as a Catholic theologian in opposition to Protestant authors, who claimed him for the Reformation; (2) Voigt's preference for the Utraquist literature of the sixteenth century over the earlier tracts of the radical Taborite faction in the Bohemian Reformation; and (3) Voigt's rejection of the Bohemian Brethren's Protestantism, while praising their literary skills.[14] Yet, it turns out that, at bottom, Slavík disapproves of the liberalizing tendencies of the Catholic Enlightenment, including the subsequent efforts of Kašpar Royko, Václav Stach, Augustin Zitte, and Johann H. Wolf to rehabilitate Hus as a Reform Catholic during the reign of Joseph II.[15] Slavík is particularly harsh in his characterization of Stach as an unscrupulous freethinker under the cover of religiosity.[16] His characterization of František Faustin Procházka, however, is somewhat less caustic.[17]

The Soviet historian Myl'nikov, though, despite his obligatory reference not only to Marx and Engels but also to Klement Gottwald,[18] avoids a strict social and economic interpretation of the awakening. On the contrary, he devotes considerable space to analyzing the intellectual currents of the Austro-Bohemian Enlightenment. Even more unexpectedly, he seems to delight in highlighting, almost in the spirit of Jeffersonian liberalism, the Bohemian tendencies toward tolerance and freedom of thought.[19] He pays considerable attention to the awakeners' interest in the Bohemian Reformation, drawing parallels between the liberal attitudes within the Reformation's moderate wing and those within the orbit of the Enlightenment. According to him, the sympathetic treatment of the moderate participants in the Bohemian Reformation began with Voigt.[20] In particular, he notes—in a much more positive light than Slavík—the rehabilitation of Jan Hus as "an Enlightened Catholic" (*prosveshchennyi katolik*) by Royko, Stach, and, especially, Wolf.[21] While noticing the similarity between the Enlightenment and the Bohemian Reformation, as well as the awakeners' interest in the Bohemian culture of the fifteenth and sixteenth centuries, he does not address the issue of a transfer of ideas and ethical values from the Reformation to the awakening.

Schamschula, Macura, and Hroch

Aside from Hugh Agnew, whose work is discussed later, among the significant works concerning the Bohemian national awakening appearing in latter part of the twentieth century were those of Walter Schamschula, *Die Anfänge der tschechischen Erneuerung und das deutsche Geistesleben, 1740–1800* (1973); Vladimír Macura, *Znamení zrodu: České národní obrození jako kulturní typ* (The Sign of Birth: The Czech National Awakening as a Cultural Type) (1995 and 1983); and Miroslav Hroch, *Social Preconditions of National Revival in Europe: A Comparative Analysis of the Social Composition of Patriotic Groups Among the Smaller European Nations*, trans. Ben Fowkes (2000 and 1985).[22] The work of Macura and Hroch originated in the Marxist period, but both of them were able to present their viewpoints subsequently during the 1990s. The three authors differ in their chronological coverage of the awakening, but all their time frames are relevant to a consideration of the relationship between the national awakening, on the one hand, and the Bohemian Reformation, or the cultural heritage of the sixteenth century, on the other. In addition, Hroch not only deals with the national awakening in Bohemia but also addresses similar movements of cultural renewal in other European lands.

Let us turn first to Schamschula. This German historian limits his period of coverage to the first major phase of the awakening before 1800, and his presentation is somewhat skewed by his declared intention to highlight German contributions to the cultural revival. Most notably, however, his voluminous work of impeccable scholarship does not touch on any substantive influence of the literature and historiography of the Czech Reformation, either on the Bohemian Enlightenment or on the Bohemian national awakening. He merely notes Tomáš Masaryk's thesis about the influence of the Bohemian Reformation in passing in his introduction without pursuing the topic further.[23] Also in the introduction, Schamschula seems to endorse the Marxist or quasi-Marxist thesis that the cultural regeneration known as the awakening was based on the demise of feudalism and the ascendancy of the urban middle class. Accordingly, he refers positively to Felix Vodička, the Czech literary historian, who applied this formula not only to Bohemia but also to several other European countries.[24] In the main body of his book, Schamschula, however, does not emphasize the sociological approach any more than he does the effect of the Bohemian Reformation.

Schamschula's treatment is basically divided into the consecutive consideration of three areas of the awakeners' interest: history, language, and literature. In addition, he periodically points out the awakeners' special concern with the culture of the sixteenth century. In part, he attributes this concern to a general interest in classicism and neo-humanism during the Enlightenment rather than a fascination with the Bohemian Reformation.[25] He does ascribe, particularly to František M. Pelcl, Josef Dobrovský, and Procházka, a high regard for the Czech language and literature during the reign of Rudolf II. Yet, he treats this interest as something superficial and almost inconsequential,[26] and thus, on the whole, he does not assign any major significance to the awakeners' concern with the literary legacy of the Utraquist period. Only in passing does he note the rehabilitation of Jan Hus by Kašpar Royko[27] or the calls during the reign of Joseph II for reincorporating the Reformation period into the narrative of Bohemian history.[28]

As for language, Schamschula considers the proposed restoration of the sixteenth-century grammatical norms as an elitist approach implying contempt for the common man's speech and thus as an experiment doomed to failure.[29] Minimizing the content value of the sixteenth-century literature, he reduces its usefulness to the linguistic aspect and traces its appreciation by the awakeners to its perfection of vocabulary, grammar, and style.[30] This in turn leads him to underappreciate the awakeners' bibliographic work, which he characterizes as an uninspiring, pedantic, and a rather pointless accumulation of dates, book lists, and authors' biographies, as well as histories of printing.[31] Consequently, Schamschula does not track the relationship between the production of such inventories and the program of reprinting the classics of the sixteenth century that was to shape the intellectual life of the coming generations in Bohemia. In general, in his assessment of the awakeners' interest in the culture of the Utraquist era, he does not draw any further conclusions concerning the relationship between the legacy of the Golden Age and the intellectual leitmotifs of the awakening.

Schamschula's presentation is further characterized by the effort to separate sources of the awakeners' inspiration according to language. Hence, he draws a sharp distinction between the German writings of the age of Dobrovský and the Czech writings of the age of Josef Jungmann. This approach obscures the importance of intellectual continuity in the process of the awakening, which was independent of language. The important point, surely, was which ideas were accepted and internalized rather than the language in which they were couched. Thus, Schamschula's approach again leads to a view that the language revival rather than the transmission of ideological values constituted the core of the awakening.[32]

Vladimír Macura in *Znamení zrodu: České národní obrození jako kulturní typ* focuses his coverage on the second phase of the national awakening, the period after 1800. Even more single-mindedly than Schamschula (or later Agnew), he assigns the position of primacy in the national awakening to the restoration of the Czech language to the status of a literary medium, leaving aside the philosophical substance or the intellectual content of the awakening. His standpoint leads him to the startling act of excluding Bernard Bolzano—who did not regard language as the primary issue—from the history of the Bohemian revival. This rejection flies in the face of Bolzano's well-known and documented role in the formation of the philosophical outlook of two generations of Bohemian awakeners.[33]

Macura directs much of his discussion of the linguistic character (*lingvocentrismus*) of the national awakening by invoking the views of the Slovak Jan Kollár, to whom he refers 101 times in the book, more often than to any other person. Such references compare with 69 references to Jungmann, 45 for František Palacký, 18 for Karel Havlíček, and merely 11 for Josef Dobrovský. The fact that the first version of Macura's book (1983) antedated the political division of Czechoslovakia in 1993 into the Czech and the Slovak republics might account for assigning Kollár—for the sake of maintaining the appearance of a Czechoslovak cultural unity—the role of a major player rather than that of an atypical, and often ridiculed, Romantic in the otherwise realist context of the Czech national awakening.[34]

In contrast, Macura does not refer to the relationship of the literature of the sixteenth century (and the Bohemian Reformation in general) to the philosophical and cultural contents of the national awakening. Thus, neither Hus nor Comenius is mentioned, and there are only two minor references to Jan Žižka and one to Jan Rokycana.[35] Despite Macura's emphasis on the linguistic aspect of the revival, neither the restoration of the lexical and grammatical norms of the sixteenth century nor the program of reprinting the sixteenth-century classics is discussed.[36]

Hroch, in his *Social Preconditions of National Revival in Europe,* takes a broad view of the national awakening, covering not only the eighteenth but also much of the nineteenth century; and above all, he is the most sociologically oriented of the three authors under consideration in this section. His approach is also characterized by a penchant for formalistic and abstract presentation (in devising mathematical formulas) and by omission of intellectual factors. In fact, Hroch's approach raises serious reservations. During their national awakenings at the turn of the eighteenth and early nineteenth centuries, the various ethnic groups may have passed through certain stages of interest in linguistics, in collection of folklore, in requests for use of their vernacular in offices and schools, or in a fair share of representation in political and administrative institutions. Some social strata might have supported the national movement earlier, others later. These forms, however, were distinct and separate from the political culture, or—if one wishes—the weltanschauung, which sought expression through them. Even the stress on revival of a language (in Hroch's phase B; phase A involved mere study of the language, and phase C, not just linguistic, but also political demands) is not the most significant phenomenon, if it is conceptually divorced from the intellectual content of the message that it seeks to disseminate. Ultimately, the crucial question is whether this content involved the assertion of a specific ethnicity in the spirit of romanticism or whether it called for embracing a universal human culture in the spirit of the Enlightenment. When two national groups engaged in similar activities, or asked for similar institutions, or mobilized social support in a similar way, all this did not mean that their purposes were the same. The Czech case indicates that two nationalisms may be not only distinctive but also virtually contradictory phenomena, depending on the prevalence of empirical realism or metaphysical monism.

Hroch appears to justify his emphasis on formal sociological aspects and his omission of philosophical and intellectual content of the national awakening by appealing to what looks like the Marxist tenet that privileges the socioeconomic base over the cultural superstructure. As he writes, "We are in any case convinced that the establishment of the general social and economic conditions governing the emergence of any national movement constitutes the necessary starting-point for a fresh interpretation of its program, its demands and its ideological superstructure."[37] On the central topic of our interest, he makes only a stray and cryptic remark about the relationship between the awakening and the Utraquist period: "The Czech national movement could gain a point of support in the cultural sphere from a well-developed ancient [sic] literature."[38]

While Hroch's English-language monograph is based mainly on his Czech writings of the Marxist-Leninist period, only lightly revised, he was able to present a post-Communist approach in a rather fresh survey of the European national movements in a Czech monograph, *V národním zájmu: požadavky a cíle evropských národních hnutí devatenáctého století ve srovnávací perspektivě* (In the National Interest: Demands and Aims of European National Movements of the Nineteenth Century in a Comparative Perspective) (1999). This recent version continues the sociological emphasis, although it departs from the explicitly Marxist form of tying the character of political and social thought tightly to particular interests of social and economic classes.[39] The centrality of the language issue is once more reasserted and articulated into a scheme of five stages.[40] Although the Basques, the Bretons, the Irish, and the Scots are frequently mentioned, the relative insignificance of the language issue in their national awakenings does not lead to an adjustment of the linguistic paradigm.[41]

The new version seeks to correct the earlier omission and also explores the intellectual content of the national movements. With Hroch's penchant for generalization, the result, however, is not a nuanced differentiation but rather a rigid ideological standardization. He ascribes to all of the movements the pursuit of a liberal program.[42] Yet, instead of the liberal principle of society in the service of the individual, Hroch uniformly attributes to the national movements a strongly collectivist view of the nation. Although he criticizes Hans Kohn's theories of nationalism,[43] he ends up with an image of the nation (which Kohn had posited for Eastern Europe) close to Herder's philosophy of history or to Hegel's metaphysical idealism as a personification that binds the individual within a collective entity or body.[44] The illiberal character of this national model is further enhanced by attributing to each nation a survival-of-the-fittest instinct that Hroch somewhat oddly derives, not from Darwin, but from the Marxist leitmotiv of capitalist competitiveness.[45]

The general schematic image of integral nationalism is, of course, inhospitable to the individualistic and realistic tenor of the Bohemian Reformation in a symbiotic relationship with the Austro-Bohemian Catholic Enlightenment. Obscuring rather than uncovering liberalizing impulses from the Utraquist heritage, Hroch tends to dismiss appeals to the past as reactionary if extolling institutions, on the one hand, or as strictly utilitarian if concerned with language, on the other.[46] As for the Josephist Enlightenment, its liberalizing tendencies are not presented as a major factor, and the phenomenon itself is depicted more as a source of confusion and resentment, instead of purification and uplift.[47]

Fin de Siècle Epitome: Hugh Agnew

Based on sources in Czech, Latin, German, and Russian, Agnew's *Origins of the Czech National Renascence* (1993) in a way represents an ecumenical summary of research on its topic toward the end of the twentieth century. Compared to the three monographs just discussed, Agnew's treatment seems to be close to Schamschula's in chronological scope and in its adoption, in its first half, of a tripartite division devoted respectively to history, language, and literature.

Agnew seeks to uphold a neutral position between two fundamental approaches to the awakening. One he defines as the traditional nationalist view, which "lauded the value of the Hussite period and Protestantism in Bohemia, and asserted a link between them and the national renascence." The other view, represented by Josef Pekař and his followers, "insisted instead on the continuity of Czech culture after the White Mountain [the Habsburg victory of the Battle of the White Mountain, near Prague, in November 1620 that opened the era of the Counter-Reformation in Bohemia], the role of Catholicism in the Czech national identity, and the connections between the national renascence and the traditions of the Czech Catholic baroque."[48] On the whole, Agnew seems to be skeptical about the influence of the Bohemian Reformation. Rather, he calls attention to the contributions of the baroque culture and views the tendencies to deny or diminish the value of the baroque as reflecting the simplistic and schematic version of historiography typical of the Marxist-Leninist ideology.

Agnew does, however, discuss at considerable length the efforts to restore the language norms of the sixteenth century. He cites Karel Ignác Thám's recommendation in that regard, as well as his scathing criticism of linguistic corruption under the Counter-Reformation.[49] Agnew further refers to Pelcl's high respect for the Czech language, which according to Pelcl had reached its perfection under Rudolf II.[50] Likewise, he quotes from Jungmann's two articles in *Hlasatel český* (Bohemian Herald) (1806), where the language of the Golden Age is represented by a resurrected Daniel Adam of Veleslavín, who is shocked by how much the Czech language had decayed by the end of the eighteenth century.[51]

Nevertheless, Agnew, like Schamschula, adopts a rather critical attitude toward the awakeners' turn to the language of the Golden Age. It appears to him as though that language was to be regarded almost as a dead tongue on a par with classical Greek and Latin.[52] It also suggests to him an attitude of snobbery vis-à-vis the contemporary speech of the common people.[53] Nevertheless, despite his skepticism about reintroducing the norms of the sixteenth century, Agnew agrees with Macura in assigning the position of primacy in the national awakening to the restoration of Czech to the status of a full-fledged literary medium. As he writes, "It was a precondition for much of the rest of the national revival, especially for the creation of an independent national culture, including literature in Czech at all levels." Essentially, Agnew sees linguistic nationalism as the core of the Czech national movement.[54]

While he also pays considerable attention to the awakeners' resurrection of the literature of the sixteenth-century period, Agnew's interest is guided by a stress on the primacy of language in this process as well. Rather than seeing in this legacy a source of ideological inspiration, he views the literary heritage as a tool of linguistic nationalism that provided a proof of the applicability of Czech to higher learning and simultaneously supplied a model for such an application. For Agnew, the awakeners did not appear to value the literary corpus of the sixteenth century per se but instead only as evidence that advanced scholarly subjects could be adequately treated in Czech.[55] Along these lines, and only in this specific context, Agnew further stresses the shocking primitivism of mid-eighteenth-century writing in comparison with the sophisticated language and style of the sixteenth century.[56]

Like Schamschula, Agnew seems skeptical about the awakeners' efforts to establish the bibliographic canon of sixteenth-century Czech literature that appeared to him as an exercise in pedantry, and he speaks of a "rather sterile collection of bibliographic data."[57] Unlike Schamschula, Agnew considered the comprehensive projects for reprinting the sixteenth-century classics at some length. Once again, however, the object and result of this activity were for him restricted to linguistic interests, namely, to revitalizing the literature written in Czech rather than to providing intellectual nourishment for philosophical, political, legal, and social thought.[58] The high linguistic standards of the sixteenth-century publications were to inspire the current writers to strive for a similar perfection of diction and style.[59] Tracing the transmission of liberal attitudes and values to succeeding generations through a structured dissemination of sixteenth-century political and philosophical literature was evidently not on Agnew's agenda.

The Twenty-First Century

After Agnew, we reach the contemporary period at the start of the third millennium. Two surveys of earlier vintage, which appeared in the post-2000 period, will be noted briefly. One was a twice-delayed work of the pre-Communist era, František Kutnar's *Obrozenské vlastenectví a nacionalismus, Příspěvek k národnímu společenskému obsahu češství doby obrozenské* (Patriotism and Nationalism in the Awakening: A Contribution to the National Social Content of Czechdom in the Revival Period) (2003);[60] the other was a new edition of Josef Haubelt's *České osvícenství* (The Bohemian Enlightenment) (1986 and 2004). Among the original publications on the era of the national awakening, I will note at greater length Jitka Lněničková's *České země v době předbřeznové, 1792–1848* (1999), and the collective work by Pavel Bělina, Jiří Kaše, and Jan P.

Kučera, volume 10 of *Velké dějiny zemí Koruny české* (Large History of the Lands of the Bohemian Crown) (2001).[61]

In the *Obrozenské vlastenectví a nacionalismus,* Kutnar follows in the footsteps of his teacher Josef Pekař in his attempt to connect the national awakening with the signs of linguistic national patriotism of the Counter-Reformation era. He is not curious about a possible connection between the awakening, on the one hand, and the ideas of Utraquist intellectual and political liberalism growing out of the Bohemian Reformation, on the other.[62] Correspondingly, he shows little concern with the Enlightenment's introduction of freedom of thought and expression or, obversely, with the release from the rigid thought control of the baroque era. Kutnar sees the use of history by the awakeners as a stimulus to national pride, not as a source of acquisition and resurrection of political or philosophical knowledge in harmony with the spirit of the Enlightenment era.[63]

Like the original edition (1986), Haubelt's refurbished version of *České osvícenství* (2004) seeks to connect the Bohemian Enlightenment with the growth of natural sciences. The main thrust of the author's conceptual scheme, however, is still aimed at a Marxist-like juxtaposition of the (for its time) progressive bourgeois Enlightenment to the reactionary feudal period of the baroque.[64] Yet, the authoritative testimony of Zdeněk Nejedlý of the Communist era is replaced in the introductory part by citing the views of Jan Patočka and Jan Fiala.[65] In viewing the attitudes of the Enlighteners toward the Bohemian Reformation, Haubelt remains critical of the efforts of Kašpar Royko, Johann H. Wolf, Václav Stach, and Augustin Zitte to separate Hus from the radicals of the Bohemian Reformation and ridicules the depiction of Hus and mainstream Utraquism as anticipations of the Enlightenment's liberalism.[66]

Lněničková devotes several parts of her book to the issues of the national awakening.[67] In discussing the revival, she notes that the welter of ideas included an awareness of a connection between the Bohemian Reformation and modern political liberalism, "particularly in the sense of tolerance, responsibility and freedom of thought for the individual, learning, etc." She considers it as one idea among many entertained by Czech politicians of the 1840s.[68] A massive transfer of ideas from the sixteenth to the late eighteenth and early nineteenth century is, therefore, not considered.[69] In any case, references to the intellectual ambience of the Bohemian Reformation are scarce, and the names of Hus, Žižka, Jan Rokycana, or George of Poděbrady do not appear in the book.

The author attributes the preoccupation with historical themes in literature and scholarship, not to a wish to learn from the past but to the fear of Austrian censorship that made dealing with contemporary topics risky.[70] Republication of authors from the period of the Bohemian Reformation by the premier academic publisher, *Matice česká* (the Bohemian Foundation), is noted in passing as something innocuous and inconsequential.[71] In the area of language revival, Lněničková does not even discuss the conspicuous return to the grammatical norms of the Utraquist age.[72]

Similarly, little attention is paid to the role of the Catholic Enlightenment in the transmission of liberal, individualistic, and realistic attitudes into the modern political culture that would subsequently steer a course against the metaphysical monism of Herder and Hegel. Instead, Catholic Enlightenment is presented as a phenomenon of minor significance without any notable relevance to the core values of the national awakening.[73] While Karl H. Seibt is mentioned, there is no reference to Josef Fesl, and Bernard Bolzano is presented as an eccentric and marginal figure despite—as noted earlier—his seminal role in the education of two generations of the awakeners.[74] In fact, the anti-Hegelianism of Bolzano and Franz Exner is deplored, together with the subsequent Bohemian distaste for philosophical idealism.[75] Rather incongruously, in view of her censure of Czech antiromanticism and anti-idealism, Lněničková goes on to attribute to the Czech awakeners a collectivist view of the nation as a hypostasis of a higher entity manifesting the common spirit of a particular society as a whole. She attributes this alleged anti-individualistic and antirealistic view to the influence of German ideas on Czech intellectual life.[76]

While the author minimizes the importance of the Catholic Enlightenment in the intellectual atmosphere of the awakening, she emphasizes the role of the Counter-Reformation in engendering, above all through the Society of Jesus, the patriotic emotions that contributed to the genesis of the national awakening. When it comes to naming particular individuals who receive this high credit, however, instead of figures of the Counter-Reformation, she lists mainly former Jesuits or Jesuits' disciples who turned from the Counter-Reformation to Josephist Reform Catholicism. The former category includes Dobrovský, František Pubička, and Stanislav Vydra; the latter includes Pelcl, Václav Kramerius, Stach, and, one may add, Jan Jeník of Bratřice.[77]

As in the case of Hroch, Lněničková pays considerable attention to the likely class origin and class character of the rank-and-file supporters of the awakening.[78] More important, she continues to embrace the language revival, defining the awakeners' aim in the 1840s as the rather imitative task of developing Czech-language literature comparable to that of Germany. Accordingly, she downplays the intellectual content of the awakening, although she does note—but only in passing—that, aside from its linguistic preoccupation, the revival in Bohemia adhered to a liberal viewpoint in politics and social thought.[79] Yet the stress on the primacy of linguistic nationalism, and hence on the Romantic over the Enlightenment tendency, is less pronounced than among her predecessors, such as Macura—partly, perhaps, because she has discarded the onus of incorporating the attitudes of the Slovaks who had avidly embraced the spirit of romanticism and idealism. In contrast to Macura in particular, the number of references in Lněničková's book to the Slovak romanticist Kollár are dwarfed by references to his more realistically inclined Bohemian colleagues, such as Dobrovský, Jungmann, Havlíček, and Palacký.[80]

Bělina in parts one and two of the tenth volume of *Velké dějiny zemí Koruny české* devotes several sections to the problems of the national awakening with a focus on the period chronologically preceding the coverage of 1792–1848 by Lněničková.[81] Unlike Lněničková, Bělina pays considerable attention to the Enlightenment and points to its interest in the Bohemian Reformation. He notes a sympathy for moderate Utraquism of the sixteenth century among the awakeners, particularly through favorable treatments of Jan Hus. According to him, the awakeners' devotion to the spirit of the Enlightenment affected their insistence on Hus's sincerity, reasonableness, and essentially orthodox Catholicism. Bělina sees the Enlightenment's attitude of tolerance projected onto Hus, particularly by Zitte, and onto the Bohemian Reformation as a whole by Otto Steinbach of Kranichstein's *Versuch einer Geschichte der alten und neuen Toleranz im Königreich Böhmen und Markgraftum Mähren* (1786).[82]

Ultimately, however, Bělina—in what appears as a volte-face—indicates a marked disapproval of the Catholic Enlightenment, as expressed through Joseph II's religious reforms, and reveals considerable sympathy for Counter-Reformation Catholicism.[83] For instance, he deplores the interposition of state authority between Rome and the national churches.[84] He also objects to much of the critique of the Jesuits' role during the Counter-Reformation. In an ultimate sally, he startlingly characterizes the Catholic Enlightenment, such as represented by Dobrovský, as being "so dangerous to the Catholic cause."[85]

Contrasting with Bělina's benign view of the Counter-Reformation are what appear to be residual signs of a Marxist interpretation. One such echo may be seen in attributing Pelcl's dislike of the radical trends in the Bohemian Reformation, not to the enlightened distaste for religious fanaticism and violence but to a fear among the propertied classes of social upheavals inspired by the outbreak and the aftermath of the French Revolution.[86] Incidentally, this opinion clashes with a less speculative conclusion only two pages earlier to the effect that—long before the revolutionary upheavals in France—the distaste for the fanaticism and violence in the early Bohemian Reformation was shared by the enlightened awakeners, such as Dobrovský and Steinbach of Kranichstein.[87] The notion of religion's dependence on economics also surfaces in the reference to Lutheran antagonism to the Unity of Brethren that is attributed to the economic interests and anxieties of the propertied classes.[88] In addition, there seems to be an echo of the Marxist approach in Bělina's attribution of the emergence of a territorial, and later an ethnic, patriotism to the acceleration of economic development in the eighteenth century.[89]

Bělina's view of the relationship between the Catholic Enlightenment and the Bohemian Reformation (in its moderate incarnation) is, therefore, paradoxical. On the one hand, he draws parallels between the two, especially for their tolerance and endorsement of peaceful discussion of controversial issues. On the other hand, he tends to depict the Josephist Enlightenment in a rather negative way, as an extremist, if not a perverse, phenomenon.[90] Consequently, Bělina's treatment does not indicate that there was a substantive transmission of ideas from the Bohemian Reformation by way of the Enlightenment to the Czech political culture that germinated during the awakening.

A Neglect of "Golden Age" Liberalism

On the whole, then, recent historiography, Marxist and non-Marxist alike, both in the Czech Republic and abroad, pays little attention, if any, to the formative role of the sixteenth-century Utraquist literature in the intellectual environment of the Bohemian national revival of the late eighteenth and early nineteenth centuries. In the historical literature, the interest in the legacy of the Bohemian Reformation is largely limited to a focus on the language revival. Accordingly, the concern with the sixteenth-century culture is made subservient to the linguistic preoccupation, while its independent role in the thought formation of the modern era tends to be neglected. The resulting image or interpretation of the relationship of the awakening to the time of the Bohemian Reformation is, therefore, more in line with Pekař's concept of ethnic nationalism than of Masaryk's view of advancing the cause of universal intellectual and moral values.

These findings suggest the need for freshly examining the actual transmission of political and cultural values over a gap of almost two centuries from the Bohemian Reformation to the national revival. The task is undertaken in the opening sections of this book. While chapter 2 discusses the liberal culture of the sixteenth-century Golden Age in Bohemia that was shaped by Utraquism, the next two chapters (3 and 4) will address the inducements, both negative and positive, for the cultural transfer during the national awakening. Chapter 5 describes the actual mechanisms of the cultural transfer. The goal of this historical probing is to shed light on the distinctive roots of Czech political culture in the modern period. The second half of the book (chapters 6–11) traces the growth of this political culture, characterized by realism, tolerance, and liberalism in the Bohemian lands under the continuing sway of the Catholic Enlightenment, personified by the stellar triumvirate of Karl H. Seibt, Bernard Bolzano, and Franz Exner.

2

Tolerance, Universalism, and Plebeianism as Legacies of the Sixteenth Century

Let us consider the major political and social ideals of the Bohemian Reformation that the Austro-Bohemian Catholic Enlightenment rediscovered and passed on to the subsequent political culture of Bohemia. In this chapter, we will focus on three relevant aspects of the political and cultural scene of sixteenth-century Bohemia, namely, tolerance, universalism, and plebeianism. The first two derived from the libertarian character and the universalist orientation of the Utraquist Church, which gained ascendancy in Bohemia in the wake of the execution of Jan Hus. The third aspect grew out of the dominant role of the urban milieu in the sustenance of the Utraquist Church and in the formation of the civic culture in sixteenth-century Bohemia. Hence, the tolerant and open-minded intellectual ambience, as well as its universalist aspirations, owed much to the spirit of the Utraquist Church with its liberal, yet traditionalist, ecclesiology; and the plebeian character of the sixteenth-century culture reflected, in large part, the effect of Utraquism as a commoner's church.

The *Via Media* of Utraquism

We begin with a brief outline of the ecclesiastical and theological developments that led to the ascendancy of the Utraquist Church and follow with a discussion of how the church and the urban society that nourished it were shaped by mutual interaction in sixteenth-century Bohemia.[1] Utraquism, which emerged from the Bohemian Reformation of the late fourteenth and early fifteenth centuries, aimed at purging the medieval church of material wealth and political pretensions, while preserving its sacramental character and historical episcopate. The formal name of the Utraquist (in Czech, *pod obojí*) Church was derived from the Latin phrase *sub utraque specie* (under each of two kinds). This appellation referred to its belief—contrary to the current rules of the Church of Rome—in the theological necessity of communion for the laity in wine, as well as bread, and not only for adults and older children but also for young children and infants.[2]

The most prominent early spokesman for the reform movement in Bohemia was Jan Hus.[3] His execution at the Council of Constance in 1415 led to an administrative separation of the Bohemian Church from the Church of Rome by 1420. The Utraquist priests, however, continued to be ordained (in a rather irregular way) by bishops in communion with the Roman See. The ordinations were performed variously by vagrant Italian bishops in Bohemia, Greek Uniate prelates in Venice, or resident bishops in neighboring dioceses.[4] The governance of the Utraquist Church was vested in the Consistory of the Archdiocese of Prague, a collegium of priests headed by an administrator officially known as *administrator et parochi consistorii archiepiscopatus Pragensis sub utraque communicantium*.[5] At different times, either the Diet of Bohemia or the Bohemian Royal Chancery chose and appointed this ruling body from the priesthood, ordained in the historical apostolic succession.

In this study, the terms *Utraquist Church* and *Utraquism* are normally used. The conventional use of the terms *Hussite Church* and *Hussitism* tends to distort the character of Bohemia's ecclesiastical history. Jan Hus was in one respect much more significant than the Bohemian Church, but in another respect much less so. As a champion of human rights in the most prominent forum of his time, he belongs, on the one hand, to all ages and all mankind. On the other hand, as a participant in the Bohemian reform movement, he did not aspire to found a new religion but rather shared with his fellow reformers a search for no more (and no less) than the standard church of the West, cleansed from what they considered the unacceptable overlay of papal monarchism. The Utraquist Church venerated Hus among the Bohemian saints as both a symbol and the prime example of its liberal stance, but he was not viewed as a principal theologian, let alone a founder. It is not surprising then that the term *Hussite Church*, which insinuated Hus's paramount role and obscured the continuity with the medieval tradition, was never adopted by the Utraquists themselves but was pejoratively applied to them by their opponents.[6] The term *Hussite* was not used for self-identification even by the more radical Bohemian dissidents, which included the Taborites, the Orebites, and the subsequent Unity of Brethren.[7] The Utraquist Church did not feel a need to make claims of originality; it conceived of itself as the continuation of the Catholic Church in Bohemia.[8]

During the Bohemian wars of religion (1420–31), the center stage was occupied by the Taborites and the Orebites, religious radicals whose enthusiasm and fighting spirit were probably indispensable in saving the Bohemian Reformation from the onslaught of five imperial and papal crusades.[9] The ecclesiastical leadership of the Utraquist Church never endorsed and ultimately rejected (after the debacle of the crusades) these "heretics," who questioned a substantial part of the medieval corpus of beliefs and rituals.[10] In contrast, the Utraquists could be classified as mere "schismatics" who rejected Roman ecclesiastical authoritarianism but retained all the instrumentalities of traditional Christianity, including the historical apostolic succession, the real presence in the Eucharist, the seven sacraments, the word of God, the law of God, saints, images, good works, and medieval liturgical books and vestments. Of course, their schism existed only in the eyes of the Roman Church. From their own viewpoint, it was Rome that was separated from the true church, so long as it failed to adopt the biblical eucharistic teaching and maintained its apparatus of enforcement and coercion.

In 1436, the legitimacy of Utraquism as a part of the Roman Church was recognized by Rome through the Compactata, negotiated by the Bohemians at the Council of Basel. Lay communion in both kinds was permitted in Bohemia and Moravia, while other controversial issues were left open.[11] The recognition, however, was subsequently revoked on questionable grounds by Pope Pius II in 1462, leaving the formal relations between Rome and the Utraquists in a perpetually unsettled state. The few remaining adherents of the Roman Curia in Bohemia continued to be administered by a separate Consistory (under an arrangement dating to 1421) and were known as communicants *sub una* (that is, under one kind, or by bread alone). Eventually, they became directly subordinate to the archbishop of Prague when the office was restored in 1561 after a lapse of more than 130 years.[12]

With the onset of the Lutheran Reformation in 1517, the Utraquist Consistory had refused to embrace the principles of *sola fide* (that is, salvation is secured by faith alone), *sola scriptura* (that is, the word of God in Scripture is sufficient for salvation), or any other Protestant innovations, and the Utraquist Church came to occupy a middle position between Rome and Wittenberg. With its attachment to scripture, scholastic rationalism, and tradition, it also foreshadowed the *via media* of the then-germinating Anglicanism.[13] As the sixteenth century progressed, a religious cleavage developed in Bohemia along social lines: the numerically weak but politically powerful nobles (barons and knights) were increasingly attracted to the Augsburg Confession, the official Lutheran creed, while the Czech commoners (townspeople and peasantry) remained loyal to the Consistory and the Utraquist faith.[14]

Devoid of legal protection for their denomination, the Lutheran nobles pressed the king of Bohemia (also the holy Roman emperor), Maximilian II, at the Diet of 1575 to grant recognition to the Augsburg Confession, somewhat modified under the name of the Bohemian Confession. It was the resolution of this demand that set the scene for Bohemia's remarkable and distinctive religious tolerance that lasted into the seventeenth century. In a paradoxical move, the Utraquist towns supported the nobles' demand for the legalization of the Augsburg Confession. Their move, however, had political rather than religious reasons. First, their main sense of threat came less from the Lutherans than from the Counter-Reformation, which had been gathering strength in the Habsburg monarchy after the Council of Trent (1545–63). Second, the Utraquist townspeople feared political isolation vis-à-vis the king and the Roman Church if they were to break the united front with the other anti-Roman dissidents by failing to support the nobles' request. Third, the nobles assured the towns that the Bohemian Confession would merely define the outer limits of religious acceptability without imposing a Lutheran conformity on Utraquism.

In the final resolution, Maximilian II insisted on overtly preserving the legal status quo according to which only Utraquism under its Consistory (together with the few remaining adherents of the Roman Church, or the party *sub una*) would be viewed as legally established. Maximilian, however, appeased the nobles with a gentlemen's agreement, which bound him as well as his son and heir (both as king and emperor), Rudolf II, to protect the existing adherents of the Bohemian Confession, provided that there were no encroachments on the current status and position of Utraquism (or those of the party *sub una*).[15] Maximilian's promise of religious freedom was to cover not only the Lutherans but also the hitherto unprotected Unity of Brethren. The Unity, a relatively small but devout and influential sect, had split from the Utraquist Church in 1457 and revived and perpetuated some of the radical tenets of earlier Taboritism.[16]

An important landmark in the development of Utraquism in the early seventeenth century was the full legalization of the Bohemian Confession, a step accompanied by the transfer of control over the hitherto Utraquist Consistory from the king and his officials to the Bohemian Diet dominated by Lutheran nobility. Henceforth, the Consistory was to administer not only the Utraquists but also the other so-called *sub utraque* (*pod obojí*), namely, the Lutherans and the Unity of Brethren. This occurred by King and Emperor Rudolf II's decision, incorporated in the famous Letter of Majesty of July 9, 1609.[17] The act of 1609 signified that the Utraquists and the Brethren formed, together with the Lutherans, a political alliance, henceforth known as the party *sub utraque*, for mutual protection against the adherents of the Roman Curia, or the party *sub una*, which was by and large favored by the monarch and his officials and viewed as the major threat by the Utraquists, the Lutherans, and the Brethren alike.

The function of the Bohemian Confession was therefore comparable to that of the English Blasphemy Act of 1650. While the Blasphemy Act defined the boundary negatively by what was prohibited, the Bohemian Confession did so positively by stating what was permissible.[18] As in 1575, so also in 1609, the political support for the Bohemian Confession was not evidence of its religious acceptance. The toleration of the "unorthodox" Bohemian Confession in 1609 by the Utraquists and the Brethren was analogous to the toleration of the "unorthodox" Compactata in 1436 and 1485 by the *sub una*. Both fit into the framework of the established Bohemian tradition of religious peace and harmony, which will be discussed in more detail later in this chapter.

In summing up the genesis of Utraquism, it should be noted that there was a direct line of progress from Jan Hus to the so-called Prague Party, led by the masters of the University of Prague that turned into mainline Utraquism. During the religious wars, extrinsic radical elements, in particular the Taborites, coexisted with mainline Utraquism. The radical militants fell away, partly from exhaustion and an ideological flameout after having performed an important military service to preserve the Bohemian Reformation.[19] That victory in 1434 permitted mainline Utraquism to perpetuate the moderate and liberal tradition of Hus and his academic precursors and associates.[20]

As noted, the doused flames of the Taborite religious radicalism (minus its militarism) had rekindled in the Unity of Brethren by 1457. With the ascent to power of the Utraquist King George of Poděbrady (1458–71)[21] and under the guidance of the Utraquist archbishop-elect Jan Rokycana (1448–71),[22] the theological self-definition of mainline Utraquism was essentially completed. Another phase of theological creativity followed in the 1530s and 1540s when Bohuslav Bílejovský and Pavel Bydžovský responded on behalf of Utraquism to the challenge of the German Reformation by rejecting Luther's teaching.[23] Their reaffirmations of Hus's legacy informed the Utraquists' stand vis-à-vis two subsequent challenges: the Bohemian Confession of 1575 and the Letter of Majesty of 1609. Hence, the church's energy and vitality would be displayed not only through its resistance to the Roman Curia on the right but also in its response to the followers of Luther who, after 1517, joined the Brethren as challengers on the left. Foremost, however, the Utraquists' positive contribution was reflected in their tolerance and intellectual liberalism that were, in turn, conditioned by a religious *via media*, or the middle position between Rome and Luther.

Tolerance and Liberalism

Utraquism's liberal ecclesiology, with its social and political ramifications, was an important legacy informing the development of the Bohemian political culture as it emerged from the Austro-Bohemian Enlightenment. Despite (or even perhaps in harmony with) their traditionalism in dogma and liturgy, which distinguished them from later Protestants, the Utraquists struck two libertarian notes in theological discourse by their insistence on an interplay between reason and authority and on a free preaching of the word of God. Furthermore, having eschewed the monarchic authoritarianism of the late medieval Roman Church, the Utraquists maintained a consensual approach in ecclesiastical administration. In addition, their abhorrence of violent methods to enforce religious conformity promoted a tolerant view of other denominations. In its intellectual openness and moderation of discourse, conditioned partly by its intermediate position between Rome and the Protestant Reformation, the Utraquist Church of Bohemia resembled the Church of England, particularly that of the Elizabethan settlement of 1558.[24]

The positive features of Utraquist ecclesiology tended to be obscured in the historical literature by a tendency to cast a jaundiced eye at the relatively laissez-faire attitude of Utraquist theology. Thus, the toleration of dissenting opinions was misinterpreted as a sign of religious indifference; avoidance of strong-arm enforcement was misjudged as excessive permissiveness or even as a condonation of immorality; openness to discussion in theology was seen as springing from a lack of intellectual rigor. We shall explore the reasons why historical discourse has tended to turn what can be viewed as real ecclesiological virtues of the Utraquist Church into alleged vices and thus to obfuscate their positive impact on the Austro-Bohemian Catholic Enlightenment.

Freedom and Consensus

Two principles constituted the cornerstones of Utraquism's liberal ecclesiology: the theological openness to rational argument and a repudiation of the administrative and judicial jurisdiction and practices of the Roman Curia. Although generated in an extended period of dramatic events, symbolically and formally these principles were enshrined respectively in the so-called Judge of Cheb (*iudex in Egra compactatus, soudce chebský*) of 1432 and the charter of ecclesiastical liberties issued by the Emperor and King Sigismund in 1436.

Intellectual openness characterized the Bohemian Reformation almost from the very start, as it was embraced in the early stages by Hus and his original colleagues. The use of magisterial command without discussion, as practiced by the Roman Church, was specifically repudiated by the Utraquists, first with reference to the witness of Hus and then collectively during the Bohemian wars of religion.[25] Safeguarding personal judgment, Hus went (in a treatise from 1410) as far as to defend the utility of reading heretical books and to oppose their burning as contradictory to sound reason, as well as the precepts of the church fathers.[26] Eventually, Hus earned a wide recognition as a pioneer and martyr of human rights by his refusal to recant at the Council of Constance, unless the judges demonstrated the error of his ideas.[27] Finally, the endorsement of a relatively free discussion of religious issues was codified in the Four Articles of Prague, the Test or so-called Judge of

Cheb in 1432, and the Compactata of the Council of Basel in 1436. The tenets of the Judge of Cheb were particularly important. The Utraquists insisted on them in 1432 before embarking on negotiations with the Council of Basel by stipulating that the Bible and opinions in conformity with the Scripture were to govern the theological discussions with the council.[28] Thus, the Utraquists were ready to respect teachings of popes, church fathers and doctors, and councils that might be extrabiblical (not specifically contained in the Bible) but not those propositions they viewed as actually contradictory to the Scripture.[29]

The atmosphere of intellectual openness was further strengthened by the Utraquists' injunction to preach the word of God freely. This stance was adumbrated by Hus's challenge to a papal edict that prohibited him from preaching in 1412. He claimed that the edict violated the Scripture by depriving him of a right guaranteed by Christ himself to the apostles and their legitimate successors.[30] The idea of preaching the word of God freely was also promoted by John Wyclif, the late-fourteenth-century Oxford scholar whose doctrines had considerable vogue in the early stages of the Bohemian Reformation.[31] The principle of free preaching passed into mainstream Utraquism through its incorporation into the basic Utraquist documents, namely, the Four Articles of Prague of 1419 (as Article One) and the Compactata (as Article Two).[32]

The Utraquists' resistance to the practice of naked magisterial authority arises partly from the academic backgrounds of the early Bohemian Reformers, as well as from the spirit of tolerance in Wyclif's theology.[33] The leadership of the Bohemian Reformation consisted mainly of university teachers and other theological academics, who were accustomed to the application of reason and reasoning, evident particularly in the freewheeling (*quodlibet*) disputations.[34] Thus, the tone of the Utraquists' discourse was set neither by folkish sectarians susceptible to emotional enthusiasms nor by organizational bureaucrats who stressed the exercise of authority. On the issue of sectarian enthusiasm, as pointed out earlier, the Utraquist Church constantly distanced itself from the theological radicalism of the Taborites.[35] On the issue of bureaucratic control, the Utraquist Church found a way of emancipation from Rome's power.

Protected by the Bohemian Diet, the Utraquist Church asserted its autonomy from Roman administrators and judges soon after the execution of Hus. In fact, from 1420 to 1431, the whole country was much of the time at war with the Holy See. Emperor Sigismund made the dismantling of Rome's administrative and judicial prerogatives official by an imperial charter of ecclesiastical liberties, dated January 6, 1436. The document reaffirmed the virtual jurisdictional independence of the Utraquist Church in Bohemia and Moravia from the Roman See. It foreshadowed the separation of the Church of England from Rome, but it was not so drastic, because the pope still retained the power to confirm the appointment of bishops, and thus a sacerdotal tie between Utraquist Prague and papal Rome was preserved.[36]

Freed from the administrative rules of the Roman Church, the Utraquists were also free to liberalize the internal governance of their church. Thus, the Utraquist Church renounced the interdicts, anathemas, excommunications, and other drastic spiritual weapons that were employed routinely by the Roman Church in the late medieval and early modern times.[37] Fittingly, in view of Hus's fate, this included an opposition to the burning of heretics.[38] Furthermore, the internal administration of the Utraquist Church stressed assent rather than passive submission. Under this approach, in particular, the appointments and transfers of priests, especially in urban parishes, were not dictated but negotiated between the Consistory and the municipal authorities, resulting in a liberal give-and-take system of consensual administration.[39] As firm adherents to the historical apostolic succession for the valid ordination of priests, the Utraquists remained episcopalians and even papalists. From the viewpoint of church governance, however, they feared the heavy hand not only of the pope but also, eventually, of the monarchic bishops, and they preferred to rely for diocesan administration and judiciary on a collegium of priests (the Consistory), so that their system of ecclesiastical organization could be called presbyterial (though, of course, not Presbyterian).

Religious Peace and Tolerance

The nonconfrontational and accommodating spirit of mainline Utraquism found its embodiment in a remarkable state of institutionalized religious toleration in sixteenth- and early seventeenth-century Bohemia.[40] The institutional milestone in the legal underpinning of this tolerance was the Peace of Kutná Hora (1485) that proscribed accusations of heresy and mutual vilification between the Utraquists and the adherents of the Roman Curia. As precedents, the agreement could build on the principles of free discussion and benign attitude toward dissenting views, which had been expressed in the Compactata and the Judge of Cheb.[41] Subsequently, the concept of tolerance was also expanded to cover the Lutherans and the Unity of Brethren, first informally by King Maximilian II's oral approval of the Bohemian Confession in 1575 and then formally by King Rudolf II's issuance of the Letter of Majesty in 1609. The Utraquist political leaders played a constructive role in both cases. Three factors may be considered to account for their relatively pacific attitude: memories of the wars of the Bohemian Reformation, the belief in free discussion and respect for unacceptable opinions, and the absence of confessionalization—the need of defining themselves vis-à-vis other religious denominations.

Remembering the destructiveness of the fifteenth-century internal and external conflicts undoubtedly helped foster a pacific religious attitude among the Utraquists. While not going as far as the Unity of Brethren's sweeping doctrine of nonresistance to evil, Bílejovský's tendency to look askance at Taborite militarism if it had gone beyond the legitimate defense of the Bohemian Reformation appears to be typical of a sixteenth-century Utraquist.[42] As another example, the Utraquist author Blažej Nožička of Votín, writing in 1566, strongly condemned religious warfare, particularly that of the 1440s, as unnecessary and purely destructive. Similarly, Daniel Adam of Veleslavín, in his edition and translation of Georg Lauterbeck's treatise on government (1584), included a stern warning against unrestrained warfare, preferring two years of negotiations to one of armed conflict.[43]

Aside from the memories of war, the moderation of the Utraquist theologians' discourse can be attributed to their centrist position, which they shared with the divines of the Church of England. The latter were likewise known for the mild tone of their polemics with their Puritan opponents.[44] An illustrative example of a curious, calm, and civil examination of Luther's doctrines by two Utraquist priests was offered by the correspondence between Šimon of Habry and Jan of Německý Brod during 1528 and 1529.[45] It is also appropriate to point out the mildness with which the archetypal Utraquist, Bydžovský, treated Luther's doctrines in the 1540s or with which he chided the alleged errors of the Brethren.[46] On the points of disagreement, such as the sacramental priesthood, solafideism, and the veneration and invocation of Mary and the saints, Bydžovský's attitude toward the Lutherans paralleled the subsequent treatment by the Anglicans of disagreements with their fellow Protestants.[47] An instructive parallel is offered by Bydžovský's characterization of Luther and Melanchton as "the most learned men in Germany [*nejučeniejši w niemcych*]" and Richard Hooker's description of Calvin as "I thinke incomparably the wisest man that ever the French church did enjoy, since the houre it enjoyed him."[48] Aside from the inherent moderation of the religious *via media*, Erasmus's influence can be cited as a common denominator in the mild, even courteous tone that we find in the religious argumentation against opponents among both the Utraquists and the early Anglican theologians.[49]

The third reason for the exceptional mildness of the Utraquists' theological discussions can be sought in their escape from the need of confessionalization in the late sixteenth and early seventeenth century.[50] They avoided the processes by which the Protestant groups had to define themselves against each other and against the Church of Rome and by which the latter had to adopt its own demarcations against the churches of the Reformation. The Utraquists were already secure in their own delimitation in relation to both Roman authoritarianism (since the period of Hus and the Compactata) and the Protestant-like biblical reductionism (through the fifteenth-century encounters with the Taborites and the Brethren). Moreover, they derived their self-definition from the standard church of Western Christendom minus the papal monarchism. Hence, there was no need to define themselves afresh. Therefore, in the sixteenth and early seventeenth centuries they were spared the process of differentiation, which often led others to cast anathemas against each other and which was the reverse of adopting tolerant attitudes.[51] Moreover, the Utraquists' sense of preserving an integrity of the doctrinal fundamentals of traditional Christianity released them from the compulsion of a militant assertion of orthodoxy.[52]

The Question of Ethics

The Utraquists' virtues of intellectual openness and tolerance paradoxically contributed to charges that they lacked moral fiber and intellectual rigor. Unlike the literary legacy of the Unity of Brethren, that of mainline Utraquism has not received credit in Czech historiography for its contribution to modern Czech political culture. The view that the clergy and laity of Bohemian Utraquism were afflicted by a low moral threshold has been relatively widespread.[53] Moreover, duplicity and toadyism were ascribed to Utraquist administrators and Consistories in dealing with the agents of the Habsburg monarchs and of the Roman

Church, especially on the issues of priestly ordinations and other relations with the Roman Curia.[54]

The image of Utraquists' lack of moral stamina resulted largely from the types of sources that have been used. The Utraquists have been traditionally depicted on the basis of the Consistory's administrative and court records, revealing primarily the seamy side in the behavior of their clergy and laity. Their historical self-descriptions, like Bílejovský's work, have been almost routinely dismissed.[55] In contrast, the Bohemian Brethren have been assessed on the basis of their self-portraits. Reliance on the Brethren's accounts of events has tended to skew the record not only in favor of the Brethren but also against the Utraquists, since the Brethren, despite their many virtues, were notoriously uncharitable toward their opponents.[56]

Aside from the Brethren, adherents of the Roman Curia had a special reason to depict Utraquist priests in an uncomplimentary way. The Utraquist Church received a steady supply of priests by transfers from the Roman obedience, and, in the eyes of those *sub una*, such converts were ipso facto tainted morally or intellectually. The dubious charges from the Roman side, which ordinarily might be dismissed as self-serving, gained in credibility when reproduced, for reasons of their own, by Protestant and secular historians.[57] Finally, some of the disparaging characterizations of the Utraquists stemmed from the reports of papal nuncios, who from the vantage point of Italian cultural refinement marveled at the crude manners and behavior of the transalpine Central Europeans.[58]

As for the willingness of historians to accept at face value the slanderous assertions against the Utraquists, Kamil Krofta supplies an intriguing insight. He has traced the disparaging image to nineteenth-century historians—particularly Václav Tomek and Josef Kalousek—who mistakenly identified sixteenth-century Utraquism with Lutheranism and further assumed that Luther's solafideism fostered immorality.[59] This view passed through the prestigious work of the French historian of Bohemia, Ernst Denis, to Tomáš Masaryk and his interpretation of the "Czech question."[60]

On a theoretical level, recent research has questioned the identification of late Utraquism with Lutheranism, or the emergence of a syncretic religion, combining the two under the label of Neo-Utraquism. On a practical level, Utraquist theology and homiletics contradicted the charges of Utraquism's inherent immorality. If Luther indeed had taught his followers not to worry—because of Christ's redemptive sacrifice—about observing religious laws and commandments, the Utraquists to the contrary held the observance of "the law of God" among their highest priorities and looked askance at Lutheranism's denial of the soteriological value of works.[61] Far from indifference to moral values, examples of fervent exhortation to virtue and good works can be found in surviving homiliaries from each of the three centuries of Utraquist preaching.[62] Likewise, contrary to the Brethren's assertion, Utraquist priests held a particularly exalted view of their calling and duties.[63]

The Utraquists' intellectual openness or latitudinarianism, combined with liberal ecclesiology, was the mark of a crucial distinction from the posttridentine Roman Church, with its relatively closed intellectual world and institutional authoritarianism. It also tended to distance them further from the Lutheran and Calvinist denominations that evolved in the direction of increasing dogmatization as the process of confessionalization advanced during the sixteenth century.[64]

Universalism

A second important legacy of Utraquism to the modern political culture of Bohemia was its universalist aspiration. This statement may appear paradoxical in view of the strong national accent attributed to the Bohemian Reformation, especially during the fifteenth-century religious wars. The assumption of national exclusiveness led to Rome's misguided efforts to satisfy the Bohemians with an exceptional ecclesiastical status, by the Compactata at the Council of Basel (1434–36), and then through the grant of lay chalice for the Bohemians by Pope Pius IV (1564). These tactics of appeasement, however, failed because they ignored the basic fact that the Bohemians' goal was to reform the (Western) church as a whole, not to assert a peculiar set of ethnically grounded beliefs in isolation. This outlook would later be harmonized with the cosmopolitan character of the Austro-Bohemian Catholic Enlightenment and with the subsequent opposition in Bohemia to Herder's and Hegel's ontic cultural pluralism. In what follows, the Utraquists' universalism will be discussed in terms of their continued, albeit qualified, attachment to the Roman Church, as well as their relationship to other groups that sought to reform Western Christendom along the lines of liberal Catholicism.[65] The ambition to reform the Church of Rome has elicited the charges of sycophancy, idiosyncrasy, and megalomania against the Utraquists.

The Fallacy of a Uniate Solution

The chiliastic vision of the Bohemians as God's chosen people, reaching back to Hus's precursors, particularly Jan Milíč of Kroměříž and Matěj of Janov, gained currency during the wars of the Bohemian Reformation, particularly among the Taborites, who could view destruction as a new creation. After the calming of radical passions, the idea of an eschatological mission turned—in the Utraquists' agenda—into a moderate, yet firm, aspiration to serve as a model for a universal ecclesiastical reform.[66] Although not aspiring to establish the apocalyptic Kingdom of God on earth, the Utraquists remained convinced that their church had preserved, on behalf of all Western Christianity, the true traditional Catholic and apostolic faith against the deviations of the Roman Curia, which would eventually come around to the Utraquists' point of view.[67]

The Utraquists, therefore, never aimed at establishing a separate national church provided with special features. As a result, the Compactata were viewed not as a solution but as a step in the right direction. The ultimate goal was not limited even to transforming certain aspects of liturgy, such as instituting communion for infants and veneration of Jan Hus. It aimed more broadly at a recognition and *universal* adoption of the liberal Utraquist ecclesiology by Rome for the entire Western church. The Council of Basel's attempt to marginalize the Utraquists revealed an incompatibility with their universalist stance. Although the council was willing to offer communion *sub utraque* as a special privilege for the Bohemians, the Utraquists refused to reciprocate by recognizing the validity of lay communion *sub una* for the rest of the Western Church.

On theological grounds, therefore, the Utraquists reacted calmly to Pope Pius II's revocation of the Compactata. Their response, written by Martin Lupáč, argued that the abrogation was a loss for Rome and not for Utraquism, in line with the Utraquists' established position. Although recognizing the papacy as a guarantor of the apostolic succession for their priesthood, they held that on the issue of papal teaching authority the Scripture (that is, the law of God) stood above the pope's edicts in the cases of conflict.[68] Furthermore, despite the revocation of the Compactata, the Utraquist Church continued to maintain its sense of belonging to the universal or catholic (*obecná*) church. The insistence on this connection, as well as the endorsement of liberal ecclesiology with the reservations regarding the papacy, was reiterated by Administrator Václav Koranda the Younger, Rokycana's successor as the leading figure of Utraquism (1471–97).[69]

The mature position on the universalist aspirations of Utraquism was most clearly postulated by Bílejovský, in his *Kronika česká* (Bohemian chronicle) of 1537.[70] Despite his emphasis on the historical Bohemian roots of Utraquism, Bílejovský did not view his church simply as a national religion. Instead, he saw the Utraquist Church as a receptacle for, and guardian of, an uncorrupted Western Christianity, one that was endowed with a global mission. Above all, he saw the recovery of lay communion in both kinds as symptomatic of Utraquism's objective to inspire and lead Western Christendom back to the authentic forms of Christian faith and worship.[71] As a confirmation of the outward thrust, influences of the Bohemian Reformation were felt in neighboring lands like Poland and Hungary, and even Romania.[72] Likewise, Bílejovský's learned colleague Pavel Bydžovský illustrated a broad geographic vista when discussing the adoration of the host with his examples ranging from Bohemia to Italy, the Netherlands, and France.[73]

While not despairing of the rehabilitation of the Church of Rome in the future, for the time being Bílejovský openly invited the communicants *sub una* to join the Utraquists, independently of the Curia, assuring them that Utraquism, in fact, represented the uncorrupted form of Roman Christianity.[74] With a similarly proselytizing intent, Bydžovský sponsored and published German translations of sermons and other theological works by Utraquist classic writers, namely, Hus, Jakoubek, and Jan Příbram. There was, in fact, some evidence of German interest in Utraquism.[75]

The Question of Sycophancy

Just as the liberal ecclesiology of Utraquism has been criticized as a sign of moral corruption, so also has the universalist aspiration been widely misinterpreted. Standard historical literature has usually viewed the umbilical cord of canonical priesthood, which tied the Utraquists to the Roman Church, as an obstructing, and even shameful, liability.[76]

It has also regarded the Utraquist insistence on maintaining their conceptual belonging to the Roman Catholic Church as a rather demeaning enterprise.[77] Let us now review the entire issue of the awkward and unresolved ties between Utraquism and the Roman Curia, which reflected the universalist thrust of Bohemian reformism.

Contrary to conventional historiography, the Utraquists' insistence on forming an integral part of the Roman Catholic Church may be viewed as a mark of empowerment rather than liability.[78] While in the short run this link might have presented a dilemma, in the long run the claim to Roman Catholic identity signaled the transcendent scope of Utraquism's historical mission. It gave the church in Bohemia a standing, or an inside track, in seeking to reform the largest body in Western Christendom from within instead of attacking it from the outside. Unlike the (otherwise kindred) Church of England, which had for all practical purposes retreated into national isolation,[79] the Utraquist Church of Bohemia clung to its universal mission, of which the sacerdotal link with the Roman Church was a concrete practical sign. Lapsing into Hegelian terminology, we could say that staying within the Roman Church (and serving as its Socratic gadfly) endowed Utraquism with a world-historical role, which would be lost if it remained an isolated provincial movement or if it simply merged with mainstream Protestantism. It can also be argued that remaining attached to the Roman Church—rather than turning Protestant—served as a potentially useful function in the cosmic division of labor. After all, Rome was more in need of a liberal leavening than the reformed churches were, and thus the Utraquists avoided carrying coal to Newcastle, as the proverb goes.

Contrary to conventional historiography, the Utraquists did not approach Rome as humble beggars. From their own point of view, the heirs of Hus adopted the self-confident stance of the prophets of righteousness, whom God had commissioned to exhort the Roman Curia to recognize its failings and make amends. They did not plead with the Roman Church to admit them; rather, they challenged the Church to listen and respond constructively to what they considered a divinely sanctioned critique.[80] In their witness, the Utraquists saw themselves as a voice of conscience on behalf of the entire Western Christendom, representing a constant reproach to Rome for its errancy. The issue was not whether Rome was willing to readmit the Utraquists but whether the Roman Church was willing to reform according to the Utraquist ecclesiological prescriptions. Looking at the relationship in another way, the Utraquists did not accept that they were in schism from the true Christian church; they saw the schism on the part of the Roman Church, which had repudiated the Compactata in 1462.[81] To the Utraquists, Rome had not rehabilitated them by its approval of the Compactata, but by adopting the Compactata the Church of Rome might have been able to rehabilitate itself. As mentioned earlier, the Utraquists thought of themselves as exemplary Roman Catholics.[82]

The Question of Idiosyncrasy

Contrary to conventional historiography, the Utraquists' stand was neither idiosyncratic nor quixotic. In fact, they may be viewed as participants, albeit distinctive ones, in a more general phenomenon on a European scale, sometimes called humanist Catholicism, and associated especially with Desiderius Erasmus. Unlike the proponents of anathemas and exclusions who prevailed at the Council of Trent, these reformers were advocates of dialogue and liberal moderation as a path to renewal.[83] Let us now situate the Utraquists within the landscape of these antitridentine reformist trends in the Roman Catholicism of the sixteenth century.

To a considerable extent, the Utraquist stance paralleled the reforms that were proposed by Georg Witzel and endorsed by Ferdinand I and his son and successor, Maximillian II.[84] His proposed remaking of the Roman Church included a liberal ecclesiology (based on patristics and eschewing scholastic formulas), lay communion *sub utraque*, vernacular liturgy, and deemphasis on the veneration of saints.[85] More surprisingly, the Utraquist prescription was likewise akin to the liberal (or populist) ecclesiology of Thomas More, who—according to Brendan Bradshaw—also opposed "the institutionally oriented ecclesiology of late medieval clericalism," which would triumph at Trent.[86] Paradoxically, in view of subsequent developments, More had cautioned Henry VIII to be less emphatic in stressing papal primacy. Specifically, he did not consider the pope superior to the general council.[87] The views of More, and also his fellow martyr John Fisher, were influenced by the liberal ecclesiology of Erasmus.[88] Erasmus himself, of course, was the most conspicuous figure among the liberal advocates within the Roman Church whose impact radiated through a circle of correspondents, usually called the Erasmians.[89]

To the company of liberalization's later advocates, whose views were akin to the Utraquists, belonged the group of the Italian *spirituali*, including Cardinal Gasparo Contarini and the poet Vittoria Colonna, who hoped for a reform of the institutional church and grouped around Cardinal Reginald Pole during his exile in Italy.[90] There was also a group of Erasmus's followers in France, the so-called "critical Catholics," who, aside from rejecting the authoritarian ecclesiology of the Roman Curia, devised under the leadership of Bishop Monluc Utraquist-like reforms of the liturgy, including lay communion in both kinds and use of the vernacular in the mass.[91]

Far from being idiosyncratic, the Utraquists represented, above all numerically, the most significant group of participants within this welter of liberal, yet loyalist and orthodox, criticism of the Roman Church. Moreover, Utraquist authors were familiar with their liberal counterparts abroad. Utraquist Bohemia showed an active interest in Christian humanism, and the great vogue of Erasmus was reflected in the numerous editions of his works in Czech translation.[92] He also found correspondents in Bohemia. One of them, the humanist Jan Šlechta of Všehrdy, provided him with authentic information about the religious conditions in Bohemia, which Erasmus, in turn, shared with Thomas More.[93]

Other orthodox proponents of the Roman Church's renewal were known in Bohemia and could supply support and authentication for the Utraquist *via media*. For instance, in 1554, Bydžovský published a treatise in which he praised Witzel and exhorted any evangelicals or Lutherans (*Euangelicastros, intelligo Luteranos*) who might be in Bohemia to listen to Witzel's voice.[94] In the same pamphlet, Bydžovský included eulogies of More and Fisher as exemplary Christian martyrs. The Utraquist translator of Robert Barnes's *Vitae Romanorum Pontificum* (1535) and Bydžovský's contemporary, Šimon Ennius Klatovský, was likewise familiar with Witzel's irenic position. In addition, he expressed an admiration for More[95] and received support from another Erasmian, Friedrich Nausea, the bishop of Vienna.[96]

The Question of Megalomania

Even if from the viewpoint of *Realpolitik*—their mutual power relations—the confrontation of Rome by the Utraquists perhaps did not make much sense, it was nonetheless significant as a clash of ideas. Utraquism offered to the Roman Church an alternative model of reform to that which the Protestants embraced at Trent, and it was taken seriously by other proponents of such reforms. It was a service that an outright Protestant movement could not provide and, indeed, would not have cared to undertake, because of the Protestants' rejection of the institutional church as it had developed during the first millennium.

Among those for whom the experience with Utraquism provided a usable model for Rome's accommodation with the German Reformation, particularly notable was (once again) Erasmus, as well as his close Italian friend, Cardinal Jacopo Sadoleto. Erasmus emphasized a "Hussite" solution in his correspondence with Sadoleto in 1530.[97] Sadoleto eventually (after 1535) participated in the commission on church reform, headed by Cardinal Contarini, another Erasmian, which sought a modus vivendi with the Lutheran challenge on behalf of Rome.[98]

As a way of averting a disastrous confrontation, Erasmus wished to see Rome replicate the approach the Council of Basel had earlier taken toward Utraquism in its dealings with Lutheranism.[99] With much interest, he followed the negotiations with the Utraquists at Buda in the spring of 1525, conducted by his friend, Cardinal Lorenzo Campeggi, as a papal legate.[100] In addition to those who saw Utraquism as procedurally useful in finding a modus vivendi instead of a confrontation, others proposed using Utraquism substantively, leading to a lesser or greater degree of "Utraquistization" of the Roman Church. According to Peter Fraenkel, it was particularly Charles V who—with the advice of the Bishop of Augsburg, Christoph von Stadion—aimed at such a solution in 1531–32, including lay communion *sub utraque*, vernacular mass, married clergy, and a deemphasis, if not an outright abolition, of monasticism.[101] Similarly, Ferdinand I pressed in the same direction even at the time of the Council of Trent.[102] Nevertheless, during the course of the 1530s and 1540s, the Utraquist formula proved inadequate for a settlement between Rome and Wittenberg. As Fraenkel suggested, the Lutherans' differences from Rome were not only ecclesiological but also dogmatic.[103]

Ultimately, all the proponents of Roman renewal who preferred the scriptural theology illuminated by the insight of the Greek fathers were defeated at Trent, which rehabilitated the scholastic doctors and their authoritarian ecclesiology.[104] Instead of embracing the patristic ecclesiological tradition, Rome decided at the Council of Trent to perpetuate and reaffirm the unreconstructed model of the late medieval church.[105] Within the sixteenth-century context, the Roman Curia rejected the Utraquist model with its liberal ecclesiology and consensual governance, which offered a non-Protestant approach to renewal in line with similarly rejected ideas of humanist Catholicism, represented by figures such as Erasmus, More, and Witzel.

Plebeianism

A third major intellectual legacy of Utraquism to the nineteenth-century political culture of Bohemia was its plebeian character. The downgrading of social privilege was once more in harmony with the spirit of the Enlightenment and eventually with that of political liberalism. In Utraquist Bohemia, cultural and scholarly creativity was carried on by the townspeople, and its products reflected primarily their concerns and interests.[106] This section will also address the criticism of the culture of the Utraquist burghers for its alleged provincialism and low intellectual and artistic levels.

The character of Utraquism as a commoners' church fully crystallized during the religious discussions of 1575 around the so-called Bohemian Confession, which revealed the contrast between the quasi-democratic, plebeian culture of the townspeople and the culture of aristocratic privilege of the nobles. On one side stood the nobles with their Lutheran (and a few Calvinist) chaplains, the sectarians (mainly the Unity of Brethren), and the Lutherans of the German enclaves. On the other side stood the bulk of the Czech-speaking nation of Bohemia, which remained attached to Hus and to Utraquism, as defined in basic confessional documents from the Four Articles of Prague of 1419 to the Consistory's critique of the Bohemian Confession.[107]

Utraquism as a Plebeian Church

The religious division between the commoners and the nobles had historical and social roots reaching into the formative period of the Utraquist Church. Historically speaking, the Utraquist Church had maintained from the start a special relationship with the towns of Bohemia, particularly those of Prague.[108] Thus, already the original Four Articles of Prague of 1419, in a version cited by Vavřinec of Březová, were proclaimed: "We the mayor and the councillors and elders, as well as the entire community, of our capital city of the Kingdom of Bohemia, declare in our names and those of all the faithful in this kingdom. . . ."[109]

During the wars of the Bohemian Reformation, the towns of Prague held the top rank among the estates of the realm, followed by the barons, the Taborite community, and the knights, in that order. The political ascendancy of the towns was subsequently reflected in their participation in the parliamentary process when their estate joined the other two estates (those of the barons and the knights) as a third component of the Bohemian Diet. The one Utraquist king, George of Poděbrady, was crowned in 1458 at the city hall of the Old Town of Prague.[110] The Church of Our Lady before the Týn, the chief sanctuary of Utraquism (dubbed the "Utraquist Cathedral"), had traditionally been the principal church of the Prague townspeople since at least the turn of the thirteenth century. It is little wonder, therefore, that the city of Prague continued to play a special role as a champion of Utraquism and as a protector of the Consistory. The inhabitants of Prague and other towns strongly opposed the teaching of Luther as early as the 1520s, while the nobles wavered in their loyalty to Utraquism.[111]

The protectiveness of the Bohemian towns toward the Utraquist Church was reciprocated by the church's special concern for, and dedication to, the urban and other plebeian strata of society. This mutuality was rooted in Wyclif's teaching and in the early egalitarianism of the Bohemian Reformation, as among the radical Orebites. It contrasted not only with the predilection of Lutheranism and the Roman Church for the Bohemian nobility, both higher and lower, but also with the streak of social snobbery in the Unity of Brethren.[112] The respect for the religious convictions of, particularly, the rural population was guaranteed under the Peace of Kutná Hora, which safeguarded their denominational allegiance, even if it differed from that of their manorial masters.[113]

Reflecting the special concern of the Utraquist clergy for the commoners, Vavřinec Leander Rvačovský of Rvačov, in his famous *Masopust* (Mardi Gras) of 1580, clearly stressed the biblical injunctions concerning the dignity of the poor and ordinary people and ranked himself with the townsmen and the common people [*měšťané aneb lid obecní*] in relation to their feudal superiors [*vrchnosti*].[114] As if to underline further the plebeian character of his church, Jan Václav Cykáda, a member of the Utraquist Consistory (1605–1609), portrayed in his *Hody křesťanské* (Christian Feast Days) (1607) an antagonistic relationship between the Utraquist priests and the manorial lords.[115]

As a special bonus, the liberal ecclesiology of the Utraquists offered to the ordinary faithful the enjoyment of their favorite liturgies without the financial burden of supporting the luxuriant clerical and monastic apparatus or the threat of terrifying spiritual penalties that the Roman Church would impose.¹¹⁶ On the other side of the ledger, the Utraquists could avoid the discipline of catechization and ban on secular festivities customarily imposed by the Protestant Reformation.¹¹⁷ Thus it might be said that the Czech commoners had the best of all possible worlds.¹¹⁸

The Aversion of the Nobles to Utraquism

While the reasons for the special ties of the townspeople and other commoners to the Utraquist Church are clear, the more puzzling question is the strong attraction of Lutheranism for the Bohemian nobles. Part of the answer may be traced exactly to the symbiosis between the towns and Utraquism. Some of the nobles' low regard for the common man also affected their view of the Utraquist Church. The social standing of the Utraquist ecclesiastical leadership was not likely to impress the nobility. The Roman Church, particularly in the Counter-Reformation phase pioneered by the Jesuits in the mid-century, focused its interest on the aristocracy and gentry.¹¹⁹ While the Roman archbishops were usually drawn from aristocracy, the higher Utraquist clergy was generally of nonnoble origin. Moreover, the authority of the Utraquist ecclesiastics was based on theological learning and scholarship, not on political, diplomatic, or military skills that the nobles cherished and practiced.¹²⁰

The gradual increase in transnational loyalties and in the national heterogeneity of Bohemia's nobility also widened their social distance from the towns, which acted as guardians of local national traditions.¹²¹ An indication of the social distance was the nobles' apparent inability to deal courteously with the Utraquist authorities. Thus, in 1571 Maximilian II reprimanded the nobles for rudeness toward the Consistory.¹²² Several incidents from later periods are illustrative of the nobles' skewed interaction with the personnel of the Utraquist Church. In particular, there is on the record the uncivil treatment of Administrator Václav Dačický by the Chancellor Zdeněk of Lobkovice in 1604, when Dačický tried to object to the chancellor's describing his two daughters as "bastards" (*pankhartice*).¹²³

Part of the reason for the nobles' aversion to Utraquism lay in the *via media*, or the ecclesiological centrism. On the one hand, unlike the Roman Church, the Utraquist Church could not provide employment consistent with a noble status, inasmuch as it embraced the ideal of clerical poverty. None in its clerical establishment could expect to lead lives worthy of nobles, as the prelates of the Roman Church were able to do.[124] On the other hand, the Utraquist authorities and their priests were unsuited for the same degree of seigneurial domination as their Lutheran counterparts, inasmuch as they enjoyed the shield of a sacramental status, of the ecclesiastical rules of canon law, and of the constitutional guarantees of royal protection. Although the Utraquist Church had repudiated clerical pride and ostentation, it had preserved much of the aura of "sacredness" of the Roman Church.[125]

Lutheranism, to the contrary, vested ecclesiastical power in secular authorities, with Luther himself having demonstratively burned the book of canon law together with the papal bull of his excommunication in 1520.[126] Hence, the noble laymen came to enjoy a greater pliability and a wider scope for assertion in the ecclesiastical field. Thus, Vojtěch of Pernštejn (1532–61) aspired to become a lay bishop of a Moravian Lutheran Church. Similar ambitions for personal aggrandizement and ecclesiological inventiveness could not be accommodated in the traditionalist Utraquist Church.[127] In short, the aristocracy could neither use the Utraquist Church as a welfare safety net (for its junior members) nor treat its clergy as its feudal subjects.

In a prophetic way, Jan the Elder of Valdštejn saw the onset of an even more radical split between the Czech nobility and the rest of the Czech nation at the Bohemian Diet of 1575. Raising his solitary voice to warn his fellow aristocrats against embracing the Augsburg Confession, he argued that the hundreds of thousands of Bohemian Christians would not welcome a new and alien religion but would rather cling to the established religious order sanctified by an ancient tradition.[128]

The Ascendancy of the Towns in Culture

In the long run, the shift in religious orientations, made evident by the events of 1575, may be viewed as symptomatic of a more fundamental watershed in Czech history, namely, the passing of intellectual leadership from the nobility to the middle classes.[129] Subsequently, it would be difficult to find much of intellectual or inspirational value in the legacy of the various noble Lichtenštejns, Pernštejns, or Rožmberks or even in the literary production of a more attractive figure like Karel the Elder of Žerotín.[130] Most young nobles registered at universities abroad not to engage in scholarship but to acquire social contacts. Aside from a few exceptions, which seem to confirm the rule, literary or artistic creativity was relatively rare even among the members of the lower nobility.[131]

In comparison, the cultural legacy of the unpretentious public-spirited men and mild-mannered scholars of the towns was much more impressive and subject to subsequent emulation during the Czech national awakening. The urban creators of lasting intellectual values included the champions of Utraquism at the Diet of 1575, Sixt of Ottersdorf and Pavel Kristián of Koldín, and many others.[132] Starting in the late fifteenth century and extending throughout the rest of the Utraquist period, the urban middle classes established their leadership in the intellectual and literary life of the country.[133] The towns, especially Prague, had at their disposal—in their chancelleries, schools, and churches—more intellectuals, professionals, and experts in law and the several academic disciplines than even the wealthiest of nobles could assemble on their manors. The University of Prague was entirely in the service of the urban intellectual establishment.[134] Moreover, the critical mass of the urban intellectual potential was increasing as the sixteenth century progressed. Not only Prague but other Bohemian towns as well supported scholarship and historical writing.[135] Accordingly, in Rudolf II's reign, "it was easy to find in Czech towns burghers who could read Virgil, Ovid, Horace, even Homer, Anakreon, etc., and were themselves able to compose poems in Latin and Greek."[136] Their concern with political theory and political science is reflected, for instance, in their translations and editions of Jean Bodin, Georg Lauterbeck, and Hieronymus Weller.[137]

Vernacular Language

An important aspect of the plebeianism in the Utraquist age was the cultivation of the vernacular language. While the liberalism and universalism of the Utraquist century provided a supranational guide for the collective behavior, the Golden Age also offered an example for guarding the specificity of the national community. A culture should be universal or international in content, but national in form. To this effect, a recurrent theme in the literature of the sixteenth century was the praise for Czech language and the desideratum of using it as a literary medium. Unlike their *sub una* counterparts, who were interested mainly in aristocratic audiences, the Utraquist adherents to humanism frequently used the Czech language to maintain contact with the common people.[138]

The Utraquist Church typically favored the use of the Czech language. Administrator of the Consistory Václav Koranda the Younger devoted an entire section of his major treatise of 1493 to liturgy in Czech. Early in the sixteenth century, the Utraquist priest Jan Bechyňka urged parents to lead children to know and love their native tongue and to avoid communicating in an alien speech.[139] In his *Bohemian Chronicle*, Bílejovský argued strenuously against the Church of Rome's opposition to the vernacular, referring to a long tradition of liturgy allegedly sung in Czech since the beginning of Christianity until the reign of Emperor Charles IV (1346–78).[140]

Later in the century, the clamor for the rights of the Czech language intensified.[141] Adam of Veleslavín argued the case with particular force in his preface to Eusebius of Caesarea's *Historie církevní* (Ecclesiastical History). Noting the use of Czech language in the official record keeping in Bohemia, Adam praised the edict of Charles IV, ordering the inhabitants of Prague to teach their children Czech and conduct municipal affairs in that language. He also referred to Hus's admonition to the Czechs to preserve their language.[142] The Utraquist clergy's concern with religious books in Czech for the use of the common people (*lidé prostější*) was illustrated by Cykáda's plea in the introduction to his *Hody křestanské* (Christian Feast Days) (1607).[143]

The actual liturgical use of the vernacular by the Utraquist Church had a rather checkered history. In the early phase of the Bohemian Reformation in the fifteenth century, Czech penetrated into various sections of the mass.[144] An intermediate resurgence of liturgical Latin in the early sixteenth century, temporarily reversing the trend, was probably due to the infatuation with the classical languages aroused by the humanist vogue in Bohemia's educational system from the University of Prague down to the local grammar schools. At last, by the later sixteenth century Czech had surpassed Latin in Utraquist liturgical texts.[145]

The Question of Aesthetics

A major reason for neglecting the legacy of Utraquism and the Golden Age was the opinion of modernist aesthetes of the late nineteenth and twentieth centuries, who—disregarding didactic political, legal, and social values—looked askance at the intellectual heritage for its alleged lack of literary sophistication and rejected the reverence shown to it by the national awakeners in the late eighteenth century.[146] Arne Novák, in his influential history of Czech literature, trivialized the worth of the sixteenth-century writings thus: "The real Renaissance spirit rarely penetrates this literature; mere practical considerations prevail. There are very few works reflecting the creative poetic gifts of observation, imagination, or expression." He preferred the aesthetic qualities of the baroque culture during the Counter-Reformation.[147] René Wellek also entertained a dim view of the humanist period in Czech literature, considering it imitative of Latin models and thus unoriginal.[148]

From a somewhat different angle, the historian Josef Pekař joined the ranks of the critics when he saw the cultural thrust of the Bohemian Reformation forsaking the high level of the Romance-Catholic culture for the much lower Germanic-Protestant one. According to this view, the achievements of fourteenth-century Bohemia were much higher than those of the subsequent two centuries.[149] Curiously, the disdainful attitude toward the literature of the Utraquist era—evidently for its "bourgeois" setting—found an echo in Czech historical writing of the Marxist period.[150]

Yet, voices to the contrary—although apparently less influential—were not entirely silenced. Krofta, albeit Pekař's disciple, was convinced that the image of shallowness and poverty of sixteenth-century culture, which "has been taught and believed," was entirely mistaken, stating,

> I have studied the fruits of this culture from various aspects ... and I am convinced that it is the peak of our cultural development, that at that time we, as a nation, lived the fullest and richest life ... and that this period is to us today intrinsically much closer than what preceded and what followed.... and I am firmly convinced ... that this will be generally recognized, once these matters become better known.[151]

While the aesthetes and some others decried the low level of Czech *belles lettres,* defenders called attention to the Europe-wide contribution of scientific and sociopolitical literature, inspired by the humanist and humanitarian spirit in Bohemia. There were even those brave souls who took up the cudgels for a respectable aesthetic status of *belles lettres* in the Utraquist age. Thus, Jaroslav Kolár has argued that the Bohemians had virtually come to terms with the most advanced currents of contemporary Europe in the fifteenth and sixteenth centuries, citing as an example "the fruitful encounter of Czech literature with the work of Giovanni Boccacio."[152]

The Question of Provincialism

Another reason for deprecating the intellectual and cultural heritage of the Utraquist era was the *a priori* assumption of a cultural isolation and consequent mediocrity of Bohemia, following the wars of the Bohemian Reformation.[153] Actually, the sixteenth-century Utraquist culture, like the culture of the national awakening, although couched in the vernacular idiom, was open to outside influences, was tolerant of intellectual diversity, and pursued universal, not provincial, ideals. Bohemian Utraquism did not adopt a position of religious exclusivity, a retreat into a ghetto.

Bohemian scholars and intellectuals maintained lively contacts throughout Europe. Erasmus, whose contacts with Bohemia were mentioned earlier, listed the country among the few lands where the humanities were valued and flourished.[154] The breadth of cultural horizons was exemplified by the Utraquist author Řehoř Hrubý of Jelení, who translated Erasmus's works as well as those of Petrarch and the Greek fathers.[155] Two erudite Utraquist ecclesiastics, Jan Hortensius Zahrádka and Jindřich Dvorský z Helfenberka, each of whom held the top office in the Utraquist Church as administrator (respectively in 1541 and 1572–81), enjoyed high international reputation. Hortensius, a prominent mathematician, also won fame as a specialist on St. Paul's epistles. Dvorský had entered into scholarly communication in the early 1540s with no less a figure than the "praeceptor Germaniae," Philipp Melanchton, on the classics of antiquity.[156] During the opening years of the seventeenth century, Martin Bacháček, astronomer and rector of the University of Prague, was a respected colleague of such luminaries as Johannes Kepler and Tycho de Brahe. In their work, both Brahe and Kepler used astronomical observations made earlier in Prague by Šimon Proxen of Sudety, Cyprian Lvovský, and Tadeáš of Hájek.[157]

The breadth of vision was not limited to a few top intellectuals; it applied also to the rank-and-file levels. Utraquism's status as a religion of the commoners did not involve a decline of standards to the primitive level of unsophisticated folkish religions, usually associated with the Waldensian or Lollard ministers. Utraquist ecclesiastics remained loyal to the roots of the Bohemian Reformation, which were firmly planted in the academy. Their publications show these men to be learned, theologically sophisticated, and academically minded scholars who continued to infuse Utraquism with a spirit of reasonableness. Their engagement with the patristic and scholastic writers was based not on mere citations from compendiums of excerpts (florilegia) but on creative intellectual engagement with their text. Thus, for instance, the Second Book of Bílejovský's *Bohemian Chronicle* indicates theological erudition documented by sixty-eight references to the opinions of at least twenty-four fathers and doctors of the church, and other distinguished theologians.[158] Bílejovský's colleague, Bydžovský, demonstrated a substantial command of patristic literature (both Greek and Latin), the medieval doctors of the church, decrees of both ancient and medieval church councils, provisions of canon law (specifically the Decretum of Gratian), and the classics of Utraquism, as well as Luther's and Melanchton's doctrines.[159] The tradition of learned clergy continued into the early decades of the seventeenth century. Pačuda, in his *Spis v němž se obsahuje* (Treatise . . . on Events Preceding the Advent of Christ) of 1616, not only cited profusely from the fathers and doctors of the church but also displayed a working knowledge of Latin and Greek classical authors, such as Homer, Herodotus, Euripides, Plutarch, and Plautus.[160]

The Utraquist University of Prague, despite the common decline of universities in Central Europe in the fifteenth and sixteenth centuries, maintained an effective network of secondary schools in the towns of Bohemia, culminating during the rectorate of Martin Bacháček.[161] No less a figure than Kepler expressed his admiration for this institution of learning. Moreover, as a result of the symbiosis between the university and the urban milieu, the scope of educated townsmen's intellectual interest reached beyond practical knowledge of law, medicine, and technology to the sphere of pure science and scholarship in philosophy, classics, theology, linguistics, and history.[162]

The Plebeian Legacy of Utraquism

In greater historical perspective, the cultural achievements of Bohemia's commoners helped compensate for the political and military shortcomings of the Bohemian nobility. The mismanagement of the Bohemian uprising (1618–20) demonstrated further the dysfunctional character of the Bohemian nobility by revealing its incompetence in the direction of both diplomatic and military affairs.[163] The nobles' failure, which led to the disappearance of the Bohemian sovereign state and the suppression of its political culture in the aftermath of the Battle of White Mountain in 1620,[164] did not destroy the intellectual and cultural legacy of the Utraquist sixteenth century or the Golden Age. After the hiatus of the Counter-Reformation, the Golden Age revived in harmony with the ensuing era of the Enlightenment of the late eighteenth century. Its endorsement of unshackled learning, tolerance, and attachment to the society of commoners—in contrast to the baroque intolerance, militancy, and aristocratism—essentially provided the ingredients, in a symbiosis with the Enlightenment, for the formation of the nineteenth-century political culture in Bohemia. Hence, the wisdom embodied in the literary legacy of the urban statesmen and searchers after truth had not perished but in a reborn state helped provide the guidelines for further political and cultural development.

3

The Counter-Reformation and the Catholic Enlightenment: An Acute Antithesis

As noted earlier, the relationship between modern Czech political culture, which emerged in the nineteenth century, and the Bohemian Reformation of the fifteenth and sixteenth centuries has constituted a perennial problem in Czech historiography. The intermezzo of the 1622–1781 Counter-Reformation posed an additional complication. The historiographic discussions led to interpretations of continuity or discontinuity in the national development, which was often viewed as a metahistorical process with the nation figuring as a real entity.[1] Such hypostatizing notions have been deconstructed and discounted by recent theoreticians of nationalism like Ernest Gellner and Eric J. Hobsbawm, who see nationalism as a nineteenth-century "invention."[2] This study aims at reconsidering the transmission of national self-identification from a distant past by adopting a fresh approach, which is free of the "Romantic" or "metaphysical" view of nationality.[3] The continuity, or discontinuity, is not treated as a metahistorical process but as a mundane transmission of texts, which is empirically verifiable. The narrative is based not on the assumption of a national essence or a primordial national character but simply on an empirical tracking of the suppression and reemergence of written texts. It eschews reification or hypostatization of abstract notions. Perhaps the one overarching connection was the impact of the Gutenberg revolution, which released the power of the printed word, the effectiveness of which spans centuries.[4] With respect to recent Czech historiography, the interpretation offered in this study is countercyclical. From the 1990s on, the prevalent tendency has been to integrate the Counter-Reformation as a positively constructive element into the virtually seamless web of cultural development.[5] This study tends to support the opposite view—that the Counter-Reformation interrupted an intellectual elite in its search for universal liberal propositions and institutions. Another group of intellectual pacesetters could deliberately resume this search once that blockage was lifted.

To substantiate the claim that there was a transmission of political and cultural values over a gap of almost two centuries from the Bohemian Reformation to the national revival, we must consider the mechanism of this transfer, namely, through the reprinting of sixteenth-century classics, the reproduction of the sixteenth-century writings in school and university textbooks, the celebration of the Bohemian Reformation in history and literature, and the embrace of the historical rights of the pre-1620 Bohemian state as a political program. The impact of sixteenth-century writings was even more significant at the beginning of the nineteenth century than in its own time because of modern literacy rates, and the lower cost of printing that made literature more accessible. To illuminate the process of transfer, we may find it helpful to refer to R. G. Collingwood's "theory of reenactment." The British historian and philosopher has argued that in reading sources of the past the reader literally thinks the very thoughts of the writer.[6] The reenactment, according to Collingwood, brings the past to actuality in the present, and by being reenactable, the past "is not something that has finished happening." In other words, past thought becomes alive in the present.[7] Within the context of the Czech national awakening, that concept would mean that the intellectual paradigms and value systems of the sixteenth-century authors could have reemerged in the minds of the nineteenth-century Awakeners.

Within the historiographical and methodological characteristics just discussed, this study aims at demonstrating a link between the Bohemian Reformation and the Czech national awakening after a major disruption caused by the Counter-Reformation. Like the Italian humanists in the fifteenth century, the Czech awakeners at the turn of the eighteenth century felt that a cultural revival had to be based on the achievements of an earlier age. The Italians looked back to Greco-Roman antiquity for intellectual inspiration; the Bohemians looked to the Golden Age of the sixteenth century, which was religiously nurtured by the Utraquist Church, deriving from the Bohemian Reformation. The Italians were inspired by the influx of Greek books after the fall of Constantinople, while the Bohemians rediscovered Utraquist books from the hitherto closed collections after the fall of the Jesuit Order in 1773, when Pope Clement XIV—mainly under pressure of the Bourbon monarchs—paradoxically dissolved one of the pillars of Tridentine Catholicism.[8]

The revival process linked with the Bohemian Reformation, however, resulted in a paradox: the Czech national awakening resurrected the Utraquist sixteenth century in its civic culture but without its religious dimension. The world that the Bohemian Reformation had created was revived as a secular order, not as a theological system. Two factors help clarify this oddity. First, the Counter-Reformation and the Reformation alike worked, albeit from opposite directions, to destroy the credibility and authenticity of a Christian *via media*, which Utraquism theologically represented. For the Counter-Reformation, the mainline Bohemian religion had a deficiency of traditional orthodoxy; for the Evangelical and the Reformed, it had an excess. Second, initially the Josephist Reform Catholicism, in the name of which the Counter-Reformation was overthrown in Bohemia, held out a promise for the revival of Utraquism or something like Utraquism, both being subspecies of liberal Catholicism.[9] The retridentization of the Roman Church, starting in 1800 and moving full speed ahead (or perhaps backwards) after 1848 toward the authoritarian model, removed the possibility that the Austrian renewal of Catholicism might provide a surrogate institutional basis for the reemergence of theological Utraquism, or quasi-Utraquism.[10]

This chapter will examine three principal elements of the conflict between the Counter-Reformation and the Catholic Enlightenment, with a focus on Bohemia: (1) the character and the infrastructure of the cultural revolution brought on by the Josephist Enlightenment; (2) the rejection of the previous culture of the Counter-Reformation by the Bohemian Awakeners; and (3) the nature of the new religious outlook that emerged from the clash between the Josephist Enlightenment and the Counter-Reformation as a form of liberal Catholicism.

The Cultural Revolution

The onset of the cultural revolution of the Austro-Bohemian Catholic Enlightenment, which replaced the rigidity of the Counter-Reformation in the Habsburg monarchy with the more liberal Reform Catholicism of Joseph II, was dramatically signaled by the dissolution of the Jesuit Order. The transition to a new intellectual climate was prepared under

Joseph's mother and precursor, Maria Theresa (1740–80), by a group of advisers known as the "Greats of Vienna" (die *Grossen in Wien* or *Grossen der Erde*) and included the empress's physician Gerhard van Swieten, her confessor Ignaz Müller, Auxiliary Bishop of Vienna Ambros Simon Stock, and the jurist Karl Anton Martini.[11] The repudiation of tridentine Catholicism was symbolized by a statement of Wenzl A. Kaunitz, the leading ideologue of what became known as Josephism. In a ruling of June 21, 1773, he agreed with barring the Jesuits' system of teaching because, in particular, history had to be taught "purely from genuine sources and without ideological prejudice."[12]

The intellectual mainspring of the Austro-Bohemian Enlightenment was Catholic rather than Protestant.[13] An important ingredient was Jansenism, emanating from the Austrian Netherlands since the first half of the eighteenth century.[14] Another input was the early Italian Enlightenment, represented particularly by the theologian Lodovico Antonio Muratori through his writings of the 1730s and 1740s. A translation of his famous *Della regolata divozione d'Cristiani* appeared not only in a German translation in Vienna in 1762 but also in a Czech version in Prague in 1778. It launched a vehement attack against the ritualism of baroque religious devotions.[15] A treatise by Jacques Bossuet, the famous French bishop considered friendly to the Jansenists, appeared in Czech in Prague also in 1778. The Jansenist objection to ultramontanism was seconded by an influential treatise *De statu ecclesiae et legitima potestate Romani Pontificis* (1763). Under the pseudonym of Justus Febronius, the author, Johann N. von Hontheim, Bishop of Trier, argued that the pope lacked power in secular affairs and that the general church councils circumscribed his authority in ecclesiastical matters. Thanks to the efforts of Gerhard van Swieten, Hontheim's treatise was published in 1779 in Vienna and other cities of the Habsburg Empire.[16]

The revolution was consummated by the entourage of Joseph II, which included statesmen Josef A. Riegger and Kaunitz, and university professors Paul J. Riegger, Josef V. Eybel, Karl A. Martini, and Josef Sonnensfels. An important aspect that symbolized the Catholic slant of the Austro-Bohemian Enlightenment was the prominent role of high ecclesiastics such as Bishop Jan Leopold Hay of Hradec Králové and Abbots Franz S. Rautenstrauch and Otto Steinbach of Kranichstein.[17] After the abolition of the Jesuit Order, Rautenstrauch was put in charge of reforming the curricula of seminaries and theological faculties in the

Habsburg Empire. Josef Dobrovský was among the first beneficiaries of the reforms when he studied at the University of Prague from 1773 to 1777.[18]

The new academic establishment was staffed in part by foreigners and in part by adaptable scholars from the abolished religious orders. An exemplary exponent of free scholarship was Kašpar Royko (a Slovene born near Maribor), who was appointed professor of church history in Graz in 1774 and then in Prague in 1782.[19] The dedicated and energetic reformers included a considerable number of former Jesuits and Jesuits' disciples who turned away from the Counter-Reformation to embrace Josephist Reform Catholicism. The former category included Dobrovský, Johann Heinrich Wolf, František Pubička, and Stanislav Vydra; the latter included František M. Pelcl, Václav Matěj Kramerius, Václav Stach, and Jan Jeník of Bratřice.[20]

Institutions of higher learning, especially those for the training of clergy, were henceforth to serve the new cultural revolution and diffuse the ideas of the Catholic Enlightenment. Like the universities and seminaries, some were restaffed and transformed. Diocesan and monastic seminaries were replaced by "general seminaries," one in each province (*Land*) of the empire, and supervised not by the ecclesiastical hierarchy but by the imperial government.[21] Augustin Zippe, who served as the rector of the general seminary in Prague (1783–85), was elevated by Joseph II to the position of the director of theological studies in Vienna after Rautenstrauch's death in 1785. His secular counterpart was Franz K. Kresl of Qualtenberg (1720–1801) as head of the Court Educational Commission in Vienna. Dobrovský directed the reformed Catholic seminary in Olomouc, first as a vice-rector (from August 1787) and then as rector (from August 1789 to July 1790), and in that capacity he was under direct supervision of Emperor Joseph, who viewed the general seminaries as a prime instrument of ecclesiastical reform.[22]

Still other institutions were newly established, like the learned societies modeled on the examples of France and Britain, which were to disseminate the new philosophical and cultural outlook. New publication programs were encouraged, whose purpose was to promote an openness in philosophy, religion, and history through textbooks for secondary and university students, as well as through books for the general public.[23] The most prominent among these institutions was the Bohemian Learned Society, established in 1784, in which Dobrovský again was one of the leading lights. The participants in the promotion of the Josephist Enlightenment had a sense of solidarity and group loyalty in their common endeavor.²⁴

As the chief promoter and protector of the cultural revolution that ushered in the Catholic Enlightenment, Emperor Joseph II enjoyed a high respect, indeed affection, among the Bohemian national awakeners.²⁵ The latter were thus willing to minimize the Germanizing impact of the Josephist regime. In the preface to his two-volume *Básně v řeči vázané* (Poems in Verse) (1785), Václav Thám called the emperor "a special and ardent lover of the language of his Czech people." The Bohemians should be grateful to him for helping preserve the Czech language, when in 1781 he ordered that all books in Bohemia—hitherto prohibited by the Counter-Reformation—were to be gathered in the state library in Prague.²⁶ Karel Ignác Thám in his *Kurzgefasste böhmische Sprachlehre* (Brief Textbook of Czech) (1785) and again in his *Deutsch-böhmisches Nationallexikon* (German-Czech Dictionary) (1788) also lauded Joseph II for introducing the study of Czech into several institutions of higher learning in the Habsburg monarchy. He noted that Rautenstrauch, one of the chief executors of Joseph's educational policy, prescribed the teaching of pastoral theology in Czech in the seminaries.²⁷ In addition, in his *Über den Karakter der Slawen* (On the Character of the Slavs) (1803), Karel Ignác Thám emphasized the emperor's interest in the Czech-language theater in Prague in 1786. Jan Jeník of Bratřice claimed that the emperor would have saved the symbolically charged Bethlehem Chapel in Prague (where Hus had preached), had he known of the plans to destroy it in 1786.²⁸

In a more general way, Václav Thám eulogized Joseph II as a hero who was determined to root out all that interfered with learning and that spread ignorance in his lands. The emperor was on the way to gaining immortality in the hearts of the Bohemians.²⁹ Johann H. Wolf, professor of history at the University of Prague, acclaimed Joseph's grant of the freedom of the press, which permitted any publications except those attacking religion, the state, or good morals. He also credited the emperor with endorsing measures consonant with the early stages of the Bohemian Reformation, such as an unfettered reading of the Bible and limitations on papal judicial and administrative power.³⁰ Karel R. Ungar praised Joseph for ending the suppression of literature in the Czech language and suppressing instead the Index of Prohibited Books.³¹ Augustin Zitte—under the pseudonym F. A. Zieger—was the probable author of *Das Buch Joseph* (Book of Joseph), which endorsed and sought to justify on theological grounds Joseph II's religious reforms.[32] Pelcl declared that the inhabitants of Bohemia and other Hereditary Lands would forever bless the memory of the emperor, who terminated the state of religious oppression.[33] Kašpar Royko similarly lauded Joseph's benevolence and added that "thereby many millions of people will become enlightened and the enlightened nations will happily rejoice."[34] Moreover, according to Royko, the religious toleration that Joseph had introduced would prevent victimization of virtuous men by selfish bishops and perverse monks in the future. He referred to the emperor as a patient and kind father of his peoples.[35]

Leapfrogging the Counter-Reformation

Before examining the mechanism of the cultural transmission in Bohemia from the sixteenth to the eighteenth century, we should address two main reasons for the cultural return to the past. One was a negative one, the aversion to the Counter-Reformation; the other positive, the attraction of the Bohemian Reformation's legacy. This chapter discusses the negative perception that the imposed literature of the Counter-Reformation was irrelevant in the era of the Enlightenment. The positive appeal of the Utraquist culture of the Golden Age is treated in chapter 4.

In summing up the Bohemian awakeners' condemnation of the legacy of the Counter-Reformation, Robert Pysent has observed that they dismissed "almost all of Czech literature, except for a few historiographical and émigré works, between 1620 and the last decades of the eighteenth century."[36] One of the important organs of the cultural revolution, *Prager Gelehrte Nachrichten* (Prague Learned Reports), already in the 1770s connected the Counter-Reformation with what they called derogatorily "scholasticism" and other medieval "superstitions," as well as with the fanaticism of the Jesuits. This herald of the Enlightenment proclaimed an adherence to the contrary principles of free press, free scientific investigation, and religious tolerance.[37] The dim view of the Counter-Reformation was shared by both the clerical and the lay champions of Josephist Enlightenment in Bohemia.

If we start with Dobrovský, the outstanding figure of the Catholic Enlightenment, we note that for him the Counter-Reformation brought about a steep decline in the state of the Czech language and imposed a medieval-like intellectual darkness in Bohemia. In the literature of the Counter-Reformation, he saw an instrument of obscurantism and superstition. According to him, "The Battle of White Mountain in 1620 crippled and enfeebled the entire Bohemian nation in both body and soul."[38] This was his assessment in 1791 of the Counter-Reformation's intellectual heritage: "The heresy hunters . . . tried for so many years, albeit in vain, to suppress the sound human reason in Bohemia. They wanted to compensate for the damage wrought by allowing the publication and distribution of a few dozen booklets about miraculous sacred images. Nevertheless, the larger part of the people did not find them to their taste."[39] Dobrovský's colleague František Faustin Procházka joined him in condemning the literary products of the Counter-Reformation as "monkish superstitions," "stupidities," and "idiocies."[40] Elsewhere, Procházka referred to the imprisonment of human reason in a "dark cell" during the period of religious intolerance.[41]

Among other clerical promoters of the Josephist Enlightenment, Augustin Zitte claimed that during the Counter-Reformation, volumes of Czech-language books "languished in chains" in Jesuit libraries.[42] Already in the late sixteenth century, Abbot Otto Steinbach of Kranichstein saw the Jesuits, especially those of Spanish background, as inciting hatred against the Lutherans and the Unity of Brethren, particularly in Moravia.[43] He condemned even more harshly the imposition of religious uniformity after the Battle of White Mountain, which led to forcible conversions and expulsions of nonconformists. Steinbach assigned a particularly sinister role in the suppression of religious freedom to two Spanish generals in the imperial service, Don Martin von Huerda and Don Balthasar. According to him, the religious intolerance instituted a reign of terror in Bohemia for over a century and a half, during which the remaining nonconformists had to live in fear of their lives and hide their religious books from the emissaries of the official church.[44]

Likewise, Kašpar Royko harshly criticized the Jesuits and the Counter-Reformation regime, the mainstays of which were "excommunication, Inquisition and the Index."[45] Many of the anathemas issued by the Council of Trent had the flimsy basis of "Verbo Dei . . . non scripto" (unwritten word of God). As for specific examples of outrages, Royko referred to the bloody proceedings in England during the reign of Queen Mary (1553–58) and the cruelties of the Duke of Alba in the Netherlands (1566–73).[46] Johann H. Wolf in his *Geschichte des König-*

reichs Böheim (History of the Kingdom of Bohemia) (1783) accused the Jesuits of destroying the earlier flourishing Bohemian classical tradition by eliminating the teaching of Greek and introducing their own inferior Latin during the Counter-Reformation. Thus the whole country sank into a "barbaric" condition (*Barbarei*).[47] Elsewhere, he charged that the Jesuits had arbitrarily confiscated and destroyed Czech-language books, considering them indiscriminately heretical. According to Wolf, the Counter-Reformation proscribed reading of the Bible and introduced inquisitorial practices that he labeled as "an invention of the devil."[48]

Among the lay champions of Josephist Enlightenment, Karel Ignác Thám, in his *Kurzgefasste böhmische Sprachlehre* (1785), denounced the Counter-Reformation for the innumerable Bohemian books that the "simple-mindedness and fanaticism" (*Einfalt und Schwärmerei*) had committed to the flames.[49] In his *Über den Karakter der Slawen* (1803), he noted that all Bohemian books written between 1414 and 1635 were suspected of containing heretical ideas and largely subject to destruction by Jesuit missionaries during the ensuing Counter-Reformation.[50] Karel's bother, Václav Thám, in the preface to the two volumes of his *Básně v řeči vázané* (1785), had accused the Counter-Reformation of cultivating superstition and demeaning devotionalism in contrast to the learning and understanding of the Utraquist era.[51] As a result, the memory of the high achievements of the past was suppressed, and the Bohemians were kept in a state of ignorance. The priestly "monster" (*stvůra*) had placed on the Index of Prohibited Books the whole gallery of prominent sixteenth-century writers.[52] Having burned or censored the best work of the Bohemians past, the ecclesiastical cultural apparatus, according to Thám, turned to a corruption of the Czech tongue. The earlier noble and expressive language was denounced as "Hussite"—an expression glorious to the Bohemians but abominable to the ecclesiastical censors. In Thám's opinion, these misguided clerical dictators disfigured the revered tongue "by transforming it into their own Jesuitical language, one that was ignoble and interlaced with awkward expressions."[53] Toward the end of his preface Thám responded to those who fought a rearguard battle to preserve the system of thought control and wallowed "in the darkness of insane ignorance" (*ve tmách šílené nevědomosti*). These benighted individuals opposed reading imported books, considering them heretical; yet such literature, according to Thám, contained immeasurably more sound reason and wise judgment than all their "monkish trifles, confused, mixed up and interlaced with hypocritical pieties."[54]

Pelcl expressed his contempt for the Counter-Reformation culture, asking rhetorically, "And what kind of learning could one expect from a teacher in the dingy monastery, where prejudice, simony, hypocrisy, frauds and the highest degree of ignorance prevailed?"[55] Even more gruesomely, he claimed that Jesuit missions, preaching on the horrors of purgatory, were likely to leave three or four individuals insane—out of dread of eternal punishment—in any given locality. Pelcl attributed specifically to Antonín Koniáš (1691–1760), a Jesuit missionary, the ability to drive weak individuals to insanity, through graphic description of the horrors of purgatory and inferno.[56] He deplored the hunt for and destruction of old books in Czech, describing the process and its consequences in the following way:

> Old Czech publications were taken away and burned, whereby the missionaries caused more damage to literature than, if the land had been for many years devastated by the Tartars or other barbarians .... Disguised, they would often intrude on the townsmen and peasants, and search every corner in their homes. Their exertions caused many thousands of people to be cast into misfortune, and innumerable volumes were burned.[57]

According to Pelcl—aside from Koniáš—another famous member of the Jesuit Order, Matěj V. Šteyer (1630–92), tore thousands of books out of the hands of their helpless owners.[58]

At the turn of the century, František X. Němeček in his extensive excoriation of the Counter-Reformation spoke of the saddest period of "cultural deprivation" (*Kulturabnahme*).[59] Bohemia's flourishing conditions of the sixteenth century terminated in the disastrous regime change (*"unter den Flammen der böhmischen Staatsumwälzung"*) during the Thirty Years' War. There was a decline in learning, speech, morals, well-being, and population; and history (as a record of significant achievements) virtually ceased in Bohemia. Instead of an active intellectual life, ignorance and pedantry prevailed: the Jesuit-dominated educational system idealized tastelessly florid rhetoric without significant underlying thought. The network of outstanding secondary schools erected in the sixteenth century disappeared, and the few existing Latin schools focused on the rudiments of Latin and theology, as preparation for monastic service.[60] The zeal of religious intolerance inspired missionaries, who, operating in every region of the country, entered private homes and confiscated books suspected of dissident views or those written by Utraquists. Thus, the most valuable and substantive literature in Czech disappeared or became extremely rare, and this inquisitorial process further contributed to the decline of the Czech language and literature. For Němeček, the cultural degradation wrought by the Counter-Reformation had not spared music, which, although required for liturgical purposes, was pursued mechanically, without feeling or genuine inspiration.[61]

In the younger generation, Kramerius used particularly strong language in the preface to his translation of Josef Valentin Eybel's *Christkatholische nützliche Hauspostille*, in which he counseled guarding against products of the baroque literature of the Counter-Reformation, such as certain lives of saints, which were like "an infectious wound" or "a poison stealthily consuming the human brain."[62] Jeník of Bratřice, educated by the Jesuits in Prague in the 1760s, agreed that the Jesuits' objective was to keep people in ignorance, deplored their suppression of allegedly heretical books, and labeled the whole period of their ascendancy from Ferdinand II to Maria Theresa as one of tyranny, lifted only by Joseph II.[63] Furthermore, Jeník ridiculed the legends of saints, which were read to the students at meals in the Jesuit College. He claimed that this early education almost deprived him of common sense in his tender years; in particular, the youngsters in the Jesuit College were traumatized by graphic descriptions of eternal punishments after death.[64]

Subsequently, František L. Čelakovský blamed the harshness of the Jesuits for the cultural disaster following the Battle of White Mountain.[65] Jungmann, who shared in the admiration for the Golden Age of the sixteenth century, deplored the era of the Counter-Reformation, noting in no uncertain terms that "the Bohemian nation excelled all other Europeans in the arts during the beautiful age when it defied the papacy; it never sank so low as when Jesuitism scored a victory over it."[66] In 1823, young František Palacký added his condemnation of the cultural policy of the Jesuits. At the onset of the Counter-Reformation, the Jesuits hated Czech national literature as an instrument of inimical policy and consigned books massively to the *auto da fé*.[67] In 1831, Palacký characterized the post-1620 period with equal harshness as "the saddest in Czech language and literature" when "the nation so quickly sank from remarkable cultural heights into lowest barbarism."[68]

Catholic Enlightenment

Although adamantly opposed to the Counter-Reformation spirit and procedures growing out of the tridentine tradition, the Austro-Bohemian Enlightenment remained Catholic.[69] Its Reform Catholicism proceeded not only from the state officialdom of the Habsburg Monarchy but also from ecclesiastical figures who were genuinely convinced about the necessity to move beyond the outdated Catholicism of the baroque era to save the monarchy from an irretrievable intellectual retardation. Some were already mentioned among the "Greats of Vienna." Others included the Archbishop of Salzburg Jerome Count Colloredo and the Bishop of Ljubljana (Laibach) Johann Karl Count Herberstein, who actively promoted the new religious agenda, especially after 1780. An early harbinger of the reformist tendency within the ecclesiastical hierarchy of the monarchy was the Archbishop of Vienna Johann Count Trautson, who intimated the new approach in a pastoral letter of 1752.[70]

Among the most conspicuous characteristics of Josephist Reform Catholicism belonged a strong aversion to asceticism and intolerance. The skeptical stance toward asceticism in particular covered priestly celibacy, monasticism, and quasi-mystical devotional exercises.[71] From the governmental side, asceticism and celibacy were sharply criticized by Kaunitz and his right-hand man for Bohemian religious affairs, Franz J. Heinke.[72] From the ecclesiastical side, Zippe, inveighing against a number of Jesuit practices, also singled out asceticism as contrary to moral teaching and out of harmony with human nature. Man was neither an angel nor an animal, but if he attempted to be an angel, he would turn into an animal. He denounced explicitly the mystical asceticism of Gerhard von Zütphen, Johann Rusbrochius, and Johann Tauler.[73] Zippe attacked elaborate ritualism; religious rites that did not lead to moral improvement were, in his view, mere "pantomimes." He included in that category confessions, pilgrimages, donations to monasteries, repetitious uttering of certain prayers, and the wearing of scapulars. Finally, Zippe excoriated casuistic moral teaching as contrary to the sound admonitions of the Gospel and the church fathers. The casuist left the ground of true morality to seek ways of excusing the sinner's moral lapses.[74]

On the positive side, Zippe emphatically endorsed religious tolerance, the fruits of which were beneficent, just as those of intolerance were harmful. This was true in the experience of both the Catholic and the

Protestant sides. Zippe likewise stressed the Enlightenment principle of cultural universalism. A Christian could not limit his affection to the people of a certain territory; the object of his love had to encompass every human being, without distinction of estate, country, or way of thinking. Zippe characterized a proper Christian thusly: "He is a citizen of the world . . . which consists of all the states, as if of so many families."[75]

Zippe's more radical fellow Josephist, Zitte, in one of his sermons condemned with exceptional harshness such ascetic practices of the past as mortification, suppression of desires, crucifixion, and self-torture, calling them criminal acts. According to him, penances involving ashes and tears, as described in the Old Testament, were of alien Egyptian origin, and the New Testament never endorsed them. Similarly, it was wrong to translate the word *disciplina* as a whip (*Geissel*) to justify self-flagellation.[76]

The new spirit of toleration and stress on pastoral care over dogmatic controversies was exemplified by Abbot Rautenstrauch.[77] He deplored the suppression of the non-Catholics in Bohemia after the Battle of White Mountain, condemning the coercion of conscience and of religion as contrary to the teachings of Christ.[78] He favored Bishop Hay's famous letter of November 20, 1781, in support of religious toleration.[79] His reading included prominent thinkers of the Enlightenment such as Voltaire, Leibniz, and Joseph Priestley.[80] His interest in Priestley indicated his broader concern with Anglophone liberalism. Thus, he followed with sympathy the struggle of the United States for independence and the development of the American political system.[81] On the issue of censorship, he advocated a reform according to the British model.[82]

Abbot Steinbach, as a member of Joseph II's Religious Commission for Bohemia, undertook a systematic defense of religious tolerance in 1785. According to him, religious freedom was a natural right of man, enabling him to worship the Supreme Being, or the ineffable Creator, according to his innermost conviction. In the past, intolerance, through the practices of the Inquisition, had led to outrages that sought to suppress religious dissent through fire and sword. He argued that toleration had a long early tradition in Bohemia and had been practiced toward the pagans under Duke St. Wenceslaus in the tenth century and then toward the Jews from the eleventh century onward.[83] He saw the beginnings of intolerance in the reigns of Charles IV and Wenceslaus

IV, when the Waldensians were threatened with execution and a Dominican prior received a special inquisitorial authority, starting with an edict of 1376.[84] He deplored the unpunished pogrom against the Jews (for alleged offense against the Eucharist) in Prague in 1390 and Ferdinand I's intent to expel the Jews from Bohemia in 1547.[85] Finally, Steinbach applauded the end of the religious oppression that had lasted for over 150 years prior to 1781 and exhorted both the Catholics and the Protestants to set aside the old prejudices, " so that [all] might soon taste the flourishing fruits of the hallowed (*geheiligten*) tolerance in its full glory and extent."[86]

In a similar vein, Royko in his history of the Council of Constance observed that the Catholics should regard the Protestants not as opponents but as brethren.[87] In his other writings, he lauded Henry IV for issuing the Edict of Nantes (1598), just as he deplored its revocation by Louis XIV (1685).[88] Likewise, he noted with approval Elizabeth I's efforts to mitigate the religious strife in England and particularly the relative toleration introduced by the Glorious Revolution in 1689. His highest praise was, of course, reserved for Joseph II's Patent of Religious Toleration for the Hereditary Lands of the Habsburg Monarchy.[89]

Much of Rautenstrauch's reformatory thinking can be gleaned from his proposals for the establishment of the general seminaries and the regulation of theological education in the universities.[90] The seminaries had to be cleansed of two principal blemishes: the reign of superstitious beliefs and the ultramontane interference from the Roman Curia.[91] The main thrust of the future priests' education was to be directed toward refining personal morals and implanting an active love for others. The ultimate model and teacher was to be "the universal educator of mankind, Jesus Christ, whose morals were as pure, as they were full of the warmest love for one's neighbor."[92] On a more mundane level, Rautenstrauch prescribed the study of the earlier promoters of Catholic Enlightenment, in particular Pierre Nicol, Bossuet, Jacques Duguet, and Muratori. To the contrary, the seminary rectors were enjoined to keep out any works teaching monastic asceticism or stressing extreme virtue, inasmuch as these writings led either to unhealthy mysticism or to misanthropy.[93]

In his guide book for the reform of theological teaching in the universities, Rautenstrauch returned to censures of asceticism and ultramontanism. He banished from the curricula the teaching of mystics, whom he blamed for perverting moral theology into a sweeping enmity against sensual pleasures.[94] In a pamphlet on the pope's visit to Vienna, he reemphasized his opposition to the overcentralized administration of the Roman Church. According to him, every bishop, being instituted by the action of the Holy Spirit, possessed adequate power to grant dispensations in his own diocese, without depending on the authority of the pope.[95]

Royko wholeheartedly endorsed Rautenstrauch's and Zippe's liberal reforms of theological education. He pointed to Bossuet and Muratori as exemplary theologians who combined profound learning with religious moderation.[96] Royko likewise took up the themes of asceticism and ultramontanism. On the former, he endorsed the monastic reforms of Joseph II. On the latter, he favored the defenders of the Gallican liberties in the French church and, closer to home, the ideas of Bishop Hontheim on ecclesiastical authority, as well as Joseph II's curtailment of papal power in his own realms.[97] Other Josephists acclaimed Rautenstrauch's reform of theological schooling that, according to Johann Wolf, stressed pastoral theology and "consistently removed unnecessary subjects," focused on pointless theological speculation.[98]

The Austro-Bohemian Catholic Enlightenment did not seek to eliminate the supernatural, merely to sanitize its concepts.[99] A characteristic book in that respect was Johann van Opastraet's *Pastor Bonus*, which appeared in Prague in 1777 and denounced the exaggerated baroque cult of the Virgin Mary and other saints.[100] As another example, Kramerius, in the preface to his Czech edition of *Das Buch Joseph* (*Kniha Josefova*) in 1784, praised Joseph II's religious reformism as purifying "our Roman Catholic religion,"[101] although he condemned the prejudices, superstitions, and errors of the Counter-Reformation. Writing to his friend Augustin Helfert, Dobrovský declared his stand for Enlightenment, reason, philosophy, and Christianity and his opposition to Roman centralism, monasticism, subordination of reason, and blind faith.[102]

Dobrovský exemplified the basic balance at the heart of Josephist Reform Catholicism, consistent with the spirit of the Enlightenment. This liberal Catholicism sought to preserve the essentials of the Christian faith, which would be purged of the peculiar authoritarian, ascetic, and quasi-mystical features stressed by the Counter-Reformation. The tenets of Dobrovský's liberal Catholicism were gathered in his *Lectures Concerning the Practical Side of the Christian Religion* that he delivered when teaching in the general seminary in Hradiště u Olomouce (1787–90) and in which he drew to some extent on the teaching of Zippe at the general seminary of Prague (1783–85).[103] Zippe had defined for him the imperial religious policy, as aimed at combining thorough theological knowledge with "true Enlightenment based on sound foundations."[104] According to Dobrovský, moral happiness was the goal of religion, which instructed the believer to use his life joyously and rationally in the expectation of an eternal life.[105] In line with the outlook of Reform Catholicism, he deplored fasts, superstitions, outdated beliefs, and fanaticism, as well as the various forms of asceticism: "denials" of the world, of joy, of self-love, of reason. His condemnation of fanaticism was especially stern as it had led to the Inquisition tribunals, intolerance, religious wars, and other flagrant perversions. [106] As the bottom line, however, he wished to preserve the essentials of the Christian faith. He emphasized that morality had to be rooted in the belief in Providence or in a grand order of nature.[107] In other words, Reform Catholicism was not supposed to become a cover for the repudiation of Christian orthodoxy.[108]

Dobrovský shared his liberal religious views with other important representatives of Josephist Reform Catholicism. In 1779, he had reprinted parts of Rautenstrauch's reform program, *Anleitung und Grundriss zur Systematischen Dogmatischen Theologie*, in his own journal *Böhmische Litteratur auf das Jahr 1779* (1779).[109] In the mid-1780s, Dobrovský was in contact with Rautenstrauch and Van Swieten.[110] His circle of acquaintances increased with the establishment of the general seminary in Prague in 1783. In addition to Zippe, especially after he became director of theological studies in Vienna, Dobrovský was in close contact with bishops Hay and Josef F. Hurdálek of Litoměřice.[111] Before his appointment as head of the general seminary in Olomouc in 1787 with the help of Hay and Zippe, Dobrovský served as consultant to Zippe on other possible candidates for leadership in the new ecclesiastical establishments.[112] Dobrovský also worked closely with Václav Stach (1754–1831), professor of pastoral theology in the general seminary in Olomouc, helping him with Czech translation of textbooks in the new spirit.[113] Dobrovský's disciple Antonín J. Puchmajer, later a prominent awakener in his own right, also sought to apply the Enlightenment criteria to the Roman Catholic religion, steering it away from the baroque asceticism and mysticism.[114]

A generation of priests following Dobrovský and educated in the spirit of Josephist Enlightenment believed—against the spirit of the Counter-Reformation—in the feasibility of reconciling theology with the advancement of knowledge and modern progress, as well as in a positive tolerance toward other Christian churches.[115] Dobrovský himself held that what was imposed on Bohemia after 1620 was not real Catholicism but a perverse form of "Ultra-Catholicism." He proclaimed that a new era was opening for literature with the abolition of the Jesuit Order in 1773 and rejoiced that the Enlightenment (*Aufklärung*) would sweep out the darkness from human minds.[116]

4

Catholic Enlightenment and Utraquism: A Liberal Symbiosis

Aside from the two negative reasons for a return to the intellectual heritage of the Utraquist sixteenth century—the distaste for the Counter-Reformation and the need to fill the cultural vacuum—a third and decisive reason was the positive appeal of the legacy of the Golden Age.[1] It was a way to deal with this cultural *tabula rasa* that the government in Vienna had created within the Habsburg Empire when it discredited, and in a way proscribed, the expressions and products of the baroque and Counter-Reformation mentality and practice.[2] Early national awakeners—such as Mikuláš Adaukt Voigt, Karel R. Ungar, Johann H. Wolf, František F. Procházka, Ignác Cornova, František M. Pelcl, and Karel and Václav Thám—who had seen Bohemia's cultural nadir during the Counter-Reformation, located the acme of Czech culture in the sixteenth century. Their successors, like Josef Dobrovský, Jan Jeník of Bratřice, Václav Kramerius, Josef Jungmann, Karel Vinařický, and Vincenc Zahradník, all agreed that the new culture of the Enlightenment needed the literature of the sixteenth century as its foundation.[3] These considerations help explain why, at the dawn of the nineteenth century, Czech national awakeners turned to the revival of the Utraquist literary legacy of the sixteenth century through reprinting, teaching, and other dissemination.

Happily, the cultural heritage of the Golden Age had become accessible after the downfall of the Counter-Reformation. With the suspension of the Index of Prohibited Books and the massive closing of monasteries, the hitherto proscribed literature of the Bohemian Reformation was transferred into the academic libraries, and duplicates were sold on the open market.[4] Early in the process of rediscovery in 1776,

Leopold Johann Scherschnik exulted in the flourishing of literature and book publishing in fifteenth- and sixteenth-century Bohemia. Intellectual leaders of the Austro-Bohemian Catholic Enlightenment like František Faustin Procházka judged that no country in sixteenth-century Europe was superior to Bohemia in its writers and scholars. František M. Pelcl stressed the cosmopolitan Bohemian contacts at that time with cultural centers outside the country.[5] František X. Němeček considered the sixteenth-century musical accomplishments of the Bohemian literary brotherhoods much superior to those of the contemporary German *Meistersänger*.[6] The intellectual freedom of the Austro-Bohemian Enlightenment permitted the awakeners to explore freely the previously proscribed literature of the Utraquist century. They were fervently interested in the literary and political features of the Golden Age, but the religious aspects also came to their attention. From the long-term perspective, the awakeners' promotion of the secular aspects of the past bore lasting fruit, while their interest in the recovery of the ecclesiastical features was eventually frustrated.

Admiration for the Utraquist Century: Secular Aspects

As devotees of the Enlightenment, Dobrovský and his colleagues highly valued the principle of freedom of thought and expression during the Golden Age of the Bohemian Reformation.[7] Their endorsement of the cultural achievements of the Utraquist era, which was the obverse of their denunciation of the Counter-Reformation's cultural depredations, began shortly after 1780. Generous and enthusiastic, their endorsement was prompted by the virtual lifting of press censorship, one of the hallmarks of the liberal spirit of the Josephist Enlightenment.

As an example of praise for the virtues of the Reformation era, Johann H. Wolf in his textbook on Bohemia's history, published in 1783, extolled the flourishing of town schools, classical languages, and book publication.[8] Procházka, in his *De saecularibus liberalium artium in Bohemia et Moravia*, characterized the publishing program of Daniel Adam of Veleslavín and the highlights of Rudolf II's reign as models of cultural creativity and discussed in considerable detail the accomplishments of individual writers and scientists.[9] Similarly, Pelcl, in his historical and grammatical works, maintained that Czech culture in arts and sciences reached its highest point—a golden age—in the second half of the sixteenth century during the reign of Rudolf II; the literature of the period was seen as classic, a model to be followed by current writers. The University of Prague was staffed by scholars and scientists of international reputation; even women attained high distinction in literature.[10] Němeček, Wolf's successor in the chair of history at the University of Prague, presented another glowing characterization of the sixteenth century as the "beautiful period of Bohemian learning" (*schöne Periode böhmischer Gelehrsamkeit*) when outstanding scholars gave their nation a reputation that had not been seen since the ravages of the Thirty Years' War and the following political repression. Němeček pointed out, once again, that Bohemian culture had reached its peak in the arts and sciences during the reigns of Maximilian II and Rudolf II, when its fame reached abroad and attracted foreign scholars into the country. Commerce and industry flourished amid peace and prosperity. Printing reached a high standard of perfection, rivaling the graphic arts of Germany and the Netherlands in its elegance and accuracy, as well as in the quality of illustrations. Education for women was promoted. According to Němeček, thanks to a diffusion of culture, a number of towns became seats of higher learning, and scholars took part in municipal governments.[11]

The literary masterpieces of the Golden Age were held up as models for emulation in the current cultural revival of Bohemia. Václav Thám, in the *Básně v řeči vázané* (1785), called attention to the impressive number of exemplary writers who flourished in Bohemia from the reign of Ferdinand I to that of Rudolf II.[12] Celebrating the quality and style of the Czech language in the sixteenth century, Pelcl urged contemporary authors to use the writings of Adam of Veleslavín, Jan Kocín of Kocinét, Václav Hájek of Libočany, and Jan A. Komenský as their models.[13] He went on to list altogether a hundred distinguished authors of the period as evidence of the high quality of literary culture, in which both men and women participated. In addition, Pelcl claimed that, by the end of the sixteenth century, 1,312 Bohemian book titles had been published and estimated that more than 1 million volumes were in circulation. Because of the great demand, Czech-language books were printed not only in Bohemia and Moravia but also in Venice, Nuremberg, Dresden, Wittenberg, and Leipzig.[14] In his patriotic lecture of 1803, Karel Ignác Thám, brother of Václav Thám, cited the names of forty-six distinguished Czech authors and thirty-one translated texts from Greek and Latin in history, literature, and theology among the sixteenth-century Bohemian classics worthy to be followed as models.[15]

The high degree of language development also appealed to the awakeners. Matěj V. Kramerius, for instance, expressed his pride in the Czech language in the introduction to his reprint of *Letopisové Trojanští* (1790):

> The Germans and other nations began to cultivate their language only in this our century but have not yet brought it to perfection.... Our dear mother tongue, on the contrary, three hundred and more years ago, had reached such a perfection that it can not only equal Greek and Latin languages, but surpasses all others by its expressiveness, fulness, and plentiful vocabulary.

He added that anyone reading Czech books of that period would be impressed by the excellence of their style.[16] His newspaper, *Krameriovy noviny*, returned to the topic the next year, claiming that the Czech language had reached the highest form of perfection two hundred years earlier, before its pathetic decline.[17] Dobrovský inspired his disciples to regard the sixteenth-century literature as a model for future development. In the mid-1830s, one such disciple, Vincenc Zahradník, claimed that the only way to avoid writing in the corrupted language inherited from the early eighteenth century was for the writer to immerse himself in the tongue of the old Czechs. He praised the linguistic work of Jungmann and his associates in restoring the norms of the Golden Age.[18] His example and exhortation influenced other Catholic priests.[19] Jan Jeník of Bratřice, too, joined in praising the literary culture of the sixteenth century.[20]

It was primarily Dobrovský, however, who defined the rationale for further advance through a return to the past. He celebrated the Utraquist sixteenth century (1520–1620) for its augmentation of Czech language and literature and its spread of humanism and printing as culminations of Czech intellectual development. According to him, "The entire mass of the nation was stimulated to read and summoned to think. The cultivated part thought and wrote freely."[21] Still, in 1823, Palacký proclaimed the period 1500–1620 as the most brilliant epoch in the literature of Bohemia.[22] As late as 1829–33, František L. Čelakovský aspired to emulate the language of Veleslavín in his own translation of Augustine's *City of God*.[23] Hence, the return to the sixteenth century and resumption of its ways were the clearly implied direction of further progress.[24] It may be noted that tying the national awakening to the liberal culture of a remote past was not a uniquely Czech phenomenon.[25]

The elements that made the Utraquist century on (a secular level) particularly compatible with the century of the Enlightenment in the minds of the awakeners will be next considered more specifically under the rubric of three issues: (1) liberalism, free discussion, and tolerance; (2) language preservation; and (3) plebeianism. The cultural return to the sixteenth century tended to reinforce these values in Czech society. The awareness of this connection also helps to account for the relative popularity of the Josephist Enlightenment. According to the observation of the famous *philosophe* Honoré de Mirabeau, Bohemia boasted the highest number of the Enlightenment's adherents among all the Habsburg lands.[26]

Liberalism, Free Discussion, and Tolerance

Dobrovský recognized the liberalism of the Utraquist sixteenth century as a special virtue and considered its culture, therefore, superior to the earlier phases of the Bohemian Reformation in which he deplored the manifestations of Taborite and other religious radicalism and intolerance.[27] He was attracted to the atmosphere of "free thinking and writing" in the sixteenth century when common people were also drawn to reading and urged to think for themselves. The introduction of printing allowed the writings of authors ancient and contemporary, domestic and foreign, to be widely available. For Dobrovský, it was "the beautiful or golden age" of Czech literature.[28] Like other awakeners, Dobrovský drew equations between the states of religious toleration under Utraquism and the Enlightenment. According to him, Emperor Maximilian II instituted virtual religious freedom in 1567, which encouraged independent thinking (*das Selbstdenken befördert wird*).[29] Pelcl compared the state of religious toleration under Ferdinand I to that just introduced by Joseph II. Kaunitz, like Dobrovský, invoked Maximilian II's name when seeking to convince Maria Theresa to favor religious tolerance.[30]

The spirit of toleration was broadly attributed to the Bohemian Reformation by Otto Steinbach of Kranichstein's "Versuch einer Geschichte der alten und neuen Toleranz im Königreich Böhmen und Markgraftum Mähren" (1786). He applauded the mutual tolerance of the Utraquists and the communicants *sub una*, recognized by the Compactata of 1436 and the Peace of Kutná Hora of 1485. He highlighted the liberality of Maximilian II, who broadened religious tolerance to include the Protestants in Bohemia, particularly the Unity of Brethren, and ignored the reprimands of Pope Pius V, who threatened him with anathema or even with revocation of his imperial dignity.[31] Steinbach's reference to Maximilian II's trouble with Pius V could be interpreted as an allusion to Joseph II's problem with Pope Pius VI over the 1781 Edict of Religious Toleration. Likewise, assessing the situation prior to the Counter-Reformation, Steinbach endorsed the reaffirmation of religious freedom in Moravia in 1608 by King Matthias and in Bohemia by Rudolf II with the grant of the Letter of Majesty in 1609.[32]

The awakeners were also eager to point out the parallels between the liberal and tolerant values of Utraquism and those of Josephist Reform Catholicism. The spirit of toleration, akin to that of the Enlightenment, was found in Hus, particularly by Augustin Zitte (1750–85). Zitte, in his *Lebensbeschreibung des Magisters Johannes Huss von Hussinecz* (1789–90), published posthumously, pointed out that Hus opposed the burning of heretical books. Appealing to church fathers (such as Augustine, Jerome, and Ambrose), canon law, and sound reason, he maintained that heretical writings could contain truth as well as error. According to Hus, that was true of the works of Wyclif, as well as those of Aristotle and Peter Lombard. Kašpar Royko sought to clear Hus of the charge of heresy in his lengthy critical history of the Council of Constance. The book was greeted by Dobrovský as a "thorough and liberal" document in which the Czechs should take pride for saving the honor of their outstanding countryman.[33]

Likewise, Jeník of Bratřice called attention to the spirit of toleration in the Bohemian Reformation and perceived the remarkable kinship between the liberalism of the Utraquist sixteenth century and the Austro-Bohemian Enlightenment. Similarly, Palacký saw the crux of the Czech national revival in a merger between sixteenth-century Czech culture and modern European thought of the Enlightenment. In paying tribute to Jungmann, Palacký noted that he had taught his countrymen to think and speak as old Czechs and modern Europeans at the same time.[34] Karel Havlíček Borovský exhorted his countrymen in April 1848 to reject the condition of humiliation imposed by the Battle of White Mountain and "remember the older times when the glory of your name blossomed brilliantly."[35]

Language Preservation

The national awakeners were, of course, aware of the insistence on the use of the Czech language as part of the fifteenth- and sixteenth-century political culture in contrast to its downgrading in the Counter-Reformation era. Pelcl stressed that, in the sixteenth century, Bohemian scholars wrote their books in Czech, and the government used the Czech language in its operations.[36] The language had thereby reached the highest level of perfection, so that even in Pelcl's time, whoever wished to write good Czech needed to use the sixteenth-century texts as his model.[37] In his *Obrana jazyka českého*, Karel Ignác Thám also pointed out the high degree of language development displayed in Czech publications of the sixteenth century and likewise reflected on the felicitous translations of such Latin works as *Encomion moriae* of Erasmus. In his *Kurzgefasste böhmische Sprachlehre* (1785), he went on to enumerate a large number of other classical works successfully translated from either Greek or Latin in the same period.[38]

In *Über den Karakter der Slawen* (1803), Thám cited at length from the decree passed by the Bohemian Diet in 1615 that obliged immigrant foreigners (both nobles and townspeople) to learn Czech and see to it that their children could speak it as well.[39] The flowering of the language resulted from its use at the highest levels of cultural activity.[40] Němeček praised King George of Poděbrady for introducing Czech into the official dealings of the government. He also noted the exceptional purity of the Czech language used in the Utraquist worship of the sixteenth century and the common use of Czech by Bohemia's political leaders and social elites. He credited Adam of Veleslavín in particular with the development and promotion of the Czech language through his work as a publisher.[41]

Dobrovský indicated his approval of the Bohemian Diet's decree of 1530, stipulating that proceedings before the Court of the Land (*zemský soud*) had to be conducted in Czech, even if the parties were foreigners. In an intriguing suggestion, Dobrovský argued that the Czech language was to serve as an aid in extending Habsburg power over the Poles and other Slavs during Rudolf II's reign. He also applauded Karel of Žerotín's admonition to the city fathers of Olomouc in 1610 not to be ashamed of Czech but to use it consistently in their official correspondence. Like Karel Ignác Thám, Dobrovský called attention to the 1615 decree of the Diet, which sought to curb the spread of German at the expense of Czech in Bohemia.[42] Subsequently, Palacký joined in lauding the use of the Czech language during the period 1500–1620.[43]

Thus, the Czech awakeners could find inspiration in the sixteenth-century writers as like-minded advocates of the revival, fortification, and preservation of the Bohemian vernacular. Conversely, the sixteenth-century authors had already acted as awakeners clamoring for the use of Czech in literature and in public life. In addition, the very existence of advanced literature in the sixteenth century showed that the Czechs had considerable cultural and intellectual accomplishments to their credit, which in turn entitled them to a resumption of scholarship and culture in their own language.[44] In view of the cosmopolitan outlook of the Enlightenment, however, it is essential to point out that the awakeners did not attribute to language an autonomous power to create or advance the culture of the nation. It merely served as an instrument for expressing values that were of universal validity and could be expressed in any other language.

As discussed subsequently, especially in chapter 6, this pragmatic attitude toward language use persisted past the zenith of the Josephist Enlightenment. Thus, Jungmann emphasized the same theme in a lead article that he provided for the Czech-language scientific journal *Krok* in 1821, dwelling especially on his countrymen's right to make contributions to the common cultural treasury of humanity in their own tongue.[45] Palacký expressed himself in a similar vein in reviewing the objectives of the *Časopis českého musea* in 1837:

> Now then let us spread, cultivate and perfect the various branches of knowledge, and let us bring pure and God-pleasing sacrifices not only on the altar of our homeland, but also humanity. A time has surely begun in the world history, when all local barriers in the intellectual life of individual nations are always further sinking and disappearing, and when a free, constant and rapid exchange of thoughts, ideas, and sentiments occurs among the advanced nations of Europe everywhere, establishing in this manner, although through divers tongues, only one higher literature that is European and at times also universal.[46]

Plebeianism

Like the culture of the Utraquist age, the cultural revival of the awakening depended on individuals of middle-class origin or status.[47] The awakeners were also convinced that it was the towns, rather than the nobles, that brought about the flourishing of Bohemian culture in the sixteenth century.[48] By and large, the nobles did not directly engage in the cultural and scholarly revival of the late eighteenth and early nineteenth centuries. Although they may have contributed financially to several publication projects, the nobles seemed to see the awakening as something outside, or perhaps beneath, their personal concern or involvement. Except for a few families (Šternberks, Kinskis, Choteks), the nobles focused on their agrarian interests and reduced their scientific and artistic interests to a collection of decorative objects.[49] In the late eighteenth century, the aristocrats dominated the prestigious honorary membership (*Ehren-Mitglieder*) of the Royal Bohemian Society of Sciences, while the ordinary members (*Ordentliche Mitglieder*), who made genuine contributions to science and scholarship, were almost entirely commoners. Thus, in 1788, all of the six honorary members were aristocrats, while only one figured among the fourteen ordinary members.[50] Under the nobles' leadership, the society stagnated in the opening decades of the nineteenth century. A revival followed in the 1830s when the commoners gained the administrative ascendancy.[51]

In noting major Bohemian authors of the sixteenth century in his *Obrana jazyka českého*, Karel Ignác Thám cited the striking preponderance of townspeople over nobles. Among the prepublication subscribers to the epochal two volumes of *Básně v řeči vázané* (1785), edited by Václav Thám, there were only three nobles. Dobrovský confidently predicted and expected the vanishing of noble privileges.[52] At the coronations of Leopold II (1791) and Francis I (1792), representatives of the urban and rural middle classes, not the nobles, pleaded for Czech-language rights. A recently compiled list of 135 notable awakeners who were born before 1830 includes only three nobles.[53]

For their part, the awakeners were highly critical of the nobles' indifference. Jungmann, nursing memories of humiliation from earlier work as a tutor in noble families, resented the aristocrats' lack of concern for the national revival.[54] František Čelakovský and Josef Kamarýt commented on this indifference in connection with the *Matice česká* in 1831.[55] The new historical prose of the awakening typically portrayed the aristocracy in a negative light and favored the townspeople and the lower country gentry. Josef K. Tyl celebrated the struggle of the townspeople in the fourteenth century against the nobility's power in his drama *Staré Město a Malá Strana* (1851).[56] Karel J. Erben also ranked himself among the defenders of the poor and destitute.[57] Karel Havlíček, a member of the awakeners' culminating generation, ridiculed what he considered futile attempts to convert the Bohemian aristocracy to the support of Czech cultural endeavors.[58]

Havlíček would sum up the awakeners' feelings in an article of 1850, in which he maintained that the nobles not only failed to help but even became a hindrance both in public life and in their private demeanor. He asked, "How could the Czech language flourish, if the higher estates did not use it among themselves, when they neither wrote nor read anything in Czech, when they considered and declared the cultivators of the national language as fools and eccentrics?"[59] In Havlíček's opinion, the aristocrats abdicated the honorable duty of leading the nation, with the task falling to the patriots-commoners who gained the trust of their fellow citizens. Despite their limited means and modest social standing, the lowly patriots reached the goal of ensuring the existence and perpetuation of a national culture. In short, the nation advanced without the assistance of the nobles, and even against their will.[60]

Some half a century later, Tomáš Masaryk largely agreed with Havlíček, whom he generally admired, in his own 1895 retrospective on the national awakening. While elsewhere the nobility eagerly participated in the national culture, in Bohemia the nobles evidently could not make up their minds whether they were foreigners or Czechs.[61] Although individual aristocrats provided some monetary support to Czech literary work, there was virtually no creative contribution by the blue bloods to the awakening's cultural renaissance.[62]

The three characteristics shared by the sixteenth century and the national awakening—liberal universalism, language cultivation, and plebeianism—were interrelated. The stress on the cultivation of the vernacular was related to the plebeian character of Bohemia's culture. While the nobles could read in Latin or French, the common people needed their literature in Czech.[63] Above all, while the use of the Czech language was emphasized, it was not an aim in itself. Rather, it was to serve primarily as a medium for expressing all human values, transcending the national community. This penchant for universalism may be traced to the main thrust of the Bohemian Reformation.[64]

Reform Catholicism and Utraquism: Theological Aspects

With their focus on the Golden Age of the sixteenth century, the awakeners were interested in exploring not only the framework of its literature and politics but also the character of its religion, which had grown out of the Bohemian Reformation. Although the sympathetic assessment of the secular culture of the Golden Age was fairly unproblematic, the assessment of the religious aspect encountered the contrast between mainstream Utraquism and radical trends, especially Taboritism. The pioneers of the Catholic Enlightenment were naturally inclined to resent the intolerance and violence of the radicals, while mainstream Utraquism appealed to them in its tolerance and moderation as kindred to their own Reform Catholicism.

It is, therefore, not surprising that the Austro-Bohemian Catholic Enlightenment continued to treat Taborite radicalism with deep misgivings, if not outright aversion. Thus, Pelcl found what he considered the fanaticism of the Taborites and the subsequent intolerant religious zeal of the Jesuits almost equally repugnant. Procházka highlighted the literature of the Utraquist period, at the same time expressing reservations about the bloody activities of Žižka and the Taborites early in the Bohemian Reformation.[65] Voigt similarly commented on the horrors of the religious wars, when force took over control from legality and Bohemia became a scene of "gruesome inhumanity, robberies, murders, and arson." He did, however, contrast the (mis)behavior of the Taborite hosts with the subsequent period of Utraquist predominance. In particular, the Utraquist King George of Poděbrady—when not distracted by foreign wars—introduced laws serving as models of justice and equity.[66] Steinbach and Royko likewise deplored the religiously inspired violence, particularly the harshness of Žižka, but stressed that denominational hatreds were to a large extent inflamed by the provocations of the Roman Church, especially by the crusades of Pope Martin V and Emperor Sigismund, as well as by the acts of the Council of Constance. Not just the Taborites but also the Roman side had committed outrages.[67]

Similarly, Dobrovský disapproved of the religious radicalism of the Taborites and others for its violence and intolerance in the early phases of the Bohemian Reformation, which he contrasted with the later sixteenth century and its adherence to political and social values like those cherished by the Enlightenment.[68] He specifically denounced the Taborites' battle hymn "Kdož jste Boží bojovníci" (All ye warriors of God) for its message of vengeance and cruelty.[69] Also Antonín Puchmajer concluded his otherwise celebratory ode on Žižka's victories with disapproval of the warrior's inhuman shedding of blood and unrestrained wrath toward the enemy.[70]

Despite some initial confusion about the actual focus of the Bohemian Reformation, the awakeners before long clearly identified Utraquism as the mainstream religious element of the Bohemian Reformation from Hus on and distinguished it from the extraneous radicalism of the Taborites. Eventually, this Utraquism, including the teaching of Hus, was interpreted by the awakeners as orthodox and Catholic. Thus, Royko stressed that in his view the Taborite extremism meant a pronounced deviation from the moderation of Hus and the mainstream of the Bohemian Reformation.[71] The sharp distinction between violent Taboritism and moderate Utraquism was, in fact, historically justified.[72] The assertion of the orthodoxy of Hus and Utraquism was, of course, another matter and represented a drastic departure from the official teaching of the Counter-Reformation period.

The awakeners challenged the standard theological view of the Jesuits, according to which not just the radicals but also Hus and the Utraquists were considered heretical on a par with the Lutherans and the Calvinists. As an example, Josef Kaukal titled his important textbook, used at the University of Prague, *Tribunal Polemicum adversus atheistas, theistas et omnes Christiani nominis hostes, sycretistarum, Lutheranorum, Hussitarum errores* (1738).[73] A professor of biblical studies at the University of Olomouc, Franz Wolff (1728–after 1785) in his *Commentarium in Sacram scripturam* (1765–68) criticized the Utraquists in a more nuanced way for their papal minimalism, for their communion *subutraque*, for allowing the participation of laity in administration of church properties, and for their rejection of monasticism.[74] As late as 1777, there appeared a Czech extract from Florimond de Remond's *Histoire de la naissance, progrès et décadence de l'herésie de ce siècle* (1605), under the title *Husitského v Čechách kacířství počátku, zrůstu, a pádu vejtah* (An Extract Concerning the Origin, the Growth, and the Fall of the Hussite Heresy in Bohemia).[75]

Important exceptions to the routine damning of Hus and the Utraquists, however, were the textbooks of church history written by the Jesuit Ignaz Popp and published in the 1750s. Popp, a professor at the University of Olomouc, conceded that Hus had rejected most of Wyclif's heretical opinions and went on to view favorably the acceptance of the Compactata by the Utraquists and the Council of Basel.[76] Most strikingly, he drew fundamental contrasts between Hus and Luther. Hus accepted an orthodox interpretation of the Eucharist, auricular confession, and extreme unction, but it was especially from the moral standpoint that Luther could not be compared to Hus. In short, according to Popp, Luther by his lifestyle and teaching was as remote from Hus as the Saxon Pathmos was from the place of the exiled angel from the Apocalypse.[77]

Despite distinguishing Hus clearly from both Wyclif and Luther, Popp, however, could not bring himself to exculpate Hus entirely, and thus he still attributed to him serious errors, such as his flouting of papal authority and appealing symbolically from the pope to Christ in his defiance of papal excommunication. In a survey of Bohemia's history, Popp also questioned the legitimacy of George of Poděbrady, a Utraquist, as the King of Bohemia.[78] Nevertheless, Popp saw Hus and Utraquism as lesser evils than Luther and Lutheranism, in the same way that early sixteenth-century Roman propagandists such as Johannes Cochlaeus, Hieronymus Dungersheim, Hieronymus Emser, and Johann Faber did, as they entertained hopes of reconciliation between Rome and the Utraquists.[79] At the very least, by his elevation of Hus's moral character, Popp paved the way for his total rehabilitation by the Catholic theologians of the Josephist Enlightenment.

Turning to the early awakeners, Voigt, in his *Effigies* (1773–75)—in the process of the rehabilitation of Utraquism—continued along the lines developed by Popp and maintained that the Protestants had improperly attempted to co-opt Hus, who was essentially an orthodox Catholic. František Pubička, in his *Chronologische Geschichte Böhmens* (1770 on), also went to great lengths to refute the idea that Hus's religious views were Protestant, although he still claimed that Hus was justly sentenced at the Council of Constance because his act of questioning the church's authority formally constituted heresy.[80] Procházka's *De saecularibus liberalium artium* (1782) represented a further step forward, although he still remained rather cautious, given the ambiguous attitude toward heresy lingering from Maria Theresa's reign. On the one hand, he was noncommittal toward Hus himself and often relied on accounts of such pillars of Roman orthodoxy as Aeneas Sylvius Piccolomini's (Pope Pius II) *Historia Bohemica*, and Václav Hájek of Libočany's *Kronyka česká*.[81] On the other hand, he sought to present a clear distinction between what he now considered the near-orthodox positions of the Utraquists and the errors of their Taborite opponents. He referred to Jan Příbram's defense of the Eucharistic doctrine of transubstantiation against Peter Payne who, on behalf of the Taborites, upheld Wyclif's heretical doctrine of remanence.[82] In describing the events around the Council of Basel, Procházka again stressed the difference between the positions of Jan Rokycana, Příbram, and Křišťan of Prachatice, on the Utraquist side, and those of Payne and Mikuláš of Pelhřimov, on the Taborite side.[83] Concerning the relative orthodoxy of the Utraquist doctrinal positions, Procházka, indeed, sought support from the Roman advocate of the lesser-evil theory, the earlier-mentioned Johannes Cochlaeus.[84]

While there was still some hesitation on this subject under Maria Theresa, during the reign of Joseph II the floodgates had lifted, and the rehabilitation of Hus and Utraquism was in full swing within the Catholic Enlightenment.[85] Abbott Franz S. Rautenstrauch deplored the persecution of the Bohemian dissidents from Rome after the Battle of White Mountain and expressed an interest in viewing mementos of Žižka during a visit in Tábor on September 21, 1782.[86] As noted earlier, Popp, Voigt, and Pubička had broached the subject that Hus's religious views were not Protestant but—at least by implication—Catholic.[87] According to Abbott Steinbach, Hus was the most learned among the Bohemians of his time. Both he and Jerome of Prague incurred Rome's hostility because of their cogent criticism of clerical and papal abuses and were unjustly sentenced and executed in Constance. Alexius Pařízek, in his history textbook for secondary schools (1781), maintained that after the adoption of the Compactata by the Council of Basel (1436), the Utraquists were as much Catholics as the communicants *sub una*.[88]

In a culmination of the rehabilitation campaign, overt calls for a reintegration of Utraquism with the Reform Catholicism of the Enlightenment issued from the writings of Royko, Johann H. Wolf, and Pelcl.[89] As professor of church history at the University of Prague, Royko (1744–1819) displayed the liberal viewpoint of the Catholic Enlightenment in his history of the Council of Constance (1780–85). Supporting conciliarism against authoritarian tendencies, he proceeded to examine the original conciliar documents to determine whether Hus was convicted either because of outright falsehoods or because of a partial suppression of truth.[90] He concluded that Hus's teaching was not erroneous (much less heretical) and that he was therefore unjustly labeled and sentenced as a heretic.[91]

Turning to contemporary times, Royko pointed out that Joseph II corrected a number of the clerical abuses that Hus and the Bohemian Reformation had censured; in particular, he terminated the practice of simony and limited monasticism and the powers of ecclesiastical courts.

Royko expected that additional reforms were forthcoming, such as an introduction of clerical marriages, of lay communion in both kinds, and of Czech language in the liturgy, which would further emulate the practices of the Utraquist era. Above all, he relished the thought of how happy Hus would have been had he lived in the reign of Joseph II, when his views would have found protection, since he did not deviate in any substantial way from the Catholic faith.⁹² It is, therefore, not surprising to hear an unfriendly critic charge that Royko was, in fact, a "Utraquist" seeking to revive the spirit of the Bohemian Reformation.⁹³

Royko's magnum opus was also published in part in the Czech translation by Václav Stach as *Historie velikého sněmu kostnického* (A History of the Great Council of Constance) (1785, 1786). Stach, a professor in the general seminary of Olomouc, was himself a fervent devotee of Hus, as he wrote to Dobrovský on August 20, 1786: "Entire Moravia knows that I love Hus."⁹⁴ Like the original, Stach's translation presented Hus not only as a faithful Catholic but also as precursor of Joseph II's Reform Catholicism.⁹⁵ Dobrovský likewise endorsed Royko's interpretation. In fact, he was convinced that Hus was "an innocent victim of ecclesiastical tyranny."⁹⁶

Another explicit identification between Utraquism and Reform Catholicism of the Josephist Enlightenment came from Johann Heinrich Wolf, who in his book *Leben, Lehre, Wandel und Tod des im J. 1415 lebendig verbrannten Johann Hus* (1784), asserted that the Utraquists were neither heretics nor Protestants, but good and genuine Catholics. The Utraquists were unjustly persecuted by the Roman Curia and pitilessly abandoned by the Protestants. He wrote:

> The fate of the Hussites, our brethren and compatriots, was almost the same as that of the flying mice that are pecked on by birds, and bitten by mice. So they [Utraquists] are suppressed by the Catholics, and do not arouse the sympathy of the Protestants. Indeed, this was unjust. If one wishes to confirm it, one should turn to history and especially to their origins. Then it would be found, that the Hussites, particularly the disciples and adherents of Jan Hus, were neither heretics, nor Protestants, but good, authentic and proper Catholics.⁹⁷

Wolf distinguished clearly between the orthodox Utraquists on the one hand and the Protestant-like radicals (the early Taborites and the later Unity of Brethren) on the other hand.⁹⁸ In Wolf's opinion, Hus himself was "a true and pious teacher of the Catholic Church." Even his insistence on the limits of papal judicial and administrative power was legitimate, and this view was adopted not only in the Protestant states but also in the enlightened Catholic ones, as was currently happening under Joseph II in the Habsburg monarchy.[99] According to Wolf, the Bohemians—as the Utraquists maintained—had been accustomed to lay communion in both kinds from the beginning of Christianity and only later were deprived of it willfully by Rome.[100]

Pelcl, likewise, recognized the Utraquists as orthodox Catholics and carefully distinguished them from the heterodox Protestants, in particular the Lutherans. In his history of Wenceslaus IV, Pelcl signified his agreement with Royko's detailed discussion and characterization of the proceedings at Constance.[101] He himself maintained that Hus was not guilty of the heresies of which he was accused. Instead, he adhered to orthodox positions on the seven sacraments (including auricular confession), on the binding character of the church tradition, on good works such as fasting, and on the veneration of saints. What Hus opposed, according to Pelcl, was the misuse of papal and conciliar powers, in particular the grant of indulgences for unjust wars, imposition of arbitrary penalties (against which he appealed from the pope to Christ), and the condemnation of Wyclif, whom he considered a saintly personage.[102]

As for Utraquism, Pelcl was familiar with the fundamental works of sixteenth-century Utraquist theology and Bohuslav Bílejovský's *Kronyka česká* and considered the Utraquists to be "believing Christians" who followed traditional Catholic practices, such as the veneration of the Virgin Mary.[103] The Utraquists wished to negotiate, not to separate from the Roman See, and the Council of Basel recognized the Utraquists as true sons of the Church.[104] In his *Geschichte der Böhmen,* Pelcl asserted that there were two types of Catholics in the sixteenth century: the Utraquists and those communicating *sub una specie*. The Utraquists continued to consider themselves part of the Roman Church, but this position became increasingly precarious with the implementation of the edicts of the Council of Trent.[105] Despite the disfavor of Rome, the Utraquists maintained an orthodox Catholic position, which clearly distinguished them from the Protestants (the Lutherans, the Brethren, and the Calvinists) as of 1602.[106]

Augustin Zitte defended Hus's Catholic orthodoxy on two fronts: against the charges of heresy from the Jesuits and against Protestants' tendency to appropriate him. On the one hand, in his biographies of

Hus's precursors (1786), Zitte argued against the Jesuit Bohuslav Balbín (1621–88) that Hus's views represented a sharp break with previous Bohemian theology. Referring to Konrád Štěkna, Jan Milíč of Kroměříž, and Matěj of Janov, Zitte pointed out that Hus, like them, continued within the earlier theological tradition.[107] He remained within the historical teachings of the Church, and he followed only what had been taught by the most upright and irreproachable Catholic theologians.[108] On the other hand, in his biography of Hus (1789–90), Zitte sharply rebuked German Protestants for misrepresenting Hus as a witness and teacher of their faith. Hus, in fact, had not deviated from the proper teaching of the Roman Church and died as a true Catholic, even performing the sacramental rite of confession before his execution. The real reason for his persecution was not theological error but his campaign against clerical abuses.[109] In his biography of Wyclif (1786), Zitte maintained that Hus was not affected by Wyclif's erroneous or heretical propositions. The prime example was Hus's continued adherence to the doctrine of transubstantiation.[110]

Other champions of Catholic Enlightenment recognized the kinship between Reform Catholicism and Utraquism. Abbot Steinbach agreed that the Utraquists adhered to Catholic orthodoxy and applauded the proceedings of the Council of Basel, confirmed by Pope Eugene, that recognized in the Compactata (1436) the Utraquists as "the first sons of the Church" (*die ersten Söhne der Kirche*) and as equal to the communicants *sub una* (*die einfach Kommunicirenden*).[111] Němeček sharply distinguished the Utraquist form of worship from that of the Protestants. In particular, their religious songs contrasted with the "tastelessness" (*Abgeschmackheiten*) of the German Lutheran hymns.[112] It may be noted for its symbolic significance that the prominent leader of Josephist Reform Catholicism, Abbot Rautenstrauch, was in contact with the Old Catholics of Holland, grouped in the Union of Utrecht. These Old Catholics were, like the Utraquists, representatives of liberal Catholicism, although—unlike the Utraquists—they did not recognize the pope's priestly role within the church.[113]

Lingering Religious Symbiosis

In general, Catholic clergy educated in the enlightened spirit under the guidance of Karl H. Seibt, Dobrovský, Josef F. Hurdálek, Jan L. Hay, Rautenstrauch, and Augustin Zippe had no qualms about endorsing the

Utraquist Reformation and its heroes. Despite Václav Thám's preface, which contained a trenchant critique of the Counter-Reformation's cultural depredations, twenty-two Catholic priests constituted the largest group among the prepublication subscribers to his *Básně v řeči vázané* (1785).[114] Under the sway of the Catholic Enlightenment, the Roman clergy could participate in the liberal spirit of the national revival with relatively little concern, and writers such as Royko, Stach, Johann H. Wolf, Zitte, and Pelcl could seek to equate Bohemian Utraquism with the Reform Catholicism of the Enlightenment. Staying within the framework of the Catholic Enlightenment, they defended the Catholic orthodoxy of Hus and the lay communion in both kinds, as well as admitting the fallibility of the popes and the ecumenical councils.[115] Although in 1790 Kramerius ran into censorship difficulties when he planned to publish a Czech translation of Friedrich Eckhart's biography of Žižka, Puchmajer (a Catholic priest) published his "Ode on Jan Žižka of Trocnov" in 1802, in which he celebrated his subject as a national liberator and a patriot who avenged the martyrdom of Hus against the papal and imperial crusaders.[116]

After the turn of the century, a divergence would develop between the civic culture revived by the awakening and the increasingly rigorous stance of the Roman Church, which was returning to the tridentine spirit of rigidity and authoritarianism. Nevertheless, a degree of symbiosis between Reform Catholicism and sixteenth-century Utraquism persisted well into the nineteenth century. The quintessential representative of the Josephist Enlightenment, Václav Stach, continued to teach at the Olomouc seminary throughout the 1790s.[117] Another one, Kašpar Royko, continued to hold influential positions until his voluntary retirement in 1814.[118] Augustin Zippe, yet another emblematic figure of Josephist Reform Catholicism—who served as the rector of the general seminary in Prague (1783–85) and was subsequently elevated to the position of director of theological studies in Vienna—continued, after the abolition of that office, as a member of the educational commission of the imperial government until his death in 1816.[119] Johann Heinrich Wolf's textbook *Geschichte des Königreichs Böheim* (1783), written in the spirit of the Catholic Enlightenment, continued in use into the 1820s, and a Czech translation was published in 1819.[120] At the same time, the liberal Josef Dittrich, who had helped resurrect the Utraquist literature of the sixteenth century, still taught theology at the University of Prague in the early 1820s.[121]

A bastion of the Catholic and Utraquist symbiosis was the seminary of Litoměřice, where Hurdálek served as bishop (1815–22) and where Dobrovský could influence the seminarians during periodic visits.[122] His star disciple there was Zahradník, whom he supplied with Utraquist literature such as Rokycana's sermons. Deeply immersed in the spirit of Reform Catholicism, Zahradník became an enthusiastic devotee of sixteenth-century Czech writings.[123] Likewise, priests in rural Bohemia could propagate with impunity publications in the spirit of the Enlightenment, such as Jan Nejedlý's *Hlasatel český* (1806–1807, 1818–19).[124]

Among the laity, Jeník of Bratřice valued the liberal Catholicism of Bernard Bolzano and Michael Fesl and objected to their persecution in 1819. He also agreed with Royko's irenic interpretation of Hus and the Bohemian Reformation.[125] Čelakovský did not see any contradiction between his admiration for Hus and his continued participation in the rites of the Roman Church, although he was at the same time highly critical of the hierarchy and an adamant opponent of the defenders of the Counter-Reformation. Most of his literary associates were liberal Catholic priests and even a nun. Jungmann, although indifferent to orthodox Christianity, likewise maintained that Hus did not mean to establish a new religion and did not differ from the Roman Church in any dogmas; he questioned only the extent of papal authority. In his dogmatic orthodoxy, he thus differed in principle from Luther and subsequent Protestantism.[126]

The revolutionary year 1848 would briefly revive expectations of returning the liberal spirit of Utraquism to the Roman Church. The aftermath of 1848, however, would put a final end to the hopes that a Reform or liberal Catholicism might return the Roman Church to a Utraquist-like state. Thus, in the end, the liberal influence was eliminated from the area of ecclesiology, and the spirit of the Enlightenment continued to flourish in the secular sphere alone.[127]

5

The Czech National Awakening as a Renaissance

This chapter considers the transmission of political and cultural values over a gap of almost two centuries from the Bohemian Reformation (1415–1622) to the national revival (1773–1848). This transfer is traced through the reprinting of sixteenth-century classics, the reproduction of sixteenth-century writings in school and university textbooks, the celebration of the Bohemian Reformation in history and literature, and the embrace of the historical rights of the pre-1620 Bohemian state as a political program.

The Infrastructure of Restoration

It was František M. Pelcl in Prague who started the tradition of reprinting sixteenth-century Czech literature, issuing *Příhody Václava Vratislava z Mitrovic* (The Adventures of Václav Vratislav of Mitrovice) in 1777. He defined the rationale behind the project in the preface to this edition, praising the standard of sixteenth-century Czech literature and excoriating the executors of the Counter-Reformation, especially the Jesuit missionaries, for the work of cultural destruction. He exclaimed, "It is a wonder that here and there a Czech book turns up."[1] Karel Raphael Ungar similarly complained about the scarcity of books in the Czech language, which was caused by the zeal of "pious literary storm troopers" who annihilated entire volumes or obliterated their parts. In revulsion against the *Index librorum prohibitorum,* in 1782 Josef V. Zlobický proposed to Emperor Joseph II that the index itself be prohibited.[2] The recovery of the thought of the age of Utraquism presupposed, first, bibliographic identification of the publications of the sixteenth century; second, establishment of editorial and publication programs; and, third, a return to the language norms of the sixteenth century.

Bibliographic Record

Although, as Pelcl pointed out, the depredations of the book burners hampered the restoration of the bibliographic record, the work was also facilitated by the influx of publications from the hitherto proscribed collections after the demise of the Jesuit Order in 1773. Leopold J. Scherschnik published an early survey of the holdings of the library of the formerly Jesuit St. Clement's College in 1776, noting carefully the works of Hus and Jerome of Prague.[3] In addition to Pelcl, Mikuláš Adaukt Voigt (1733–87) and František Faustin Procházka (1749–1809) contributed greatly to the restoration of the literary bibliography.[4] In his *Acta litteraria Bohemiae et Moraviae* (1774–84), Voigt stresses the previously proscribed works (in both Czech and Latin) of the period of the Bohemian Reformation, especially the publications of the sixteenth century.[5] Procházka's thorough intellectual history *De saecularibus liberalium artium in Bohemia et Moravia* (1782) emphasizes the period of sixteenth-century humanism and eighteenth-century Enlightenment, and it influenced not only Josef Dobrovský but also Josef Jungmann. His subsequent collections, *Miscellaneen der Böhmischen und Mährischen Litteratur* (1784–85), likewise laud the humanist literature but do not neglect the religious writings of the Bohemian Reformation.[6]

Another outstanding bibliographer was Karel Raphael Ungar, who directed the university library in Prague. František X. Němeček expressed his deep gratitude to him for salvaging suppressed books from episcopal consistories and placing them into public libraries, and Karel Ignác Thám credited him with collecting some 2,500 sixteenth-century volumes.[7] Ungar's bibliographic compendium, *Allgemeine böhmische Bibliothek* (1786), listed not only holdings of the university library but also those of private libraries in Prague and abroad. Moreover, he searched booksellers' catalogs and various editions of the Index of Prohibited Books for additional entries.[8] In general, Ungar deplored the scarcity of Bohemian books, especially from the period 1414–1635, which were automatically subject to the inquisitorial zeal of the Counter-Reformation. If not completely destroyed, publications were mutilated by obliteration of passages or entire pages. The zeal of the censors affected even literature by authors *sub una*, such as so-called Dalimil, Václav Hájek, and Johann Ferus. Ungar continued to publicize his bibliographic findings beyond the initial compendium.[9]

The eminent Dobrovský had special words of praise for the bibliographic accomplishments of František Faustin Procházka, which would bring the Czech-language publications of the Utraquist era to the awareness of the reading public.[10] Dobrovský himself contributed to the identification of the corpus of this literature, incorporating the results in three early collections of literary history.[11] He was especially interested in describing the holdings of libraries both in Prague and elsewhere in Bohemia, focusing on important manuscripts and rare books. He sought to enlist the cooperation of other scholars in gathering the bibliographic data, promising them acknowledgment in his journal.[12] In the same vein, he exhorted Bohemian libraries, particularly those in Prague, to prepare and publish catalogs of their collections. Paradoxically, he also found a major aid in the *Index Bohemicorum Librorum Prohibitorum* by Antonín Koniáš, the third edition of which appeared in 1770. Dobrovský's contributions to the allied field of the history of printing appeared particularly in his *Über Einführung und Verbreitung der Buchdruckerkunst in Böhmen* (Introduction and Diffusion of the Art of Printing in Bohemia) (1782) and in several editions of his *Geschichte der böhmischen Sprache und Literatur* (History of the Czech Language and Literature) (1791, 1792, 1818).[13] He was able to build on the work of his Enlightenment predecessors, such as Voigt's *Beiträge zur Buchdruckerkunst in Böhmen* (Contributions to the Art of Printing in Bohemia) (1772) and Ungar's edition of Bohuslav Balbín's *Bohemia docta* (1776–80). Dobrovský, in turn, found his most important successor in Jungmann with his comprehensive *Historie literatury české* (History of Czech Literature), first published in 1825, which in a way crowned this work of bibliographic archeology.[14]

Publication Programs

As for publication programs, Dobrovský praised the publishers who, in the early 1780s—immediately after the abolition of the index in 1782—began to reprint the hitherto proscribed Czech books. He cited the example of Comenius's *Labyrint světa* (The Labyrinth of the World), which appeared as early as 1782. Václav Thám, who himself edited reprints of Czech poetry in the two volumes of *Básně v řeči vázané* (Poems in

Verse) (1785), was a dedicated advocate of restoring to circulation the fruits of the literary past.[15] Before the republication process, sixteenth-century literature was difficult to find. In the 1760s and 1770s, Pelcl, for instance, had depended on the private libraries of the Šternberks and the Nostices.[16] Pelcl himself considered reprinting sixteenth-century classics and encouraged others, like Jan B. Dlabač, to do the same. The republication activity was also supported by Jan Jeník of Bratřice, with the express wish to make up for the void created by the Jesuit censorship in Bohemia's literary heritage.[17]

After a brief start, Pelcl yielded the field of reprints to Procházka, whose publication program became emblematic for the transmission of sixteenth-century knowledge.[18] Procházka conceived an ambitious design to restore the materials that had perished during the Counter-Reformation and had not yet been reprinted in new editions. Launching his project in 1786, he envisioned four series: (1) histories and chronicles of the Czechs; (2) histories of other nations; (3) treatises on arts and sciences; and (4) nonpolemical religious literature. In the first series, he published the Dalimil or Boleslav Chronicle and that of Pulkava; in the second, Oldřich Prefát of Vlkanov's travelogue and Hosius's *Moscow Chronicle*; in the third, Kopp's treatise on health,[19] the collection by Jan Češka, *Příkladné řeči a užitečná naučení vybraná z knih hlubokých mudrců* (Exemplary Speeches and Useful Instructions, Selected from the Books of Wise Men),[20] and Erasmus's *O připravení k smrti* (Preparation for Death)[21] and *Enchridion*; in the fourth, Pseudo-Augustine's *Samotné rozmlouvání duše* (The Soliloquies of the Soul). All were published in 1786 except for Erasmus's *Enchiridion* (1787).[22] In a preface to that book, Procházka defended his publication program against the rearguard of the Counter-Reformation whose champions blamed him for disregarding the Index of Prohibited Books.[23] The stress on Erasmus was particularly significant, inasmuch as his Catholic humanism served as a bridge between Utraquism and the Catholic Enlightenment.[24] The awakeners, in fact, were as fond of Erasmus as their Utraquist predecessors had been. Royko called Erasmus "a man miraculously schooled in Greek and Latin writings, born to expel barbarism from the earth."[25] Dobrovský drew on Erasmus for opposition to ascetic religious practices. Subsequently, the writer František V. Hek also belonged among his admirers.[26]

Those who followed in Procházka's footsteps included František Jan Tomsa (1753–1814) and Václav Matěj Kramerius (1753–1809). Pelcl admonished Tomsa to observe Procházka's high linguistic standards in his own re-publication of sixteenth-century classics.[27] Kramerius's notable reprintings included *Letopisové trojanští* (The Chronicles of Troy) (1790), Šimon Lomnický of Budeč, *Krátké naučení mladému hospodáři* (A Brief Instruction for a Young Householder) (1794), *Ezopovy básně* (The Poems of Aesop) (1791), *Jana Mandyvilly, znamenitého rytíře cesty po světě* (World Travels of John Mandeville, the Famous Knight) (1796), *Krátká historie o válce židovské z knih Josefa Flavia* (A Short History of the Jewish War by Josephus Flavius) (1806), and *Příhody Václava Vratislava z Mitrovic* (1807).[28] Another important republisher of sixteenth-century literature was Johann Ferdinand of Schönfeld, whose printing house issued, among others, *Perlička dítek božích* (A Little Pearl of God's Children) (1782) by Sixt Palma Močidlanský,[29] Pseudo-Augustine's *Samotné rozmlouvání duše* (1784),[30] *Vzdychání nábožná* (Pious Aspirations) (1786) by Jan A. Komenský, and above all the sizable *Kronika česká* (Bohemian Chronicle) (serially, 1819–23) by Václav Hájek of Libočany.[31] Schönfeld employed the literary, editorial, and historical skills of Josef Linda (1789–1834). Finally, Václav Hanka (1791–1861) received high credit for republishing old Czech texts.[32]

Language Norms

Finally, the national awakening involved the reestablishment of the sixteenth-century grammatical norms for the new literary language. Václav Fortunát Durych and František Faustin Procházka laid the foundation for the restoration of the language by relying on old editions and manuscripts in their republication of the Bible in 1778–80. Along these lines, in 1785 Václav Thám denounced the campaign that the Jesuits had carried on during the Counter-Reformation against the exemplary Czech language of the sixteenth century. They sought to downgrade it by ascribing to it the adjective *Hussite*—a word odious to them but glorious to the Czechs.[33] Two Counter-Reformation diehards, the grammarians Jan V. Pól and Maximilian Šimek, had voiced objections to restoring the language to its sixteenth-century purity in the 1770s and 1780s. Their characterization of the old Czech language as "heretical," however, seemed irrelevant, and they acquired the reputation of mischievous, if not comical, busybodies.[34] For instance, Tomsa denounced Pól's linguistic work in the introduction to his own *Vollständiges Wörterbuch* (Complete Dictionary) (1791) for violating the classical norms in the two editions of his *Grammatica linguae Bohemi-*

cae, published in Vienna in 1773 and 1783.[35] Pelcl was also harsh in his assessment of Pól's work, charging that his grammar book contained "a multitude of newly coined words, which a Bohemian could not possibly understand," as well as much incorrect spelling. He went on to describe Pól's manual of Czech orthography (1786) as "entirely false and incorrect" (*ganz falsch und fehlerhaft*).[36] Pelcl's aversion to the linguistics of the Counter-Reformation era is further illustrated by his comment on the *Alphabetum Bohemicum* (1718): "The author is unknown and his rules are mostly false and ungrammatical." As for Šimek, Dobrovský freely expressed his skepticism about his knowledge of Czech grammar.[37]

In furthering the work of language restoration, Pelcl inventoried the sources for an authoritative dictionary of the Czech language in 1793 and characteristically cited, not the imprints of the Counter-Reformation, but such sixteenth-century classics as the works of Václav Hájek, Veleslavín, Sixt of Ottersdorf, and Komenský; the translations of Jan Kocín of Kocinét; and the texts of parliamentary documents. For that purpose, he proposed the establishment of a society, *Hromada*, the members of which would excerpt words from the sixteenth-century literature.[38] In the introduction to his own book on Czech grammar (1795, 1798), Pelcl maintained that the Czech language reached its perfection in the second half of the sixteenth century when it had become as regular and expressive as Latin or Greek. The rules of grammar were best derived from the literature of the outstanding writers of that age. He singled out for special praise the grammar of Vavřinec Benedikt z Nudožer, published in 1603.[39] Likewise, Jiljí Bartoloměj Chládek, a member of the Premonstratian Order and rector of the University of Prague, based the rules for his textbook on Czech grammar (1795) on the literature of the Utraquist age. This work was held in unusually high regard by Pelcl.[40]

Dobrovský, even in his histories of literature, was always interested in the character of language itself, stressing the importance of the art of translation, dictionaries, and grammar books.[41] In 1786, he praised Kramerius's translation of Bishop Hay's pastoral letter for its special virtue of keeping "very close to the Bohemian literary language as it [appeared] in the best writers of the sixteenth century—in the Golden Age of our mother tongue."[42] On the same basis, Dobrovský formulated the rules of Czech prosody (1794) and of Czech grammar (1809, 1819).[43] Relying heavily on Dobrovský's advice, Tomsa also by and large followed the linguistic model of the sixteenth century in his early lexicographic and grammatical works, culminating in the *Vollständiges Wörter-*

buch (1791). In particular, he lauded *Lexicon symphonum* by Sigismund Gelenius (1537), which he thought deserved to be republished with only minor revisions.[44] Dobrovský prepared an introduction in which he confirmed that Tomsa had frequently consulted him in Prague.[45] In his newspaper, *Krameriovy noviny*, in June 1791 Kramerius extolled the perfection of the Czech language of two hundred years earlier, deplored its subsequent decline, and rejoiced in its current revival.[46] In October 1791, Kramerius enthusiastically welcomed Tomsa's grammatical texts for having "collected only those rules which have a solid basis in the works of our classical Czechs."[47]

In comparison with the philological work of Pelcl, Dobrovský, and Tomsa, that of Karel Ignác Thám became more controversial, although he also sought to remain within the linguistic paradigms of the sixteenth century. In the introduction to the first edition of his dictionary, *Deutsch-böhmisches Nationallexikon* (German-Czech National Dictionary) (1788), he listed among his sources numerous sixteenth-century texts, including original Czech works, translations of foreign authors, law books, and town charters.[48] He succeeded in obtaining a preface from the distinguished linguist Johann Christoph Adelung, the librarian of the elector of Saxony in Dresden. In the preface, Adelung supported the Bohemian awakeners' linguistic restoration, pointing out that contemporary Italy was experiencing a similar Renaissance and that Greece was soon to follow.[49] In line with the linguistic return to the sixteenth century, Thám acknowledged—in the first volume of the 1805 edition of his own dictionary—his substantial indebtedness to the dictionary *Sylva quadrilinguis,* published by Veleslavín in 1598.[50]

Sharp criticism of Thám's lexicographic work came from Dobrovský, who deplored the lack of accuracy. A fairly acrimonious exchange of views between the two scholars ensued in the spring of 1798 over the forthcoming second edition of Thám's German-Czech dictionary, published in 1799–1800.[51] Possibly as a consequence of this critique, the publisher omitted Thám's name from the second volume of the next edition (1805–7), though his name was fully restored in the edition of 1814.[52] Thám's book of Czech grammar *Böhmische Grammatik zum Gebrauche der Deutschen* (Czech Grammar for the Use of Germans) (1798) also encountered sharp criticism, this time from Pelcl. Pelcl charged Thám with plagiarism and fictitious entries.[53] Nevertheless, Thám's grammar appeared subsequently in a fourth and a fifth edition (1801, 1804).[54]

All along, Dobrovský was leisurely preparing his own dictionary, largely with the assistance of Antonín J. Puchmajer. Puchmajer also relied heavily on the literature of the Utraquist period, noting in his letter to Dobrovský on February 9, 1798, that twenty-seven of his sources were published in the sixteenth century and only one in the first half of the eighteenth.[55] The second volume of Dobrovský's *Deutsch-böhmisches Wörterbuch* (German-Czech Dictionary), published in 1821, was mostly Puchmajer's work.[56] In the preface to the first volume, originally published in 1802, Dobrovský had returned to his critique of inaccuracies in the second edition of Thám's dictionary.[57] Dobrovský maintained that in comparing Thám's dictionary with the earlier one by Tomsa, whenever the former was wrong, the latter was correct.[58]

The views of Dobrovský, Kramerius, and Pelcl were embraced by Jan Nejedlý (1776–1834), Pelcl's successor as professor of Czech at the University of Prague and editor of the first modern Czech journal, *Hlasatel český*.[59] Voicing the consensus of the awakeners, *Hlasatel český* endorsed the linguistic norms of Veleslavín on its opening page (1806).[60] Issues of modernizing the sixteenth-century orthography, raised especially by Tomsa and Karel Ignác Thám, were settled in a generally conservative direction under Dobrovský's authority.[61] Jungmann, in his important "Dvojí rozmlouvání o jazyku českém" (Two Disquisitions about the Czech Language) (1803) considered, in the second disquisition, Veleslavín to be a paragon of the language culture at its highest.[62] The revival of sixteenth-century language as a medium for literary work was characteristic not only of the elite but also of such rank and file authors as František V. Hek.[63] Moreover, Vincenc Zahradník maintained that the old Czech could express philosophical concepts more substantively and concretely than contemporary German could. Not only the lexical side but also the syntactical side should observe the old norms.[64] This injunction was followed most notably by František Palacký (1798–1876), who successfully emulated not only the vocabulary but also the style of sixteenth-century Czech in his literary work.[65]

Reprinting the Classics

To establish the link between the Utraquist century and the awakening, let us examine the record of republishing the classic sixteenth-century works during the period from 1781 to 1881. It was at this time that Bohemia's modern political culture was taking shape. As noted earlier, the principal reason for reprinting and disseminating sixteenth-century Utraquist literature was a recognition of its intrinsic didactic, historical, or entertainment value. Subsidiary reasons were the insufficiency of current writings in Czech and the intellectual or linguistic irrelevance of the literature of the Counter-Reformation period.[66] We shall mark the character and extent of this republication process, excepting legal texts and legal literature, which are considered in a separate section. This inventory is not intended to be comprehensive or exhaustive but rather suggestive of the variety and richness of the reprints.[67]

Initially, the reprints tended to appear in serial publications. While Dobrovský devoted his journals (published 1779–86) largely to bibliographies and reports on current publications and academic affairs, Voigt and Procházka opened their pages to smaller pieces of fifteenth- and sixteenth-century Bohemian literature. In his *Acta litteraria*, for instance, Voigt included brief texts of Adam Rosacius of Carlsperg, Adam Zalužanský of Zalužany, and Václav Hájek, as well as manuscripts, in particular "Acta Bohemica Concilii Basilensis" (c. 1433) and "Statuta Collegii Caroli Quarti" (1528).[68] In his *Miscellaneen*, Procházka, among others, published minor works of Viktorin Kornelius of Všehrdy and Bohuslav Hasištejnský of Lobkovice, as well as manuscripts concerning the Taborites and, more broadly, the Bohemian Reformation. Procházka stopped issuing his journal in 1785, when he turned to his master plan—mentioned earlier—of systematically reprinting, in several series, a substantial part of the Czech fifteenth- and sixteenth-century classics. At that time, he concluded an agreement for his publication program with the bookseller Caspar Windtmann and the printer Jan J. Diesbach.[69]

Thus, it was the reprints of books that prevailed over those in journals. Of special interest is the transmission (thanks to Josef Dittrich) of a quintessential Utraquist text, namely, Bohuslav Bílejovský's *Kronika česká* (1537), under the title of *Kronika církevní* in 1816. Dittrich, an alumnus of the reformed general seminary in Vienna in the 1780s and professor of church history at the University of Prague since 1803, also prepared new editions of two works by Tomáš Bavorovský in 1822, an irenic theologian from the Roman side who advocated friendly coexistence between the *sub una* and the Utraquists.[70] Dittrich's use of Czech pseudonyms, Skalský and Klíč, reflected his association with the national awakening. Another example of religious literature was John Chrysostom's *Kniha o napravení padlého* (Book about the Correction of a Fallen Man), translated and provided with a patriotic preface by Viktorin Kornelius of Všehrdy, originally published in 1495 (second edition, 1501), which reappeared in 1820.[71] As noted earlier, Oldřich Velenský of Mnichov's Czech translation of *Enchiridion militis Christiani* by Erasmus, originally published in 1519, and Erasmus's *O připravení k smrti*, originally published in 1563–64, were reprinted by Procházka in 1786–87.[72] In a revival of religious and didactic literature, Veleslavín's work *Čest a nevina pohlaví ženského* (Honor and Innocence of the Female Gender) (1585) reappeared in 1823 with an appended treatise by Kocín, *Abeceda pobožné manželky a rozšafné hospodyně* (The Alphabet of a Pious Spouse and a Prudent Housekeeper).[73]

In the field of history, Procházka reissued the Chronicle of so-called Dalimil and the *Kronika česká* by Příbík Pulkava of Radenín in 1786, both of which were especially popular in the sixteenth century.[74] In 1817, Kramerius made available for Czech readers the historical writings of Veleslavín and Martin Kuthen through the republication of *Dvě kroniky o založení země České* (Two Chronicles about the Founding of the Bohemian Land). As noted earlier, *Kronika česká* (1541) by Václav Hájek was serially reprinted during 1819–23 by the publisher Johan Ferdinand of Schönfeld.[75] The reprints in the field of history profoundly influenced the new literary production of the awakening period. Thus, in 1828 the playwright Václav V. Klicpera looked at Hájek's chronicle as an inexhaustible source of themes for Czech poetry. In the 1830s, the famous Karel Hynek Mácha praised Hájek's work as an outstanding piece of Czech *belles lettres*.[76] Other reprints of historical works from the sixteenth century include a collection of documents edited by Jan B. Dlabač and published in 1821.[77] Furthermore, Prokop Lupáč of Hlaváčov's *Historie o císaři Karlovi IV*, originally published in 1584, was reissued by Hanka in 1848, and *Kronika Pražská* by Bartoš Písař, written in the 1530s, was published by Karel J. Erben in 1851. All of Veleslavín's original works, which dealt mostly with historical themes, were included in a collected edition of 1853.[78]

From the rich historical and geographic literature of non-Bohemian countries, Matouš Hosius's translation of *Kronika Moskevská* (Muscovite Chronicle) by Aleksander Gwagnin (Alessandro Guagnini), which had appeared in 1589, was reissued around 1786 in Prague with an introduction by František Faustyn Procházka.[79] In 1805, Ladislav Bartolomeides republished in Levoča Flavius Josephus's *Jewish War*, translated by Pavel Aquilinas (Vorličný) under the title *Flavia Jozefa o válce židovské knihy sedmery* (originally published in 1553). In 1806, another version, based on the edition by Mikuláš Stypacius of 1591, was published again by Kramerius in Prague.[80] Jan Kocín's translation of Eusebius's *Ecclesiastical History* (1594) appeared under the title *Desatery knihy Eusebiovy církevní historie* in 1855 in a new edition by J. E. Krbec.[81] From the favorite genre of travel literature, one of the earliest republications was *Příhody Václava Vratislava z Mitrovic*, prepared, as noted earlier, by Pelcl in 1777. The volume was published again by Kramerius in 1807.[82] It was again Procházka, who reissued Oldřich Prefát of Vlkanov's *Cesta z Prahy do Benátek* (A Journey from Prague to Venice) (originally printed in 1563) in Prague in 1786.[83] Kramerius published the fictitious travelogue *Jana Mandyvilly, znamenitého rytíře cesty po světě* (The World Travels of John Mandeville, the Illustrious Knight) in 1796; the original Czech edition had appeared in Plzeň in 1510.[84]

Among the reprints of popular sixteenth-century *belles lettres*, *Historijí dvanácte o bratru Janu Palečkovi* (Twelve Stories about Brother Jan Paleček) (1567), ranked especially high, and the component stories appeared several times in various journals at the turn of the eighteenth century.[85] In 1790, Kramerius issued anew *Letopisové Trojanští*, a book published three times previously (after 1476, 1487, and 1603),[86] as well as *Ezopovy básně* in 1791.[87] Šimon Lomnický of Budeč enjoyed new popularity; Tomsa republished his tale, *Tobolka zlatá* (A Golden Purse), in 1791, and Kramerius republished a didactic piece, *Krátké naučení mladému hospodáři* (A Brief Instruction for a Young Householder), in 1794.[88] Dobrovský, collaborating with Antonín Pišely, published a collection of folk sayings and proverbs by Jakub Srnec of Varvažov in 1804 under the title *Českých přísloví sbírka* (A Collection of Bohemian Proverbs).[89] *Rada všelikých zvířat* (The Counsel from Divers Animals) originally published in Plzeň (1528) and in Prague (c.1573 and 1578) was republished in 1815 with an introduction by Dobrovský.[90] Selections from Vavřinec Leander Rvačovský of Rvačov's *Masopust* (The Mardi Gras)—such as *Klevetník* (A Gossip) and *Všetýčka* (A Busybody)—were reprinted several times in late eighteenth and early nineteenth century.[91] Václav Dobřenský's didactic work, *Vrtkavé štěstí* (Fickle Fortune) (1583), reappeared in Prague in 1824 in an edition by Václav R. Štěpán.[92] The play *Historia o jednom sedlském pacholku a poběhlém židu* (Story of a Peasant and a Wandering Jew) by Tobiáš Mouřenín of Litomyšl, originally published in 1604, was reprinted at least eleven times in the nineteenth century, the last time in 1877. One of its central themes was used by Josef Kajetán Tyl in his play *Strakonický dudák* (The Bagpiper of Strakonice).[93] The story of *Meluzína* (Mélusine), published in 1595, was converted into a play by Klicpera and published in 1848.[94]

Finally, the linguistic heritage of the sixteenth century was successfully retrieved. The most massive recovery occurred through the reappearance of the thesaurus of the Czech language, based on the work of Veleslavín. In 1805, Karel Ignác Thám published his *Neuestes ausführliches und vollständiges deutsch-böhmisches synonymisch-phraseologisches Nationallexikon oder Wörterbuch* (1805–7), based on Veleslavín's *Sylva quadrilinguis vocabulorum et phrasium Bohemicae, Latinae, Graecae et Germanicae linguae* (1598). A second revised edition, also by Thám, appeared in 1814, under the same title. In line with the restoration and celebration of the Czech linguistic norms of the sixteenth century, in 1818 Dobrovský reprinted Václav Písecký's encomium of 1512, entitled "The Merits of the Czech Language."[95]

As a result of the program of reprinting, Czech readers in the period of the national awakening had available to them a large portion of the corpus of literature that had intellectually nourished their sixteenth-century ancestors. The process was aided by cheaper printing and the spread of literacy, especially in the rural areas, under the influence of the Enlightenment.[96]

Transmission in Textbooks

The second approach to documenting the revival of sixteenth-century values is to look at what nationally conscious Czech students studied and what shaped their world outlook. Pelcl, on his appointment as the first professor of Czech language and literature at the University of Prague in 1792, already had his students reading sixteenth-century authors and parliamentary documents.[97] The same was true of his successors in this academic chair: Jan Nejedlý (1801–34), who was particularly insistent on fidelity to the sixteenth-century norms of the Czech language, followed by Čelakovský (1835–36), Jan Vávra (1836–39), and Jan P. Koubek (1840–54). In the opening decades of the nineteenth century, students depended on the reprinted works or original editions, as was the case with Zahradník, who studied, among others, Veleslavín, Kocín, Koldín, Plácel of Elbing, Sixt of Ottersdorf, Hájek, and Komenský.[98] The reintroduction of the sixteenth-century modes of thought was later facilitated by textbooks, which provided relatively easy access to a great variety of authors.

A modest beginning to the publication of anthologies of old Czech literature was the sample of texts in Karel Ignác Thám's *Kurzgefasste böhmische Sprachlehre* (A Brief Textbook of Czech) (1785), reprinted in the fourth (1801) and fifth editions (1804) of his *Grammatik*.[99] This was followed by the "Chrestomathie" in Tomsa's *Über die Veränderungen der čechischen Sprache* (On the Changes in Czech Language) (1805), which contained literary texts mainly from the fifteenth through the early seventeenth centuries plus—characteristically skipping over the baroque era—a number of texts from the post-1770 period.[100] Initially, the two major transmission channels of literature from the sixteenth century to the nineteenth century were the anthologies, published successively by Josef Jungmann and Alois V. Šembera. Jugmann's textbooks included his *Slovesnost* (Literature) (1820) and his *Historie literatury české* (1825). His textbooks were followed by Šembera's two-volume anthology *Dějiny řeči a literatury československé* (History of Bohemian Slav Language and Literature) (1858–68).[101] The second volume, covering the period from 1409, was published serially, beginning in 1861. Characteristically, Šembera keynoted the second volume of the textbook with a quotation from Sixt of Ottersdorf embracing those values that the Bohemian nineteenth century shared with the sixteenth: free discussion and tolerance.[102] Among many witnesses in the 1820s, Václav S. Štulc provides testimony on the intensive use of Jungmann's *Slovesnost*, and Josef F. Šumavský on that of his *Historie literatury české*. Josef Kalousek stressed the deep influence of Jungmann's and Šembera's textbooks on the student youth in the 1850s.[103]

The third major reader of Czech literature was *Výbor z literatury české* (Anthology of Czech Literature). Volume one (1845), *Od nejstarších časů až do počátku XV. století* (From Earliest Times till the Early Fifteenth Century), was edited by Josef J. Jungmann with František Palacký and others, and volume two (1868), *Od počátku XV až do konce XVI. století* (From the Early Fifteenth to the End of the Sixteenth Centuries), was edited by Karel J. Erben.[104] In his introduction to volume two, Erben justified the focus on the Utraquist period by stressing its literary merits and contrasting them with the mediocrity and corrupted language of most of the seventeenth- and eighteenth-century writings. This volume started appearing in installments in 1857 and was completed in 1868. The eleven-year hiatus between the appearance of the first volume (1845) and the resumption of the work on the second (1856) was caused by the revolutionary events of 1848 and their aftermath. According to Erben, the main purpose of the textbook was to provide an inventory of Czech literary achievements and to serve as a basis for further development of literature in the Czech language.[105]

The *Výbor z literatury české* contained a rich and varied selection from the writers of the Bohemian Reformation. Volume one, published in 1845, excerpted five works of Tomáš of Štítné: *Rozmluvy nábožné* (Discussions about Religion), *Knihy učení křesťanského* (Books of Christian Teaching), *Řeči sváteční* (Holiday Sermons), *O sedmi stupních* (Seven Steps), and *Sv. Augustina samomluvenie* (St. Augustine's Soliloquy).[106] Volume two contained a plethora of works by the theological luminaries of the Utraquist Church, beginning with selections of Jan Hus's *Postilla* (Homiliary), *Dcerka* (A Daughter), and *Listové ze žaláře* (Letters from Prison) and of Jerome of Prague's *List panu Lackovi z Kravař* (A Letter to the Lord Lacek of Kravaře).[107] The textbook also presented the account of Poggio Bracciolini to Leonhard of Aretin about the trial and execution of Jerome in 1416 in a Czech translation by Veleslavín.[108] The stormy atmosphere in Bohemia following the death of Hus was captured in the proceedings of the Diets of Prague (September 1415 and November 1423) and that of Čáslav (June 1421), as well as in the records of the council meetings of the Old Town of Prague in July 1420, July 1421, February and May 1422, and January 1429.[109]

Works by other theologians of the fifteenth-century included Jan of Příbram's *Život kněží táborských* (The Lives of Taborite Priests),[110] Prokop of Plzeň's *Veřejné napomenutí Čechům i Moravanům* (A Public Admonition to the Bohemians and Moravians),[111] and three selections from the works of Peter of Chelčice, including his homiliary (*Postilla*).[112] The two leading figures of fifteenth-century Utraquism are included. Jan Rokycana, the archbishop elect, is represented by a *List proti Pikartóm* (A Letter against the Pikharts) (1468) and selections of his homiliary *(Postilla)*,[113] and Václav Koranda the Younger, the Utraquist administrator, by his *Poselstvie krále Jiřího do Říma k papeži* (An Embassy of King George to the Pope in Rome) (1462).[114] The report *O sněmu kutnohorském po smrti krále Jiřího* (The Diet in Kutná Hora after King George's Death) (1471) captured the spirit of Utraquist resistance to the crusades elicited by renewed papal anathemas.[115] The student reader also contained selections from three prominent fifteenth-century personages who were not professional theologians—Vavřinec of Březová,

Jan Žižka,[116] and Ctibor Tovačovský of Cimburk. Tovačovský's *Hádání pravdy a lži* (A Dispute between Truth and Falsehood) (written in 1467, published in 1539) is quoted at considerable length.[117]

Volume two of *Výbor z literatury české* proceeded to cover several of the prominent Utraquist intellectuals involved in the Czech urban culture of the sixteenth century. The earliest was Viktorin Kornelius of Všehrdy's appeal to Bohemian patriotism, taken from the introduction to his translation of John Chrysostom's *Kniha o napravení padlého*.[118] Among the historians of the early sixteenth century, the reader covered Mikuláš Konáč of Hodiškov, Bartoš Písař, and Martin Kuthen of Šprinsberk. The sample of Konáč's writing was taken from his Czech adaptation of Aeneas Sylvius Piccolomini's (Pope Pius II's) *Historia Bohemica* (1510).[119] Bartoš was represented by passages from his *Kronika pražská* (Prague Chronicle) (1530s)[120] and Kuthen by his inspirational *Kronika o Žižkovi* (Žižka Chronicle) (1564).[121] Pavel Aquilinas (Vorličný)'s translation of Flavius Josephus's *Jewish War*, under the title *Flavia Jozefa o válce židovské knihy sedmery* (1553), was a fourth notable historical work of the mid-sixteenth century to be showcased.[122] In addition, the anthology featured two eminent Utraquist statesmen and authors, Sixt of Ottersdorf and Pavel Kristián of Koldín. Sixt discussed the unsuccessful resistance to Ferdinand I's Schmalcaldic War in his *Knihy památné o nepokojných letech 1546 a 1547* (Memoirs of the Troubled Years, 1546–47).[123] The anthology also offered an opportunity for students to savor the legal lore of Koldín from the preface of his famous *Práva městská království českého* (The Municipal Laws of the Bohemian Kingdom) (1579), as well as the section *O spravedlnosti a právu (De justicia et jure)* from the same work.[124]

The textbook devoted considerable space to the author and printer Veleslavín, who presided over the great Czech literary flowering during the last quarter of the sixteenth century, as noted earlier. The *Výbor* credited him with authorship of more than twenty books in Czech, and with many more Czech publications that he edited, revised, or printed. Among the included excerpts were those from Veleslavín's *Život Eneáše Sylvia*, a life of Pius II, which he published in his edition of *Kroniky dvě o založení země české* (Two Chronicles of the Foundation of the Bohemian Land) (1585), containing Pius's *Kronika Česká* and Kuthen's *Kronika o založení země české* (A Chronicle of the Foundation of the Bohemian Land). A specimen of events for January 1 was taken from Veleslavín's *Kalendář historický* (A Historical Calendar) (1578, 1590), which had arranged significant occurrences of Czech and world history by the days of each month.[125] Featured also were two other scholars, Prokop Lupáč of Hlaváčov and Jan Kocín, who had been involved in Veleslavín's publication projects. Lupáč was introduced through his *Historie o císaři Karlovi IV* (History of Emperor Charles IV), originally published in 1584, and Kocín through the introduction to his translation of Eusebius's *Ecclesiastical History* (*Historia církevní Eusebia*), published by Veleslavín in 1594.[126] Veleslavín also revised and published the Czech translation of Aleksander Gwagnin's *Kronika Moskevská* (The Moscow Chronicle) by Matouš Hosius, which appeared in 1589 and is represented in the *Výbor*.[127]

Independently of Veleslavín and his associates, the *Výbor* introduced two authors of the last quarter of the sixteenth century, Václav Dobřenský and Leander Rvačovský. It features excerpts from Dobřenský's didactic work, *Vrtkavé štěstí* (1583). Rvačovský, a notable Utraquist priest, was represented by his entertaining *Masopust* (1580).[128]

Czech scholarly journals, in particular *Časopis českého muzea* starting in 1828, also served as conduits for the appreciation of the literature of the Utraquist sixteenth century, which was highlighted in their coverage. These publications were avidly read by the student youth, as attested by František Cyril Kampelík in 1829. Students, in fact, constituted the largest group of subscribers to such periodicals, between 20 and 30 percent, during the 1830s and 1840s.[129]

Exalting the Bohemian Reformation in History and Literature

A third way of linking the nineteenth with the sixteenth century was through a historical interpretation highlighting the period of the Bohemian Reformation and implicitly, if not explicitly, condemning the heritage of the Counter-Reformation period as irrelevant, obscurantist, and harmful. In a way, the task at hand was to restore the image of Bohemia's history for the country's inhabitants. Jan Jeník of Bratřice, in fact, claimed that the history of Bohemia was entirely ignored during his Jesuit schooling up to the early 1770s.[130]

By a deliberate assault on the "darkness" of the Counter-Reformation, the Catholic Enlightenment facilitated the rearmament of the Bohemian national awakening by rehabilitating features of the distinctive past that largely reflected the drama of the Bohemian Reformation. In the area of history, the new interpretation can be documented, for instance, from the official textbook for secondary schools, the *Geschichte des Königreichs Böheim* (1783). Its author, Johann H. Wolf, the first professor of history at the University of Prague, characterized the events following the Battle of White Mountain (1620) as the deplorable results of the intolerance of the times. Jan Hus and also in a way the Bohemian Utraquist King George of Poděbrady (1458–71) were depicted as victims of excessive, often ruthless, religious zeal.[131] The process of rehabilitation was set in motion in the area of literature and drama as well. Evidence of this trend was the publication of the play *Johann Žižka, chevalier von Trocznow*, by Franz Guolfinger Steinsberg, soon after 1780.[132]

An important protagonist in the campaign to rehabilitate the Utraquist past was Pelcl, who stated on January 16, 1781, in his memoirs: "Every Bohemian who reads Czech-language books and knows the history of his country is already a bit of a Hussite."[133] In his *Kurzgefasste Geschichte der Böhmen* (1774), as well as in his study *Lebensgeschichte des römischen und böhmischen Königs Wenzeslaus* (1788–89), Pelcl sought to establish a correspondence between Hus's reformist critique and outlook and the liberal religious and sociopolitical views of the Enlightenment. Hus's sentencing for heresy by the Council of Constance appeared to him an unjustified and imprudent act. Moreover, according to Pelcl, the violence of the wars of the Bohemian Reformation was less an expression of religious fanaticism than a need to defend against the intolerance of Rome and its implementation by Emperor Sigismund.[134]

The Bohemian Enlightenment produced other vindications of the Bohemian Reformation and critical assessments of authoritarian ecclesiology. A number of Catholic theologians also shared in the rehabilitation, even glorification, of the Bohemian Reformation by applying to it the criteria of the Catholic Enlightenment. As early as the 1750s, Gelasius Dobner began to draw on Utraquist historians such as Veleslavín and Prokop Lupáč of Hlaváčov for his own study of Bohemian history.[135] František Pubička wrote his *Chronologische Geschichte Böhmens* in the spirit of Reform Catholicism. Receiving a whole-hearted approval from Ungar, he objected to the copious ascription of miracles to saints in the hagiographic writings of the Counter-Reformation. Although not entirely uncritical of Hus, Pubička spoke with respect about Hus's efforts at moral regeneration of the clergy and his opposition to granting indulgences for secular ends. He also took pride in the bravery of the Taborite warriors.[136] Voigt, too, endorsed that legacy and noted with satisfaction Hus's great vogue, shown by the marking of his feast day on Bohemian sixteenth-century calendars.[137] Ungar himself wrote an essay on Jan Žižka, whom he presented as a national hero of unusual military skill.[138] As for *belles lettres,* plays celebrating Žižka and the Taborites were staged in Prague in the 1780s.[139]

Subsequently, in 1798 Ignác Cornova emphasized the political wisdom of George of Poděbrady, shown in his ability as a Utraquist to maintain a Catholic orthodoxy according to the Compactata, which recognized the Utraquists as true Catholics and sons of the church.[140] Along the same lines, Dlabač celebrated Žižka, the Taborites, and George of Poděbrady in pamphlets written during the Napoleonic Wars of 1808–13, calling them brave defenders of Bohemia's independence and emphasizing that during the wars of Bohemian Reformation, no outsiders were able to defeat the Czechs.[141]

Perhaps most to the point in the work of rehabilitating the Utraquist Age was Dobrovský's *Geschichte der böhmischen Sprache und Literatur* (1792), which praised the Bohemian Reformation as coinciding with the flourishing of Bohemian literature, extolled the Utraquist theologians for their discussions of the limits and misuse of ecclesiastical authority, and condemned the Counter-Reformation for its cultural vandalism.[142] It was Dobrovský—and Pelcl—who had paved the way for the emergence of Palacký. A connecting link was provided by Jeník of Bratřice, who, inspired by Pelcl, cooperated with both Dobrovský and Palacký in historical research.[143] Palacký's monumental *Dějiny národu českého v Čechách a na Moravě* (History of the Czech Nation in Bohemia and Moravia), begun in 1832, made the Bohemian Reformation the centerpiece and acme of Czech history.

While during the Enlightenment period the Bohemian Reformation could be portrayed positively, during the restoration era of Metternich absolutism (1815–47) or the Pre-March [*Vormärz*] period (preceding the March 1848 Revolution), not only the Roman Church but also the Austrian state began to look askance at certain aspects of the Bohemian past. The censorship targeted mainly the allegedly radical and revolutionary tendencies connected with the names of Hus, Žižka, and Tábor.[144] In 1796, the first two volumes of Royko's history of the Council of Constance could still reappear with their passionate defense of Hus, and in 1798, Jeník of Bratřice, as an Austrian officer, could exhort a company of Czech soldiers to emulate the military prowess of Žižka and Prokop Holý.[145] By 1818, however, Čelakovský had been barred from study in České Budějovice for reading Hus's *Postila*.[146] In contrast, historical texts were relatively immune to the censor's whims, and the reprinting of sixteenth-century publications could continue even after the shadow of the restoration had replaced the era of the Enlightenment within the Habsburg Empire. The desire to disseminate prohibited notions probably supplied the incentive to forge "historical texts" that contained ideas that otherwise would have been unacceptable to the censor. Thus emerged the poems of the Králodvorský and Zelenohorský manuscripts "discovered" in 1817–18 but actually forged by Hanka and Linda. Ironically, these poetic collections, distinctly patriotic and libertarian, came to constitute the first Czech romanticist works of lasting literary value.[147]

A loosening of censorship followed in 1848, and the apotheosis of the Bohemian Reformation again came into the open. Tyl typically glorified persons and events of the period, such as in his plays *Jan Hus* and *Žižka z Trocnova* and his story "Dekret kutnohorský" (The Decree of Kutná Hora). The performance of *Jan Hus* in 1848 aroused sweeping enthusiasm among the theatergoing public.[148] In 1850, Augustin Zitte's eulogistic biography of Hus appeared in a Czech translation by J. V. Sommer.[149]

Historical Rights of the Bohemian State

Yet another way of gauging the reintegration of sixteenth-century precepts into the nineteenth-century context of Bohemia's political culture is to examine the (often ridiculed) emphasis on the historical rights of the Bohemian state. Bohemian constitutional and municipal law of the sixteenth century again reflected a highly developed sense of political pragmatism and dedication to civic society.[150] The legal and constitutional system of Bohemia, benefiting from the skills of the erudite legislators, stood high in comparison with general European standards and those prevalent in neighboring countries. The Confederation of 1619 was in a sense the first modern constitution of Europe.[151]

While a tendency to look back at pre-absolutist constitutionalism appeared elsewhere in Europe in the early nineteenth century, in Bohemia it was particularly significant because of the abrupt and arbitrary abrogation of the country's traditional constitution in consequence of the Battle of White Mountain. The largely ornamental Bohemian Diet, an impotent relic from the pre-1620 period, cautiously attempted to assert its legislative powers and resurrect the principles of the Bohemian constitutional law in its *Desideria* of 1790–91, during a brief relaxation in royal absolutism. These principles appeared to harmonize with the tenets of emerging modern parliamentarianism.[152] Similar tendencies to revive the historical rights of the Bohemian state reappeared, after a long lapse, at the Diet's sessions in the mid-1840s. The campaign to create a parliamentary body on the basis of the moribund feudal assembly culminated in the Diet's approval of the so-called *Dedukce o právní nepřetržitosti práv a svobod českých* (Deduction about the Legal Continuity of the Rights and Liberties of Bohemia) in 1847.[153]

Bohemian awakeners looked fondly back at the legislative system in the Golden Age. Like his cohorts, Pelcl was deeply impressed by the famous classic of Pavel Stránský, *Respublica Boiema* (first printed by Elzevier in Holland in 1634), which he found in the library of the Šternberk family in the 1760s.[154] Voigt included a panegyric on the Bohemian constitution, as it had existed before 1620, in his treatise *Über den Geist der Böhmischen Gesetze* (1788).[155] He selected for special praise the sixteenth-century legal treatises by Viktorin Kornelius of Všehrdy, *O právách, o soudech i o deskách země české knihy devatery* (Nine Books about the Laws, Courts, and Registers of the Bohemian Land) (1508, 1564) and Brikcí of Licko's *Práva městská* (Municipal Law) (1536, 1579, 1590). According to Voigt, before it was distorted by Ferdinand II's Renewed Land Ordinance in 1627, the legal and constitutional system of Bohemia resembled the British political and legal order as it had evolved by the eighteenth century. In the sixteenth century, Bohemia's statecraft was similar to that of contemporary France, and it stood midway between the anarchy of the Polish political order and the absolutism of tsarist Russia.[156] Jeník of Bratřice praised the constitutional norms of the sixteenth century for providing a wide range of civil rights. He valued the advanced character of the Bohemian Confederation of 1619. On the other side of the coin, Jeník fiercely denounced as traitors those—like Jaroslav Bořita of Martinice, Vilém Slavata, and Albrecht Wallenstein—who assisted in abrogating Bohemia's political independence.[157]

Documents and treatises of sixteenth-century Bohemian law (administrative and constitutional) appeared both in new editions and in early nineteenth-century textbooks and readers, which, as pointed out earlier, shaped the minds of the upcoming generations. These re-editions included Viktorin Kornelius of Všehrdy's *Z kněh o právích země české* (From the Books of Legal Rights in the Bohemian Land) (1515), which was published by Hanka with a preface by Palacký in 1841. Excerpts from five parts of this fundamental treatise were also reprinted in volume two of *Výbor z literatury české* (1868).[158] The text of the St. Wenceslaus' Day Contract, concluded in 1517 by the three estates of the Kingdom of Bohemia (*Smlouva všech tří stavů Svatováclavského sněmu*), was reprinted in the journal *Právník* (1861) and appeared in volume two of *Výbor z literatury české*.[159] As early as 1792–1803, Cornova published a German translation of Stránský's *Respublica Boiema* as *Staat von Böhmen* in seven volumes.[160] Only the first four volumes contained Stránský's original work; volumes five through seven were written by Cornova himself. In the notable volume seven, Cornova discussed the history of Bohemian institutions: rulers, courts, officials, law, and diets.[161] He treated the Bohemian Diet of the sixteenth century as both a necessary and a wholesome institution that provided the mechanism for consultation and for securing the consent of the population for the policies of the state. He deplored Ferdinand I's interference with the Diet in the wake of the Schmalkaldic War in 1547 and particularly the emasculation of the Diet by Ferdinand II in 1627 in the wake of the Battle of White Mountain. Finally, he called for the restoration of the Bohemian Diet as it had existed before the reign of Ferdinand II.[162] Even earlier, in 1790 Cornova had published a brief extract from Stránský's work, under the title *Von den böhmischen Landständen, Landtagen und Landesämtern*.[163]

In addition, volume one of *Výbor z literatury české* (1845) contains the first 42 out of 100 articles of *Řád práva zemského* (The Rules of the Law of the Land); these articles, which describe court procedures, were prepared between 1348 and 1355.[164] The volume also contains a collection of Bohemian legal documents from 1380 to 1402, under the title *Nejstarší listiny české* (The Oldest Bohemian Charters),[165] and a treatise, *Výklad na právo země české* (An Exposition of the Laws of the Bohemian Land), which Ondřej of Dubá had prepared for King Wenceslaus IV.[166] Volume two (1868), moving into the fifteenth century, contains the records of the Bohemian Diets of 1415, 1421, and 1423 and of the Diet of Kutná Hora in 1471, which followed the death of George of Poděbrady.[167] As for law literature and documents of the sixteenth century, the *Výbor* begins with the preface by Matouš of Chlumčany to the *Zřízení privilegií koruny a království Českého* (Privileges of the Crown and the Kingdom of Bohemia), submitted to King Vladislav in 1501. Further, the anthology covers the articles adopted by the General Diet of the Kingdom of Bohemia held in January 1547[168] and excerpts from the law code of the Kingdom of Bohemia, *Práva a zřízení zemská království českého* (Constitutional Laws and Institutions of the Kingdom of Bohemia), adopted by the Diet in 1549 and printed in 1550.[169]

In the area of local and municipal law, the widely used fifteenth-century text of Ctibor Tovačovský of Cimburk, the so-called *Kniha Tovačovská* (The Book of Tovačov) (written in the 1480s), was published in excerpts in *Mährischer Magazin* in 1789. The entire work was printed in Brno in 1858 in an edition by Karel J. Demuth and again in Brno in 1868 in an edition by Vincenc Brandl. Volume two of *Výbor z literatury české* also gives lengthy citations from the *Kniha Tovačovská*.[170] Incidentally, Koldín's *Práva městská království českého* (The Municipal Laws of the Kingdom of Bohemia) (1579) was available at the beginning of the nineteenth century in a relatively recent reprint (1755).[171] In addition, in the area of municipal law, the *Výbor z literatury české* offers samples of the proceedings of Prague city councils in the areas of public, as well as private, law between 1418 and 1435. Aside from its attention to the *Kniha Tovačovská* and excerpts from Koldín's *Práva městská království českého*, the textbook contains the preface to Brikcí of Licko's *Práva městská* (The Rights of Towns), originally published in Litomyšl in 1536.[172]

A Reincarnation of *Das schöne oder goldene Zeitalter*

Thus, a way of assessing the Czech national awakening is to view it as an odyssey moving back in time from the culture of the Counter-Reformation to the culture formed by sixteenth-century Utraquism. The revived spirit of Utraquism was celebrated through the work and achievements of the nineteenth-century awakeners. Eventually, it would be the civic aspect of Utraquist liberalism, universalism, and plebeianism without its theology that would prevail in Bohemia's modern political culture.[173] And although the awakeners stressed the importance of the vernacular, language was primarily an instrument to advance universal human values, not an assertion of ethnic distinctiveness and peculiarities.

The obstacles to a fair assessment of the role of the sixteenth century have been duly noted (mainly in chapter 2). It may be argued that, leaving aside the defenders of the Counter-Reformation, the aspersions cast by a coalition of modernist aesthetes, on the one hand, and intellectual and moral rigorists, on the other, were stimulated by, and in turn themselves reinforced, the unfavorable image of the age in Czech historiography as a civilization doomed to annihilation. Already the traditional label for the historical period, "Pre–White Mountain Era" (*doba předbělohorská*), implied that its significance—or perhaps lack of significance—was predetermined (as something ephemeral or transient) by the denouement of the Battle of White Mountain in 1620. This premonition interfered with the evaluation of its long-term role in Bohemia's political and national culture. It obscured the way in which the Bohemian society of the sixteenth century could be said to have foreshadowed, and in its legacy fostered, the liberal values of Bohemian national awakening in its tolerance, constitutional politics, dominance of middle-class culture, and freedom of thought. Far from being doomed, these values proved imperishable and indestructible.[174]

In conclusion, it is important to stress once more the process by which ideas were transmitted from the sixteenth to the late eighteenth century, as discussed in chapters 3 through 5. As we have seen, for the awakeners, the attachment to the values of the Utraquist sixteenth century was a matter of conscious, personal, and voluntary decision. In part, they based that decision on a conviction that it had the moral, or even official, support of the governmental apparatus of the Habsburg monarchy. Therefore, as noted at the start of chapter 3 in this volume, it is neither necessary nor useful to assume that a continuity between the Bohemian Reformation and the national awakening would require ipso facto the action of a hidden metaphysical force that would incite the historical actors to a certain type of behavior or, conversely, that the awakeners must have behaved as epiphenomena of a reified national spirit. This can also serve as a response to the postmodern critics of the allegedly metaphysical presupposition of a historical continuity in national societies.

6

The Bohemian Fate of Johann Gottfried Herder

The Czech national awakening is habitually linked with the influence of Johann Gottfried Herder as a Romantic and anti-Enlightenment figure. This study argues the opposite. It contradicts, at least in the Czech case, the idea originally articulated by Hans Kohn that European nationalism —especially in the center and the east of the continent—was an expression of a particularist self-assertion that verged on (or passed into) xenophobia. It defied the realistic and cosmopolitan outlook of the Enlightenment.

The objective of this chapter is, first, to show that the pacesetters of the Czech national awakening functioned within the realistic cosmopolitan Enlightenment rather than within the emotional self-centeredness growing out of the romanticist ethos. Rather than relying on Herderian sources, the awakeners drew primarily on the ideals of the Josephist Enlightenment and the subsequent liberal Catholicism epitomized by Karl H. Seibt (1735–1806) and Bernard Bolzano (1781–1848). The assumptions to the contrary were based on several issues: (1) a confusion with the Slovak national romanticism; (2) the allegedly antinational character of the Enlightenment; (3) a distaste for liberal Catholicism by both the official Roman Church and the secularists; and (4) the assumption of an obvious ascendancy of German culture, which was inspired by romanticism and philosophical idealism.

The second objective is to highlight the relevance and significance of intellectual substance over institutional forms and to expose the limitation of an extrinsic approach to the understanding of nationalism, as evident, for instance, in the taxonomic approaches of Miroslav Hroch.[1]

The various ethnic groups during their national awakenings at the turn of the eighteenth and early nineteenth centuries may have passed through certain stages of interest in linguistics, folklore, use of their vernacular in offices and schools, or a fair share of representation in political and administrative institutions. These forms, however, were distinct and separate from the political culture, or—if one wishes—the weltanschauung that sought expression through them. The crucial question is whether such forms were the assertion of a specific ethnicity in the spirit of romanticism or whether they partook of a universal human culture within the spirit of the Enlightenment. When two national groups engaged in similar activities, or asked for similar institutions, it did not mean that their purposes were the same. The Czech case indicates that two national agendas may even be contradictory.

The Czech preference for empirical realism over metaphysical idealism can be placed into broader contexts. Projecting into the past, their preference can be related to the Thomistic realism of the Bohemian Reformation in contrast to the anti-Aristotelian stance of Luther and the German Reformation. Projecting into a later period, the Bohemian preference can be related to the dichotomy between the realistic "Austrian" and the speculative "German" philosophical tradition.[2]

Herder's Proto-Romanticism and Idealism

The dark features of East European nationalism are usually viewed as both caused and epitomized by the German Romantic and idealist current of thought in the late eighteenth and early nineteenth centuries. The crucial role in inspiring this process is normally assigned to Johann Gottfried Herder, whose impact was magnified and continued by German philosophical idealism, which culminated in the philosophical and metaphysical system of Hegel. A recent authoritative source has characterized the pivotal function of Herder's thought:

> It would be difficult to underestimate [sic] the influence of the German philosopher Johann Gottfried Herder (1744–1803) on the first, romantic or proto-nationalistic phase of nationalism in Eastern Europe. . . . He also popularized the idea that each people or "folk" had a unique "soul" or "spirit" [*Volksgeist*] that manifested itself in its language, poetry, literature, music, customs, and history.[3]

It has been common practice to emphasize the influence of Herder on the Czech national awakening, particularly with respect to its inspirational Slavic context. Eugen Lemberg, for example, considered Czech national feeling and historical self-image fixated at Herder's outlook.[4] According to Alexander Gillies, "The Czechs were affected first and most fundamentally" by Herder. Frederick M. Barnard echoed this view: the Czechs "were the first to proclaim Herder's gospel of national self-determination."[5] Walter Schamschula saw a paradigm-altering influence of Herder on the Czech national awakening.[6] Alexandr S. Myl'nikov spoke of "the great Herder, one of the most popular figures of the [Czech] national awakening." Robin Okey speaks of growing Herderian influence on the Czechs in the period 1800–30.[7] Such august figures as Tomáš G. Masaryk, and after him Jan Patočka, considered the Czech awakening in large part an offspring of Herderian protoromanticism. Patočka wrote: "Herder provided the intellectual underpinning for our awakening . . . .Early, he affected Dobrovský, then the national topology of Kollár and Šafařík, the humanism of Palacký, the Slavism of the entire coterie of Jungmann. All these intellectual leaders were influenced, above all, by Herder's motive of the Slavs' European cultural mission."[8]

Herder's philosophy of history in its national collectivism, determinism, and particularism indeed contradicted the tenets of the Enlightenment in several ways. Under the influence of Johann G. Hamann, Herder rejected the concept of "mankind," born out of the rationalism and universalism of the Enlightenment.[9] His view was that a nation had a peculiar spirit and that it must advance not through the imitation of others but through the cultivation of its individual characteristics, particularly language, folklore, and national customs. Thus, there was no universal culture, but each nation was to develop its own consciousness: "Every nation carries within itself the central point of its own happiness, just as every ball contains its own center of gravity."[10] It has been suggested that Herder's motivation derived in part from a concern over the fragmented state of the German-speaking area during the eighteenth century. This he wished to remedy through the fostering of a German national ideology that would unite Germany and, based on language and literature, produce a distinct national character. Truth for Herder tended to be more the property of a linguistic entity than a bearing of universal character. The Herderian stress on the unbreakable bond between language and culture was perpetuated by Wilhelm Humboldt.[11]

It was also true that there was a genetic relationship between Herder's philosophy and German philosophical idealism. Herder's weltanschauung, in an anticipation of German romanticism and idealism (especially Schelling and Hegel), embraced the idea of an organic development of the entire world, reflected in nature and in human society in several stages of a single cosmic organism.[12] This connection with Herder was particularly pronounced in Johann Fichte's *Addresses to the German Nation* and in the *Ideen zu einer Philosophie der Natur* (Ideas for a Philosophy of Nature) of Schelling, who enjoyed the reputation of being "an avid reader of Herder."[13] It has also been said that Hegel combined "transcendental idealism with a sense of historical relativity" by bringing together Herder (and Wilhelm Humboldt) with Kant.[14] Moreover, Herder shared with the idealist philosophers the murky roots in German mysticism, which had crystallized in Jacob Boehme's theosophy and was perpetuated by the Pietist tradition.[15] In its further development, however, philosophical idealism tended to outgrow the Romantic framework.[16] In particular, Hegel did not subscribe to the Herderian notion that different norms in different societies that expressed a peculiar national spirit were ipso facto legitimate.[17] Conversely, it is unfair to Herder—as has often happened—to hold him responsible for the peculiarities of subsequent German philosophy of history.[18]

Illusion of Herder's Influence

The Slovak Question

Perhaps the most important source of attributing a key role to Herder in the Czech case stemmed from confusion between the intellectual content of the Slovak national awakening and that of the Czech. A typical expression of this merging can be found in Masaryk's *The Czech Question*, which characterized Ján Kollár (1793–1852) as a seminal figure in the Czech national awakening.[19] On closer examination, this conventional view appears highly questionable. While Kollár's philosophical orientation toward Herder and German romanticism was typical of the Slovak national awakening with its Lutheran Protestant basis, it was not characteristic of the intellectual climate of Bohemia, which had nourished the national awakening of the Czechs. Inappropriately, Kollár has been viewed as representative of Czech intellectual culture. [20]

German-style romanticism and idealism sought to infiltrate Czech thought largely through Slovak intellectuals who, undoubtedly assisted by their Protestant Lutheran background, were drawn to contemporary German academic thought. In this, they followed in the footsteps of intellectuals of other Slav nations, especially the Poles and the Russians.[21] This fascination with German philosophical idealism was in contrast to the leading figure among the early Czech awakeners, Josef Dobrovský (1753–1829), who represented the more sober Enlightenment spirit in scholarship.[22]

The Czech awakeners seemed to regard Slovaks' quasi-mystical vision of the destiny of the Slavs as something like a puerile infatuation.[23] Under Herder's influence, Kollár, in particular, elevated the nation to the level of humanity and divinity.[24] The Czechs' view of the Slavic connection was more sober and modest, free of cosmic or apocalyptic overtones. Thus Josef Jungmann (1773–1847) envisaged the Czech national mission with respect to other Slav nations as a mundane aid in transmitting the values of Western civilization to the East free of imperialistic garb. A similar deflation of the Slavic idea, differing from Jungmann's in degree but not in kind, is also pronounced in Karel Havlíček's (1821–1856) writings.[25]

The Enlightenment Question

Another incentive to exaggerate, or even invent, a romanticist input in the national awakening was the presumption of the Enlightenment's hostility to the Czech vernacular. František V. Krejčí's assessment of the enlightened reforms of Maria Theresa and especially of Joseph II is typical: "A special irony of fate, however, was that what brought such a political and intellectual liberation, at the same time endangered the nationality and language to such a degree that the threat of Germanization was never—since the battle of the White Mountain—so horrifying, as exactly then."[26] The tendency to pit the Enlightenment against the national awakening and instead credit romanticism was also reflected in a recent compendium of the history of Czech literature.[27]

For the purposes of contextualization, it may be pointed out that a similar problem emerged in Finnish historiography involving a reluctance to credit the Enlightenment with a role in stimulating nationalism or a national awakening because of its alleged aversion to the vernacular language. Instead, the roots were spuriously sought in German romanticism and Hegelianism.[28] There was a failure to distinguish between the two basic components of the awakening: its ideological (liberal) substance and its linguistic form. Actually, the Enlightenment was not in itself opposed to national patriotism. For instance, the Dutch experienced their national awakening under the label of the Dutch national enlightenment of the 1760s and 1770s.[29]

Thus also in the Czech case, the sour view of the Enlightenment favored the assumption that romanticism provided the principal inspiration for the culture of the awakening and that Herder—albeit a German—served as the guru of the awakeners. Josef Kaizl formulated this image of Herder's role with particular directness: "The powerful fructifying current of Western humanistic rationalism was channeled in our case very effectively into nationalism and the bridge, carrying this development, was—in my judgment . . . Johann Gottfried Herder."[30] The assumption of a contradiction between the Enlightenment and the national revival was, in fact, based on what was in itself a Herderian tenet of an inextricable unity—or of confusion—between language and culture. The fact that the awakeners at the turn of the eighteenth century and early decades of the nineteenth used German to read and write did not mean that they adopted German cultural values. The language served as a medium to reach the culture of Western Europe or to recall, revive, or maintain the historical national ethos by relating mainly to the liberal values of the Golden Age of the sixteenth century, to a society, which, in turn, stemmed largely from the Bohemian Reformation.

The Herderian view of the relationship between the language revival and the national awakening involved a double error. First, the one-sided emphasis on language obscured the more significant aspect of the philosophical and cultural content of the awakening. Second, this one-sided emphasis confused cause and effect. Under the influence of the Enlightenment, the revival of language emerged as a byproduct of the revival of the Utraquist and humanistic culture of the sixteenth century, not vice versa. This revival of respect for the Utraquist and humanistic culture almost automatically led to a revival of respect for the Czech language in which the sixteenth-century culture was cast. This explains the seeming paradox that the attachment to the Czech past preceded the propagation of the language. This attitude was reflected even in the work of the most ardent champions of the Czech language like Jungmann, whom František Palacký (1798–1876) credited with linking the old Czech culture with the Enlightenment.[31]

The function of the sixteenth-century culture as a driving force behind the revival of the Czech language was strengthened by the fact that German had played only a minor, if any, role in the development of Czech theology, law, science, literature, or philosophy in the era of the Bohemian Reformation. This militated against the permanent adoption of German during the national revival. The Bohemophone prevalence was, of course, characteristic of the literary production emanating from the Utraquist milieu, but more surprisingly, in the sixteenth century, the use of the German language was also circumscribed among the partisans of Rome—the *sub una* or communicants in one kind. The prominent Czech Jesuit author, Václav Šturm, can serve as an example. When the Unity of Brethren charged that he wrote in Czech (rather than Latin or German) to avoid a dispute with the supporters of the Augsburg Confession, the Jesuit disarmingly replied that he did not know German.[32]

The primacy of the historical culture over language helps integrate Dobrovský and other awakeners of the Enlightenment era who might have had doubts about the future use of the language. And, more importantly, the contributions of German speakers such as Bernard Bolzano and Michael J. Fesl (1788–1863) can be recognized without a sense of incongruity. With the revival of a distinct culture, the Czechs could remain a distinct nation, even if the unthinkable had happened and German prevailed as the language of communication in Bohemia. To make the separability of language and nationality concrete, let us consider the survival of nationalities that have lost (or largely lost) their language. In the contemporary world, the Basques have not turned into Spaniards, the Irish or—to take a more startling example, the Zimbabweans—have not become English; Bretons and Corsicans have not turned into Frenchmen.[33] Conversely, it is possible to point to the distinct difference in political culture between the Czechs and the Slovaks despite a great linguistic proximity. Looking at the matter from yet another angle, if the language had revived without the distinct historical patterns of thought and memories, the inhabitants of Bohemia would just have become Czech-speaking Germans.[34] Hence, the result is a distortion rather than an illumination if, on account of the language factor, the Enlightenment is replaced by romanticism (or Karl H. Seibt by Herder) in order to explain the core values of the Czech national awakening credibly.[35]

To make matters worse, there has been a tendency to exaggerate the Germanizing influence of the Enlightenment and its agents in Bohemia. Thus, Seibt has often been depicted not only as a German speaker but also as an avid Germanizer of Bohemia. Walter Schamschula, in his otherwise remarkable monograph on the Bohemian national awakening, portrayed the cosmopolitan Seibt, who was oriented toward French and British Enlightenment thought, as an enthusiastic German nationalist and the purveyor of an exclusively German culture. He even blamed the "*Seibtkreis*" (Seibt's circle) for making Dobrovský feel at home with the German language.[36] Similarly, disregarding August G. Meissner's (1753–1807) reputation for spreading English and French ideas, Schamschula presents him only as a devotee of German culture.[37] Actually, Seibt demonstrated his ultimate linguistic neutrality when he took considerable risk in his capacity as censor to approve the publication of Bohuslav Balbín's eulogy of the Slavic tongues, the *Dissertatio apologetica pro lingua Slavonica praecipue Bohemica* (Defense of the Slavic Language, Particularly the Czech) (1775).[38] Similarly, his colleague, Ferdinand Kindermann (1740–1801), although he preferred German as the language of school instruction, did not wish to suppress the use of Czech.[39] Even Bernard Bolzano was not indifferent to the rights of the Czech language, regarding it, however, as a transient instrument and not as a permanent value in itself.[40] Similarly, Fesl welcomed an opportunity to improve his knowledge of Czech and in 1815 expressed satisfaction with the increasing use of Czech in Prague.[41]

At the other end of the intellectual spectrum, the linguistic resurrectionist Václav Thám (1765–1816) was willing to give the Austrian Enlightenment the benefit of the doubt for its alleged Germanizing tendency.[42] Others, taking the Enlightenment's raison d'état at face value, argued against the superficial utility of a single state language. Instead, they maintained that, on strictly utilitarian and rationalistic grounds, large states did better in balancing heterogeneous populations than in facing the people of a single language, as the French royalty had. Kramerius and Dobrovský argued along these lines at the time of Leopold II's coronation in 1791.[43] Fundamentally, in the Czech national awakening, both the pioneers of the liberal philosophical substance (like Bolzano) and those of the national linguistic form (like Jungmann), although they can be separated and distinguished, shared common roots in the realistic and empirical Enlightenment. Despite his attachment to the Czech language, Jungmann shared Bolzano's view of the cosmopolitan character of human culture.[44] When Jungmann expressed a certain bitterness about Bolzano, it was for personal rather than for ideological reasons.[45]

There were other reasons for questioning the role of the Enlightenment in the Czech national awakening. Masaryk decried the French or "Voltairian" Enlightenment for its presumably irreligious character. Projecting his preferences into the Czech milieu, he preferred Kollár's Herderianism because of its religious tinge over Jungmann's secularism despite its humanitarian and enlightened tenor. He characterized Jungmann thus: "Voltaire's great adherent, he is an uncritical and blind advocate of the Enlightenment of the previous century and of Josephism."[46] Actually, Masaryk's view of the liberal Enlightenment was rather ambiguous; while on the one hand condemning its secularist spirit, he maintained on the other hand that "the [eighteenth-century] Enlightenment—German, English, and French—was merely a continuation in the spirit of the Bohemian Reformation's principal ideas."[47] Joining the critics, Patočka deemed the influence of the Enlightenment as negative for its jejune quality that overlooked the deeper layers of human experience. In other words, the Enlightenment was shallow and superficial while, in contrast, romanticism was deep and profound.[48] Along the same lines, Seibt has been subjected to criticism for the superficiality of his learning.[49]

An additional complication was introduced by those, like Kaizl and Patočka, who claimed that Herder was, in fact, an Enlightenment thinker. Their stand was based on the grounds that he was not a full-fledged romanticist, like, for instance, Fichte.[50] This claim, of course, did not alter the fact that he had opposed the basic ideas of the Enlightenment, nor did it detract from his role as a key progenitor of romanticism or from the fact that he is commonly considered in revolt against the Enlightenment.[51] Patočka stressed Herder's deviation from the Enlightenment standard in his philosophy of history in which he posited "deeper and more harmonious rules than the human uni-linear intellect of the Enlightenment reason." Thus, according to Patočka, Herder paved the way for the philosophy of history offered by German idealism. In epistemology, Herder stood closer to Boehme's mysticism than to English empiricism; sense perceptions, for him, were not mere factual data but revealed an immanent soul.[52] Nevertheless, the arguable contamination of Herder's romanticism by the Enlightenment may call for a certain caution and make a virtue out of calling him a proto-romanticist. Carleton Hayes put the case most succinctly: "Herder was not only a child of the eighteenth century but also a father of the nineteenth century ... here speaks a voice from two centuries ... its 'Patriotism' is not the eighteenth-century plaster replica of antique city patriotism; it is the brand-new marble statue of the national patriotism which is the idol of the nineteenth century."[53]

The Religious Question

The identification of Herder as a major inspirer of the Czech national awakening was also motivated by an interest in linking the awakening with a Protestant past and thus highlighting the revival's repudiation of the Counter-Reformation. This was again, above all, Masaryk's opinion. His identification of Herder's role rested on two questionable propositions: first, that Herder provided a bridge between the awakening and the Czechs' Protestant past; and, second, that Kollár, who mainly supplied the Herder connection, was a typical representative of the awakening. [54]

The distinguished philosopher and statesman was correct in linking the awakening with the disrupted intellectual development of a previous age—with the Bohemian Reformation. The mainstream Bohemian Reformation, however, was not Protestant but Utraquist, and Utraquism was a peculiar *via media* that was actually closer to Rome than to Luther.[55] The repudiation of the Counter-Reformation and its works and heritage actually occurred under the auspices of the liberal or reform Catholicism of the Josephist era. The Catholic Enlightenment condemned the intellectual ambience of the Counter-Reformation period as one of obscurantism or "darkness." The Austrian Catholic Enlightenment had its non-Protestant inspirational roots in Jansenism.[56]

The Catholic Enlightenment—represented in Bohemia particularly by the theologians and philosophers Seibt, Bolzano, and Fesl—had a seminal effect on the character of the national awakening, performing a double service. First, as a variant of liberal Catholicism, Utraquism exhibited a certain kinship with the reform Catholicism of the Josephist Enlightenment. Hence it was actually the liberal Catholicism of the Enlightenment that could provide a link with the *via media* of the Bohemian Reformation. Hence, the awakening did not need the services of Herder to link it with an allegedly Protestant past.[57] Second, the input of liberal Catholicism helped immunize the awakening against the appeal of the somber tenor of the emotional romanticism of the Herderian type. Instead, it helped keep the Czech philosophical mind in the sunny realm of Enlightenment sobriety. From the position of Bolzano's liberal Catholicism, romanticism represented a perversion of ethics, whereas philosophical idealism represented a pantheist view and a denial of individual responsibility.[58]

Masaryk's search for the roots of awakening in Herderian romanticism was paradoxical, since his own intellectual roots were in the Enlightenment and its universalism.[59] For Herder, the primary reality was the individual nations that pursued their individual destinies.[60] In a rather abstract sense, Masaryk viewed Herder as a link with one subordinate element within the Bohemian Reformation, namely, the Unity of Brethren, which he esteemed highly in contrast to his low opinion of mainstream Utraquism. According to Masaryk's overoptimistic view, Herder, as a disciple of the Unity's internationally famous bishop John A. Comenius (Jan Amos Komenský) (1592–1670), was actually transmitting ideas from the Bohemian Reformation back into the Czech intellectual milieu.[61] Even if Comenius's influence on Herder were significant, which is doubtful, Herder would be sending the wrong signal to the Czech awakeners.[62] Comenius was in the tradition of secularized eschatology or mystical collectivism, which anticipated the core philosophy not only of Herder's proto-romanticism but also of subsequent absolute idealism. Comenius's theologized historiography, identifying human progress with the process of divinization, implied the obverse of the realism and ontic individualism that the awakeners drew from the intellectual context of the Enlightenment and recaptured from the Utraquist tradition of the Bohemian Reformation.[63] The Europe of the Enlightenment tended to look askance at Comenius's secularized eschatology, and the leading figures of the Czech national awakening shared this negative view, among them Mikuláš Adaukt Voigt (1733–87), František M. Pelcl (1734–1801), František Faustin Procházka (1749–1809), and Karel Ignác Thám (1763–1816, brother of Václav).[64]

The Question of a German Model

Sometimes, Herder's seminal role in the national awakening was asserted on the assumption of an inevitable German ascendancy in Czech intellectual development. Thus, Patočka has written: "The influence of the German cultural milieu on the beginnings [of national awakening] was so overpowering that it is virtually impossible to speak about a cultural distinctiveness."[65] Hence, if Herderian romanticism laid the foundation for modern German nationalism, it performed the same role in the Czech case, which was imitative of the German model. We have found this notion in Patočka as well. The view, however, dissolves if examined against a more nuanced analysis of Czech receptivity to intellectual impulses from the camp of rising German nationalism: it is based on a confusion between linguistic form and intellectual content. The Czech awakeners did not follow the German example of turning their back on the Enlightenment and embracing ethnically centered exclusivism.[66] In a more general sense and more recently, Kateřina Bláhová has maintained that "Czech humanistic scholarship ... has developed in connection with German scholarship ... and has grown firmly not only geographically and geopolitically, but also in its philosophical anchoring and methodology in the Central European space."[67] In a way, Patočka and Bláhová were right in speaking about a deep "German" influence, but the latter stemmed from Austria, not from Germany proper. It bore the stamp of the Enlightenment and rationalism, not of romanticism and idealism.

The Slovaks' Romantic Idealism

There is no doubt about Herder's key role in the Slovak national awakening. The susceptibility of Slovak Lutherans to the influence of German thought dated back to the impact of Pietism, which emphasized an austere life style and an inward devotion and exaltation over intellectual doctrine. The search for, and stress on, an internalized and immediate relation to God bordered on mysticism.[68] Subsequent progenitors of modern nationalism in Slovakia were deeply influenced by German Lutheran universities—Jena, in particular, but also Leipzig and Göttingen.[69] In Jena alone, the number of students from Hungary increased tenfold between 1780 and 1810. The graduates of the German universities subsequently diffused their knowledge among younger students through the network of secondary schools.[70] The illusion of Slovak national romanticism as part of the Czech national awakening was amplified by the Slovak Lutherans' attachment (through the mid-1840s) to the Czech language as their literary medium. Thus, they seemed an integral part of the Czech cultural scene. Given that the opposite was true, there was an indication that language alone was not a reliable index of cultural identity. The wrapping of the package was less important than its contents.

The transmission of German philosophical romanticism and idealism into the Slovak intellectual milieu occurred initially thanks to Kollár and Pavel J. Šafařík (1795–1861) and then through L'udovít Štúr (1815–56) and Jozef Hurban (1812–88). Prior to them, Bohuslav Tablic (1769–1823) had studied in Germany at the University of Jena from 1790 to 1792 and Jiří Palkovič (1769–1850) in 1792–93. Jena, a town in the Grand Duchy of Saxony-Weimar, was the home of Schiller, Fichte, and Schlegel; and Hegel taught there at the turn of the century.[71] Palkovič became an influential proponent of national ideas in the spirit of Herder, particularly after his appointment as a professor at the Evangelical Lyceum in Bratislava in 1803.[72] A telling testimony of the nexus among Luther, Herder, and the Slovak national awakeners is the fact that Palkovič arranged for an edition of Luther's catechism with extensive commentaries by Herder. The text was intended for use in Slovak Lutheran schools.[73]

Kollár pursued theological studies at Jena from 1817 to 1819, in an atmosphere of a fierce German nationalism that was fueled by a detestation of everything French.[74] There he witnessed the nationalist frenzy of the Wartburg Festival of October 1817, and he was still in Jena when August Kotzebue was assassinated by a German nationalist.[75] Together with his fellow students at Jena and budding Slovak awakeners such as Samuel Ferjenčík (1793–1855) and Ján Benedikti (1796–1847), Kollár was exposed to the ideas of Kant, Schelling, and Fichte by his professors. Šafařík had preceded Kollár at the University of Jena, where he studied from 1815 to 1817, and joined the learned society, Societas Latina Ienensis. He studied avidly the writings of Herder and Fichte, as well as those of Lessing. He had already been introduced to Herder's ideas at the Evangelical Lyceum of Kežmarok (1810–14) by Johann Genersich (1761–1825), his favorite professor and another alumnus of Jena (1782–85).[76]

Thus, both Kollár and Šafařík could be considered Herder's disciples.[77] According to Robert B. Pynsent, almost everything that the two Slovak scholars wrote about the Slav character derived directly or indirectly from Herder's *Ideen zur Philosophie der Geschichte der Menschheit* (Outlines of a Philosophy of the History of Mankind), in which several pages of book 16, chapter 4, are devoted to a sympathetic depiction of the Slavs. Pynsent's conclusion was based mostly on comparative textual analysis.[78] Kollár, in fact, celebrated Herder in one of the sonnets of his *Slávy dcera* (The Daughter of Sláva), a lengthy and expanding poetical work that praised the benefactors of the Slavs and excoriated their opponents.[79] Kollár was profoundly impressed and influenced by Herder's philosophy of history—particularly his concept of "humanity" as an ordering principle and goal of the world process—while he still maintained some distance from the German idealist philosophy.[80] Most of Kollár's references to Herder appeared in his *Ueber die literarische Wechselseitigkeit* (On Reciprocity in Literature).[81] Šafařík focused on Herder's philological and pedagogical principles and, in 1819, proposed to apply them through his office as a principal of the Serbian gymnasium in Novi Sad.[82]

Kollár's adaptation of Herder's general theories was, however, more significant than the impact of the German philosopher's few rather sparse remarks about the Slavs. Kollár adopted the characteristic view of history as a gradual working out of a divine purpose through mankind,[83] which involved a recognition of cultural pluralism as an operating principle in the advancement of world history.[84] Within the framework of Herder's historical philosophy, Kollár believed that the Slavs would usher in a "third age," "the age of humanity," which would follow the current so-called second age, dominated by nations whose inhabitants spoke Romance and Teutonic tongues.[85] In particular, according to Kollár, the Slavs were destined to reconcile the epochal clash between the objectivism of the first (or ancient) age and the subjectivism of the second (or Romance-Teutonic) age, and thus create a setting for a more balanced and fuller realization of the ideal humanity.[86] Although this procedure resembled the operation of Hegel's dialectic, Kollár considered Hegelianism an example of the defective "objectivist" Romance-Teutonic age. For Kollár, Herder was one of the few who anticipated the truly balanced synthesis of the future; the others were, curiously, Wilhelm Humboldt and Walter Scott.[87]

After Kollár, L'udovít Štúr and his associates pushed to new extremes the notion of the impressive future of the Slavs that Kollár had erected on the basis of Herder's philosophy.[88] Štúr, who studied at the University of Halle in 1838–40, and his principal associates Hurban and Michal M. Hodža (1811–70) would connect Herder's ideas with Hegelianism.[89] Štúr proclaimed his fervent faith in the dominant role of the Slavs in Europe's future in a letter of 1847 to Ljudevit Gaj (1809–72), the leader of the Croat Illyrian Movement.[90] On behalf of the Slav ideal in the 1840s, he maintained wide contacts with cultural leaders of other Slav nations, not only with Croats, Serbs, and Slovenes within the Habsburg monarchy but also abroad, with Russians and Ukrainians.[91] The impact of German-style idealism on Štúr and his group dovetailed with their exposure to Polish messianism and Russian Slavophilism.[92] If Kollár sought to replace Hegel's historical scheme with Herder's, Štúr and his school wished to continue the process within the historical and philosophical paradigms of Hegel.[93]

The dissonance between Kollár's view of Slavdom and that of the Czech awakeners was noted earlier. Masaryk himself had observed with some dismay Kollár's aggressive and vengeful attitude toward the enemies of the Slavs, which he contrasted with Dobrovský's tolerant and understanding attitude toward the alleged national antagonists.[94] There was, however, considerable reluctance to dwell on this cultural disjunction between the Slovaks and the Czechs.[95] Calling attention to the differences seemed "politically incorrect." A notable illustration of this tendency was Masaryk's exhortation to the Czechs not only to sing Slovak songs but also to learn to feel and think in a Slovak manner.[96] Actually, it may be suggested—turning to the Nietzschean distinction between the Apollonian and the Dionysian spirit—that the dose of the Romantic-Dionysian element was higher in the national awakening in Slovakia than in Bohemia.[97] If adherence to Herderian romanticism be considered an evil in contemporary historiography of nationalism, it might be said that the sins of the Slovaks fell inadvertently on Czech heads. As noted earlier, the appeal of philosophical romanticism and idealism to the Slovak awakeners was evidently related to their Lutheranism, which helped condition them intellectually to Herder's and subsequently to Hegel's weltanschauung.[98]

Limitation of Herder's Influence in Bohemia

Czech awakeners' attitude toward Herder was one of a pleasant surprise that he—as a German—would recognize the merits of Slavs, although his attitude specifically to the Czechs was questionable. They did not derive any positive inspiration from his substantive ideas on the nature, behavior, and destiny of nations, which he based on a need to cultivate national peculiarities and to assert oneself vis-à-vis other nations. Their own dedication to the national revival was fueled instead by the serene and sunny confidence justified by the memory of past achievements. As for Herder's inspiration specifically for the Czech awakening, his effectiveness was limited by his identification of the Czech historical past as

"German," considering not only Comenius but also Hus as sharers in Teutonic culture.[99] Not even the most hard-boiled adherents of the Enlightenment, despite their real or alleged penchant for Germanization, would go that far.

There is little evidence of the Czech intellectual leaders' interest in Herder's writings during the formative stages of the national awakening. It was Seibt, the highly influential teacher of philosophy and literature at the University of Prague and admirer of the English and French Enlightenment—not Herder, representing the German Lutheran strand of romanticism—who was the chief guru and intellectual pacesetter of the Bohemian national revival.[100] In particular, Herder's Romantic nationalism was alien to Dobrovský. Among the latter's rare references to Herder, there is one to the *Ideen zur Philosophie der Geschichte der Menschheit* in his letter to Václav Fortunát Durych (1735–1802) of May 9, 1792.[101] Durych used Herder primarily as a foil to oppose other German scholars' demeaning views of the Slavs, in particular those of Johann Peter von Ludwig (1668–1743) and Joseph Benedikt Heyrenbach (1738–79).[102] Earlier, in June 1783, his younger friend and correspondent, Augustin Helfert, tried to get Dobrovský interested in Herder's work on Hebrew poetry.[103] Hugh Agnew has called attention to Karel Ignác Thám's (1763–1816) knowledge of Herder's writings. Agnew referred to Thám's quotations from two of Herder's works in the address that Thám gave upon assuming his position as teacher of Czech in the gymnasium of the Old Town of Prague, published in 1803 as *Über den Karakter der Slawen* (Character of the Slavs). The two works of Herder were *Ideen zur Philosophie der Geschichte der Menschheit* and *Briefe zur Beförderung der Humanität* (Letters for the Advancement of Humanity). From the latter, he quoted a lengthy passage on the value of a native tongue, the varieties of which were granted by God and should be protected by secular sovereigns.[104] In the same published lecture, Thám also referred to Herder's *Abhandlung über den Ursprung der Sprache* (Treatise on the Origin of Language) on the issue of a universal criterion for evaluating languages and included a long quotation from the work. By the time Thám called attention to Herder's ideas, the intellectual parameters of the Czech national awakening, however, were already established, and Thám's discussion of Herder could hardly have exerted a seminal influence. Agnew likewise dismissed the claim that Herder's ideas played an authentic role in the Czech awakening.[105]

Likewise, there seems little evidence of Herder's formative influence on the Czech awakeners' views on the Slav issue. Certainly, they did not need Herder to call their attention to the existence of Slavdom and its numerical and geographic potential. This had already been spelled out by Bohuslav Balbín (1621–88) and after him by Dobrovský in his address of 1791 before Emperor Leopold II. Dobrovský, not Herder, was the progenitor of the Czech awakeners' interest in Slavdom.[106] Dobrovský himself, in particular, did not need Herder to spark his interest in Slavdom, although his ideological dependence on Herder has been asserted.[107] Dobrovský had become a devotee of the Slav question through the influence of Durych long before he heard about Herder. He had also then recognized the value of Slavic studies for the purposes of national awakening.[108]

Balbín's *Dissertatio apologetica pro lingua Slavonica praecipue Bohemica* (Defense of the Slav Language, Particularly the Czech) was published as early as 1775 by Pelcl, and the awakeners were well aware of the Jesuit scholar's arguments. Although not a Slavic enthusiast, Havlíček highlighted Balbín's sense of Slavic relatedness in 1850.[109] Even before Balbín, Czech writers in the sixteenth century had seized on the wider implications of the Slavic character of their language, in particular Daniel Adam of Veleslavín (1546–99).[110] In fact, an awareness of the relationship to other Slavs had been appearing in Czech writings since the fourteenth century. Pynsent cited the example of Martin Kabátník, "who came across a Serbian mameluke in Cairo."[111] Similarly, the Czechs did not need Herder to teach them about the importance of language preservation.[112] Czech literature of the sixteenth century was permeated with this idea, which the Bohemian Enlightenment revived and reasserted.[113]

Interest in or even enthusiasm for Russia came about during the period of the Enlightenment, partly through retrospective immersion in sixteenth-century literature and partly through to the tsarist empire's involvement, as a Habsburg ally, in the Turkish wars of the 1780s and later in the wars of the French Revolution and the Napoleonic period. As another sign of rising interest in Russia, Dobrovský's contemporary, Procházka, republished in 1786 Matouš Hosius's translation of *Kronika Moskevská* (The Muscovite Chronicle) by Aleksander Gwagnin (Alessandro Guagnini), originally published in Czech in 1589 with a new laudatory preface that rather improbably praised the high level of Russian art, morals, and politics. Czech newspapers, published by Schönfeld and later by Kramerius, devoted exceptional attention to Russia's military successes against the Turks and later the French.[114] Paradoxically, it was exactly Russia's alliance with Austria against the French that soured Herder in the 1790s on his earlier vision of Russia's future world-class historical role and led him to anticipate George Kennan in advocating a policy of "containment" toward Russia.[115]

On the issue of Slavdom, the identification as Slavs had a greater significance to the Slovaks than to the Czechs. Hence Kollár and even Šafařík would be responsive to the appealing power of Herder's theories. The Slovaks in the past had identified substantively with Slavdom. For Kollár, in particular, the Slavs formed a single nation.[116] The small size of the Slovak national community was also conducive to seeking psychological and physical support from the large entity of Slavdom.[117] For the Czechs, the sense of a distinct nationality was a matter of fact, and, therefore, the Slav attribute was rather extrinsic, not intrinsically needed to bolster national self-confidence. This view would crystallize most sharply in Havlíček's attitude of the 1840s. Jungmann's correspondence with Marek likewise ridicules the concerns of the Habsburg government that the Czech awakeners had adopted Panslav ideas and wished to merge Bohemia with Russia.[118]

Sporadic references to Herder also appeared in the later stages of the national awakening. The role of his ideas, however, was less that of original inspiration than that of supporting arguments against derisive attitudes toward the Slavs. Jungmann, in his speech opening his lectures on Czech language at the Litoměřice seminary, in November 1810, referred to Herder, Bernhardt Jenisch (1734–1807), August L. Schlözer (1735–1809), and Johann S. Vater (1771–1826) as those sensible (but rare) Germans who could shed the typical contempt for Slavic languages. Thus, Herder was presented in the role of a perceptive student and the Czechs and other Slavs in the role of his intellectual mentors, rather than vice versa. Jungmann, in fact, placed more emphasis on Schlözer than on Herder, citing the former's forecast that in the future Europeans would study Slavic languages, especially Russian, as eagerly as they studied French at the time. In 1813, he translated and printed in the *Prvotiny* (First Fruits) Herder's statements defending the Slav character against his own compatriots' low opinions and predicting a bright future for the Slavs.[119] In general, the interest of Czech awakeners focused on the few instances of Herder's positive depiction of the Slavs, particularly in *Ideen zur Philosophie der Geschichte der Menschheit*, rather than on the general ramifications of his philosophy of history or metaphysics. The marginal character of the Slav theme in Herder's teaching is indicated by its usual omission in the general discussions of his philosophy.[120]

Still later, there was some awareness of Herder's work. Čelakovský translated his *Blätter der Vorzeit* (Pages from Antiquity) as *Listy z dávnověkosti* in 1823 as an exercise in poetical style rather than in connection with the issues of nationality, with which Herder's largely biblical themes had little to do. Vincenc Zahradník, noting that his bookshelves were adorned by the works of Goethe, Schiller, Herder, and Lessing, observed: "These volumes are of great benefit to me, even if I do not read them. Alone a glance at them teaches me, it teaches me humility." In his writings, he cited from German authors like Lessing and Wieland but not Herder.[121] Also in a letter of October 24, 1831, Josef Jaroslav Langer praised Herder to Vinařický.[122] Herder's name, however, did not come up in Jungmann's, Václav Hanka's (1791–1861), and Palacký's published correspondence with Kollár.[123] Typically, the historian Jeník of Bratřice found little appeal in Herder's interpretation of Slavdom's role or other German historiography on the Slav question. He derived inspiration and emotional satisfaction from West European liberals' respect for the Bohemian Reformation, such as that reflected in the celebration of Hus, Žižka, and George of Poděbrady by John Bowring in his *Cheskian Anthology* (1832).[124]

Bernard Bolzano, whose pedagogical influence, after Seibt's, was particularly profound in Bohemia, can be viewed as Herder's very antipode.[125] Representing the epitome of the cosmopolitan Catholic Enlightenment, Bolzano was immune to the appeal of Herder's view of nations as ontic entities.[126] Moreover, Bolzano also lacked interest in Herder because he was not a strong logician, referring to Herder only in passing in his famous *Wissenschaftslehre* (Theory of Science) in that connection.[127] In his philosophical diary for 1817–27, Bolzano compared Herder's *Abhandlung über den Ursprung der Sprache* unfavorably with Johann N. Tetens's *Über den Ursprung der Sprachen und der Schrift* (On the Origin of Language and Letters).[128] As an opponent of Romantic idealism, Bolzano firmly rejected the Herderian view presented by Friedrich H. Jacobi that the purpose of history was to reveal the idea of a metaphysically monistic humanity. He rejected a trajectory according to which the development of mankind in time was a single process and particular and distinct groups served only as harmonious members of one body. Bolzano condemned this "mystical-theosophic" view on the grounds that it attempted to mingle human with divine matters.[129]

A wild card in the Czech group was Palacký, whose background was, indeed, Lutheran Protestant—and he had received his higher education in Slovakia. He could be, therefore, presumed to share the Romantic and quasi-utopian enthusiasm of Kollár, Štúr, or Hurban.[130] Unlike his Slovak cobelievers, however, Palacký had missed an exposure to the Herderian and other idealist teachings of the German Protestant universities where, more so than in Slovakia, the Slovaks acquired their Romantic and idealistic enthusiasm. Kollár, for instance, claimed that his philosophical awakening occurred in Jena, after he escaped the intellectual wasteland of the Bratislava "mummy."[131]

Palacký's intellectual outlook, on the contrary, was formed in the more realistic intellectual atmosphere of the Hungarians' Anglophilia in the Slovak capital on the Danube. Symptomatic of his distance from Slovak Lutheran intellectuals was his paradoxical discovery of Herder through an English-language source. He found the substance of Herder's teaching in Hugh Blair's *The Rise and Progress of Language*.[132] Subsequently, in 1818, he did receive a copy of Herder's *Briefe zur Beförderung der Humanität* from his Hungarian benefactress in Bratislava, Nina Zerdahely, but he was then intellectually more involved with the works of Madame De Staël. De Staël might also have passed onto him her rather sketchy but unenthusiastic impressions of none other than Herder.[133] Paradoxically, while Palacký benefited from the cultural symbiosis between the Hungarians and the English, the Slovak awakeners, in particular Kollár, resented what they considered a British friendship for the hostile Magyars. Ultimately, it led Kollár to regard the British as enemies of the Slavs.[134]

Palacký's intellectual formation derived from the British, primarily Scottish, Enlightenment, not from Herderian romanticism. As a historian, the mature Palacký, in fact, considered himself a pupil of two Scottish mentors, David Hume and William Robertson.[135] He did acknowledge his indebtedness to Herder, not in the philosophy of history but in his early study of aesthetics (1819), and even in the area of aesthetics he credited two Britishers, HughBlair and Francis Bacon, as his primary inspirers. Elsewhere, he noted that he found the work of German aestheticians unsatisfactory.[136] Characteristically, cumulative indexes to *Časopis českého musea* (Journal of the Bohemian Museum) for the first twenty years, 1827–1846, when Palacký was the editor for much of the time, do not show any references to Herder, except to one of his poems on a theme from Czech history that appeared in 1832.[137]

As for the Slav issue, Palacký's focus was on the cultural revival of the Czechs, and his interest in other Slav nations was distinctly limited. In the first half of the nineteenth century, when Kollár and Štúr were embracing Russia, Palacký did not see in tsardom an embodiment of Slavic characteristics but rather an alien mixture of Tartar and Germanic principles of autocracy. This view appeared in his famous letter to Frankfurt of 1848, and his attitude softened only in the early 1860s as he became aware of Russia's post-Crimean liberalization.[138] In his letter to Pogodin in 1871, he later explained his stand on the issue of Slavdom. In his view, a Czech revival was the most significant contribution to the interests of all Slavs that he could have undertaken.[139] He did not credit Herder with the theory of Slav character, which he employed in his history of Bohemia. Herder's name was also missing from the roster of authorities at the start of his monumental *History of the Czech Nation*.

Among Palacký's contemporaries, Havlíček likewise signified his opposition to Herderian cultural pluralism. Endorsing Leibniz's concept of the unity of human culture, he wrote in 1846: "What can be more dignified than the idea of intellectually joining all of humanity into a single nation which would grasp by reason everything in the realm of speech, and would be able to think and communicate in the same purity the truth flowing out of the intellect."[140] Writing in the same year, the historian and literary critic Václav B. Nebeský (1818–82) maintained that if the Slavs were to score major achievements in the future, it would happen freely and spontaneously, not according to the laws of the Herderian or Hegelian philosophy of history.[141]

Havlíček's contemporary, author and philosopher Karel B. Štorch (1812–68), clearly articulated the view of cultural monism in his article in *Časopis českého musea* in 1848. He postulated a fundamental distinction between poetry and philosophy in the development of human society. Poetry was typical of a more primitive state; hence poetry flourished more in Poland than in Bohemia. As society advanced, philosophy gained ascendance over poetry. While poetry remained attached to a nation, philosophy of necessity escaped national limitation, and the concept of a "national philosophy" was a contradiction in terms. Truth was just one, valid for everyone anywhere. Hence, philosophy dealt with problems that were by definition of universal significance, such as matter and spirit, the individual and the collective, the temporary and the eternal, or the realm of necessity and the realm of freedom. The development of philosophy depended on dealing with those common problems, not on contributions from particular national cultures.[142]

The most daring assertion against ontologically based cultural pluralism was Štorch's prognosis that the current surge of individual nationalities was just a superficial and temporary manifestation on the way to a global unity. "It [is] true," he wrote, "that our time is sometimes called—and not in vain—a time of Awakening and asserting nationalities." The nature of this phenomenon, however, was largely rhetorical and without a solid foundation. According to Štorch, "the character of our age is exactly that the particular yields to the common, and above the exclusivity of the individual nationalities the unity of mankind vaults its temple."[143]

Cultural Input from German Nationalism

In general, the Czech scholars were rather selective in seeking intellectual inspiration in German sources for the advancement of the national awakening. Their close contact with the world of German-language literature was not in fact conducive to adopting the line of German nationalism that stemmed from the proto-romanticism of Herder and would pass onto the metaphysical idealism of Fichte, Hegel, Schopenhauer, and Nietzsche, eventually bifurcating into right- and left-wing variants. Already Jungmann was exposed by his university teachers Seibt and August G. Meissner to the study of English and French thought, and he would display a full proficiency in both languages.[144] Subsequently, the substance of political culture, which appealed to the Czech awakeners, stemmed rather from the Western liberal tradition, which was in harmony with their initial Enlightenment outlook. Anglophone liberalism characteristically held sway over Palacký, as well as over the younger generation of the awakeners like Čelakovský, Josef V. Kamarýt (1797–1833), and Havlíček.[145]

Even the use of German to gain access to world culture was considered more an embarrassment than an advantage, and the awakeners sought to acquire knowledge of other languages. Thus, as a student Jan B. Koubek studied French, Italian, Polish, and Russian.[146] Those who did not know English preferred to read Scott's novels in Polish rather than in German translations.[147] In a review of Kollár's *Slávy dcera* in

1831, Čelakovský maintained that Czech writers did not care about what German reviewers thought: "I will omit what here and there has been mentioned about *Slávy dcera* in German journals, which for some time have started voicing opinions about Slav literature—although it is not anything to care about."According to Čelakovský, much more significant for the Czechs was the positive view of the British, especially John Bowring. Further on, he made a deprecatory reference to German literature, while he proudly quoted the English translation of one of Kollár's sonnets.[148] In 1834, a reviewer (apparently Palacký) of Edward Robinson's *Historical View of the Slavic Language in Its Various Dialects* (1834) in *Časopis českého musea* favorably compared the level of Anglophone Slavic studies with that of German scholarship. He stressed that it was not the immediate neighbors to the west who produced the best foreign survey of the Slavs but a writer beyond the Atlantic.[149] In 1847, František M. Klácel extolled Shakespeare above Goethe and Schiller in *Časopis českého musea* in an article announcing the publication of *Romeo and Juliet* in Czech by Matice česká (the Bohemian Foundation), a learned society.[150] Much later, Havlíček quipped that German offered much that was original and much that was useful but that which was original was not useful and that which was useful was derived from French and English sources that were preferable to study in the original rather than in German translations.[151] Havlíček's sympathy for the empiricist approach to philosophy by the English-speaking peoples had also its political analog in his sympathy for Anglophone liberalism. Through reports of his visit to the British Isles in the summer of 1850, František L. Rieger strengthened Havlíček's interest in the British political system and inspired Havlíček to start a series of articles on the topic.[152]

A more general and reliable index of the relatively small role played by German texts in the national awakening was provided by the contents of the leading intellectual medium, *Časopis českého musea*. During its first two decades, 1827–46, covering the heyday of the revival, the highbrow journal published altogether sixty-two translations. The largest blocks of twenty each were from classical tongues and from other Slavic languages. Even the nine translations from English (three American and six British) outdistanced the seven translations from German. (Among the rest, four were from modern Romance languages, one from Danish, and one from Hindi.)

The idea of ascendancy of German culture and its function as the main (or perhaps the sole) source of cultural revival in Bohemia during the national awakening was not entertained by the awakeners themselves but rather fostered by the Austrian imperial bureaucrats and various German commentators. One might cite the opinions of the earlier-mentioned professor of Austrian and world history at the University of Prague, Josef Linhart Knoll, in 1833, when he stressed the importance of German culture. According to him, it was through German initiative that science, art, and industry began to flourish in Bohemia in the eighteenth century. Without the German contribution, he contended, there would not have been any progress in art, science, and civilization in Bohemia.[153] Rudolf Glaser, former editor of the journal *Ost und West* (East and West), wrote in a memorandum to the National Museum committee on March 26, 1844, that any impartial observer would agree that the Slavs gained civilization from the Germans. The Germans still in Bohemia represented the more highly cultured part of the population. While he (unlike Knoll) welcomed the advance of the Czech population, he made it depend exclusively on the German example and education.[154] Needless to say, such ideas were alien to Czech awakeners.

As for Herder's position, specifically on the Czech national awakening, he was regarded more as a curiosity than a mentor, and his contribution did not lie in the field of positive inspiration but in that of defensive argumentation. He was a shield against Germanization rather than a positive stimulus to national aspirations. His name could be invoked and thrown in the faces of the Teutonic detractors. His views were cited for that purpose, for instance, in a landmark document, the statement by *Matice česká* of April 10, 1832, in support of the Czech language in the schools of Bohemia. In this document addressed to Count Karel Chotek, the Supreme Count Palatine of Bohemia, its principal author, Vinařický, included references to Herder's tenets on the importance of a mother tongue in the development of culture.[155]

In a sense, that tendency would continue when some hundred years later—under more sinister circumstances—Patočka dwelt on Herder's praise of the Slavs in the face of the Nazi ascription of subhuman qualities to the Czechs and their linguistic kinsmen.[156] Along similar lines, anti-Nazi German writers in Czechoslovakia, wishing to promote a Czech-German rapprochement, tended to chide the Nazis and their precursors for their doctrine of Slav inferiority by dwelling on the alleged influence of Herder on the Czech national awakening. Franz Werfel (1890–1945), writing before the end of World War I, quoted from Herder's

Humanitätsbriefe where Hus was praised as a pioneer of the Reformation who surpassed anything that happened in Germany.[157] In the 1930s, the writer Rudolf Fuchs (1890–1942), who belonged to the circle of Egon Erwin Kisch, presented Herder as a fighter for the national emancipation of the Slavic nations. He claimed that Herder helped the Bohemian national awakeners establish an independent Czech culture and that he was, therefore, held in highest esteem by such figures as Dobrovský, Jungmann, and Kollár.[158] Hence, the portrayal of the Czech national awakening as an essentially German creation, either to fend off or daunt the Nazis, or for other dubious purposes, also helped create the illusion of Herder's crucial role in the Czech national awakening.

The Light of Reason versus the Heat of Emotion

The awakeners' attitude toward their western neighbors was not one of hatred or xenophobia. That attitude differed from German nationalism, which achieved a major impetus from the humiliation inflicted by Napoleonic France and was bent on self-assertion and retribution in the proclamations of Fichte, Ernst Arndt, Friedrich von Schlegel, and Friedrich Schleiermacher.[159] The Czech awakeners derived sufficient inspiration from the cultural attainments of Czech literature of the sixteenth century not to need Herder to tell them how good they were or to resort to force to make others acknowledge their worth.

The Czech awakeners' rather understanding and tolerant attitude toward their Teutonic neighbors was in itself an indication that they remained unaffected by the spirit of Herderian Romantic nationalism, which preached the stern assertion of a national individuality. Such an easygoing approach contrasted, as noted earlier, with the attitude toward national enemies displayed by Kollár, the Slovak adherent to Herder's philosophy, the harshness of which has continued to dismay Western commentators from John Bowring to Robert Pynsent.[160] The Slavs are cast in the role of victims, having been historically tormented by the Huns, the Goths, the Avars, the Franks, and the Magyars. An everlasting and determined hatred is attributed to the traditional enemies of the Slavs, in particular the Teutons and the Magyars.[161] The characterization of national enemies by Kollár included "deceiving German, Teutonic cannibals, inhuman Germans, and descendants of Cain."[162] The animus against national enemies derived its force from the Herderian maxim that crime against a good nation was a grave sin against humanity, inasmuch as harm was done to entire mankind.[163] The Germans, in particular, were portrayed by Kollár as implacable opponents of the Slavs. Their greatest transgression was the Germanization of the formerly Slav Central Europe, turning the inhabitants into helots to fight other Slavs. The Slavs had done nothing to merit such a fate.[164]

The expressions of hatred toward the Magyars would further escalate among Slovak awakeners. In 1841, Hurban referred to the Magyars as a "Bashkirian race," which for its bestiality was incapable of "lawfulness, virtue, or justice."[165] L'udovít Štúr agreed with Šafařík a year later that "the spiritually and morally defective Magyars" (*duchovně a mravně nemohoucí Maďaři*) represented an intrusion of "Uralic barbarity" (*uralská surovost*) in the midst of Slavdom and that their destiny was to disappear from Europe, following the example of the Mongols, the Tartars, and the Turks.[166]

Expressions of such ferocious feelings toward another nationality would be hard to find in Dobrovský, Havlíček, Palacký, or later Masaryk. The Teutonic neighbors tended to be treated with humor rather than hatred, mainly for their conceited pedantry that should not be taken too seriously.[167] Typical of this approach is Palacký's reference to them as those "who pompously declare themselves in front of the whole world as know-it-alls and learn-it-alls."[168] Elsewhere, he viewed the German literati as hopelessly conceited, unable to appreciate the value of Slavic literature because of the conviction of their own incomparable superiority.[169] The Germans were more pitied than hated for their pride. The self-confidence vis-à-vis the Germans rested in the sense of historical achievements, in particular in conducting a religious Reformation a hundred years before Luther. The high degree of language development was also cited, for instance, by Kramerius in the introduction of his 1790 reprint of *Letopisové Trojanští* (The Annals of Troy).[170]

There are several reasons why Herder's formative influence in the Czech national awakening has been exaggerated, if not entirely invented. First, the Slovak awakeners studied him, and there has been a tendency to assign to Slovak intellectuals a disproportionate role in the Czech national awakening. Second, the penchant of philosophers like Masaryk and Patočka for schematization and abstract solutions tended to overshadow concrete historical research. Third, notions about the Protestant character of the Bohemian Reformation made plausible—as we saw in Masaryk—the appeal of a Lutheran-based romanticism and idealism (and hence of Herder) for the Czech national awakeners. This approach obscured the fact that the actual *via media* of Bohemian Utraquism placed the Czech intellectual tradition more in the orbit of reform or liberal Catholicism and the Josephist Enlightenment. Fourth, the aversion to recognizing the ascendancy of the Enlightenment—and hence highlighting the role of Herder's linguistic nationalism—stemmed, moreover, from an unbalanced stress on linguistic form over intellectual substance in the national awakening. Fifth, for modern theoreticians of nationalism, Herder provided an attractive point of departure for the genesis of Czech nationalism, especially after it had become customary to view the existence of a national tradition as a post-1780 invention that had no meaningful relationship to earlier cultural development.[171] More recently, however, this view has been contradicted by situating the beginning of nationalism in the sixteenth century.[172] And sixth, because of the ascendancy of the Romantic and idealistic trend in German thought, Herder's key role appeared logical to those who were convinced of Bohemia's overwhelming dependence on German culture. We saw this coupling in Patočka. Actually, to the extent that there was a major input in the Czech national awakening from German-language sources, it did not come from the dominant metaphysical trend of romanticism and idealism (Herder to Hegel) but from the subordinate intellectual current of empirical realism (Seibt and Bolzano to Brentano).

The Czech awakeners on closer examination were not drawn to German romanticism but continued to construct a modern political culture in the spirit of the Enlightenment, which related to Bohemia's historical past. The low opinion of Czech culture often appearing in German sources was attributed to ignorance. It inspired regret rather than calls for revenge. On the contrary, West European, particularly Anglophone, literature was noted with particular gratification when it reflected respect for Czech cultural achievements—above all, those connected with the Bohemian Reformation. This awareness of Western respect helped bolster the Czechs' national self-confidence and made it independent of Herder's praise of the virtues of the Slav character. The sense of past accomplishments also mitigated the need for bellicose self-assertion or for exacting revenge on the national oppressor. Patočka, among others, has singled out the sense of past accomplishments as a positive element in the national awakening.[173] The attitude was also in line with certain bonhomie and tolerance embedded in the legacy of the Bohemian Reformation, as it reached its full fruition in sixteenth-century Utraquism. The Enlightenment had revived the memory of and respect for the civilizational values derived from the Bohemian Reformation. As Nietzsche might have said, the Apollonian spirit prevailed over the Dionysian one.[174]

The resistance to romanticism conditioned the further development of a Czech political culture independent of German philosophical idealism, while the intellectual roots, remaining in the ideals of the Austro-Bohemian Enlightenment, aimed logically at embracing the Western European style of liberalism.[175] It was a trend against collectivistic, deterministic, and particularist tendencies toward individualistic, open-ended, and universalistic ones.[176] The aversion to Herder and romanticism, in turn, related to the traditions of the Bohemian Reformation revived by the Enlightenment.[177]

7

The Roots of Resistance to German Idealism

With their philosophical roots in the Austro-Bohemian Catholic Enlightenment, the mainstream of Bohemian intellectuals chose a line of philosophy that was ontically individualistic, epistemologically empirical, and open-ended and unpredictable in historiography and that adhered to the ethics of individual responsibility. In line with the indifference to Herder's philosophy of history and to his metaphysically based national particularism (discussed in chapter 6), the leaders of the national awakening turned decisively against the metaphysics of German idealism. This attitude markedly distinguished the cultural landscape in Bohemia from that of its neighbors in Central and Eastern Europe.[1]

While it can be plausibly argued that the speculative effervescence of German idealist philosophy and its ontically pluralistic view of national cultures did inspire the Slovak awakeners, it left their Czech counterparts by and large cold. It clashed with the realistic weltanschauung derived from the Austro-Bohemian Enlightenment and strengthened by the revival of the Utraquist heritage. This empirical and realistic orientation was transmitted to the older generation (Václav Stach, Josef Dobrovský, Antonín J. Puchmajer, Bernard Bolzano, and Josef Jungmann) primarily by Karl H. Seibt[2] and to the younger generation (Vincenc Zahradník, František L. Čelakovský, Karel A. Vinařický, and Karel Havlíček) by the heirs of the Catholic Enlightenment, Bernard Bolzano and Franz Exner. This chapter traces the relevant intellectual trends in Bohemia under Seibt, his contemporaries, and his followers. The paramount role of Bolzano will be discussed in the next chapter.

Existence over Essence

Let us first examine the broader philosophical context of Bohemian resistance to speculative philosophy. Why was it that absolute idealism, so highly fashionable in Central and Eastern Europe, did not take root in the intellectual climate of Bohemia? Two major factors will be explored. One is the role of the Austro-Bohemian Catholic Enlightenment, which restored the Aristotelian emphasis on individual existence as opposed to collective essence; it preferred the study of particular causes to the study of occult relationships.[3] The other factor is the corresponding rejection of essentialist metaphysical views that would undermine ontological individuality. The rejected essentialist metaphysics had intruded in two variants. The first, the more proximate trend, was characteristic of the late, so-called baroque or second scholasticism that was fostered by the Counter-Reformation. The other, the more remote trend, was rooted in the secularized eschatology of Lutheran Protestantism and flourished in the several forms of metaphysical idealism. Ultimately, as I will show, the two trends were related, not only formally but also causally. The intellectual leaders of the Austro-Bohemian Catholic Enlightenment could oppose the "essentialism" of late (baroque or second) scholasticism in two ways, which were not mutually exclusive. Some, mainly the ecclesiastics, promoted a renewed respect for the early scholasticism of the thirteenth century and hence an adherence to Thomistic moderate realism.[4] Others, mainly laymen, tended to turn outright to the French rationalism of Descartes or to the English empiricism of Locke.[5]

Eschewing the "Essentialism" of Late or Baroque Scholasticism

If Reform Catholicism was for the Czech awakeners a crucial factor in resisting the enticements of romanticism and later philosophical idealism, it was because the Catholic Enlightenment in the Austro-Bohemian area involved a rejection of the late or baroque scholasticism with its "essentialism" and reinstituted the sway of realism in the Aristotelian tradition. It was the Enlightenment's realist philosophy that promoted the liberal and individualist stance of the national awakening in Bohemia, while at the same time it blunted the appeal of romanticism and idealism with their monistic ontology and collectivist tendency. Let us first explore the character of the late or baroque scholasticism. The nature of this philosophical current may also help explain why Hegelianism became attractive not only in Lutheran areas but also in certain Catholic countries other than Bohemia, especially in Poland.

The essentialism of baroque scholasticism—also called Suárezian scholasticism after its seminal thinker, Francisco Suárez—was attributed to an overreliance (compared to medieval Thomism) on the metaphysics of Avicenna and Duns Scotus, which prompted a departure from the Aristotelian realism of Thomas Aquinas.[6] While Thomism searched for concrete individuality, late scholasticism, developed particularly by the Jesuits, looked for general principles.[7] Abandoning the solid ground of Aristotelian realism—largely under the influence of Suárez, Pedro da Fonseca, and Benito Pereira—baroque scholasticism tended to foreshadow the appearance of philosophical idealism by elevating collective essences over individual existence.[8] The Austro-Bohemian Enlightenment, like the original Thomism, restored the emphasis on the primacy of concrete individual existence. That stress, in turn, provided the ontological underpinning for the primacy of the individual and its rights, in contrast to the stress on the primacy of the collective abstract essence that baroque scholasticism and metaphysical idealism alike fostered.[9]

The stark contrast between Thomism and Suárezian scholasticism was defined with particular force by Étienne Gilson; but it was not an idiosyncratic perception of his, for it had been argued as well by earlier interpreters of the Catholic Enlightenment, such as Sebastian Merkle.[10] According to Gilson, Suárez, "lost sight of Aquinas's vision of being as the concrete act of existing and tended to reduce being to essence."[11] According to Suárez, essence was real independently of its embodiment (*essentia realis*) or existence in actual being (as *essentia actualis*); hence, existence was merely a particular state of essence.[12] As a result, existence became irrelevant or a mere attribute of essence in the ontological explanation of being. Being, defined as actual essence, no longer required the supplement, which Aquinas and his followers called "existence."[13] In sum, as Gilson stated: "Suárezianism has consumed Thomism."[14] Moreover, although Suárez overtly denied the reality of Plato's "eternal ideas," the hallmarks of philosophical essentialism, he in fact admitted them through the back door as *essentiae reales*, which could survive independently of their embodiment in actual finite being.[15] The Spanish reworking of scholasticism was introduced into Central Europe mainly through Gregory of Valencia at the University of Ingolstadt and Roderigo Arriaga at the University of Prague.[16] The Jesuit attachment to Suárezian scholasticism was so strong that Jan Bock, who attempted to teach Thomism in Prague, incurred persecution in 1684.[17]

There was a causal relationship between baroque or late scholasticism with its "essentialism," on the one hand, and German metaphysical idealism, on the other. While dominating Catholic schooling, late scholasticism also exerted an influence on the educational establishment of the Protestant world. By the late sixteenth century, representatives of late scholasticism like Fonseca, Pereira, and Suárez had become standard references in the German Lutheran universities.[18] Suárez, in particular, was highly valued by Christian Wolff, and subsequently Hegel spoke of him with approval.[19] It has in fact been suggested that Hegel became one of the legatees of Suárez's metaphysical antirealism and metaphysical anti-individualism.[20] In sum, Gilson observed that Hegel's absolute idealism was "an overhauling of ancient essentialism."[21]

The principal intermediary between the metaphysics of Spanish late scholasticism and that of German idealism was Wolff, whose notion of "being" was basically the same as that of Suárez, "whom he ... not only read, but analyzed, and whom he proclaimed as the deepest among Scholastic metaphysicians."[22] This led to a counterintuitive Ibero-Jesuit and Luthero-Teutonic interaction or cross-fertilization that some might consider philosophical and theological miscegenation.[23] From Wolff, the essentialist philosophy entered the world of German idealism through Kant, who considered the pedestrian Wolff the ultimate metaphysician and—curiously—a philosopher superior to Spinoza, Leibniz, or Descartes.[24] Moreover, Hegel preferred Wolff's metaphysics to Kant's critical idealism.[25]

As a further step in this chain of relationships, it was not surprising that the late representatives of Suárezian scholasticism would also find Wolff's metaphysics congenial.[26] Appointed in 1752 as the last Jesuit in charge of philosophical studies at the University of Prague, the astronomer Joseph Stepling (1716–78), advocated the use of Wolff, whose textbook had been approved by the Inquisition censorship in Verona. At his behest, Ignác Frantz, the head of the Jesuit Province of Bohemia, composed a textbook of philosophy in 1752 that treated Wolff favorably.[27] The promoters of the Austro-Bohemian Catholic Enlightenment, such as Franz Steinsky and František X. Němeček, in contrast, saw in German idealism a variant of the fantastic visions (*Schwärmerei*) and mysticism of the late baroque.[28]

Embracing the Realism of the Austro-Bohemian Catholic Enlightenment

The Catholic Enlightenment in the Austro-Bohemian area, to the contrary, purged philosophy from the tendency of late scholasticism to idealize "essentialism," which departed from the ontological individualism of Thomistic-Aristotelian realism.[29] By restoring the latter, the Enlightenment fortified its followers against the appeal of idealistic and collectivistic notions that characterized romanticism and metaphysical idealism.[30] The assertion of realistic Thomism in the Austrian Catholic Enlightenment has not been fully appreciated as a seminal paradigm shift that was to influence philosophical thinking for centuries to come. In the first place, historical literature tended to trivialize the discrediting of Suárezian scholasticism as merely a manipulative move to combat the disliked Jesuits.[31] In other words, the change in philosophical paradigms was not presented as a matter of fundamental intellectual significance but instead as a rather ludicrous quarrel among the monks.[32] In the second place, the assault on baroque or Suárezian scholasticism was also characterized as a struggle against "Aristotelianism," while, in fact, the opposite was true.[33] The Thomistic realism that it promoted was actually Aristotelian, while Suárezian essentialism, which was superseded, had—in its stress on universals—gravitated in the anti-Aristotelian Platonic direction. To underscore the liberal significance of the Thomistic revival, we note that pristine Thomistic realism is seen as an ingredient in the philosophical underpinnings of English empiricism and liberalism, with the influence of Aquinas having reached John Locke[34] partly through the Anglican Thomist Richard Hooker.[35]

The process of installing Aquinas in place of Suárez in the teaching of philosophy and theology was initiated in the reign of Maria Theresa (1740–80). As noted in chapter 3, the empress relied on a group of advisers, among whom Bishop Simon A. Stock was prominent.[36] The major turning point came on September 10, 1759, with the royal decree that removed the Jesuits from controlling the faculties of theology and philosophy at the universities of Prague and Vienna.[37] As far as the Habsburg hereditary lands were concerned, the Dominican Pietro Maria Gazzaniga was the key figure in opposing Jesuit scholasticism with the Thomistic scholasticism of the Catholic Enlightenment. Invited from Italy at Stock's behest to teach theology at the University of Vienna in 1760, Gazzaniga embodied the affirmation of Thomistic realism against

Jesuit essentialism in a four-volume opus, *Praelectiones theologicae* (1763–66), as well as in the subsequent *Theologia dogmatica in systema redacta* (1776).[38] He acknowledged Bishop Stock's role in restoring the teaching of theology, according to Thomas Aquinas, in the dedication of the third volume of *Praelectiones theologicae*. For the same reason, he eulogized Maria Theresa.[39] In line with the spirit of the Enlightenment, he referred positively to Erasmus and John Locke, while, in line with the Thomistic ontic pluralism, he censured Spinoza and Wolff for their alleged pantheism.[40]

Turning specifically to Bohemia, the battle was initially carried on at the theological schools of Hradec Králové and Olomouc. Even in the first half of the eighteenth century, there was an intimation of the coming return to Aquinas at Olomouc, where a Jesuit maverick, Šiminský (Schiminski) surreptitiously preferred to teach Thomism rather than the mandated Suárezianism, comparing the latter to a crayfish that bites and the former to a bun of Haná (*Hannatica Buchta*) that nourishes.[41] Hilibert Lebeda, canon of the diocese of Hradec Králové, took up the cudgels for Thomism and against Suárezianism in his book, published in 1751.[42] The idea of promoting Thomism had definitely prevailed by 1754 under Maria Theresa, with Bishop Stock again playing a crucial role.[43] After the university reform of 1759, the Dominicans, as well as the Augustinians, in Prague and Olomouc were authorized to lecture according to their own textbooks.[44] Accordingly, Dominican Ignác Světecký was appointed professor of theology in Olomouc in 1760, and a fellow Dominican, Qualbert (Jan) Reidinger (1725–78), became the most prominent opponent of Suárezian scholasticism in the Bohemian lands upon his appointment as professor at the University of Olomouc in 1767. Furthermore, Reidinger combined the restoration of Thomist realism with interest in Cartesian rationalism, further bolstering the anti-essentialist tendency in the philosophical underpinnings of the Catholic Enlightenment in Bohemia.[45] In the Bohemian lands, the milestone of the renewed Thomism was the publication of the volume *Hieronymi ordinis Praedicatorum episcopi Aemoniensis de D. Thomae Aquinatis doctrina et scriptis libri duo* by the Dominicans of Olomouc in 1763.[46] In a preface signed by Světecký and Reidinger, the Dominican authors dedicated the volume to Maria Theresa and outlined the program of the Thomistic restitution. They thanked the empress for her directive that Dominicans, the guardians of St. Thomas's legacy, were to lecture on theology in each university of the monarchy. Prior to this—the preface claimed—the teaching of Aquinas was confined to private study in all of Central Europe (*in tota Germania*).[47] In their teaching of theology, the Olomouc Dominicans relied primarily on Gazzaniga's textbooks. In another major development, after 1762 the direction of the Olomouc University was entrusted to a commission that excluded the Jesuits and was headed from 1762 to 1775 by Abbot Pavel F. Václavík, the Dominicans' friend.[48]

What was particularly important about the Thomist revival was its effect on the Bohemian awakeners as it shaped their philosophical outlook in the matrix of Aristotelian realism. Reidinger, the leading proponent of Thomism and opponent of Jesuit essentialism, became the intellectual hero of Josef Dobrovský, Mikuláš A. Voigt, Ignaz A. Born, and František M. Pelcl.[49] Pelcl and Voigt, in their *Abbildungen Böhmischer und Mährischer Gelehrten und Künstler*, highlighted Reidinger's defense of Aquinas in his *Hieronymi Vielmii*, mentioned earlier.[50] Another member of this coterie, Leopold Scherschnik, was eager to point out works on Aquinas in his early survey (1776) of the holdings in the Prague University Library.[51]

While the philosophical underpinning of the Catholic Enlightenment derived mainly from the Thomistic revival in the reign of Maria Theresa, later in the reign of Joseph II, during the culmination of the Enlightenment, even a more radically antimetaphysical approach had gained prominence. As noted in chapter 3, the theological leadership of Reform Catholicism was assumed by Abbot Franz S. Rautenstrauch, who replaced Bishop Stock as the chief *spiritus movens* in religious education. He was charged with transforming theological education in all the universities of the empire and in the early 1780s formulated the operating rules for the government-supervised general seminaries. Rautenstrauch opposed any intrusion of philosophical speculation—whether Augustinian, Thomistic, or Scotist—into the realm of theology. He was convinced that human reason could not comprehend the mysteries of faith. According to Rautenstrauch (sounding like a logical positivist), attempts to answer questions such as "How does God know what he knows?" or "To what extent can God foresee the future?" could generate only meaningless phrases.[52] The intellectual underpinnings of theology were to be mainly the Scripture and tradition. He followed the approach of his fellow Benedictine Martin Gerbert.[53] Due to Rautenstrauch, the influence of Gazzaniga diminished after the Dominican left Vienna in 1782.[54]

Despite Rautenstrauch's doubts about the role of philosophy in theological education, the Thomistic influence continued in the higher theological schools of the Habsburg Empire. That continuity was evident from the experience of Bolzano, who received his theological and philosophical training in institutions reformed under Rautenstrauch's guidance.[55] In theology, Bolzano relied on the works of Gazzaniga, particularly their affirmation of Thomistic realism against Jesuit essentialism, embodied in the four volumes of *Praelectiones theologicae* (1788–94). Still, in 1844 he would share his interest in Gazzaniga's work with Exner.[56] Earlier, he had recommended to his own students Gazzaniga's *Praelectiones theologicae*, as well as *Theologica Polemica* (1778–79), together with Johann M. Sailer's *Grundlehren der Religion* (1832) and Beda Mayr's *Verteidigung der natürlichen, christlichen und katholischen Religion nach dem Bedürfnisse unserer Zeit* (1787–90).[57]

The Protestant Lutheran Factor

As discussed in chapter 3, the intellectual basis of the Bohemian national awakening was a symbiosis of the Catholic Enlightenment, on the one hand, and the intellectual legacy of sixteenth-century Utraquism, on the other, which had represented a non-Protestant religious *via media*. From that point of view, the Bohemian readiness to resist German idealism may be seen as a parallel or an analogy to the Utraquist resistance to Lutheranism. While the Utraquists retained respect for medieval scholasticism with its Aristotelian foundation of individualizing realism,[58] Luther repudiated Aristotelian realism and moralism as part of his frontal attack on the scholastics' teaching. Among the Utraquists, the currency of the original pre-Renaissance Thomism was, in fact, reinforced at the University of Prague in the mid-fifteenth century by the vogue of Johannes Versor's teaching. The popularity of his approach is attested by the numerous writings and commentaries of this scholastic philosopher that were brought to Prague from the University of Paris in the 1440s by Bohemian students, the most zealous of whom was Václav of Vrbno.[59] The Aristotelian realism of Thomas Aquinas and his teacher Albertus Magnus thus prevailed at the University of Prague during the sixteenth-century Utraquist era.[60]

Unequivocally rejecting the medieval scholasticism of the Aristotelian tradition, Luther maintained that certain medieval doctors had spun many artificial mental constructs that even they could hardly understand. In addition, their ratiocinations tended to obscure the fact that the word of God contained in the Bible was entirely sufficient for salvation.[61] The main culprit in Luther's eyes was Thomas Aquinas, who placed Aristotle on a pedestal of virtual equality with Christ, and, as a result, the Greek philosopher's worldly wisdom encroached on divine truth.[62] As far as medieval philosophy was concerned, Luther endorsed the line that led through St. Bonaventura to St. Francis of Assisi, which rejected the Thomistic "unmoved mover" and substituted "God who acts": in other words, God as Being became God as Person.[63]

A distinct intellectual relationship between Lutheranism, on one hand, and German idealism/romanticism, specifically Hegelianism, on the other hand, has of course been frequently discussed. An example is the view of Ernst Troeltsch:

> In the development of German metaphysics, from Leibnitz and Kant to Fichte, Schelling, Hegel, and Fechner, the influence of the Lutheran background is recognizable in the direction of speculation towards the unity and interconnection of things, towards the inner rationality and logical consistency of the conception of God, towards general principles, ideal points of view, and the intuitive sense of the inward presence of the Divine. Indeed, even in the thought-world of Goethe and Schiller . . . the influence of this background is clearly recognizable . . . a proof of how deeply German metaphysics is rooted in Lutheranism.[64]

Tomáš Masaryk likewise called Kant a philosopher of Protestantism. Although Kant's philosophy contradicted orthodox Lutheranism, Masaryk argued, "his thought was rooted in Lutheran subjectivism and emphasis on morality." Walter Kaufmann cited the view of Hegel as "Germany's most Protestant, most Lutheran philosopher."[65] Hegel himself did not try to conceal his Lutheran roots. In fact, he seemed to flaunt them. In a letter to Friedrich A. Tholuck, he wrote: "I am and always was a Lutheran."[66] Yet in 1816, for instance, he spoke openly about the conversion of Christian theology into a philosophy in his absolute idealism and added, "Our universities and schools are our churches."[67] In the *Vorlesungen über die Philosophie der Religion*, he stated: "Philosophy has the aim of knowing the truth, of knowing God, because His is the absolute truth," and "In philosophy, which is theology, there is but one task to be accomplished, to show the rationality of religion."[68]

It is important to consider, in addition to the influence of official Lutheranism, the effect of irregular Protestant sources that evolved within German Lutheranism. Heinrich von Treitschke discerned the connecting link between Lutheranism and German classical philosophy in the Pietist movement, represented by Jakob Spener and Hermann Franke, which recovered the purely moral content of Christianity, freed from the intellectual shackles of dogma. Hence, the Germans conducted another Reformation leading to free and unprejudiced intellectual life. With justified national pride, they could claim to be at once "pious and free," creating a literature that was Protestant but not tainted with dogma.[69] In the light of this link, it can be assumed that the Slovak susceptibility to romanticism and metaphysical idealism, noted earlier,[70] was enhanced by the presence of a Pietist strand in Slovak Lutheranism.[71] Slovak students had already appeared in the Pietist university newly erected by August H. Franke in the Prussian Halle, and books in Slovak were published there.

Aside from Pietism, a notable of the esoteric sources was the theosophy of Jacob Boehme. Boehme's influence on the main assumptions of Hegel's metaphysics or "ontotheology" has been viewed as particularly pronounced. Thus, Cyril O'Regan pointed to Hegel's triple use of Boehme's theology of image: "its narrative quality, the movement of actualization as a process of divinization, and the image's communitarian nature."[72] According to James Collins, Hegel relied "on the theosophical language of Jacob Boehme to describe the turbulent inner life of the primal ground of being."[73] According to Frederick Copleston, "Boehme's triadic schemes and his idea of self-unfolding of God reappear, indeed, in Hegel, though minus Boehme's intense piety and devotion."[74] The theologian Friedrich C. Oetenger (1702–82) presumably served as the main conduit of Boehme's ideas to his own Swabian compatriots, Schelling and Hegel.[75] In searching further for the "mystical impulse in German Idealism," O'Regan points beyond Boehme to Meister Eckhart, whose fairly static ontological view of God's image Boehme historicized and thus made the concept suitable for a dialectical process.[76] In addition, Hegel's historical views bore an imprint of the theosophical ideas of Joachim of Fiore and his school.[77]

As for the long-range relationship of Lutheranism and German idealism, a Lutheran background was also seen as a factor in the philosophy of Nietzsche.[78] In his *Antichrist*, Nietzsche openly stated: "The German Protestant minister is the grandfather of German philosophy."[79] Sidney Hook made the point rather bluntly: "A disguised metaphysical theology has been the bane of the whole history of German idealism from Kant to Heidegger."[80] Recently, Marie Bayerová has hinted that the "Protestant" factor had played a role in rousing Austrian resistance to the speculative aspects of German idealism.[81] The Lutheran angle is highlighted in reverse by the philosophical journey of Heidegger from his native Catholicism to his distinctive brand of idealism. He denounced Catholic scholasticism based on the Aristotelian precept that was "to take its bearings from the natural world rather than the domain of inner life." The cultivation of the inner self (*Innewerden*) and the advent of self-consciousness was, according to Heidegger, the characteristic of German Pietism that Hegel had absorbed into his philosophical outlook.[82] To take a view from the other shore, the logical positivist of the Vienna Circle, Otto Neurath, maintained that Lutheranism was particularly conducive to metaphysical speculation because—unlike in Catholicism—the line between philosophy and dogma was not sharply drawn but blurred instead.[83]

Seibt, Catholic Enlightenment, and Anti-Idealism

Against considerable odds—in view of the reactionary turn of Habsburg politics after 1792—the liberal and cosmopolitan tenor of the Catholic Enlightenment continued to permeate the philosophical life of Bohemia during the first half of the nineteenth century.[84] The aversion of the Austrian imperial government to the intellectual developments in German Lutheran universities considerably assisted this continuity. The Romantic and idealist trends (from Herder to Hegel) were considered inconsistent with the political culture of the Empire, not only because their roots were Protestant (as discussed earlier) but also because their emphasis on the ontic national-cultural differences clashed with the multinational character of the empire.[85] Already Herder "denounced multinational empires in favor of national entities founded on an affinitive culture of their own."[86] The balance, albeit uneasy, permitted a perpetuation of the liberal trend with its empirical and realistic outlook, partly inherited from the Bohemian Utraquist tradition.

The pedagogical role of Seibt was of major importance for affirming the intellectual commitment to the Catholic Enlightenment in Bohemia. He strengthened the Thomistic-Aristotelian empirical and realistic outlook with his appeal to French, and particularly British, modes of thought. Moreover, in his teaching of liberal arts at the University of Prague, he sought to link the Catholic faith with the temper and philosophy of the Enlightenment. Maria Theresa had appointed him an extraordinary professor of humanities at the university in 1763. After the abolition of the Jesuit Order in 1773, he assumed the post of director of philosophical studies at the university in 1775 and oversaw all the gymnasia (academic secondary schools) in Bohemia. Finally, he served as a professor of philosophy from 1784 to 1801.[87]

Seibt was an exceptionally well liked and respected teacher. His teaching left profound marks on the intellectual development of at least two generations of students.[88] Students were fascinated by both the content and the style of his lectures, which also attracted a wide range of listeners from the educated public. His colleague and successor from 1802 to 1821, František X. Němeček, thus described Seibt's extraordinary effectiveness as a teacher: "All that came out of his mouth appeared so new, so intelligible and so attractive; therefore all who had the intelligence and the desire to learn flocked into his lecture hall. His words and his teaching were received with enthusiastic eagerness."[89] His numerous disciples, sometimes called the "Seibtianers," were to dominate Bohemia intellectually in the latter part of the eighteenth century.[90] Johann H. Wolf placed Seibt on the list of the most distinguished promoters of liberal arts [*die schöne Wissenschaften*] in the history of Bohemia, and František F. Procházka, in his *De saecularibus liberalium artium* (1782), praised Maria Theresa for her wisdom in appointing Seibt to the influential university post.[91]

As an adherent of the realistic and empirical outlook, Seibt shied away from Herder's and Kant's teachings, which were then gaining popularity in Germany, and favored the writings of Hume, Montesquieu, Voltaire, and Johann B. Basedow.[92] His promotion of the ideas of Basedow (1724–90) was particularly significant. As an individualist and realist, Basedow was a decisive opponent of the collectivist idealism of Herder. In pedagogy and ethics, Basedow upheld the Enlightenment ideal of individual happiness against Herder's ideal of an overriding obligation to a particular national society.[93] In his exchanges with Basedow, Herder, in turn, ridiculed the concept of an all-human cosmopolitan happiness, maintaining that each individual could be happy only according to his national characteristics.[94] Against Herder's cultural particularism, Seibt sided with Basedow's cosmopolitanism and honored him in a stirring eulogy: "I am filled with high respect and thankfulness by the name of Basedow; his memory will be blessed and celebrated by a grateful posterity."[95]

Seibt upheld the principle of individualism not only in the philosophical but also in the political setting. For him, the happiness of the individual (*Glück des Einzelnen*) constituted the foundation of the state. In his inaugural lecture of 1771, he argued that the state did not impose its own goals on the private lives of its citizens but depended on the autonomous satisfaction of each individual within the civil society (*die bürgerliche Gesellschaft*). In turn, civil society's achievement of its objectives ensured the welfare of the state.[96] Seibt resorted to quoting his favorite philosophers concerning the political and military strength that derived from civic individualism. Thus, he cited the "sagacious" (*scharfsinnig*) Hume on the prevalence of relatively few Greeks over the multitudes sent by Xerxes against them.[97] Seibt also referred to the "great" Montesquieu on the importance of education, which—more than material possessions—determined the stamina of a state's citizens.[98]

His main field of teaching was ethics (oddly called *Klugheitslehre* or sagacity),[99] in which he focused on the character development of the individual. The teaching of sagacity covered two sides: the inner or moral one and the outer or civic one (*bürgerliche Klugheit*).[100] Overall, Seibt's ethical approach to statecraft was utilitarian. The goal of earthly life was the pursuit of happiness, which could be achieved by obtaining intellectual and material goods such as honor, leisure, friendship, family, good manners, property, or commercial success.[101] His lecture course, as reflected in his textbook *Klugheitslehre, praktisch abgehandelt, in akademischen Vorlesungen*, can best be described as essentially one in the humanities, typical of the liberal arts. He combined coverage of selections from religion, philosophy, and literature with a special emphasis on ethics and etiquette. A basic reading list of nine items was highlighted in the textbook: (1) biblical citations; (2–3) citations from the Greek and Roman classics; (4) Christina, Queen of Sweden, *Works, Containing Maxims and Sentences* (1753); (5) François de la Rochefoucauld, *Réflexions ou sentences et maximes morales* (1665); (6) Madeleine de Souvré, marquise de Sablé, *Maximes* (1678); (7) Amelot de la Houssaie, *L'homme de cour* (1707), an adaptation of Baltasar Gracián, *El oráculo manual y arte de prudencia* (1647); (8) Samuel Richardson, *Teaching of*

Virtue and Good Manners[102]; (9) *The Rule of Life, in Select Sentences Collected from Greatest Authors, Ancient and Modern* (1742).[103]

In addition to these sources, Seibt referred in his lectures to a number of other authors, almost exclusively French or British. The former included further writers on morals and polite demeanor, such as Jean-François Cardinal de Retz, Marie de Rabutin-Chantal (Madame de Sévigné), and Jean de La Bruyère; the philosopher Michel de Montaigne; and the playwrights Jean Racine and Pierre Carlet de Chamblain de Marivaux.[104] Marivaux was a prominent figure of the Enlightenment, a friend of Montesquieu, who sought to pursue journalism in the British style, in particular using as a model Joseph Addison's *Spectator*. Among British authors, Seibt highly valued Shakespeare, who "distinguished himself with an unreachable excellence" in exemplifying the rules of human conduct,[105] and Lord Chesterfield, from whose *Letters to His Son* he drew liberally for maxims.[106] In addition, Seibt referred to the writings of another dramatist and poet, Edward Young, as well as to the theologian Thomas More and the philosopher Francis Bacon.[107]

In his teaching of philosophy proper, especially after 1784, Seibt relied on the textbook of an advocate of British empiricism and determined opponent of German idealism, Johann Georg Feder (1740–1821). The textbook appeared originally in 1769 as *Lehrbuch der Logik und Metaphysik* and was later translated into Latin as *Institutiones Logicae et Metaphysicae* (1777).[108] Feder's principal work, *Untersuchungen über den menschlichen Willen* (1779–93), was to be a discussion of human will along the lines of Locke's discussion of human reason. He was the first one in Germany to inform the public about the economic theories of Adam Smith's *An Inquiry into the Principle and Causes of the Wealth of Nations*. As for German idealism, Feder subjected Kant's *Kritik der reinen Vernunft* to a devastating critique. In a review in the *Göttinger gelehrten Anzeigen*, he compared Kant's idealism contemptuously to Berkeley's.[109]

Seibt, in the spirit of liberal Catholicism, defended the philosopher's right to the freedom of thought, independently of theological dogmas.[110] At the same time, he was neither a deist nor an atheist but adhered to the Reform Catholicism of the Josephist era.[111] He corresponded and shared his religious outlook with Rautenstrauch, the leading theologian of the Austro-Bohemian Enlightenment.[112] The two cooperated in the publication of a journal, *Neue Literatur*, and Rautenstrauch defended Seibt when the latter was accused of heterodox views in 1779.[113] After the inquiry into his religious faith, Seibt affirmed an attachment to Catholic theology by producing a sizable prayer book, *Katholisches Lehr- und Gebetbuch*, for the student youth, published in 1779.[114] Aside from numerous prayers for varied occasions, such as times of the day, the mass, confession, communion, and special holidays, there were more practical instructions on the proper use of time, on the duties toward oneself and one's neighbors, and on the wise management of earthly goods.[115] Perhaps as the ultimate seal of Seibt's Catholic orthodoxy, there was a brief discussion of the concept of hell.[116] The empress was thoroughly pleased with the prayer book and rewarded Seibt with a diamond ring with a holograph note: "Meinem lieben Seibt zum Andenken, Maria Theresa" (To my dear Seibt as a souvenir, Maria Theresa).[117]

As noted earlier, Seibt has been routinely portrayed by both Czech and German (especially Sudeten German) writers as an avid Germanizer and enemy of the Czech language.[118] It can be pointed out, to the contrary, that Seibt demonstrated his linguistic open-mindedness when he took considerable risk—in his capacity as censor—to approve the publication of the famous defense of the rights of the Czech language, *Dissertatio apologetica pro lingua Slavonica preacipue Bohemica* (1775), which had been written by Bohuslav Balbín a century earlier but had until then remained only in manuscript.[119] Although he lectured in German, virtually all the authors whom he assigned or discussed—judging from his textbooks—were either French or English. As a supervisor of the former Jesuit gymnasia in Bohemia, he opposed the total elimination of Czech and Latin as languages of instruction from these secondary schools and asked for continuation of their use at least at the gymnasia of Hradec Králové, Jičín, Jindřichův Hradec, and Klatovy. The empress's patent for the gymnasia in Bohemia and Moravia, issued in October 9, 1777, however, ignored his request and the German language prevailed.[120]

Seibt's Contemporaries and Followers

Eminent representatives of the Catholic Enlightenment, such as Dobrovský, Václav Thám, Matěj V. Kramerius, Puchmajer, Jan Nejedlý, Bolzano, and Jungmann, expressed their indebtedness to Seibt as their mentor.[121] Seibt also played an important role in the promotion of Dobrovský's academic career,[122] in 1783 supporting his candidacy for a professorship at the University of Prague and intervening in his favor with Rautenstrauch.[123] Seibt's intellectual orientation was shared by learned priest-scholars, in particular Mikuláš Adaukt Voigt (1733–87), Ignác Cornova (1740–1822), Stanislav Vydra (1741–1804), Karel R. Ungar (1743–1807), Johann H. Wolf (1745–84), and František Faustin Procházka (1749–1809). As noted in chapter 4, these devotees of the Josephist Enlightenment and champions of Reform Catholicism also saw a special correspondence between the Austro-Bohemian Enlightenment and the free discussion, humanism, and tolerance of the Utraquist age stemming from the Bohemian Reformation.[124] Those who more particularly passed on the realistic, individualistic, and cosmopolitan tenets of Josephism as professors at the University of Prague included František Martin Pelcl, professor of Czech language and literature; František Steinský (1752–1816), professor of auxiliary historical sciences; František X. Němeček (Niemetschek, 1766–1821), Seibt's successor; and Aloys Klar (1763–1833), professor of ancient philosophy, as well as Wolf and Cornova.[125]

The preference for Thomistic existentialism over Suárezian essentialism in the Catholic Enlightenment forearmed the early Czech awakeners to confront specifically the challenge of philosophical idealism. They saw this intellectual current as promoting either an unacceptable amalgamation of the natural with the supernatural, usually in a variant of pantheism, or a return to baroque-like irrationalism with its fantastic visions (*Schwärmerei*) and mysticism that were rejected as part and parcel of the Counter-Reformation.[126] Thus, Rautenstrauch embraced a stark philosophical realism that militated against the metaphysical concepts of secularized eschatology, characteristic of German idealism. The grasp of the inner meaning and potentialities of the universe, according to him, exceeded human understanding.[127] Also, Dobrovský opposed Fichte's and Schelling's systems of philosophical idealism, calling them *Hirngespinst* (whim, chimera, bogey).[128] He showed some interest in Kant but indignantly disavowed any plans to teach his philosophy.[129] In his lectures on religion at the General Seminary, he referred to Locke, Anthony Shaftesbury, and especially to Pascal but neither to Herder nor to Kant. His knowledge of English psychological empiricism stemmed in part from the writings of his friend Johann C. Adelung.[130] Václav Stach, as Dobrovský's colleague at the Olomouc General Seminary, opposed the philosophy of Kant as well.[131] Němeček, according to Král, followed Seibt in interpreting philosophy according to Kant's opponent Feder.[132]

In the longer run, other Bohemian writers—aside from Bolzano, whose magisterial opposition to Kant, Fichte, and Schelling will be discussed in chapter 8—produced philosophical works, mainly in the 1840s, that perpetuated the tendency stemming from the Austro-Bohemian Enlightenment toward realism and cosmopolitanism and away from idealism and metaphysical speculation. As an example, the outstanding disciple of the theological school of Litoměřice, Zahradník (1790–1836), whom Michael J. Fesl had taught in the early 1810s, adopted philosophical realism and an anti-Romantic orientation with a weltanschauung governed by the application of "common sense" (*zdravý rozum*). His favorite philosopher was Christian Garve (1742–98), a student of British empiricism.[133] The poet and later professor of Czech language at the University of Prague, Jan Pravoslav Koubek (1805–54), likewise voiced his distaste for "the German philosophy" during his studies in Prague in the 1820s.[134]

Jungmann's colleague, Antonín Marek, in his pioneering Czech textbook of philosophy, *Základy filosofie: Logika. Metafysika* (Foundations of Philosophy: Logic, Metaphysics) (1844), relied primarily on the text of Wilhelm Traugott Krug, *System der theoretischen Philosophie* (1818).[135] In analyzing the epistemological approach of Fichte, Marek reproduced Krug's equation, according to which "consistent Idealism" (*konsequente Idealismus*) resulted in "absolute Nihilism" (*absolute Nihilismus*).[136] Aside from their shared opposition to idealism, Marek was probably attracted by Krug's avowed cosmopolitan leaning, which made him proud to see his works disseminated in translation among the Greeks, the Hungarians, and the Poles.[137] Occasionally, Marek cited other philosophers, particularly Jakob F. Fries, Johann Herbart, and Karl L. Reinhold, who had parted ways with post-Kantian idealism.[138] Fries was a personal as well as philosophical enemy of Hegel, whose speculative idealism—as well as that of Fichte and Schelling—he opposed. He viewed the results of their speculative idealism as a construction of empty artificial concepts (*leere Begriffskünstelei*).[139] According to Fries, philosophy should be primarily descriptive, not speculative.[140]

Marek's preference for Reinhold and Herbart, as well as Krug, coincided with Bolzano's intellectual orientation. As discussed in chapter 8, Krug in particular was among the opponents of idealist logic most frequently cited in Bolzano's *Wissenschaftslehre.* Bolzano also noted with satisfaction Fries's departure from Kant's basic propositions, such as his categories and antinomies.[141] Likewise, Palacký had early on voiced a high opinion of Krug, whose aesthetics he considered an improvement over Kant's.[142] The endorsement of the German opponents of speculative philosophy was undoubtedly shared by Jungmann, who was a *spiritus movens* behind Marek's textbook of philosophy. Jungmann had won his philosophical credentials by assessing in 1842, together with Exner, Bolzano's treatise on aesthetics for the Royal Bohemian Society of Sciences.[143]

The other major philosophical work published in Bohemia under the auspices of *Matice česká* and with Jungmann's blessing was *Duševloví zkušebné* (Experimental Psychology) in 1844. The author, Ferdinand Hyna, also adopted an anti-Kantian orientation,[144] depending heavily on the views of Johann Peithner von Lichtenfels, a follower of Herbart. Lichtenfels had published the *Grundriss der Psychologie, als Einleitung in die Philosophie* in 1824, and had taught philosophy at the University of Prague in 1827–31. As a student (like Exner) of Leopold Rembold at the University of Vienna, Lichtenfels was imbued with the philosophy of Herbart, who had sought to develop a realistic alternative to the philosophy of Kant, Fichte, Schelling, and Hegel. Hyna was probably Lichtenfels's student in Prague in 1827–28.[145] Aside from dependence on Herbartism through Lichtenfels and possibly through Exner's unpublished lectures, Hyna relied heavily on the philosophical and psychological works of Gottlob E. Schulze (1761–1833), especially on his *Psychische Anthropologie* (1819).[146]

Schulze had early been influenced by Hume's skepticism, then by Reinhold's logical realism. From the start, he opposed Kant's epistemology, particularly the unity of sensory and *a priori* cognition. Kant, according to him, expected to transcend experience, while at the same time postulating that it was impossible to proceed beyond experience without succumbing to some form of dogmatism.[147] Schulze's frontal attack on metaphysical idealism in *Kritik der theoretischen Philosophie* (1801), in which he questioned existence of an absolute or any supersensory realm, became an object of scathing critique by Schelling and Hegel.[148] Opposing Schelling with the same vigor with which he had opposed Kant, Schulze set out to safeguard realism in logic against Schelling's absolute system of identity (*absolutes Identitätssystem*). He defended the power of reason to systematize the perception of objects or classes of objects without resorting to *a priori* concepts.[149] Moreover, Hyna referred directly to Krug, whose work was also the main source for Marek's *Základy filosofie*.[150] Finally, Hyna mentioned the writings of Karl F. Burdach (1776–47), Fries, and the well-known figure of the Bavarian Catholic Enlightenment, Johann M. Sailer.[151]

The articulate critics of metaphysical idealism in the late 1840s also included Václav B. Nebeský, Karel B. Štorch, and František Čupr. In his article in *Časopis českého musea* in 1846, Nebeský viewed Kant as more or less obsolete, with only a few adherents remaining. Fichte had made himself an object of ridicule, according to Nebeský, with his "*ich / nicht ich*" dichotomy and the extremist metaphysics that had obscured his real virtues of personal courage, deep moralism, and concern for the public well-being.[152] Nebeský was much harder on Schelling. Schelling started with postulating a special relationship between nature and creative art that, according to Nebeský, led his youthful followers to the intoxicating idea of identifying nature with the human spirit. A devastating critique from the viewpoint of empirical natural sciences resulted in the conclusion that Schelling presented metaphors rather than concepts. Renouncing his initial system as a part of "negative" philosophy, Schelling offered a new "positive" one, but Nebeský doubted that the latter could arouse a comparable enthusiasm, evidently being just a recycling of the old Gnostic teachings. Accordingly, his followers had plunged into medieval mysticism. The resulting obscurity contradicted the very raison d'être of philosophy: to seek clarity and understanding.[153]

In an article in 1847, Štorch characterized German idealist philosophy as being primarily a response to Kant's assertion that human knowledge was necessarily limited to phenomena. His successors insisted that the real purpose of philosophy was to know the absolute. Štorch saw an exception to this trend of German thought in the figure of Lessing, who stood close to British empiricism, thus avoiding lush speculation and confusing displays of erudition.[154] Writing a year later, Štorch saw an unfortunate tendency in German idealist philosophy to move between the extremes of "the highest degree of abstraction" and "the highest degree of subjectivity." This tendency resulted in fierce partisanship on one hand and in the passion for coining peculiar new vocabularies on the other.[155] In an article of the same year, Čupr characterized Kant's subjectivist epistemology as a philosophical dead end and considered Fichte's and Schelling's efforts to get around this predicament through reconciling subjectivity and objectivity in the concept of the self unconvincing.[156]

Separately from, but in harmony with, the realistic outlook of liberal Catholicism, Palacký exhibited an aversion to the metaphysics of German idealism. In fact, his Lutheranism was a rather superficial one. Jiří Koralka ventures the opinion that Palacký's family tradition was not really Lutheran but more specifically rooted in the Bohemian Reformation, possibly in the Unity of Brethren.[157] Moreover, Palacký was not attracted to theology. As noted in chapter 6, instead of attending the classes at the Bratislava Evangelical Lyceum, he devoted himself to the study of the literature of the British Enlightenment and liberalism from the libraries of Hungarian gentry, in whose houses he worked as a tutor.[158] His lyceum teachers condoned this substitution of Enlightenment philosophy of the West European style for Lutheran theology.

His weltanschauung can best be characterized as deriving from the Scottish Enlightenment, which he imbibed during his student days in Bratislava from the Hungarians' Anglophilia.[159] Happily, the Scottish Enlightenment—in its realism, individualism, and cosmopolitanism—shared the characteristics of the Austro-Bohemian Enlightenment. In that respect, it was significant that Bolzano also drew on Dugald Stewart's philosophy of common sense.[160] As for philosophical idealism, beginning with Kant, it was alien to Palacký's intellectual taste, and his youthful aversion to the "dogmatic conundrums" of idealist metaphysics was affirmed by Dobrovský's influence after 1823.[161] Thus, Palacký shied away from Schelling's philosophy and that of kindred philosophers like Schlegel and Fichte. Apparently, he did not read either Fichte or Schelling in the original, but he had early learned about the substance of their philosophy from the unflattering characterizations in Anne Staël's *De l'Allemagne*. According to Madame de Staël, Fichte and Schelling had produced systems that were remarkable for their one-sidedness and detachment from real life—referring to Fichte's extreme idealism and Schelling's pantheism.[162] In March 1819, Palacký wrote to Jungmann that he had included certain passages in his book on aesthetics "in order to warn young gullible Bohemians against the error and nonsense of the German critique, especially the Fichte-Schelling-Schlegel sect and others."[163] He also had serious reservations about Kant.[164] Ultimately, he signaled a lack of interest in Kant's basic epistemological problem—the relationship of noumena and phenomena—

dismissing it from practical consideration as an issue that would forever remain controversial in philosophy.[165] He was even dissatisfied with Kant's aesthetics, and, as noted earlier, he considered the aesthetics of the anti-idealist Krug an improvement on Kant's.[166] To sum up, Palacký generally expressed a preference for the British empiricists Bacon, Locke, Hobbes, and Hume against the (mainly German) metaphysical and transcendental thinkers.[167] At best, he considered idealistic philosophy defective or one-sided,[168] and, after all, it was the *Časopis českého musea*—the journal that he had founded—that published Vilém Gábler's epochal attack on idealist metaphysics in 1847.[169]

8

Bolzano:
Against Kant, Fichte, and Schelling

Bernard Bolzano was the key figure in Bohemian philosophy during the first half of the nineteenth century, and a number of testimonies have acknowledged the lasting significance of his intellectual legacy. Karel Havlíček noted that Bolzano had strengthened freedom of thought in Bohemia and provided a model of enlightened humanism with his enthusiasm for the general welfare, justice, and civil rights. In a way, Havlíček was the main conduit for bringing Bolzano's philosophical, political, and social ideas into the mainstream of Czech intellectual life.[1] According to Eugen Lemberg, Bolzano's profound influence on university students and more broadly on the Bohemian educated public prevented German-style romanticism from taking root in Bohemia. Later, Josef Durdík, professor of philosophy at the University of Prague, compared Bolzano's role in Bohemia to that of Socrates in Athens. The distinguished twentieth-century literary critic and historian Arne Novák credited Bolzano with helping steer Czech literature from ecstatic emotionalism in an "ethical and humanistic" direction.[2]

Bolzano's Influence

After the impact of Karl H. Seibt and his contemporaries on the early generations of the Bohemian awakeners in the latter part of the eighteenth century, the influence of the Catholic Enlightenment's ideology —which in turn had been affected by sixteenth-century Bohemian Utraquism—continued into the first half of the following century. That influence was due largely to the ascendancy of Bolzano and to a degree to his colleagues Michael J. Fesl (1788–1864) and František Příhonský (1787–1859). Bolzano was the quintessential representative of Reform Catholicism[3] and clearly the outstanding personage in perpetuating philosophical realism, utilitarian ethics, and a cosmopolitan view of culture. This chapter covers his rejection of German idealism from Kant to Schelling, as well as his endorsement of German and British empirical realists from Karl L. Reinhold to John Locke. Bolzano's resolute opposition to Hegel's idealism is treated in chapter 9.

Bolzano's own education was firmly rooted in the legacy of the Josephist Enlightenment. During his study of philosophy at the University of Prague (1796–99), he was taught logic, metaphysics, and ethics by Seibt and literature and aesthetics by August Gottlieb Meissner. His youthful religious reading excluded baroque otherworldliness and emotionalism and focused on more sober literature like Muratori's *Wahre Andacht* (True Devotion) and Seibt's prayer book.[4] During his four years at the Theological Faculty of the University of Prague (1800–1804), he studied from textbooks written at the peak of the Enlightenment in Joseph II's reign, and five out of seven of his professors had been active prior to 1790 in the Josephist General Seminary of Prague. He remembered fondly the professor of pastoral theology, Johann Marian Míka (1754–1816), who held that religious revelation was not important per se but as a way of inspiring moral edification.[5] Bolzano fully assimilated the tenor of the Catholic Enlightenment and also relied theologically on its earlier representatives, such as Pietro M. Gazzaniga; Beda Mayr (1742–94), the Benedictine of Donauwörth; and Johann Michael Sailer, professor of theology in Bavaria (1784–1821). The Dominican Gazzaniga remained his main authority in theology, and through him he thus drew indirectly on the thought of Thomas Aquinas.[6] Bolzano did not show much enthusiasm for Aquinas's own writings or for that matter for any scholastics or lay philosophers active before the eighteenth century.[7] In this regard, he may also be seen as a true child of the Enlightenment.

Bolzano assumed the role of a premier educator, which Seibt had played before him, with his appointment in 1805 to the newly created chair of Catholic religious studies in the Philosophical Faculty of the University of Prague. His famous *Erbauungsreden* (Edification Lectures) could be considered a continuation of Seibt's seminal lectures (*Kollegien*) on ethics and politics.[8] The weekly *Erbauungsreden* attracted close to a thousand listeners on Sundays,[9] and the audiences, which included not only students and academics but also intellectually inclined burghers and military officers, could not be accommodated even in the largest of the university lecture halls; the nearby church of St. Salvator had to be used as early as 1806.[10] The regular academic course of religious instructions that Bolzano taught for fifteen years (1804–19) was required of all students in the Philosophical Faculty. Inasmuch as the Philosophical Faculty was, in turn, a prerequisite for the other divisions or faculties of the university, he thus had taught most of the future teachers, lawyers, civil servants, physicians, and priests who would dominate scholarship, science, culture, and public affairs in Bohemia during the second quarter of the nineteenth century and beyond.[11]

According to Marie Pavlíková's calculations, Bolzano had an opportunity to influence some 5,100 students by his lectures and sermons during his teaching at the University of Prague.[12] According to Jiří Kořalka, his disciples more specifically included the scientists Jan Evangelista Purkyně (1787–1869), Jan S. Presl (1791–1849), and Karel B. Presl (1794–1852); the German poet Karl Egon Ebert (1801–82); and the Czech writers and scholars Josef Linda (1789–1834), Václav Hanka (1791–1861), Josef V. Kamarýt (1797–1833), Josef K. Chmelenský (1800–39), and František L. Čelakovský (1799–1852).[13] More than 300 of Bolzano's students attained significant positions in public life.[14] Čelakovský testified to the great enthusiasm his fellow students felt for Bolzano as a guru in Prague in the 1810s. Suppression of Bolzano was greeted with much indignation.[15] This is also illustrated, for instance, by the experience of Josef Linda, or that of Josef Franta Šumavský, who abandoned his theological studies because of Bolzano's persecution.[16] Čelakovský privately placed Bolzano's removal from the University of Prague side by side with the martyrdom of Jan Hus in Constance.[17] Accused of heterodoxy, Bolzano was removed from his university position in January 1820, victimized by a temporary surge in ecclesiastical conservatism in the Habsburg monarchy.

Among the older generation, Jeník of Bratřice admired the liberal Catholicism of Bolzano and that of his disciple and colleague Fesl.[18] Within the younger generation, the priests-poets Karel A. Vinařický (1803–69), Boleslav Jablonský (1813–81), and Václav S. Štulc (1814–87) and the writers Josef Wenzig (1807–75) and even Karolina Světlá (1830–99) considered themselves his intellectual and ethical disciples.[19] Subsequently, Světlá left a testimony to the fundamental influence of Bolzano in shaping the intellectual outlook of the Czech awakeners who had received their education in the opening decades of the nineteenth century.[20]

Bolzano's Liberal Catholicism

Bolzano's philosophy was the epitome of the Catholic Enlightenment. Like his own teacher Seibt, he believed that the happiness of the individual rather than the interest of the state was the primary concern of social existence. For Bolzano, as for Seibt, the purpose of human life was the cultivation of individual personality to pursue autonomous goals. It was not to participate in a social enterprise with goals generated from outside that, at best, the individual might internalize.[21] The emphasis on educating the individual in developing his moral personality and in embracing enlightened humanitarian objectives reflected the educational philosophy of Franz S. Rautenstrauch, who reformed the theological education of which Bolzano was a beneficiary.[22]

Like Seibt, Bolzano clearly preferred enlightened humanism to Romantic nationalism.[23] He traced the inspiration for the Romantic weltanschauung to the German idealists, particularly to the teaching of Schelling, and he perceived this philosophy as something fantastic and murky that postulated a mysterious world-spirit, projecting its powers into the visible world.[24] He was particularly critical of Friedrich Schlegel for attempting to propagate the ideal of nationalism in the German Romantic style in the multinational Habsburg Empire.[25] His own emphasis was on general human values and the promotion of universal knowledge, not on particular ethnic values and the development of peculiar national philosophies.[26] Human equality was grounded both in religion and in natural reason; consequently, there were no preferred, or ontologically distinct, nations with ontologically distinct destinies.[27]

Bolzano, like Seibt before him, however, was not indifferent to the rights of the domestic tongue, although—in line with his cosmopolitan view of human culture and destiny—he regarded Czech as a practical instrument, not as a value in itself. Within this framework, he urged equal rights for both the Czech and the German languages in Bohemia and wished as many German speakers as possible to learn Czech.[28] His friendship and cooperation with Palacký in the Bohemian Society of Sciences during the 1830s and 1840s pointed to an interest in the development of Czech.[29] Although he admitted only an imperfect knowledge of the "Bohemian language," he would show, in 1839, a lively interest in Vinařický's introductory reader for Czech schoolchildren, praising particularly its design and style.[30]

Like Seibt, Bolzano did not believe that a political community was to be built around the collective spirit of a nation. In ethics, he was a rare adherent (for Central Europe) of utilitarianism of the Benthamite type, focusing on the measure of pleasure and pain as an objective foundation for morals and legislation, opposed to other criteria like moral sense, law of nature, law of reason, right reason, or good order.[31] Bolzano defined the highest ethical principle in Bentham's terms,[32] convinced that Bentham's criterion was not selfish pleasure but also a concern for the well-being of others.[33] Bolzano's utilitarianism was consonant with the tradition of the Austro-Bohemian Catholic Enlightenment. Already the quintessential Josephist, Rautenstrauch was seriously interested in the writings of the early American initiator of utilitarianism in politics, Joseph Priestley.[34]

In addition to his rejection of metaphysical idealism, his Benthamite inclination further distanced Bolzano from the bulk of German-speaking philosophers, who generally looked askance at utilitarianism. In particular, his Benthamite ethics inevitably led him to clash with Kant's moral rigor. Bolzano opposed Kant's idea of an unconditional demand for virtue, postulating instead the normative character of those dealings that serve the happiness of many individuals. According to Bolzano, moral activity was not firmly grounded in the divine will that had to be followed, as Kant maintained, but man was able to enjoy his own free will so that the divinity could not directly participate in either his good or his evil deeds.[35] In his critique of Kant's supreme moral law in his *Lehrbuch der Religionswissenschaft* (Textbook of Religious Science), the famous categorical imperative (that one should do what all others in the given situation should do) appeared to him trite and empty.[36] He further questioned what he considered a Kantian notion that only through submission to duty could a man become free.[37] Bolzano, therefore, opposed any collectivist or deterministic views of ethics. He also reproached Kant for not wanting to hear anything about the Enlightenment ideal of happiness (*Glückseligkeit*) in ethics.[38]

Like Seibt (whose prayer book he had used in his youth), Bolzano remained a devotee of the liberal brand of Catholicism that the ecclesiastical reformers of the Austro-Bohemian Enlightenment had developed.[39] He held that religion was to be less a matter of theological speculation and more a source of moral edification. In his *Lehrbuch der Religionswissenschaft*, he defined religion primarily as the collection of those beliefs that enhanced the virtue and happiness of human beings.[40] He advocated a society with complete religious freedom, without any established religion.[41] In matters of discipline, he considered the requirement of priestly celibacy "harmful and purposeless."[42] He questioned the practice of ecclesiastical censorship and book prohibition; such an interference hampered the advancement of knowledge and tended to discredit the Roman Church in the eyes of reasonable people.[43]

In his ecclesiological views, Bolzano maintained a position reminiscent of sixteenth-century Bohemian Utraquism. His aim was to liberalize ecclesiastical administration from within, not to destroy the historical hierarchical structure.[44] He also maintained the individualistic and realistic view typical of the Austro-Bohemian Enlightenment and thus he opposed the romanticist interpretation of the church as an organic entity or the living body of Christ. In other words, he argued that the church had no metaphysical reality of its own beyond the sum of the individual believers.[45] This aspect of his individualistic approach again owed much to Seibt's religious outlook.[46] As a part of his liberal approach, Bolzano also favored church services in vernacular languages,[47] and he privately sympathized with the schism of Johann Ronge, a Catholic priest in Germany who was excommunicated in 1844 and established a liberal German Catholic Church in Wrocław in 1845.[48] He also rejoiced over František Náhlovský's report in 1845 of cordial relations between Catholic and Protestant clergy in Bautzen as a palpable sign of religious toleration.[49]

Despite his liberal religious views, Bolzano again followed Seibt in not questioning the core values of Catholic orthodoxy. In particular, he remained convinced of the necessity for divine revelation. Natural religions, according to him, had historically led to many errors, and even the most learned of men could arrive at unacceptable conclusions in the religious realm on such issues as the origin and purpose of evil, the immortality of the soul, and the remission of sins.[50] On the ground of moral effectiveness or enhancement (*sittliche Zuträglichkeit*), Bolzano argued for the authenticity of the biblical narrative and its accounts of miracles.[51] Thus, he did not abandon basic Catholic beliefs. Accordingly, in his notes to the second edition of his *Lehrbuch der Religionswissenschaft*, he reproved both Hegel and Schelling for denying personal immortality.[52] Likewise in the *Lehrbuch*, he objected to the viewpoints of agnostics, Deists, materialists, and those philosophers who denied the existence of evil.[53]

Bolzano and Metaphysical Idealists

In philosophy, therefore, Bolzano opposed not only Fichte, Schelling, and Hegel, whose speculation he considered superficial and obscure,[54] but also Kant and his *Critiques*.[55] As of 1811–17, he was widely read in Kant, as well as in Fichte and Schelling.[56] Even earlier, in 1806, he had to defend himself resolutely against the bizarrely groundless insinuations of sympathy for Kant and Schelling by ecclesiastical censors.[57] At the time of his removal from the university in 1820, his religious views, as expressed in the *Erbauungsreden*, were likewise fancifully related to Kant's *Die Religion innerhalb der Grenzen der blossen Vernunft* (1794) in a secret report by Adolph Koppmann (1781–1835), professor of theology at the University of Prague, to Archbishop Leopold Chlumčanský of Prague.[58]

Kant's "Critical" Philosophy

Bolzano's reactions to Kant's "critical" philosophy were consistently negative. Altogether, he was one of the most acute critics of both Kant and German idealism.[59] According to his later recollections, his discovery of Kant's errors dated to the age of eighteen, when he first read Kant's *Critique of Pure Reason*, having prepared himself by studying Alexander Baumgarten's *Metaphysik* at the age of sixteen.[60] In his *Lehrbuch der Religionswissenschaft*, he gave four principal reasons for the need to combat so-called critical philosophy, of which Kant was the prime mover: (1) its continuing attraction for a large number of intellectuals; (2) its undeniable shrewdness (*Scharfsinn*); (3) its seeming thoroughness and finality; and (4) its influence on subsequent German philosophy.[61] In his opinion, German idealism, beginning with Kant, introduced obscurity rather than clarity into philosophical issues.[62] He went as far as to signify his agreement with the negative judgment of German idealist philosophy by Ludwig Feuerbach, the famous materialist philosopher. He cited with satisfaction Feuerbach's view that what was currently called "the speculative philosophy" was "the shadiest, most uncritical thing in the world."[63] Inasmuch as his negative judgment applied not only to Kant's followers but to Kant himself, he considered absurd the call of Joseph Schram (in 1836) for overcoming the subsequent idealism by a return to Kant's philosophy.[64]

Bolzano's objective was to correct the mistakes of Kantian philosophy.[65] Thus, he dealt with Kant's assertions that causal relations existed only among sensory perceptions but not among matters that were not subject to such a perception[66] and that *a priori* truth did not exist in time and space and, hence, had no ground in the existing being.[67] Bolzano felt that the basic flaw of idealism was a confusion between an object of the imagination and imagination itself. Moreover, he charged Kant with inconsistency, because Kant claimed both that there were no objects (*Dinge*) and that these objects had an effect on us.[68] He also condemned Kant's distinction (which Schelling also upheld) between the freedom of the intelligible world and the determinism of the empirical one. A distinction between two such worlds was untenable.[69]

Opposing Kant's concepts of "pure intuition" and "theory of the *a priori*," he concentrated on the more semantic theory of meaning, which included the theory of concepts (*Begriffe*), judgments (*Urteile*), and propositions (*Sätze*). Bolzano devoted a sizable excursus to critiquing Kant's epistemology in the *Lehrbuch der Religionswissenschaft*. His summary verdict about the weakness of Kant's approach was that it rested on his inconsequential assertion "about the subjectivity of all our judgments." Opposing this subjectivist approach, Bolzano found the proper philosophical starting point in the assumption that existing truths were objective and behaved as causes and consequences. There was no reason for the intrusion of the self as a thinking being into this process. Instead, the philosopher should present a system of these truths in their objective relationships and thus eventually arrive at an explanation of so-called empirical truths. According to Bolzano, Kant's *a priori* question of what justified the self (the "I") in forming judgments was absurd. It made no sense to seek to ascertain whether one's judgments were objectively true, if one did not assume his own ability to form true judgments.[70] Similarly, Kant's assertion that we could not make judgments about the causes of phenomena (the so-called noumena) contained contradictions inasmuch as it already contained two judgments: (1) that such noumena existed; and (2) that judgments could not be made about them.[71]

It was above all his principal work, *Wissenschaftslehre*,[72] written during the 1820s, that was dedicated to refuting and replacing Kant's "critical" philosophy and to indicting its direct and indirect influence on the subsequent development of nineteenth-century German philosophy.[73] Bolzano objected particularly to Kant's assertion that a judgment merely involved manipulation of different imagined concepts instead of objectively existing true concepts.[74] According to Bolzano, a judgment (*Urteil*) included holding for true a proposition in itself (*Satz an sich*). The propositions in themselves enjoyed an abstract existence independent of concrete spoken or mental objects. Thus, they differed from mere thoughts (*Denken*) or subjective images (*subjektive Vorstellen*). According to Bolzano, knowledge or perception (*Erkenntnis*) resulted when the abstract "proposition in itself" became concrete as matter (*Stoff*) in the mind of a person.[75] Although Kant severely condemned ontological and epistemological skepticism, Bolzano maintained that the former's philosophical approach in fact undermined the possibility of arriving at true or real knowledge, since according to his own admission the things in themselves (*Dingen an sich*) or noumena could not be experienced.[76] Although he thereby denied knowledge above sense perceptions, Kant was inconsistent and admitted the reality of the self that was not a mere appearance.[77] Similarly, his insistence on unchangeable human nature appeared to violate the divide between noumena and phenomena.[78]

While he admitted the usefulness of Kant's distinction between analytic and synthetic judgments (*Urteile*), Bolzano maintained that Kant's assertion of *a priori* synthetic judgments was a fundamental error.[79] He pointed out that Kant failed to differentiate properly between perceptions (*Anschauungen*) and concepts (*Begriffe*). According to Bolzano, "perception" covered only what was strictly individual; any common characteristics belonged to the realm of "concepts" in representations (*Vorstellungen*). To him, the outcome of Kant's approach would have been a gross essentialism, subsuming specific individuals under general entities. Thus, persons like Socrates or Plato would thereby be deprived of their specificity and "belong under the concept of man, and the perception of them would be subsumed under the concept of man."[80] A similar concern with "essentialist" tendencies underlay Bolzano's rejections of Kant's distinction between ideas (*Vorstellungen*) that relate to their object in a "mediated" (*mittelbar*) way and those that relate in an "unmediated" (*unmittelbar*) way.[81] He sought to focus on the refutation of those doctrines of Kant's logic and ontology that were still commonly accepted by philosophers in Germany (*allen Weltweisen Deutschlands*). Thus, he tackled with particular zest Kant's concept of a single infinite space, inasmuch as for Kant it is not an empirical datum but a perception (*Anschauung*) *a priori*.[82] He quoted Salomon Maimon on Kant's odd inversion of the traditional concept of the relationship between form and matter.[83]

As for Kant's famous twelve categories, Bolzano considered them grounded in metaphysics, not in logic, and by and large arbitrary and useless.[84] Kant's equally famous distinction between *a priori* and *a posteriori* knowledge could be more simply viewed, according to Bolzano, as a difference between two kinds of propositions as such (*Sätze an sich*) according to their content (*Inhalt*): concept sentences (*Begriffssätze*), when the content consisted only of concepts (*Begriffe*); and perception sentences (*Anschauungssätze*), the content of which did not entirely consist of concepts.[85] Similarly, Kant's distinction between concepts (*Begriffe*) *a priori* and those based on experience (*Erfahrung*) was invalid; all concepts derived from experience and differed between pure and mixed ones.[86] Likewise, antinomies of reason, which Kant had postulated in his *Critique of Pure Reason*, were more apparent than real, and there was no reason to worry about such an error-producing mechanism in our minds, simply because the impossibility of this mechanism had not been proved.[87] In a concentrated critique in paragraph 305 of the *Wissenschaftslehre*, Bolzano attacked Kant's doctrines of analytic judgments, empirical (as distinct from *a priori*) judgments, and *a priori* intuitions.[88] He also unequivocally rejected the Kantian division of syllogisms into categorical, hypothetical, and disjunctive.[89] He was not satisfied with Kant's explanation of the cause of error or erroneous judgments, which he ascribed to an interference of sense perceptions (*Sinnlichkeit*) with sound reason (*Verstand*). This explanation failed to address the mix-up between merely subjective grounds and objective grounds of error or to resolve the confusion between mere appearance of truth and actual truth.[90]

In addition, Bolzano was concerned with the deficiencies of Kant's teaching in the areas of the philosophy of history and of aesthetics. On the first topic, he commented in his diary of 1817–27: "How one-sided are all his concepts of the purpose of history!"[91] On the second topic, he claimed that Kant had no genuine interest in aesthetics[92] and that when he had to deal with the subject of beauty, he applied his favorite categories mechanically and in an ill-fitting way, particularly the four criteria (*Gesichtspunkten* or *Momenten*) of quality, quantity, relation, and modality.[93] No matter how defective (*unvollkommen*) his pronouncements about beauty were, his idiosyncratic (*eigentümliche*) ideas nevertheless had considerable influence.[94]

On semantic issues, Bolzano rejected Kant's distinction between "object" and "*Gegenstand*," stating that the latter was simply "our German word" for the former. He further disputed Kant's assertion that an "object" could mean both "something" and "nothing"; a concept (*Begriff*) of nothing could be an object or a "*Gegenstand*" but not "nothing as such" (*Nichts an sich*).[95] He considered incorrect Kant's logical maxim of affinity: "that intermediate attributes (*Zwischenarten*) could exist between two adjacent attributes (*Nebenarten*)."[96] In discussing the "matter" and the "form" of a conclusion, he also found obscure Kant's explanation (*dunkle Erklärung*) of the form.[97] Bolzano considered false Kant's assertion that an idea (*Vorstellung*) without an object that was represented was nonsensical. It was correct only in the case of a perception (*Anschauung*).[98] Eventually, in its afterlife, Bolzano's *Wissenschaftslehre* was used as a basis by his younger colleague, František Příhonský, for his own critique of Kant's philosophy (1850).[99]

While Bolzano's main criticism in the 1820s was aimed at Kant, he did not neglect to give trenchant and, at times, caustic critiques of other German idealists. In his view, German philosophers—after Kant and under his influence—acquired a number of bad habits, vitiating the subsequent course of intellectual life and development. Among them was a liking for metaphorical expression, a corresponding avoidance of concrete statements, a passion for discovering similarities (or even identities) among dissimilar objects, a love of paradox, and a copious employment of tautologies with complete disregard for their inanity. The root problem—and here again the prime fault could be traced to Kant—was a disregard for the rules of logic. Kant took a dim view of the study of logic, which, according to him, had stagnated since Aristotle, and in any case he believed that a strict logical method, while applicable in mathematics and natural sciences, was not useful in philosophy.[100]

Two Post-Kantian Idealists, Fichte and Schelling

Among the post-Kantian idealists, Bolzano paid specific attention to Fichte and Schelling. For both of them, according to Bolzano, the absolute represented an identity of the ideal and the real, of the subjective and the objective, of history and nature.[101] While Leibniz could already be accused of such an unwarranted conflation, the case was even clearer with Kant, Fichte, Schelling, and Hegel, whose systems rested on the constant confusion of the concept as a thought and the thought's object.[102] He also criticized Fichte and Schelling for holding that a thing can be a causation of itself.[103] In 1815, he noted with satisfaction the uncomplimentary assessment of post-Kantian speculation in Germany, especially that of Schelling, by an anonymous author as "a mystical philosophy."[104] In his diary of 1817–27, he cited a reviewer's opinion that Fichte and Schelling developed their systems from the principle of identity either by trickery or misinterpretation.[105]

In the introduction to his *Wissenschaftslehre*, Bolzano noted that Fichte had used the same book title, *Wissenschaftslehre*, for the exposition of his own subjective idealism. Bolzano, however, stressed that he did not invest the title with Fichte's extravagant expectations and looked forward to an attainable goal, instead of becoming involved, like Fichte, in contradictions.[106] Bolzano maintained that he failed to comprehend Fichte's promised new way of looking at the world and experienced the same difficulty with the works of "Schelling, Hegel and other writers, philosophizing in a similar manner."[107] In his diary of 1827–44, he traced the cause of the aberrations in contemporary philosophy to Fichte's assertion that "philosophy must begin with the presupposition that only the One is, and outside of this One there is nothing."[108] He found most puzzling how Fichte could describe judgments "as an arbitrary activity and *reason* (*Vernunft*) as the freest power of men."[109] He saw the same problem in his *Lehrbuch der Religionswissenschaft*, where he attempted to analyze Fichte's supreme moral law, namely, that every being should bring its freedom under the concept of absolute autonomy (*der absoluten Selbstständigkeit*). He viewed Fichte's concept of freedom as just a form of tyranny, inasmuch as human freedom was merely an instrument for the realization of a moral law in the sensory world, which was to be ruled by reason. Hence, everything that depended on human freedom had to be strictly regulated by the prescripts of reason.[110]

Among Fichte's errors in logic, Bolzano singled out the assertion that the "I" was a subject that was its own object. Against this concept of "subject-object," Bolzano pointed out that an idea of self was not the same as the self itself, adding, "no more than an image in the mirror is not the man himself, and after all this is something a philosopher should know."[111] Noting Fichte's objection to the separation of concepts, judgments, and conclusions in logic as a violation of the organic unity of knowledge, Bolzano quipped that such an insipid observation betrayed that Fichte "had not studied logic with any diligence."[112] Bolzano also faulted Fichte for following Kant in the opinion that space was a perception (*Anschauung*) and thus lacked objective reality.[113] In a summary judgment on Fichte in 1843, Bolzano maintained that Fichte lacked in the highest degree the ability to express his thoughts clearly despite his great fame as a philosopher.[114]

In an early treatise on *Logische Vorbegriffe* from 1815–16, Bolzano noted that Schelling lacked a concept of objective truth (*Wahrheit*). For Schelling, truth or falsehood was a mere attribute of cognition, that is, an agreement between the perception and what was perceived, but that for him what was perceived had no independent reality.[115] In his diary of 1817–27, Bolzano noted a satirical review of the effect of Schellingian philosophy on German literature that registered its contradictions,[116] and he cited with aspersion the use of Schellingian language in literary criticism. The citation begins, "Life as such is the unconditional, eternally building and determining itself. As determining it is free, as determined it is necessary; consequently it is free and necessary at the same time."[117] In a similar context, Bolzano focused on Schelling's "great discovery" that God was freedom rather than reason. Freedom here stood in opposition to necessity, and the latter was, in turn, defined as that which could not "not exist." Bolzano wondered about the ontological meaning of the word "could" in this context.[118] The freedom of God or the absolute consisted in its ability to remain in the state of potentiality, or to realize itself, or to return to the original state; these processes gave rise to a supernatural world. Bolzano considered this intellectual exercise an awkward attempt to reintroduce the concept of the Trinity, and he dismissed the image of a supernatural world as a pointless idea.[119] In addition, Bolzano saw a contradiction in Schelling's positing the individual human as immanent in the absolute yet possessing his own substance.[120] Concerning the reality of the objective world, Bolzano disagreed with Schelling that a material object was not a substance but a combination of forces. Force could not be insubstantial; it had to be either a substance or the attribute of a substance.[121]

In the *Wissenschaftslehre,* Bolzano excoriated Schelling's assertion of complete identity of being and thought.[122] Schelling's definition of the absolute as neither a combination nor an annihilation of the real and the ideal but as an identity of both struck Bolzano as full of contradictions. According to Schelling, the absolute could be both real and not real, as well as ideal and not ideal.[123] Consequently, Bolzano objected to Schelling's trivializing the law of contradiction as applying only to ordinary circumstances while, in the realm of speculation, change had its beginning in the reconciliation of opposites.[124] Bolzano was likewise critical of Schelling's idea of "intellectual perception" (*intellectuelle Anschauung*), by which the soul entered into an immediate relationship with the absolute and became one with the absolute. According to Bolzano, conceptual verities (*Begriffswahrheiten*) became known through reason (*Vernunft*) without any need to resort to Schelling's epistemological construct.[125] Turning to the subject of aesthetics in 1843, Bolzano commented that Schelling had changed his concepts so often in substantial ways that their future mutations could not even be guessed at.[126] More generally, he concluded that what Schelling called philosophy was something arbitrary that led to the results that he favored at a given time.[127] Bolzano's diaries indicate that his harsh critique of Schelling's philosophy was not based on a superficial examination but on a rather substantial probing.[128]

While he viewed Fichte and Schelling as tricksters or incompetents, Bolzano still considered them worthy of serious attention. Thus, within the realm of German idealism, he ranked them above Schopenhauer, whom he viewed as mentally deranged. In his diary of 1817–27, Bolzano referred to Schopenhauer's *The World as Will and Representation* (1819) and commented that the author was "evidently insane."[129] Elsewhere in the same diary, he characterized the book as "deliriums that encompass a full system of philosophy."[130] In a letter to Příhonský of June 1837, he quipped that, if Schopenhauer's philosophy had any value, it was only in Schopenhauer's own imagination.[131]

Bolzano and Empirical Realists

While adamantly opposed to German idealists from Kant onward, whose epistemological and ontological concepts, he felt, could not be taken seriously, Bolzano found kindred spirits in the advocates of realistic and empirical approaches in philosophy, particularly in Karl L. Reinhold, Christoph Bardili, and Wilhelm T. Krug. Even if he did not agree with some of their propositions, he subjected them to detailed analysis. Already in 1814–15 he cited Reinhold, Bardili, and Krug for their work in logic, in defiance of Kant's assertion that logic exhausted its function with Aristotle and had no value for modern thought.[132] In fact, he had studied the writings of Reinhold as early as 1802.[133] Bolzano was aware of yet another prominent German opponent of the Fichte-Schelling-Hegel phase of philosophy: Friedrich Eduard Beneke (1798–1854), Hegel's competitor at the University of Berlin in the late 1820s.[134] In 1838, he hoped to enlist Beneke for a jury to assess his own philosophical and theological views, based mainly on the *Wissenschaftslehre*.[135]

Reinhold and the Heritage of the Enlightenment

Reinhold (1757–1823), like Bolzano, began his intellectual career as a priest in the Austrian Catholic Enlightenment. However, after an enthusiastic participation in the Josephist campaign for Reform Catholicism in Vienna, he defected to Protestant Saxony in 1783. Initially infatuated with Kant and later idealists, he broke with transcendental philosophy after an acrimonious conflict with Schelling and Hegel. He subsequently turned for inspiration to Christoph Bardili's logical realism, as well as to the Scottish common sense philosophy of Thomas Reid and Dugald Stewart, and he crowned his scholarly career with work in the analysis of language. Reasserting the heritage of the Enlightenment, he assumed the existence of a primal language with a natural system of universal meanings that had been obscured by a deposit of historically developed linguistic usages. Once excavated, this universal language would be generally recognized and accepted. In his philosophy of language, he was eventually seen as a precursor of Gottlob Frege (1848–1925) and Ludwig J. Wittgenstein (1889–1951). In the meantime, however, he had become an "unperson" to the philosophical canon of Central Europe, due to the strong bias of Neo-Kantians and Neo-Hegelians.[136]

Referring to Reinhold's work from this later period, Bolzano noted with satisfaction in the *Wissenschaftslehre* that Reinhold agreed with him that *Wahrheit an sich,* as a true sentence, provided the matter (*Stoff*) for a concrete judgment or *Erkenntnis*. Bolzano particularly appreciated Reinhold's fundamentally anti-idealist view that there was no question of identity between the mental image of an entity (*Vorstellung eines Wesens*) and its being (*Seyn*).[137] Bolzano, however, asserted against Reinhold that *Wahrheit an sich* not only could be independent of an existing entity but also could never serve as the matter of an existing entity.[138] Reinhold likewise impressed Bolzano by his studies of the philosophy of language, especially his work *Grundlegung einer Synonymik*.[139]

Bardili and Rational Realism

Christoph Bardili (1761–1808) also turned against the transcendental philosophical tradition from Kant to Hegel. Embracing the approach of rational realism that he outlined in his seminal work *Outline of the First Logic; Purged of the Errors of Logicians in General, and Kantian Ones in Particular* (1800), Bardili also opposed the identification of thought with being.[140] He helped inspire Reinhold's logical realism and joined him in the publication of a series entitled *Beiträge zur leichteren Uebersicht des Zustandes der Philosophie* (Contributions to an Easier Overview of the Conditions of Philosophy) (six issues, 1801–3). In the *Beiträge*, they published an unfavorable review of Schelling's system of transcendental idealism, and Schelling retaliated harshly in the "Einleitung zum Kritischen Journal"(Introduction to a Critical Journal) (1802). Bardili and Reinhold responded in "Correspondence about the Substance of Philosophy and the Nullity of Speculation" (1804).[141] Bolzano refers to Bardili's *Outline of the First Logic* in his *Wissenschaftslehre*.[142]

Krug, an Early Opponent of Idealism

As an early opponent of idealism, Wilhelm T. Krug (1770–1842) directed a treatise, *Briefe über die Wissenschaftslehre* (Letters about the Theory of Science) (1800), mainly against Fichte,[143] and his *Briefe über den neuesten Idealismus* (Letters about the Most Recent Idealism) (1801), mostly against Schelling.[144] According to Krug, "consistent Idealism" (*konsequente Idealismus*) resulted in "absolute Nihilism" (*absolute Nihilismus*).[145] Although often called a disciple of Kant, Krug himself resolutely denied that he ever was a "Kantian."[146] In his textbook *Handbuch der Philosophie und der philosophischen Literatur* (Manual of Philosophy and Philosophical Literature) (1828) Krug often polemicized against German idealists, again mainly against Fichte and Schelling, and referred favorably to philosophers of the opposite camp—the anti-Kantian realist Johann R. Herbart and the English empiricists and the Scottish common sense philosophers.[147]

In the *Wissenschaftslehre*, Bolzano quoted with satisfaction Krug's attack on Schelling's assertion of a transcendental identity between the subject and the object.[148] He agreed with Krug that the issue of the origin of thoughts was not the most important one, since the relationships among thoughts could be explored anyway. Bolzano added, however, that these relationships also had to include an assessment of their correctness.[149] Bolzano, in fact, found Krug's criterion of logical truth (*Wahrheit*) in the mere lack of contradiction between the mental image (*Vorstellung*) and the object of knowledge (*Erkenntnis*) inadequate.[150] However, he was pleased to establish that what Krug called "Denkobject" was exactly the same as Bolzano's own "Vorstellung an sich," as in Krug's statement "zwei Begriffe, die wirklich gleich wären, im Grunde nur ein Denkobject ausmachen würden" (Two concepts, which would be really equal, would basically constitute only one object of thought).[151]

Bolzano was also critical of Krug's definition of the three maxims of logical ordering (*Grundsaetze der logischen Anordnung*), in which he thought Krug followed Kant.[152] He did appreciate Krug's efforts to make more sense of Kant's twelve categories.[153] He had only a few emendations to add to Krug's teaching on the being of unmediated conclusions (*das Daseyn unmittelbarer Schlüsse*), and he maintained that Krug, on the whole, had advanced the matter conscientiously and solidly beyond his predecessors.[154] Krug, for his part, reacted in his *Antidoton* (1836) to Bolzano's *Lehrbuch der Religionswissenschaft* (1834), but Bolzano considered the critique insubstantial.[155] His friend Johann A. Zimmermann prepared a rebuttal.[156]

Locke and the Scottish Philosophers

In opposing Kant, Bolzano paid attention to the empiricism of John Locke[157] and to a lesser extent the Scottish philosophy of common sense in the works of Dugald Stewart, Thomas Reid, and James Beattie.[158] In a section in his *Wissenschaftslehre* in which he seeks to define his concept of "proposition in itself" (*der Satz an sich*), Bolzano cites (in English) Locke's basic definition of knowledge.[159] He also explores Locke's criterion of truth (*Wahrheit*).[160] Elsewhere, he disagrees with Locke's distinction between "mental and verbal" truths,[161] and also, unlike Locke, he maintains that there could be "clear ideas" of not just perceptible objects but also of those that were not perceptible, such as moral and physical qualities (courage, weight, and the like).[162] On the whole, he praised Locke for grasping correctly the distinction between concept sentences (*Begriffssätzen*) and perception sentences (*Anschauungssätzen*), the former expressing full certainty, the latter only probability.[163] Locke, according to Bolzano, defined the meaning of analytical sentences more appropriately in his "trifling propositions" than Kant did in his "*Analytische Sätze.*"[164] He agreed with Locke in rejecting the concepts of "inborn ideas" but felt that Locke did not carefully specify "how experience brought forth certain ideas."[165] In his discussion of empiricism, Bolzano referred to Beattie and Reid, as well as to Locke. In this connection, he likewise wrote an analysis of the second volume of Dugald Stewart's *Elements of the Philosophy of the Human Mind* in his philosophical diary in 1820.[166] He agreed with the empiricists that judgments had to be preceded by action of certain external objects on us that result in perceptions. For him, however, the empiricists did not adequately account for the criteria of judgments by their appeal to "instincts."[167]

The French Empiricist Destutt

Bolzano adopted a more ambivalent stance in the *Wissenschaftslehre* toward the French empiricist who was influenced by Locke, Antoine L. Destutt de Tracy (1754–1836). He found Destutt wanting, like Krug, in his lack of stress on assessing the correctness of ideas and of course was particularly taken aback by Destutt's assertion that the rules of logic were useless.[168] He approved of Destutt's view that the task of judgment was not merely to draw equations between objects,[169] but he questioned his use of the term *sensation* for perception. Bolzano equated *sensation* with the German emotive *Empfindung*, and he felt that perceptions were more appropriately designated by terms close to the intellect, as either ideas (*Vorstellungen*) or thoughts (*Denken*).[170]

Bolzano has been called the greatest logician between Leibniz and Frege, thanks mainly to the *Wissenschaftslehre*.[171] It has been suggested that he was indebted to Leibniz for his starting point, but he vehemently denied any suggestion of dependence on Leibniz.[172] He objected specifically to the reference by Ernst E. Reinhold (the son of his favorite Karl L. Reinhold) to his *Wissenschaftslehre* as "an eclecticism derived from the Leibniz-Wolff school."[173] In fact, he treated the suggestion as a slur on his independence catering to the wishes of the Austrian imperial authorities that favored Leibniz's philosophy.[174] More seriously, in his opinion, Leibniz was in part the fountainhead of the epistemological morass, which subsequently afflicted German idealism.[175] He evidently did not follow Fesl's suggestion in a letter of December 12, 1842, to discuss the relationship between his philosophy and Leibniz's before the Royal Bohemian Society of Sciences in Prague.[176]

Seibt and Bolzano versus Herder and Kant

Thanks to the charisma and influence of Seibt and Bolzano, the philosophical tenor of the Catholic Enlightenment, combined with the legacy of the Bohemian Reformation, would receive an indefinite lease on life. What Seibt had implanted in the intellectual soil of Bohemia in the late eighteenth century, Bolzano nurtured in the early nineteenth. His disciples and like-minded philosophers, in turn, would adopt and perpetuate the tradition of realism, empiricism, individualism, and utilitarianism in the Habsburg monarchy, especially in Bohemia and Austria. Hence it was Seibt, relying on English and French Enlightenment—not Herder, representing the German Lutheran strand of quasi-mystical nationalism—who was entitled to the symbolic position of chief inspirer or intellectual pacesetter of the Bohemian national revival.[177] Similarly, it was Bolzano, who relied on the realism and individualism of the Austro-Bohemian Catholic Enlightenment, and not Kant (or Schelling, or Fichte), who shaped the philosophical outlook of the following generations of Bohemian intellectuals.

9

Hegel's Collision with the Catholic Enlightenment in Bohemia

The Bohemian opposition to the teaching of Hegel in the 1830s and 1840s had the same intellectual basis as the rejection of romanticism and Hegel's precursors in the German idealist tradition from Kant through Fichte to Schelling (see chapters 7 and 8). The negative attitude toward German idealism in Bohemia culminated with the rejection of Hegel's philosophy, which in the 1830s and 1840s came to dominate much of the intellectual scene not only in Prussia but also in Slovakia, Poland, Hungary, and Russia. Hegelianism contradicted the realistic and cosmopolitan viewpoint embedded in the Catholic Enlightenment in Bohemia. As an adherent of ontically based cultural pluralism, Hegel thought that the world spirit, as it advanced through history, would be realized through embodiment in a particular folk spirit at a particular time. The people to which such a folk spirit belonged would be, for one epoch, the dominant nation in world history. Hegel considered his present era that of the German spirit and nation, stating, "The German spirit is the spirit of the new world. Its aim is the realization of Absolute Truth."[1] Despite his metaphysical monism (the singularity of the absolute as the sum total of reality), Hegel did not favor a cosmopolitan solution that would lead to an eventual absorption of the nation-state into a global polity. This was because—as Anthony Kenny has pointed out—"it would take away the opportunity for war, which he thought had a positive value of its own as a reminder of the transitory nature of finite existence."[2]

The Issue of Hegel's Influence

The realistic and empirical orientation of philosophical thinking in Bohemia, however, was more consonant with Lockian individualistic liberalism than with Hegel's metaphysics, which tended to encase the individual in a metaphysical monism and social collectivism.[3] While Bohemian anti-Hegelianism was obviously a legitimate position, it was variously deprecated and obscured in historical literature. It was maligned by a coalition of devotees to German idealism and opponents of the Enlightenment in both its secularist and its Catholic variants. In addition, its existence was confused by references to Slovak intellectual preferences.

The Question of Prestige

In many cultural quarters, German idealism was viewed as the highest achievement of philosophical speculation. This was particularly true in Prussia, even during Hegel's lifetime, as illustrated by the case of the philosopher Friedrich E. Beneke (1798–1854). Beneke was an empiricist in the tradition of Locke, who incurred the displeasure of the absolute idealists, entrenched in the philosophical and governmental establishment in Berlin. He was forbidden to lecture, and the reason given by the minister of culture (1817–38), Karl von Altenstein, a Hegelian, was that Beneke's book "was not so much wrong on particular points as that it was *unphilosophisch* in its totality because it did not attempt to derive everything from the Absolute."[4] In fact, it was said that under Altenstein, Hegelianism became, in practice, the official philosophy of the Prussian state.[5] Still, in 1842 Beneke complained to his English correspondents that in his home country he could not find sympathetic collaborators. Idealist philosophy held complete sway, and empiricism was deemed to be unworthy of German thought.[6] Another German philosopher whose academic career in Prussia was ruined by his opposition to Hegelianism was Paul de Lagarde (1827–1891).[7] Later, the Neo-Kantian Friedrich A. Lange, writing in the 1870s, although not particularly fond of post-Kantian idealism, considered Germany the citadel of philosophy, while the English had produced no great philosopher since Hume, and the French none between Diderot and Comte.[8] This attitude persisted, and Sidney Hook recalled in 1930 that philosophers in Germany regarded idealism "not as one of a number of possible logical alternatives but rather as a national possession, the blazing jewels in Germany's cultural crown."[9]

Since Kant, philosophy had been considered essentially a domain for German idealism, with subsequent development representing variations on the themes of Kant, Fichte, Schelling, and Hegel. British empiricism, from Locke to John Stuart Mill, and the American pragmatism of William James were not considered worthy of serious attention.[10] Not just foreigners but also German observers noted this phenomenon: "There was a strong tendency to overrate 'German idealism' and to minimize British, French, and American philosophical trends," Philipp Frank observed.[11] Even long after World War II, the West Germans felt a strong preference for the "old Platonic dream of absolute knowledge from pure reason" and contempt for "the merely empirical" (*blos Empirischen*), as represented by the Vienna Circle.[12] The view of philosophy as knowledge superior to science because it rose above merely empirical understanding was characteristic of Hegel, as well as post-Kantian idealism in general.[13]

Therefore, the Bohemian awakeners' tendency to reject German idealism in general and Hegelianism in particular was considered intellectually gauche. Later critics viewed this rejection as evidence of a deplorably practical bent of the Czech mind or a lack of philosophical sophistication—a kind of intellectual primitivism.[14] This view was particularly true of the modernist aesthetes of the late nineteenth and early twentieth centuries and of the post–World War II Marxist-Leninist adherents for whom the official genealogy assigned to Hegel the role of the John the Baptist of Marxism.[15] The founders of Marxism, of course, themselves claimed the heritage of German philosophy, above all Hegel. Engels declared in 1891: "We German socialists are proud that we derive not only from Saint-Simon, Fourier and Owen, but also from Kant, Fichte and Hegel."[16] Lenin likewise considered Hegel's dialectic his most valuable contribution to Marxist idelogy.[17] Zdeněk Nejedlý, the intellectual arbiter of the postwar Communist regime, condemned, from a Marxist point of view, the Czech philosophers of the first half of the nineteenth century for ignoring the great German thinker and contrasted their failings with his own mistaken belief in František Palacký's Hegelianism.[18] As another example of the Marxist-Leninist critique of the logical realism in the Czech philosophical tradition, in 1958 Milan Machovec deplored Bolzano's writings as purely formalistic and thus without substantial content because of their lack of speculative metaphysics.[19]

Others, however, were also critical of the early anti-Hegelianism in Bohemia. Thus, the prewar historian of philosophy Josef Král, for example, called the attitudes of the anti-Hegelians, especially Gabler, as unprofessional or unscholarly and shallow.[20] Another condescending explanation was that the lack of sophisticated philosophical terminology in the Czech language hampered the comprehension of Hegel's ideas by Bohemian readers.[21] By the middle of the twentieth century, independently of Marxism-Leninism (and rather paradoxically), the famous dissident Jan Patočka belonged among Hegel's admirers.[22]

The more radical criticism equated the Bohemian awakeners' anti-Hegelianism with hostility to all of philosophy and conjured up the image of a "tragic antiphilosophical tradition." This view, of course, accepted the earlier-mentioned assumption that German idealism represented the acme of philosophical thought and, therefore, that the questioning of its value equaled disrespect for philosophy as such.[23] Applied consistently, this stance would lead to excluding from philosophical acceptability all the alternative trends, in particular the Catholic Enlightenment (including Bernard Bolzano), British empiricism, and French positivism. While Tomáš Masaryk considered Karel Havlíček's reliance on "common sense" philosophically respectable,[24] within the Bohemian context, such a stance involved much scoffing at the typical "Czech positivism."[25] Karel Mácha viewed the Bohemian anti-idealism of the first half of the nineteenth century as a unique case of philosophical gaucherie in Europe.[26] Jitka Lněničková, commenting on the views of Havlíček and Gabler, claimed that Czech philosophy in the first half of the nineteenth century had failed to reach a level of professional respectability.[27]

Most tellingly, attempts to salvage a degree of reputability for the nineteenth-century Czech thought led to the spurious attribution of Hegel's influence to Karel Hynek Mácha and to Palacký and, more generally, to the ideology of the Czech national awakening, particularly through Kant's alleged influence on Bolzano.[28]

The Question of Progressivism

Bohemian philosophers and political thinkers were also criticized by Marxists and other champions of historical determinism for resisting the trend toward romanticism and absolute idealism, inasmuch as these revolts against the individualism and empiricism of the Enlightenment were viewed as harbingers of "modernity and progress." In this context, the Bohemian opponents of Hegelianism were seen as old-fashioned, if not outright reactionary, because of their adherence to the individualist-realistic orientation of Austrian Catholic Josephism, stemming from the late eighteenth century. Not only did their stand seem pedestrian and unexciting,[29] but also the opposition to German idealism was viewed as a sign of intellectual retardation.[30] The Bohemian aversion to Hegel was attributed to two principal factors. The first was the pressure of the Austrian imperial government, which was allergic to any intellectual initiatives from the Lutheran Protestant milieu. The second was the extension of the Austro-Bohemian Catholic Enlightenment, which, instead of the progressive teaching of Hegel, promoted what was considered the second-rate and static philosophy of Johann Herbart in the Habsburg monarchy.[31]

Zdeněk Nejedlý concluded that, as a result of the Czech aversion to metaphysical speculation (including dialectical materialism), the country lacked any competent Marxist philosophers as it entered the Socialist era in the late 1940s.[32] Against the Czechs' Western-style individualism, Nejedlý highlighted the romanticism of the Slovaks (Jan Kollár), the Poles (Adam Mickiewicz), and the Russians (Leo Tolstoy) as paving the way for collectivist socialism and eventually Marxism.[33] The rejection of German idealism was attributed to the general intellectual backwardness of the Habsburg monarchy that corresponded to its lack of economic development.[34] The philosophy of Johann Herbart, which had prevailed over that of Hegel in the Bohemian academy by the mid-nineteenth century, was considered static because it tended to eliminate the metahistorical role of contradictions, while Hegel's dialectical method served as a motor of change.[35] More recently, Josef Haubelt, the ranking historian of the Bohemian Enlightenment, has also presented Hegel's historical outlook as progressive.[36]

An assessment of positive or even progressive features of the Catholic Enlightenment, including the place of Bolzano's philosophy, was hampered by the complex and often contradictory attitudes toward the influence of the Roman Church. There was a reluctance to acknowledge the positive or "progressive" role of the Catholic Enlightenment, despite its having overthrown the intellectual constraints of the Counter-Reformation and despite the liberalizing influence of Reform Catholicism from its inception under Joseph II to its intellectual extension under Bolzano.[37] If German idealism, culminating in Hegel's teaching, was viewed as a philosophical advance over any other previous system of thought, then Bolzano's outlook could be called ipso facto outdated and old-fashioned.[38] Bolzano could be charged with following obsolete concepts of eighteenth-century static rationalism and, therefore, with lagging behind the development of European thought that had progressed from Kant through Fichte and Schelling to Hegel.[39]

If Bolzano's liberal Catholicism was not considered progressive enough, the view of Franz Exner, who perpetuated the Catholic Enlightenment's anti-Hegelian line at the University of Prague in the 1830s and 1840s, was even more negative. He was deemed an instrument of the Austrian government in promoting Herbart's anti-Kantian realism as a barrier not only to the "progressive" trend of German idealism and its offspring but also to liberal Catholicism.[40] In that sense, it was symptomatic to juxtapose Exner not only to Hegel and his school but also to Bolzano. Actually, Exner could not be viewed as a stooge of the Habsburg reactionaries; he had, in fact, been under suspicion by the imperial authorities for deviation from Christian orthodoxy, causing him to be passed over for a university professorship in Vienna in 1829.[41] During his lifetime, Bolzano was also regarded as a reactionary opponent by the German nationalists on the specious ground that his adherence to all-human cosmopolitan values provided support to the decrepit multinational Habsburg monarchy.[42] Along this line of reasoning, the German nationalists considered Bolzano's Enlightenment empiricism banal and insipid (*seicht*).[43]

The Puzzle of the Catholic Enlightenment

A powerful coalition opposed a recognition of the value or even the very existence of the Catholic Enlightenment and its progeny, Reform Catholicism.[44] The partisans of the official Roman Church suspected the role of Reform Catholicism because its character was in stark contradiction to the subsequent retridentization of the Roman Church that was carried out initially in response to the French Revolution and that accelerated after 1848. Therefore, their attitude toward Josephist Reformists and to the Bolzano school was ambivalent at best and condemnatory at worst. Bohdan Chudoba, for instance, categorically dismissed both the Enlightenment and liberal Catholicism. He characterized the Josephist Enlightenment—instead of the Bohemian Counter-Reformation—as the real period of intellectual "darkness" (*temno*).[45] As another example, Bedřich Slavík, in his *Od Dobnera k Dobrovskému* (1975), questioned the intellectual honesty of the Reform Catholics, imputing to them a hypocritical attitude of freethinkers operating under the cover of religiosity.[46] The principles of free discussion and liberal polity were seen as threats to tridentine ecclesiology and hence (perhaps quite illogically) to traditional Christian orthodoxy.[47] According to another tridentine critic, Bohemian Catholic priests were in danger of losing the sense of their sacerdotal vocation because the Enlightenment pressed them to preoccupation with economic development and with the cultural tasks of the national awakening.[48]

At the other side of the ledger, Protestant and secularist observers and commentators tended to view the tenor of Reform Catholicism as no more palatable than the stance of the official church. The very idea of the Catholic Enlightenment was viewed as a contradiction in terms.[49] For instance, Arnošt Kraus reprimanded Kašpar Royko for his inconsistency, if not insincerity, since he—a Catholic theologian—wrote as if the Council of Trent had never happened, disregarding the council's injunctions against the freedom of expression on issues of theology and ecclesiology.[50] Kraus also equated Josef Dobrovský's and Augustin Zitte's religious tolerance with religious indifference.[51] Josef Král characterized Bolzano's outlook as "an inconsistent mixture of rationalist metaphysics with Catholic dogma."[52] Actually, Bolzano explicitly denied that there was a contradiction between the Enlightenment (*Aufklärung*) and genuine religious beliefs,[53] and he looked askance at the Catholic theologians who were reluctant to avow the supernatural for fear of being ridiculed by the Hegelians.[54] Jiří Rak points out that the skepticism about an accommodation of the Roman faith with Enlightenment thinking led to widespread neglect of the pioneering work on the Reform Catholicism of the Josephist era by Eduard Winter in Czech historiography.[55]

The Austro-Bohemian Catholic Enlightenment was also criticized for retarding intellectual progress because it sought to replace, in the curricula of universities and Catholic seminaries, the baroque scholasticism of Francisco Suárez with the teaching of Thomas Aquinas. The critics considered Suárez's essentialist ontology more progressive than Aquinas's existentialist one. The essentialist approach of baroque scholasticism was seen as paving the way—through the mediation of Christian Wolff's teaching—for the metaphysical concepts of Kant and his successors (see chapter 7).[56] The deprecatory view of Reform Catholicism was in a way a reprise of the jaundiced attitude toward the Utraquist *via media* in modern Czech historiography held by both the Roman and the Reformation sides.[57]

The Slovak Factor

At times, a degree of confusion about Bohemian attitudes toward Hegel was created by the misleading impression that Slovak romanticism and Hegelianism constituted a part of the Czech cultural milieu. The misconception gained ground, perhaps, because Slovak Lutherans, initially through the mid-1840s, showed a special attachment to the Czech language as a literary medium.

The views of Slovak intellectual pacesetters, in fact, contrasted with Czech anti-Hegelianism. The difference can be traced to their roots in Lutheranism, which produced a high degree of susceptibility to the appeals of not only Herderian German-style romanticism but also Hegelian absolute idealism. Both romanticism and idealism had grown out of the Lutheran religious tradition as well. The Slovak Lutherans were profoundly affected by their studies at German Lutheran universities, in particular Jena but also Leipzig and Göttingen.[58] In Jena alone, the number of students from Hungary (the Slovaks' wider homeland) increased tenfold between 1780 and 1810, and graduates of German universities subsequently diffused their knowledge to younger students through the network of secondary schools.[59] (See also chapter 6 in this volume.)

Early Encounters with Hegel

The realistic and empirical orientation of the Austro-Bohemian Catholic Enlightenment—strengthened by the revival of Utraquist thought, which militated against the adoption of German philosophical idealism—continued in Bohemia from the end of the eighteenth into the nineteenth century and eventually turned against Hegel's philosophy. While Dobrovský had disapproved of Fichte and Schelling,[60] Jungmann had already turned his attention to Hegel, especially dismayed by the Hegelian infatuation of the young František M. Klácel.[61] He urged Antonín Marek to expand his proposed philosophical textbook by an inclusion of realistic metaphysics in order to forestall a possible spread of Hegelianism.[62] Jungmann considered England to be the country most worthy of intellectual emulation and shared Bolzano's unflattering view of idealist philosophy. Jungmann regarded that philosophy and its antecedents as phenomena bordering on mental confusion, if not insanity.[63] His judgment could not be attributed to a lack of philosophical sophistication as was often the case in the criticisms leveled at anti-Hegelians: in his preface to Marek's *Základy filosofie: Logika. Metafysika* (1844), Jungmann indicated his solid interest in philosophy and familiarity with Hegel's opponents, Wilhelm T. Krug, Johann G. Kiesewetter, and, above all, Josef N. Jäger, on whose views Marek had particularly relied in his textbook.[64]

In Marek's correspondence with Jungmann in 1815, both had agreed not to feature the idealists in the planned Czech textbook of philosophy.[65] In the actual textbook, *Základy filosofie: Logika. Metafysika* (1844), Marek was critical of Hegel's obscure ways of expressing his ideas and was opposed to his pantheism that denied personal immortality, and substituted perpetuity of the human species.[66] As noted earlier, Marek drew heavily on the *System der theoretischen Philosophie* by Wilhelm T. Krug, a staunch opponent of Hegel's idealism.[67] As early as 1802, Krug had conducted an exchange of critical articles with Hegel on the subject of "collective human reason" (*gemeine Menschenverstand*)[68] and directed that same year a pamphlet *Der Widerstreit der Vernunft mit sich selbst* (The Conflict of Reason with Itself) against both Hegel and Schelling.[69] Krug also devoted his 1809 inaugural lecture at the University of Leipzig, *De poëtica philosophandi ratione*, to a strident rejection of Hegel's phenomenology.[70] In addition, Marek cited Hegel's opponents, Jakob F. Fries and Karl L. Reinhold, in his textbook. Hegel had denounced Fries in his *Philosophy of Right* as a shallow thinker and a sentimentalist for advocating a constitutional and representative government and praising the political wisdom of the common man.[71] He had charged Reinhold with an intention to conduct an intellectual revolution through reduction of philosophy to logic in the footsteps of Christoph G. Bardili's *Grundriss der ersten Logik* (1800).[72]

Another of Jungmann's associates in philosophy, Vincenc Zahradník, in his book on logic (1836), scathingly denounced the hypostatizing of abstract terms by Hegel and related philosophers.[73] Opposed to subjectivism in epistemology, he valued Christian Garve (1742–98), a follower of English empiricism, above Kant.[74] As the basis of his own weltanschauung, Zahradník adopted a philosophical realism that was governed by the application of "common sense" (*zdravý rozum*).[75] He considered Hegel's philosophy "a sheer insanity" and explained: "Fichte, Hegel and similar philosophers are vain and worthless as philosophers, if for no other reason than that they indulge in a mystical language, where the most specific words and the most definite language should be used."[76] He found Hegel's idea that God reaches consciousness through natural and historical processes to be absurd.[77] Among philosophers, he endorsed the English rationalist William Wollaston (1659–1724) and the German skeptic Johann Andreas Wendel, who opposed Fichte and Schelling.[78] In the area of moral and political philosophy, he relied heavily, like Bolzano, on the utilitarian approach.[79]

Yet another member of Jungmann's entourage, Karel A. Vinařický, reacting to Klácel's articles in *Časopis českého musea* in 1843, felt that it was more effective to use satire than serious arguments in discrediting Hegelianism. In any case, according to Vinařický, Hegel's philosophical legacy had been disintegrating even in Germany into several competing schools, and the youthful advocates of Hegelianism in Bohemia were just pathetic epigones. Anyway, it was doubtful that this bizarre and tiresome material could have had much influence. What was true of Hegel was also true of Fichte.[80] Vinařický responded to his correspondent Jan Körner, who had denounced Klácel's articles and described Hegelianism, as "the most despicable error of rationalism, which makes God out of frail and malodorous man and lets him again disintegrate into dust, and which denies that [God] in whom we live and who is the wisest originator of all things."[81] Another of Vinařický's correspondents, Václav Štulc, who participated in the debate about Klácel's articles in 1843, however, considered the impact of Hegelianism a more serious matter.[82]

Bolzano and Hegel

Above all, however, Bolzano was the paradigm-setting figure of the prevailing Bohemian anti-Hegelianism. He embodied the role of Catholic liberalism and Enlightenment in fostering the Bohemian opposition to German idealism in general and to Hegelianism in particular. His tremendous influence on Czech students and the educated public was noted earlier (in chapter 8). His magisterial teaching provided a direct bridge between Josephist realism and positivist individualism in Bohemia, thus avoiding submergence in the metaphysical stream of Herder's and Hegel's historicist and collectivist ideologies.[83] Bolzano's sternly critical attitude toward Hegel was a direct extension of his dim view of Kant's subjectivistic epistemology, against which he waged a life-long struggle (see chapter 8). He was even less impressed by the speculative constructs of those whom he regarded as Kant's followers, namely, Fichte, Schelling, and Hegel,[84] as he wrote in a letter of November 1, 1841, to Michael J. Fesl, his former pupil and younger colleague: "A number of otherwise good heads thanks to the Schelling-Hegelian fashion will be entirely lost to thinking."[85]

Contrast in Politics

At the start, it is important to point out that Bolzano's utilitarian view of the character and function of the state was almost diametrically opposed to Hegel's view of the state as the most perfect phenomenon in the world—"the Divine Idea as it exists on earth."[86] Bolzano counseled constant watchfulness against the state's attempts to impose its own purposes and thus replace the particular agendas of the individual citizens. From his utilitarian point of view, individuals were of prime political and social importance and needed to be protected against the encroachments of the state even to the point of civil disobedience.[87] For Bolzano, civil society was meant to provide space for the development of individual initiatives; for Hegel, civil society was an instrument for surreptitiously manipulating (through the "cunning of reason") individual and social actions toward the interest of the state. On the philosophical level, Bolzano's ontic individualism and liberalism clearly contrasted with Hegel's phantom individualism, the purpose of which was to dissolve the individual in perfect collectivism, reflecting Hegel's ontic monism. As Isaiah Berlin summed up, Hegel celebrated "the authority and the power and the greatness of the State as against the whims or individual inclinations of this or that citizen or subject."[88]

Comments in Notebooks

Turning to Bolzano's critical comments on Hegelianism, in his philosophical diaries for 1811–17 and for 1817–27 there are numerous references to what he considered the flaws of Hegel's logic.[89] Concerning the third volume of Hegel's *Wissenschaft der Logik* (1812–16), Bolzano noted that for Hegel, being and knowing are absolutely identical (*Seyn und*

Wissen ist absolut identisch). On another topic, Bolzano pointed out that Hegel's concept of theology involved its drastic secularization and reduction to a concept of teleology. He agreed with the reviewer of Hegel's volume about his confusing use of the predicate "is" (*ist*), which did not always denote equality and thus caused inconsistency and contradiction.[90] In examining Hegel's *Encyklopädie der philosophischen Wissenschaften im Grundrisse*, he paused over Hegel's assertion that becoming was a unity of being and nothing. Presumably not without a touch of irony, he noted an extremely eulogistic reference to the same work by Thaddäus Rixner that, after Hegel, to write philosophy was like attempting to compose another Iliad after Homer.[91]

In his diary for 1827–44, the focus of Bolzano's critique of idealist philosophy shifted to Hegel from Kant. He launched into a lengthy analysis of Carl Fortlage's *Die Lücken des Hegelschen Systems der Philosophie* (1832). Bolzano noted that Fortlage, who was formerly Hegel's disciple, had ended up disillusioned with the teaching of his mentor.[92] Thus, Fortlage deplored Hegel's exaggerated promises of teaching a higher truth while, in the end, he offered a disappointingly banal assertion that his definitions taught the true being of things. Bolzano also noted Fortlage's censure of Hegel's assertion that any later philosophy represented a development and advancement of all earlier philosophy with the implicit assumption that Hegel's own system represented a culmination of known philosophy.[93]

In a letter to Fesl of July 17, 1834, referring to his readings in recent philosophy, Bolzano confided that he experienced great difficulty in understanding Hegel: "I often read many pages without being able in the least to guess, what he wishes with all this to say, what he here wants to praise or reprimand and how it all relates to the title." When he could understand partly or completely what Hegel was saying, then he found it wrong—for example, Hegel's statements about physiognomy and phrenology, about revelation and Christianity, the Trinity, the Incarnation, and the like, in the *Phänomenologie des Geistes*.[94] In another letter to Fesl of September 8, 1837, he wrote in a similar vein: "What will you say when I admit that for the last six weeks I have done almost nothing else than read Hegelian and other nonsense?"[95]

On the basis of Hegel's *Phänomenologie des Geistes* (1832), Bolzano made scathing observations about Hegel's system of logic in his philosophical diary for 1827–44. He called attention to Hegel's explicit statement that no sentence was fully true except in the context of all other sentences. He considered the expression "fully true" a pitiful confusion of concepts (*elende Verwechslung der Begriffe*); moreover, the proposition meant that an entire system could be true only within itself but that outside of itself, it was false. Bolzano added: "With such a thought we are to console ourselves."[96] Similarly, Bolzano questioned Hegel's assertion that a substance remained forever unknown; all that could be known were accidents or properties. Knowing the properties of a thing and claiming not to know its substance was, according to Bolzano, a *contradictio in adjecto*. The being of an object consisted in the aggregate of its properties; nothing more could be expected.[97] On another point of Hegel's logic, Bolzano noted that the validity of Hegel's fundamental proposition that thinking and being were identical (*dass Denken und Seyn an sich identisch wären*) had never been proved by Hegel or his followers. Referring to an article, published in 1839 by the professor of philosophy at the University of Kiel, Heinrich M. Chalybäus (1796–1862), he expressed satisfaction that this was as open an admission of the weakness of Hegel's logic as one could wish for from a Hegelian.[98]

Critique in The Theory of Knowledge

In the *Wissenschaftslehre*, Bolzano continued his critique of Hegel's concept of logic.[99] He confessed that he could never make sense of Hegel's assertion that a thought of an object and the object itself were the same thing. This was so, even if the object was another thought, because: "Because here after all there is still a thought which is not the same as my [original] thought, but another thought."[100] Likewise, he questioned Hegel's definition of judgment (*Urtheil*), writing, "I do not flatter myself to fully understand what Hegel presents in all the individual words of his highly peculiar declaration." It appeared clear to him that Hegel did not consider judgment a proposition in itself but the transaction of the spirit (*Handlung des Geistes*). While for Bolzano a judgment was indivisible, for Hegel it was a kind of concept that could be divided into parts.[101] He questioned even more emphatically Hegel's refutation of epistemological skepticism: "I myself must admit that I do not understand it at all. How could doubt through doubting alone disappear!"[102] Likewise, Bolzano disagreed with Hegel's dialectical logic of the reconciliation of opposites, whereby Hegel maintained that a contradiction involved an even deeper relationship than identity. He claimed that Hegel, in offering illustrations of this point, had fabricated or invented (*erdichtet*) examples of contradictions where none actually existed.[103] Along the same lines, Hegel's postulation of a dialectical relationship among concept (*Begriff*), judgment (*Urtheil*), and conclusion (*Schluss*)—as representing a positing, a negation, and a cancellation (*Aufhebung*) of the negation—appeared to him a frivolous game (*Spielerey*).[104]

Bolzano noted that Hegel, contrary to all the previous logicians, maintained that a concept (*Begriff*) could not be complex (composed of several parts) and wondered on what grounds Hegel would consider such a view "barbaric" (*barbarisch*).[105] He returned to the subject in his *Über den Begriff des Schönen* (The Concept of Beauty) (1843), wondering why Hegel would deny a truth (calling it *Barbarei*), which was so obvious and could be illustrated by copious examples.[106] In the *Wissenschaftslehre,* Bolzano also contested Hegel's assertion that "nothing" was a real entity ("Das Nichts ist seiner Natur nach dasselbe als das Seyn"). "Nothing" could be imagined only as a concept (*Begriff*); it could not be imagined as an object (*Gegenstand*).[107] Hegel in his *Wissenschaft der Logik*, according to Bolzano, merely reworked the table of Kant's arbitrary and useless "categories."[108] He further contested Hegel's concept of "truth" (*Wahrheit*), which the latter confused with "being" (*Seyende*). Truth was not a being that "was" or "existed," but the attribute (*Beschaffenheit*) of a sentence *(Satz).*[109] In general, Hegel reified words, such as "representation," "concept," and "idea" (*Vorstellung, Begriff und Idee*), into monstrosities that moved around like living beings, and, before one knew what had happened, they mutated into their opposites.[110]

According to Bolzano, what Hegel discussed about "concept in general" (*Begriff im Allgemeinen*) in thirty-two pages of his *Logik* was incomprehensible.[111] He was puzzled by Hegel's opposition to elucidating "obscure concepts" (*dunkeln Begriffe*).[112] He sought to attribute Hegel's popularity, in part, to the perverse taste of the German public, which, in terms of philosophy, was fascinated by half-understandable statements, respected those who expressed themselves in riddles, and regarded obscurities cloaked in fashionable words as the most profound truths. Clarity and comprehensibility, in contrast, were held in contempt. Bolzano, therefore, appealed to Germans to forsake the aberration that supported an erudition unpalatable and laughable in the eyes of their neighbors.[113] In the *Wissenschaftlehre*, he once more concluded that Hegel "knew nothing about the uses of logic."[114]

The notes that Bolzano kept in the 1830s when he worked on the

Wissenschaftlehre contain additional critiques of Hegel.[115] He questioned Hegel's assertion in *Philosophie des Rechts* that monarchy was "the most perfect government, the creation [*Verfassung*] of the developed reason, which had to be affirmed through heredity."[116] The term *concept* meant something different for Hegel from what it meant to all other logicians. It included a real content so that a real being corresponded to our thought; in other words, the real was identical to the ideal.[117] This position led Hegel to the absurd assertion that "nothing" was a real object, instead of an objectless concept.[118] Once more, he doubted the validity of Hegel's dialectic, this time on two grounds. First, if the initial positive was to overcome its contradiction and return to the original "immediacy" (*Unmittelbarkeit*)—through the negation of a negation—there would be no progress. Second, Hegel's examples of the dialectical movement involved no real contradictions.[119] As a reversal of Socrates' estimate of Herakleitos, Bolzano suggested that what one could assume about Hegel was that if what one *could* understand was wrong, then what one could *not* understand was wrong also.[120]

Essays on Aesthetics, Epistemology, and History

Indeed, in *Über den Begriff des Schönen*, Bolzano once more wondered how a man like Hegel who had spent twenty-five years unable to grasp a simple mathematical proof could have reached such a high reputation in the field of philosophy.[121] Likewise, he held that a number of Hegel's statements in the *Vorlesungen über die Ästhetik* were amazingly banal and commonplace.[122] In this area, as in his entire philosophy, Hegel borrowed his main theses from Schelling but altered them fundamentally, so that Schelling complained that Hegel had corrupted them. Yet, Hegel's devoted disciples continued to regard him as one who had "discovered the fountain of all wisdom" (*Stein der Weisen gefunden*).[123] The very opening of his discussion of aesthetics contained the error that served as the leitmotiv of his philosophy, namely, a confusion of the concept of a thing (*Begriff einer Sache*) with that thing itself (*mit dieser Sache selbst*).[124] In general, Bolzano often linked Schelling with Hegel in his strictures.[125]

In *Über den Begriff des Schönen*, Bolzano further elaborated on this theme. He took as his basis Hegel's pronouncement that "idea in general is nothing else than a *concept*, the *reality* of the concept, and the *unity* of the two" [emphasis in original]. He pointed out that the reality of a concept referred simply to the concept and could not create an object of the concept. Hence to speak about the unity between the concept and its reality was a mere tautology.[126] Furthermore, Hegel's assertion that "the concept as an ideal unity and universality negates itself, and—what this [that is, unity] includes in itself—is released as a real independent objectivity" Bolzano considered as something that could be neither rationally understood nor intuitively imagined, but merely uttered as words.[127] In sum, Bolzano considered Hegel's treatise on aesthetics a compound of three elements: (1) many idiosyncrasies that were evidently false; (2) borrowings from others that he did not amend; and (3) some correct observations that were cast in an obscure language and did not offer new knowledge.[128]

Bolzano also dealt with the view that Hegel's philosophical system was ultimately grounded in mysticism. He approached the topic through his note-taking on Joseph Willm's (1793–1853) *Essai sur la philosophie de Hegel* (1835–37). Hegel's tendency to see the infinite in everything finite could be generally described as mysticism. Hegel falsely assumed that all the mysteries of Christianity tended to show the identity of God with the universe in symbols. Bolzano quoted Willm as saying that Hegel held "his own teaching for an absolute Gospel."[129] With a marked irony, Bolzano stated elsewhere that Hegel died "believing that through his philosophy the good Lord was for the first time brought up to a full consciousness of Himself."[130]

Two of Bolzano's philosophical essays were devoted specifically to the criticism of Hegel's philosophy. Although written in the 1830s, their publication was delayed until 1851, when František Příhonský was responsible for their posthumous appearance.[131] In the first one, "Über Hegel's berühmten Spruch: Alles wirkliche ist vernünftig und alles Vernünftige ist wirklich," which he derived from Hegel's *Philosophie des Rechts,*[132] Bolzano maintained that Hegel's pronouncement that "what is rational is real; and what is real is rational" was defensible only by maintaining that all that was irrational, such as moral evil and pain, had no true lasting reality but only an apparent transient one.[133] The saying then became quite trite and could be equated with the statement "what God has done, is well."[134] The maxim, if taken seriously, however, would be conducive to passivity on the assumption that the world spirit (presumably embodied in the prevalent majority) knew best. There would be no demand for individuals, including philosophers, to generate new ideas.[135]

The second essay was devoted to Hegel's concept of history, especially the history of philosophy.[136] According to Bolzano, even that part of the educated public for whom Hegel's ideas were beyond comprehension paid attention and respected his idiosyncratic views of history in general and the history of philosophy in particular. History depicted, or was in itself—Hegel confused the concept of history as a narrative and as a development—the perfect unfolding of the *Weltgeist* in time, whereby the latter was attaining its own self-consciousness and freedom. Every situation of mankind was at its core nothing other than a stage in the progress of the rational and necessary course of this *Weltgeist*. Similarly, the history of philosophy was to be nothing other than an expression of its own development and progress, and a subsequent system was indubitably (even necessarily) a perfection of the immediately preceding one. Moreover, every philosophical system that gained substantial currency was to be regarded as already perfect for its own time, not simply as a preparatory stage in the solution of the master problem that was philosophy's ultimate task. From the global point of view, the entire history of philosophy was, moreover, divisible into clear groups of three systems, in which the earliest posited something, the second one opposed that something, and the third one combined the two earlier ones into a higher unity.[137]

Bolzano found all these historiographical concepts in defiance of common sense. It was disturbing to assert that the ideas of certain philosophers, no matter how dubious or even foolish, should be accepted as a rational and even necessary step forward on the path of progress. It was an offensive hubris to identify one system as the most perfect philosophy of the present. The Hegelian reasoning proceeded on the assumption that the Europeans were undoubtedly the most cultivated part of humankind; in Europe no one philosophized better than in Germany and, within Germany, in Berlin (or possibly Munich). It was then concluded that the Hegelian (or Schellingo-Hegelian) philosophy was the true philosophy of the present and that all other systems of philosophy were of no account.[138] Actually, it was impossible to determine what the philosophy of a certain age was, since historically several systems had coexisted at a time.[139]

As for the metaphysical core of the historical process, the concept of an initially unconscious absolute or deity that needed to develop through the totality of the world and reached consciousness through humanity appeared to Bolzano most improbable, if not absurd. The concept presupposed a monistic and deterministic development of the physical universe and of human thought. It ignored the evidence of chance and diversity in natural and historical phenomena. On the grounds of individualism, Bolzano also objected to the Hegelian view that the thinking of the plethora of living individuals could be melded into the thought of a single absolute that was becoming conscious of itself.[140] The meaning of the absolute coming into self-consciousness was trivial, if one took into account the assertions of Hegel and his disciples that "to know and to be was identical." It was profoundly amoral, if the result was defined as "the entering into being of always more possible forms through man and the world," and no distinction between good and evil forms was made.[141] Under this theory, whatever foolishness the "great ones of the world" (*die Grossen der Erde*) had begun, or what crimes against humanity they had committed, all that was to be seen "as a *rational* and *necessary* step forward" [emphasis in original].[142]

In Bolzano's opinion, Hegel's triadic pattern of historical development (thesis, antithesis, synthesis) was an artificial construct that had little or no support in reality. The pattern did not correspond to the actual development of philosophical systems in the past. It could be constructed only through a distortion by the arbitrary selection and elevation of some systems and the equally arbitrary rejection of others, which did not fit the Procrustean bed of the dialectical pattern. In its very basis, the dialectical reconciliation of two opposites, as the finding of a middle way between two exaggerated claims, appeared unsound. While Hegel himself boasted that he preferred to exaggerate his position, Bolzano cautioned that the adoption of extreme stands was not a normal way of advancing knowledge (as, for instance, in mathematics).[143]

Equally artificial and unsubstantiated, according to Bolzano, was Hegel's often repeated assertion that "every nation on earth was predetermined to realize a particular stage in the development of the *Weltgeist*." Bolzano objected particularly to the ontologically monistic collectivism that Hegel's vision presupposed and questioned the assumption that entire nations advanced historical progress rather than individual human beings. He resolutely opposed the view that historical progress had to occur through national entities rather than through individuals, regardless of their national allegiance. Bolzano found Hegel's definition of the necessary stages of historical development equally arbitrary. In this context, he criticized Hegel's assertions that initially and necessarily no one felt free among the Orientals, then among the Greeks some (the citizens) felt free, and eventually among the Christian nations *all* felt free.[144] Another of Hegel's capricious tenets, according to Bolzano, was that a nation could become world-historical only at a single time. Aside from the difficulty of defining the "world-historical" role, nations could return to the forefront of history after a period of obscurity.[145]

Final Assessment of Hegel

Bolzano asked how Hegel's set of ideas, full of errors and woven together into a pattern of errors, could enjoy such a high degree of popularity, acceptance, and authority, when a dispassionate examination revealed that his doctrines were not an advance but a regression in philosophy. There was a presumption that what was new was an improvement over its precedents, which was what Hegel himself had maintained. For Bolzano, this might have been a presumption but not ipso facto an ensured result, as the case of Hegel had demonstrated. Bolzano enumerated a number of reasons that might account for an undeserved fame of a personage such as Hegel: (1) the philosopher was endowed with a prominent university chair, which secured him a wide and respectful audience; (2) the philosopher had an attractive personality and was provided with high credentials; (3) he acted in such a way as to convince the student youth that he had been fortunate enough to have discovered the key to all knowledge (*Stein der Weisen . . . glücklich gefunden*); (4) he invented a new vocabulary that provided an easy means for giving the impression of profound thought, without engaging in a deeper probing, just by employing certain rhetorical devices; (5) he borrowed terms from other fashionable fields of knowledge (such as theology, jurisprudence, and aesthetics) and from the empirical sciences to give his pronouncements an additional weight of authority; (6) he employed emotionally charged propositions that appealed to human pride, love of comfort, and other passions; (7) and he found favor with government authorities that considered the spread of his ideas to their advantage. While any one of these reasons would be effective, the combination of them all in their synergy, as in Hegel's case, created a well-nigh irresistible impact.[146] At the same time, Bolzano pointed out that even Hegel's most devoted disciples did not agree that his writings contained philosophy in its most perfect state. He referred to the views of Chalybäus and of the Polish philosopher August Cieszkowski (1814–94).[147] His opposition to Hegel's philosophy also turned Bolzano against the Catholic romanticism of the restoration or *Vormärz* era that Anton Günther and his followers propagated in the Habsburg monarchy.[148] As early as 1832, Bolzano had criticized Günther's *Vorschule der spekulativen Theologie* because it was oriented toward Hegel's idealism. It represented "a bad sign of our times," following the retrograde direction of Hegel.[149]

Toward the end of his life, Bolzano decided that Hegel was not really a conscious deceiver who intended to mislead his readers by his philosophical constructs. He changed his mind under the impact of the biography of Hegel by Karl Rosenkranz (1844). In a questionable rehabilitation, Bolzano decided to view Hegel as a silly prattler, "who always assumed that the most recent views were the truest ones and did not deceive, but was himself deceived."[150]

10

Bohemian Anti-Hegelianism: Slovak Contrast and Polish Paradox

In the spirit of the realism and empiricism of the Austro-Bohemian Catholic Enlightenment, Bolzano's influence fortified and perpetuated the Bohemian aversion to German idealism in general and to Hegel's philosophical system in particular. That influence established a lasting break with the Slovak intellectual tradition that was grounded in the spirit of Lutheran idealism. In an apparently paradoxical outcome, the Bohemian anti-Hegelianism also led to a contrast with the prevalent Polish intellectual outlook.

The Demise of Hegelianism in Bohemia

Directed against the champions of Hegel, František Klácel (1808–82) in particular, the great debate on German philosophy was symptomatic of the Bohemian intellectual orientation in the late 1840s. The initial phase took place in 1843 and involved Josef Jungmann, Karel A. Vinařický, and their associates (see chapter 9). The second and more decisive phase began in 1845 when Karel Havlíček, a pupil of Franz Exner and an admirer of Bernard Bolzano, became a leading participant.[1] Havlíček opened the campaign with an article in *Česká včela* (1845) that was highly critical of idealist philosophy:

> God may correct me, if I admit that I do not like to talk or hear the talk about the philosophical standpoint, about profound opinions, about a penetration into the ultimate substance of concepts, as I would in any case when philosophy, as often happens, does not agree

with sound reason, rather side with this good gift of God against the philosophers.[2]

Subsequently, Havlíček pointed out the low opinion of German idealism that had prevailed in contemporary England and in France, the two countries he considered intellectually more advanced than Germany.[3]

As a champion of common sense and empiricism, and thus opposed to flights of speculative imagination in philosophy, Havlíček sided with the like-minded Vilém Gabler,[4] who had entered the great battle in the *Časopis českého musea* in 1847 with the article "Něco o filosofii" (A Bit about Philosophy).[5] In an article in *Česká včela* in 1847, Havlíček agreed with Gabler that all knowledge should be based on an experience of the real world and that its formation should progress in a modest manner from one experience to another. Sounding like a twentieth-century logical positivist, he condemned the philosophers, "particularly numerous in Germany, [who have] formulated for themselves a special scholastic language, incomprehensible to others, in which their wisdom appears from afar very worthy and rare. When, however, the words are put aside, immediately the substance disappears with the words."[6] When Hegel's opponents were attacked in the Prague German journal, *Ost und West*,[7] Havlíček pledged to continue his defense of the rights of "normal reason" against the idealist philosophers. The latter caused more harm than the overt enemies of reason: "pretending to have an exclusive competence to care for it, they cripple it and thwart it by their [sophistic] entanglements from its natural path of progress."[8] Responding to Augustin Smetana's accusation, Gabler denied that he was denouncing the philosophy of Johann F. Herbart, who was dear to his teacher Exner; rather, his critique was explicitly directed against the school of German idealism.[9] During 1847, Havlíček made several other satirical observations concerning idealist metaphysics, which culminated in his remark: "English scholars had pronounced the following verdict on German philosophy from Kant to Hegel: 'A mere jargon of meaningless sounds—*vox praeterea nihil.*'"[10]

The prominent authors Václav B. Nebeský and Karel B. Štorch, both of whom had studied philosophy in Prague during Exner's professorship in the early 1830s, also participated in the great anti-Hegelian debate. In his article in *Časopis českého musea* in 1846, Nebeský traced Hegel's rise to fame to his appointment to a university chair in Berlin that caused him to identify with the Prussian state and led to an apotheosis by his devotees. These followers claimed that Hegel had inaugurated a new era in world history—an age of joy with fullness of life and beauty. This historical acme supposedly reached its expression in Hegel's philosophy and German cultural achievement.[11] The celebratory tone was absent earlier, when there was considerable uncertainty about the meaning of Hegel's statements and he himself was difficult to approach personally.[12] Again, after his death the philosophical movement disintegrated into at least three schools. The virtual incomprehensibility of Hegel's writings to the common reader facilitated their fragmentation; their difficult style and idiosyncratic terminology rendered them esoteric. Their interpreters evolved several competing systems and dazzled their audiences with the philosopher's most unusual ideas. According to Nebeský, their extremism and mutual strife led an Englishman to comment that the Hegelians represented "a substantial step toward satanization" (*notným krokem ke zd'ábleni*).[13]

Štorch, in an article in *Květy* of 1847, saw Hegel at the end of idealist philosophy's quest for the absolute, responding to Kant's challenge that only phenomena were knowable. Štorch considered the entire process a naive *petitio principii* that resulted in Hegel's pretentious claim that Germany's philosophy provided all of Europe with the perfect metaphysics.[14] In that connection, he referred to an ironic comment in an article in the *Edinburgh Review*, whose author wrote, "It is curious to mark the triumph with which Hegel proclaims that all Europe has left to Germany the sole cultivation of metaphysics: 'We have the exalted vocation,' he says, 'of guarding the holy fire, as the Eumolpids were the sole guardians of the Eleusinian Mysteries in Athens.'"[15] Štorch returned to the topic in *Časopis českého musea* a year later. In his view, Hegel's philosophy had the pretension of being the Babylonian Tower of modern speculation. A few years after the founder's death, it disintegrated into several contending schools without turning into a formal German or just Prussian ideology. This denouement showed, according to Štorch, how false the claims were about the finality and perfection of Hegelianism.[16]

A peculiar case in the story of Czech resistance to Hegel was that of František Palacký, that *rara avis* of a full-blooded Czech with a Lutheran background. However, as noted earlier (see chapter 7), his education did not involve the study of Lutheran theology at the German academic institutions as was the case with the Slovak awakeners, and thus he could avoid indoctrination in the philosophical idealism rampant at Lutheran universities in Germany.[17] During his studies in Bratislava, young Palacký was instead exposed to the literature, history, and philosophy of the British—and more specifically Scottish—Enlightenment, thanks to the Anglophilia of the Hungarian gentry, who were drawn to Bratislava as the traditional capital of Hungary. Palacký had found employment as tutor in their houses together with access to their libraries.[18] Consequently, the assertion of Hegel's influence on Palacký's philosophy of history proved unconvincing.[19] His philosophical outlook was firmly established in his youth before he encountered Hegel, whose influence, if any, would be minimal.[20] Moreover, according to the testimony of Josef V. Frič, Palacký admitted to Exner that he had never been concerned with Hegel's philosophy.[21] In 1838, Palacký, in reviewing recent Slovak literature—particularly Kuzmany's "Lučatínská Víla"— deplored the Hegelian spirit that he had already found objectionable in the romanticism of the Czech poet Karel H. Mácha.[22] As noted later in this chapter, in a private reference to Hegel in 1846, Palacký also expressed regret about the German philosopher's influence on Štúr.[23] Fundamentally, of course, Palacký's philosophical grounding was in the Scottish Enlightenment, not in German idealism.[24]

Even the late attempts of the 1840s to implant Hegelianism in Bohemia were short-lived and did not establish a line of continuity. Ignác J. Hanuš (1812–69), Augustin Smetana (1814–51), and František M. Klácel are often named as promoters of Hegelianism in Bohemia.[25] On closer examination, this judgment requires serious qualification in the case of Hanuš and Smetana, both of whom were students of Exner and were, therefore, affected by Herbartism.[26] In the case of Hanuš, his preoccupation with Hegel dated mainly—and characteristically—to his teaching appointment at the University of L'viv (Lwow, Lemberg) (1838–47), where he was in contact with Polish Hegelians, including Mickiewicz.[27] Otherwise, the effect of Hegel's philosophy on him has been characterized as only superficial: "[It] played for him more the role of inspiration for positing new questions than guides to resolving problems."[28] Smetana ultimately reached the conclusion about the one-sidedness and rigidity of Hegel's system, which he proposed to alleviate and open up by resort to Herbart's realism and empiricism, as well as an abandonment of the monistic viewpoint.[29] It may be said, therefore, that Klácel was the one authentic Hegelian. He was to Czech philosophy what Mácha was to Czech literature: an exception that confirmed the rule of Bohemian realistic sobriety that had developed under the aegis of the Catholic Enlightenment.[30]

On the whole, Hegelianism remained an alien lore for Bohemian philosophers and intellectuals. Not even in specialized areas such as the philosophy of history (except for Smetana) did Hegel's thought leave any traces on Czech intellectual life. Czech historiography eschewed teleological perspectives and adopted an austerely positivist methodology.[31] As noted in chapter 9, eventually the lack of interest in Hegel would be ultimately blamed for hampering the emergence of a Marxist-Leninist tradition.[32] In any case, by 1847–48 there was virtually no sign of Hegelianism left in Bohemia.[33]

Slovak Contrast

The distinctiveness of Bohemian anti-Hegelianism comes into sharp relief when contrasted with Slovak enthusiasm for Hegel. This Slovak preoccupation can be considered an extension of the earlier interest in Herder and the German romanticism that derived from the Lutheran religious background of the leading Slovak intellectuals and their training in the Lutheran universities of Germany.[34] Slovak Protestants were specifically proud of their Lutheranism, convinced that it was a progressive religion in contrast to the stagnant Calvinism of their Magyar Protestant compatriots.[35] By the 1830s and 1840s, the University of Halle attracted more Slovak students than the other German Lutheran universities, such as Jena, Leipzig, Halle, and Göttingen.[36]

Slovaks and German Lutheran Universities

The Slovak reception of Teutonic philosophical influences began through Jan Kollár (1793–1852) and Pavol Jozef Šafárik (1795–1861). With their attachment to Herder's philosophy of history and ontologically based nationalism, they created the intellectual precondition for an advancement to philosophical idealism that culminated in the Hegelian enthusiasm of L'udovít Štúr (1815–56) and his colleagues.[37] As noted earlier (see chapter 6), Kollár was a student of theology in Jena from 1817 to 1819; Šafárik before him, from 1815 to 1817. Paradoxically, Kollár and Šafárik themselves, despite their fascination with Herder, refused to make a full-fledged transition from Herder to Hegel. Kollár, in particular, claimed to detest Hegel's philosophy, as well as its influence on Štúr and his circle, as both intellectually and morally repugnant.[38] Nevertheless, as Masaryk pointed out, while Kollár may have found Hegel's metaphysics unacceptable, he actually followed Hegel's philosophy of history. He did so by assigning to a particular nation a leading historical role at any given time to the exclusion of other nations. Like Hegel, Kollár also accepted an artificial Teutonic-Romance national entity and the idea that the task of a leading nation was to reconcile the preexisting cultural contradictions generated by the historical process.[39]

It was, however, mainly Kollár's and Šafárik's successors in the Slovak national movement who developed a whole-hearted attachment to Hegelianism that they connected with Herder's idea of *Humanität*.[40] The chief protagonists were L'udovít Štúr (1815–56), Josef M. Hurban (1817–88), Michal M. Hodža (1811–70), Štefan Launer (1821–51), Benjamín P. Červenák (1816–42), Petr Záboj Kellner-Hostinský (1823–18), and Samuel Ormis (1822–75).[41] While earlier generations of Slovak Lutheran theologians had studied in Jena, by and large Štúr and his contemporaries attended the University of Halle. Halle was a domain of German idealism and sheltered its students from an exposure to British empiricism or French positivism.[42] By the 1830s and 1840s, the vogue for Kant, Fichte, and Schelling had faded, while that for Hegel remained. Hegel had then reached the peak of his early fame with his collected writings, which appeared in eighteen volumes (1832–45), and his disciples were staffing the chairs of philosophy in German universities. At Halle, the guardians of Hegel's legacy were professors Johann E. Erdmann and Julius S. Schaller.[43] Incidentally, it was Erdmann's book, *Grundriss der Psychologie für Vorlesungen* (1840), that Exner would use as one of his targets in the sharp critique of Hegelian psychology, *Die Psychologie der Hegelschen Schule* (1842).[44]

Slovak students at Halle became interested in the application of Hegelianism to the philosophy of politics, history, and art. They were fascinated by Hegel's stress on the absolute idea or world spirit, which revealed itself in history and whose possible, even necessary, realization determined the destiny of all nations.[45] Their teachers at Halle taught, according to Hegel's philosophy of history, that in every period there was a leading nation that represented the world spirit. It advanced above all other nations, passed through a life cycle, died, and was replaced by another nation. The absolute spirit, however, was immortal, and as it advanced, its current state subsumed all the earlier stages. In addition,

Professor Erdmann stressed Hegel's stark cultural pluralism, according to which a national language was the main mark of the world spirit's realization in a given nation.[46]

It was primarily Štúr who most clearly exemplified Hegel's direct influence. He had studied at the University of Halle from 1838 to 1840, where he came to regard the Hegelian philosophical system as "the highest attainment of the human mind."[47] In addition to Štúr, other well-known Slovak intellectuals studied at the time in Halle under the spell of Hegel's philosophy, in particular Jonáš Záborský, Benjamín P. Červenák, Gustáv Grossmann, Mirko Blaškovič, the brothers Ludovít and Samo B. Hroboň, and Ján Benko.[48] Somewhat later, in the mid-1840s, they were followed to Halle by Andrej Sládkovič, Štefan Launer, Jozef Horváth, Ján Raffay, Ján Kalinčiak, Ondrej H. Lanštják, Ludovít A. Gál, August Šulek, and Karol Hrenčík.[49]

Štefan Launer

An important and distinctive member of the younger group was Štefan Launer, who studied theology and philosophy in Halle in 1843–44. Like other Slovak adherents of Hegel, relying on *The Philosophy of History* and *Phenomenology of the Spirit*, he accepted the proposition that a rational spirit expressed itself through world history and used nations as its instruments.[50] This world spirit advanced its cause sequentially through a series of chosen nations, which were, in their substance, "organs for the expression and realization of that part of the concept of man that the spirit desired to reveal to humankind at a given stage." Launer focused on Hegel's tenet that only one nation at a given time could lead and thus be dominant; such a nation was called upon to be the absolute purveyor of the rules of behavior, thought, and law, because it expressed the spirit of the time. It legitimately subordinated and dominated "through thought and sword" all other nations that were properly instruments of the elect nation and attained to spiritual worth only to the extent of participation in the forms of the latter's intellectual expressions.[51]

On the one hand, according to Launer, ideas that in the past had represented an expression of the world spirit continued to remain in force after the demise of the nations that had produced them. On the other hand, current ideas that did not emanate from the world spirit remained irrelevant, like stillborn children. The chosen nations of the Christian era were the Italians, the French, the English, and the Germans; they realized within humankind the objectives of the world spirit in the realms of beauty, goodness, truth, and freedom. The Slavs had to learn from those nations or otherwise just passively rotate around them like the planets around the sun. Contrary to most other Slovak Hegelians, Launer did not believe in a world-historical role of Slavic nations that would have them produce the spirit's additional global ideas.[52] Instead, the Slavs were to adopt the fruits of the world spirit from the more advanced European nations.[53] According to their national temperament, the Croats were to gravitate to the Italians, the Poles to the French, the Russians (with grave reservations) to the English, and the Czechs and Slovaks to the Germans.[54] According to this formula, Launer saw the Lutheran Reformation as an instrument of the German philosophical and theological ascendancy among the Slovaks. Lutheranism had initiated the formation of the Slovak intellectual culture exclusively by the German spirit.[55] Launer did allow (in a very remote future) for only one exception among the Slavs. There was the possibility of a world-historical role for the Russians because of their extreme isolation from Europe, their current drastic backwardness, and the eventual exigency of the world spirit to manifest itself further in a novel way, beyond the four existing chosen nations.[56]

L'udovít Štúr

In contrast to Launer, Štúr connected Herder's alleged views on the future of Slavdom with Hegel's philosophy of history without any reservations.[57] Along with his immediate followers, Štúr viewed Hegel's historical dialectics as a way of realizing what he considered to be Herder's idea about the historical mission of the Slavs.[58] Štúr's philosophy of history for both the Slavs and the Slovaks was based directly on Hegel's teaching about a national spirit and its development and gradual unfolding in the national culture. This development was to be based on the specific problems and forms of spiritual life of the Slovak nation.[59] Just as there were laws of nature, there were also laws of history. Indeed, Štúr did not shirk from embracing an ontic monism, as he wrote in his "Prednášení historická" (Historical Lectures): "This Idea, this Reason manifests itself in the world and nothing else but it manifests itself in the world."[60] Štúr believed, with Hegel, that the idea was an absolute subject that used the world, nature, and history as a medium for realizing and affirming its creativity and infinitude.[61] The absolute idea was the creator and lawgiver of all being. Its involvement in the historical process filled Štúr with optimism that progress in the world, and in history, was guaranteed.[62] Štúr also accepted Hegel's political and social collectivism (*pospolitost*), although he saw the realm of realization of human freedom in the nation rather than in the state. As the spirit was superior to the body, so the nation was superior to the family. Without the nation, a human being could not develop spiritually. The nation offered the opportunity for individuals to rise from their limitations to the higher level of general interests.[63]

Štúr sought to indoctrinate his own students in Hegel's philosophy and urged them to define national destiny within the Hegelian parameters.[64] While teaching at the Lutheran lyceum in Bratislava from 1840 to 1843, he based his lectures in history on Hegel's *Philosophie der Geschichte* and *Philosophie des Geistes*. Like Bolzano in Bohemia before him—albeit in an entirely different direction—he played a dominant role in shaping the outlook of the future intellectual class.[65] In 1842, he sought to calm the scruples of his younger colleague Samo B. Hroboň, who complained that Hegel's philosophy was undermining his religious faith. Štúr admonished Hroboň that the Slovak national cause could be advanced only "on the basis of the great thinker Hegel."[66] Štúr also tried to get Czech intellectuals such as Josef V. Frič interested in Hegel's ideas.[67]

Inasmuch as Hegel paid scanty attention to the Slavs and their creative potential in his own writings, Štúr and his school sought to make up for this lacuna by connecting Hegelianism with Herder's ideas on the destiny of the Slavs. Thus, the Slav cause could be interpolated into Hegel's historical scheme, and the Slavs, taking their cue from the great German thinker, could foresee their own future as the coming expression of the world spirit on the basis of his philosophy.[68] In 1853 in this expectation, Štúr wrote his final work, *Das Slawenthum und die Welt der Zukunft* (Slavdom and the World of the Future), in German, first published in Vladimir I. Lamanskii's Russian translation in 1867.[69] In their comments on the book, Josef Jirásek and Albert Pražák identified numerous parallels between Hegel's *Philosophie der Geschichte*, as well as his *Ästhetik*, and Štúr's work.[70] In particular, Štúr repeatedly endorsed Hegel's concept of history as an expression of the absolute idea.[71]

Expressing his ultimate views in *Das Slawenthum und die Welt der Zukunft,* Štúr's vision went far beyond Kollár's ideal of Slav cultural cooperation. The book rejected the civilization of the West as corrupt and assigned the Slavs the task of a cultural rebirth of Europe, from which, moreover, the Czechs and the Poles were largely disqualified for being excessively tainted by the mores of the West.[72] The virtues of the Slavs were characterized according to the Slavophile teaching of Aleksei S. Khomiakov and Ivan Kireevskii, but the political outcome of the future reflected more the program of the contemporary Russian Panslavs, such as Stepan P. Shevyrev and Mikhail P. Pogodin. Štúr envisaged the fulfillment of the Slavs' destiny in a single political and administrative system, with a single language and religion, under the aegis of Russia's autocracy.[73]

Jozef M. Hurban

After Štúr, Jozef M. Hurban was perhaps the most prominent of the Slovak Hegelians although, unlike most of them, he had not actually studied at Halle.[74] Originally, he was inspired by Fichte's militant patriotism, thanks to the *Reden an die deutsche Nation*, but soon—after discussions with Štúr—he shifted his intellectual focus to Hegel. He acquired Hegel's collected works, and, as he later recalled, all that he himself "produced, thought, wrote, and spoke" bore the imprint of the German philosopher.[75] In addition, his Hegelianism was fortified by the influences of Polish scholars August von Cieszkowski (1814–94) and Bronisław F. Trentowski (1800–1869).[76] In 1842, Hurban wrote of Hegel's teaching as "something uplifting and heavenly" and added that "every Slav [had to] submit to it in order to fly higher."[77] The task of philosophy was to reveal the proper course of social development and then provide appropriate guidance for the continuation of that process. Along the lines of Hegel's philosophy, the Slovaks could, in the company of the other Slavs, participate in advancing the purpose of world history toward its ultimate fruition.[78] According to Hurban, the Slovaks were in special need of assistance from Hegel's philosophy to help their belatedly awakening nation become conscious of its special destiny and historical mission.[79]

Like Štúr, Hurban embraced an ontic monism, according to which the absolute idea realized itself through a dialectical process in concrete being.[80] The idea had to penetrate all the distinct individual phenomena and reveal itself as the substance of life and as penetrating life in its entirety.[81] Like Štúr, Hurban also embraced a cultural pluralism that was metaphysically based. According to the Hegelian laws of being, a nation pursued its specific role in the articulation and individualization of the absolute.[82] Or conversely, the spirit reified, or incarnated, itself in that nation, the history of which signified the entering of the spirit from its own self into the objective world.[83] The spirit within the nation was "a single subject, like one human being, one person." It acquired a voice through the pronouncements of the nation's great men in the social, political, ecclesiastical, and literary spheres of life.[84]

Hurban accepted Hegel's triadic concept of the development of world history, involving the ages of the Orient, the Greco-Roman antiquity, and the modern Germanic West. He asserted, however, that yet another stage, realized through the Slavs, was inevitable because of the decline of the contemporary West, where religion, art, and science were in decay.[85] The Slavs were the obvious candidates to maintain the further progress of mankind. Moreover—possibly based on the teaching of the Slavophiles—the Slavs were in possession of "a spiritual vision of truth in its entirety" and were thus capable of achieving a harmonious integration of all aspects of knowledge and art in a Slavic culture of the future.[86]

Hurban opened to the promotion of German idealism the pages of the cultural review *Slovenskje pohladi na vedi, umeňja a literatúru* (Slovak Outlook on Science, Art, and Literature), which he edited first in Skalica and then in Trnava from 1846 to 1852. In 1847, Hurban emphatically defended German idealism in general, and Hegel's philosophy in particular, against Eugen Gerometta, a Slovak Catholic priest. The latter poked fun at the Germans' fascination with philosophy, saying that among such philosophers "the names of Kant, Krug, Schelling and Fichte are well known, and most recently that of Hegel, who enjoys a large number of followers, so that at present every writer is considered a disciple of Hegel, who wrote so incomprehensibly that no one can understand him." In his rebuke, Hurban maintained that those who fashionably and ignorantly maligned Hegel typically had never studied him, much less Kant, Schelling, or Fichte. In addition, Hurban undertook to excuse Hegel's rather embarrassing lack of interest in the Slavs in general and the Slovaks in particular. Although Hegel had not been directly concerned with the Slavs, Hurban said, Hegel's concepts could be fittingly applied to them, and Slovak philosophy could not be constructed without an informed input from Hegel's system. Finally, Hurban highlighted as especially impudent the accusation that Hegel denied the existence of God. Such detractors, he said, ignored the numerous references to God in Hegel's writings.[87]

The following issue of Hurban's journal, *Slovenskje pohladi*, carried an article, "Prvot'ini vedi slovanskej"(The Rudiments of Slavonic Science), the author of which was hidden under the acronym P. Z. H. The author actually proceeded to outline the integration of Slavic destiny with the philosophical and historical concepts of Hegel. First of all, he applied the Hegelian triadic pattern of thesis-antithesis-synthesis to world history as a whole. On the universal scale, it involved three chronological ages: Asian or Pre-Christian, European or Christian, and Slavic or Humanistic-Christian.[88] On the scale of modern history, the pattern encompassed three stages of knowledge, namely, the Romance stage of empirical science, the Germanic stage of metaphysical science, and the Slavic stage of real science. The Romance nations discovered nature, the Germanic ones the spirit, and the Slavs would supply the comprehensive vision, integrating the preceding stages of knowledge.[89] Since the Slavs were the last group in the history of humanity to step to the forefront, they were destined to play a climactic role in the history of mankind: "The Slav is the last son in human history, and the Slav learning is the 'amen' of all human knowledge." In the course of modern history, the archetypal man will have, therefore, appeared successively as a Frenchman, a Prussian, and a Slav, representing respectively the philosophy of "empiricism, idealism, and absolutism."[90]

In 1851, Jan Kalinčiak, a Slovak novelist and another alumnus of the University of Halle, also defended Hegel against attack by the journalist Daniel Lichard (1812–82), an opponent of the Slovak-Czech language schism. In Hurban's *Slovenskje pohladi*, Kalinčiak claimed that Lichard did not really understand Hegel[91] and in particular that he incorrectly interpreted Hegel's concept of nations, confusing it with Herder's folkloristic interests.[92] Hurban himself added comments to Kalinčiak's critique, rebuking Lichard for his impudence in questioning the value of Hegel's teaching, as if he himself were a professor of philosophy.[93]

Michal M. Hodža

The last member of the dominant intellectual triumvirate of the Slovak national awakening, Michal M. Hodža, like his colleagues Štúr and Hurban, adopted the characteristic teaching of German idealism, namely, the principles of the metaphysically based national pluralism and the singularity of universal being, or ontic monism. Since his youth, he had avidly studied and analyzed the philosophy of Hegel, as well as that of Kant and Schelling.[94] According to his philosophical outlook, the single world spirit was attaining its self-realization through the distinct cultures of particular nations. The formation of each distinct national culture, in all its departments, required the national language as the indispensable instrument. Hodža maintained that the Slavs together were destined to form the appropriate national unit for the next stage of the world-historical process.[95]

Like Štúr and Hurban, Hodža also envisaged the necessity of a leading role for the Slavs in the next stage of world-historical development because of the current moral and cultural decay of Western Europe.[96] According to Hodža, the Slavs were, in fact, well suited to achieve a new synthesis of the positive achievements of past civilizations. Like Hurban, he believed that the Slav nature was endowed with an all-embracing spirit. Surprisingly, he saw that kind of spirit also manifested in the thought of Leibniz, Kant, and Hegel. In Hodža's opinion, the Slovaks would fulfill their historical destiny not by themselves but within the general Slav community. Aside from the social and historical theories of Russian Slavophiles, he conspicuously relied on the tenets of Adam Mickiewicz's Polish messianism.[97]

Significantly for the nexus among Luther, Hegel, and the Slovak national awakeners, Štúr and his entourage resisted claims that Hegel's teaching tended to spread corruption within the Lutheran faith by undermining its fundamental tenets. Trying to shield Hegel, they sought to de-emphasize the Hegelian doctrine of God's dependence on humanity, namely, that the absolute idea (God) reached self-awareness only through human minds.[98] At the other end of the spectrum, they demonstrated a firm attachment to Lutheranism and staunchly opposed the idea of a union of the Lutherans with the Calvinists in Hungary.[99] Hurban went as far as to maintain that Lutheranism and Calvinism contrasted with each other like light and darkness. Historically, according to him, the Reformation in Slovakia had gravitated to Lutheranism in the crucial sixteenth century.[100] Lutheranism suited the national character of the Slovaks, as Calvinism suited that of the Magyars.[101] The Calvinist religion supported social privilege and, therefore, was favored by the Hungarian feudal nobility. Moreover, Calvinism was often used as a cover for unbelief.[102] The Hungarian Calvinists, in turn, countercharged that it was the contemporary Slovak Lutherans who had abandoned Christianity by turning into pantheistic Hegelians.[103]

The Divisive Hegel

The Czech awakeners felt uneasy about their Slovak colleagues' fascination with romanticism and idealism. Their dismay over Herder's influence on Slovak romanticism was noted earlier in chapter 6. It was even stronger with respect to what was considered the Slovaks' infatuation with Hegel and with German idealism. In 1846, Palacký privately regretted that Štúr embraced Hegel's ideas during his studies at the University of Halle. He felt that it was the German philosopher's influence that led the Slovak awakener to embark on the road toward a separate Slovak language.[104]

The language schism was overtly blamed on Hegel's influence on Štúr and Hurban by Vendelín Grünwald, writing in *Květy* in 1845. Grünwald objected to Hurban's adoption of Hegel's essentialist idea of nationhood, which claimed that "whatever nations have accomplished, that had its source in their own truth, in their substance, in their spirit and principle; their spirit [expressing itself] had stepped out of its nothingness." Grünwald also considered the Slovaks' adulation of Hegel inappropriate because of the German philosopher's low opinion of the Slavs.[105] Hurban took up Hegel's defense in *Květy* that same year. According to him, it was to the Slovaks' credit that they accepted Hegel as their intellectual guide. Hurban went on to deplore the Czech critics' alleged slander of Hegel, whom he called "that great man" who "dwelt, as if in an eternal castle, in his perennial system." Hegel, for Hurban, completed the great historical cycle of Western intellectual development begun by Aristotle who contemplated the nature of thought. Hegel had made the great epistemological discovery that concept and object were identical, as were thought and being (or becoming).[106] Hurban rejected the charge of Hegel's contempt for the Slavs by citing what he considered Hegel's neutral comment in the *Philosophie der Geschichte* that the Slavs had not yet manifested the workings of the world spirit in history. He justified Hegel's reluctance to assess the Slavs because in the German philosopher's views, the effects of the spirit could be seen only after its manifestation was completed and not while it was in progress.[107] Incidentally, Václav B. Nebeský shortly thereafter (in 1846) returned to questioning the appropriateness of the Slovaks' search for a place in Hegel's scheme of history to accommodate the Slavs.[108]

Hurban shifted from a defense of Hegel to an offensive against the Czech intellectuals and excoriated the philosophical empiricism that represented a legacy from the Austro-Bohemian Enlightenment. In his opinion, a reliance on "the common sense" (*všední rozum*) was an inadequate epistemological instrument to attain to genuine truth. Such truth could be attained only by higher speculation, which—shining like the sun—could illuminate the character of universal being. Hurban further claimed that it would be a disaster for science and the more lofty areas of human life if only what could be validated by common sense should be considered true. According to him, such an approach had led to the superficial rationalism that had created terrible distortions in the ecclesiastical, political, and social life of Europe, and he expressed a hope that the Slavs would be spared falling under similar philosophical misconceptions.[109] This superficial rationalism also thwarted the understanding of what was the inner spirit in the life of a nation—what was "the organism of the internal factors of the national life."[110]

In another mark of the Slovak and Czech division over Hegel, that rare Czech Hegelian Klácel found sympathy in Slovakia after his exclusion from teaching in Bohemia in institutions under the Catholic Church's control on the basis of his "pantheism." Characteristically, he gained support in Slovak Lutheran circles, with L'udovít Štúr trying to secure an academic position for him.[111] Likewise, Hurban praised Klácel for appreciating the essentialist distinctiveness of individual national cultures.[112] In addition, Štúr had a friendly interest in Ignác J. Hanuš, who—as noted earlier—was fascinated by Hegelianism in the Polish intellectual ambiance in L'viv.[113]

A Polish Paradox?

The distinction between the realistic and the individualistic outlook of the Bohemians and the Austrians and the quasi-mystical collectivist Hegelian outlook of the Slovaks cannot be viewed simply as deriving from the Catholic-Lutheran dichotomy. It stemmed from the specific conditions of the region. There was a close and distinct relationship between the Austro-Bohemian realistic-empirical orientation and the Josephist Catholic Enlightenment, on the one hand, and Hegelianism and the Lutheran theological milieu of Central Europe specifically, on the other.

Adherence to the Roman Church alone did not, of course, create a barrier against the appeals of Hegelianism. Thus, the Catholic Poles embraced absolute idealism just as eagerly as the Slovak Lutherans did.[114] As early as January 1812, Samuel Bandtke reported to Josef Dobrovský from Cracow his displeasure over the overwhelming interest in German metaphysics, particularly in Fichte and Schelling, which overshadowed empirical studies in history and philology.[115] The leading Polish intellectuals came to regard Hegel as the acme of German and universal philosophy by the 1840s, just as they had regarded Schelling's philosophy previously. As early as 1830, W. Chłędowski, editor of the journal *Haliczanin*, summed up this attitude by calling German idealism from Kant to Hegel "the noblest achievement in the history of the human mind."[116] Conversely, an adherence to Lutheranism was not a necessary prerequisite for an ardent embrace of Hegelianism, as the case of the Orthodox Russians indicates.[117]

In the Polish case, the powerful appeal of Hegelianism was partly due to the absence of a liberal Catholicism that would have been an equivalent of the outcome of the Josephist Enlightenment in Austria and Bohemia.[118] As noted earlier in chapter 7, the latter restored in philosophy the purity of Aristotelian realism characteristic of early scholasticism and rejected the scholasticism of the sixteenth and seventeenth centuries.[119] In Poland, the Jesuit or baroque scholasticism[120] was not countered by the restoration of pristine Thomism; on the contrary, the essentialist tendency was reinforced by a vogue of the metaphysics of Christian Wolff.[121] Wolff's ideas were popularized by Wawrzyniec Mitzlof de Kolof (1705–70) and his two successors, Antoni Wiśniewski (1718–74) and Piotr Świtkowski (1744–93).[122] The synergy of Suárezian scholasticism and Wolff's metaphysics most likely facilitated through its "essentialism" the adoption of German idealism. Among the Bohemians, the Catholic Enlightenment acted as a barrier against philosophical idealism and as a bridge to logical positivism. Among the Poles, Catholic philosophy could act not as a barrier but as a bridge to Hegelianism. Needless to say, Hegelianism and German idealism, especially in the 1830s and 1840s, did not favor liberal thought in Poland.[123]

The opposition to the realistic and empirical orientation of the Enlightenment became apparent with the turn to philosophical idealism, in the first instance to Kant, whose thought was popularized by Józef

K. Szaniawski (1764–1843).[124] Subsequently, the turn to romanticism occurred under the philosophical aegis of Schelling with Maurycy Mochnacki (1804–34), glorifying feeling and intuition, and Józef Gołuchowski (1787–1858), delving into Schelling's metaphysics.[125] The main impact of Hegelianism was felt after 1830, and it was often combined with the idea of Polish messianism and intensified by interest in theosophic currents represented by Jacob Boehme, Louis-Claude de Saint-Martin, and Andrzej Towiański. The most famous among the Polish Hegelians were August Cieszkowski (1814–94) and Bronisław F. Trentowski (1800–1869), who attempted to combine Hegelian procedures with theistic views and a messianic philosophy of history.[126] Along these lines, Józef Kremer, professor at the University of Cracow, later on attempted to reconcile Hegel's metaphysics with Catholic theology.[127]

Bolzano, in his analysis of Hegel's history of philosophy, subjected Cieszkowski's theories of history to severe criticism, based on the latter's *Prolegomena zur Historiosophie*.[128] According to Bolzano, Cieszkowski pushed Hegel's ideas to extreme conclusions by applying the triadic pattern (thesis, antithesis, synthesis) not only to intellectual developments but also to history in general, which he saw as a totality of past, present, and future. According to Cieszkowski, the first phase was antiquity, ruled by beauty; the second was the Christian-Germanic world, dominated by truth; and the beginning of the last one was in the present, to be governed by deed. Furthermore, philosophy had reached its highest point at present and henceforth could not but abandon the height of theory for the lowlands of practice, and its fate was to become popularized, or to spread itself flat in a nether region (*sich in die Tiefe zu verflachen*). Another bizarre aspect of Cieszkowski's elaboration of Hegel's philosophy of history was, according to Bolzano, the view that the "great men" represented the universal historical idea, as well as the distinct and specific character of their nations. Consequently, the history of entire nations could be narrated through the lives of their great men (or leaders).[129]

Even more startling, according to Bolzano, was Cieszkowski's explication of the necessary stages of Hegel's historical theory as having not merely an intellectual content but also particular characteristics of the physical world. Thus, the Chinese spirit represented mechanism, while Athens and Sparta, respectively, represented dynamic and static electricity. The last two united in the electromagnetic system of the Macedonian Empire that was antithetical to the light religion of the Persians.

Finally, the two were subsumed by the expansive and absorbing power of warmth, which was the symbol of Rome.[130]

For the sake of contextualization, it should be noted that among the Poles' Slavic kinsmen, the Russians, the enormous vogue of German idealism was perhaps even stronger than in Germany itself. Moreover, there was a lively intellectual exchange reinforcing the enthusiasm for German philosophy between the Russian section of Poland (the Grand Duchy) and Russia proper.[131] The appeal of Hegelianism affected almost all the luminaries of Russia's nineteenth-century intellectual firmament, including Petr I. Chaadaev, Ivan V. Kireevskii, Mikhail Bakunin, Vissarion G. Belinskii, Alexander Herzen, Nikolai G. Chernyshevskii, and Georgii V. Plekhanov.[132] The notable religious and cultural historian Nikolai Berdiaev has suggested that this vogue was rooted in an accidental preestablished harmony between Hegel's philosophy of history and Eastern Orthodox apocalypticism.[133] Another and a more direct role may be sought in eighteenth-century Russia's fascination with German mysticism and theosophy, particularly Jacob Boehme,[134] which also had found reflection in Hegel's metaphysics. Boehme himself was highly regarded not only by Hegel but also by other stalwarts of German idealism such as Schelling and Schopenhauer.[135] In addition, Masaryk has pointed out that after the Napoleonic Wars—as a reaction to Napoleon's aggression—Russian students tended to flock to German universities and to avoid French ones. Belinskii, for instance, expressed his low regard for French philosophy in the 1840s and praised Germany as the spiritual Jerusalem of modern man, adding, "The philosophy of the Germans . . . is the clear and precise development and explanation of Christian teaching, as a teaching that is founded on love and on the idea of uplifting man through his consciousness all the way to divinity."[136] As a final observation, in the first half of the nineteenth century Russian intellectuals came strangely to resemble their Polish counterparts in their devotion to Hegel, despite the Orthodox-Catholic divide.[137]

The anti-idealist analytical tradition would eventually be implanted in the Habsburg part of Poland. Its pioneering representative was Kazimierz Twardowski (1866–1938), a pupil of Robert Zimmermann and Franz Brentano in Vienna. After a stay as *Privatdozent* in Vienna, Twardowski served as professor of philosophy at the University of L'viv (1895–1930). As an empiricist in the Austrian philosophical tradition, he thus became its representative in that part of Poland, which tellingly formed a part of the Habsburg Empire.[138] During the first half of the nineteenth century, however, even Austrian Poland or Galicia had felt the strong influence of Hegel. Thus, it was at the University of L'viv, in 1838–47, that Ignác J. Hanuš, a former disciple of Exner in Prague, had come under the spell of Hegelianism.[139]

The German Issue

The Czech awakeners did not reject Hegelianism because it represented a German philosophy, as has been often claimed.[140] It was not shunned because it was German but because the Hegelian and other constructions of absolute idealism were considered misguided, fantastic, and even—in anticipation of the logical positivism and analytical philosophy of the turn of the second millennium—nonsense.[141] To counter the charge of philosophical xenophobia, two observations can be made. First, that the rejection of metaphysical idealism was not a Czech idiosyncrasy is shown by analogous judgments of critics from other nations, such as that of the British Bishop Connop Thirlwall.[142] Second, Czech critics of Hegel also relied on the views of German-speaking writers, beginning with Bolzano and Exner and continuing with Brentano.[143]

In 1842 Exner himself pointed out that not only the English and the French but also many Germans opposed Hegel's philosophy.[144] In particular, the Prussian philosopher Friedrich E. Beneke expressed a negative view of German idealism in no uncertain terms as early as 1822: "It is finally the time that we Germans abandon the unnatural stilted speculation, for which other nations ridicule us, while we pity them with a self-loving pride, that they have no inkling of true philosophy."[145] He further mocked those who desired "the Universal Absolute" (*Absolut des Weltalls*), in which they would be merged with "worm and angel, birch tree and crystalline crusts, and—with God (?!)—."[146] His endorsement of empiricism brought him in contact with English scholars, especially William Whewell (1794–1866), professor of moral philosophy at Cambridge, who in turn was a friend of Bishop Thirlwall.[147] Along the same lines, in 1851 Václav Nebeský noted that even among the Germans, critical voices had been raised against philosophical idealism and literary romanticism; these Teutonic voices favored instead the more down-to-earth intellectual outlook à la the English, particularly as reflected in the dramas of Shakespeare.[148]

Moreover, in the Bohemian case, a negative view of Hegelianism did not imply contempt for philosophy as such, as has been maintained (see chapter 9). Disrespect for philosophy certainly could not be attributed to Bolzano. Similarly, Jungmann, who stood close to Bolzano's views in his assessment of German idealism—he considered its tenets as something bordering on insanity—expressed the highest regard for philosophy. In his preface to Antonín Marek's textbook, he referred to philosophy as a necessary background for "the growth and full development of all literature."[149] Moreover, Ignác J. Hanuš credited Jungmann with having aroused, as his gymnasium teacher, a deep interest in philosophy.[150] Similarly, Havlíček admired the philosophy not only of Bolzano but also of Leibniz, whose teaching he studied under his university professor, Exner, as well as from Exner's treatise *Über Leibnizens Universal-Wissenschaft* (1845).[151] J. Fidrmuc, an early participant in the great debate about philosophy, recognized the value of logic and psychology (then considered a part of philosophy).[152] Nebeský, an avowed opponent of metaphysical idealism, proclaimed the indispensability of philosophy, albeit of the empirical and realistic orientation.[153] Even Vilém Gabler, the most scathing critic of metaphysical speculation, did not deny the need for logic and "common sense" philosophy.[154] As a bottom line, the awakeners, who participated in the anti-Hegelian debate of the 1840s, had received their training in philosophy at the University of Prague from Bolzano, František Příhonský, Johann Peithner von Lichtenfels, and Exner. None of them, therefore, could be casually accused of either a philosophical primitivism or an inability to understand Hegel's German.

Finally, in considering the German issue, we should note that the term *German philosophy* was actually a shorthand designation for philosophical idealism in general and Hegelianism in particular. The opposing *Austrian* philosophical school, which the Bohemians tended to embrace, was also linguistically German. Likewise, the eventual flourishing of the Austrian school in the Vienna Circle and the Society for Empirical Philosophy was also linguistically German, with the society located, of all places, in Hegel's final citadel—Berlin.[155] During the great anti-Hegelian debate, František Čupr, Gabler, and Nebeský indicated their respect for the philosophy of Herbart, and Štorch for the philosophy of Lessing.[156] In the latter part of the nineteenth century, Josef Durdík, the heir of Exner's and Zimmermann's Herbartism at the University of

Prague, affirmed that—while rejecting German idealism—the Czech university embraced (in Herbart's philosophy) a "realism" that was more a product of German than of British or French philosophy.[157]

To the extent, therefore, that the awakeners drew on Teutonic sources, it was not the Romantic-idealist mainstream but the subsidiary realistic-empirical one, which, so to say, played second fiddle to the main current in German political culture. For the Czechs, the latter was epitomized at the time of the national awakening by Seibt and Bolzano and later (in Masaryk's time) by Brentano. The choice of the Austrian tradition, of which Bolzano is considered a founder, over the German philosophical tradition had long-range consequences for Czech intellectual and political orientation.[158] In addition, the distinction between the Austrian and the German philosophical traditions places the Bohemian case into a wider Central European and, perhaps by extension, Euro-Atlantic context. Conversely, the Bohemian case study helps illuminate the character of the two philosophical paradigms.

11

Liberal Thought and the Authoritarian Church

The charisma and teaching authority of Bernard Bolzano, above all, extended and reaffirmed in the intellectual life of Bohemia the liberal spirit of the Catholic Enlightenment, engendered partly by the legacy of Bohemian Utraquism. This philosophical orientation, based on empirical realism and explicitly opposed to idealist speculation and conceptualization, continued at the University of Prague, through Bolzano's successors as professors of philosophy, František Příhonský (1818–24), Johann Peithner von Lichtenfels (1827–31), and especially Franz Exner (1832–48). Bolzano's liberality was also shared by his contemporaries, in particular Antonín Marek (1785–1877), Ferdinand Hyna (1802–81), Karel B. Štorch (1812–68), Václav B. Nebeský (1818–82), and František Čupr (1821–82), who provided intellectual leadership to the national awakening in the 1840s. As of midcentury, the end result was, on the one hand, the lasting success of the Catholic Enlightenment's heritage in the intellectual life of Bohemia, as evidenced by the prevalence of realism and empiricism over idealism and speculative metaphysics. On the other hand, the Catholic Enlightenment suffered a defeat in the area of ecclesiology. Instead of a return to the ecclesial liberalism of the Utraquist Church advocated by the champions of the Enlightenment, the Roman Church gradually and relentlessly reasserted tridentine rigidity in a process that reached its culmination (or perhaps, its nadir) in the aftermath of 1848. In consequence of this growing split, the liberal tenor of intellectual life was becoming directly opposed to the ecclesiastical structure with its authoritarian character.

A New Counter-Reformation?

The disjunction between Austro-Bohemian Reform Catholicism and the Roman Church after 1790 was rather slow in developing, allowing the Catholic Enlightenment in its philosophical aspect to dominate Bohemia's intellectual scene into the mid-nineteenth century and, in a secularized form, beyond.[1] It is true that the reaction against Josephist reforms was sharply articulated by the papal nuncio to Vienna, Antonio Severoli (appointed in 1801), who wrote about "the damage done by Joseph II's diabolical laws" and wished to see religious conditions return to those in the time before Maria Theresa.[2] The Roman offensive was, however, an uphill battle partly because of the jealousy of the Habsburg bureaucracy and partly because of the entrenched advocates of Reform Catholicism.[3] The Austrian state apparatus mounted significant opposition to papal intervention into the ecclesiastical affairs of the empire.[4] Moreover, the Austrian state sympathized with the Catholic Enlightenment's opposition to the currents of metaphysical idealism originating and spreading from the Lutheran states of Germany.[5]

The precarious congruity between the Enlightenment and the elements of liberalism in the Roman Church survived even the severe setback of the persecution of Bolzano and Michael J. Fesl in Prague and Litoměřice, respectively.[6] Bolzano was not only removed from his university post in 1820 but also prohibited from preaching.[7] A breve of Pope Pius VII dated December 18, 1819, instructed Josef F. Hurdálek, bishop of Litoměřice, to remove Fesl from all ecclesiastical offices. A commission from Vienna ordered Fesl's arrest in the spring of 1820 and investigated his colleagues, including Vincenc Zahradník. Soon afterward, in October 1822, under pressure from the pope, Bishop Hurdálek himself had to resign his office "voluntarily" for earlier condoning the subversive activities of Fesl and his associates.[8]

Ironically, the success in removing Bolzano, Fesl, and Hurdálek was followed by a reversal of the process of retridentization as the Austrian bureaucrats, jealous of Rome's authority, provided a temporary reprieve for the Josephist ecclesiastical policy.[9] The adherents of Reform Catholicism remained active in the philosophical and theological faculties of the University of Vienna and in the imperial commission for religious literature, headed by the Archbishop of Vienna, Sigismund Anton von Hohenwart.[10] As a mark of the continuity in liberal Catholicism, Dobrovský's intervention with the Archbishop of Prague, Václav Chlumčaský, on behalf of Bolzano helped the philosopher continue his scholarly activity relatively unhampered, even preserving his right to publish.[11]

Exner and Liberal Catholicism's Triumph in Philosophy

After his dismissal from the university post in 1820 on suspicions of religious heterodoxy, Bolzano was free to pursue his research and writing as a private scholar, and his influence continued to spread.[12] It was at this time that he established contact with František Palacký, mainly through the Royal Bohemian Society of Sciences, of which he had been a member since 1815. For a number of years, Bolzano served as secretary of the mathematical section and, in 1843, as the society's director. Writing his famous history of Bohemia, Palacký consulted Bolzano on theological issues of the Bohemian Reformation, with which Bolzano, as a liberal Catholic, evidently sympathized.[13] Bolzano's disciples Fesl, Příhonský, and Anton Slivka remained active into the 1850s and in contact with Bolzano and each other.[14] Among his other students, Johann A. Zimmermann (1793–1869) and František Schneider (1797–1858) continued to teach religion and philosophy in secondary schools in the spirit of Reform Catholicism.[15] Bolzano even received a measure of support from the authorities of the state and the church, which were staffed by his former students. Remarkably, Vinzenz Fiebrich, a high official in the imperial police in Vienna, enabled him to publish his major works abroad in the 1830s.[16] Alois F. Schrenk, archbishop of Prague from 1838 to 1849, respected Bolzano as his own teacher and was himself a Catholic liberal.

The realist and cosmopolitan tenor of Bohemia's intellectual life, originally inspired by the Catholic Enlightenment, continued at the University of Prague even after Bolzano's dismissal. His first successor, as professor of philosophy, was his disciple, Příhonský (1788–1859), from 1819 to 1824.[17] Subsequently, Příhonský remained a friend of Bolzano when he was appointed head of the Sorbian Seminary (Lužický Seminář) in Prague (1824–39). After his own transfer as canon to Bautzen (Budyšín) in Saxon Lusatia, he surveyed Bolzano's *Wissenschaftslehre* (Theory of Knowledge) for criticism of Kant's epistemology in his *Neuer Anti-Kant*, published in Bautzen in 1850.[18] The line of Reform Catholicism continued through Příhonský's successor as head of the Sorbian Seminary (1839–48), František Náhlovský (1807–53), a devoted adherent of Bolzano's philosophy. He would become the leading spokesman for liberal Catholicism during the revolutionary years 1848–49.[19]

In the long run, the key successor to Bolzano as a teacher at the University of Prague was Professor Franz Exner (1802–53), who lectured there from 1831 to 1846. Also a consistent opponent of German idealism, especially that of Hegel, Exner initiated in Bohemia what would be the long-lasting vogue of the German philosopher Johann Herbart (1776–1841).[20] He saw the main task of philosophy as the clarification and rectification of concepts from the viewpoint of logical noncontradiction. Exner had been introduced to Herbart by his own teacher at the University of Vienna, Leopold Rembold (1786–1842), who, after an initial fascination with Friedrich Jacobi's critique of the Enlightenment, had become a champion of Herbart's anti-idealism.[21] Eventually, Exner was able to set the tone of philosophical education in the entire Habsburg monarchy. In 1848, he was summoned from Prague to the imperial Ministry of Education in Vienna and saw to it that Herbart's philosophy and pedagogical doctrines were adopted throughout the Austrian Empire.[22]

Like Bolzano, and Karl H. Seibt before him, Exner was a charismatic teacher for his university audiences, and a number of important intellectuals paid tribute to his influence. He substituted dialogues with his students for plain lecturing, raising the method of teaching to a higher level. He would frame major philosophical questions and encourage his students to think independently about them. He also spread his influence beyond the university walls to the established intellectual circles of Prague by holding informal seminars at his house. Participants included František Palacký, the historian Josef Linhart Knoll, the physicist J. C. Doppler, and the aristocratic member of Bolzano's circle, Count Leo Thun.[23] Among his star students was Karel Havlíček, who steeped himself in the ambience of Catholic Enlightenment by studying philosophy under Exner, and František Schneider, another of Bolzano's disciples. Havlíček was also familiar with the writings of Bolzano himself, whom he respected highly and was able to meet several times in his retirement retreat at the country estate of Těchobuz.[24] Other prominent Czech intellectuals like František Čupr and Václav Nebeský came to favor Herbart's philosophy as a result of Exner's influence.[25] In addition, Exner's students included the future philosophers Robert Zimmermann, Fridolin W. Volkmann, Gustav A. Lindner, Vilém Gabler, Ignác J. Hanuš, and Augustin Smetana; the writers Anton Springer, Karel H.

Mácha, Karel Sabina, and František Girgl; and the statesman František L. Rieger.[26] Exner's disciple and assistant Josef W. Nahlowsky continued to teach Herbart's philosophy at the University of Prague from 1845 to 1848.[27]

Exner, relying heavily on Herbart, taught philosophy in the spirit of Aristotelian realism and in opposition to German idealism,[28] thus continuing the realistic tradition that had originated in the Catholic Enlightenment. Herbart—although initially a pupil of Fichte—repudiated the subjective starting point of post-Kantian dialectical idealism and adopted the position of ontological realism.[29] Another criterion of distinction was that he stood for metaphysical pluralism, as opposed to the ontic monism of the German idealists.[30] Like Bolzano, he developed a realistic alternative to the philosophies of Kant, Fichte, Schelling, and Hegel, and his resistance to idealism and its method was grounded in a prior education in mathematics and physical sciences. Against Kant (who claimed that only the substance of experience is received while the form is produced subjectively) and Fichte (who claimed that the substance was also a product of the subject), Herbart held that the subject received both the form and the substance from the outside as "an expression of certain objective relations of the things in themselves."[31] Moreover, Herbart adhered to a cultural monism that was in harmony with Bolzano's universalist stand, denying that there were inherent cultural differences among nations.[32] Herbartism, therefore, was not in opposition to the realistic and cosmopolitan philosophy of the Austro-Bohemian Enlightenment but rather dovetailed with it.[33]

Thus, Exner's teaching and writing perpetuated the intellectual dominance of the Catholic Enlightenment as it had been consolidated by Bolzano's work and influence and stood for a belief in universal human culture, political utilitarianism, and liberal Catholic theology. He saw the advance of humankind as a single universal process from a primitive to an advanced state. Free from the ethnic attributes of ontic cultural pluralism, this view saw the historical process inspired by universal moral values that could be characterized as a pursuit of the Platonic trinity of goodness, truth, and beauty.[34] Like Bolzano, he applied utilitarian principle to political life: the objective of politics was the pursuit of happiness by individual citizens.[35]

As a champion of liberal Catholicism, Exner shifted the emphasis from discipline and dogma to moral aspirations and actions. The universal pursuit of moral improvement was inspired by God, as exemplified by the exhortations of the prophets of the Old Testament. Exner opposed thought control, because its effect was to distort the work of reason that was a God-given instrument for human advancement. Yet Exner remained within the bounds of Catholic orthodoxy. For him, it was wrong, indeed a foolishness (*Tollheit*), to assume that reason could function independently from God; no matter how much one could learn through reason, there was an area beyond its reach that provided a space for faith. If religious faith were abandoned, the void would be filled by superstition, as the absence of light is filled by darkness. According to Exner, true knowledge led to God, not away from him, and the existing age was fortunate to be an age of Christ.[36] The presence of different faiths in society required religious tolerance. The truth of any one faith should be supported by rational arguments, not by suppression of other religious denominations.[37]

Exner and German Idealism

As a disciple of Herbart, Exner also adopted a consistently critical attitude toward Hegel's teaching. In his principal study, *Die Psychologie der Hegelschen Schule* (1842), Exner based his analysis of Hegel's psychology on "Der Subjective Geist," a section in Hegel's *Enzyklopädie der philosophischen Wissenschaften*,[38] and the interpretation of this text by members of Hegel's school: Johann Karl Rosenkranz (in 1831), Karl Ludwig Michelet (in 1840), and Johann E. Erdmann (in 1840).[39] Since there was a great similarity between the three treatments, he focused mainly on the work of Rosenkranz. At the start, Exner insisted that the basic elements of psychology, as a field of knowledge, must be a clear and unambiguous description and explanation of mental states. Furthermore, these must not violate the principles of experience, such as the distinction between thought and perception.[40] According to Exner, this distinction was discarded by Rosenkranz's dictum that in perception "the spirit [was] in its immediate identity with nature"[41] or, more concretely, a thought was the negation of what was perceived; it was no longer separate from the perceived, but it became the perceived.[42]

Using the example of visual perception, Exner illustrated how Hegel and his followers conceived of the identity of spirit and nature. He referred to Hegel's view that the optical nerve, as an intermediate term between the spirit and the color, was in itself a spirit and that it was also the color, or at least a light, an inner organic light. Exner then quoted Hegel as saying that "only because the eye itself is light, can it see, and the dictum of Empedocles, that we perceive the light outside of us only through the light within us, is entirely correct." Exner suggested that this interpretation was utterly unacceptable to contemporary physicists or physiologists and worthy of the tricks of the fictitious comical hero Baron Münchhausen. According to Exner, a further extension of the Hegelians' argument was the proposition that we perceive the earth, the air, and the water outside of us, through the earth, the air, and the water within us.[43] On a more abstract level, Exner denounced the Hegelian mechanism of the identity between the perceiving subject and the object of perception. He labeled as unmitigated nonsense (*ein Knäuel von Unsinn*) the assertion that the object was a negation of the subject and that the subject, through its consciousness, negated the negation. According to Exner, if the objects were identical with the subject, as Hegel maintained, they could not contradict the subject; if they did so, as Hegel also maintained, then they could not be identical with the subject.[44]

Turning to group psychology, Exner was nonplussed and repelled by Hegel's insistence that to acquire their consciousness, nations needed to engage in bellicose encounters with other nations and that slavery was morally justifiable. In the latter case, the slaves were responsible for their own state of subjugation because they lacked sufficient pugnaciousness and thus were unworthy of freedom.[45] More broadly, Exner pilloried the rigidly collectivist approach of Hegel's school of philosophy to social entities, in which the spirit in its objectivity established the absolute criteria of right and wrong, which the subjective spirits—that is, each individual—in a given community (family, civil society, or the state) had to obey. For Exner, this abhorrent principle embodied the dictum "might is right" (*Macht ist Recht*).[46] The vagaries in application of the Hegelian dialectical method to human development were illustrated, for Exner, by Rosenkranz's approach to the question of race. According to Rosenkranz's dialectical trichotomy, the yellow race was a necessary negation of the black one, and the white race represented "a unity and truth" (*die Einheit und Wahrheit*) of the other two. Not surprisingly, Exner considered such an interpretation fanciful and arbitrary.[47] Likewise, he found the Hegelian definition of freedom a mere play on words, as a will that was neither determined nor undetermined but the truth of both types of will at the same time. In his opinion, an author who engaged in this type of reasoning in any other field of knowledge would be forever branded with the marks of "intellectual incapacity and shameless impudence." Indeed, the Hegelian school was largely responsible for the disrespect of most empirical scientists for philosophy.[48]

In his *Über Nominalismus und Realismus* (as *Abhandlungen der Königlichen bömischen Gesellschaft der Wissenschaften* for 1843), Exner once more opposed Hegel's identification of thought and being. He further pursued this theme in *Über die Lehre von der Einheit des Denkens und Seins*, which appeared as *Abhandlungen der Königlichen bömischen Gesellschaft der Wissenschaften* for 1847.[49] As was the case elsewhere, Exner contrasted the teaching of Herbart with that of the so-called Young Hegelians and the materialists. Thanks to Exner, Herbart's philosophy, which related to the tradition of Enlightenment realism, henceforth determined the tone of Czech academic philosophy.[50] Likewise, Bolzano's critical assessment of Hegel continued to be taught to students in Bohemia and Austria through the obligatory textbook *Philosophische Propädeutik* (1853), in which Robert Zimmermann presented the discipline of logic according to Bolzano's teaching (without mentioning his name).[51] The anti-Hegelian orientation also prevailed in academic philosophy in Bohemia among its German-language practitioners.[52]

Bolzano and Exner

From the viewpoint of the basic philosophical continuity from Bolzano to Exner, it is important to reemphasize that Exner did acknowledge his indebtedness to Bolzano, with whom he was in cordial personal contact soon after his own arrival in Prague in 1832.[53] Exner continued to maintain friendly relations with Bolzano, who advised his successor on how to defend himself against accusations of heterodoxy, particularly when Exner was requested to answer to Archbishop Schrenk for allegedly suggesting, in one of his university lectures, the eternity of creation.[54] In the 1830s, moreover, Exner shared with Bolzano an aversion to the Austrian Catholic romanticists under Anton Günther. Bolzano objected to Günther's followers, as he did to all who were affected by Kant and the subsequent idealism or by romanticism.[55] Both Bolzano and Exner defended the Austro-Bohemian Reform Catholicism of the Enlightenment era and its legacy of philosophical realism, which the Güntherianers challenged with their idealism.[56]

Bolzano remained linked with Exner and his successors by their uncompromising opposition to Hegel's philosophy. Exner privately supported Bolzano's continuing research, although he did not wish to publicly flaunt his relations with the officially tainted philosopher.[57] He was particularly helpful to Bolzano in clarifying concepts in his magnum opus, *Die Wissenschaftslehre*, which Bolzano had completed in manuscript by 1830 but kept revising thereafter before its publication in 1837.[58] Their disagreements on philosophical issues in the period of 1833–34 were minor, revolving mainly around the epistemological status of objectless ideas.[59] Another disputed point was Bolzano's insistence that simple ideas (*einfache Vorstellungen*) or perceptions (*Anschauungen*) can have only one real object.[60] Their differences thus remained within the shared realm of objective logic, or "moderate scientific rationalism," as Exner put it.[61] They gloried in their common opposition to German idealism.[62] Exner assured Bolzano, as early as December 1833, that Hegel, as well Schelling and Fichte, struck him as arbitrary and useless dreamers and that he found almost comical Hegel's readiness to reverse meanings of concepts contrary to the existing rules of logic.[63] In 1839, Bolzano objected to Fesl's insinuation that Exner was actually opposed to him.[64] Bolzano and Exner also shared a religious background in the Austro-Bohemian Catholic Enlightenment. This can be seen, for instance, in their common interest in the Dominican Pietro Maria Gazzaniga's four volumes of *Praelectiones theologicae* (1788–94), which affirmed Thomistic existentialism against Jesuit essentialism.[65] In agreement with Bolzano's ontic cultural universalism, Exner likewise rejected the Hegelian school's attempts to construct metaphysical bases for differentiation among races or nations.[66]

Bolzano himself indicated to Fesl that Exner virtually agreed with his own philosophical concepts and in particular accepted his teaching about "propositions" (*Sätze an sich*) and "truths" (*Wahrheiten an sich*),[67] although he preferred to call them "thoughts as such" (*Gedanken an sich*).[68] Bolzano, in turn, expressed his sympathy with Exner's philosophical endeavors and in particular in 1843 applauded Exner's determination to defend formal logic "against the attacks of Hegel, Schleiermacher and other formidable opponents."[69] In his letters to Fesl and Příhonský, Bolzano reiterated his high regard and sympathy for Exner, and he promoted professional contacts between Exner and his own pupils Johann A. Zimmermann and František Schneider. In 1841, he sponsored Exner's membership in the Royal Bohemian Society of Sciences, in which he served as secretary of the philosophical section.[70] Thus, assertions of Exner's hostility to Bolzano, and vice versa, are obviously wrong.

Bolzano and Herbart

Likewise, the promotion of Herbart's philosophy at the University of Prague by Exner and his disciples did not happen in opposition to Bolzano but in harmony with his teaching. Bolzano himself had been familiar with Herbart's writings at least since 1814 and was actively interested in them from that time on.[71] He also had been aware of the publication of Herbart's *Psychologie als Wissenschaft* in 1824[72] and commented on Herbart's theory of aesthetics as a branch of morality.[73] Above all, he pointed out the similarities in their philosophical approaches such as that between his and Herbart's epistemological proposition concerning the source of imagination (*Vorstellung*).[74] Bolzano added: "It seems to me that the difference between mine and his teaching in this matter rests in mere wording."[75] In this sense, in his correspondence with Exner in 1833, he claimed that Herbart's distinction between *Anschauungen* (perceptions) and *Begriffen* (concepts) was the same as his own between subjective and objective *Vorstellungen* (ideas).[76] His acknowledgment of agreement with Herbart in this area is particularly significant since the issue of epistemology lay at the heart of his critique of Kant and subsequent German idealism.[77] In the *Wissenschaftslehre,* he contrasted the clarity of Herbart's thought favorably with what he called the obscurantism of Fichte, Schelling, Hegel, and other idealists.[78] He referred to Herbart's *Lehrbuch zur Einleitung in die Philosophie* (1813) as profound (*tiefsinnig*).[79] Again in his manuscript "Ein Vorschlag zur Vermeidung vieler Missverständnisse in der Philosophie" (A Proposal for the Avoidance of Many Misunderstandings in Philosophy) (about 1839), he called Herbart "one of the most thoughtful and broadly educated philosophers."[80] He also noted Herbart's agreement with him that judgment involved more than just a state of mind but something objective like his own *Satz an sich* (proposition as such).[81] Hence, psychology played no role in logic.

Bolzano further pointed out that Herbart shared his view of the singularity of concepts, although the thought (*Denken*) of the same concept could be repeated many times.[82] According to him, they agreed that the same concept could not be simple at one time and complex at another.[83] In a case of an apparent disagreement with the "profound" Herbart, Bolzano observed courteously: "It is not my opinion that Herr Herbart would have answered this question affirmatively; therefore, I will rather assume that I did not understand him."[84] He spoke appreciatively of Herbart's definition of distinctions among "species" and "genus,"[85] and he considered Herbart's treatment of the concept of ideas in their subjective setting incomparably superior to Hegel's.[86] Bolzano likewise referred to Herbart's *Lehrbuch zur Psychologie* (Textbook of Psychology) in discussing the manner in which ideas (*Vorstellungen*) originated.[87] He found particularly ingenious, if not entirely convincing, the way Herbart explained the origin of the concepts of time and space.[88] Finally, he sought to amend Herbart's definition of philosophy as not just "processing and justifying of concepts for the use in cognition of factually given data" but also as "classifying their objective foundation."[89] Bolzano's wide-ranging interest in Herbart's teaching comes to light through his remark to Příhonský in 1837 that he owned several of Herbart's works, and the rest, as well as secondary works about the philosopher, he could borrow from Exner.[90]

The highpoint in the relationship between Bolzano and Herbart was an attempt to enlist Herbart in a grandiose assessment of Bolzano's philosophy.[91] In December 1838, Fesl had proposed the announcement of a prize in 1839 for an evaluation of Bolzano's philosophical and theological views, based mainly on the *Wissenschaftslehre*. The prize would be financed by Bolzano's publisher, and scholars such as Herbart, Christoph F. Ammon, professor of theology in Erlangen, and Benedikt A. Pflanzpastor in Moosheim would participate as judges.[92] Bolzano, in addition, suggested as members of the jury Friedrich E. Beneke of Berlin University; Immanuel H. Fichte, professor in Bonn and son of the famous philosopher; and Johann K. Rosenkranz, professor in Halle.[93] Herbart, however, failed to reply to the invitation, and the project was abandoned.[94] In any case, Herbart died two years later, but Bolzano's concern with his work continued. In 1841, he advised Příhonský on sources for a survey of Herbart's philosophy that the former was planning.[95] Robert Zimmermann claimed that Bolzano relied on Herbart's aesthetics in his own *Über den Begriff des Schönen* (On the Concept of Beauty) (1843).[96]

Although some critics would find Herbartism dull and tedious, others discerned that "the Herbartians made Czech thought more factual, sober, and precise and prepared the ground for a later positivism."[97] Other unfriendly critics have argued that pressure from the Austrian government was responsible for the demise of Kantian and Hegelian philosophy in the Habsburg monarchy. Catholic Austria was, in fact, conspicuously free from the influence of the German Protestant idealism of Kant, Hegel, Fichte, and Schelling, which came to occupy a central place in the intellectual life of Germany proper.[98] This line of argument viewed Herbartism as the philosophy favored by the rulers of the Austrian Empire because it could oppose not only German idealism but also the liberal Catholicism of Bolzano that was under suspicion for its alleged radicalism.[99] Two observations may be made with respect to these criticisms.

First, the charge that the Habsburg government forced Herbart's philosophy on the hapless Czechs in the nineteenth century in opposition to German idealism curiously parallels the charge that the Habsburg government had forced Utraquism on the Czechs in the sixteenth century in opposition to German Lutheranism. That charge simply dismisses the likelihood that the Czech intellectual leadership might have preferred Hus to Luther, or Herbart to Hegel. An argument for the genuine appeal of Herbart's philosophy was strongly developed by Josef Durdík in the late nineteenth century and recently by Josef Zumr.[100] The fact that in 1835 the Austrian imperial authorities removed from his professorship Exner's teacher and the first supporter of Herbart— Leopold Rembold—for excessive rationalism and for being a threat to religious faith diminishes the suspicion that Herbart's antiromanticism and anti-Hegelianism were coordinated with, or served the interests of, the backward-looking political philosophy of the Habsburg dynasty.[101]

Second, the claim that Herbart stands in opposition to Bolzano, as has often been made,[102] is discredited by the already mentioned close relationship of Bolzano and the coryphaeus of Herbart's philosophy, Exner.[103] Herbart's philosophical orientation paralleled rather than contradicted that of Bolzano. After Exner, Bolzano's philosophical teaching was carried on more directly into the mid-1850s by Robert Zimmermann (1824–98).[104] Zimmerman considered the differences between Bolzano and Herbart insignificant in the crucial area of logic.[105] In his inaugural lecture at the University of Prague in 1852, he, in fact, defined the Bohemian philosophical tradition as a line connecting Seibt, Bolzano, and Exner.[106] He taught at the University of Prague from 1852 to 1861 and then at the University of Vienna from 1861 to 1898. As noted earlier, Zimmermann's textbook *Philosophische Propädeutik*, first published in 1853, was based on Bolzano's concepts and subsequently used widely throughout the Austrian gymnasia.[107] In addition, Bolzano's own seminal textbook, *Beiträge zu einer begründeteren Darstellung der Mathematik* (1810),[108] was used by a whole student generation in Bohemian and Austrian universities and equipped them with solid instruction in logic and the philosophy of science. It prepared the ground for the spread of analytical philosophy in the school of Franz Brentano.[109] Interest in Bolzano's teaching would, in turn, receive another impetus from Brentano, whose influence further strengthened the adherence to realism and empirical philosophy at the universities of Vienna, Prague, and others in the Habsburg monarchy.[110] Otto Neurath, one of the founding fathers of the famed Vienna Circle, subsequently defined the Austrian line of philosophical progression as proceeding from Bolzano through Herbart to Brentano.[111]

Thus, the late flowering of the Catholic Enlightenment under Bolzano's direct disciples and Exner helped fortify the Czech attachment to Aristotelian realism and a corresponding aversion to the Platonic or Neo-Platonist modes of thought incarnated in German romanticism and metaphysical idealism. More important, as a part of the Austrian philosophical tradition, these developments in Bohemia would eventually lead—on a global scale—to the flourishing of logical positivism and analytical philosophy.[112]

Liberal Catholicism's Demise in Ecclesiology

While the Catholic Enlightenment established a legacy in the prevailing realistic tradition of philosophy in Bohemia, the story was entirely different in the sphere of ecclesiology. It is true that the champions of Josephist Reform Catholicism managed to survive the repressions of the 1820s through the 1840s to reemerge during the 1848 revolutionary period.[113] Bolzano himself felt encouraged by what were considered liberal pronouncements of the new Pope Pius IX from 1846 to early 1848.[114] On November 27, 1846, he wrote to Fesl that the new pope appeared "a very broadly educated, enlightened and well meaning man who—rara avis in terra (that is, in sede apostolica)—wishes for modern improvements."[115] The onset of the revolutionary events in Central Europe, triggered by the February Revolution of 1848 in France, initially escalated the hopes of ecclesiastical liberalization. On March 19, 1848, even Archbishop Alois Schrenck hinted at the church's renewed liberality by celebrating a mass in the main square in Prague for the success of Bohemian national aspirations.[116] Partly under Bolzano's influence, attempts were launched to reform the Roman ecclesiastical organization in Bohemia in the spirit of liberal Catholicism. Prominent among these proponents were the priest František Schneider and the journalist Havlíček.[117] Sympathizing with the reformist trend among the Catholic clergy in Prague during the spring of 1848, Havlíček put forward his own request for church reform on June 7, 1848, in the newspaper *Národní noviny*, which he edited.[118]

The active leadership of the reform movement was assumed by František Náhlovský, Bolzano's disciple in philosophy and theology, who organized a convocation of priests in the Sorbian Seminary in May 1848. The meeting celebrated Bolzano, Fesl, and Hurdálek as heroes. Proposals for liberalization included, among other things, participation of laity in ecclesiastical administration, local election of bishops and other dignitaries (with a high degree of autonomy from Rome), and the abolition of the requirement of priestly celibacy.[119] In economics, the demands were to lessen the differences in income between the bishops and the priests and to keep only those monasteries engaged in advanced education, while abolishing others as bastions of backwardness. These proposals echoed the eighteenth-century ecclesiastical reforms of Joseph II, as well as Bolzano's ideas in ecclesiology as expressed in his *Perfektabilität des Katholicismus* (Perfectability of Catholicism) (1845).[120]

At that point, however, the Bolzanists were challenged by the Catholic romanticists, or the Güntherianers. In particular, their newspaper, the *Wiener Kirchenzeitung*, launched an attack on Fesl as a proponent of state control over the church along the lines of Joseph II's ecclesiastical policy.[121] The Bolzanists, in turn, found the Güntherianers objectionable mainly on two grounds. First, their ultramontanism threatened to restore to full power the papal monarchy, which had been curbed by Joseph II's reforms. Second, the romanticist spirit exhibited a kinship with the mysticism of the baroque and was suspected of reviving "superstitions" of the earlier era, which Reform Catholicism had likewise sought to exorcise in the spirit of the Enlightenment.[122] Thus, the story of liberal Catholicism arrived at a peculiar conundrum, which, however, would be rendered irrelevant by Rome's post-1848 reaffirmation of the authoritarian ecclesiology. As early as June 1848, Náhlovský was removed from his post in the Sorbian Seminary by Bishop J. Dittrich and was temporarily replaced by Příhonský, who—to Bolzano's chagrin—had been too cautious to join Náhlovský's public call for ecclesiastical reforms.[123]

Any possibility of a rapport between Bohemian Utraquism (partially resurrected in Josephist Reform Catholicism) and the Roman Church would be terminated after 1848 with Rome's uncompromising turn to the past, which amounted to a virtual second Counter-Reformation in intent, if not in result.[124] In his statements on religious reform in 1850–51, Havlíček no longer expected much from the formal ecclesiastical organization and appealed to the reform-minded among the lower clergy to keep the idea of reform alive. His main targets were what he considered the haughtiness and low moral standard of the hierarchy and the harmfulness of enforced clerical celibacy.[125] In the 1870s, Jan Neruda, the Czech writer and poet, would ruefully reflect on the vanished species of Catholic clergy among the awakeners to whom, according to him, Prague was closer than Rome and the crown of Bohemia dearer than the papal tiara.[126]

The ultimate outcome of this disjunction was that the national awakening revived Utraquist liberal culture without Utraquism as a religion. By the late eighteenth century, however, patriotism provided a secular basis for national self-definition that made possible a separation of the cultural, political, and social aspects from the religious milieu that had originally nourished them. The political, social, and cultural values generated by the Bohemian Reformation could be revived without reviving its theological dimension.[127] While the effect of the liberal Reform Catholicism was doomed in the area of ecclesiology, the liberal tendency of the Austro-Bohemian Catholic Enlightenment continued into the nineteenth century and beyond in philosophy, where it was implanted, thanks especially to Bolzano. It did so in the form of realistic anti-idealistic philosophy, particularly that of Herbart. As the Catholic Enlightenment had philosophically dovetailed with the heritage of Bohemian Utraquism, so also Herbartism related harmoniously to Bolzano's logical realism.

Religious Void in Bohemia

On the one hand, this realistic and anti-idealistic trend reached its apogee in the Bohemian rejection of the philosophy of Georg Hegel, which enjoyed a widespread vogue elsewhere, mainly in the neighboring countries of Central and Eastern Europe.[128] On the other hand, the chances of reviving—under the aegis of Reform Catholicism—the theological heritage of Utraquism was doomed by the full-fledged suppression of liberal Catholicism in the ecclesiastical structure in 1848–49. The dream of the late eighteenth-century Catholic theologians—in particular Kašpar Royko, Václav Stach, Johann H. Wolf, and Augustin Zitte—would remain unrealized.[129] The contrast between a liberal political culture and an authoritarian church introduced a fundamental dichotomy, if not schizophrenia, into the intellectual life of Bohemia.[130]

As a result, the Bohemian Reformation was rehabilitated and celebrated as a revolt against intellectual coercion and as a rejection of intolerance but not in the religious substance of its traditional theology. Commentators, in particular Tomáš G. Masaryk, have noted this paradox in modern Czech political culture, which combined extolling the liberalism of the Bohemian Reformation with indifference to its religious content.[131] Masaryk blamed the young Czech liberals for this inconsistency.[132] While advancing secularism undoubtedly played a major role in promoting religious indifference, a difficulty was also posed by the theological centrism of the Bohemian Reformation. Once the liberal orientation was officially rejected by the Roman Church, the religious *via media* of the Bohemian Reformation lost the chance for an institutional sponsor. It could not find sympathy either from the tridentine Catholicism on the Right or from the Protestant churches on the Left. Thus, the Czechs lost a chance to recover their authentic religious past.

Epilogue: The Global Legacy of Bohemian Anti-Hegelianism

The Bohemian anti-Hegelianism of the early nineteenth century, which was based on the Bohemian Enlightenment and more remotely on the sixteenth-century Utraquist legacy, can be seen as the prime source of the Austrian philosophical tradition and, through it, of modern analytical philosophy. The Austrian tradition was marked by philosophical realism and an insistence on the empirical basis of all synthetic knowledge. Defined against the German philosophical tradition, the Austrian school rejected Kantianism with its concept of synthetic *a priori* truths and the subsequent German idealism as formulated by Fichte, Schelling, and Hegel.[1] Beyond a merely formal resemblance between modern analytical philosophy and Bernard Bolzano's logical realism, stemming from the Austro-Bohemian Enlightenment, there was actually a clear intellectual lineage from Bolzano to Otto Neurath, Alfred J. Ayer, and Willard V. Quine, although Bolzano had long been remembered in intellectual history mainly for his allied interest in mathematics, before his role as precursor of logical positivism became widely recognized.[2]

The important contribution of Bohemian thinkers to subsequent philosophical development was obscured in Czech historiography. Their anti-Hegelianism had been denounced as evidence of intellectual immaturity or lack of philosophical sophistication The attitude of the critics reflected the high respect for the attainment of philosophical idealism prevalent in Central and Eastern Europe.[3] Criticism of Bohemian anti-Hegelianism came from the Marxist side as well, inasmuch as Marx founded his own philosophy on Hegel, whom he viewed as the ultimate word in previous philosophical development. Marx insisted that Hegel's doctrines—standing on their head—merely needed to be set on their feet to become the foundation of his own dialectical materialism.[4] The Leninist aversion to the Austrian school was then canonized by Lenin's anathema of Ernst Mach and his "empirio-criticism," which—prior to the Vienna Circle—was considered the last word on the Austrian philosophical school.[5]

The Austrian School and Analytical Philosophy

Three leitmotifs connected the late Austro-Bohemian Enlightenment in the early nineteenth century and the emergence of analytical philosophy in the mid-twentieth. The first was the repeated episodes of Bolzano's influence. The second was the opposition to metaphysical idealism, particularly to Hegel's teaching. The third and rather discreet connection was the legacy of the Catholic character of the Austro-Bohemian Enlightenment, which involved the reaching out of Catholic Neo-Thomists to the logical positivists, on the one hand, and the reaching out, by the latter, to the scholastic philosophy, on the other.

The first phase of Bolzano's direct influence has already been discussed at length in chapter 11. As noted, the realistic, empirical, and individualist Aristotelian approach to philosophy launched by Bolzano continued at the universities of Prague and Vienna under his associates Franz Exner and Robert Zimmermann.[6] The second phase of Bolzano's influence received a major boost at the University of Vienna from Franz Brentano, who taught there from 1874 to 1895.[7] Originally a Catholic theologian, Brentano turned lay professor of philosophy, showing his allegiance to Bolzano's concepts in his lecture course on logic during the 1880s.[8] Like Bolzano, he was an empiricist in the Aristotelian sense, who claimed that "nothing is in the intellect which is not previously in the senses."[9] Like Bolzano before him, Brentano considered Kant's epistemological system entirely misguided. According to him, Kant's concepts of *"a priori"* and "synthetic judgment" could not withstand even elementary criticism. Moreover, in postulating the unknowability of the "thing in itself," Kant was, in effect, imposing a fanciful barrier to the expansion of human knowledge.[10] In addition, Brentano's methods for language analysis were, to a considerable extent, similar to those employed by English philosophers at the start of the twentieth century.[11] Under his guidance, Austrian universities became bastions against philosophical idealism.[12]

Brentano's disciples—Anton Marty, Alexius Meinong, Kazimierz Twardowski, and Carl Stumpf—developed some of their own philosophical views under the impact of Bolzano's *Wissenschaftslehre* (Theory of Knowledge).[13] Aside from Brentano's teaching, their familiarity with Bolzano's ideas stemmed from Zimmermann's textbook, *Philosophische Propädeutik*, generally used in the academic secondary schools (gymnasia) of the Austrian Empire.[14] Twardowski (1866–1938) later served as professor of philosophy at the University of L'viv (then Lwów or Lemberg) from 1895 to 1930. As an empiricist in the Austrian philosophical tradition, he thus became its representative in that section of the Polish area that tellingly had formed a part of the Habsburg monarchy.[15] Among Brentano's other distinguished students, Edmund Husserl developed the initiatives, originating from Bolzano's work, in a different direction from the mainstream logical positivists of the later Vienna Circle—namely, toward phenomenalism.[16] Husserl paid the highest tribute to Bolzano in his *Logical Investigations,* first published in 1900–1901, calling Bolzano's *Wissenschaftslehre* "a work which in its treatment of the logical 'theory of elements,' far surpasses everything that world-literature has to offer." Furthermore, he defined the excellence of Bolzano's achievement by contrasting it with the flaws of German idealism: "Of the ambiguous profundity of that systematic philosophy, which rather aimed at thinking out world-conceptions and a world-wisdom, and which hindered the progress of scientific philosophy so badly by unholy blend of discordant intentions, Bolzano—the contemporary of Hegel—shows no trace."[17] Husserl also claimed that his own *Logical Investigations* had received a "crucial" stimulus from Bolzano's work.[18]

Eventually, the Austrian school of philosophy forged an alliance with philosophy in England. It was particularly at Cambridge, where, under the guidance of Bertrand Russell and George E. Moore, the return to the British empirical tradition became pronounced after the turn of the nineteenth century.[19] Some date the emergence of analytical philosophy to Ludwig Wittgenstein's arrival from Austria to Cambridge to study with Russell in 1912.[20] Just like Bolzano and Brentano before them, Moore and Russell defined their empirical and analytical positions in contrast to the Hegelian speculative and metaphysical tradition as it was represented at that time in Britain by the idealist school connected with Thomas H. Green (1836–82), Francis H. Bradley (1846–1924), and Bernard Bosanquet (1848–1923). Moore's and Russell's stance involved "a wholesale rejection, for example, of the doctrine of 'internal relations' and of 'organic wholes,' of knowledge considered as 'synthesis' or dialectic, and of reality conceived as fundamentally monistic, one and absolute."[21] The third phase of Bolzano's influence was manifest in the Vienna Circle and related groups. The original logical positivists gathered in the Vienna Circle under Moritz Schlick at the university in 1929 and included Rudolf Carnap, Herbert Feigl, Kurt Gödel, Hans Hahn, Karl Menger, Otto Neurath, and Friedrich Waismann. Another center was in the Society for Empirical Philosophy of Berlin (*Berliner Gesellschaft für Empirische Philosophie*), gathered around Hans Reichenbach in 1926, which included Walter Dubislav, Kurt Grelling, and Carl Hempel. Although not formally members of either group, Wittgenstein and another Austrian philosopher, Karl Popper, were at times closely associated with logical positivism.[22] Also the L'viv-Warsaw school of logical analysis, founded by Twardowski, maintained as a whole and through its individual members, particularly Alfred Tarski, close contacts with the Vienna Circle.[23] The founding manifesto of the Vienna Circle traced the lineage of logical positivism explicitly to Bolzano.[24] Bolzano's name was frequently mentioned by speakers at the major meeting that was organized by the logical positivists, the First International Congress for the Unity of Science, held in Paris in 1935.[25]

There is also the testimony of Ayer, the British philosopher, from the 1930s that the Vienna Circle looked back at Bolzano as a revered precursor.[26] A link to British and American analytical philosophy was forged even then. Both Ayer and Quine, who studied in Austria in 1933, participated in the meetings of the Vienna Circle.[27] Ayer henceforth considered himself an apostle of logical positivism to Britain, although his radically empiricist ideas, based mainly on Hume and Russell and the reading of Wittgenstein, predated his encounter with the Vienna Circle. Ayer, however, credited his Oxford tutor, Gilbert Ryle, with having encouraged his interest in the Vienna Circle even then.[28] As early as the fall of 1933, Ayer announced that he would be teaching a course at Oxford on philosophical analysis, which covered, in addition to Russell and Wittgenstein, the writings of Carnap, who then taught at the German Charles University (Karls-Universtät) of Prague.[29] The Austrian logical positivists combined two philosophical traditions: the positivistic-empirical and the logical. While Comte and the American pragmatists had rejected metaphysics as useless or superfluous, the logical positivists went further by claiming that the propositions of metaphysics were, strictly speaking, meaningless.[30] Carnap specifically mentioned Hegel's system and those of Fichte, Schelling, Bergson, and Heidegger as examples of meaningless metaphysics.[31] He targeted Hegel by pointing out Hegel's statement that "pure Being and pure Nothing, therefore, are one and the same" as nonesense, and he criticized Heidegger for adopting "many peculiarities of the Hegelian idiom along with their logical faults."[32] According to Carnap, Hegel's teaching and other metaphysical systems, in the light of the new logic, proved themselves "to be not merely materially false, as earlier critics maintained, but logically untenable and therefore meaningless."[33] As a young disciple of Austrian logical positivism, Ayer wrote in a similar vein in an article of 1934. He maintained that if metaphysics claimed that it was concerned with reality beyond empirical experience, then it affirmed, by its own admission, that all its assertions were senseless. He therefore concluded that "it [was] not necessary to take a list of metaphysical terms such as the Absolute, the Unconditioned, the Ego and so forth, and prove each of them to be meaningless."[34] In discussing the relationship between logical positivism and analytical philosophy, Rudolf Haller, the contemporary historian of philosophy, highlighted the role of the Vienna Circle in banishing "the Central European obscurantism of Hegelian-Marxist derivation."[35]

A notable link to the primeval origins of analytical philosophy in the Catholic Enlightenment—and in a way, a closing of the circle—was the interest of a group of Neo-Thomists, particularly in France under Charles Ernest Vouillemin, in logical positivism. Thus logical positivism, which had its roots in the Catholic Enlightenment of Austria, found recognition in the Catholic liberalism of the mid-twentieth century. It was in a way a reprise of the connection between the early anti-Hegelianism and the liberal Catholicism represented by Bolzano and Exner and later by Brentano. Although the logical positivists were not inclined to support theological propositions any more than metaphysical ones,[36] their school could serve as an ally against German idealism.[37] It could annihilate the philosophical obstacles that had interfered with an unencumbered consideration of theology. By clearing the jungle of the secularized supernatural that idealism presented in its metaphysical constructs (such as Schelling's and Hegel's pantheism), logical positivism, so to say, opened the space for the consideration of the theological supernatural on its own merits.[38] Moreover, to Vouillemin—relying mainly on Carnap's epistemology—the concept of "notion" and "being" according to "logical empiricism," which cleared away all *a priori* preconceptions, was perfectly consistent with "Christian realism."[39] Jacques Maritain similarly praised logical positivism for its ability to "disontologize science," thus opening up the door for other types of (in his view) legitimate ontic explorations.[40]

At the other side of the ledger, the Vienna Circle was significantly influenced by the French Neo-Thomist Pierre M. M. Duhem (1861–1916), a philosopher and physicist. According to Philipp Frank, Duhem's stern effort to purge the scientific approach to knowledge of any tinge of metaphysics was considered a most valuable contribution to the new positivism. In particular, Ernst Mach endorsed him most warmly.[41] Moreover, the logical positivists looking for their own distant intellectual ancestors tended to point to the medieval scholastics, in contrast to early Lutheran theologians. Already the founding manifesto of the Vienna Circle had called attention to Brentano's background in scholastic theology, which was credited with his emphasis on logical rigor and with having forearmed him against "Kant and the systematic idealist philosophers."[42]

Along these lines, later in 1933 Otto Neurath praised the theological and philosophical system of the Roman Church for subverting the premises of idealist metaphysics and facilitating a shift to logical empiricism.[43] He maintained that, in particular, a direct road led to logical positivism from late medieval nominalism, from William of Ockham at Oxford to Russell at Cambridge.[44] According to Neurath, the empirical and logical trend, partly rooted in scholasticism, flourished in Habsburg Austria under Catholic auspices, often thanks to philosophers with clerical background—Bolzano first and after him Brentano. This trend contradicted the work of great system-making from Kant to Hegel that had prevailed in most of Germany. Protestantism blurred the line between theology and philosophy and found it easier to transpose metaphysical speculation from theology to social relations and problems.[45] According to Neurath, the main lines of development in Catholicism led from Ockham to logical positivism, in Protestantism from Luther to German idealism.

In agreement with Neurath's interpretation, Brentano even after his formal break with Christianity preserved a high esteem for the philosophical tradition of the Catholic Church and also retained a distaste for Protestantism, as well as for the politics of Protestant Prussia exemplified by Bismarck.[46] His thorough knowledge of scholastic philosophy, especially that of Thomas Aquinas, is attested to by his star disciple and later colleague, Carl Stumpf.[47] Stumpf himself, as a student in the Catholic Seminary of Würzburg in the late 1860s, had received a firm grounding in Aquinas and the Scholastics.[48]

In a development parallel to the interest of French Neo-Thomists in the epistemology of the Vienna Circle, German Catholic philosophers sought to establish a relationship between the Aristotelian realistic tradition and Husserl's school of the phenomenologists in order to enlist phenomenology as an ally against the prevalent German idealism.[49] Somewhat whimsically, the Vienna Circle was seen as linked to medieval scholasticism not only through Brentano's teaching but also through "the method of a communal philosophical argument" that Brentano shared with medieval scholastics, and that Schlick practiced in the Thursday evening discussions of the Vienna Circle, and that even Wittgenstein entered into with an entourage in his "cell in Cambridge."[50]

The Prague Connection

Even after the era of Bolzano, Bohemia continued to play a significant role in the development of the philosophical empiricism that eventually led to the flourishing of analytical philosophy. Some of the prominent members of the Austrian school of philosophy were German-writing philosophers who lived and worked in Bohemia. Mach, one of the spiritual ancestors of the logical positivism of the Vienna school (and Vladimir Lenin's notorious *bête noire*), taught at the University of Prague from 1867 to 1895. If, as specified by Otto Neurath, the main line in the process of defining the Austrian opposition to Kantianism and metaphysical idealism proceeded from Bolzano through Herbart and Brentano,[51] then the University of Prague supplied an important link, inasmuch as the ideas of Herbart and Brentano dominated the teaching of philosophy there.

After the division of the Charles University of Prague (Universitas Carolina) into two institutions in 1882, Herbart's philosophy continued to prevail at the Czech Charles University (Univerzita Karlova) and Brentano's at its German counterpart. The followers of Brentano at the German Charles University (Karls-Universität) included Stumpf (1848–1936) and Anton Marty (1847–1914), who taught in Prague from 1879 to 1884 and from 1880 to 1914, respectively.[52] In addition, Otto Philip

Willmann (1839–1920) lectured on philosophy at the German university, according to Herbart, from 1882 to 1903.[53] At the Czech university, the Herbart tradition, established by Exner and Zimmermann, culminated in the work of their disciple Josef Durdík (1837–1902), who had an allied interest in modern British and French philosophy, especially Comte's positivism.[54]

As the key opponent of German idealism in the Czech University of Prague, Durdík characterized Herbart as an advocate of realism, pluralism, individualism, and nominalism in philosophy[55] and as one who, in contrast to Hegel's obscurantism and national exclusivity, expressed himself in normal language and whose outlook was cosmopolitan.[56] According to Durdík, Hegel had raised national intolerance and assertiveness to the level of a philosophical system by teaching that in any given historical epoch there was only one "chosen" nation in which the world spirit was incarnated.[57] He thus violated the spirit of philosophy, which should have a wider applicability than the focus on just one nation. Durdík pointed out that Hegel's philosophy was also inappropriate for natural science, where his dialectical method in particular proved useless.[58] Superficially, its schemata might appear useful in social science, but even there it was preferable not to force the narrative into preestablished patterns. Hegel's national exclusivity also affected his theory of aesthetics, which was applicable to romanticism at most. National limitation was evident even in Hegel's style of expression, where certain statements were untranslatable from German into other languages.[59] Not only idealism but also its spin-offs in the form of Schopenhauer's or Eduard von Hartmann's pessimism had failed to produce a clarity of thought that was the purpose of philosophy.[60] If it were claimed that Hegel's philosophy was the ultimate system, it would merely mean that it stood at the end of a forlorn line of previous mystical indulgences.[61]

According to Durdík, Herbart's philosophy, in contrast to that of Hegel and his followers, had an international global scope; it was valid for all of humankind. It was an expression of intellect that sought rational precision, unbounded by national distinctions.[62] Czech philosophy was fortunate to have embraced Herbart's realistic orientation at the start and avoided the pitfalls of Schelling and Hegel, as well as the subsequent pessimism prevalent in much of German philosophy in the second half of the nineteenth century.[63] Against insinuations that Herbart's philosophy was implanted forcibly in the Habsburg Empire by the imperial government in the post-Napoleonic restoration era (*Vormärz*, 1815–48), Durdík pointed out that Herbartism had proved its own worth in the latter part of the nineteenth century by flourishing on its own.[64]

Other professors who taught philosophy at the University of Prague (before and after its division in 1882) adopted Herbart's philosophical positions in a determined resistance to speculative idealism, particularly in its Hegelian version. They included disciples of Exner, such as Josef Dastich (1835–70), Fridolin Wilhelm Volkmann (1821–77), and Gustav A. Lindner (1828–87), as well as professor of aesthetics Otakar Hostinský (1847–1910), who was himself a disciple of Volkmann.[65] Thus, evidently suiting the Austrian and particularly the Bohemian mind, Herbart's empirical realism dominated philosophy at the University of Prague for seventy years from Exner through Zimmermann to Durdík.[66] The roots of the empirical and realistic tradition, as Durdík also pointed out, went back to Bolzano and eventually to Seibt.[67]

The vogue of Herbartism also created an affinity between the University of Prague and an exceptional bastion of philosophical realism in the German Empire—the University of Leipzig. There the philosophical faculty in the latter part of the nineteenth century was critical of metaphysics, abhorred idealism, and endorsed empiricism. For Prague philosophers, the main figure of attraction at the University of Leipzig was Gustav T. Fechner (1801–87), professor of philosophy and psychology. Young Tomáš G. Masaryk, an early disciple of Brentano, was drawn to him during his own studies at the University of Leipzig in 1876–78,[68] and Lindner popularized Fechner's theories in his *Textbook of Empirical Psychology*, which was used in classes of philosophy in the Austrian gymnasia.[69]

The next generation of Brentano's disciples at the German University of Prague was represented by Oskar Kraus (1872–1942), who established the Brentano Society and the Brentano Archives in Prague.[70] The philosophical interest of Hugo Bergmann's (1883–1975) combined the studies of Brentano and Bolzano before his departure for Jerusalem in 1920. While in Prague, he involved Franz Kafka in the Brentanist discussion group. Kraus deplored the continued sway of idealism in German universities in the twentieth century, inasmuch as the "scientific" character of Schelling's thought and the validity of Hegel's dialectic had been discredited in the previous century.[71] Masaryk, as a professor of philosophy at the Czech University of Prague since 1882, established a friendly rapport with Marty and Stumpf. Although he was firmly rooted in the Austrian philosophical tradition, his own attachment to Brentano's philosophy was not so rigorous as Marty's and Stumpf's.[72] Masaryk also supported the younger generation of Brentano's pupils who taught in Prague, particularly Kraus and Christian Ehrenfels (1850–1932). Among other disciples of Brentano with whom he had studied in Vienna, Masaryk maintained contact with Alexius Meinong, professor at the University of Graz.[73]

It may be noted that opposition to Hegel's teaching in Bohemia was not limited to philosophy but also encompassed the social sciences. The political theorist at the law school of the Czech University of Prague, František Weyr (1879–1951), comments in his memoirs that he considered Hegel's political and legal philosophy a primary source of the modern political systems that elevate the concept of comprehensive collectivism at the expense of the individual.[74] Parenthetically, it may also be noted that the anti-idealist tradition at the University of Prague in the 1920s and 1930s led to a significant later contribution in aesthetics, particularly the theory of literature, thanks to Herbartian objectivism. Czech aesthetics, developed by the Prague Linguistic Circle and epitomized by Roman Jakobson and Jan Mukařovský, could become "richly psychological without falling into the trap of subjectivism or into metaphysical speculation."[75]

Turning to logical positivism, a link with the Vienna school continued in Prague from 1931 with the appointment of Carnap to a philosophy professorship in the German university. Carnap still cooperated with Neurath and Hahn in publishing the series *Einheitswissenschaft* and with Reichenbach of the Berlin Society in publishing the journal *Erkenntnis*. Carnap developed the case against metaphysics at the time of his arrival in Prague in his *Elimination of Metaphysics through Logical Analysis of Language*.[76] He also provided a bridge to American analytical philosophy as a teacher of Quine (1908–2000) of Harvard and Charles W. Morris (1901–79) of the University of Chicago.[77] During his study tour of Europe in 1933, Quine found Prague, after Vienna, the most stimulating place for the study of logical positivism.[78] Even earlier, the American philosophical community had become aware of the work of the Vienna Circle, which had close ties with the academia of Bohemia.[79] This became evident when the preparatory preconference (*Vorkonferenz*) for the worldwide gathering of logical positivists, the First International Congress for the Unity of Science, in Paris in 1935, had been held in Prague a year earlier.[80] Moreover, Dubislav (1895–1937), the last chairman of the Society for Empirical Philosophy of Berlin, sought refuge from Nazi persecution in Prague in 1936.[81]

Thus, after the annexation of Austria by Germany, Bohemia briefly became heir to the Austrian philosophical tradition that had been suppressed by the Nazis in Austria itself. Bohemia, in turn, served as a significant transit point of this tradition to Western Europe and the United States. After suppression in Germany, Austria,[82] and Bohemia by the Nazi regime—which fiercely, even lethally, disliked logical positivism[83]—many of the opponents of metaphysical idealism found refuge in English-speaking countries. Of the Bohemian contingent, Kraus left for England in 1939 and Carnap for the United States in 1936. Kraus died at Oxford in 1942; Carnap continued teaching in the United States until his retirement in 1961. Hans Reichenbach, founder of the Berlin Society for Empirical Philosophy, followed Carnap to the United States in 1938.[84] Logical positivism found a receptive audience within the pragmatic, empirical, and logically minded philosophical context represented by Ernst Nagel and Carnap's disciples, Quine and Morris. Carnap later commented on the philosophical situation in the United States upon his arrival in 1936: "The movement of German Idealism, in particular Hegelianism . . . had by then almost completely disappeared. . . . Thus I found in this country a philosophical atmosphere which, in striking contrast to that in Germany, was very congenial to me."[85] Transplanted into the Anglophone world, "analytic philosophy" exerted a powerful influence, particularly in the United States.[86] In the English-speaking countries, analytical philosophy continued its sway under the guise of symbolic logic, theory of descriptions, and linguistic analysis.[87] As Peter Hylton has maintained, if analytical philosophy is "taken broadly, as including both those who define themselves in opposition to [it] and those who see themselves as modifying [it], the tradition has been and continues to be dominant in the leading English-speaking universities."[88] Indeed, analytical philosophy after 1950 attained a global status and has been cultivated outside the Western world, particularly in Japan but also in Russia, China, India, Latin America, and Africa.[89]

Returning to the Bohemian national awakening, we can view retrospectively the intellectuals who were inspired by Bolzano and Exner as respectable or—if one wishes—"progressive" thinkers, in line with the evolving Austrian school of philosophy and anticipating the flourishing of analytical philosophy in the Anglophone world and elsewhere. In a way, they were intellectually ahead of their times, despite (or perhaps because of) their association with the Catholic Enlightenment of Austria. In their aversion to Hegelianism in particular and German idealism in general, the Bohemian philosophers and public intellectuals of the 1830s and 1840s (such as J. Fidrmuc, Vilém Gabler, Vendelín Grünwald, Karel Havlíček, Karel F. Hyna, Marek, Václav B. Nebeský, Karel B. Štorch, Václav V. Tomek, Karel A. Vinařický, and Vincenc Zahradník)[90] can also be viewed, with their commitment to common sense, in a variant of František Šmahel's apt phrase, as logical positivists and analytical philosophers before logical positivism and analytical philosophy existed.[91] In fact, as noted earlier, their teacher, Bolzano, has been commonly considered one of the forefathers of the Vienna Circle.[92] As the leaders of the Catholic Enlightenment in Bohemia could look at the Utraquist intellectuals as their precursors, so could the analytical philosophers of the early twenty-first century view the anti-Hegelians of the national awakening.

In addition, the rejection of Hegel by the early nineteenth-century Czechs in the name of liberal Catholicism can also be seen as a parallel to the rejection of Luther by the sixteenth-century Bohemians in the name of Utraquism, the values of which the Enlightenment revived in the intellectual circles of Bohemia. The rejection of Hegel's views, like the earlier rejection of those of Luther, was not based on their Teutonic origin but on a conviction of their erroneous and irrational character. Their choice made a difference to the subsequent development of Czech political culture. As pointed out in the introduction, the distinction between the Austrian and the German philosophical traditions, moreover, places the Bohemian case into a wider Central European, and (by extension) Euro-Atlantic, context and the Bohemian case study helps illuminate the character of the entire paradigm.

Local Legacy of Anti-Hegelianism: Bohemia's Political Culture

Relating to the toleration, universalism, and plebeianism of the sixteenth-century Golden Age (which stemmed from the Bohemian Reformation),[93] the national awakening revived these values and merged them with the ideals of the Austro-Bohemian Catholic Enlightenment in the formation of the modern Czech political culture. Employing the criteria of the Enlightenment, philosophical realism, and universalism, on one hand, and romanticism, idealism, and nationalism, on the other, Bohemia's political culture belonged to the former rather than to the latter. The preponderant influence came from Seibt, not Herder; from Bolzano and Herbart, not Hegel; and later from Brentano, not Nietzsche. In other words, Czech political culture moved along the trajectory of the Austrian, not the German, philosophical tradition. The impact of the Catholic Enlightenment and the related Austrian Reform Catholicism, instead of the Lutheran-based German romanticism and idealism, was not due only to the constellation of existing political and cultural circumstances. It is the argument of this book that the choice also related to its consonance with the echoes of Bohemia's historical tradition, stemming consciously from the Bohemian Reformation.[94]

The dichotomy within this choice was a local Bohemian illustration of what at a higher level constituted a general European, if not universal, tendency of contrast between existence and essence, realism and idealism, universalism and particularism, and individualism and collectivism. At the same time, the choice was made deliberately by the intellectual leaders of the national awakening, not dictated either by a primordial character or by a metaphysical essence of the nation.

As a result, the Czech national awakening embraced, on the one hand, the idea of a monistic culture, one of universal validity for all of humankind, as opposed to the cultural particularism governing the Herderian-Hegelian philosophy of history that postulated an essentialist separateness of nations. On the other hand, the Bohemians adhered to an ontic pluralism of being, which served as a philosophical underpinning for individualism in political and social relations, in contrast to the tendency toward highlighting collective social interests in the Herderian-Hegelian approach, based on the idea of a metaphysical unity of being. The outcome was a cultural monism combined with ontic pluralism, in other words, a cosmopolitan culture with political and social individualism. Cultural monism served as a protection against xenophobia; ontic pluralism, as a protection against utopian dreams. This correlation may shed light on the often noted fact, pointed out in the introduction to this volume, of the exceptional tenacity of liberal democracy in Czechoslovakia, which retained a democratic form of government even in 1918–38, while its neighbors adopted authoritarianism, if not totalitarianism.

Appendix: Philosophy Professors at the Charles University (Universitas Carolina) of Prague

Prior to the University's Division, 1753–1882

Josef Stepling, 1753–62 (1716–78)[1]
Karl Heinich Seibt, 1763–1801 (1735–1806)
August Gottlieb Meissner, 1785–1804 (1753–1807)
František X. Němeček, 1802–20 (1766–1849)
Bernard Bolzano (in the Department of Religion), 1804–20 (1781–1848)
Alois Klar, 1806–33 (1763–1833)
Josef Georg Meinert, 1806–11 (1773–1844)
František Příhonský, 1820–24 (1788–1859)
Anton F. Spirk, 1823–26 (1787–1847)
Johann Peithner von Lichtenfels, 1826–31 (1793–1868)
Franz Exner, 1831–48 (1802–53)
Joseph Wilhelm Nahlowsky, 1848–50 (1812–85)
František Čupr, 1848–50 (1821–82)
Ignác Jan Hanuš, 1849–52 (1812–69)
Hermann Karl Leonhardi, 1849–75 (1809–75)
Robert Zimmermann, 1852–61 (1824–98)
Fridolin Wilhelm Volkmann, 1856–77 (1821–77)
Josef Dastich, 1861–70 (1835–70)

A note on the sources: Information for this appendix is drawn from *Slovník českých filozofů*, ed, Jiří Gabriel (Brno: Masarykova Univiverzita, 1998); *Dějiny Univerzity Karlovy, 1348–1990,* ed. František Kavka and Josef Petráň, 4 vols. (Prague: Karolinum, 1995–98); *Personalstand der Deutschen Universität in Prag zur Anfang des Studienjahres* (Prague: Der Akademische Senat, 1906/07–1925/26); Jan Zouhar, Helena Pavlincová, and Jiří Gabriel, *Demokracie je diskuse . . . : Česká filosofie, 1918–1938* (Olomouc: Nakladatelství Olomouc, 2005).

Ernst Mach, 1867–82 (1838–1916)
Josef Durdík, 1869–82 (1837–1902)
Otto Philip Willmann, 1872–82 (1839–1920)
Carl Stumpf, 1879–82 (1848–1936)
Anton Marty, 1880–82 (1847–1914)

Czech University (Univerzita Karlova), 1882–1939[2]

Josef Durdík, 1882–1902 (1837–1902)
Gustav A. Lindner, 1882–87 (1828–87)
Tomáš G. Masaryk, 1882–1914 (1850–1937)
Otakar Hostinský, 1883–1910 (1847–1910)
František Drtina, 1891–1925 (1861–1925)
František Čáda, 1896–1918 (1855–1918)
František Krejčí, 1898–1928 (1858–1934)
Emanuel Rádl, 1904–39 (1873–1942)
Josef Král 1920–24, 1932–39 (1882–1978)
Karel Vorovka, 1921–29 (1879–1929)
Vladimír Hoppe, 1922–27 (1882–1931)
Jan B. Kozák, 1927–39 (1888–1974)
Ferdinand Pelikán, 1929–39 (1885–1952)
Ladislav Rieger, 1931–39 (1890–1958)
Albína Dratvová, 1932–39 (1882–1969)
Jan Patočka, 1936–39 (1907–77)
Josef Beneš, 1938–39 (1901–70)

German University (Karls-Universtät), 1882–1939

Carl Stumpf, 1882–84 (1848–1936)
Ernst Mach, 1882–95 (1838–1916)
Otto Philip Willmann, 1882–1903 (1839–1920)
Anton Marty, 1882–1914 (1847–1914)
Friedrich Jodl, 1885–96 (1849–1914)
Christian von Ehrenfels, 1896–1929 (1850–1932)
Alfred Kastil, 1902–9 (1874–1950)
Josef Eisenmeyer, 1906–26 (1871–1926)
Samuel Hugo Bergmann (in the university library), 1909–20 (1883–1975)
Oskar Kraus, 1916–39 (1874–1942)
Rudolf Carnap, 1929–35 (1891–1970)
Emil Utitz, 1934–39 (1883–1956)

Notes

Chapter 1

1. The term was favored by Josef Dobrovský: "das schöne oder goldene Zeitalter der böhmischen Sprache." See Josef Dobrovský, *Dějiny české řeči a literatury v redakcích z roku 1791, 1792 a 1818*, ed. Benjamin Jedlička (Prague: Melantrich, 1936), 46. See also Jan Mukařovský, ed., *Dějiny české literatury* (Prague: Nakladatelství Československé akademie věd, 1959–95), 2:114; Josef J. Jungmann, *Historie literatury české*, 2d ed. (Prague: Řivnáč, 1849), 125.

2. An odd case is Josef Haubelt, who was considered a hard-core Marxist-Leninist; yet his book on the Enlightenment in Bohemia was republished in 2004 only with omissions of quotations from Marx and Lenin; see Josef Haubelt, *České osvícenství*. 2nd rev. ed. (Prague: Rodiče, 2004); 1st ed. (Prague: Svoboda, 1986).

3. Klement Gottwald, "Znachenie tvorchestva Aloiza Iraseka," in his *Izbrannye proizvedeniia* (Moscow: Gos. Izdatel'stvo politicheskoi literatury, 1957), 2:279–80.

4. Earlier post–World War II works—Albert Pražák, *České obrození* (Prague: E. Beaufort, 1948) and Felix Vodička, *Cesty a cíle obrozenské literatury* (Prague: Československý spisovatel, 1958)—are not synthetic monographs but loose collections of essays on specific topics. Their focus is almost entirely on literary history.

5. Josef Kočí, *České národní obrození* (Prague: Svoboda, 1978), especially pages 5, 24–66. See also Aleksandr S. Myl'nikov, *Epokha Prosveshcheniia v cheshskikh zemliakh: Ideologiia, natsional'noe samosoznanie, kul'tura* (Moscow: Nauka, 1977), 349.

6. Kočí, *České národní obrození*, 450.

7. Antonín Robek, *Lidové zdroje národního obrození*, Acta Universitatis Carolinae, Philosophica et historica, Monographia, 48 (Prague: Univerzita Karlova, 1974), 8.

8. Ibid., 8

9. "Zesocializováním myšlenek poddanské vesnice." See Antonín Robek, *Městské lidové zdroje národního obrození*, Acta Universitatis Carolinae, Philosophica et historica, Monographia, 69 (Prague: Univerzita Karlova, 1977), 9.

10. Josef Petráň and others, *Počátky českého národního obrození: Společnost a kultura v 70. až 90. letech 18. století* (Prague: Academia, 1990), 10.

11. Ibid., 9.
12. Finally, there is also a brief treatment; see Aleksandr S. Myl'nikov, *Kul'tura cheshskogo vozrozhdeniia* (Leningrad: Nauka, 1982).
13. Bedřich Slavík, *Od Dobnera k Dobrovskému* (Prague: Vyšehrad, 1975), 6.
14. Ibid., 115.
15. Ibid., 178–81, referring to Kašpar Royko, *Geschichte der grossen allgemeinen Kirchenversammlung zu Kostniz*, 4 vols. Vols. 1–2, 2nd ed. rev. (Vienna and Graz: In Commission der Weingand, 1782); vol. 3 (Prague gedruckt. In Commission der Ferstlischen Buchhandlung zu Graz, 1784); vol. 4 (Prague: im Verlage des Verfassers, 1785); Royko, *Historie velikého sněmu kostnického*, trans. Václav Petryn (pseudonym of Václav Stach), 2 vols. (Prague: Diesbach, 1785); Augustin Zitte, *Lebensbeschreibung des Magisters Johannes Huss von Hussinecz*, 2 vols. (Prague: W. Serle, 1789–90); and Johann H. Wolf, *Leben, Lehre, Wandel und Tod des im J. 1415 lebendig verbrannten Johann Hus* (Rome [Prague], 1784).
16. Slavík, *Od Dobnera k Dobrovskému*, 178–79.
17. Ibid., 182–85.
18. He refers to Gottwald's placing the Awakening, together with the Taborite "revolutionary" radicalism, among the highlights of Czech history; Aleksandr S. Myl'nikov, *Epokha Prosveshcheniia v cheshskikh zemliakh: Ideologiia, natsional'noe samosoznanie, kul'tura* (Moscow: Nauka, 1977), 7, citing Gottwald, "Znachenie tvorchestva Aloiza Iraseka," 2:279.
19. Aleksandr S. Myl'nikov, *Vznik národně osvícenské ideologie v českých zemích 18. století* (Prague: Univerzita Karlova, 1974), 173; Myl'nikov, *Epokha Prosveshcheniia v cheshskikh zemliakh*, 67, 82.
20. Ibid., 73, like Slavík, refers to Mikuláš A. Voigt, *Acta litteraria Bohemiae et Moraviae*, 2 vols. (Prague, 1774–83).
21. Myl'nikov, *Epokha Prosveshcheniia v cheshskikh zemliakh*, 78–79, referring to Royko, *Geschichte der grossen allgemeinen Kirchenversammlung zu Kostniz*; Royko, *Historie velkého sněmu kostnického*, trans. Stach; and Wolf, *Leben, Lehre, Wandel und Tod des im J. 1415 lebendig verbrannten Johann Hus*. Myl'nikov (p. 78) cites Wolf (p. 3) as stating "the disciples and adherents of Jan Hus, were neither heretics, nor Protestants, but good, genuine and proper Catholics." As a consequence, the Utraquists received no pity from the Protestants when the Church of Rome persecuted them.
22. Hroch's English-language work is based on older research, namely, Miroslav Hroch, *Die Vor kämpfer der nationalen Bewegung bei den kleinen Völkern Europas: Eine Vergleichende Analyse zur gesellschaftlichen Schichtung der patriotischen Gruppen*, Acta Universitatis Carolinae Philosophica et Historica, Monographia 24 (Prague, 1969); and Hroch, *Obrození malých evropských národů: I. Národy severní a východní Evropy* (Prague: Univerzita Karlova, 1971).
23. Walter Schamschula, *Die Anfänge der tschechischen Erneuerung und das deutsche Geistesleben, 1740–1800* (Munich: Fink, 1973), 10.
24. Ibid., 11, n. 11, refers to Vodička, *Cesty a cíle obrozenské literatury*, 14–22.
25. Schamschula, *Die Anfänge der tschechischen Erneuerung*, 256.
26. Ibid., 234–35.
27. Royko, *Geschichte der grossen allgemeinen Kirchenversammlung zu Kostniz*; see Schamschula, *Die Anfänge der tschechischen Erneuerung*, 87.
28. Schamschula, *Die Anfänge der tschechischen Erneuerung*, 305.

29. Against these snobbish attitudes, he posits the preference for the speech of simple Moravian folks of Joseph Vratislav E. von Monse, professor at the University of Brno; see Schamschula, *Die Anfänge der tschechischen Erneuerung*, 235–37.

30. Ibid., 248.

31. Ibid., 253–54.

32. Ibid., 13–15.

33. Vladimír Macura, *Znamení zrodu: České národní obrození jako kulturní typ*, rev. ed. (Prague: H & H, 1995), 170.

34. See ibid., 251–55. The first edition, which is not cited in this chapter, appeared as *Znamení zrodu: České národní obrození jako kulturní typ* (Prague: Československý spisovatel, 1983). On the contrast between Kollár's romanticism and the realism of Havlíček and Palacký, see, for instance, Josef Kaizl, *České myšlenky*, 2nd ed. (Prague: Edvard Beaufort, 1896), 40.

35. Macura, *Znamení zrodu*, 74, 183.

36. For an English-language summary of his views, see Vladimír Macura, "Problems and Paradoxes of the National Revival," in Mikuláš Teich, ed., *Bohemia in History* (New York: Cambridge University Press, 1998), 182–97.

37. Miroslav Hroch, *Social Preconditions of National Revival in Europe: A Comparative Analysis of the Social Composition of Patriotic Groups among the Smaller European Nations*, trans. Ben Fowkes (New York: Columbia University Press, 2000), 30.

38. Ibid., 61.

39. For instance, Miroslav Hroch, *V národním zájmu: požadavky a cíle evropských národních hnutí devatenáctého století ve srovnávací perspektivě* (Prague: Lidové noviny, 1999), 100.

40. Ibid., 59–71.

41. For instance, ibid., 21, 42–43, 54, 73, 85, 115, 119, 128.

42. For instance, ibid., 173. This is strangely at odds with his critique of "many liberals from J. S. Mill on" for questioning the justification for the existence of 11 "small nations"; ibid., 140.

43. See a curious reference to Kohn as "an American Zionist stemming from Bohemia" [*americký sionista pocházející z Čech*] in ibid., 10; see also ibid., 74.

44. Ibid., 75, 166, 177.

45. Ibid., 140.

46. Ibid., 62, 85, 104.

47. Ibid., 34.

48. Hugh L. Agnew, *Origins of the Czech National Renascence* (Pittsburgh: University of Pittsburgh Press, 1993), 6.

49. Karel Ignác Thám, *Obrana jazyka českého proti zlobivým jeho utrhačům* (Prague: Schönfeld, 1783), 21, 24–26, cited by Agnew, *Origins of the Czech National Renascence*, 57–58.

50. Agnew, *Origins of the Czech National Renascence*, 75, cites from introduction to František M. Pelcl, *Grundsätze der böhmischen Grammatik* (Prague: Jeřábek, 1793).

51. Josef Jungmann, "O jazyku českém rozmlouvání první," *Hlasatel český* 1, no. 3 (1806), cited by Agnew, *Origins of the Czech National Renascence*, 65.

52. Agnew, *Origins of the Czech National Renascence*, 75; Walter Schamschula, "Dobrovskýs und Pelzels Beiträge zu den 'Lieferungen für Böhmen von Böhmen,'" in Alois Schmaus and Ilse Kunert, eds., *Aus der Geisteswelt der Slaven. Dankesgabe an Erwin Koschmieder* (Munich: Sagner, 1967), 157.

53. Agnew, *Origins of the Czech National Renascence*, 75–76.
54. Ibid., 90–91; page 91, n. 141, refers to the first edition of Vladimír Macura's work, for which see note 34 above.
55. Ibid., 58–59, citing from Thám, *Obrana jazyka českého proti zlobivým jeho utrhačům*, 43–44.
56. Agnew, *Origins of the Czech National Renascence*, 68, 70.
57. Ibid., 126.
58. Ibid., 93. The narrow formalistic purpose, rather than a transfer of ideas, is defined in the following way: "Publishing works of early Czech literature helped to make important sources for the study of the language more easily available to linguists and literary historians, but it did more than this. It also provided Czech authors who were starting to create modern Czech literature with a model from which to learn good Czech usage, and helped to fill the pressing need for Czech reading material of a high standard." Ibid., 126.
59. Ibid., 103, 125.
60. First by Nazi censorship in 1941, then by the onset of the Communist regime in 1948; František Kutnar, *Obrozenské vlastenectví a nacionalismus*, 9, 15.
61. In addition, a recent survey of the period from the viewpoint of literary history is offered by the collective work of Jan Lehár, Alexandr Stich, Jaroslava Janáčková, and Jiří Holý, *Česká literatura od počátků k dnešku* [Czech Literature from Its Beginnings to the Present] (Prague: Lidové noviny, 1998). Chapter 15, on the period of the Awakening, "Osvícenský klasicismus a jeho ústup. Působení romantismu a národních snah" [The Enlightened Classicism and Its Retreat. The Effect of Romanticism and the National Aspirations], pp. 151–76, is written by Alexandr Stich. It makes no mention of the enthusiasm for the sixteenth-century literature, the restoration of the language norms of the Veleslavín era, or any other sign of interest in the ideological or religious legacy of the Bohemian Reformation.
62. Kutnar, *Obrozenské vlastenectví a nacionalismus*, 18; see also Jiří Rak, "Doslov" [Epilogue], ibid., 346.
63. Kutnar, *Obrozenské vlastenectví a nacionalismus*, 86–88, 131–33.
64. Haubelt, *České osvícenství*. 2nd rev. ed. (Prague: Rodiče, 2004), 184–85, 547. Compare Haubelt, *České osvícenství* (Prague: Svoboda, 1986); see especially, 28–30, 150–51, 450–51.
65. Jan Patočka, "Bolzanovo místo v dějinách filosofie," in *Filosofie v dějinách českého národa*, Protokol celostátní konference o dějinách české filosofie v Liblicích ve dnech 14.–17. dubna 1958 (Prague: Nakladatelství ČSAV, 1958), 111.
66. Haubelt, *České osvícenství*. 2nd rev. ed., 549–550.
67. The relevant sections are "Politické dění v českých zemích," 73–95; "Vlast, národ a jazyk," 113–65; "Krásná literatura," 311–35; and "Vědecký život," 390–401, in Jitka Lněničková, *České země v době předbřeznové, 1792–1848* (Prague: Libri, 1999).
68. She does not treat the matter as of fundamental significance, constituting an ideological core of the awakening; Lněničková, *České země v době předbřeznové*, 80–81.
69. This could be explained, in part, by the chronological scope of the book, considering that much of the theoretical and practical foundation for the transmission was laid in the 1770s and 1780s. There is only a brief coverage of these decades; Lněničková, *České země v době předbřeznové*, 113–25.

70. Ibid., 141–42.
71. Ibid., 145, 399.
72. See, for instance, the discussion of language norms, Lněničková, *České země v době předbřeznové*, 119–20; a minor exception is the innocuous remark concerning Jan Nejedlý; ibid., 137.
73. Lněničková, *České země v době předbřeznové*, 252.
74. On Bolzano, presented as an advocate of a fusion of Czech and German nations in Bohemia (rather than of a civil society covering both nations), see Lněničková, *České země v době předbřeznové*, 80, 104, 393, 395; for Jungmann's characterization of Bolzano as "an enemy of the Czech nation," see ibid., 131.
75. Lněničková, *České země v době předbřeznové*, 394.
76. Ibid., 114.
77. Ibid., 116.
78. Ibid., 145, 148, 398–99.
79. Ibid., 80.
80. Ibid., 438–52.
81. The relevant sections are "Auguři a haruspikové," 155–94; "Josefinismus a jeho myšlenkové zdroje," 220–43; "Počátky organizace vědeckého života v českých zemích," 427–38; and "Počátky vědecké historiografie a odvozených disciplín," 439–52, in Pavel Bělina, Jiří Kaše, and Jan P. Kučera, *Velké dějiny zemí Koruny české*, vol. 10, 1740–92 (Prague: Paseka, 2001).
82. He attributes a special sympathy for the Bohemian Reformation also to Voigt, Pelcl, and Royko; see Bělina, Kaše, and Kučera, *Velké dějiny zemí Koruny české*, 10:242–43.
83. This attitude is expressed by the regretful tone over the suppression of monasteries, religious brotherhoods, choral societies [*literátská bratrstva*], and tertiary monastic orders; Bělina, Kaše, and Kučera, *Velké dějiny zemí Koruny české*, 10:105.
84. Ibid., 10:230.
85. "Tak nebezpečném věci katolické." See Bělina, Kaše, and Kučera, *Velké dějiny zemí Koruny české*, 10:225. See also ibid., 10:223.
86. Bělina, Kaše, and Kučera, *Velké dějiny zemí Koruny české*, 10:244.
87. Ibid., 10:242.
88. Ibid., 10:227.
89. Ibid., 10:12.
90. See the suggestion of Josephism's kinship with twentieth-century totalitarianism; Bělina, Kaše, and Kučera, *Velké dějiny zemí Koruny české*, 10:252.

Chapter 2

1. For overviews of the Bohemian Reformation, see Howard Kaminsky, *A History of the Hussite Revolution* (Berkeley: University of California Press, 1967); Thomas A. Fudge, *The Magnificent Ride: The First Reformation in Hussite Bohemia*, St. Andrew's Studies in Reformation History (Brookfield, Vt.: Ashgate, 1998); Ferdinand Hrejsa, *Dějiny křesťanství v Československu* (Prague: Husova Československá evangelická fakulta bohoslovecká, 1946–50), vol. 2–6; Zdeněk V. David, *Finding the Middle Way: The Utraquists' Liberal Challenge to Rome and Luther*

(Washington, D.C.: Woodrow Wilson Center Press; Baltimore: Johns Hopkins University Press, 2003).

2. For the significance of Utraquist eucharistic reforms, see three articles by David R. Holeton, "Sacramental and Liturgical Reform in Late Medieval Bohemia," *Studia Liturgica* 28, no. 1 (1987): 94; "The Communion of Infants and Hussitism," *Communio Viatorum* 27 (1984): 217–19; and "The Communion of Infants: The Basel Years," *Communio Viatorum* 29 (1986): 35–36.

3. On Hus, see Matthew Spinka, *John Hus: A Biography* (Princeton, N.J.: Princeton University Press, 1968); Václav Novotný, *Jan Hus: Život a učení*, I. *Život a dílo* (Prague: Laichter, 1919–21); Ernst Werner, *Jan Hus: Welt und Umwelt eines Prager Frühreformators*, Forschungen zur mittelalterlichen Geschichte, 34 (Weimar: Böhlau, 1991); Peter Hilsch, *Johannes Hus (um 1370–1415): Prediger Gottes und Ketzer* (Regensburg: Pustet, 1999).

4. In particular, the dioceses of Passau, Olomouc, Wrocław, Poznań, and later Nitra. Occasional transfers of Roman priests also continued to replenish the ranks of the Utraquist clergy; see Klement Borový, *Antonín Brus z Mohelnice, arcibiskup pražský; Historicko-kritický životopis* (Prague: Dědictví sv. Prokopa, 1873), 195; Julius Pažout, *Jednání a dopisy konsistoře pod obojí způsobou přijímajících, 1562–1570* (Prague: Historický spolek, 1906), 120–21, 246. On the vagrant bishops, see David R. Holeton, "Church or Sect: The *Jednota bratrská* and the Growth of Dissent from Mainline Utraquism," *Communio Viatorum* 38 (1996): 26; on ordinations in Venice, see Anna Skýbová, "Le ordinazioni dei sacerdoti utraquisti a Venezia nella prima metà del XVI secolo," in *Italia e Boemia nella cornice del rinascimento europeo*, ed. Sante Graciotti (Florence: Leo S. Olschki, 1999), 51–65.

5. See, for instance, *Sněmy české od léta 1526 až po naši dobu*, vols. 1–11, 15 (Prague: Zemský výbor, 1877–1941), 5:516.

6. "Hussiti" seemed to be a term of opprobrium favored by the Curia; see *Die Hauptinstruktionen Clemens' VIII. für die Nuntien und Legaten an den europäischen Fürstenhöfen, 1592–1605*, ed. Klaus Jaitner, Tübingen, 1984, i. 59, ii. 10; *Nuntiaturberichte aus Deutschland, nebst ergänzenden Aktenstücken*, Abt. 2, 1560–72, viii, ed. Johann Rainer, Graz 1967, 46–47; Abt. 3, 1572–85, vi, ed. Helmut Goetz, Tübingen 1982, 154, 365, 369; Abt. 3, vii, ed. Almut Bues, Tübingen 1990, 49, 88. The courteous designation was "'communicantes sub utraque'"; see ibid., Abt. 3, vi. 467; Abt. 3, vii. 98, 376. A more neutral unofficial designation was '*Calixtini*', used, for instance, by Bishop John Dubravius in 1544; see his *Ad collegium Pragense de ecclesiae oeconomia epistola* printed in *Ioanis, Dei gratia episcopi Olomucensis, In psalmum ordine quintum ecclesiae deprecantis typum gerentem, cuius initium est: Verba mea auribus percipe, Domine, enarratio . . .* (Prostějov: Ioannes Guntherus, 1549), 3. The Utraquists were, in fact, offended by the designation of themselves as Hussites.

7. Ferdinand Seibt, "'Hussiten' als historischer Begriff," in his *Hussitica: Zur Struktur einer Revolution* (Cologne: Böhlau, 1965), 10–15.

8. Just as Anglicanism viewed itself as a continuation of the Catholic Church in England; Urban T. Holmes III, *What Is Anglicanism?* (Harrisburg, Pa.: Morehouse, 1982), 11.

9. For characterizations of the Taborites and the Orebites, see Frederick G. Heymann, *John Žižka and the Hussite Revolution* (Princeton, N.J.: Princeton University Press, 1955), 75–91; Jan B. Lášek, "Priest Ambrož and East-Bohemian Utra-

quism: Hradec and Oreb," *Bohemian Reformation and Religious Practice* 3 (2000), 105–18. On the crusades, see Frederick G. Heymann, "The Crusades against the Hussites," in *A History of the Crusades*, ed. Kenneth M. Setton (Madison, Wisc.: University of Wisconsin Presss, 1969–89), 3:586–646.

10. František M. Bartoš, *The Hussite Revolution, 1424–1437*, ed. John M. Klassen (Boulder, Colo.: East European Monographs, 1986), 112–18.

11. František Šmahel, "Husitské artikuly a jihlavská kompaktáta," in *Jihlava a Basilejská Kompaktáta: Sborník příspěvků z mezinárodního sympozia k 555. výročí přijetí Basilejských kompaktát, 26–28. červen 1991*, ed. Zdeněk Jaroš and Dana Nováková (Jihlava: Muzeum Vysočiny, 1992), 11–28; Bartoš, *The Hussite Revolution, 1424–1437*, 73–111. For the text of the Compactata, see *Archiv český* III (Prague, 1844), 398–444.

12. Josef Macek, *Víra a zbožnost jagellonského věku* (Prague: Argo, 2001), 173–88; Veronika Macháčková, "Církevní správa v době jagellonské na základě administrátorských akt," *Folia Historica Bohemica* 9 (1985): 235–90; Veronika Macháčková and AntonínMařík, "Praha v činnosti administrátorů pod jednou v letech 1450–1550," pt. 2, *Documenta Pragensia* 9 (1991): 409.

13. On the *via media* of Utraquism, see Zdeněk V. David, "The Strange Fate of Czech Utraquism: The Second Century, 1517–1621," *Journal of Ecclesiastical History* 46 (1995): 641–68.

14. David, *Finding the Middle Way*, 170–78.

15. The events of the Diet of 1575 are described in considerable detail, above all, in Ferdinand Hrejsa, *Česká konfesse: Její vznik, podstata a dějiny* (Prague: Česká akademie pro vědy, slovesnost a umění, 1912), 86–94; Hrejsa, *Dějiny křesťanství v Československu*, 6:274–323; Kamil Krofta, "Boj o konsistoř podobojí v l. 1562–75 a jeho historický základ," *Český časopis historický* 17 (1911): 404–6, 411–16; and Jaroslav Pánek, *Stavovská opozice a její zápas s Habsburky, 1547–1577* (Prague: Academia, 1982), 101–11; see also David, *Finding the Middle Way*, 190–94.

16. On the Unity of Brethren and its origins, see Rudolf Říčan, *The History of the Unity of Brethren: A Protestant Hussite Church in Bohemia and Moravia*, trans. C. Daniel Crews (Bethlehem, Pa.: Moravian Church in America, 1992); Peter Brock, *The Political and Social Doctrines of the Unity of Czech Brethren in the Fifteenth and Sixteenth Centuries* (The Hague: Mouton, 1957); and Murray L. Wagner, *Petr Chelčický: A Radical Separatist in Hussite Bohemia* (Scottsdale, Pa.: Herald Press, 1983).

17. The edict of 1609 established the legitimacy of the Bohemian Confession as a comprehensive umbrella for religious dissent from the Roman Church but not as a specific confessional creed of all those supporting its legitimization; Anton Gindely, *Geschichte der Ertheilung des böhmischen Majestätsbriefes von 1609* (Prague: Carl Bellmann's Verlag, 1858); Kamil Krofta, *Majestát Rudolfa II* (Prague: Historický klub, 1909); Julius Glücklich, "Koncept Majestátu a vznik Porovnání," *Český časopis historický* 23 (1917): 110–28; Hrejsa, *Česká konfesse*, 437.

18. On the Blasphemy Act, see John Spurr, *English Puritanism, 1603–1689* (New York: St. Martin's Press, 1998), 120.

19. On the field armies of the Taborites and Orebites, see Fudge, *Magnificent Ride*, 170.

20. Utraquism perpetuated the original character of the Bohemian Reformation. For the misleading but widespread view of the Bohemian Reformation's

"degeneration" into Utraquism, see, for instance, Robert Kalivoda, *Husitské myšlení* (Prague: Filosofia, 1997), 68–69.

21. Frederick G. Heymann, *George of Poděbrady: King of Heretics* (Princeton, N.J.: Princeton University Press, 1965); Otakar Odložilík, *The Hussite King: Bohemia in European Affairs, 1440–1471* (New Brunswick, N.J.: Rutgers University Press, 1965).

22. Frederick G. Heymann, "John Rokycana: Church Reformer between Hus and Luther," *Church History* 28 (1959): 240–80; František Šmahel, *Husitská revoluce* (Prague: Karlova Univerzita, 1993), 4:97–105.

23. Concerning Bohuslav Bílejovský, see David, *Finding the Middle Way*, 80–103; and on Pavel Bydžovský, ibid., 111–33.

24. On the similarity, see ibid., 103–10. See also Holmes, *What Is Anglicanism?* 12.

25. On the open-mindedness and tolerance in Utraquism, see also Zdeněk V. David, "Central Europe's Gentle Voice of Reason: Bílejovský and the Ecclesiology of Utraquism," *Austrian History Yearbook* 28 (1997): 33–37.

26. Jaroslav Čechura, *České země v letech 1378–1437: Lucemburkové na českém trůně* (Prague: Libri, 1999–2000), 2:124.

27. Brian Tierney, *The Idea of Natural Rights: Studies on Natural Rights, Natural Law and Church Law, 1150–1625* (Atlanta, Ga.: Scholars Press for Emory University, 1997), 32, 214.

28. Bohuslav Bílejovský, *Kronika církevní*, ed. Josef Skalický (Prague: Fetterl z Vilden, 1816), 17. On the principle of the Judge of Cheb (*soudce chebský*), see also Amadeo Molnár and others, *Soudce smluvený v Chebu*, Sborník příspěvků přednesených na symposiu k 550. výročí (Cheb: 1982), 9–36; on the Utraquists' refusal to obey popes or councils, if contradicting the Bible, see also František Bartoš, *Husitská revoluce* (Prague: Academia,1965–66), 2:49, 66, 113, 181–82; or the partial English translation, Bartoš, *The Hussite Revolution, 1424–1437*, 79–82; and Heymann "John Rokycana: Church Reformer between Hus and Luther," 246.

29. Thus, Jakoubek of Stříbro, the early authoritative theologian of Utraquism, affirmed in 1420 that liturgical ceremonies were to be retained even though not found in Scripture unless they were directly contrary to the law of God. See Holeton, "Church or Sect?," 9, n. 52. Holeton cited from Jakoubek's *Egressus Ihesus* (Sermons on Matthew 24) in Prague MS NK X G 20, ff. 98v, 100r. The Utraquists shared the principle of noncontradiction with the Anglicans (see Holmes, *What Is Anglicanism?* 13) and clearly rejected the Lutherans' and other Protestants' principle of *sola scriptura*.

30. Václav Novotný, *M. Jana Husi korespondence a dokumenty* (Prague: Komise pro vydávání pramenů náboženského hnutí českého, 1920), 135; Jiří Spěváček, *Václav IV, 1361–1419* (Prague: Svoboda, 1986), 448–49.

31. Although ultimately the Bohemians refused to follow him in his departures from the orthodoxy of medieval theology; see David, *Finding the Middle Way*, 34–37.

32. Rudolf Říčan, ed., *Čtyři vyznání* (Prague Komenského evangelická bohoslovecká fakulta, 1951), 39; Hrejsa, *Dějiny křesťanství v Československu*, 2:271; Miloslav Kaňák, *John Viklef: Život a dílo anglického Husova předchůdce* (Prague: Blahoslav, 1973), 37.

33. Stephen Lahey, "Toleration in the Theology and Social Thought of John

Wyclif," in *Difference and Dissent: Theories of Tolerance in Medieval and Early Modern Europe*, ed. Cary J. Nederman and John C. Laursen (Lanham, Md.: Rowman and Littlefield, 1996), 53–58.

34. This was typical of late medieval universities. See, for instance, Howard Kaminsky, "The University of Prague in the Hussite Revolution: The Role of the Masters," in *Universities in Politics: Case Studies from the Late Middle Ages and Early Modern Period*, ed. John W. Baldwin and Richard A. Goldthwaite (Baltimore: The Johns Hopkins University Press, 1972), 79–80, 104–105; Jiří Kejř, *Kvodlibetní disputace na pražské universitě* (Prague: Univerzita Karlova, 1971).

35. Already, Jakoubek of Stříbro in the 1410s and Jan of Příbram in the 1430s were impatient with the folkish religious thinkers' lack of theological erudition; see Božena Kopičková, *Jan Želivský* (Prague: Melantrich, 1990), 28; Kamil Krofta, "O některých spisech M. Jana z Příbramě," *Časopis českého musea* 73 (1899): 213.

36. František Šmahel, *Husitská revoluce* (Prague: Historický ústav, 1993), 4: 100–01. For Sigismund's decree see *Archiv český*, 3 (1844), 427–31. See also Winfried Eberhard, *Konfessionsbildung und Stände in Böhmen* (Munich: Oldenbourg, 1981), 4445; Diarmaid MacCulloch, *Thomas Cranmer: A Life* (New Haven, Conn.: Yale University Press, 1996), 116.

37. Kamil Krofta, "Václav Koranda mladší z Nové Plzně a jeho názory náboženské," *Listy z náboženských dějin* (Prague: Historický klub, 1936), 258.

38. Jiří Kejř, "The Death Penalty during the Bohemian Wars of Religion," *Bohemian Reformation and Religious Practice* 6 (2007): 143–63.

39. The consensual system of administrative discipline was stipulated, for instance, in the Candlemas Day Articles of 1524, points 1–6; see Bartoš Písař, *Kronika pražská*, ed. Josef V. Šimák (Prague, 1907) (Fontes rerum Bohemicarum, vol. 6), 21–22; David, *Finding the Middle Way*, 211, 214, 301.

40. This notable state of legalized religious pluralism has by and large escaped the attention of Euroatlantic historical literature. For instance, there is no mention of Bohemia in N. M. Sutherland's "Persecution and Toleration in Reformation Europe," in *Persecution and Toleration*, Studies in Church History, 21, ed. W. J. Sheils (Oxford: Blackwell, 1984), 153–62; or in Randolph C. Head, "The Transformations of the Long Sixteenth Century," in *Beyond the Persecuting Society: Toleration before the Enlightenment*, ed. John Christian Laursen and Cary J. Nederman (Philadelphia: University of Pennsylvania Press, 1998), 95–106. For the late sixteenth century, the emphasis has usually been placed on toleration in Poland, the Dutch Republic, and France (1598–1685). See Perez Zagorin, *How the Idea of Religious Toleration Came to the West* (Princeton, N.J.: Princeton University Press, 2003).

41. Thomas A. Fudge, "The Problem of Religious Liberty in Early Modern Bohemia," *Communio Viatorum* 38 (1996): 67–70; Ernest Denis, *Fin de l'indépendance bohême*. 2nd ed. (Paris: Librairie Leroux, 1930), 1:208–209; Jaroš and Nováková, eds., *Jihlava a Basilejská Kompaktáta*, especially, 11–27. For the text of the Peace of Kutná Hora, see *Archiv český* 5 (Prague, 1862), 418–27. See also Václav Koranda, Jr., *Traktát o velebné a božské svátosti oltářní* (Prague: Tiskař Korandy, 1493), f. A3v–A4r.

42. Bílejovský, *Kronika*, 53, 55.

43. Blažej Nožička z Votína, *Knížka proti bludům některým před tisíci lety odsouzeným* (Prague: Jan Kantor, 1566), f. K(v); Georg Lauterbeck, *Politica historica: O*

vrchnostech a správcích světských knihy patery, trans. Daniel Adam of Veleslavín (Prague: Daniel Adam of Veleslavín, 1584); see Milan Kopecký, *Daniel Adam z Veleslavína* (Prague: Svobodné slovo, 1962), 25.

44. See Spurr, *English Puritanism, 1603–1689*, 57, 61–62; and literature cited in Sheila Lambert, "Richard Montagu, Arminianism and Censorship," *Past and Present* 124 (1989): 68, n. 118. Like the Anglican authors in the tradition of John Jewel, Richard Hooker, or Richard Montagu, so also the Utraquist Church of Bohemia fostered discussion rather than edicts and preserved a nonconfrontational, even cordial, tone in discussion with religious interlocutors. See Richard Montagu, *A Gagg for the New Gospell? No, a New Gagg for an Old Goose* (London: T. Snodham, 1624), f. *3v.

45. See the complaint by priest Šimon about the excesses of Luther's polemical language, particularly his insults of Henry VIII in *Contra Henricum regem Angliae* (1522), in *Dopisy kněží Šimona z Habru a Jana faráře Německo-Brodského o rozdílech ve víře, 1528–1529*, ed. František Dvorský, in *Archiv český*, 14 (1895), 335. The text of Luther's letter is published in Luther, *Werke: Kritische Gesammtausgabe* (Weimar: Böhlau, 1883–1996), 10, Zweite Abteilung, 178–79.

46. Zdeněk V. David, "Pavel Bydžovský and Czech Utraquism's Encounter with Luther," *Communio Viatorum*, 38 (1996), 42–53.

47. It is summed up by the famous statement of Richard Hooker: "As farre as they followe reason and truth, we feare not to tread the selfe same steppes wherin they have gon, and to be theire followers. Where Rome keepeth that which is ancienter and better, others whome we much more affect leavinge it for newer and changinge it for worse; we had rather followe the perfections of them whome we like not, than in defects resemble them whome we love." Richard Hooker, *Folger Library Edition of the Works* (Cambridge, Mass.: Harvard University Press, 1977–98), 2:121 [*LEP* V.28.1].

48. Pavel Bydžovský, *Tento spis ukazuje, že Biskupové Biskupa a Biskup kněží, a kněží od řádných Biskupů svěceni, Těla a Krve Boží posvěcovati mají* (N.p., 1543), 11; Hooker, *Folger Library Edition of the Works*, 1:3 [*LEP* Preface 2.1].

49. Thus, Erasmus referred to the examples of Christ, St. Paul, and St. Augustine as masters of gentle polemics. Accordingly, he endorsed the power of civil discourse in dealing with religious dissensions, noting that "the spirit of Christ in the Gospels has a wisdom of its own, and its own courtesy and meekness." See Desiderius Erasmus, *The Correspondence* (Toronto: University of Toronto Press, 1974–92), 8:203, see also 8:81–82, 155–57, 202–205; and 9:398. Concerning Erasmus's influence on Jewel, see R. J. Schoeck, "From Erasmus to Hooker," in *Richard Hooker and the Construction of Christian Community*, ed. Arthur S. McGrade (Tempe, Ariz.: Medieval and Renaissance Texts and Studies, 1997), 66–67; 69–73. See also Bruce Mansfield, *Erasmus in the Twentieth Century, c. 1920–2000* (Toronto: University of Toronto Press, 2003), which includes references to Erasmus's influence on John Jewel; and Robert K. Faulkner, *Richard Hooker and the Politics of a Christian England* (Berkeley: University of California Press, 1981), 53. Erasmus's vogue in Bohemia is discussed later in this chapter.

50. On the concept of "confessionalization," see Robert Bireley, *The Refashioning of Catholicism, 1450–1700: A Reassessment of the Counter Reformation* (Washington, D.C.: Catholic University of America Press, 1999), 6–8.

51. A similar moderation developed in the Anglican Church with relative avoidance of "tests of orthodoxy, heresy trials, censorship of thought" as "generally alien to the Anglican ethos." See Holmes, *What Is Anglicanism?* 12.

52. Although using nautical similes more suitable for seafaring Britain than for landlocked Bohemia, Diarmaid MacCullough has pointed out an analogous religious situation in England in the 1530s: "Evangelicals [Cranmerian Lutherans] were often more bitter about religious radicalism [the sectarians] than the traditionalists [high churchmen] were, because it revealed the insecurity of their own position: were not the radicals seeking to capsize a boat which the evangelicals themselves were already rocking?" MacCulloch, *Thomas Cranmer*, 145.

53. Kamil Kofta, "Nový názor na český vývoj náboženský v době předbělohorské," in his *Listy z náboženských dějin českých*, 380–81. Kamil Krofta provides a comprehensive overview of these charges in his *Nesmrtelný národ: Od Bílé Hory k Palackému* (Prague: Laichter, 1940), 344–429. For a more recent characterization of the Utraquist age as one of "social and moral laxity and abulia," see Zdeněk Rotrekl, *Barokní fenomén v součastnosti* (Prague: Trost, 1995), 129. See also František Kameníček, "Pod obojí (utrakvisté)," *Zemské sněmy a sjezdy moravské, 1526–1628* (Brno: Zemský výbor Markrabství moravského, 1900–1905), 3:418–19.

54. On the Consistory's abject and evasive dealings with archbishops Brus and Medek and papal nuncios, see, for instance, Krofta, "Boj o konsistoř," 386, 391, 401–403; Josef Matoušek, "Kurie a boj o konsistoř pod obojí za administrátora Rezka," *Český časopis historický* 37 (1931): 23, 27–28, 31, 252, 274, 281; Karel Stloukal, "Počátky nunciatury v Praze: Bonhomi v Čechách, 1581–84," *Český časopis historický* 34 (1928): 15–16, 256; Zikmund Winter, *Život církevní v Čechách: Kulturně-historický obraz v XV. a XVI. Století* (Prague: Česká akademie pro vědy, slovesnost a umění, 1895), 1:182–83, 330–34. On the topic of diplomatic deception see David, *Finding the Middle Way*, 156–58.

55. The typical sources for the treatment of the Utraquists have been Klement Borový's *Jednání a dopisy konsistoře katolické a utrakvistické* (Prague: I. L. Kober, 1868); or Julius Pažout's *Jednání a dopisy konsistoře pod obojí způsobou přijímajících, 1562–1570* (Prague: Historický spolek, 1906), see especially p. v. Aside from Zikmund Winter, the cases of priestly transgressions were pilloried by Antonín Podlaha in " 'Úpadek' strany podobojí na sklonku XVI. století," *Sborník historického kroužku* 5 (1904): 29–36, 65–69, 161–64, 219–27.

56. For instance, even the sympathetic historian Kamil Krofta demurs at the Brethren's unsubstantiated characterization of the Utraquist Administrator Martin Mělnický as "a dishonourable man, a liar, a drunkard, an obvious whoremonger" [člověk nevážný, lhář, ožralec, kurevník zjevný]; see Krofta, "Boj o konsistoř," 302, n. 2. On the Brethren's expressions of vengefulness, see Winter, *Život církevní*, 1:495–96. One is tempted to apply to them the critical characterization of the Puritans as those "who delighted in nothing so much as the contemplation of their own virtue and the condemnation of the supposed vices of others." See Peter Lake, *Anglicans and Puritans? Presbyterianism and English Conformist Thought from Whitgift to Hooker* (London: Unwin Hyman, 1988), 5.

57. Kameníček, *Zemské sněmy a sjezdy moravské*, 3:419.

58. For instance, nuncios Cesare Speciano and Giovanni Dolfin; see Matoušek, "Kurie a boj o konsistoř," 31, 267; *Nuntiaturberichte aus Deutschland. Dritte*

Abteilung, 1572–1585, 8. Band: Nuntiatur Giovanni Delfins, 1575–1576, ed. Daniela Neri (Tübingen: Max Niemayer, 1997), 74; also Anna Skýbová, "Cesta po Čechách v roce 1561," *Český lid* 63 (1975): 99; Hrejsa, *Česká konfesse*, 58.

59. Otakar Josek, *Život a dílo Josefa Kalouska* (Prague: Historický spolek, 1922), 292, cited by Krofta, *Nesmrtelný národ*, 350–51; Jaroslav Čechura and Jana Čechurová, eds., *Korespondence Josefa Pekaře a Kamila Krofty* (Prague: Karolinum, 1999), 87.

60. Hence, for Masaryk, Bohemian Utraquism ended in a moral morass and intellectual chaos in the sixteenth century. This led him to conclude that only the radical Taborites and the Unity of Brethren had left behind a worthy legacy of the Bohemian Reformation; Tomáš G. Masaryk, *Česká otázka. Naše nynější krize. Jan Hus*, Spisy 6 (Prague: Masarykův ústav, 2000), 150–55; Doubravka Olšáková, "Český překlad Denisova díla v kontextu sporu o smysl českých dějin," *Dějiny a součastnost* 23/5 (2001): 28–32. Despite his opposing view on the Bohemian Reformation, Josef Pekař agreed with Masaryk that sixteenth-century Bohemia was morally corrupt except for the Unity of Brethren; see Josef Pekař, "Tři kapitoly z boje o sv. Jana Nepomuckého," in *Postavy a problémy českých dějin*, ed František Kutnar (Prague: Vyšehrad, 1990), 249. Palacký similarly favored the Taborites over the Utraquists, whom he considered a party of "stagnation" [*utkvělost*]; see František Palacký, *Dějiny národu českého* (Prague: Bursík a Kohout [1893]), 5:514.

61. See the evidence presented in Zdeněk V. David, "The Integrity of the Bohemian Reformation: The Problem of Neo-Utraquism," in *The Bohemian Reformation and Religious Practice*, 5, pt. 2 (2005): 329–51. On the Utraquist views of the good works, see the attitudes of Pavel Bydžovský and Vavřinec Leander Rvačovský of Rvačov in David, *Finding the Middle Way*, 118–19, 223–24.

62. For instance, Václav Koranda, Jr., in 1489 to Valentin Polon in 1589 and Jan Cykáda in 1607; see Krofta, *Nesmrtelný národ*, 381–82; Jan V. Cykáda, *Hody křesťanské na které Bůh Otec skrze Syna svého zve* (Prague: Impressí Šumanská, 1607), f. B1(r)–(v); Valentin Polon, *Pomni na mne: Knijžka obahujíci v sobě kratičká spasidedlná Naučení a sebrání*. . . . (Staré Město Pražské: Buryan Valda, 1589); see his exhortations to priests (f. A6–2a–b), parents and youth (f. K5–3a–L5–1a), and to laity in general (f. B2a–b).

63. Polon summed up his view of the glory and duty of priesthood stipulating the following for the clergy: "They should conscientiously tend to their office, remain steady in their calling, lead the people in goodness and morality, follow Christ in his footsteps and [follow] the holy Fathers in their salvific teachings, point the way to good order and Christian piety, provide examples of virtue, avoid scandal, shine like lights and radiate virtue among the faithful (Matthew 5), and resist the sins and temptations of the world." Polon, *Pomni na mne*, f. A7r; see also A8r–v. Regarding the priests' duties, see also Vavřinec Leander Rvačovský of Rvačov, *Masopust* (Prague: Jiří Melantrich, 1580), f. D2v.

64. Zdeněk V. David, "Utraquists, Lutherans, and the Bohemian Confession of 1575," *Church History* 68 (1999): 331–35.

65. In this section I drew on my previous work in David, *Finding the Middle Way*, chap. 10.

66. Rudolf Urbánek, "Český mesianismus ve své době hrdinské," in *Od pravěku k dnešku: Sborník k 60. narozeninám J. Pekaře,* ed. Josef Klik, 1:262–84, especially 263–64 (Prague, 1930).

67. František Palacký, *Obrana husitství*, trans. and ed. František M. Bartoš (Prague: Blahoslav, 1926), 41.
68. Macek, *Víra a zbožnost jagellonského věku*, 58.
69. Václav Koranda, Jr., *Manualník*, ed. J. Truhlář (Prague, 1888), 50ff.; Koranda, *Traktát o velebné a božské svátosti oltářní*, f. 98a, 128a. See also Noemi Rejchrtová, "Obrazoborecké tendence utrakvistické mentality jagellonského období a jejich dosah," *Husitský Tábor* 8 (1985): 66; Winfried Eberhard, "Zur reformatorischen Qualität und Konfessionalisierung des nachrevolutionären Hussitismus," in *Häresie und vorzeitige Reformation im Spätmittelalter*, Schriften des Historischen Kollegs Kolloquien 39, ed. František Šmahel (Munich: Oldenbourg, 1998), 223. The humanist Václav Písecký summed up the grievance against Rome: "They never wanted to grant . . . what they had promised in Basel and confirmed with their seals." Bohumil Ryba, "Václav Písecký, Eneáš Sylvius a Lukianos," *Listy filologické* 57 (1930): 145.
70. Born around 1480 in Malín near Kutná Hora, Bílejovský was ordained as a priest in Italy (probably in Venice) and served in Mělník, Čáslav, and Kutná Hora. Except for a brief mission to Tábor, he lived from 1532 in Prague, where he was elected to the Consistory in 1534 and died in 1555. See Josef V. Šimák, "Bohuslava Bílejovského Kronika česká," *Český časopis historický* 38 (1932): 92–93.
71. Bílejovský, *Kronika*, 39–41; Kamil Krofta, "Slovo o knězi Bohuslavu Bílejovském," *Listy z náboženských dějin*, 296–97.
72. See, for instance, Ewa Maleczyńska, *Ruch husycki w Czechach i w Polsce* (Warsaw: Ksiazka i Wiedza, 1959); Richard Pražák, "Zu den Beziehungen zwischen den Böhmischen Ländern und Ungarn zu Zeiten Matthias Corvinus," in *Matthias Corvinus and the Humanism in Central Europe*, ed. Tibor Klaniczay and József Jankovics (Budapest: Balassi Kiadó, 1994), 193–202; Josef Macůrek, "Husitství v rumuských zemích," *Časopis Matice moravské* 51 (1927): 1–98.
73. Pavel Bydžovský, *Odvolání jednoho Bratra z Roty Pikhartské*, 2nd ed. (Prague: Jan Jičínský, 1588), f. C5r–D1v.
74. Bílejovský, *Kronika*, 27, 39–41.
75. Josef Jireček, *Rukověť k dějinám literatury české* (Prague: Tempsky, 1875–76), 1:116. See also the Consistory's response of July 28, 1548, to a noble's request to replace the Lutheran minister on his estate with a German-speaking Utraquist priest; Borový, *Jednání a dopisy konsistoře katolické a utrakvistické*, 1:229.
76. See, for instance, Noemi Rejchrtová, "Role utrakvizmu v českých dějinách," in *Traditio et Cultus, Miscellanea historica bohemica Miloslao Vlk, archiepiscopo Pragensi, ab eius collegis amicisque ad annum sexagesimum dedicata*, ed. Zdeňka Hledíková (Prague: Univerzita Karlova, 1993), 75.
77. Josef Pekař, for instance, depicted the Utraquists as standing at the Curia's door like humble petitioners asking to be tolerated or like beggars imploring the authorities for their indulgence. See Josef Pekař, *Žižka a jeho doba* (Prague: Vesmír, 1927–33), 3:327.
78. Macek, for instance, has characterized as benighted or retarded [*zpozdilá*] the continuing Utraquist ambition to reform the Roman Church; see Macek, *Víra a zbožnost jagellonského věku*, 59.
79. For Hooker, as well as for his successors like Archbishop Laud, the focus on the contemporary national church tended to mute the global perspective; see Diarmaid MacCulloch, *The Later Reformation in England, 1547–1603* (New York: St.

Martin's Press, 1990), 99; Anthony Milton, *Catholic and Reformed: The Roman and Protestant Churches in English Protestant Thought, 1600–1640* (New York: Cambridge University Press, 1995), 303.

80. Bílejovský, *Kronika církevní*, 13–14; Vavřinec z Březové, *Husitská kronika*, ed. Marie Bláhová (Prague: Svoboda, 1979), 88–89. See also Kopičková, *Jan Želivský*, 94.

81. Amedeo Molnár, "Martin Lupáč: Modus disputandi pro fide," *Folia Historica Bohemica* 4 (1982): 161–77.

82. Polon, *Pomni na mne*, f. Club 5–1b, A6–2b, A6–3a, A6–3b. Bílejovský states literally that "we Czechs *sub utraque* are the true Romans" [. . . my Čechové pod obojí jsme praví Římané], *Kronika církevní*, 27. In the ecclesiastical area, their resistance was comparable—in its tenor, if not in its results—to the political opposition of the North American colonies to the British monarch claiming to defend the rights of Englishmen.

83. Peter Matheson, *Rhetoric of the Reformation* (Edinburgh: T&T Clark, 1998), 215–37.

84. Witzel, an ordained priest, married and served as a Lutheran minister in Saxony in the 1520s. After the adoption of the Augsburg Confession in 1530, he rejoined the Roman Church as a married lay preacher and lived mainly in Dresden, Berlin, and Mainz. See Winfried Trusen, *Um die Reform und Einheit der Kirche: Zum Leben und Werk Georg Witzels* (Münster: Aschendorffsche Verlagsbuchhandlung, 1957), 22–26, 48–83.

85. On Witzel's theology, see Barbara Henze, *Aus Liebe zur Kirche Reform: die Bemühungen Georg Witzels (1501–1573) um die Kircheneinheit* (Münster: Aschendorff, 1995), 23, 91–151. Another figure who sought to mediate between Rome and Wittenberg was Hermann von Wied, archbishop of Cologne, who corresponded with Archbishop Thomas Cranmer in the mid-1540s. The Curia, however, removed him from office in 1546; see August Franzen, *Bischof und Reformation: Erzbischof Hermann von Wied in Köln vor der Erscheidung zwischen Reform und Reformation* (Munster: Aschendorff, 1971), 80–81; MacCulloch, *Thomas Cranmer: A Life*, 393.

86. Brendan Bradshaw, "The Controversial Sir Thomas More," *Journal of Ecclesiastical History* 36 (1985): 564.

87. See his comments on Henry VIII's critique of Luther, *Assertio septem sacramentorum* (1521); Thomas More, *Complete Works* (New Haven, Conn.: Yale University Press, 1963–97), 5, pt. 2:721; John Guy, *Thomas More* (London: Arnold, 2000), 115, 178; William B. Patterson, "Hooker on Ecumenical Relations: Conciliarism in the English Reformation," in *Richard Hooker and the Construction of Christian Community*, ed. Arthur S. McGrade (Tempe, Ariz.: Medieval and Renaissance Texts and Studies, 1997), 289.

88. On Erasmus's liberal ecclesiology see, for instance, Erasmus, *The Correspondence*, 8:207–209; 415, no. 46; Hilmar M. Pabel, "The Peaceful People of Christ: The Irenic Ecclesiology of Erasmus of Rotterdam," in *Erasmus' Vision of the Church*, ed. Hilmar M. Pabel (Kirksville, Mo.: Sixteenth Century Journal Publishers, 1995), 57–93; Ernest E. Reynolds, *Thomas More and Erasmus* (New York: Fordham University Press, 1965).

89. More and Fisher likewise shared Erasmus's interest in Greek patristics, as well as in the ecclesiological ambiance of the first millennium; see Irena Backus, "Erasmus and the Spirituality of the Early Church," in *Erasmus' Vision of the Church*,

ed. Pabel, 95–114; Wilhelm Maurer, "Erasmus und das Kanonische Recht," in *Vierhundertfünfzig Jahre lutherische Reformation, 1517–1967: Festschrift für Franz Lau zum 60. Geburtstag,* ed. Helmar Junghans and others (Göttingen: Vanderhoeck and Ruprecht, 1967), 222–32; Maria Dowling, *Fisher of Men: A Life of John Fisher, 1469–1535* (New York: St. Martin's Press, 1999), 30–40. Recently, even Henry VIII has been added to the faction that was inspired by Erasmus's program of ecclesiastical reform; see George W. Bernard, *The King's Reformation: Henry VIII and the Remaking of the English Church* (New Haven, Conn.: Yale University Press, 2005), 236–37, 644 n. 58.

90. The cardinal himself is said to have adhered to a Catholic humanism, and he belonged among Erasmus's correspondents. See Francesco Gui, *L'attesa del concilio: Vittoria Colonna e Reginald Pole nel movimento degli "spirituali"* (Rome: Editoria Università Elettronica, 1997); see also Dermot Fenlon, *Heresy and Obedience in Tridentine Italy: Cardinal Pole and the Counter Reformation* (Cambridge: Cambridge University Press, 1972), 21–23; Thomas F. Mayer, "'Heretics be not in all things heretics': Cardinal Pole, His Circle, and the Potential for Toleration," in *Beyond the Persecuting Society,* ed. Laursen and Nederman, 107–24.

91. Thierry Wanegffelen, *Une difficile fidelité: Catholiques malgré concile en France, XVIe–XVIIe siècles* (Paris: Presses Universitaires de France, 1999), 152–62. Among later Catholic reformers in the second decade of the seventeenth century, the erratic Marco Antonio De Dominis, archbishop of the Croatian Split, sought to purge the Western Church of the papal monarchism and restore it to the episcopal collegiality of the first millennium. His critique of papal monarchism appeared in Czech translation in 1619. See Mercantonio de Dominis, *Ohlášení a zpráva* (Prague: Daniel Sedlčanský, 1619). See also Noel Malcolm, *De Dominis (1560–1624): Venetian, Anglican, Ecumenist and Relapsed Heretic* (London: Strickland and Scott Academic Publications, 1984).

92. *Chvála bláznovství* [Praise of Folly] (1513), *Enchiridion militis Christiani* (1519), and *Výklad na Otčenáš* [Explanation of the Lord's Prayer] (1526) were translated early. Eight more of his works were published in Czech 1519–95, some in several editions. See Kolár, *Návraty bez konce,* 120, 141, 175–77; *Knihopis českých a slovenských tisků,* vol. 2 in 9 pts. (Prague: Nakladatelství Československé akademie věd, 1925–67), nos. 2348–69. See also Mirjam Bohatcová, "Erasmus Roterdamský v českých tištěných překladech 16.–17. století," *Časopis národního muzea,* Řada historická 155 (1986): 37–58.

93. Erasmus, *The Correspondence,* 6:321–23. See also ibid., 7: 89–95, 119–28; More, *Complete Works,* vol. 6, pt. 1, 192; pt. 2, 658. Another Czech correspondent, Arkleb of Boskovice, supplied Erasmus with information on Bohemia's religious situation in 1520. He also assured Erasmus of the popularity of his writings and of the high respect for his opinions in the country; Erasmus, *The Correspondence,* 8:75–76.

94. Kolár, *Návraty bez konce,* 179; Pavel Bydžovský, *Historiae aliquot Anglorum martyrum, quibus Deus suam ecclesiam exornare sicut syderibus coelum dignatus est* (Prague: J. Cantor, 1554), f. Br.

95. Robert Barnes, *Kronyky. A životů sepsání nejvrchnějších Biskupů Římských jináč Papežů,* trans. Ennius Glatouinus (Nuremberg: Woldřich Nejber and Jan Montán, 1565), f. 195v, 198r–198v. More's and Fisher's advocacy of a diminished papacy pointed to their formal kinship with the Utraquists. On the Utraquist view

of the papacy, see Zdeněk V. David, "A Brief Honeymoon in 1564–1566: The Utraquist Consistory and the Archbishop of Prague," *Bohemia* 39 (1998): 269–70.

96. On Nausea's relations with the Utraquists, see also Josef Hejnic and Jan Martínek, eds., *Rukověť humanistického básnictví v Čechách a na Moravě od konce 15. do začátku 17. století* (Prague: Academia, 1966–82), 2:103. Henze, *Aus Liebe zur Kirche Reform*, 50, 81. On Nausea's relations with Erasmus; see Erasmus, *The Correspondence*, 11:322–23.

97. Richard M. Douglas, *Jacopo Sadoleto, 1477–1547: Humanist and Reformer* (Cambridge, Mass.: Harvard University Press, 1959), 74, 80–81, 116. Erasmus's letter to Sadoleto is cited in Douglas, *Jacopo Sadoleto, 1477–1547*, 115.

98. In particular, Contarini tried to find a common ground with the Lutherans on justification during negotiations at the Diet of Regensburg in 1541; see Elisabeth G. Gleason, *Gasparo Contarini: Venice, Rome, and Reform* (Berkeley: University of California Press, 1993), x, 241–45; James Atkinson, "Die römisch–katholische Kirche und die Reformation in anglikanischer Sicht," in *Vierhundertfünfzig Jahre lutherische Reformation*, ed. Junghans and others, 14–15.

99. Josef Macek, "Osudy basilejských kompaktát v jagelonském věku," *Jihlava a Basilejská Kompaktáta*, 199–200. See also Alain Dufour, "Humanisme et Reformation," in his *Histoire politique et psychologie historique* (Geneva: Librairie Droz, 1966), 54.

100. Letter from Floriano Montini (secretary to Cardinal Campeggi) to Erasmus, February 22, 1525, from Buda, in Erasmus, *The Correspondence*, 11:48–49; on Erasmus's friendship with Campeggi, see ibid., 11:84, 323.

101. Peter Fraenkel, "Utraquism or Co-Existence: Some Notes on the Earliest Negotiations before the Pacification of Nuernberg, 1531–1532," *Studia theologica* 18, 2 (1964): 130, 132–34. See also Euan Cameron, "The Possibilities and Limits of Conciliation," in *Conciliation and Confession: The Struggle for Unity in the Age of Reform, 1415–1648*, ed. Howard P. Louthan and Randall Zachman (Notre Dame, Ind.: University of Notre Dame Press, 2004), 76–77.

102. Fraenkel, "Utraquism or Co-Existence," 135–36, 140, 144; Miloš Pojar, *Jindřich Matyáš Thurn: Muž činu* (Prague: Ivo Železný, 1998), 14.

103. Fraenkel, "Utraquism or Co-Existence," 137, 150.

104. Douglas, *Jacopo Sadoleto, 1477–1547*, 93.

105. Bradshaw, "The Controversial Sir Thomas More," 563–64.

106. Zdeněk V. David, "The Plebeianization of Utraquism: The Controversy over the Bohemian Confession of 1575," *The Bohemian Reformation and Religious Practice* 2 (1998): 131–35, 156–58.

107. The proportion of Utraquists in the Czech-speaking population of Bohemia on the eve of the Battle of White Mountain (totaling 1,200,000) can be estimated at between two-thirds and three-quarters. Refining further the figures for religious affiliation in Bohemia, the number of Utraquists would be between 780,000 and 936,000, the number of Czech Lutherans and Brethren each between 60,000 and 120,000, and the number of Czech *sub una* between 144,000 and 180,000. See David, *Finding the Middle Way*, 328, n. 126. The size of religious groups within the German-speaking population of Bohemia, probably 500,000 strong, can be similarly estimated. According to an analogous calculation, the number of German *sub una* would be 60,000–75,000, and the number of German Brethren 25,000–50,000. This would leave 375,000–415,000 German Lutherans. The undoubtedly small num-

ber of German Utraquists, if once approximated, should be subtracted from the number of Lutherans.

108. See, for instance, Frederick G. Heymann, "The Role of the Bohemian Cities during and after the Hussite Revolution," in *Tolerance and Movements of Religious Dissent in Eastern Europe*, ed. Bela K. Kiraly (New York: Columbia University Press, 1975), 27–28. The urban complex of Prague consisted of three main components: Old Town, New Town, and Lesser Town.

109. Cited by Říčan, ed., *Čtyři vyznání*, 39, n. 1; see also *Od nejstarší doby do sloučení pražských měst, 1784*, vol. 1, of *Dějiny Prahy*, ed. Pavel Bělina (Prague: Paseka, 1997), especially 225. On the link between towns and Utraquism, see also Kalivoda, *Husitské myšlení*, 65–68.

110. Pravoslav Kneidl, "Městský stav v Čechách v době předbělohorské" (Ph.D. diss., Univerzita Karlova, 1951), 10; Daniel Adam z Veleslavína, *Kalendář historický: To jest krátké poznamenání všech dnuov jednokaždého měsíce přes celý rok* (Prague: Daniel Adam z Veleslavína, 1578), 131.

111. Josef Šusta, *Král cizinec*, České dějiny, vol. 2, pt. 2 (Prague: Laichter, 1939), 219; Hrejsa, *Dějiny křesťanství v Československu*, 4:256–57.

112. On Wyclif's concern for the poor, Anne Hudson, "Poor Preachers, Poor Men: Views of Poverty in Wyclif and His Followers," in *Häresie und vorzeitige Reformation*, 43–44, 47, 52–53; Fudge, *Magnificent Ride*, 173–74. The Brethren resembled the English Puritans, whose moral rigor served as a mark of distinction from the poverty stricken and as a license for reprimanding the poor for their promiscuous and slothful ways. See Spurr, *English Puritanism, 1603–1689*, 76.

113. In contrast to the subsequent period, central European peasantry enjoyed considerable bargaining powers vis-à-vis its feudal lords in the sixteenth century, if backed by the right of appeal to the royal officials or the monarch; see Kalivoda, *Husitská epocha a J. A. Komenský* (Prague: Odeon, 1992), 25; Ladislav Soukup, "Poddaní a jejich právní postavení v zemských zřízeních doby předbělohorské v Čechách," *Vladislavské zřízení zemské a počátky ústavního zřízení v Českých zemích, 1500–1619*, ed. Karel Malý and Jaroslav Pánek (Prague: Historický ústav Akademie věd České Republiky; Ústav právních dějin Právnické fakulty Univerzity Karlovy, 2001), 244; Kamil Krofta, *Dějiny selského stavu*, dílo sv. 3, ed. Emanuel Janoušek (Prague: Laichter, 1949), 143–52. For comparative purposes, see Govind Screenivasan, "The Social Origins of the Peasants' War of 1525 in Upper Swabia," *Past and Present* 171 (May 2001): 40–55.

114. "Let there be not among you any difference; listen well to the little one as to the great one, to the poor one as to the rich one, without any regard for the person," or "God himself, when he wishes to punish or to show mercy, shows no regard for the status of the person." Citing 2 Moses 23, 5 Moses 1; Rvačovský of Rvačov, *Masopust*, f. 273r; see also f. 273v–274r.

115. Such nobles seized parish grazing lands, gardens, and ponds and refused to pay the tithes from their produce; Cykáda, *Hody křestanské*, f. B1v–B2r, p. 222. For similar charges of noble embezzlements, see the Utraquist Consistory's letter to Rudolf II of August 8, 1578, in *Sněmy české*, 5:301. As noted later on, the populist strand was also exemplified by the Utraquist clergy's concern with religious books in Czech for the use of the common people [*lidé prostější*], as, for instance, Cykáda expressed in the introduction to his *Hody křestanské*.

116. The costly clerical lifestyle and the cloistered ideal had been pruned away

by the early Utraquist reforms; see Zikmund Winter, *Zlatá doba měst českých* (Prague: Odeon, 1991), 167–68; Winter, *Kulturní obraz českých měst: život veřejný v XV. a XVI. věku* (Prague: Matice česká, 1890–92), 2:576–77; David R. Holeton, "The Evolution of Utraquist Eucharistic Liturgy: A Textual Study," *The Bohemian Reformation and Religious Practice*, 2 (1998): 103. The Utraquist Church had renounced interdicts, anathemas, excommunications, and other dreaded spiritual weapons employed routinely by the contemporary Roman Church; Kamil Krofta, "Václav Koranda mladší z Nové Plzně a jeho názory náboženské," *Listy z náboženských dějin*, 258.

117. On the Puritan stress on "discipline," see Spurr, *English Puritanism, 1603–1689*, 52. Concerning the dread engendered by the Calvinist stress on predestination, see Alexandra Walsham, "The Parochial Roots of Laudianism Revisited: Catholics, Anti-Calvinists and 'Parish Anglicans' in Early Stuart England," *Journal of Ecclesiastical History* 49 (1998): 629.

118. The Czech Lutheran minister Jan Štelcar Želetavský confirmed the people's attachment to the Utraquist faith, even as he ridiculed it as a blind attachment to ancestral beliefs; Jan Štelcar Želetavský z Želetavy, *Kázání dvoje* (Prague: Jiří Dačický, 1586), f. B8v.

119. Walsham, "The Parochial Roots of Laudianism Revisited," 630.

120. The plebeian bias of Utraquism might have been, in part, inspired by Wyclif, as a critic of ecclesiastical riches; see Hudson, "*Poor Preachers, Poor Men*," 43–44, 47, 52.

121. The aristocrats' sojourns abroad, particularly exposures to foreign Protestant and Catholic universities, were also a factor. See Marie Koldínská, *Každodennost renesančního aristokrata* (Prague: Paseka, 2001), 10–11; Jiří Kovařík, "Proměny feudální třídy v Čechách v předbělohorském období," in *Proměny feudální třídy v Čechách v pozdním feudalismu*, ed. Josef Petráň (Prague: Univerzita Karlova, 1976), 137–64, especially 138–41.

122. Such as addressing Utraquist Administrator Martin of Mělník in a discourteous way, denying him his proper title; see Krofta, "Konsistoř pod obojí," 395, n. 4.

123. *Sněmy české*, 11, pt. 1:76; Vilém Slavata, *Paměti nejvyššího kancléře království českého*, ed. Josef Jireček (Prague: Kober, 1866–68), 1:47.

124. On the appeal of Catholic priesthood to the nobles during the Counter-Reformation, see, for instance, Gregory Hanlon, "The Decline of a Provincial Military Aristocracy: Siena 1560–1740," *Past and Present* 155 (1997): 106–108; Bohumil Navrátil, *Biskupství olomoucké 1576–1579 a volba Stanislava Pavlovského* (Prague: Česká společnost nauk, 1909), 198.

125. See the complaint of priest Jan Facilis, pastor of the church of St. Jiljí in Prague, in January 1594 against the intrusion of secular authorities into the parish house as a violation of the canons and ecclesiastical immunities [*contra canones et immunitates spirituales*]; *Sněmy české*, 11 pt. 1:70, n. 293.

126. Along these lines, Ralph Keen, *Divine and Human Authority in Reformation Thought: German Theologians on Political Order, 1520–1555* (Nieuwkoop: De Graaf, 1997), 6, characterized the Lutheran attitude toward political power: "When the Reformers appealed to secular authorities, they did so with a conception of authority that secularized the ecclesiastical order and subordinated it to the political order"; "Martin Luther," *New Catholic Encyclopedia*, 8:1088.

127. Even the Unity of Brethren looked askance at Pernštejn's entrepreneurship in ecclesiology; Jan V. Novák, "Spor Bratří s p. Vojtěchem z Pernštejna a na Prostějově r. 1557 a 1558," *Časopis českého musea* 65 (1891): 44, 48, 54 n. 9; *Knihopis českých a slovenských tisků*, vol. 2, pt. 6:91. Also the Utraquist Consistory voiced its distaste over the zest of "the great lords" for manipulating religious concepts to their liking, as in composing the text of the Bohemian Confession in May 1575; *Sněmy české*, 4:412; Hrejsa, *Česká konfesse*, 128, cf. 120–21.

128. *Sněmy české*, 4:393.

129. Janáček, "Královská města česká na zemském sněmu r. 1609–1610," 251.

130. See, for instance, Noemi Rejchrtová, "Listy osamělého politika," in Karel starší ze Žerotína, *Z korespondence* (Prague: Odeon, 1982), 7–38. More recently, Kalivoda has assigned to Žerotín's political stance the prime responsibility for the failure of the Bohemian uprising against the Habsburgs in 1618; Kalivoda, *Husitská epocha a J. A. Komenský*, 42–43, 59–60. The nobility had customarily remained at the level of bare literacy without any ambition for juridical or classical learning; see Jiří Pešek, *Měšťanská vzdělanost a kultura v předbělohorských Čechách, 1547–1620* (Prague: Karolinum, 1993), 129.

131. Koldínská, *Každodennost renesančního aristokrata*, 10. Notable exceptions included Václav Budovec of Budov or Kryštof Harant of Polžice and Bezdružice. On the former, see Noemi Rejchrtová, ed., in Václav Budovec of Budov, *Antialkorán* (Prague: Odeon, 1989), 10; see also Václav Bůžek, "Literární mecenát nižší šlechty v předbělohorských Čechách," *Husitství, Reformace, Renesance: Sborník k 60. narozeninám Františka Šmahela*, ed. Jaroslav Pánek and others (Prague: Historický ústav, 1994), 3:837, 839.

132. In particular, Daniel Adam of Veleslavín, Martin Bacháček, Brikcí of Licko, Marek Bydžovský of Florentin, Mikuláš Dvorský, Jan Kocín of Kocinét, Mikuláš Konáč of Hodiškov, Martin Kuthen of Šprinsberk, Prokop Lupáč of Hlaváčov, Jakub Srnec of Varvažov, Jan Straněnský, Adam Zalužanský of Zalužany, and Václav Zelotín of Krásná Hora.

133. Kolár, *Návraty bez konce*, 25, 139–40.

134. See, for instance, Jiří Pešek, "Kultura českých předbělohorských měst, 1547–1620," *Česká města v 16.–18. století: Sborník příspěvků z konference v Pardubicích 14. a 15. listopadu 1990*, ed. Jaroslav Pánek (Prague: Historický ústav, 1991), 208–209; Petr Čornej, *Rozhled, názory a postoje husitské inteligence v zrcadle dějepisectví 15. století* (Prague: Univerzita Karlova, 1986), 5–6; Josef Hejnic, "Daniel Adam von Veleslavín: Zu den gegenseitigen Beziehungen zwischen der tschechischen und lateinischen Literatur im letzten Viertel des 16. Jahrhunderts," in *Studien zum Humanismus in den böhmischen Ländern*. Schriften des Komitees der Bundesrepublic Deutschland zur Förderung der Slawischen Studien, 11, ed. Hans-Bernd Harder and Hans Rothe (Cologne: Böhlau, 1988), 270–72.

135. Such as Hradec Králové, Kouřim, Louny, Písek, Rakovník, and Žatec; see Michal Svatoš, "Humanismus an der Universität Prag im 15. und 16. Jahrhundert," in *Studien zum Humanismus in den böhmischen Ländern*, 203–205; Jiří Pešek, "Měšťanská kultura a vzdělanost v rudolfínské Praze," *Folia Historica Bohemica* 5 (1983): 174–76. Václav Ledvinka, "Feudální velkostatek a poddanská města v předbělohorských Čechách," Jiří Pešek, "Kultura českých předbělohorských měst, 1547–1620," and Petr Vorel, "Města jako sídla feudálních vrchností," all in *Česká města v 16.–18. století*, ed. Pánek, 101, 123–24, 204.

136. Josef J. Jungmann, *Historie literatury české*, 2d ed. (Prague: Řivnáč, 1849), 120, cited by Antonín Rejzek, *Blahoslavený Edmund Kampián, kněz Tovaryšstva Ježíšova, pro sv. víru mučeník ve vlast své* (Brno: K. Winiker, 1889), 123.

137. Hieronymus Weller, *Kniha utěšená a velmi potřebná, zavírajíc v sobě naučení o povolání všech správců*, trans. Mikuláš Dvorský (N.p., 1591), *Knihopis*, no. 16.690; Jan Kocín z Kocinétu, *Ioannis Bodini Nova distributio iuris universi . . . explicata a Ioanne Cocino* (Prague: J. Negrin, 1581); see *Rukověť humanistického básnictví*, 3:53; Lauterbeck, *Politica historica: O vrchnostech a správcích světských knihy patery*. See also Mirjam Bohatcová and Josef Hejnic, "O vydavatelské činnosti Veleslavínské tiskárny," *Folia Historica Bohemica* 9 (1985), 291–388.

138. Walter Schamschula, *Geschichte der tschechischen Literatur* (Cologne: Böhlau, 1990–96), 1:225–26.

139. Koranda, *Traktát o velebné a božské svátosti oltářní*, f. T1r–V6r; Jan Bechyňka, *Děkování z večeře Dorotě Řehové*, cited in Noemi Rejchrtová, "Jan Bechyňka: Kněz a literát," in *Praga Mystica: Z dějin české reformace*, vol. 3 of *Acta reformationem bohemicam illustrantia*, ed. Amedeo Molnár (Prague: Kalich, 1984), 8, 23.

140. Bílejovský, *Kronika církevní*, 20–22.

141. See, for instance, introductions to Flavius Josephus, *Historie židovská. Na knihy čtyři rozdělená*, trans. and intro. Václav Plácel z Elbingu. (Prague: Daniel Adam of Veleslavín, 1592), f. (*) 2v; and Flavius Magnus Cassiodorus, *Historie cýrkevní*, trans. Jan Kocín z Kocinétu (Prague: Daniel Adam z Veleslavína, 1594), f.) (ii.

142. Eusebius of Caesarea (Pamphilus), *Historie církevní*, trans. Jan Kocín z Kocinétu (Prague: Daniel Adam z Veleslavína, 1594), f. A5v. See also Bedřich Spiess, "Jan Kocín z Kocinétu co historik církevní," *Časopis českého muzea* 46 (1872): 69–70. Veleslavín further noted that all significant areas of knowledge should be available in the Czech language; see his preface to Lauterbeck, *Politica historica*, 2nd ed., f. 6v.

143. Introduction to Cykáda, *Hody křestanské*, f. B1v–B2r, 222.

144. Holeton, "The Evolution of Utraquist Eucharistic Liturgy,"123–24; David R. Holeton, "The Role of Jakoubek of Stříbro in the Creation of a Czech Liturgy: Some Further Reflections," in *Jakoubek ze Stříbra. Texty a jejich působení*, ed. Ota Halama and Pavel Soukup (Prague: Filosofia, 2006), 49–86.

145. See, for instance, Schamschula, *Geschichte der tschechischen Literatur*, 1:219; Zikmund Winter, *Děje vysokých škol pražských od secessí cizích národů po dobu bitvy bělohorské, 1409–1622* (Prague: Česká akademie pro vědy, slovesnost a umění, 1895), 23–30; Winter, *Život a učení na partikulárních školách v Čechách*, 517–99; Winter, *Zlatá doba měst českých*, 141–42. Writing in 1589 and 1592, respectively, nuncios Antonio Puteo and Antonio Caetano already found the spread of liturgical Czech in Bohemia quite pronounced; Matoušek, "Kurie a boj o konsistoř pod obojí," 27, 32.

146. František X. Šalda, "O krásné próze Máchově," in *Torso a tajemství Máchova díla*, Sborník pojednání Pražského linguistického kroužku, ed. Jan Mukařovský (Prague: Borový, 1938), 183.

147. Arne Novák, *Stručné dějiny literatury české*, ed. R. Havel and A. Grund (Olomouc, 1946), 61, cited by Eduard Petrů, *Vzdálené hlasy: studie o starší české literatuře* (Olomouc: Votobia, 1996), 227; Vojtěch Jirát voiced the same opinion; see

Jirát, "O klasicismu, zvláště pak o klasicismu českém," in Jirát, *Portréty a studie* (Prague: Odeon, 1978), 13. For mild dissent, see also Milan Kopecký, "Tradice a její žánrová modifikace," in *Speculum medii aevi: Zrcadlo středověku*, ed. Lenka Jiroušková (Prague: Koniasch Latin Press, 1998), 80–81.

148. René Wellek, *Essays on Czech Literature*, intro. Peter Demetz (The Hague: Mouton, 1963), 23.

149. Čechura and Čechurová, *Korespondence Josefa Pekaře a Kamila Krofty*, 86.

150. For instance, Zdeňka Tichá, *Cesta starší české literatury* (Prague: Panorama, 1984), 203–205.

151. Čechura and Čechurová, *Korespondence Josefa Pekaře a Kamila Krofty*, 87. Earlier, Palacký insisted on the high aesthetic, not only linguistic, level of the sixteenth-century literature in Bohemia; see František Palacký, *Gedenkblätter* (Prague: F. Tempsky, 1874), 31.

152. Kolár, *Návraty bez konce*, 119, 121. Subsequently, Viktor Viktora has also testified to the richness of Czech sixteenth-century literature, see Viktora, *K pramenům národní literatury* (Plzeň: Fraus, 2003), 74–116.

153. See, for instance, *Dějiny zemí koruny české* (Prague: Paseka, 1992), 1:289. See Josef Kalousek, "O vůdčích myšlénkách v historickém díle Palackého," *Památník na oslavu stých narozenin Františka Palackého* (Prague: Matice česká, 1898), 177–232.

154. Erasmus, *The Correspondence*, 6:174.

155. Francesco Petrarca, *Knihy dvoje o lékařství proti štěstí a neštěstí* (Prague: Jan Severýn z Kapí Hory, 1501); see *Knihopis*, no. 7049. His son, Zikmund Hrubý of Jelení (Gelenius), assisted Erasmus in editing ancient authors; see *Lexikon české literatury: Osobnosti, díla, instituce*, ed. Vladimír Forst and others (Prague: Academia, 1985–2008), 2, pt. 2:339.

156. *Ottův slovník naučný* (Prague: Otto, 1888–1908), 8:275; 11:642–43. Bohemian editions of the Bible were noted internationally for their attention to Greek texts; Josef Dobrovský, *Dějiny české řeči a literatury v redakcích z roku 1791, 1792 a 1818*, ed. Benjamin Jedlička (Prague: Melantrich, 1936), 153.

157. Josef Hanzal, "Martin Bacháček z Nauměřic a městské školy ve středních Čechách před Bílou Horou," *Středočeský sborník historický* 10 (1975): 141–42; František Palacký, *Dílo*, ed. Jaroslav Charvát (Prague: Mazáč, 1941), 4:13. The legal system of Bohemia met the highest European standards, and the Confederation of 1619 could be regarded as the first modern constitution; Karel Malý, "Právní kultura v českém stavovském státě," in *Vladislavské zřízení zemské a počátky ústavního zřízení v Českých zemích*, 55–66.

158. Bílejovský, *Kronika církevní*, 88–104. For their names and the number of references to each, see David, *Finding the Middle Way*, 15.

159. For instance, Pavel Bydžovský, *Děťátka a neviňátka hned po přijetí křtu sv. Tělo a Krev Boží, že přijímati mají* (Prague: Bartoloměj Netolický, 1541), f. B4r; his *Knížky o přijímání Těla a Krve Pána našeho Ježíše Krysta. . . .* (Prague, 1539), 52–55; Bydžovský, *Tato Knížka toto try ukazuje. . . .* (N.p., 1542), 14–16; Bydžovský, *Tento spis ukazuje, že Biskupové Biskupa a Biskup kněží*, 12–15; Jireček, *Rukověť k dějinám literatury české*, 1:114–15. He cited from recent authoritative editions, such as Pseudo–Dionysius, *Theologia vivificans. Cibus solidus. Dionysii coelestis hierarchia. Ecclesiastica hierarchia. Divina nomina. Mystica theologia. Undecim epistolae. Ignatii undecim epistolae. Polycarpi epistola una*, edited by Jacques Le Fèvre d'Étaples.

In alma Parisiorum academia, Per Henricū Stephanū, 1515, see Bydžovský, *Děťátka a neviňátka*, f. B2r. Even a regular Utraquist priest, Vavřinec Leander Rvačovský of Rvačov, is praised for his "unusual linguistic, historical, and theological knowledge." See Antonín Rybička, "Rvačovský Vavřinec Leander," *Časopis českého musea* 45 (1871): 326.

160. Matauš Pačuda, *Spis v němž se obsahuje které věci (z stran lidského pokolení) předešly příchod a narození mesiáše pravého Krista* (Prague: Matěj Pardubický, 1616). For a full list of these theologians and classical authors, see David, *Finding the Middle Way*, 331.

161. *Od nejstarší doby do sloučení pražských měst, 1784*, vol. 1 of *Dějiny Prahy*, 223–24; Viktora, *K pramenům národní literatury*, 13; Zikmund Winter, *O životě na vysokých školách pražských: kulturní obraz XV. a XVI. století* (Prague: Matice česká, 1899), 564; and Winter, *Děje vysokých škol pražských*, 60–62. On the diminution of international membership and decline to an undergraduate or "finishing school" level, see Rainer C. Schwinges, *Deutsche Universitätsbesucher im 14. und 15. Jahrhundert: Studien zur Sozialgeschichte des Alten Reiches* (Stuttgart: Franz Steiner, 1986), especially, 470–72, 495–96.

162. Hanzal, "Martin Bacháček z Nauměřic," 142; Pešek, *Měšťanská vzdělanost a kultura*, 26–28.

163. Josef Janáček, "České stavovské povstání, 1618–20: Otázky a problémy," *Folia Historica Bohemica* 8 (1985): 20–26, 30–32. Concerning military leadership, see František Hrubý,"Nové příspěvky k historii bitvy na Bílé hoře," *Časopis českého musea* 27 (1922): 277–88. See also František. J. Kroiher, "Nevlastenectví českých stavů nekatolických v době předbělohorské," *Sborník historického kroužku* Sešit 3 (1894): especially 69; Jaroslav Pánek, "Stavovství v předbělohorské době," *Folia Historica Bohemica* 6 (1984): 172.

164. Jaroslav Pánek, "Republikánské tendence ve stavovských programech doby předbělohorské," *Folia Historica Bohemica* 8 (1985): 49. On the failures on the diplomatic front, see Jonathan Israel, *The Dutch Republic: Its Rise, Greatness, and Fall, 1477–1806* (Oxford: Clarendon Press, 1995), 469.

Chapter 3

1. On the question of cultural transmission from the Bohemian Reformation into modern political culture, a major dispute developed in the Czech intellectual arena starting in the 1890s. The protagonists were, on one side, Tomáš G. Masaryk and his school, including historians like Jaroslav Vančura and Kamil Krofta; and on the other side were the historian Josef Pekař and his colleagues. See the Preface to this volume, n. 3.

2. Ernest Gellner, *Nations and Nationalism* (Ithaca, N.Y.: Cornell University Press, 1983), especially 43–50; Eric J. Hobsbawm, *Nations and Nationalism since 1780*, 2nd ed. (New York: Cambridge University Press, 1992). For a summary statement, see Anthony D. Smith, *The Ethnic Origins of Nations* (Oxford: Blackwell, 1987), 7–13. For a critical comment on Gellner and Hobsbawm, see Gregory Jusdanis, *The Necessary Nation* (Princeton. N.J.: Princeton University Press, 2001), 36–39. For additional literature, see Hugh Seton-Watson, *Nations and States* (London: Methuen, 1977); Benedict Anderson, *Imagined Communities: Reflections on*

the Origin and Spread of Nationalism (London: Verso, 1991); and Anthony Smith, *National Identity* (Reno: University of Nevada Press, 1991).

3. More recently, however, there has been a questioning of the "antigenealogical" perspective on the study of nations, see Elías José Palti, "The Nation as a Problem: Historians and the 'National Question,'" *History and Theory* 40 (2001): 324–46.

4. On the subject, see "AHR Forum: How Revolutionary Was the Print Revolution?" *American Historical Review* 107 (2002): 84–128.

5. The benign attitude toward the Counter-Reformation can be deduced, for instance, from the critical reaction that greeted the appearance of Jan Fiala's *Hrozné doby protireformace* (Heršpice: Eman, 1997). See Tomáš Knoz, review of Miloš Pojar, *Jindřich Matyáš Thurn* (Prague, 1998), in *Časopis Matice Moravské* 119 (2000): 306.

6. R. G. Collingwood, *The Idea of History*, rev. Jan van der Dussen (Oxford: Clarendon Press, 1993), especially, 215–19, 282–302, 441–50.

7. Cited by Jan van der Dussen, "Editor's Introduction," to Collingwood, *The Idea of History*, xxxviii. On Collingwood's theory of reenactment, see also Christopher Parker, *The English Idea of History from Coleridge to Collingwood* (Burlington, Vt.: Ashgate, 2000), 185–86, 201, 212; Jan W. van der Dussen, *History as a Science: The Philosophy of R. G. Collingwood* (The Hague: Martinus Nijhoff, 1981), especially, 93–109, 312–24; and Rex Martin, *Historical Explanation: Re-enactment and Practical Inference* (Ithaca, N.Y.: Cornell University Press, 1977), 58–60.

8. I owe the suggestion of the parallel between the Italian Renaissance and the Bohemian national awakening largely to John W. Brennan. On the proscribed books from the Jesuit libraries, see, for instance, Josef Polišenský and Ella Illingová, *Jan Jeník z Bratřic* (Prague: Melantrich, 1989), 86, 164. Outside Bohemia, in Lower and Upper Austria there was also a certain, more limited, harkening during the Enlightenment to the pre–Counter-Reformation period, particularly the spirit of religious toleration, epitomized by Emperor Maximilian II; see R. J. W. Evans, "Über die Ursprünge der Aufklärung in den habsburgischen Ländern," in *Das achtzehnte Jahrhundert und Österreich*, Jahrbuch der Österreichischen Gesellschaft zur Erforschung des achtzehnten Jahrhunderts 2 (Vienna: Böhlaus, 1985), 18–19.

9. On the rendering of the German terms *Josephinismus* and *josephinistisch* into English as *Josephism* and *Josephist*, see Derek E. Beales, *Enlightenment and Reform in Eighteenth-Century Europe* (New York: I. B. Tauris, 2005), 287–91.

10. See chapter 11 in this volume.

11. Eduard Winter, *Der Josefinismus: die Geschichte des österreichischen Reformkatholizismus, 1740–1848* (Berlin: Rütten & Loening, 1962), 34; Pavel Křivský, "Korespondence Jana Leopolda Haye, Josefa Františka Hurdálka a Augustina Zippa s Josefem Dobrovským," *Literární archiv: Sborník Památníku národního písemnictví* 5 (1970): 138. František X. Němeček dated the onset of the cultural revolution to Maria Theresa's reign (after 1760) with van Swieten as the principal moving spirit; see Němeček, "Züge aus der Geschichte der Wissenschaften und des Geschmackes in Böhmen; geschrieben im Jahre 1794," *Libussa*, eine vaterländische Vierteljahrschrift, ed. J. G. Meinert, vol. 2 (Prague: Calve, 1804), 56.

12. Franz A. J. Szabo, *Kaunitz and Enlightened Absolutism, 1753–1780* (New York: Cambridge University Press, 1994), 245. See also Peter Hersche, ed., *Der aufgeklärte Reformkatholizismus in Oesterreich* (Bern: Herbert Lang, 1976), 10, 14.

13. Jan Patočka, "Bolzanovo místo v dějinách filosofie," in *Filosofie v dějinách*

českého národa (Prague: Nakladatelství ČSAV, 1958), 111. As an exception to this view, Harm Klueting sees the primary source in the writings of the two German Lutheran law professors, Christian Thomasius (1655–1728) and Justus Henning Böhmer (1674–1749); see Klueting, "Kaunitz, die Kirche und der Josephinismus. Protestantisches landesherrliches Kirchenregiment, rationaler Territorialismus und theresianisch-josephinisches Staatskirchentum," in *Staatskanzler Wenzel Anton von Kaunitz–Rietberg, 1711–1794,* ed. Grete Klingenstein and Franz A. Szabo (Graz: Andreas Schneider, 1996), 187.

14. On Jansenism in the Austrian Netherlands, see Jan Roegiers, "Jansenisme en katholieke hervorming in de Nederlanden," in *Geloven in het verleden: studies over het godsdienstig leven in de vroegmoderne tijd, aangeboden aan Michel Cloet,* ed. Eddy Put, Juliette Marinus, and Hans Storme, Symbolae Facultatis Litterarum Lovaniensis. Series A, vol. 22 (Leuven: Universitaire Pers Leuven, 1996); and Craig Harline and Eddy Put, *A Bishop's Tale: Mathias Hovius among His Flock in Seventeenth-Century Flanders* (New Haven, Conn.: Yale University Press, 2000). On Jansenism in the Habsburg Empire and its relationship to Josephism, see Peter Hersche, *Der Spätjansenismus in Österreich* (Vienna: Verlag der Österreichischen Akademie der Wissenschaften, 1977), especially 313–55. On Jansenism in Bohemia, see Milan Machovec, *Josef Dobrovský* (Prague: Svobodné slovo, 1964), 26–36.

15. Lodovico Antonio Muratori, *O pravé křesťanské pobožnosti* (Prague: Pravidelní školská knihtiskárna, 1778). Dobrovský recommended reading Muratori to his theology students about the necessary role of reason in religion; see Josef Dobrovský, *Přednášky o praktické stránce v křesťanském náboženství,* ed. Josef Volf, Miloš B. Volf, and Josef Vraštil, Spisy a projevy, vol. 16 (Prague: Melantrich, 1948), 64; James V. Melton, "From Image to Word: Cultural Reform and the Rise of Literate Culture in Eighteenth-Century Austria," *Journal of Modern History* 58 (1986): 113–15; and Derek E. Beales, *Joseph II: In the Shadow of Maria Theresa, 1741–1780* (New York: Cambridge University Press, 1987), 62–63.

16. Jacques Bénigne Bossuet, *Učení katolického v těch věcech, o kterých rozepře jsou, vyložen* (Prague: C. k. školní knihtiskárna, 1778); and Pavel Bělina, Jiří Kaše, and Jan P. Kučera, *Velké dějiny zemí Koruny české* 10, 1740–92 (Prague: Paseka, 2001), 229. Erasmus's irenic *Ratio seu methodus compendio perveniendi ad veram theologiam* was published in Prague (by Joann Mangoldt) in 1786.

17. František Faustin Procházka, *De saecularibus liberalium artium in Bohemia et Moravia satis commentarius* (Prague: Litteris Scholae normalis, Schmadl factore, 1782), 411; Adam Wandruszka, "Der Reformkatholizismus des 18. Jahrhunderts in Italien und in Österreich," in *Festschrift Hermann Wiesflecker zum sechzigsten Geburtstag,* ed. Alexander Novotny and Othmar Pickl (Graz: Selbstverlag des Historischen Instituts der Universität Graz, 1973), 231–40; Erich Zöllner, "Bemerkungen zum Problem der Beziehungen zwischen Aufklärung und Josephinismus," in *Österreich und Europa: Festgabe für Hugo Hantsch zum 70. Geburtstag* (Graz: Styria, 1965), 203–19; and Patočka, "Bolzanovo místo v dějinách filosofie," 111.

18. František Palacký, "Josefa Dobrovského život a vědecké působení," *Česká včela* 4 (1837): 262. However, Rautenstrauch, as well as van Swieten, initially felt that Dobrovský's temperament made him unsuitable for positions in academic institutions, see ibid., 269; Procházka, *De saecularibus liberalium artium in Bohemia et Moravia,* 412. Concerning Rautenstrauch, see Josef Hanzal, "F. Š. Rautenstrauch ve světle svých deníků," *Český časopis historický* 93 (1995): 86–97; Beda Franz

Menzel, *Abt Franz Stephan Rautenstrauch von Břevnov-Braunau: Herkunft, Umwelt und Wirkungskreis*. Königstein/Ts: Königsteiner Institut für Kirchen-und Geistesgeschichte der Sudentenländer, 1969; and Josef Müller, *Das pastoraltheologischdidaktische Ansatz in Franz Stephan Rautenstrauchs "Entwurf einer besseren Einrichtung theologischen Schulen,"* Wiener Beiträge zur Theologie, 25 (Vienna: Herder, 1969).

19. *Knihopis českých a slovenských tisků* (Prague: Nakladatelství Československé akademie věd, 1925–67), 2: pt.7, 449.

20. Jitka Lněničková, *České země v době předbřeznové, 1792–1848* (Prague: Libri, 1999), 116.

21. See Bělina, Kaše, and Kučera, *Velké dějiny zemí Koruny české*, 10:79.

22. Pavel Křivský, "Korespondence Jana Leopolda Haye, Josefa Františka Hurdálka a Augustina Zippa s Josefem Dobrovským," *Literární archiv: Sborník Památníku národního písemnictví* 5 (1970): 133 n.1, 151; Palacký, "Josefa Dobrovského život a vědecké působení," 270, 276. Having guided the reform of theological education in Austria and Bohemia, Rautenstrauch turned his attention to Hungary, but he died in 1785, less than a year later in Rožňava in present-day Slovakia.

23. The leaders of this cultural revolution, which was to reorganize intellectual and social life along the principles of the Enlightenment, had much in common philosophically with such founding fathers of the United States as Thomas Jefferson, John Adams, and James Madison. In fact, there was a measure of inspiration from the American political philosophy surrounding the War of Independence; see Josef Hanzal, "F. Š. Rautenstrauch ve světle svých deníků," *Český časopis historický* 93 (1995): 87 n.7, 93.

24. Palacký, "Josefa Dobrovského život a vědecké působení," 277. After its foundation in 1818, Dobrovský served on the board of the Bohemian National Museum; see ibid., 294. Karel Ignác Thám prepared a list of the Bohemian adherents of the Enlightenment, including, in the 1780s, Pelcl, Dobner, Pubička, Aleš Pařízek, Voigt, Ungar, Dobrovský, Jiljí Chládek, Stanislav Vydra, Ignác Cornova, Durych, and Procházka; see Karel Ignác Thám, *Obrana jazyka českého proti zlobivým jeho utrhačům* (Prague: Schönfeld, 1783), 40–41. Another list can be found in Procházka, *De saecularibus liberalium artium in Bohemia et Moravia*, 410–15, adding Vratislav Monse and Karl H. Seibt; and in the preface to Václav Thám, *Básně v řeči vázané*, První sebrání (Prague: U Rosenmüllerských dědiců, 1785), f. A5r–v.

25. In recent literature there has also been a tendency to lift from Joseph the opprobrium of being an "enlightened despot" like Catherine II of Russia and Frederick the Great of Prussia; see Jonathan Israel, "Enlightenment! Which Enlightenment?" *Journal of the History of Ideas* 67 (2006): 534–35.

26. Václav Thám, *Básně v řeči vázané*, A3v. Already under Empress Maria Theresa, the Czech language was, in fact, introduced as an obligatory subject in the military academy at Wiener Neustadt. Czech was to be taught immediately after German, on the grounds that its grammar facilitated the subsequent study of Latin and the rigors of its pronunciation the study of any other languages; Tomáš Burian, "Český jazyk v Novém městě za Vídní," *Časopis českého musea* 12 (1843): 526. The teaching of Czech was suspended in 1807 and restored in 1824; see ibid., 530–31.

27. Karel Ignác Thám, *Kurzgefasste böhmische Sprachlehre* (Prague: Schönfeld, 1785), iv; and Karel Ignác Thám, *Deutsch–böhmisches Nationallexikon* (Prague: Schönfeld, 1788), xv–xvi; Karel Ignác Thám, *Obrana jazyka českého proti zlobivým*

jeho utrhačům 45. In the preface to the fourth edition of his grammar (1801), Thám escalated his praise of the great emperor, who "as the king of Bohemia according to the ground rules of the grammar learned and spoke Czech, gaining thereby the confidence, high respect, sympathy and love of the entire Slav nation." Karel Ignác Thám, *Böhmische Grammatik zum Gebrauche der Deutschen*, Vierte Auflage (Prague: Diesbach, 1801), cited in Karel Ignác Thám, *Böhmische Grammatik zum Gebrauche der Deutschen*, Fünfte Auflage (Prague: Diesbach, 1804), xii.

28. On September 19, 1786, the emperor also attended a Czech-language performance in the Prague theater; see Karel Ignác Thám, *Über den Karakter der Slawen, dann über den Ursprung, die Schicksale, Volkommenheiten, die Nützlichkeit und Wichtigkeit der bömischen Sprache* (Prague: Johann Diesbach'schen Buchhandlung, 1803), 35–36, see also 13; Jan Jeník z Bratřic, *Z mých pamětí*, ed. Josef Polišenský (Prague: ELK, 1947), 25–26.

29. Václav Thám, *Básně v řeči vázané*, První sebrání, f. A3v–A4r.

30. Johann Heinrich Wolf, *Geschichte des Königreichs Böheim zum Gebrauche der Studierenden Jugend in der K.K. Staaten* (Vienna: Johann Thomas von Trattner, 1783), 235; and Arnošt Kraus, *Husitství v literatuře zejména německé* (Prague: Česká akademie, 1917–24), 2:185.

31. Karel Raphael Ungar, *Allgemeine böhmische Bibliothek* (Prague, Schönfeld, 1786), 9–10.

32. The tome [F. A. Zieger], *Das Buch Joseph* (Prague: Wolgang Gerle, 1783) was translated and published in Czech by Kramerius, as *Kniha Josefova. Sepsaná od jistého spatřujícího osmnácté století. Dílem již stalé věci a dílem proroctví. Na způsob Biblí* (Prague: Kramerius, 1784); see Jan Novotný, *Matěj Václav Kramerius* (Prague: Melantrich, 1973), 33. On Zitte's presumed authorship, see František M. Bartoš, *Tajemství knihy Josefovy; Knihy a zápasy* (Prague, 1948); Novotný, *Matěj Václav Kramerius*, 32. Incidentally, Augustin Zitte, a secular priest and writer in Prague, needs to be distinguished from his more illustrious contemporary, the earlier mentioned Augustin Zippe. The two appear to be confused, for instance, in Josef Haubelt, *České osvícenství*. 2nd rev. ed. (Prague: Rodiče, 2004), 364–65; in František Kutnar, *Obrozenské vlastenectví a nacionalismus, Příspěvek k národnímu společenskému obsahu češství doby obrozenské* (Prague: Karolinum, 2003), 128, and even in *Slovník českých filozofů*, ed., Jiří Gabriel (Brno: Masarykova Univiverzita, 1998), 210.

33. František M. Pelcl, *Geschichte der Böhmen von den ältesten bis auf die neuesten Zeiten*, 4th ed. (Prague: Schönfeld, 1817), 2: 965.

34. Kašpar Royko, *Geschichte der grossen allgemeinen Kirchenversammlung zu Kostniz*. Vols. 1–2, 2nd rev. ed. (Vienna and Graz: In Commission der Weingand, 1782), 1: f. 2v.

35. Kraus, *Husitství v literatuře zejména německé*, 2:161.

36. Robert B. Pysent, "The Baroque Continuum of Czech Literature," *Slavonic and East European Review* 62 (1984): 323, n. 5.

37. Aleksandr S. Myl'nikov, *Vznik národně osvícenské ideologie v českých zemích 18. století* (Prague: Univerzita Karlova, 1974), 173.

38. "Die Schlacht am weiszen Berge 1620 lähmte und entkräftigte die ganze böhmische Nation an Leib und Seele." Josef Dobrovský, *Dějiny české řeči a literatury v redakcích z roku 1791, 1792 a 1818*, ed. Benjamin Jedlička (Prague: Melantrich, 1936), 58, 160, 166; Jan Lehár and others, *Česká literatura od počátků k dnešku* (Prague: Lidové noviny, 1998), 162; Bedřich Slavík, *Od Dobnera k Dobrovskému*

(Prague: Vyšehrad, 1975), 264 ; and Josef Macůrek, "Dobrovského pojetí českých dějin a stanovisko k našemu historickému vývoji," *Slavia* 23 (1954): 183–84.

39. Dobrovský, *Dějiny české řeči a literatury*, 54–55. In a lighter vein, Dobrovský also noted the ineptitude of monastic librarians, who would have been better suited "for the kitchen or the wine-cellar"; Josef Dobrovský, *Böhmische und Mährische Litteratur auf das Jahr 1780* (Prague: Mangoldische Buchhandlung, 1780), 6.

40. Jan Jakubec, ed., *Literatura česká devatenáctého století*, with Josef Hanuš, Jan Máchal, and Jaroslav Vlček, 2nd ed. (Prague: Jan Laichter, 1911–17), 1: 369–70. Jan Jakubec, *Dějiny literatury české*, 2nd ed. (Prague: Jan Laichter, 1929–34), 2: 13–14.

41. František Faustin Procházka, *Miscellaneen der Böhmischen und Mährischen Litteratur, seltener Werke, und verschiedenen Handschriften*, vol. 1, 3 pts. (Prague, 1784–85), 1, pt. 2:253.

42. Augustin Zitte, *Lebensbeschreibung der drei ausgezeichnetsten Vorläufer M. Joh. Huss von Hussinec, bekanntlich: des Konrad Stiekna, Johann Milicz und Mathias von Janow, nebst einer Übersicht der böhmischen Religionsgeschichte bis auf seine Zeit* (Prague: Wolfgang Gerle, 1786), 3.

43. Otto Steinbach of Kranichstein, "Versuch einer Geschichte der alten und neuen Toleranz im Königreich Böhmen und Markgraftum Mähren," *Abhandlungen de Böhmischen Gesellschaft der Wissenschaften zu Prag auf das Jahr 1785* Zweite Abteilung (1786), 221.

44. Ibid., 230. He located the depredations of Don Martin von Huerda and Don Balthasar in the areas of Kutná Hora, Litoměřice, Bydžov, and Hradec Králové.

45. Kašpar Royko, *Synopsis historiae religionis et ecclesiae christianae: methodo systematica adumbratae* (Prague: Ioann Mangoldt, 1785), 118–19.

46. Ibid., 107–109.

47. Wolf, *Geschichte des Königreichs Böheim*, 233.

48. Kraus, *Husitství v literatuře zejména německé*, 2:185.

49. Thám, *Kurzgefasste böhmische Sprachlehre*, iv–v.

50. He credited one of these missionaries, Antonín Koniáš, with having 60,000 Bohemian books burned; see Thám, *Über den Karakter der Slawen*, 12–13.

51. Václav Thám, *Básně v řeči vázané*, První sebrání, f. A3r–v; Novotný, *Matěj Václav Kramerius* 76; Polišenský and Illingová, *Jan Jeník z Bratřic*, 35, 67.

52. He listed Václav Dobřenský, Jan Gryll of Gryllov, Jiří Hanuš Landškronský, Matěj Kollin z Chotěřiny, Jan A. Komenský, David Krynýt of Hlaváčov, Šimon Lomnický of Budeč, Jan Rozácius Sušický, Tomáš Soběslavský, Sixt of Ottersdorf, Jan Táborský, Jiří Tesák, Daniel Adam of Veleslavín, and "many others," referring to the *Index bohemicorum librorum prohibitorum et corrigendorum*, jussu Antonii Petri Archiepiscopi Pragensis editus Anno 1767 (Pragae: Typis Archiepiscopalibus, 1767). See Václav Thám, *Básně v řeči vázané*, První sebrání, f. A2v–A3r.

53. Václav Thám, *Básně v řeči vázané*, První sebrání, f. A3r–v.

54. Ibid., f. A6r. We find here another reference to "temno."

55. František M. Pelcl, *Grundsätze der böhmischen Grammatik*, 2nd ed. (Prague: Jeřábek, 1798), 252; František M. Pelcl, *Paměti*, trans. Jan Pán (Prague: Státní nakladatelství kràsné literatury, hudby a umění, 1956), 55.

56. František M. Pelcl, *Böhmische, mährische und schlesische Gelehrte und Schriftsteller aus dem Orden der Jesuiten von Anfang der Gesellschaft bis auf gegenwärtige Zeit* (Prague, 1786), 184.

57. Pelcl, *Paměti*, 39.

58. Pelcl, *Böhmische, mährische und schlesische Gelehrte*, 75. By faint praise, Pelcl ridiculed the Jesuits' alleged penchant for asceticism; see Zuzana Urválková, "František Martin Pelcl o Jezuitech," in *Bůh a bohové: Církve, náboženství a spiritualita v českém 19 století*, ed. Zdeněk Hojda and Roman Prahl (Prague: KLP, 2003), 125.

59. Němeček, "Züge aus der Geschichte der Wissenschaften und des Geschmackes in Böhmen," 19.

60. Ibid., 39–40, 43.

61. Ibid., 45, 47.

62. Cited in Novotný, *Matěj Václav Kramerius*, 38. Josef Valentin Eybel, *Christkatholische nützliche Hauspostille auf alle Sonn–und Feiertage* (Linz, 1784) was published in Czech translation as *Křesťanská katolická užitečná domovní Postyla* (Prague: Kramerius, 1785). Eybel was professor of canon law at the University of Vienna and, in turn, a disciple of Paul J. Riegger; see Manfred Brandl, *Der Kanonist Joseph Valentin Eybel, 1741–1805: sein Beitrag zur Aufklärung in Österreich* (Steyr: Ennsthaler, 1976), 19–20, 24.

63. Jan Jeník z Bratřic, *Z mých paměti*, ed. Josef Polišenský (Prague: ELK, 1947), 27; Polišenský and Illingová, *Jan Jeník z Bratřic*, 81–82, 85–86, 90.

64. Jeník z Bratřic, *Z mých paměti*, 22–23, 25; he claimed that the fear of diabolical beings kept him in his youth from visiting the toilet at night; ibid., 29.

65. Jakubec, ed., *Literatura česká devatenáctého století*, 2:589, 594.

66. Josef Jungmann, *Zápisky*, ed. Radek Lunga (Prague: Budka, 1998),43.

67. František Palacký, *Gedenkblätter* (Prague: F. Tempsky, 1874), 33–34.

68. František Palacký, *Böhmische Sprache und Literatur* (1831), cited by Josef Hanuš, *O pobělohorské protireformaci: Úvodem k českému obrození*, Universita Komenského. Bratislava, Filosofická fakulta, Sborník, 4, n. 39 (Bratislava, 1926), 6.

69. On the concept of Catholic Enlightenment, see also Alois Křišťan, *Počátky pastorální teologie v českých zemích* (Prague: Triton, 2004), 29–34. On questioning the tridentine decrees, see W. Zeil, "Der Briefwechsel J. Žurs und F. J. Loks mit J. Dobrovský, 1778–1797," *Lětopis: Jahresschrift des Instituts für sorbische Volksforschung*, Reihe B, Geschichte, 15 (1968): 79. For a critique of the postmodernist debunking of the very concept of the Enlightenment, see Israel, "Enlightenment! Which Enlightenment?" 523–45.

70. Peter Hersche, ed., *Der aufgeklärte Reformkatholizismus in Oesterreich* (Bern: Herbert Lang, 1976), 3–5. On this neglected theme, see David Sorkin, "Reform Catholicism and Religious Enlightenment," *Austrian History Yearbook* 30 (1999): 187–219, with "Comments" by T. C. W. Blanning and R. J. W. Evans, ibid., 221–35; Dale K. Van Kley "Piety and Politics in the Century of Lights," in *Cambridge History of Eighteenth-Century Political Thought*, ed. Mark Goldie and Robert Wokler (New York: Cambridge University Press, 2006), 119–31; Derek E. Beales, *Enlightenment and Reform in Eighteenth-Century Europe* (New York: I. B. Tauris, 2005), especially 79–82; and T. C. W. Blanning, "The Enlightenment in Catholic Germany," in *The Enlightenment in National Context*, ed. Roy Porter and Mikuláš Teich (New York: Cambridge University Press, 1981), 118–26. For older works on Catholic Enlightenment, see Sebastian Merkle, *Die katholische Beurteilung des Aufklärungszeitalters* (Berlin: K. Curtius, 1909); Sebastian Merkle and Bernhard Bess, *Religiöse Erzieher der katholischen Kirche aus den letzten vier Jahrhunderten* (Leipzig: Quelle und Meyer, [1922]); and Sebastian Merkle, *Die kirchliche*

Aufklärung im katholischen Deutschland (Berlin: Reichel, 1910). For a later discussion, see Jonathan Sheehan, "Enlightenment, Religion, and the Enigma of Secularization," *American Historical Review* 108 (2003): 1061–80.

71. Jaromír Plch, *Antonín Marek* (Prague: Melantrich, 1974), 99. In fact, Bishop Josef Hurdálek of Litoměřice may have proposed the introduction of married clergy; see Vincenc Zahradník, *Filosofické spisy*, edited by František Čáda (Prague: [Česká akademie pro vědy slovesnost a umění,] 1907–8), 1: 88–89. Some priests seem to have repudiated celibacy de facto, if not de jure. Thus Marek had three sons, see Plch, *Antonín Marek*, 100; see also the discussion of Dobrovský's point of view by Pavel Marek, "A Discussion on Celibacy in the History of the Catholic Modernist Movement, 1900–1908," in *Živý odkaz modernism,* ed. Zdeněk Kučera, Jiří Kořalka, and Jan B. Lášek (Brno: L. Marek, 2003), 116–18.

72. Interestingly, they highlighted fiscal consequences: celibacy interfered with the increase of population and productive taxpayers; S. Santoli, "Wirtschaftliche Grundlagen des Josefinismus," *Österreichisches Archiv für Kirchenrecht* 13 (1962): 213–32, cited by Bělina, Kaše, and Kučera, *Velké dějiny zemí Koruny české*, 10:231.

73. "Der Mensch is weder Engel noch Thier: und das Schicksal will, wer den Engel spielen will, Thier wird." See Augustin Zippe, *Sechs Predigten, gehalten, auf Veranlassung der in Böhmischkamnitz errichteten Armenversorgungsanstalt* (Prague: Anton Elsenwanger, 1782), 50, 52.

74. Ibid., 71–72. He called Caramuel, although not a Jesuit, "Corriphaeus der Casuisten." See ibid., 75.

75. Augustin Zippe, *Von der moralischen Bildung angehender Geistlichen in dem Generalseminario in Prag* (Prague: Wenzel Peskaček, 1784), 64, 96–97.

76. Augustin Zitte, *Neun neue Exhorten*, oder Ermahnungen bei Gelegenheit einer alten Noven; gehalten bei St. Salvator, an erzbischöflichen Priesterhause in der Altstadt Prag, von 23.–31. Juli, im Jahre 1781 (Prague: Mangoldt, 1783), 103, 104–105.

77. Křišťan, *Počátky pastorální teologie*, 34–51.

78. Franz Stephan Rautenstrauch, *Diarium eruditum*, Státní ústřední archív, Prague, MS Benediktini Břevnov, ŘBB 89, f. 247r.

79. Franz Stephan Rautenstrauch, *Diarium privatum*, Státní ústřední archív, Prague, MS Benediktini Břevnov, ŘBB 88, f. 161r.

80. Franz Stephan Rautenstrauch, *Diarium eruditum*, Státní ústřední archív, Prague, MS Benediktini Břevnov, ŘBB 89, f. 22r, 162r–169v (his comments on Priestley's *Letters to a Philosophical Unbeliever*, pt. 1, 1780), 252r–253r. See also Joseph Priestley, "Letters to a Philosophical Unbeliever. Part 1," in Priestley, *The Theological and Miscellaneous Works*, ed. John Towill Rutt, 25 v. in 26 (London: G. Smallfield, 1817–32), 4:317–411. Reprint: vol. 4, 317–411 (New York: Garland, 1983).

81. Franz Stephan Rautenstrauch, *Diarium eruditum*, Státní ústřední archív, Prague, MS Benediktini Břevnov, ŘBB 89, f. 140r, 226r.

82. Ibid., f. 259r–259v.

83. Steinbach of Kranichstein, "Versuch einer Geschichte der alten und neuen Toleranz," 201, 204–205.

84. Against Pelcl, Steinbach held the alleged edict of Charles IV for authentic; Steinbach of Kranichstein, "Versuch einer Geschichte der alten und neuen Toleranz," 206–208.

85. Ibid., 208, 219.
86. Ibid., 233.
87. Kašpar Royko, *Geschichte der grossen allgemeinen Kirchenversammlung zu Kostniz*, vol. 4 (Prague: im Verlage des Verfassers, 1785), 214, cited by Kraus, *Husitství v literatuře zejména německé*, 2:160.
88. Royko, *Synopsis historiae religionis et ecclesiae christianae*, 106, 107, 136.
89. Ibid., 104.
90. Franz Stephan Rautenstrauch, *Entwurf zur Einrichtung der Generalseminarien in den k. k. Erblanden* (Vienna: Sonnleithner and Hörling, 1784); and Franz Stephan Rautenstrauch, *Entwurf zur Einrichtung der theologischen Schulen in den k. k. Erblanden*, 2nd ed. (Vienna: Sonnleithner and Hörling, 1784) [1st ed. 1782].
91. Rautenstrauch, *Entwurf zur Einrichtung der Generalseminarien*, f. A2r–A2v. The general seminaries were to be located in Vienna, Prague, Olomouc, Graz, Innsbruck, and Freiburg and two in Lviv (Latin and Uniate); ibid., 8–9.
92. Ibid., 12.
93. Such literature was to be excluded forever ["auf ewig versagen"]; Rautenstrauch, *Entwurf zur Einrichtung der Generalseminarien*, 22.
94. Rautenstrauch, *Entwurf zur Einrichtung der theologischen Schulen in den k. k. Erblanden* 2nd ed., 121.
95. Franz Stephan Rautenstrauch, *Warum kömmt Pius der VI. nach Wien? Eine patriotische Betrachtung* (Pressburg: Landerer, 1782), 19.
96. Kašpar Royko, *Einleitung in die christliche Religions-und Kirchengeschichte* (Prague: Joh. Jos. Diesbach, 1788), 53, 88; and Royko, *Synopsis historiae religionis et ecclesiae christianae*, 114–15. He refers to Muratori as "vir doctissimus, et moderationis theologicae commendator." Ibid., 114.
97. Royko, *Synopsis historiae religionis et ecclesiae christianae*, 114, 120–121.
98. See, for instance, Wolf, *Geschichte des Königreichs Böheim*, 238. On Václav Fortunát Durych's liberal Catholicism, see Walter Schamschula, *Die Anfänge der tschechischen Erneuerung und das deutsche Geistesleben, 1740–1800* (Munich: Fink, 1973), 178. While considering Durych a Reform Catholic, Schamschula questions Eduard Winter's view of Durych as a Jansenist, ibid.; and Winter, *Der Josefinismus und seine Geschichte*, 82.
99. Merkle, *Die katholische Beurteilung des Aufklärungszeitalters* 7, offers the following characteristic of the Catholic Enlightenment: "von einem Kampf gegen den Supernaturalismus an sich keine Rede ist, sondern nur gegen unberechtigte, aus ihm gezogene Konsequenzen, namentlich gegen krankhafte Auswüchse des Wunderglaubens: Wundersucht und Aberglauben, Front gemacht wird."
100. Eduard Winter, *Der Josefinismus und seine Geschichte: Beiträge zur Geistesgeschichte Österreichs, 1740–1848* (Brno: Rohrer, 1943), 159.
101. Novotný, *Matěj Václav Kramerius*, 33.
102. Letter to Helfert of November 5, 1784, in Josef Dobrovský, *Dopisy Josefa Dobrovského s Augustinem Helfertem*, ed. Josef Wolf and F. M. Bartoš, Spisy a projevy, vol. 22 (Prague: Melantrich, 1941), 123. Concerning Dobrovský's adherence to Reform Catholicism, see Milan Machovec, *Josef Dobrovský* (Prague: Svobodné slovo, 1964), 90. Dobrovský demonstrated his liberalism by his solicitude for Josef Fesl in his Austrian exile in the 1820s; see Stanislaus Hafner, "Aus B. Kopitars römischen Briefen an Josef Fesl," in *Studia Slovenica Monacensia: In honorem Antonii Slodnjak septuagenarii*, ed. Hans–Joachim Kissling (Munich: Trofenik, 1969), 30.

103. Augustin Zippe, *Von der moralischen Bildung angehender Geistlichen in dem Generalseminario in Prag* (Prague, 1784), cited in Dobrovský, *Přednášky o praktické stránce v křesťanském náboženství*, 6. Aside from Zippe, Dobrovský relied on the writings of Christian Salzmann, ibid., 11–12.

104. "Wahre heilsame gegründete Aufklärung," see Zippe's letter of November 16, 1787, to Dobrovský in Křivský, "Korespondence Jana Leopolda Haye, Josefa Františka Hurdálka a Augustina Zippa s Josefem Dobrovským," 152.

105. Dobrovský, *Přednášky o praktické stránce v křesťanském náboženství*, 14, 19. In his teaching of morality, he stressed interpersonal relationships rather than obligations toward the state; ibid., 11. In that sense he came close to the utilitarianism of Bernard Bolzano's *Vom besten Staate*. See chapter 8 in this volume.

106. Dobrovský, *Přednášky o praktické stránce v křesťanském náboženství*, 48–52, 55.

107. Jiří Černý, "K některým problémům osvícenského filosofického myšlení v Čechách," in *Filosofie v dějinách českého národa* (Prague: Nakladatelství ČSAV, 1958), 103–104.

108. Thus, Deistic or Unitarian views were clearly out of bounds in Joseph II's general seminaries, as well as wearing of secular garments; see Křivský, "Korespondence Jana Leopolda Haye, Josefa Františka Hurdálka a Augustina Zippa s Josefem Dobrovským," 152–55.

109. Josef Dobrovský, *Böhmische Litteratur auf das Jahr 1779* (Prague: Mangoldische Buchhandlung, 1779), 32–41.

110. See, for instance, the reference to his visit in Vienna in 1784; Dobrovský, *Dopisy Josefa Dobrovského s Augustinem Helfertem*, 105; see also 71–72.

111. Dobrovský, *Dopisy Josefa Dobrovského s Augustinem Helfertem* 7; Křivský, "Korespondence Jana Leopolda Haye, Josefa Františka Hurdálka a Augustina Zippa s Josefem Dobrovským," 133 n.1.

112. Křivský, "Korespondence Jana Leopolda Haye, Josefa Františka Hurdálka a Augustina Zippa Josefem Dobrovským," 149, 151. Dobrovský received priestly ordination from Bishop Hay only on December 17, 1786, just before the Olomouc appointment; Dobrovský, *Dopisy Josefa Dobrovského s Augustinem Helfertem*, 9.

113. He revised Stach's translation of Franz Giftschütz's *Leitfaden für Vorlesungen über Pastoraltheologie* (Vienna, 1785); the translation appeared in 1789–90; see Křivský, "Korespondence Jana Leopolda Haye, Josefa Františka Hurdálka a Augustina Zippa s Josefem Dobrovským," 155–56.

114. Viktor Viktora, *K pramenům národní literatury* (Plzeň: Fraus, 2003), 199. See also Viktor Viktora, "Antonín Jaroslav Puchmajer homiletik," *Mezi časy; kultura a umění v českých zemích kolem roku1800*, Sborník příspěvků z 19. ročníku sympozií k problematice 19. století, Plzeň, 4.–6. března 1999, ed. Zdeněk Hojda and Roman Prahl (Prague: KLP, 2000), 208–13.

115. Zahradník, *Filosofické spisy*, 1:76–79; Palacký, "Josefa Dobrovského život a vědecké působení," 262.

116. John Bowring, *Cheskian Anthology: Being a History of the Poetical Literature of Bohemia* (London: Rowland Hunter, 1832), 76–77. Josef Dobrovský, *Böhmische Litteratur auf das Jahr 1779* (Prague: Mangoldische Buchhandlung, 1779), 10. Among other things, he pointed to the beneficial effects of the university reform in 1774 that established new academic chairs and rid theological and philosophical studies of the previous misuse; ibid., 4.

Chapter 4

1. On the poverty of culture in the late eighteenth-century Bohemia, see the typical account of František X. Němeček, "Züge aus der Geschichte der Wissenschaften und des Geschmackes in Böhmen; geschrieben im Jahre 1794," *Libussa, eine vaterländische Vierteljahrschrift*, ed. J. G. Meinert, vol. 2, 1804 (Prague: Calve), 19–21; see also Josef Petráň and others, *Počátky českého národního obrození: Společnost a kultura v 70. až 90. letech 18. století* (Prague: Academia, 1990), 240; Jan Novotný, *Matěj Václav Kramerius* (Prague: Melantrich, 1973), 75; Josef Johanides, *František Martin Pelcl* (Prague: Melantrich, 1981), 149.

2. Only the lowest level of literature, the tales and fairy tales, remained relatively unscathed by Counter-Reformation censorship, and their republication continued from the sixteenth century into the mid-nineteenth century; see Jaroslav Kolár, *Česká zábavná próza 16. století a t. zv. knížky lidového čtení* (Prague: Nakladatelství Československé akademie věd, 1960), 87–89.

3. Vincenc Zahradník, *Filosofické spisy*, ed. František Čáda (Prague: Česká akademie pro vědy slovesnost a umění, 1907–1908), 1:73–74; Josef Polišenský and Ella Illingová, *Jan Jeník z Bratřic* (Prague: Melantrich, 1989), 109; Novotný, *Matěj Václav Kramerius*, 183–84. Josef F. Šumavský shared their opinion in the 1820s; Miloslav Kaňák, *Josef Franta Šumavský* (Prague: Melantrich, 1975), 41–42.

4. Polišenský and Illingová, *Jan Jeník z Bratřic*, 164.

5. Leopold Johann Scherschnik, "Über den Ursprung und die Aufnahme der Bibliothek am Clementinischen Collegium zu Prag," *Abhandlungen einer Privatgesellschaft in Böhmen zur Aufnahme der Mathematik, der vaterländischen Geschichte und der Naturgeschichte* 2 (1776): 259; František Faustin Procházka, *De saecularibus liberalium artium in Bohemia et Moravia satis commentarius* (Prague, 1782), 333–34; František M. Pelcl, *Geschichte der Böhmen von den ältesten bis auf die neuesten Zeiten*, 4th ed. (Prague: Schönfeld, 1817), 2: 615–18.

6. In his argument with Mikuláš Adaukt Voigt, see Němeček, "Züge aus der Geschichte der Wissenschaften," 31.

7. Bedřich Slavík, *Od Dobnera k Dobrovskému* (Prague: Vyšehrad, 1975), 114–15, 208–9, 282; Polišenský and Illingová, *Jan Jeník z Bratřic*, 66, 81.

8. Johann Heinrich Wolf, *Geschichte des Königreichs Böheim zum Gebrauche der Studierenden Jugend in der K.K. Staaten* (Vienna: Johann Thomas von Trattner, 1783), 233–35.

9. *De saecularibus liberalium artium in Bohemia et Moravia*, 306–34.

10. František M. Pelcl, *Grundsätze der böhmischen Grammatik* (Prague: Jeřábek, 1795), "Vorrede," iii–iv; also 2nd ed. (Prague: Jeřábek, 1798), "Vorrede," v–vi; Pelcl, *Geschichte der Böhmen von den ältesten bis auf die neuesten Zeiten*, 4th ed. (Prague: Schönfeld, 1817), 2: 674–76, 677, 679.

11. Němeček also recommended Procházka's *De saecularibus liberalium artium* as a survey of sixteenth-century accomplishments. See Němeček, "Züge aus der Geschichte der Wissenschaften," 25–26, 32–34, 37–38. On the exceptionally high standards of education in sixteenth-century Bohemia, see also Karel B. Štorch, "Komenského snahy pansofické," *Časopis českého musea* 25, no. 3 (1851): 87.

12. Václav Thám, *Básně v řeči vázané, První sebrání* (Prague: U Rosenmüllerských dědiců, 1785), f. A2r.
13. Pelcl, *Grundsätze der böhmischen Grammatik*, 2nd ed., 263.
14. Ibid., 248–53.
15. Karel Ignác Thám, *Über den Karakter der Slawen, dann über den Ursprung, die Schicksale, Volkommenheiten, die Nützlichkeit und Wichtigkeit der bömischen Sprache* (Prague, 1803), 14–15.
16. Novotný, *Matěj Václav Kramerius*, 336.
17. *Krameriovy noviny*, 1791, no. 26 (June 25): 205.
18. Antonín Rybička, "Vzpomínka na Vincence Zahradníka," *Časopis českého musea* 45 (1871): 34–35; Jungmann, *Historie literatury české*, 359–60; also letter from Zahradník to Hanka, dated May 28, 1835, in Zahradník, *Filosofické spisy*, 1:121.
19. In particular, the later bishop of České Budějovice, Jan Jirsík. Ibid., 1:37.
20. Zahradník, *Filosofické spisy*, 1:25. Jeník of Bratřice voiced special respect for authors like Martin Bacháček; see Polišenský and Illingová, *Jan Jeník z Bratřic*, 59, 63, 66–68, 81–82. The novelist Prokop Chocholoušek (1819–64) likewise lauded the high level of Bohemia's educational system in the sixteenth century; Magdaléna Pokorná, *Milován a sledován: Český spisovatel Prokop Chocholoušek, 1819–1864* (Prague: Práh, 2001), 118–19.
21. "Die ganze Masse der Nation wird zum Lesen gereizt und zum Denken aufgefordert. Der kultivirteste Theil denkt und schreibt frei." Josef Dobrovský, *Dějiny české řeči a literatury v redakcích z roku 1791, 1792 a 1818*, ed. Benjamin Jedlička (Prague: Melantrich, 1936), 46 and also 148–49, 152; František M. Bartoš, "Dobrovského pojetí husitství a reformace," *Slavia* 23 (1954): 198–99. Dobrovský's, as well as Pelcl's, interpretation of Bohemia's history was also endorsed by Kašpar Royko, *Einleitung in die christliche Religions-und Kirchengeschichte* (Prague: Joh. Jos. Diesbach, 1788), 318.
22. František Palacký, *Gedenkblätter* (Prague: F. Tempsky, 1874), 30; František Kutnar and Jaroslav Marek, *Přehledné dějiny českého a slovenského dějepisectví*, 2nd ed. (Prague: Lidové noviny, 1997), 164.
23. Artur Závodský, *František Ladislav Čelakovský* (Prague: Melantrich, 1982), 272.
24. Dobrovský, *Dějiny české řeči a literatury*, 171.
25. For instance, in the case of the Icelanders, the "golden age" was placed even further back (to 930–1262) than in the Czech case; see Sigríður Matthíasdóttir, "The Renovation of Native Pasts: A Comparison between Aspects of Icelandic and Czech Nationalist Ideology," *Slavonic and East European Review* 78 (2000): 693, 701, 703.
26. Pavel Bělina, Jiří Kaše, and Jan P. Kučera, *Velké dějiny zemí Koruny české*, vol. 10, 1740–92 (Prague: Paseka, 2001), 179.
27. Kutnar and Marek, *Přehledné dějiny českého a slovenského dějepisectví*, 163; in the following generation, Antonín Marek also preferred the moderate spirit of sixteenth-century Utraquism to Taborite radicalism, which he considered almost as detrimental to Czech national interests as the Counter-Reformation; Jan Jakubec, *Antonín Marek: Jeho život a působení i význam v literatuře české* (Prague: Bačkovský, 1896), 201.

28. "Das schöne oder goldene Zeitalter der böhmischen Sprache," Dobrovský, *Dějiny české řeči a literatury*, 46; Jan Mukařovský, ed., *Dějiny české literatury* (Prague: Nakladatelství Československé akademie věd, 1959–95), 2:114.
29. Dobrovský, *Dějiny české řeči a literatury*, 47.
30. Pelcl, *Geschichte der Böhmen von den ältesten bis auf die neuesten Zeiten*, 4th ed., 2:615; Karel Stloukal, *V předvečer tolerančního patentu*, 315, cited by Bělina, Kaše, and Kučera, *Velké dějiny zemí Koruny české*, 10:239–40.
31. Otto Steinbach of Kranichstein, "Versuch einer Geschichte der alten und neuen Toleranz im Königreich Böhmen und Markgraftum Mähren," *Abhandlungen de Böhmischen Gesellschaft der Wissenschaften zu Prag auf das Jahr 1785*, Zweite Abteilung (1786): 215–17, 220.
32. Ibid., 223.
33. Augustin Zitte, *Lebensbeschreibung des Magisters Johannes Huss von Hussinecz* (Prague: W. Gerle, 1789–90), 1:115, 118–19; Slavík, *Od Dobnera k Dobrovskému*, 178, and see also 177–83; Kašpar Royko, *Geschichte der grossen allgemeinen Kirchenversammlung zu Kostniz*. Vols. 1–2, 2nd rev. ed. (Vienna and Graz: In Commission der Weingand, 1782); vol. 3 (Prague: gedruckt. In Commission der Ferstlischen Buchhandlung zu Graz, 1784); vol. 4 (Prague: im Verlage des Verfassers, 1785).
34. "Naučil Čechy myslet a mluvit staročesky a novoevropsky zároveň." František Palacký, *Spisy drobné*. Edited by Bohuš Rieger (Prague: Bursík a Kohout, [1898–1902]), 1:383–84, cited by Jiří Kořalka, *František Palacký, 1798–1876: Životopis* (Prague: Argo, 1998), 526. See also Polišenský and Illingová, *Jan Jeník z Bratřic*, 66, 111, 119.
35. Karel Havlíček Borovský, "Úvodník," *Národní noviny*, April 5, 1848, cited by Jitka Lněničková, *České země v době předbřeznové, 1792–1848* (Prague: Libri, 1999), 161. Earlier in 1845, he maintained that the national greatness and importance lay in the past and that the future must be built on it; see Karel Havlíček, "Literatura: *Časopis českého musea*. 1845. 4tý svazek," *Česká včela* 12 (1845): 382.
36. Pelcl, *Grundsätze der böhmischen Grammatik*, 1st ed., "Vorrede," iii–iv; also 2nd ed.,"Vorrede," v–vi.
37. Pelcl, *Grundsätze der böhmischen Grammatik*, 2nd ed., 253–54.
38. Karel Ignác Thám, *Obrana jazyka českého proti zlobivým jeho utrhačům* (Prague: Schönfeld, 1783), 40–41; Karel Ignác Thám, *Kurzgefasste böhmische Sprachlehre* (Prague: Schönfeld, 1785), v–vi.
39. Karel Ignác Thám, *Über den Karakter der Slawen*, 13–14, citing from *Artykulové na sněmu obecném Generálním, kterýž držán... Léta Páně 1615* (Prague: v Impressí Šumanské, [1615]); see *Knihopis českých a slovenských tisků* (Prague: Nakladatelství Československé akademie věd, 1925–1967), no. 370. Pelcl likewise cited at length from the same decree; see Pelcl, *Geschichte der Böhmen von den ältesten bis auf die neuesten Zeiten*, 4th ed. 2:681–82.
40. Karel Ignác Thám, *Über den Karakter der Slawen*, 10–11.
41. Němeček, "Züge aus der Geschichte der Wissenschaften," 23, 27, 35–36.
42. Dobrovský, *Dějiny české řeči a literatury*, 47–49, 148, 159.
43. František Palacký, *Gedenkblätter* (Prague: F. Tempsky, 1874), 30, 33.
44. Josef Kočí, *České národní obrození* (Prague: Svoboda, 1978), 189.
45. Josef Jungmann in *Krok* 1 (1821): 7–9, cited in Jaromír Plch, ed., *Antologie*

z české literatury národního obrození (Prague: Státní pedagogické nakladatelství, 1978), 190–91.

46. František Palacký, "Předmluva k vlasteneckému čtenářstvu," *Časopis českého musea* 11(1837): 7.

47. Josef Hanzal, *Od baroka k romantismu: Ke zrození novodobé české kultury* (Prague: Academia, 1987), 89, and review by Pavel Bělina in *Folia Historica Bohemica* 13 (1990): 503; Josef Johanides, *František Martin Pelcl* (Prague: Melantrich, 1981), 90; Alexandr S. Myl'nikov, *Vznik národně osvícenské ideologie v českých zemích: Prameny národního obrození* (Prague: Univerzita Karlova, 1974), 238. Hugh L. Agnew, *Origins of the Czech National Renascence* (Pittsburgh, Pa.: University of Pittsburgh Press, 1993), 171–72, calls attention to the plebeian character of the awakening; he sees the origin of this phenomenon negatively because of the nobility's desertion and positively because of the Enlightenment's interest in the "common man."

48. Němeček, "Züge aus der Geschichte der Wissenschaften," 33–34.

49. Jiří Černý, "K některým problémům osvícenského filosofického myšlení v Čechách," in *Filosofie v dějinách českého národa* (Prague: Nakladatelství ČSAV, 1958), 109; Walter Schamschula, *Die Anfänge der tschechischen Erneuerung und das deutsche Geistesleben, 1740–1800* (Munich: Fink, 1973), 291. Even the counts Šternberks, Klebelsberg, and Antonín Libsteinský of Kolovraty eschewed a Czech national orientation in planning the National Museum; see Kaňák, *Josef Franta Šumavský*, 38–39; Hanzal, *Od baroka k romantismu*, 89.

50. *Abhandlungen der böhmischen Gesellschaft der Wissenschaften zu Prag* (Prague, 1785–88), 4 (1788): 19–20.

51. Lněničková, *České země v době předbřeznové*, 396.

52. Karel Ignác Thám, *Obrana jazyka českého*, 14–17; Václav Thám, *Básně v řeči vázané*, Sebrání druhé (Prague: Schönfeld, 1785), 83; Novotný, *Matěj Václav Kramerius*, 82; Rudolf Holinka, "K Dobrovského koncepci českých dějin," *Slavia* 23 (1954): 203–4.

53. František Josef Kinský, Kašpar Šternberk, and Karel Marie Drahotín Villani; see Jiří Fiala, *Chronologický přehled dějin české literatury národního obrození* (Olomouc: Univerzita Palackého, Filozofická fakulta, 1992), 51–54. Certain members of the vanishing lower nobility identified with the urban commoners; an example was Jeník of Bratřice; see Polišenský and Illingová, *Jan Jeník z Bratřic*, 77, 97, 110. On Leopold II's coronation, see Novotný, *Matěj Václav Kramerius,* 145–46, 157.

54. Karel Tieftrunk, *Dějiny Matice české* (Prague: Řivnáč, 1881), 5; Josef J. Jungmann, *Zápisky*, ed. Radek Lunga (Prague: Budka, 1998), 34–35; see also Jan Jakubec, ed., *Literatura česká devatenáctého století*, with Josef Hanuš, Jan Máchal, and Jaroslav Vlček. 2nd ed. (Prague: Jan Laichter, 1911–17), 1:688.

55. František Ladislav Čelakovský, *Korespondence a zápisky*, Sbírka pramenů ku poznání literárního života v Čechách, na Moravě a ve Slezsku, Skupina 2, Číslo, 14, ed. František Bílý (Prague: Česká akademie pro vědy, slovesnost a umění, 1910), 2:188, 197. See also Marek's letter to Jungmann, dated January 10, 1846, Josef Emler, ed., "Listy Antonína Marka k Josefu Jungmannovi," *Časopis českého musea* 66 (1892): 477.

56. See, for instance, Pokorná, *Milován a sledován*, 25, 37, 114–15; Josef K. Tyl,

"Staré Město a Malá Strana," in Tyl, *Historická dramata,* Spisy 20 (Prague: Státní nakladatelství kràsné literatury, hudby a umění, 1954), 451–53; see also Antonín Měšťan, *Geschichte der tschechischen Literatur im 19. und 20. Jahrhundert* (Cologne: Böhlau, 1984), 93.

57. Stanislav Souček, "Příspěvek k poznání Erbena básníka," *Časopis matice moravské* 39 (1916): 220.

58. In his critique of Tyl's novel *Poslední Čech,* see Karel Havlíček, "Literatura: *Poslední Čech.* Novela Jos. Kajetana Tyla," *Česká včela* 12 (1845): 212.

59. "Nynější postavení české šlechty," *Slovan,* October 26, 1850, cited in Karel Havlíček, *Politické spisy,* ed. Zdeněk V. Tobolka (Prague: Laichter, 1900–1902), 3:429.

60. "Nynější postavení české šlechty," *Slovan,* October 26, 1850, cited in Havlíček, *Politické spisy,* ed. Tobolka, 3:429–30. Concerning Palacký's disappointment with the Bohemian nobility's role in the national revival, see Jaroslav Goll, "František Palacký," *Český časopis historický* 4 (1898): 233–34. See also Kočí, *České národní obrození,* 451.

61. Tomáš G. Masaryk, *Česká otázka. Naše nynější krize. Jan Hus,* Spisy 6 (Prague: Masarykův ústav, 2000), 76.

62. For an opposite point of view, see Josef Hanuš, *Národní museum a naše obrození: k stoletému jubileu založení Musea* (Prague: Národní museum, 1921–23), vol. 1; for instance, 1:101. Josef Pekař largely agreed with Hanuš; see Josef Hanzal, *Josef Pekař: život a dílo* (Prague: Karolinum, 2002), 123. On Hanuš and the nobles' role, see also Schamschula, *Die Anfänge der tschechischen Erneuerung,* 19.

63. Jungmann signaled the cultural divorce between the awakeners and the aristocracy. For all he cared, the nobility might adopt Chaldean as its language of communication. It would not affect the attachment of his colleagues to the Bohemian tongue of the commoners; Josef Jungmann, "O jazyku českém rozmlouvání druhé," *Hlasatel český* 1, no. 3 (1806): 344.

64. See chapter 2 in this volume. This cultural universalism also became the guiding principle of the nineteenth-century heirs of the Catholic Enlightenment. A relevant example is the essay of Josef Durdík, professor of philosophy at the University of Prague, who—admitting that national differences might have a meaning in the area of folk art—insisted that they had no place in higher intellectual activity, like art music, *belles lettres,* or philosophy; see his "O významu nauky Herbartovy," *Časopis českého musea* 50 (1876): 317.

65. František M. Pelcl, *Paměti,* trans. Jan Pán (Prague: Státní nakladatelství krásné literatury, hudby a umění, 1956), 17; Johanides, *František Martin Pelcl,* 164–65. Pelcl was particularly severe in his condemnation of "certain fanatics," who after the death of King Wenceslaus IV "dreamed up a new religion and incited the populace to a frenzy against each other." See František M. Pelcl, "Historische Nachrichten von dem Litthauischen Prinzen Siegmund Koribut," *Abhandlungen der böhmischen Gesellschaft der Wissenschaften zu Prag* 2 (1786): 360. For a summary of Pelcl's critique of the Taborites' excesses, see also Arnošt Kraus, *Husitství v literatuře zejména německé* (Prague: Česká akademie, 1917–24), 2:148–54; Procházka, *De saecularibus liberalium artium,* 197–99.

66. Mikuláš Adauctus Voigt, *Über den Geist der böhmischen Gesetze in den verschiedenen Zeitaltern* (Dresden: Waltherische Hofbuchhandlung, 1788), 177–78, 180.

67. Steinbach of Kranichstein, "Versuch einer Geschichte der alten und neuen Toleranz," 211; on the Roman side, he called attention to the mass immolation of Utraquists in the mines of Kutná Hora in 1420; ibid., 214; Kraus, *Husitství v literatuře*, 2:162. Němeček condemned Taborite violence as the period of what he considered "the most dreadful religious war," fought amid "the vain squabbles of scholastic theologians." See Němeček, "Züge aus der Geschichte der Wissenschaften," 23.

68. "One must be ashamed of earlier times, when such mischief was carried on in the name of religion." Josef Dobrovský, *Litterarisches Magazin von Böhmen und Mähren* 1 (1786): 77; see also Agnew, *Origins of the Czech National Renascence*, 36.

69. Dobrovský, *Dějiny české řeči a literatury*, 128; Kraus, *Husitství v literatuře*, 2:181. See also Jiří Černý, "K některým problémům osvícenského filosofického myšlení v Čechách," 104; Josef Táborský, *Reformní katolík Josef Dobrovský* (Brno: L. Marek, 2007), 90. Dobrovský was not particularly fond of the Unity of Brethren, considering Petr Chelčický an uninteresting visionary; see Milan Machovec, "František Palacký," in *Slovník českých filozofů*, ed. Jiří Gabriel (Brno: Masarykova Univerzita, 1998), 432.

70. Viktor Viktora, *K pramenům národní literatury* (Plzeň: Fraus, 2003), 205–8.

71. Kraus, *Husitství v literatuře*, 2:162.

72. The Utraquists themselves through their spokesmen, such as Bohuslav Bílejovský, had in no uncertain terms censured, and distanced themselves from, the teaching and excessive violence of the Taborites and other radicals during the Bohemian religious wars. See, for instance, Zdeněk V. David, *Finding the Middle Way: The Utraquists' Liberal Challenge to Rome and Luther* (Washington, D.C.: Woodrow Wilson Center Press; Baltimore: Johns Hopkins University Press, 2003), 92–97.

73. Rudolf Zuber, *Osudy moravské církve v 18. Stoletî* (Olomouc: Matice cyrilometodějská, 1987–2003), 2:58–59, n. 229.

74. Franz Wolff, *Commentarium in Sacram scripturam*, 4 pts. (Olomouc: Typis J. Hirnlianae, 1765–68), 1:120–21; 4: 83, 137–39. Wolff evidently was not aware that the Utraquists insisted on the communion *sub utraque* also for infants, 4:137; and wrongly attributed to them the belief in predestination, 2:262. On the other hand, he did not charge them with the Protestant position either on the justification by faith alone, 4:81; or on the rejection of mass as a sacrifice, 1:134. These issues are also discussed by Zuber, *Osudy moravské církve v 18. stoletî*, 2:70, n. 278.

75. Florimond de Remond, *Husitského v Čechách kacířství počátku, zrůstu, a pádu vejtah* (Prague: Jan K. Hraba, [1777]).

76. Ignaz Popp, *Ecclesiae sanctae epitome historica* (Olomouc: Melchior Windhauer, 1755), 290, 293.

77. "Luterus doctrina fidei et morum, tum et vita tantum fere abest ab Husso, quantum Pathmus Saxonica ab exilio Angeli Apocalyptici," Popp, *Ecclesiae sanctae epitome historica*, 296–98. Also cited by Zuber, *Osudy moravské církve v 18. stoletî*. 2:67.

78. Popp, *Ecclesiae sanctae epitome historica*, 290; Popp, *Romani imperii ab urbe condita, tum ab sua origine rerum Austriae, Bohemiae, Moraviae, Epitome Historica* (Olomouc: Melchior Windhauer, 1753), 287–88.

79. Zdeněk V. David, "Confessional Accommodation in Early Modern Bohemia: Shifting Relations between Catholics and Utraquists," in *Conciliation and Confession: The Struggle for Unity in the Age of Reform, 1415–1648*, ed. Howard P.

Louthan and Randall Zachman (Notre Dame, Ind.: University of Notre Dame Press, 2004), 176–77.

80. Mikuláš Voigt, *Effigies virorum eruditorum atque artificum Bohemiae et Moraviae* (Prague: Gerle, 1773–75), cited by Kraus, *Husitství v literatuře*, 2:147; Jiří Štaif, *Historici, dějiny a společnost: Historiografie v českých zemích od Palackého a jeho předchůdců po Gollovu školu* (Prague: Filozofická fakulta Univerzity Karlovy, 1997), 1:25–26; Kamil Krofta, "František Pubička předchůdce Palackého v zemském dějepisectví českém," *Časopis společnosti přátel starožitností* 51–53 (1943–45), published in 1946, 22–23.

81. Procházka, *De saecularibus liberalium artium*, 169–87. See Aeneas Sylvius Piccolomini (Pope Pius II), *Historia Bohemica* (Rome: Johannes N. Hanheymer and Johannes Schurener, 1475); new ed. (Basel: Michael Furter [?], ca. 1489); and Václav Hájek z Libočan, *Kronyka česká* (Prague: Severyn and Kubeš, 1541).

82. Procházka, *De saecularibus liberalium artium*, 205–7.

83. Ibid., 208–9.

84. Despite the fact that Cochlaeus's book, *Historiae Hussitarum*, had been placed on the index by Pope Sixtus V in the late sixteenth century; see Johannes Cochlaeus, *Historiae Hussitarum libri duodecim* (Mainz: Franciscus Behem, 1549); Theodor Kolde, "Cochlaeus," *Realenzyklopaedie fuer protestantische Theologie und Kirche* (Leipzig: Hinrichs, 1896–[1913?], 4:200.

85. Writing during Maria Theresa's reign in 1771, Gazzaniga still maintained an unfavorable attitude toward Hus and Jerome; see Pietro Maria Gazzaniga, *Praelectiones theologicae*, secundis curis emendatae et auctae (Vienna: Typis Joannis Thomae de Trattnern, 1770–71), 3:298–301, 601.

86. Franz Stephan Rautenstrauch, *Diarium eruditum*, Státní ústřední archív, Prague, MS Benediktini Břevnov, ŘBB 89, f. 247r; Rautenstrauch, *Diarium privatum*, Státní ústřední archív, Prague, MS Benediktini Břevnov, ŘBB 88, f. 184v.

87. Štaif, *Historici, dějiny a společnost*, 1:25.

88. Steinbach of Kranichstein, "Versuch einer Geschichte der alten und neuen Toleranz," 208, 210; Alexius Pařízek, *Versuch einer Geschichte Böhmens für den Bürger* (Prague, 1781); 2nd ed. (Prague, 1782), cited by Kraus, *Husitství v literatuře*, 2:179–80.

89. As noted in chapter 1 in this volume, the Russian scholar Aleksandr S. Myl'nikov called attention to the perception of Hus and the Utraquists as representatives of liberal Catholicism by spokesmen for the Bohemian Catholic Enlightenment; see Myl'nikov, *Epokha Prosveshcheniia v cheshskikh zemliakh: Ideologiia, natsional'noe samosoznanie, kul'tura* (Moscow: Nauka, 1977), 78–79.

90. Royko, *Geschichte der grossen allgemeinen Kirchenversammlung zu Kostniz*, 1: f. 5v.

91. Upon his analysis of Hus's recorded oral and written statements, submitted to the council; see ibid., 2: f. 1v.

92. Kraus, *Husitství v literatuře*, 2:159, 161.

93. In 1788, the critic, hidden under the pseudonym of Melchior Stoyko, charged, referring to Royko: "Jest nyní nový profesor v Praze, husita" (There is a new professor in Prague, a Utraquist). See Kraus, *Husitství v literatuře*, 2:165.

94. Kašpar Royko, *Historie velikého sněmu kostnického*, trans. Václav Petryn (pseudonym of Václav Stach) (Prague: Diesbach, 1785); Pavel Křivský, "Dopisy Vá-

clava Stacha Josefu Dobrovskému," *Časopis Vlastivědné společnosti muzejní v Olomouci* 60 (1970): 171.

95. *Husovo učení a význam v tradici českého národa*, ed. Milan Machovec (Prague: Nakladatelství Československé akademie věd, 1953), 275–82.

96. "Ein unschuldiges Opfer der hierarchischenTyrannei." Cited by Josef Tvrdý, "Vztahy Dobrovského k filosofii," *Bratislava* 4 (1930): 292. See also Josef Dobrovský, *Dopisy Josefa Dobrovského s Augustinem Helfertem*, ed. Josef Wolf and F. M. Bartoš, Spisy a projevy, vol. 22 (Prague: Melantrich, 1941), 110.

97. Johann H. Wolf, *Leben, Lehre, Wandel und Tod des im J. 1415 lebendig verbrannten Johann Hus* (Rome [Prague: Schönfeld] 1784), 3; see also Myl'nikov, *Epokha Prosveshcheniia v cheshskikh zemliakh*, 78.

98. Johann H. Wolf, *Geschichte des Königreichs Böheim*, 238.

99. Wolf, *Leben, Lehre, Wandel und Tod*, 6; Kraus, *Husitství v literatuře zejména německé*, 2:185.

100. Wolf, *Geschichte des Königreichs Böheim*, 133; Kraus, *Husitství v literatuře*, 2:189.

101. Johanides, *František Martin Pelcl*, 174. Refers to Pelcl's *Lebensgeschichte des römischen und böhmischen Königs Wenceslaus*, 2 vols. (Prague and Leipzig: Schönfeld and Meissner, 1788–90).

102. František M. Pelcl, *Neue Kronik von Böhmen* (Prague: Schönfeld, 1780–81), 102–3; František M. Pelcl, *Geschichte der Böhmen, von den ältesten bis auf die neuesten Zeiten*, 3rd ed. (Prague: Schönfeld, 1782), 1:306.

103. František M. Pelcl, *Kurzgefasste Geschichte der Böhmen, von den ältesten bis auf itzigen Zeiten*, 2nd ed. (Prague: Adam Hagen, 1779), f. 4v; see also Pelcl, *Geschichte der Böhmen von den ältesten bis auf die neuesten Zeiten*, 4th ed., 2:616. Even Jungmann welcomed the re-edition of Bílejovský's *Kronyka* by Josef Dittrich; see Josef Emler, ed., "Listy Josefa Jungmanna k Antonínu Markovi," *Časopis českého musea* 56 (1882): 173.

104. Pelcl, *Geschichte der Böhmen, von den ältesten bis auf die neuesten Zeiten*, 3rd ed., 1:306–7, 404.

105. Pelcl, *Geschichte der Böhmen von den ältesten bis auf die neuesten Zeiten*, 4th ed., 2:614, 620, 642; references to Utraquists, ibid., 2:627, 633.

106. Ibid. Pelcl, however, erroneously assumed that the Utraquists "passed over" to the Lutherans in 1605; ibid., 2:620, 642; references to Utraquists, ibid., 2:627, 633. Similarly, Johann H. Wolf implied that the exclusion of the Compactata from the laws of Bohemia in 1568 led to a prevalence of Protestantism in the country; Johann Heinrich Wolf, *Geschichte des Königreichs Böheim*, 230.

107. Augustin Zitte, *Lebensbeschreibung der drei ausgezeichnetsten Vorläufer M. Joh. Huss von Hussinec, bekanntlich: des Konrad Stiekna, Johann Milicz und Mathias von Janow, nebst einer Übersicht der böhmischen Religionsgeschichte bis auf seine Zeit* (Prague: Wolfgang Gerle, 1786), 3–4.

108. "Was lange vor ihm die untadelichsten und treuesten Diener des Wortes, die rechtschaffensten und unbescholtnesten Priester auch glaubten und lehrten," ibid., 6.

109. Zitte, *Lebensbeschreibung des Magisters Johannes Huss*, 2:284; Kraus, *Husitství v literatuře*, 2:194. Earlier (in 1784), Zitte had published a collection of Hus's writings against moral abuses in the church; Jan Hus, *Vermischte Schriften des M. J. Hus von Hussinecz. Aus dem Lateinischen*, [trans. and ed. Augustin Zitte]

(Leipzig and Prague: Wolfgang Gerle, 1784); see Dobrovský, *Dopisy Josefa Dobrovského s Augustinem Helfertem*, 112.

110. Augustin Zitte, *Lebensbeschreibung des Englischen Reformators Johannes Wiklef* (Prague: Wolfgang Gerle, 1786), 116.

111. Steinbach of Kranichstein, "Versuch einer Geschichte der alten und neuen Toleranz," 215. By the beginning of the seventeenth century, Steinbach, however, does not seem to distinguish between the Utraquists and the Protestants; ibid., 224–25.

112. The Utraquists' religious hymns were of such "a nobility and purity of language" that probably no other nation possessed; Němeček, "Züge aus der Geschichte der Wissenschaften," 27–28, 35.

113. The bishops of the Union of Utrecht sent Rautenstrauch two communications: one in 1777 and a more pressing and elaborate one, dated May 20, 1784. Rautenstrauch did not seem to respond. Perhaps he was discouraged by the Utrecht bishops' denunciation of Jansenism; see Beda Franz Menzel, *Abt Franz Stephan Rautenstrauch von Břevnov-Braunau: Herkunft, Umwelt und Wirkungskreis* (Königstein/Ts: Königsteiner Institut für Kirchen-und Geistesgeschichte der Sudentenländer, 1969), 195–96.

114. In addition, there were five Catholic seminarians among the nine student subscribers; Novotný, *Matěj Václav Kramerius*, 76, 81–82.

115. For a survey, see Jaroslav Kadlec, *Přehled českých církevních dějin* (Prague: Zvon, 1991), 2:187–90; Jakubec, *Antonín Marek*, 202; Kraus, *Husitství v literatuře*, 2:196.

116. Novotný, *Matěj Václav Kramerius*, 191–92. For Puchmajer's poem in English, see John Bowring, *Cheskian Anthology: Being a History of the Poetical Literature of Bohemia* (London: Rowland Hunter, 1832), 166–72. See also Jakubec, ed., *Literatura česká devatenáctého století*, 1:535–36.

117. Pavel Křivský, "Dopisy Václava Stacha Josefu Dobrovskému," *Časopis Vlastivědné společnosti muzejní v Olomouci* 60 (1970): 159.

118. These included the office of dean of the theological faculty at the University of Prague in 1790, rector of the same University in 1797, and an election as provost of the chapter of All Saints in Prague Castle in 1807. See Arnošt Kraus, *Husitství v literatuře zejména německé* (Prague: Česká akademie, 1917–24), 2:167; Knihopis, 2: pt.7, 449.

119. Křivský, "Korespondence Jana Leopolda Haye, Josefa Františka Hurdálka a Augustina Zippa s Josefem Dobrovským," 133 n.1.

120. Johann Heinrich Wolf, *Dějiny království českého k užívání studující mládeže v c. k. státech*, trans. Jan Putna (Vienna: C. k. školní knihosklad, 1819); the original edition: Johann Heinrich Wolf, *Geschichte des Königreichs Böheim zum Gebrauche der Studierenden Jugend in der K.K. Staaten* (Vienna: Johann Thomas von Trattner, 1783). See also Kraus, *Husitství v literatuře zejména německé*, 2:186.

121. Miloslav Kaňák, *Josef Franta Šumavský* (Prague: Melantrich, 1975), 27, 29, 32. Josef Dobrovský, *Briefwechsel zwischen Dobrovský und Kopitar, 1808–1828*, ed. Vatroslav Jagić (Berlin: Weidmann'sche Buchhandlung, 1885), 475.

122. Emler, ed., "Listy Josefa Jungmanna k Antonínu Markovi," 165, 168, 172.

123. Zahradník and his fellow seminarians in Litoměřice in the early 1810s were greatly influenced by the teaching of Michael J. Fesl, an associate of Bernard Bolzano, the latter-day apostle of Reform Catholicism in Bohemia. As for literary

works, Zahradník favored Veleslavín, Pavel Kristián of Koldín, Kocín of Kocinét, and Václav Hájek and saw a model use of the Czech language in the literary works of the Unity of Brethren. See Antonín Rybička, "Vzpomínka na Vincence Zahradníka," *Časopis českého musea* 45 (1871): 29; Zahradník, *Filosofické spisy*, 1:8–10; on Dobrovský's visits, see ibid., 1:98, 100.

124. See Kaňák, *Josef Franta Šumavský*, 12.

125. Polišenský and Illingová, *Jan Jeník z Bratřic*, 68, 114, 119. On the acceptance of Royko, see Walter Schamschula, "Der slovenische Kirchenhistoriker Kašpar Royko und die tschechische Erneuerung," in *Studia Slovenica Monacensia: In honorem Antonii Slodnjak septuagenarii*, ed. Hans-Joachim Kissling (Munich: Trofenik, 1969), 104–11.

126. Jakubec, ed., *Literatura česká devatenáctého století*, 2:593–95; Jungmann, *Zápisky*, ed. Radek Lunga, 64–66.

127. This dichotomous denouement is more fully covered in chapter 11 in this volume.

Chapter 5

1. Hugh L. Agnew, *Origins of the Czech National Renascence* (Pittsburgh, Pa.: University of Pittsburgh Press, 1993), 117. See also Zuzana Urválková, "František Martin Pelcl o Jezuitech," in *Bůh a bohové: Církve, náboženství a spiritualita v českém 19 století*, ed. Zdeněk Hojda and Roman Prahl (Prague: KLP, 2003), 123.

2. Karel Raphael Ungar, *Allgemeine böhmische Bibliothek* (Prague, 1786), 6–8; Josef Dobrovský, *Korrespondence*, Díl 3: *Vzájemné dopisy Josefa Dobrovského a Josefa Valentina Zlobického z let 1781–1807*, Sbírka pramenů ku poznání literárního života v Čechách, na Moravě a ve Slezsku, Skupina 2, Číslo 9, ed. Adolf Patera (Prague: Česká akademie pro vědy, slovesnost a umění, 1908), vii. On Zlobický's role, see also Josef Vintr and Jana Pleskalová, eds., *Vídeňský podíl na počátcích českého národního obrození. J. V. Zlobick ý (1743–1810) a současníci: život, dílo, korespondence* (Prague: Academia, 2004).

3. Josef Polišenský and Ella Illingová, *Jan Jeník z Bratřic* (Prague: Melantrich, 1989), 86, 164; Josef Johanides, *František Martin Pelcl* (Prague: Melantrich, 1981), 116–17. Leopold Johann Scherschnik, "Über den Ursprung und die Aufnahme der Bibliothek am Clementinischen Collegium zu Prag," *Abhandlungen einer Privatgesellschaft in Böhmen zur Aufnahme der Mathematik, der vaterländischen Geschichte und der Naturgeschichte* 2 (1776): 276–77.

4. Arne Novák, "Josef Dobrovský a jeho předchůdcové v českém literárním dějepise," in *Josef Dobrovský, 1753–1829: sborník statí k stému výročí smrti Josefa Dobrovského*, ed. Jiří Horák, Matyáš Murko, and Miloš Weingart (Prague: Výbor I. Sjezdu slovanských filologů, 1929), 244.

5. Mikuláš Adaukt Voigt, *Acta litteraria Bohemiae et Moraviae* (Prague, 1774–84); see also Novák, "Josef Dobrovský a jeho předchůdcové v českém literárním dějepise," 245–46.

6. František Faustin Procházka, *De saecularibus liberalium artium in Bohemia et Moravia satis commentarius* (Prague: Litteris Scholae normalis, Schmadl factore, 1782); Procházka, *Miscellaneen der Böhmischen und Mährischen Litteratur, seltener Werke, und verschiedenen Handschriften*, 3 pts. (Prague: Caspar Widtmann, 1784–85).

See also Novák, "Josef Dobrovský a jeho předchůdcové v českém literárním dějepise," 247.

7. František X. Němeček, "Züge aus der Geschichte der Wissenschaften und des Geschmackes in Böhmen; geschrieben im Jahre 1794," *Libussa, eine vaterländische Vierteljahrschrift*, ed. J. G. Meinert, vol. 2 (Prague: Calve, 1804), 46; Karel Ignác Thám, *Obrana jazyka českého proti zlobivým jeho utrhačům* (Prague: Schönfeld, 1783), iii, 46–47. See also Václav Thám, *Básně v řeči vázané*, První sebrání (Prague: U Rosenmüllerských dědiců, 1785), f. A4r, on Ungar's role in preserving the formerly prohibited books.

8. Ungar, *Allgemeine böhmische Bibliothek*, 3–4.

9. Ibid., 5–9; Karel Raphael Ungar, "Neue Beiträge zur alten Geschichte der Buchdruckerkunst in Böhmen, mit einer vollständigen Übersicht aller dazu gehörigen Daten aus dem fünfzehnten Jahrhundert," *Neuere Abhandlungen der k. böhmischen Gesellschaft der Wissenschaften* 2 (1795): 195–229. The so-called *Dalimil Chronicle* [Dalimilova kronika] was actually an anonymous text, originally written in the early fourteenth century. Bohumír Jan Dlabač also helped identify items of the humanist literature of the sixteenth century. His biographies of Jan Campanus Vodňanský and Jan Chorinnus were particularly relevant; see *Lexikon české literatury: Osobnosti, díla, instituce*, ed. Vladimír Forst, Jiří Opelík, and Luboš Merhaut (Prague: Academia, 1985–2008), 1:551.

10. Josef Dobrovský, *Dějiny české řeči a literatury v redakcích z roku 1791, 1792 a 1818*, ed. Benjamin Jedlička (Prague: Melantrich, 1936), 49. For an endorsement of Procházka's bibliographic work, see also Karel Raphael Ungar, "Von dem Zustande der Schulen und der Lateinischen Literatur in Böhmen vor Errichtung der hohen Schule zu Prague," *Abhandlungen einer Privatgesellschaft in Böhmen zur Aufnahme der Mathematik, der vaterländischen Geschichte und der Naturgeschichte* (Prague, 1775–84), 6 (1784): 128.

11. Josef Dobrovský, *Böhmische Litteratur auf das Jahr 1779* (Prague: Mangoldische Buchhandlung, 1779); Dobrovský, *Böhmische und Mährische Litteratur auf das Jahr 1780–81* (Prague: Mangoldische Buchhandlung, 1780–84); Dobrovský, *Litterarisches Magazin von Böhmen und Mähren* (Prague: Schönfeld), Stück 1 (1786), Stück 2 (1786), Stück 3 (1787).

12. Dobrovský, *Böhmische Litteratur auf das Jahr 1779*, 6–8.

13. *Index Bohemicorum librorum prohibitorum, et corrigendorum* (Prague: Johan C. Hraba, 1770); Josef Dobrovský, *O zavedení a rozšíření knihtisku v Čechách* [critical German edition of *Über Einführung und Verbreitung der Buchdruckerkunst in Böhmen*, 1782] (Prague: Nakladatelství Československé akademie věd, 1954), 10–11.

14. Dobrovský, *O zavedení a rozšíření knihtisku v Čechách*, 12; in Bohuslav Balbín, *Bohemia docta*, opus posthumum editum, notisque illustratum ad Raphaele Ungar (a.k.a. Candidus a S. Theresia) (Prague, 1776, 1778, 1780), Ungar added considerable bibliographic information, for instance, on Václav Budovec of Budov (1:226–27) and Komenský (1:207–9); Josef J. Jungmann, *Historie literatury české*, 2nd ed. (Prague: Řivnáč, 1849).

15. Dobrovský, *Dějiny české řeči a literatury*, 167; Jan Amos Komenský, *Labirynt světa a ráj srdce* (Prague: Jan Samm, 1782); Václav Thám, *Básně v řeči vázané*, První sebrání, f. A4v.

16. Johanides, *František Martin Pelcl*, 69.

17. Jan B. Dlabač, "Pamětní listové učených Čechů, Moravanů a Slezanů," *Do-*

broslav 2 (1821), cited in Johanides, *František Martin Pelcl*, 149; Jan Jeník z Bratřic, *Z mých pamětí*, ed. Josef Polišenský (Prague: ELK, 1947), 27–28.

18. Johanides, *František Martin Pelcl*, 149; Dobrovský, *Dějiny české řeči a literatury*, 169.

19. Johann Kopp of Raumenthal's books had appeared in Prague in 1536 and 1542; see *Knihopis českých a slovenských tisků*, vol. 2, in 9 pts., *Tisky z let 1501–1800* (Prague: Nakladatelství akademie věd, 1939–67), no. 4314, no. 4315. (Henceforth referred to as *Knihopis* with entry numbers.)

20. Jan Češka, *Příkladné řeči a užitečná naučení vybraná z knih hlubokých mudrců* (Prague: Jan J. Diesbach, 1786), virtually identical edition (Prague: Kašpar Widtmann, 1786), see *Knihopis*, nos. 1785–86; originally published (Plzeň: Jan Pekk, 1527), then (Olomouc: Friedrich Milichtaler, 1572), and (Prague: Burian Valda, 1579), see *Knihopis*, nos. 1782–84; see also Jungmann, *Historie literatury české*, 143.

21. *Knihopis*, no. 2359; sixteenth-century editions appeared in 1563–64 and 1579, see ibid., no. 2356–58.

22. *Knihopis*, no. 2354–2355; for sixteenth-century editions from 1519 and 1570, see ibid., no. 2351–52.

23. Josef Jireček, *Rukověť k dějinám literatury české* (Prague: Tempsky, 1875–76), 2:146–47. In addition, Erasmus's treatise, *Ratio seu methodus compendio perveniendi ad veram theologiam*, was published in Prague by Joann Mangoldt, 1786.

24. On Erasmus as a player in the Catholic Enlightenment, see Jan Patočka, "Bolzanovo místo v dějinách filosofie," in *Filosofie v dějinách českého národa* (Prague: Nakladatelství ČSAV, 1958), 111.

25. "Theologorum Sec. XVI Princeps *Desiderius Erasmus Roterdamus*, vir graecis latinisque literis ad miraculum eruditus, & ad barbariem ex orbe pellendam natus." See Kašpar Royko, *Synopsis historiae religionis et ecclesiae christianae: methodo systematica adumbratae* (Prague: Ioann Mangoldt, 1785), 113–14.

26. Josef Dobrovský, *Dopisy Josefa Dobrovského s Augustinem Helfertem*, ed. Josef Wolf and F. M. Bartoš, Spisy a projevy, vol. 22 (Prague: Melantrich, 1941), 108; František V. Hek, *Sebrané spisy*, ed. Jan Jakubec (Prague: Česká akademie pro vědy, slovesnost a umění, 1917–24), 3:149.

27. Walter Schamschula, *Die Anfänge der tschechischen Erneuerung und das deutsche Geistesleben, 1740–1800* (Munich: Fink, 1973), 200.

28. For a survey of Kramerius's republications, see Jan Novotný, *Matěj Václav Kramerius* (Prague: Melantrich, 1973), 186–88.

29. *Knihopis*, no. 6787; originally published in 1610 and 1619; ibid., nos. 6772, 6774.

30. *Knihopis*, no. 891; it preceded Procházka's reprint of 1786 (ibid., no. 893) by two years; and it had been published three times in the sixteenth century (1543, 1583, 1600), ibid., nos. 887, 888, 889.

31. Originally published in 1541, see *Knihopis*, no. 2867.

32. Jaroslav Kolár, *Návraty bez konce: Studie k starší české literatuře*, ed. Lenka Jiroušková (Brno: Atlantis, 1999), 290, 294–95; Vincenc Zahradník, *Filosofické spisy*, ed. František Čáda (Prague: Česká akademie pro vědy slovesnost a umění, 1907–8), 1:118, 121. Much of the republished literature ultimately stemmed from the printing house of Daniel Adam of Veleslavín; see Mirjam Bohatcová and Josef Hejnic, "O vydavatelské činnosti Veleslavínské tiskárny," *Folia Historica Bohemica* 9 (1985): 291–388.

33. Novotný, *Matěj Václav Kramerius*, 76. On Durych's attachment to the sixteenth-century form of Czech, see also Schamschula, *Die Anfänge der tschechischen Erneuerung*, 194–95; on Procházka's, ibid., 199.

34. Václav Zelený, *Život Josefa Jungmanna* (Prague: Matice česká, 1873), 47–49; Josef Jungmann, *Zápisky*, ed. Radek Lunga (Prague: Budka, 1998), 64–66; Dobrovský, *Dějiny české řeči a literatury*, 167–68; Arne Novák, *Josef Dobrovský* (Prague: Mánes, 1928), 31–32. For criticism of the two misfits, see also "Über den Ursprung und die Bildung der slawischen und inbesondere der böhmischen Sprache," an introduction to František J. Tomsa's *Volständiges Wörterbuch der böhmisch-deutsch-lateinischen Sprache* (Prague: Schönfeld-Meissnerische Handlung, 1791), 32. Nevertheless, at the Imperial Academy in Wiener Neustadt, textbooks by Jan V. Pól and Maximilian Šimek were used; see Tomáš Burian, "Český jazyk v Novém městě za Vídní," *Časopis českého musea* 12 (1843): 525.

35. Tomsa, *Volständiges Wörterbuch der böhmisch-deutsch-lateinischen Sprache*, 32, referring to Jan V. Pól, *Grammatica linguae Bohemicae*, originally published in Vienna in 1756.

36. Like Tomsa, Pelcl focused on the 1773 and 1783 editions of Pól's *Grammatica linguae Bohemicae*, and added an assessment of Jan V. Pól, *Wahre gegründete böhmische Schreibart* (Vienna, 1786); see František M. Pelcl, *Grundsätze der böhmischen Grammatik* (Prague: Jeřábek, 1795), xi; also 2nd ed. (Prague: Jeřábek, 1798), 325, 327.

37. "Der Verfasser ist unbekannt, und die Regeln sind meistens falsch und ungrammatikalisch." František M. Pelcl, *Grundsätze der böhmischen Grammatik*, 2nd ed. (Prague: Jeřábek, 1798), 324; Pelcl referred to *Alphabetum Bohemicum* (Prague: Karl Rosenmüller, 1718). Josef Vintr and Jana Pleskalová, eds., *Vídeňský podíl na počátcích českého národního obrození. J. V. Zlobický (1743–1810) a současníci: život, dílo, korespondence* (Prague: Academia, 2004), 52–53, 62–63.

38. Johanides, *František Martin Pelcl*, 232–33; see also Jaromír Bělič, "František Martin Pelcl a český jazyk," *Slavia Pragensia* 21 (1978): 115–32; Walter Schamschula, "Dobrovskýs und Pelzels Beiträge zu den 'Lieferungen für Böhmen von Böhmen,'" in Alois Schmaus and Ilse Kunert, eds., *Aus der Geisteswelt der Slaven. Dankesgabe an Erwin Koschmieder* (Munich: Sagner, 1967), 159–60. The project failed after an indication of Vienna's disapproval; Agnew, *Origins of the Czech National Renascence*, 76.

39. František M. Pelcl, *Grundsätze der böhmischen Grammatik* (Prague: Jeřábek, 1795), "Vorrede," iv–v; also 2nd ed. (Prague: Jeřábek, 1798), "Vorrede," v–vi; referring to Vavřinec Benedikt z Nedožer, *Grammaticae Bohemicae ad leges naturalis methodi conformatae, et notis numerisque illustratae ac distinctae, libri duo* (Prague: Otmar, 1603); see Pelcl, *Grundsätze der böhmischen Grammatik* (1798), 322–23.

40. Pelcl, *Grundsätze der böhmischen Grammatik*, 2nd ed., 327. See also Pavel Bělina, Jiří Kaše, and Jan P. Kučera, *Velké dějiny zemí Koruny české*, vol. 10, 1740–92 (Prague: Paseka, 2001), 239.

41. For instance, in the first edition of his *Geschichte der böhmischen Sprache und Literatur* (1791). See Arne Novák, "Josef Dobrovský a jeho předchůdcové v českém literárním dějepise," 249.

42. Josef Dobrovský, *Literarisches Magazin von Böhmen und Mähren*, 2 (1786): 142–43. See also Agnew, *Origins of the Czech National Renascence*, 103.

43. František Palacký, "Josefa Dobrovského život a vědecké působení," *Česká včela* 4 (1837): 308.
44. František J. Tomsa, *Vollständiges Wörterbuch der böhmisch-deutsch-lateinischen Sprache* (Prague: Schönfeld-Meissnerische Handlung, 1791), 16.
45. Josef Dobrovský, "Vorrede," in ibid., 9.
46. "Našeho slavného českého národu vždycky ta žádost byla, aby jazyk Otců jejich, kteříž jej v pravdě přede všemi jinými národy již před dvěma sty léty k největší dokonalosti přivedli, nejen zachován, alébrž i rozšířen a zveleben byl." *Krameriovy noviny*, no. 26, June 25, 1791, 205–6.
47. *Krameriovy noviny*, October 1, 1791, cited by Agnew, *Origins of the Czech National Renascence*, 77.
48. He mentioned by name nineteen original writers and eleven translated ones; see Karel Ignác Thám, *Deutsch-böhmisches Nationallexikon* (Prague: Schönfeld, 1788), xvii.
49. He highlighted Bohemian cultural achievements in the age of Rudolf II, deploring the cultural depredations of the Counter-Reformation in Bohemia; see Johann Christoph Adelung, "Vorrede," in Karel Ignác Thám, *Deutsch-böhmisches Nationallexikon* (1788), x, xii–xiii. Although he did not know Czech, Adelung assessed the German part as highly successful; Johann Christoph Adelung, "Vorrede," in Karel Ignác Thám, ibid., xiv.–] Adelung's preface was reprinted in the later editions of Thám's dictionary.
50. The title page of volume one of *Neuestes ausführliches und vollständiges deutsch-böhmisches synonymisch-phraseologisches Nationallexikon oder Wörterbuch*, 2 pts., 2nd pt: bearbeitet von Franz Tomsa (P-Ž) (Prague: Neureutter, 1805–7). *Sylva quadrilinguis vocabulorum et phrasium Bohemicae, Latinae, Graecae et Germanicae linguae* (Prague: Daniel Adam of Veleslavín, 1598) has been cherished as one of the ultimate steps in the codification of the Czech language of the Utraquist age.
51. Karel Ignác Thám, *Neuestes ausführliches und vollständiges deutsch-böhmisches synonymisch-phraseologisches Nationallexikon oder Wörterbuch*, 2 pts. (Prague: Neureutter, 1799–1800). See [Josef Dobrovský], *Zur richtigen Verurtheilung des Thamischen deutsch-böhmischen National-Lexikons*, 3 pts. (Prague: Herrlischer Buchhandlung, [1798]), and Karel Ignác Thám, *Antikritik oder Rechtfertigung*, 3 pts. (Prague, 1798); rare copies in National Library, Prague (65 D 1844).
52. *Neuestes ausführliches und vollständiges deutsch-böhmisches synonymisch-phraseologisches Nationallexikon oder Wörterbuch*, 2 pts., 2nd pt.: bearbeitet von Franz Tomsa (P-Ž) (Prague: Neureutter, 1805–1807), see *Knihopis*, no.16.157; Karel Ignác Thám, *Neuestes ausführliches und vollständiges deutsch-böhmisches synonymisch-phraseologisches Nationallexikon oder Wörterbuch*, 2 pts. (Prague: M. Neureutter, 1814); considered 3rd ed., see *Knihopis*, no. 16.158.
53. Pelcl claimed that Thám copied almost verbatim pages 122–80 from the first edition (1795) of his own *Grundsätze der böhmischen Grammatik* (The Basics of Czech Grammar) and that Thám's index of alleged Slavic gods consisted largely of fictitious names; see František M. Pelcl, *Grundsätze der böhmischen Grammatik*, 2nd ed. (Prague: Jeřábek, 1798), 328, referring to Karel Ignác Thám, *Böhmische Grammatik zum Gebrauche der Deutschen* (Prague: Diesbach, 1798); see *Knihopis*, no. 16.144. Pelcl also accused Thám of claiming falsely in his grammar of 1798 that the previous edition of his grammar, namely, Karel Ignác Thám, *Kurzgefasste*

böhmische Sprachlehre (Prague: Schönfeld, 1785), (*Knihopis*, no.16,165), had been used for twelve years in the Czech-language courses at the University of Vienna. Meanwhile, university records and the recollections of Zlobický, the professor of Czech, showed that not Thám's but Tomsa's textbook had been prescribed since 1783; Pelcl, *Grundsätze der böhmischen Grammatik* (2nd ed., 1798), 327; Thám had advanced the claim in the "Vorrede zur dritten Auflage," in *Böhmische Grammatik zum Gebrauche der Deutschen* (Prague: Diesbach, 1798), cited in Karel Ignác Thám, *Böhmische Grammatik zum Gebrauche der Deutschen*, Fünfte Auflage (Prague: Diesbach, 1804), ix.

54. Karel Ignác Thám, *Böhmische Grammatik zum Gebrauche der Deutschen*, Vierte Auflage (Prague: Diesbach, 1801), see *Knihopis* no. 16.146; Fünfte Auflage (Prague: Diesbach, 1804), see *Knihopis,* no. 16.147. There apparently never was a third edition; see *Knihopis*, no. 16.145.

55. Pavel Křivský, "Korespondence Antonína Jaroslava Puchmajera s Josefem Dobrovským," *Literární archiv: Sborník Památníku národního písemnictví,* 8 (1974): 201, 225.

56. Josef Dobrovský, *Deutsch-böhmisches Wörterbuch* (Prague: Herrlische Buchhandlung, 1802–21) [1st vol., 2nd rev. ed.,1821].

57. He complained that Thám ignored his suggestions for corrections, which had been made on the basis of the first edition; Dobrovský, *Deutsch-böhmisches Wörterbuch*, 1:1–10, commenting on Karel Ignác Thám, *Neuestes ausführliches und vollständiges deutsch-böhmisches synonymisch-phraseologisches Nationallexikon oder Wörterbuch,* 2 pts. (Prague: Neureutter, 1799–1800).

58. Dobrovský, *Deutsch-böhmisches Wörterbuch,* 1:4. Tomsa, *Volständiges Wörterbuch der böhmisch-deutsch-lateinischen Sprache.*

59. Zelený, *Život Josefa Jungmanna*, 47–49; Dobrovský, *Dějiny české řeči a literatury*, 167–68; Novák, *Josef Dobrovský*, 31–32.

60. Zelený, *Život Josefa Jungmanna*, 65–68.

61. Agnew, *Origins of the Czech National Renascence*, 80–82.

62. Walter Schamschula, *Geschichte der tschechischen Literatur* (Cologne: Böhlau, 1990–96), 1:358. The introduction of new words, particularly by Jungmann, as exemplified in his translation of Milton's *Paradise Lost* (1811), proceeded within the paradigms of the sixteenth-century language, not in violation of them. See Agnew, *Origins of the Czech National Renascence*, 84–85. These rules were identified particularly by Josef Dobrovský, especially in his *Die Bildsamkeit der Slawischen Sprache an der Bildung der Substantive und Adjective in der Böhmischen Sprache dargestellt* (Prague, 1799).

63. Hek, *Sebrané spisy*, 3:195–221.

64. Zahradník, *Filosofické spisy*,1:74. He criticized those writers who "use Czech words and correctly decline and inflect them, but bind them together in such a way . . . that a sort of a *third language* [emphasis in original] is created, which is neither German nor Czech." Ibid., 1:33.

65. Vladimír Macura, *Znamení zrodu: České národní obrození jako kulturní typ,* rev. ed. (Prague: H & H, 1995), 19.

66. Josef Petráň, ed., *Počátky českého národního obrození: společnost a kultura v 70. až 90. letech18. století* (Prague: Academia, 1990), 240.

67. For a partial survey of republished literature, see also Karel Horálek, *Studie*

o populární literatuře českého obrození (Prague: Československý spisovatel, 1990), 36–47.
  68. Voigt, *Acta litteraria Bohemiae et Moraviae,* 2 (1784): 54, 64–70, 71–79, 83–118, 175–90, 204–7.
  69. František Faustin Procházka, *Miscellaneen der Böhmischen und Mährischen Litteratur, seltener Werke, und verschiedenen Handschriften* (Prague: Caspar Widtmann, 1784–85), pts. 2–3; *Ottův slovník naučný* (Prague: Otto, 1888–1908), 20:738.
  70. Bohuslav Bílejovský, *Kronika církevní,* ed. Josef Skalický [pseudonym of Josef Dittrich] (Prague: Fetterl z Vilden, 1816); Tomáš Bavorovský, as *Kázání na Evangelium, kteréž se čte v Církvi Boží na den Božího Těla,* new ed. partial by Josef Klíč [pseud. of Dittrich] (Prague: Fetterlová, 1822), extracted from Klíč, *Postila česká* (1557); and Tomáš Bavorovský, *Zrcadlo onoho věčného a blahoslaveného života* (1561), new ed. by Josef Dittrich (Prague: Fetterlová, 1822).
  71. *Výbor z literatury české,* vol. 1, *Od nejstarších časů až do počátku XV. století,* ed. Josef J. Jungmann with František Palacký and others; vol. 2, *Od počátku XV až do konce XVI. století,* ed. Karel J. Erben, (Prague: Kronberger and Řivnáč, 1845–68), 2:1039.
  72. Desiderius Erasmus, *Ruční knížka o rytíři křesťanském,* 2nd ed., ed. František Faustin Procházka (Prague: Jan J. Diesbach, 1787); Procházka, *Kniha, v kteréž jednomu každému křesťanskému člověku naučení i napomenutí se dává, jak by se k smrti hotoviti měl* (Prague: Jan J. Diesbach, 1786); see also Dobrovský, *Dějiny české řeči a literatury,* 420.
  73. *Výbor z literatury české,* 2:1657–58. Jan Kocín z Kocinétu, *Abeceda pobožné manželky a rozšafné hospodyně* (Prague: Daniel Adam z Veleslavína, 1585), see also *Knihopis,* no. 4159.
  74. Dalimil, *Kronika boleslavská o posloupnosti knížat a králů českých* (Prague: Jan J. Diesbach, 1786), virtually identical edition (Prague: Kašpar Widtmann, 1786), see *Knihopis,* no. 1811; originally published (Prague: Daniel Karel z Karlspergka, 1620): see *Knihopis,* no.1810. Příbík Pulkava z Radenína, *Kronika česká* (Prague: Jan J. Diesbach, 1786), virtually identical edition (Prague: Kašpar Widtmann, 1786): see *Knihopis,* nos. 14.697–98.
  75. *Dvě kroniky o založení země České . . . Jedna Eneáše Senenského . . . Druhá Martina Kuthena z Krynsperku* (Prague, 1817). Veleslavín's edition had appeared as *Kroniky dvě o založení země české, Eneaše Sylvia a Martina Kuthena* (Prague: Daniel Adam z Veleslavína, 1585); Kolár, *Návraty bez konce,* 289. See also Milan Kopecký, "Poznámky k vývoji české historické beletrie předobrozenské," *Sborník prací Filozofické Fakulty Brněnské Univerzity* D 14 (1967): 63.
  76. Kolár, *Návraty bez konce,* 187, 283.
  77. Jan B. Dlabač, "Pamětní listové učených Čechů, Moravanů a Slezanů," *Dobroslav* 2 (1821), cited in Johanides, *František Martin Pelcl,* 149.
  78. *Výbor z literatury české,* 2:1537–38. The original edition appeared as Prokop Lupáč z Hlaváčova, *Historie o císaři Karlovi, toho jména čtvrtém* (Prague: Jiří Nygrin, 1584), see *Knihopis,* no. 5060; Daniel Adam z Veleslavína, *Práce původní* (Prague: Bedřich Rohlíček, 1853).
  79. Aleksander Gwagnin (Alessandro Guagnini), *Vejtah z Kroniky Moskevskéč Přidána jest Zikmunda Herbersteina dvojí cesta do Moskvy,* trans. Matouš Hosius, intro. František Faustin Procházka (Prague: Jan Diesbach, 1786); variant: pub-

lisher, Kašpar Widtmann, 1786; see *Knihopis,* nos. 2799–80. The original edition was Aleksander Gwagnin (Alessandro Guagnini), *Kronika Moskevská. Wypsání predních zemí, krajin, národuw, knízestwí, mest, zámkuw, rzek i jezer, Welikému Knizeti Mozkewskému poddanych.* . . . *Též o neslýchaném Tyranství Ivana Vasilovice Knížete Moskevského, kteréž on za pamětí naší nad poddanými svými provozoval,* trans. Matouš Hosius z Vysokého Mýta (Prague: Daniel Adam z Veleslavína, 1589); 2nd ed.: *Kronika Moskevská* (Prague: Daniel Adam z Veleslavína, 1602); see *Knihopis,* nos. 2797–98. Hosius's version is apparently based on *Sarmatiae Europeae descriptio* (Cracow: Matthias Wirzbieta, 1578).

80. Flavius Josephus, *Flavia Jozefa o válce židovské knihy sedmery,* trans. Pavel Aquilinas (Vorličný) (Prostějov: Jan Günther, 1553) [also *Knihopis,* no. 3627]; 2nd ed. (Levoča: Bartolomeides, 1805), see *Výbor z literatury české,* 2:1481–90; *Krátká historie o válce židovské z knih Josefa Flavia vytažená léta 1595 od Mikuláše Stypacia Strakovského,* new ed. (Prague: Kramerius, 1806); see also *Knihopis,* no. 3626.

81. *Lexikon české literatury: Osobnosti, díla, instituce,* ed. Vladimír Forst and others (Prague: Academia, 1985–2008), 2:756.

82. Václav Vratislav z Mitrovic, *Příhody, které on v tureckém hlavním městě viděl* (Prague: Jan M. Samm, 1777), see also *Knihopis,* no. 16.669; Josef Kočí, *České národní obrození* (Prague: Svoboda, 1978), 189.

83. Oldřich Prefát z Vlkanova, *Cesta z Prahy do Benátek, a odtud potom po moři až do Palestýny* (Prague: Jan J. Diesbach, 1786), virtually identical edition (Prague: Kašpar Widtmann, 1786); see *Knihopis,* nos. 14.354–55. The original edition (Prague: Jan Kozel, 1563); see *Knihopis,* no. 14.353.

84. John de Mandeville, *Cesta po světě, v kteréž vypisuje rozličné krajiny a města* (Prague: Kramerius, 1796); see also *Knihopis,* no. 5172. The original translation appeared in Plzeň in 1510, and other editions in 1513, 1576, 1596, and 1600; see *Knihopis,* nos. 5167–71.

85. *Výbor z literatury české,* 2:1339.

86. *Letopisové Trojanští* (Prague: V. Kramerius, 1790); see Jungmann, *Historie literatury české,* 66. For the earliest editions, see *Knihopis, Dodatky,* vol. 1 (Prague, 1994), nos. XIV–XV.

87. *Ezopovy básně spolu s jeho životem* (Prague: V Kramerius, 1791); see *Knihopis,* no. 78. For the early editions of 1556 and subsequently, see *Knihopis,* nos. 69–77.

88. Šimon Lomnický of Budeč, *Tobolka zlatá* (Prague: František J. Tomsa, 1791): see *Knihopis,* no. 4978; for original edition (1615), see *Knihopis,* no. 4977. Lomnický, *Krátké naučení mladému hospodáři* (Prague: V. V. Kramerius, 1794): see *Knihopis,* no. 4943; for original edition (1597), see *Knihopis,* no. 4941.

89. Jan Mukařovský, ed., *Dějiny české literatury* (Prague: Nakladatelství Československé akademie věd, 1959–95), 2:116. The original appeared as Jakub Srnec of Varvažov, *Dicteria sev proverbia bohemica ad phrasim latinorum accommodata* (Prague: Nigrinus, 1582); 2nd ed. (Prague: Nigrinus, 1599); see *Knihopis,* 15.642 and 15.644.

90. Jungmann, *Historie literatury české,* 64. For the early editions, see *Knihopis,* nos. 14.713–715.

91. Vavřinec Leander Rvačovský of Rvačov, *Klevetník* (N. p., end of the eighteenth or beginning of the nineteenth century); Rvačovský, *Všetýčka* (N. p., end of the eighteenth or the beginning of the nineteenth century): see *Knihopis* nos. 15.125

and 15.128. For Rvačovský, *Masopust* (Prague: Jiří Melantrich, 1580), see *Knihopis*, no. 15.127.

92. Václav Dobřenský, *Vrtkavé štěstí* (Prague: Martin Neureuter, 1824); see *Výbor z literatury české*, 2:1586; for original edition (Prague: Jiří Černý, 1583), see *Knihopis*, 2005.

93. Kolár, *Návraty bez konce*, 14; see also Jungmann, *Historie literatury české*, 141.

94. V. K. Klicpera, *Česká Melusina: Dramatická národní báchorka v pateru dějství* (Prague, 1848); see *Meluzína: An Edition of the Sixteenth-Century Czech Version of the Mélusine Romance*, ed. S. I. Kanikova and Robert B. Pynsent (London: KLP, 1996), 347. The original appeared as *Kronika kratochvílná o ctné a šlechetné Panně Meluzíně* (1595), ibid., 1. For a list of other editions, see Jaroslav Kolár, *Česká zábavná próza 16. století a t. zv. knížky lidového čtení* (Prague, 1960), 68–69.

95. Dobrovský, *Dějiny české řeči a literatury*, 409–12.

96. Literacy increased, thanks to the imperial decree of December 6, 1774, expanding the school system in Bohemia; Jungmann, *Historie literatury české*, 345.

97. *Dějiny Univerzity Karlovy, 1348–1990*, ed., František Kavka and Josef Petráň (Prague: Karolinum, 1995–98), 2:132; Johanides, *František Martin Pelcl*, 240.

98. Rybička, "Vzpomínka na Vincence Zahradníka," 29; Zahradník, *Filosofické spisy*, 1:73.

99. Karel Ignác Thám, *Kurzgefasste böhmische Sprachlehre* (Prague: Schönfeld, 1785), 135–96; Thám, *Böhmische Grammatik zum Gebrauche der Deutschen*, Vierte Auflage (Prague: Diesbach, 1801), 254–86; and Thám, *Böhmische Grammatik zum Gebrauche der Deutschen*, Fünfte Auflage (Prague: Diesbach, 1804), 265–93.

100. František Jan Tomsa, *Über die Veränderungen der čechischen Sprache, nebst einer čechischen Chrestomathie* (Prague: Tomsa, 1805), 65–263. From the Counter-Reformation period (1613 to 1763), only one item—a legal text from 1723—is cited; ibid., 208.

101. Josef J. Jungmann, *Slovesnost; aneb sbírka příkladů s krátkým pojednáním o slohu* (Prague: I. Fetterlová, 1820); Alois V. Šembera, *Dějiny řeči a literatury československé*, vol. 1 (Vienna, 1858), vol. 2 (Vienna: Nákladem spisovatelovým, 1868).

102. Šembera, *Dějiny řeči a literatury*, 2:ii.

103. Miloslav Kaňák, *Josef Franta Šumavský* (Prague: Melantrich, 1975), 41; Otakar Josek, *Život a dílo Josefa Kalouska* (Prague: Historický spolek, 1922), 33; on Štulc, see *Ottův slovník naučný*, 24:813.

104. See n. 71.

105. *Výbor z literatury české*, 2:v–vii.

106. Ibid., 1:635–790.

107. Ibid., 2:181–228.

108. Ibid., 2:1603–14.

109. Ibid., 2:365–402.

110. Ibid., 2:410–30.

111. Ibid., 2:430–38.

112. Ibid., 2:605–39.

113. Ibid., 2:733–742.

114. Ibid., 2:663–714.

115. Ibid., 2:849–62. The text was also printed in *Časopis českého musea*, pt. 2 (1847): 186 ff.
116. *Výbor z literatury české*, 2:271–82, 571–604.
117. Ibid., 2:793–804.
118. Ibid., 2:1039–48.
119. Ibid., 2:1189–1204.
120. Ibid, 2:1299–1312.
121. Ibid., 2:1511–22.
122. Flavius Josephus, *Flavia Jozefa o válce židovské knihy sedmery*, trans. Pavel Aquilinas (Vorličný) (Prostějov: Jan Günther, 1553); 2nd ed. (Levoča: Bartolomeides, 1805).
123. *Výbor z literatury české*, 2:1377–94.
124. Ibid., 2:1550–58.
125. Ibid., 2:1593–1604, 1615–22.
126. Ibid., 2:1537–50, 1657–68.
127. Ibid., 2:1567–84; for Veleslavín's editions, see *Knihopis*, nos. 2797–98.
128. Ibid., 2:1586–92, 1622–38.
129. Jan Novotný, *František Cyril Kampelík* (Prague: Melantrich, 1975), 24; Miroslav Hroch, *Social Preconditions on National Revival in Europe: A Comparative Analysis of the Social Composition of Patriotic Groups among the Smaller European Nations*, trans. Ben Fowkes (New York: Columbia University Press, 2000), 47.
130. For a brief survey, see Agnew, *Origins of the Czech National Renascence*, 31–50; Jeník z Bratřic, *Z mých pamětí*, 27. See also as a corrective, Mojmír Otruba, "Ahistorický historismus českého obrození," in *Historické vědomí v českém umění 19. století*, Uměnovědné studie, 3 (Prague: Ústav teorie a dějin umění ČSAV, 1981), 112–23.
131. Johann Heinrich Wolf's *Geschichte des Königreichs Böheim zum Gebrauche der Studierenden Jugend in den K. K. Staaten* (Vienna: Johann Thomas von Trattner, 1783), 128, 132, 152, 192.
132. Arnošt Kraus, *Husitství v literatuře zejména německé* (Prague: Česká akademie, 1917–24), 2:174.
133. František M. Pelcl, *Paměti*, trans. Jan Pán (Prague: Státní nakladatelství krásné literatury, hudby a umění, 1956), 36; see also Kamil Krofta, *K pramenům českých dějin* (Prague: Sfinx-Janda, 1948), 53–54.
134. Pelcl also expressed an admiration for the military skills of Žižka and Prokop Holý, citing with approval an Italian humanist's assessment of Žižka as a warrior above Hanibal; Johanides, *František Martin Pelcl*, 164–65, 174; František Kutnar and Jaroslav Marek, *Přehledné dějiny českého a slovenského dějepisectví* (Prague: Lidové noviny, 1997), 156–57. Dobrovský, *Dějiny české řeči a literatury*, 168.
135. Agnew, *Origins of the Czech National Renascence*, 27. Dobner, however, still clung to some Counter-Reformation concepts as his defense of Jan of Nepomuk against Dobrovský; ibid., 32.
136. Kamil Krofta, "František Pubička předchůdce Palackého v zemském dějepisectví českém," *Časopis společnosti přátel starožitností* 51–53 (1943–45), published in 1946, 13, 21–23.
137. Mikuláš Adaukt Voigt, "Über den Kalendar der Slaven, besonders der Böhmen," *Abhandlungen einer Privatgesellschaft in Böhmen zur Aufnahme der Math-*

ematik, der vaterländischen Geschichte und der Naturgeschichte (Prague, 1775–84), 3 (1777): 121, 129.

138. Karel Raphael Ungar, "Žižka's militärische Briefe und Verordnungen," *Neuere Abhandlungen der königlichen Böhmischen Gesellschaft der Wissenschaften* 1 (1790): 371–73, where he compares Žižka's skill to that of Hannibal or to that of the Greeks at Marathon.

139. By F. G. Steinsberg and J. Tandler; see Kraus, *Husitství v literatuře zejména německé*, 2:207–8.

140. Ignác Cornova, "Hat Schirach König Georgen von Böhmen . . . Religion überhaupt mit Grund abgesprochen?" *Neuere Abhandlungen der königlichen Böhmischen Gesellschaft der Wissenschaften* 3 (1798): 164.

141. Josef Haubelt, *České osvícenství* (Prague: Svoboda, 1986), 425.

142. Josef Dobrovský, *Geschichte der böhmischen Sprache und Literatur*, cited by Josef Pekař, "Masarykova česká folosofie," in *Spor o smysl českých dějin, 1895–1938*, ed. Miloš Havelka (Prague: Torst, 1995), 269–70.

143. Polišenský and Illingová, *Jan Jeník z Bratřic*, 72, 82, 103. Jeník had a high opinion of Hus, whom he called "blessed" and whom he praised for preaching the true word of God; see Jeník z Bratřic, *Z mých pamětí*, 19–20, 25.

144. Kraus, *Husitství v literatuře zejména německé*, 3:1–12; Mojmír Otruba and Miroslav Kačer, *Tvůrčí cesta Josefa Kajetána Tyla* (Prague, Státní nakladatelství krásné literatury a umění, 1961), 362; Ferdinand Čenský, ed., *Z dob našeho probuzení: Sbírka přátelských dopisů* (Prague: Urbánek, 1875), 238–39.

145. Kraus, *Husitství v literatuře zejména německé*, 2:168; Polišenský and Illingová, *Jan Jeník z Bratřic*, 221–22.

146. Závodský, *František Ladislav Čelakovský*, 25; Josef Emler, ed., "Listy Antonína Marka k Josefu Jungmannovi," *Časopis českého musea* 66 (1892): 482; Mukařovský, ed., *Dějiny české literatury*, 2:283; Kraus, *Husitství v literatuře zejména německé*, 3:104.

147. Although Dobrovský has not been suspected of involvement in the Czech case, these shenanigans provided some ground for Edward Keenan's theory of Dobrovský's authorship of the allegedly twelfth-century Russian epic, *Slovo o polku Igoreve* (The Igor Tale). He indeed had journeyed to Russia in 1792–93; see Edward L. Keenan, "Was Iaroslav of Halych Really Shooting Sultans in 1185?" *Harvard Ukrainian Studies* 22 (1998): 314–17; Keenan, *Josef Dobrovský and the Origins of the Igor's Tale* (Cambridge, Mass.: Harvard Ukrainian Research Center, 2003).

148. Otruba and Kačer, *Tvůrčí cesta Josefa Kajetána Tyla*, 363; Josef K. Tyl, "Jan Hus," "Žižka z Trocnova," *Historická dramata*, Spisy 20 (Prague: Státní nakladatelství krásné literatury, hudby a umění, 1954), 97–211, 298–371; Josef K. Tyl, "Dekret kutnohorský," Otruba and Kačer, *Historické povídky III (1841–1844)*, Spisy 9 (Prague: Státní nakladatelství krásné literatury, hudby a umění, 1961), 7–160.

149. Augustin Zitte, *Obšírný životopis mistra Jana z Husince, vůbec Hus nazvaného*, trans. J. V. Sommer (Prague: Jan Spurný, 1850).

150. Valentin Urfus, "Český historický stát: Od stavovství k absolutismu," in *VII. Sjezd českých historiků: Praha, 24.–26. září 1993* (Prague: Historický ústav, 1994), 70, 78; Urfus, "Stát v představách české národní společnosti smetanovského období," in *Povědomí tradice v novodobé české kultuře: Doba Bedřicha Smetany* (Prague, Národní galerie, 1988), 22–28.

151. Karel Malý, "Právní kultura v českém stavovském státě," in *Vladislavské*

zřízení zemské a počátky ústavního zřízení v Českých zemích, 1500–1619, ed. Karel Malý and Jaroslav Pánek (Prague: Historický ústav Akademie věd České Republiky; Ústav právních dějin Právnické fakulty Univerzity Karlovy, 2001), 63. See also Petr Kreuz, "Edice zemských zřízení a ústavně historických pramenů k dějinám českých zemí v raném novověku, 1500–1619," in ibid., 267–89; and Jaroslav Pánek, "Český stát a stavovská společnost na prahu novověku ve světle zemských zřízení," in ibid., 13–54.

152. Jitka Lněničková, *České země v době předbřeznové, 1792–1848* (Prague: Libri, 1999), 75–76.

153. The document, prepared by Palacký, sought to regain genuine legislative powers for the Bohemian Diet. Ibid., 92–94.

154. Johanides, *František Martin Pelcl*, 62–63.

155. Mikuláš Adauctus Voigt, *Über den Geist der böhmischen Gesetze in den verschiedenen Zeitaltern* (Dresden: Waltherische Hofbuchhandlung, 1788), especially, 135–203.

156. Ibid., 182–85, 200–201.

157. Polišenský and Illingová, *Jan Jeník z Bratřic*, 83–85, 119–20. The early nineteenth-century authors of the *Rukopis královédvorský* and *Rukopis zelenohorský* depicted the proceedings of old Bohemian Diets as close to modern parliamentarianism; Lněničková, *České země v době předbřeznové*, 140–41.

158. *Výbor z literatury české*, 2:1047–86.

159. Ibid., 2:1217–44.

160. Pavel Stránský, *Staat von Böhmen*, trans., rev., suppl. Ignác Cornova (Prague: J. G. Calve, 1792–1803); see *Knihopis*, no. 15.742. For earlier editions, see *Knihopis*, nos. 15.739–41.

161. Volumes 5 and 6 describe political developments in Bohemia from the reign of Joseph I (1705–11) to Leopold II (1790–92).

162. Stránský, *Staat von Böhmen*, trans. Cornova, 7:232–35, 257–58, 277.

163. Pavel Stránský, *Von den böhmischen Landständen, Landtagen und Landesämtern* (Prague: Calve, 1790); see *Knihopis*, no. 15.738.

164. *Výbor z literatury české* 1:609–26. Also reprinted in *Archiv český* 2 (1842): 76–135.

165. *Výbor z literatury české* 1:1007–60.

166. Ibid., 1:963–1008.

167. *Výbor z literatury české* 2:379–402; 849–62.

168. Ibid., 2:1359–72.

169. Ibid., 2:1467–80.

170. Dobrovský, *Dějiny české řeči a literatury*, 346; *Výbor z literatury české* 2: 803–32.

171. Pavel Kristián of Koldín, *Práva městská království českého* (Prague: František H. Kyrchner, 1755); see *Knihopis*, no. 4573.

172. *Výbor z literatury české*, 2:1315–26, 1549–58. For the original edition, Brikcí z Licka, *Práva městská* (Litomyšl: Alexandr Plzeňský, 1536), see *Knihopis*, no. 1348.

173. The special link between the awakeners and their Utraquist precursors was celebrated, for instance, in a eulogy of Zahradník, who greeted the new authors as reincarnations of such sixteenth-century paragons as Koldín, Veleslavín, and Kocín. See Rybička, "Vzpomínka na Vincence Zahradníka," 38.

174. In view of the foregoing, a modest suggestion might be in order concerning historical nomenclature. It would involve replacing the vacuous and even demeaning "Pre–White Mountain Era" with a more positive and substantive designation, such as the "Age of Utraquism" (*Doba podobojí*) or, perhaps, even with Dobrovský's earlier descriptor as the "Golden Age" (*das schöne oder goldene Zeitalter*); see Dobrovský, *Dějiny české řeči a literatury*, 46.

Chapter 6

1. Miroslav Hroch, *Social Preconditions of National Revival in Europe: A Comparative Analysis of the Social Composition of Patriotic Groups among the Smaller European Nations*, trans. Ben Fowkes (New York: Columbia University Press, 2000; originally published: Cambridge: Cambridge University Press, 1985). See also Hroch's earlier works: *Die Vorkämpfer der nationalen Bewegung bei den kleinen Völkern Europas: Eine Vergleichende Analyse zur gesellschaftlichen Schichtung der patriotischen Gruppen*, Acta Universitatis Carolinae Philosophica et Historica, Monographia 24 (Prague, 1969); and *Obrození malých evropských národů: I. Národy severní a východní Evropy* (Prague: Univerzita Karlova, 1971).

2. For the distinction, see Barry Smith, *Austrian Philosophy: The Legacy of Brentano* (Chicago: Open Court, 1994), 1.

3. Alexander Motyl, ed., *Encyclopedia of Nationalism* (San Diego, Calif: Academic Press, 2001), 1:172; see also Karl D. Bracher, *Die deutsche Diktatur: Entstehung, Struktur, Folgen des Nationalsozialismus*, 6th rev. ed. (Frankfurt/M: Ullstein, 1979), 9–10. On Herder, see Robert R. Ergang, *Herder and the Foundations of German Nationalism* (New York: Columbia University Press, 1931); Hans Kohn, *The Idea of Nationalism: A Study in Its Idea and Background* (New York: Macmillan, 1945); Alexander Gillies, *Herder* (Oxford: Blackwell, 1945); Robert T. Clark, *Herder: His Life and Thought* (Berkeley: University of California Press, 1955); Frederick M. Barnard, *Herder's Social and Political Thought: From Enlightenment to Nationalism* (Oxford: Clarendon Press, 1965); Wulf Koepke and Samson B. Knoll, eds., *Johann Gottfried Herder, Innovator through the Ages* (Bonn: Bouvier, 1982); Wulf Koepke, *Johann Gottfried Herder* (Boston: Twayne, 1987); Wulf Koepke, ed., *Johann Gottfried Herder: Language, History, and Enlightenment* (Columbia, S.C.: Camden House, 1990).

4. "Tschechische Geschichtsbild und Nationalbewusstsein auf Herderischer Stufe fixierte"; Eugen Lemberg, *Grundlagen des nationalen Erwachens in Böhmen: Geistesgeschichtliche Studie, am Lebensgang Josef Georg Meinerts, 1773–1844* (Liberec: Verlag Gebrüder Stiepel, 1932), 74.

5. Gillies, *Herder*, 130; Barnard, *Herder's Social and Political Thought*, 172; see also Robert R. Ergang, *Herder and the Foundations of German Nationalism* (New York: Columbia University, 1931), 259–60.

6. Walter Schamschula, *Die Anfänge der tschechischen Erneuerung und das deutsche Geistesleben, 1740–1800* (Munich: Fink, 1973), 13. Elsewhere, ibid., 118, n. 2, 246; however, he polemicized, against overestimating Herder's role, with Eugen Lemberg, *Nationalismus* (Hamburg, 1964), 1:175 ff. Moreover, Herder was not original in his characterization of the Slavs: "When Herder characterized the Slavic virtues as peaceful, full of joy of life, and music loving, he gave an expression to al-

ready existing ideas." ["Wenn Herder die slavischen Nationaltugenden als friedlich, lebensfroh und sangesfreudig charakterisiert, so gab er bereits bestehenden Vorstellungen Ausdruck"] (273).

7. Alexandr S. Myl'nikov, *Vznik národně osvícenské ideologie v českých zemích: Prameny národního obrození* (Prague: Univerzita Karlova, 1974), 204; Robin Okey, *The Habsburg Monarchy:From Enlightenment to Eclipse* (New York: St. Martin's Press, 2001), 116.

8. Jan Patočka, *Náš národní program*, ed. Jan Vít and Miroslav Petříček (Prague: Evropský kulturní klub, 1990), 7–8.

9. Barnard, *Herder's Social and Political Thought*, xii; Gillies, *Herder*, 12–14.

10. Johann Herder, *Zur Philosophie der Geschichte*, vol. 1. (Berlin: Aufbau Verlag, 1952), 465, cited by Ivan T. Berend, *Decades of Crisis: Central and Eastern Europe before World War II* (Berkeley: University of California Press, 1998), 54.

11. See Richard Rorty, "Dewey between Hegel and Darwin," in Richard Rorty, *Truth and Progress*, Philosophical Papers, 3 (New York: Cambridge University Press, 1998), 295. Humboldt developed his theory while studying the language of the Kawis of Java; see his *Über die Verschiedenheit des menschlichen Sprachbaues und ihren Einfluss auf die geistige Entwicklung des Menchengeschlechts* [On the Differences of the Structures of Human Speech and Their Influence on the Intellectual Development of Mankind] (1836); reprint Bonn: F. Dümmler, 1968; trans. Wilhelm Humboldt, *On Language: The Diversity of Human Language-Structure and Its Influence on the Mental Development of Mankind*, trans. Peter Heath, intro. Hans Aarsleff (New York: Cambridge University Press, 1988). Aarsleff minimizes Herder's influence on Humboldt, stressing instead that of E. B. Condillac, ibid., xxxiii–xxxv.

12. Barnard, *Herder's Social and Political Thought*, 160–62; Gillies, *Herder*, 119. Herder's influence on romanticism and German idealism, including Schelling and Hegel, was immense: see Barnard, *Herder's Social and Political Thought*, 153–59; Cyril O'Regan, *The Heterodox Hegel* (Albany, N.Y.: State University Press of New York, 1994), 51, 239; "Herder," *Concise Routledge Encyclopedia of Philosophy* (New York: Routledge, 2000), 348.

13. Dietrich von Engelhardt, "Romanticism in Germany," in Roy Porter and Mikuláš Teich, eds., *Romanticism in National Context* (New York: Cambridge University Press, 1988), 110; Gillies, *Herder*, 119; Frederick C. Beiser "Introduction: Hegel and the Problem of Metaphysics," in Frederick C. Beiser, ed., *Cambridge Companion to Hegel* (New York: Cambridge University Press, 1993), 5, n. 13.

14. There is evidence that, in fact, he also read Herder as a student. Rorty, "Dewey between Hegel and Darwin," 293. See also H. S. Harris, "Hegel's Intellectual Development to 1807," in Beiser, *Cambridge Companion to Hegel*, 27–28, n. 7. He referred to Herder in his own *Lectures on the Philosophy of History;* see Beiser, "Hegel's Historicism," in *Cambridge Companion to Hegel* (see note 13), 275, 286.

15. O'Regan, *The Heterodox Hegel*, 279–84; Kurt Leese, *Von Jacob Boehme zu Schelling: Eine Untersuchung zur Metaphysik des Gottesproblems* (Erfurt: Kurt Stenger, 1927); Heinz Burger, *Die Gedankenwelt der grossen Schwaben: Von der Klosterkultur am Bodensee bis Hegel* (Stuttgart: Steinkopf, 1978), 165–83, 190–204.

16. Engelhardt, "Romanticism in Germany," 111–12. As Rorty comments, some

rationalistically inclined followers might prefer to interpret Hegel not as "a metaphysicized Herder" but as "a historicized Spinoza"; "Dewey between Hegel and Darwin," 306.

17. Allen Wood, "Hegel's Ethics," in Beiser, *Cambridge Companion to Hegel* (see note 13), 229.

18. Paul Edwards, ed., *Encyclopedia of Philosophy* (New York: Macmillan, 1972), 3:489.

19. Miloš Tomčík, "T. G. Masaryk ako integračná osobnosť českých a slovenských novodobých dejín," *T. G. Masaryk, idea demokracie a současné evropanství*, Sborník mezinárodní vědecké konference, Praha, 2.–4. března 2000, ed. Emil Voráček (Prague: Filosofia, 2001), 45–54.

20. On Kollár as a "Czech writer," see H. Barry Nisbet, "Herder's Conception of Nationhood and Its Influence in Eastern Europe," in *The German Lands and Eastern Europe: Essays on the History of Their Social, Cultural and Political Relations*, ed. Roger Bartlett and Karen Schönwälder (New York: St. Martins Press, 1999), 128. See also František Stellner, "Slovanství v české a ruské společnosti v první polovině 19. století," *Historický obzor* 15 (2004): 207–8. Kollár's romanticism and the realism of Havlíček and Palacký are contrasted, for instance, by Josef Kaizl, *České myšlenky*, 2nd ed. (Prague: Edvard Beaufort, 1896), 40–41.

21. Dmytro Chyzhevskyi, *Hegel bei den Slaven* (Liberec [Reichenberg]: Stiepel, 1934), passim.

22. Jungmann reported that Palacký decided not to accept for publication any contributions by Kollár on the Slav question; see Josef Emler, ed., "Listy Josefa Jungmanna k Antonínu Markovi," *Časopis českého musea* 57 (1883): 58. See also Hans Kohn, *Pan-Slavism, Its History and Ideology* (Notre Dame, Ind.: University of Notre Dame Press, 1953), 13.

23. On the Czech critique of Kollár, see Hana Šmahelová, "Kollárova vize slovanské vzájemnosti," *Česká literatura* 50 (2002): 135–36, 139–40; František Pastrnek, "O starožitnických spisech Kollárových," in *Jan Kollár, 1793–1852. Sborník statí o životě, působení a literární činnosti pěvce 'Slávy dcery,'* ed. Fratišek Pastrnek (Vienna: Český akademický spolek, 1893), 231; on the reception of Kollár's etymological theories, see also Jiří Kořalka, *František Palacký, 1798–1876: Životopis* (Prague: Argo, 1998), 425; and Emler, ed., "Listy Josefa Jungmanna k Antonínu Markovi," 58 (1884), 425. On Kollár's and Šafárik's zest for collecting Slovak folk songs, see Emler, ed., "Listy Josefa Jungmanna k Antonínu Markovi," 48–49; 509.

24. Šmahelová, "Kollárova vize slovanské vzájemnosti," 146.

25. Josef Emler, ed., "Listy Antonína Marka k Josefu Jungmannovi," *Časopis českého musea* 66 (1892): 478, 480.

26. František V. Krejčí, *František Palacký, jeho význam v českém probuzení* (Prague: Svěcený, 1912), 9.

27. "Osvícenský klasicismus a jeho ústup působením romantismu a národních snah" (Enlightenment Classicism and Its Retreat under the Impact of Romanticism and the National Aspirations), in Jan Lehár and others, *Česká literatura od počátků k dnešku* (Prague: Lidové noviny, 1998), 557; the formulation is repeated in the anthology Jan Lehár and others, eds., *Česká literatura od počátků k dnešku: kniha textů* (Prague: Lidové noviny, 2000–2001), 1:419–52.

28. See Juha Manninem, *Valistus ja kansallinen identiteeti: Aatehistoriallinen*

tutkimus 1700-luvun Pohjalasta [The Enlightenment and National Identity] (Helsinki: Suomalaisen Kirjallisuuden Seura, 2000); and the review by A. F. Upton in *English Historical Review* 117 (2002): 198–99.

29. Margaret Jacob and Wijnand W. Mijnhardt, eds., *The Dutch Republic in the Eighteenth Century: Decline, Enlightenment, and Revolution* (Itaca, N.Y.: Cornell University Press, 1992).

30. Kaizl, *České myšlenky*, 21.

31. Kořalka, *František Palacký*, 526.

32. See Václav Šturm, *Krátké ozvání . . . proti kratičkému ohlášení Jednoty Valdenské neb Boleslavské* (Prague: Jiřík Dačický, 1584), 3, 19–20. As for the limited currency of German in general, Erasmus claimed that he was unable to read Luther's German tracts; Desiderius Erasmus, *The Correspondence* (Toronto: University of Toronto Press, 1974–94), 9:391–92.

33. See, for instance, Victor Kiernan, "The British Isles: Celt and Saxon," in *The National Question in Europe in National Context*, ed. Mikuláš Teich and Roy Porter (New York: Cambridge University Press, 1993), 30–31.

34. For comparison, see Richard Blanke, *Polish-speaking Germans? Language and National Identity among the Masurians since 1871* (Cologne: Böhlau, 2001).

35. As an exception, see the positive endorsement of the Enlightenment for the national awakening by Mikuláš Teich, "Bohemia: From Darkness into Light," in *The Enlightenment in National Context*, ed. Roy Porter and Mikuláš Teich (New York: Cambridge University Press, 1981), 163: "Last but not least, and interrelated with these aspects of the Enlightenment in Bohemia, was the emergence of the study of Czech history and language, and the Awakening of modern Czech national consciousness, as its product and consequence."

36. Schamschula, *Die Anfänge der tschechischen Erneuerung*, 211; see also 203, 205, 215, 247, 264.

37. Ibid., 282, 290, 293. On Meissner's emphasis on English and French culture, see Václav Zelený, *Život Josefa Jungmanna* (Prague: Matice česká, 1873), 14–15, 19.

38. The imprint was (Prague: Felicianus Mangold, 1775). Seibt received an official reprimand, and the work was temporarily proscribed; see Josef Johanides, *František Martin Pelcl* (Prague: Melantrich, 1981), 137–46; Jaroslav Prokeš, "Aféra Seibtova roku 1779," in *Českou minulostí*, ed. Otakar Odložík, Jaroslav Prokeš, and Rudolf Urbánek (Prague: Laichter, 1929), 317–30.

39. Josef Hanzal, "Jazyková otázka ve vývoji obrozenského školství," *Československý časopis historický* (1966): 322; Hanzal, "Vzdělanost a lidová osvěta," *Sborník historický* 18 (1971): 39–69. Alexandr S. Myl'nikov, *Vznik národně ocvícenské ideologie v českých zemích: Prameny národního obrození* (Prague: Univerzita Karlova, 1974), 206, saw the Born's Learned Society of the 1770s, despite its use of German, as "the starting point of Czech thought as it would develop in the following years." See also ibid., 204.

40. According to Bolzano, differences among languages were entirely arbitrary: they merely used different words for the same concepts; Bernard Bolzano, *Über das Verhältniss der beiden Volkstämme in Böhmen* (Vienna: Wilhelm Braumüller, 1849), 44–48. Masaryk's view actually was not too far from Bolzano's; in his opinion, language was just an instrument for expressing intellectual values that were universal: morality and humanity. There was no peculiar national ethics; see Masaryk, *Česká otázka. Naše nynější krize. Jan Hus* Spisy 6 (Prague: Masarykův ústav, 2000), 53–54.

Aleksandr S. Myl'nikov, *Kul'tura cheshskogo vozrozhdeniia* (Leningrad: Nauka, 1982), 4, even appropriates Bolzano for the Czech nation, calling him "original'nyi cheshskii myslitel'" [original Czech thinker]. See also Patočka, *Náš národní program*, 52–53.

41. Marie Pavlíková, "Vztah Josefa Jungmanna k Bernardu Bolzanovi a jeho žákům," *Literární archiv*: Sborník Památníku národdmího písemnictví, 8–9 (1974), 83–85, 91; Emler, "Listy Josefa Jungmanna k Antonínu Markovi," 166.

42. In 1785, he called Joseph II "a special and ardent lover of the language of his Czech people." See Jan Novotný, *Matěj Václav Kramerius* (Prague: Melantrich, 1973), 76.

43. The relevant passage from Dobrovský's address is cited in *Krameriovy noviny*, no. 1, January 7, 1792, p. 11; see also Novotný, *Matěj Václav Kramerius*, 151, 154.

44. On the two tendencies, see, for instance, Hana Šmahelová, "Bernard Bolzano a české národní obrození," *Český časopis historický* 100 (2002): 77; Pavlíková, "Vztah Josefa Jungmanna k Bernardu Bolzanovi a jeho žákům," 94, 97; Jiří Rak, "Doslov," in František Kutnar, *Obrozenské vlastenectví a nacionalismus: Příspěvek k národnímu společenskému obsahu češství doby obrozenské* (Prague: Karolinum, 2003), 354. Dobrovský also sympatizoval with Jungmann's work on the renewal of the Czech language; see, for instance, Josef Dobrovský, *Korrespondence*, Díl 2: *Vzájemné dopisy Josefa Dobrovského a Jiřího Samuela Bandtkeho z let 1810–1827*, Sbírka pramenů ku poznání literárního života v Čechách, na Moravě a ve Slezsku, Skupina 2, Číslo 8, ed. A. V. Francev (Prague: Česká akademie pro vědy, slovesnost a umění, 1906), 95, 101, 127, 131, 189.

45. Particularly in 1818–19, expressing Jungmann's disappointment about Bolzano's and Fesl's failure to support Marek for an ecclesiastical promotion; Emler, ed., "Listy Antonína Marka k Josefu Jungmannovi," *Časopis českého musea* 62 (1888): 164–66; Pavlíková, "Vztah Josefa Jungmanna k Bernardu Bolzanovi a jeho žákům," 91; see also 86.

46. Masaryk, *Česká otázka*, 39; see also 99. For a contemporary critique of Masaryk's view of Jungmann, see, for instance, Kaizl, *České myšlenky*, 33–35.

47. This ambiguity was pointed out by Kaizl, *České myšlenky*, 19. The quotation is from Masaryk, *Česká otázka*, 10. See also Zdeněk V. David, "Tomáš G. Masaryk's Ambivalent View of the Enlightenment and Political Liberalism," *Kosmas* 19, no. 2 (2006): 83–93.

48. Jan Patočka, *Náš národní program*, ed. Jan Vít and Miroslav Petříček (Prague: Evropský kulturní klub, 1990), 4–5, 25 (includes his *Česká vzdělanost v Evropě* [Prague: V. Petr, 1939]); Jan Patočka, *Dvojí rozum a příroda v německém osvícenství: Herderovská studie* (Prague: Václav Petr, 1942), 27.

49. Johanides, *František Martin Pelcl*, 123–24. See also Jiří Klabouch, *Osvícenské právní nauky v českých zemích* (Prague: Nakladatelství Československé akademie věd, 1958), 223, on "the superficiality" of the Josephist Enlightenment. Interestingly, Michel Foucault expressed a similar deprecatory attitude toward the shallowness of the Enlightenment, which he designated as the *épistémè de l'âge classique* (episteme of the classical age); see John Weightman, "On Not Understanding Michel Foucault," *American Scholar* (Summer 1989): 385, 388, 395.

50. Kaizl, *České myšlenky*, 26; Patočka, *Dvojí rozum a příroda*, 25–28; Jan Patočka, "J. G. Herder a jeho filosofie humanity," in Johann G. Herder, *Vývoj lidskosti*, trans. Jan Patočka (Prague: Jan Laichter, 1941), 452, 462.

51. Particularly, after his *Auch eine Philosophie der Geschichte* (1774); see Frederick Copleston, *A History of Philosophy* (Westminster, Md.: Newman Press, 1947–66), 6:142.

52. Patočka, *Dvojí rozum a příroda v německém osvícenství*, 28, 23–24; Patočka, "J. G. Herder a jeho filosofie humanity," 452–53, 458. According to Patočka, Herder mapped out a route from the Enlightenment, which did not lead to positivism; ibid., 462.

53. Carlton J. Hayes, "Contributions of Herder to the Doctrine of Nationalism," *American Historical Review* 32 (1927): 721, referring to Johann G. Herder, *Ideen zur Philosophie der Geschichte der Menschheit*, in Herder, *Sämmtliche Werke*, ed. Bernhard Suphan (Berlin: Weidmann, 1877–1913), 14:121. In English, see Herder, *Outlines of a Philosophy of the History of Man*, trans. T. Churchill (1800–1803); 2nd ed. (New York: Bergman Publishers, [1966]).

54. Masaryk, *Česká otázka*, 13, 15

55. Zdeněk V. David, "The Integrity of the Bohemian Reformation: The Problem of Neo-Utraquism," in *The Bohemian Reformation and Religious Practice*, 5, pt. 2 (2005): 329–51.

56. See, for instance, Manfred Brandl, *Der Kanonist Joseph Valentin Eybel, 1741–1805: sein Beitrag zur Aufklärung in Österreich* (Steyr: Ennsthaler, 1976), 23–24. For older works on the Catholic Enlightenment, see Sebastian Merkle, *Die katholische Beurteilung des Aufklärungszeitalters* (Berlin: K. Curtius, 1909); Merkle, *Die kirchliche Aufklärung im katholischen Deutschland* (Berlin: Reichel, 1910); and Sebastian Merkle and Bernhard Bess, *Religiöse Erzieher der katholischen Kirche aus den letzten vier Jahrhunderten* (Leipzig: Quelle und Meyer, [1922]).

57. There were spin-offs from the Bohemian Reformation that could be considered proto-Protestant—first Taboritism, then the Unity of Brethren—but these were marginal to the mainstream; see Zdeněk V. David, *Finding the Middle Way: The Utraquists' Liberal Challenge to Rome and Luther* (Washington, D.C.: Wilson Center Press; Baltimore: Johns Hopkins University Press, 2003), 24–32, 39–41.

58. *Antologie z dějin českého a slovenského filozofického myšlení* (Prague: Svoboda, 1981), 399.

59. It was Josef Pekař who adopted the contrary view of romanticism; Miloš Havelka, *Dějiny a smysl* (Prague: NLN, 2001), 154.

60. Masaryk was, in fact, aware that Herder elevated the nation above the individual: "In the course of history, humanity expresses itself through the individual nations; individual nations lead humanity, each for a certain time." See Masaryk, *Česká otázka,* 84. For attempts to portray Masaryk as a pupil of Herder, see Barnard, *Herder's Social and Political Thought*, 174–77; Gillies, *Herder*, 131–32.

61. According to Masaryk, "Comenius . . . still speaks to us through Leibnitz and Herder whose influence on Dobrovský and Kollár Professor [Ernest] Denis has finely demonstrated"; see Tomáš G. Masaryk, *The Making of a State: Memories and Observations, 1914–1918* (London: Allen and Unwin, 1927), 424. Denis seems rather vague about the connection to Comenius; see Ernest Denis, *La Bohême depuis la Montagne-Blanche*, pt. 2: *La renaissance tchèque vers le fédéralisme* (Paris: Ernest Leroux, 1903), 10–11. The view that Herder was, in fact, rooted in the philosophical thought of the Bohemian Reformation was later restated by Albert Pražák who, in a startling reversal of the relationship, suggested that the Czechs were Herderians "before Herder, during Herder, and after Herder" ("je možno mluvit

přímo o našem herdrovství před Herdrem, za Herdra a po Herdrovi"). This would, however, mean that the similarity between the awakeners and Herder was merely accidental. See Albert Pražák, "Herder a Češi," in Johann G. Herder, *Vývoj lidskosti* (Prague: Laichter, 1941), x; see also vi–vii.

62. Herder became familiar with Comenius's writings only in the 1790s. See Gillies, *Herder*, 131–32.

63. Comenius envisioned the attainment of a millennial kingdom through a general improvement of education leading to a fuller understanding of both humanity and divinity. The Neo-Platonic idea of lifting up the humans to the level of the divine universal harmony was expounded particularly in his *De rerum humanarum emendatione consultatio catholica*. See Jozef Pšenák and Zuzana Bugáňová, eds., *De rerum humanarum emendatione consultatio catholica a odkaz Jana Amosa Komenského pre tretie tisícročie* (Bratislava: Univerzita Komenského, 2001); Jaroslava Pešková, Josef Cach, and Michal Svatoš, eds., *Pocta Univerzity Karlovy J. A. Komenskému* (Prague: Karolinum, 1991), especially, 117–26, 185–92; Jan Patočka, *Komeniologické studie*, vol. 2, ed. Věra Schifferová (Prague: Oikúmené, 1998), 149–211. A partial edition of Comenius's opus was known to Herder, but the entire work was published only much later as *De rerum humanarum emendatione consultatio catholica* (Prague: Academia, 1966), from a manuscript rediscovered by Dmitrii Chyzhevs'ky in Halle in 1934; see also Patočka, *Komeniologické studie* 2:128–33.

64. Karel Rýdl, "Jan Amos Komenský ve vývoji evropského pedagogického a filozofického myšlení v 18. století," in *Pocta Univerzity Karlovy J. A. Komenskému*, 190–91; Jaroslav Ludvíkovský, "Dobrovský a Komenský," *Archiv pro bádání o životě a spisech J. A. Komenského* 15 (1940): 17–18; concerning criticism by Pierre Bayle and Johann C. Adelung, see also Josef Tvrdý, "Vztahy Dobrovského k filosofii," *Bratislava* 4 (1930): 287.

65. Jan Patočka, *Náš národní program*, ed. Jan Vít and Miroslav Petříček (Prague: Evropský kulturní klub, 1990), 7.

66. On the German evolution, see Hans Kohn, *Prelude to Nation States: The French and German Experience, 1789–1815* (Princeton, N.J.: Van Nostrand, 1967), 3–4.

67. Kateřina Bláhová, "Česká historiografie přelomu století v dialogu s Evropou: prolegomena k tématu," in *Komunikace a izolace v české kultuře 19. století*, Sborník příspěvků z 21. plzeňského sympozia, ed. Kateřina Bláhová (Praha: KLP, 2002), 187.

68. Ján Šurovič, "Slovenský pietizmus," *Historica Slovaca* 3–4 (1945–46): 197.

69. On the Protestant ethos of Kollár and Šafařík, see also Robert B. Pynsent, *Questions of Identity: Czech and Slovak Ideas of Nationality and Personality* (Budapest: Central European University Press, 1994), 73.

70. Jan Jakubec, ed., *Literatura česká devatenáctého století*, with Josef Hanuš, Jan Máchal, and Jaroslav Vlček, 2nd ed. (Prague: Jan Laichter, 1911–17), 2:24–25.

71. Matija Murko, "Kollárova vzájemnost slovanská," *Jan Kollár, 1793–1852. Sborník statí o životě, působení a literární činnosti pěvce 'Slávy dcery,'* ed. František Pastrnek (Vienna: Český akademický spolek, 1893), 206.

72. František Kutnar, Oldřich Králík, and Jaromír Bělič, *Tři studie o Palackém* (Olomouc: Palackého univiversita, 1949), 151–52; on Tablic, see Novotný, *Matěj Václav Kramerius*, 167; Samuel Cambel, ed., *Dejiny Slovenska* (Bratislava: Veda, 1986–88), 2:619; Pražák, "Herder a Češi," xv.

73. Martin Luther, *Katechysmus Doktora Martina Lutera, s obšírným katechetyckým výkladem vysoce osvíceného Doktora Jana Gottfrýda Herdera, bývalého generálního Superintendenta Církví ev. A. V. v knížectví Waymarském, k prospěchu škol evangelických*, trans. Jan Grýša, ed. Jiří Palkovič, 4th ed. (Prešpork [Bratislava]: Karel K. Snížek, 1825).

74. Kohn, *Pan-Slavism*, 13–14; Leander Čech, "Význam Kollárovy 'Slávy dcery' v naší básnické literatuře," *Jan Kollár, 1793–1852. Sborník statí*, 108; Šmahelová, "Kollárova vize slovanské vzájemnosti," 130.

75. Kollár, *Prózy*, Vybrané spisy, vol. 2, ed. F. R. Tichý (Prague: Státní nakladatelství kràsné literatury, hudby a umění, 1956), 169, 179, 186–87; see also *Antologie z dějin českého a slovenského filozofického myšlení*, 473; Masaryk, *Česká otázka*, 412; Matija Murko, *Deutsche Einflüsse auf die Anfänge der böhmischen Romantik* (Graz: Styria, 1897), 192 ff.

76. Josef Hanuš, *Pavel Josef Šafařík v životě a spisích* (Prague: E. Grégr, 1895), 29; Jan Novotný, *Pavel Josef Šafařík* (Prague: Melantrich, 1971), 13, 25, 66–67; Lubomíra Havlíková, "Osobnost a dílo P. J. Šafaříka v kontextu vývoje české a evropské (historické) slavistiky," *Historik v proměnách doby a prostředí 19. století*, ed. Jiří Hanuš and Radomír Vlček (Brno: Matice moravská, 2007), 136–37.

77. Samuel Št. Osuský, *Štúrova filozofia*, vol 1 of *Filozofia Štúrovcov* (Myjava: Daniel Pažický, 1926), 20–22; Karol Rosenbaum, "Die Funktion der Herderschen Humanitätsidee in der slowakischen nationalen Wiedergeburt," *Herder-Kolloquium, 1978*, ed. Walter Dietze and others (Weimar : Böhlau, 1980), 337–38. See also Walter Schamschula, *Geschichte der tschechischen Literatur* (Cologne: Böhlau, 1990–96), 2:65, 82; Jakubec, *Literatura česká devatenáctého století*, 2:366.

78. Pynsent, *Questions of Identity*, 73–86; Pynsent, "Slávy Herder," in Robert B. Pynsent, *Ďáblové, ženy a národ: Výbor z úvah o české literatuře* (Prague: Karolinum, 2008), 95–98. Masaryk likewise maintained that Kollár's treatise on Slav mutuality, *Über die literarische Wechselseitigkeit* (Pest, 1837), reflected the influence of Herder's *Ideen zur Philosophie der Geschichte*; see Masaryk, *Česká otázka*, 415; *Ottův slovník naučný* (Prague: Otto, 1888–1908), 11:160; see also Novotný, *Pavel Josef Šafařík*, 27. Another commentator, Černý, highlighted Herder's influence on Kollár's worldview: "Roste z Herdera, myslí Herderem, dýše Herderem" (He grows out of Herder, thinks with Herder, breathes with Herder). See Václav Černý, *Vývoj a zločiny panslavismu* (Prague: Institut pro středoevropskou kulturu a politiku, [1994?]), 12–13; see also 15, 17.

79. Canto 3, sonnet 61, cited in Murko, "Kollárova vzájemnost slovanská," *Jan Kollár, 1793–1852. Sborník statí*, ed. Pastrnek, 210.

80. Vladimír Macura, *Znamení zrodu: České národní obrození jako kulturní typ*, rev. ed. (Prague: H & H, 1995), 18; Pražák, "Herder a Češi," xxii–xxv.

81. These included a suggestion that the Germans would sympathize more with the Slavs if they adopted Herder's ideal of *Humanität*. See Jan Kollár, *Rozpravy o slovanské vzájemnosti*, ed. Miloš Weingart (Prague: Slovanský ústav, 1929), 94. In his *Ueber die literarische Wechselseitigkeit zwischen den verschiedenen Stämmen und Mundarten der slawischen Nation* (Pest, 1837), he referred to Herder's praise of the Slavic tongue and to the prediction of the Slavs' rightful place in the coming era of lasting peace; see Kollár, *Rozpravy o slovanské vzájemnosti*, 90, 118; the other four references to Herder are perfunctory, ibid., 40, 79, 107, 147. Elsewhere in his writings on the Slavic issue, he referred to Herder by name only once in his *Dobré vlast-*

nosti národu slovanského; see ibid., 22, 233. The brief original Czech version of "O literarnéj vzájemnosti mezi kmeny a nářečími slovanskými," *Hronka* 1–2 (1836), 39–55, lacked any mention of Herder. Similarly, Kollár did not explicitly credit Herder for inspiring him to collect folk songs; see J. Polívka, "Kollár, sběratel a vydavatel písní lidových," in *Jan Kollár, 1793–1852. Sborník statí*, 161.

82. Albert Pražák, *České obrození* (Prague: E. Beaufort, 1948), 316; Pražák, "Herder a Češi," xxi.

83. Kollár, *Rozpravy o slovanské vzájemnosti*, ed. Weingart, 95–96.

84. Elena Várossová, "Kultúrny nacionalizmus Jána Kollára," in Várossová, *Filozofia vo svete: svet filozofie u nás* (Bratislava: Veda, 2005), 158.

85. Pynsent, *Questions of Identity*, 98–99; see also Kollár, *Rozpravy o slovanské vzájemnosti*, 102.

86. "Die alternden Culturelemente verjüngen und zur *Humanität potenziiren*" [To rejuvenate the aging cultural elements and *energize them for Humanity*]; ibid., 114; see also viii, 102–7; and *Jan Kollár, 1793–1852. Sborník statí*, 209. Paradoxically, Kollár maintained that the hitherto beneficial romantic principle was being perverted, particularly in the poetry of Byron, to become opposed to nature and oversentimental, then oversatiated and overexcited, and ended up in hallucinations and emotional debility; see ibid., 104. Kollár's prediction of the Slavs' world-historical role aroused some wonderment in German intellectual circles; see anonymous article "Die slawischen Völker und ihr Verhältniss zu Deutschland," *Deutsche Vierteljahrschrift* (Stuttgart and Tubingen: Cotta), 4, no 12 (1840):104.

87. Kollár, *Rozpravy o slovanské vzájemnosti*, xlvi, 106. The others, whom he named among the modern subjectivists, were Schelling, Kant, Byron, and, with some qualifications, Schiller and Goethe; ibid., 105–7.

88. Concerning the influence of Herder on Štúr, see Josette A. Baer, *National Emancipation, Not the Making of Slovakia: L'udovit Štúr's Conception of the Slovak Nation*, St. Francis Xavier University, Center for Post-Communist Studies, Studies in Post-Communism, Occasional Paper 2 (2003), 20–24; Pražák, "Herder a Češi," xxviii.

89. *Dejiny Slovenska*, 2:791. On the transition from Herder to Hegel, see Elena Várossová, "Hegelovské inšpirácie u Štúra a Hurbana," in Várossová, *Filozofia vo svete*, 161–80.

90. L'udovít Štúr, *Listy*, ed. Jozef Ambruš and Vladimír Matula (Bratislava: Vydavateľstvo Slovenskej akadémie vied, 1954–99), 2:179.

91. In particular, Josef Rajačić, the Serbian Patriarch of Karlovci; Mikhail F. Raevskii, a priest attached to the Russian Embassy in Vienna; the Russian scholars Osip O. Bodianskii and Izmail I. Sreznevskii; Štúr, *Listy*, 4:267–71; and the Ukrainians Panteleimon A. Kulish and Nikolai A Rigel'man; ibid., 4:123–4, 245–248.

92. Osuský, *Štúrova filozofia*, 10, 23.

93. On the Slovaks' Hegelianism, see chapter 10 in this volume.

94. Masaryk, *Česká otázka*, 24, 36.

95. See for instance, František Janek, ed., *Upevňovanie vzťahov Čechov a Slovákov pri vučovaní dejepisu* (Bratislava: Slovenské pedagogické nakladateµstvo, 1961), especially 59–81. The atypical position of Kollár in Czech intellectual life does not, of course, diminish the value of his poetry or its place in Czech-language literature. Paradoxically, the work of some of the best poets in the Czech language has emerged as odd intrusions. Kollár's vengeful Slavism and Karel H. Mácha's

satanic romanticism, to which may be added Otokar Březina's collectivist mysticism, offered startling clashes with the normally placid and realistic *weltanschauung* of the Czechs.

96. "Je načase netoliko slovensky zpívat—i to se již zapomíná—ale slovensky cítit a—myslit." Masaryk, *Česká otázka*, 49.

97. Literary romanticism also left notable traces on the culture of Hungary, Poland, and Russia; see, for instance, Mihály Szegedy-Maszák, "Romanticism in Hungary," John Mersereau, Jr., and David Lapeza, "Russian Romanticism," and Donald Pirie, "The Agony in the Garden: Polish Romanticism," in Porter and Teich, eds., *Romanticism in National Context* (see note 13), 217–39, 284–316, 317–44. There is no chapter on romanticism in Bohemia. On the Dionysian and Apollonian attitudes or mentalities in Nietzsche's *The Birth of Tragedy*, see, for instance, Copleston, *A History of Philosophy*, 7:396–98.

98. A Lutheran tradition, however, was not a necessary prerequisite for Herder's appeal. He was also influential among Polish (Kazimierz Brodziński and Wawrzinec Surowiecki) and Russian (Nikolai M. Karamzin, Nikolai I. Nadezhdin, and Stefan P. Shevyrev) scholars. See Masaryk, *Česká otázka*, 47. On Brodziński and Herder, see also Ergang, *Herder and the Foundations of German Nationalism*, 261.

99. Konrad Bittner, *Herders Geschichtsphilosophie und die Slaven*, Veröffentlichungen der Slavistischen Arbeitsgemeinschaft and der Deutschen Universität in Prag, Heft 6 (Reichenberg [Liberec]: Gebrüder Stiepel, 1929), 108; Pražák, "Herder a Češi," x.

100. Masaryk, *Česká otázka*, 30; Novotný, *Matěj Václav Kramerius*, 17; Bernard Bolzano, *Vlastní životopis*, trans. and ed. Marie Pavlíková (Prague: Odeon, 1981), 28; Schamschula's *Die Anfänge der tschechischen Erneuerung*, 272, 281, 285. On his philosophical orientation, see Karl H. Seibt, *Von dem Einflusse der Erziehung auf die Glückseligkeit des Staates* (Prague, 1771), cited by Zelený, *Život Josefa Jungmanna*, 14. On Seibt's preference for Herder's rival Johann B. Basedow, see chapter 7 in this volume.

101. Josef Dobrovský, *Korrespondence*, Díl 1: *Vzájemné dopisy Josefa Dobrovského a Fortunata Duricha z let 1778–1800*, Sbírka pramenů ku poznání literárního života v Čechách, na Moravě a ve Slezsku, Skupina 2, Číslo 2, ed. Adolf Patera (Prague: Česká akademie pro vědy, slovesnost a umění, 1895), 236. There is no reference to Herder in his correspondence with Jiří Samuel Bandtke, Jiří Rybay, or Josef Valentin Zlobický; see Josef Dobrovský, *Korrespondence*, Díl 2–4 (Prague: Česká akademie pro vědy, slovesnost a umění, 1906–13). See also Havlíková, "Osobnost a dílo P. J. Šafaříka," 139.

102. Durych objected to von Ludwig's assertion that the Slavic tongue and the Slavs themselves were held in contempt as slaves or dogs in Charles IV's reign. He also opposed Heyrenbach's view that the Slavs' low culture and welfare were due to their own perverse social customs and not to German oppression; see Václav Fortunát Durych, *Bibliotheca Slavica antiquissimae dialecti communis et ecclesiasticae universae Slavorum gentis,* vol. 1 (Vienna: S. Novakovitsch, 1795), 35, 39; also cited by Schamschula, *Die Anfänge der tschechischen Erneuerung*, 32, 83.

103. Johann G. Herder, *Vom Geist der hebräischen Poesie* (Tübingen: Cotta, 1782); see Josef Dobrovský, *Dopisy Josefa Dobrovského s Augustinem Helfertem*, ed. Josef Wolf and F. M. Bartoš, Spisy a projevy, vol. 22 (Prague: Melantrich, 1941), 75. On Helfert, see FrantišekM. Bartoš, "Úvod," in ibid., 3–24.

104. Karel Ignác Thám, *Über den Karakter der Slawen, dann über den Ursprung, die Schicksale, Volkommenheiten, die Nützlichkeit und Wichtigkeit der bömischen Sprache* (Prague: Johann Diesbach'schen Buchhandlung, 1803), 8–9, 27; p. 4 has a reference to Herder's *Ideen zur Philosophie der Geschichte der Menschheit*, but not to *Briefe zur Beförderung der Humanität*. Hugh L. Agnew, *Origins of the Czech National Renascence* (Pittsburgh, Pa.: University of Pittsburgh Press, 1993), 63–64.

105. Johann G. Herder, *Abhandlung über den Ursprung der Sprache* (Berlin: F. F. Votz, 1772). See also Agnew, *Origins of the Czech National Renascence*, 63–64.

106. Pražák, "Herder a Češi," xi–xiii; Masaryk, *Česká otázka*, 30; František Kubka, "Dobrovského 'rusofilství'," in *Sborník prací věnovaných Janu Máchalovi k sedmdesátým narozeninám*, ed. Jiří Horák and Miloslav Hýsek (Prague: Klub moderních filologů, 1925), 48–49.

107. Karel Mácha, *Glaube und Vernunft: Die Böhmische Philosophie in geschichtlicher Übersicht* (Munich: Sauer, 1987), 1:119.

108. Arne Novák, *Josef Dobrovský* (Prague: Mánes, 1928), 11.

109. Havlíček, "Bohuslava Balbína obrana národu slovanského, zvláště českého," *Slovan*, May 20, 29, 1850; see Havlíček, *Politické spisy,* ed. Zdeněk V. Tobolka (Prague: Laichter, 1900–1902), 3:33–52.

110. Daniel Adam, introduction to Eusebius Pamphilus, *Historie cyrkevní*, trans. Jan Kocín z Kocinétu (Prague: Daniel Adam z Veleslavína, 1594), f. A5v. In Mercantonio de Dominis, *Ohlášení a zpráva* (Prague: Daniel Sedlčanský, 1619), de Dominis is identified on the title page as "a man stemming from the Slavic nation from which also the Czechs originate."

111. Pynsent, *Questions of Identity*, 211, n. 2.

112. Contrary to what, for instance, Okey implies in *The Habsburg Monarchy*, 295.

113. Zdeněk V. David, "Národní obrození jako převtělení Zlatého věku," *Český časopis historický*, 99 (2001), 496–98.

114. Novotný, *Matěj Václav Kramerius*, 93–95.

115. Henceforth, he wished Russia confined to its "natural sphere" of Eastern Europe and Asia; see Samson B. Knoll, "Herder," *Encyclopedia Americana* (Danbury, Conn.: Grolier, 1994 ed.), 14:136.

116. See the classic work on the rise of Slovak national consciousness, Rudo, Brtáň, *Barokový slavizmus* (Lipt. Sv. Mikuláš: Tranoscius, 1939); on Kollár, see *Antologie z dějin českého a slovenského filozofického myšlení*, 475.

117. Šmahelová, "Kollárova vize slovanské vzájemnosti," 134–35.

118. See Emler, "Listy Josefa Jungmanna k Antonínu Markovi," 57 (1883): 57–58, 511; Emler, "Listy Antonína Marka k Josefu Jungmannovi" 63 (1889): 273–74.

119. Zelený, *Život Josefa Jungmanna*, 37, 39, 78; Jan Mukařovský, ed., *Dějiny české literatury* (Prague: Nakladatelství Československé akademie věd, 1959–95), 2:236.

120. For instance, Wulf Koepke and Samson B. Knoll, eds., *Johann Gottfried Herder, Innovator through the Ages* (Bonn: Bouvier, 1982); Wulf Koepke, *Johann Gottfried Herder* (Boston: Twayne, 1987); Copleston, *A History of Philosophy*, 6: 135–49, 172–79.

121. Herder's influence is difficult to detect; see Vincenc Zahradník, *Filosofické*

spisy, ed. František Čáda (Prague: Česká akademie pro vědy slovesnost a umění, 1907–8), 1:70–71, 48.

122. Karel Alois Vinařický, *Korespondence a spisy pamětní,* Sbírka pramenů ku poznání literárního života v Čechách, na Moravě a ve Slezsku, Skupina 2, Číslo 6, 13, 19, 24, ed. Václav Otakar Slavík (Prague: Česká akademie pro vědy, slovesnost a umění, 1903, 1909, 1914, 1925), 1:202.

123. František Slavík, "Vzájemné dopis Václava Hanky a Jana Kollára," *Časopis českého musea* 71 (1897): 227–45; Antonín J. Vrťátko, "Dopisy Františka Palackého k Janu Kollárovi," *Časopis českého musea* 53 (1879): 379–481; Vrťátko, "Dopisy Josefa Jungmanna k Janu Kollárovi," *Časopis českého musea* 54 (1880): 38–59, 196–218.

124. Josef Polišenský and Ella Illingová, *Jan Jeník z Bratřic* (Prague: Melantrich, 1989), 72, 80, 115; see also Ferdinand Čenský, ed., *Z dob našeho probuzení: Sbírka přátelských dopisů* (Prague: Urbánek, 1875), 239; John Bowring, *Cheskian Anthology: Being a History of the Poetical Literature of Bohemia* (London: Rowland Hunter, 1832), 78.

125. Šmahelová, "Bernard Bolzano a české národní obrození," 74–115; Bernard Bolzano, *24 Erbauungsreden, 1808–1820*, ed. Kurt F. Strasser (Vienna: Böhlau, 2001).

126. See, for instance, Bolzano, *Vlastní životopis*, 160–62.

127. Bernard Bolzano, *Wissenschaftslehre* in *Gesamtausgabe*, ed. Eduard Winter, Jan Berg, Friedrich Kambartel, Jaromír Loužil, and Bob van Rootselaar (Stuttgart-Bad Cannstatt: Frommann Holzboog, 1969–), Reihe I, Band 11, pt. 1 (1985), 130.

128. Johann N. Tetens, *Über den Ursprung der Sprachen und der Schrift* (On the Origin of Language and Letters) (Bützow und Wismar: 1772); see Bolzano, *Philosophische Tagebücher*, in *Gesamtausgabe*, Reihe II, Nachlass, B. Wissenschaftliche Tagebücher; Band 17, *1817–1827*, 127–28, 141, 148.

129. Ibid., 87.

130. On Herder's alleged influence on Palacký, see for instance, Ergang, *Herder and the Foundations of German Nationalism*, 260–61.

131. Kollár, *Prózy*, Vybrané spisy, vol. 2, 162; cited in Masaryk, *Česká otázka*, 412.

132. František Palacký, *Korrespondence a zápisky*, Sbírka pramenů ku poznání literárního života v Čechách, na Moravě a ve Slezsku, Series 2, no. 4 (Prague: Česká akademie pro vědy, slovesnost a umění, 1898), 20, 25. For a survey of the British influences on young Palacký, see Ivan Pfaff, *Česká přináležitost k Západu v letech 1815–1878* (Brno: Doplněk, 1996), 69–72.

133. Gillies, *Herder*, 124–25; Anne L. Staël-Holstein, *De l'Allemagne* (Paris: Garnier frères, 1800), 378–81. Josef Fischer, *Myšlenka a dílo Františka Palackého* (Prague: Čin, 1926–927), 2:72–73, tried to show that Palacký's ideal of humanity derived from Herder rather than Blair; see Kutnar, Králík, and Bělič, *Tři studie o Palackém*, 54.

134. Pynsent, *Questions of Identity*, 93. Kollár did, however, exchange a friendly letter with John Bowring concerning Magyar and Slovak folk songs, on December 10, 1827; see F. Chudoba, "Listy psané Bowringovi ve věcech české a slovanské literatury," *Věstník královské české společnosti*, třída Filosoficko-historickojazykozpytná, 1912, pt. 2, 21–23.

135. Kutnar, Králík, and Bělič, *Tři studie o Palackém*, 102; Josef Polišenský,

Dějiny Británie (Prague: Svoboda, 1982), 199. As a sign of early interest in Robertson in Slovakia, Ladislav Bartolomeides had based his *Historia o Americe* (Bratislava: S. P. Weber, 1794) on Robertson's *History of America*. On the parallels of Palacký's historical views with Robertson's, see Milan Řepa, "'Ját' jsem jej příkladem Robertsona Škotského poráželi hledal.' Dílo skotského osvícenského historika jako možný vzor Palackého Dějin," in *Historik v proměnách doby a prostředí 19. století,* 52–55.

136. Kutnar, Králík, and Bělič, *Tři studie o Palackém,* 67, 161–63, 93.

137. Index for 1827–36, *Časopis českého musea* 10 (1836): 397–435; index for 1837–46, ibid., 20 (1846): 817–54. See Herder, "Kůň z hory: Česká pověst z IX. století; skládání Herderovo," *Časopis českého musea* 6 (1832): 14–17, trans. from *Stimmen der Völker,* vol. 2.

138. Kořalka, *František Palacký,* 425.

139. František Palacký, *Spisy drobné,* ed. Bohuš Rieger (Prague: Bursík a Kohout, [1898–1902]), 1:332–33.

140. Karel Havlíček, "Leibniz a jeho idea," *Česká včela* 13 (1846): n. 55, 218.

141. Václav B. Nebeský, "Několik slov o filosofii," *Časopis českého musea* 20 (1846): 241.

142. Karel Štorch, "Filosofie a naše literatura: Několik myšlenek snad včas," *Časopis českého musea* 22 (1848): pt. 1, 53–60.

143. Ibid., 61.

144. Zelený, *Život Josefa Jungmanna,* 14–15, 19. On his translation of Milton, see Josef Emler, ed., "Listy Josefa Jungmanna k Antonínu Markovi," 55 (1881): 522, 529.

145. "John Bowring and British Liberalism in the Czech National Awakening," *Slavonic and East European Review* 86 (2008), 634–64; Pfaff, *Česká přináležitost k Západu*; Simeon Potter, "Palacký a anglické písemnictví," *Časopis Matice moravské* 53 (1929): 87–141.

146. Jakubec, *Dějiny literatury české,* 2:924.

147. Antonín Měšťan, "Scott und das historische Bewusstsein der Tschechen und Deutschen in Böhmen," *Grossbritannien, die USA und die bömischen Länder 1848–1938,* Vorträge der Tagung des Collegium Carolinum, 2–6 November 1988, ed. Eva Schmidt-Hartmann and Stanley B. Winters (Munich: Oldenbourg, 1991), 232.

148. František L. Čelakovský, "Slovo o Slávy Dceři p. Jana Kollára," *Časopis českého musea* 5 (1831): 41,49, 50.

149. P. [Palacký, František], Review of Edward Robinson, *Historical View of the Slavic Language in Its Various Dialects,* Biblical Repository (Andover, Mass.: Flagg, Gould, and Newman, 1834), in *Časopis českého musea* 8 (1834): 458.

150. František Matouš Klácel, "Shakespeare, Goethe, Schiller," *Časopis českého musea* 21/1 (1847): 250–69.

151. Karel Havlíček, *Politické spisy,* ed. Zdeněk V. Tobolka (Prague: Laichter, 1900–1902), 3:196.

152. Pfafff, *Česká přináležitost k Západu,* 82. Karel Kazbunda, "Pobyt Dr. F. L. Riegra v cizině r. 1849–1850," *Zahraniční politika* 8 (1929): 1026–28; František L. Rieger, *Spisy drobné,* vol. 2 (Prague, 1915), 2:640–43.

153. In a memorandum "Betrachtungen über eine Stelle in Hornmayrs Taschenbuche" submitted to the supreme chancellor, Count Anton Friedrich Mitrovsky, on June 20, 1833; cited by Josef Hanuš, *Národní museum a naše obrození: k stoletému*

jubileu založení Musea (Prague: Národní museum, 1921–1923), 2:468–69. On the exclusion of the Slavs by *Allgemeine Zeitung* from the heritage of European civilization, see Josef Emler, ed., "Listy Antonína Marka k Josefu Jungmannovi," 63 (1889), 268; see also ibid., 66 (1892), 470–71.

154. Cited in Hanuš, *Národní museum a naše obrození*, 2:473.

155. Karel Tieftrunk, *Dějiny Matice české* (Prague: Řivnáč, 1881), 43, note *.

156. Jan Lehár and others, *Česká literatura od počátků k dnešku* (Prague: Lidové noviny, 1998), 685. In 1941, Pražák maintained that Herder thought the Czechs to be equal to the Germans and that the Bohemian awakeners were, in fact, Herder's disciples; Pražák, "Herder a Češi," in Herder, *Vývoj lidskosti*, vi, viii.

157. Paul Reimann, *Von Herder bis Kisch: Studien zur Geschichte der deutsch-österreichisch-tschechischen Literaturbeziehungen* (Berlin: Dietz Verlag, 1961), 117. See also Franz Werfel, *Nicht der Mörder, der Ermordete ist schuldig* (Leipzig, 1957).

158. Reimann, *Von Herder bis Kisch*, 119.

159. Louis Snyder, *Encyclopedia of Nationalism* (New York: Paragon House, 1990) 115; see also Arlie J. Hoover, *German Patriotic Preaching from Napoleon to Versailles* (Stuttgart, 1986); Michael Hughes, *Nationalism and Society: Germany 1800–1945* (London, 1988).

160. Šmahelová, "Kollárova vize slovanské vzájemnosti," 142. On the injuries to Slavdom by the envious "Teutonia" and on German responsibility for the burning of Jan Hus, see Jan Kollár, *Básně*, ed. Mojmír Otruba (Prague: Československý spisovatel, 1981), 21, 269.

161. If Russia's enemies were included, the following could be added to the roster of traditional opponents: Tatars, Bugri, Khazars, Pechenegs, Kumans, and Turkmens; Pynsent, *Questions of Identity*, 90–91.

162. Kaizl, *České myšlenky*, 39.

163. Jan Kollár, *Prózy*, Vybrané spisy, 2, ed. F. R. Tichý, 241, cited by Šmahelová, "Kollárova vize slovanské vzájemnosti,"142.

164. Jan Jakubec, *O životě a působení Jana Kollára* (Prague: Slavia, 1893), 32–33.

165. Albert Pražák, *Obrozenské tradice* (Prague: Svaz národního osvobození, 1928), 242.

166. Ibid., 243–44.

167. Čelakovský, "Slovo o Slávy Dceři," 41.

168. ". . . jenž tak honosně za vševědy a všeuky ve světě se prohlašují . . ." P. [Palacký, František], review of Edward Robinson, *Historical View of the Slavic Language in Its Various Dialects*, 458.

169. František Palacký, "Literní zprávy: Z Prahy," *Časopis českého musea* 2 (1828): sv. 2, 132.

170. Novotný, *Matěj Václav Kramerius*, 336. For the citation from the preface to Johann G. Herder, *Letopisové Trojanští* (Prague: Kramerius, 1790), see chapter 4 in this volume, note 16.

171. Eric J. Hobsbawm, *Nations and Nationalism since 1780*, 2nd ed. (New York: Cambridge University Press, 1992); Eric J. Hobsbawm and Terence Ranger, eds., *The Invention of Tradition* (New York: Cambridge University Press, 1983).

172. For instance, for Germany by Georg Schmidt, "Konfessionalisierung, Reich und Deutsche Nation," in *Die Territorien des Reiches im Zeitalter der Reformation und Konfessionalisierung*, ed. A. Schindling and W. Ziegler, vol. 7: *Bilanz, Forschungsperspektiven, Register* (Münster: Aschendorff, 1997), 179 ff.

173. Jan Patočka, *Co jsou Češi? Malý přehled fakt a pokus o vysvětlení*, ed. Ivan Chvatík and Pavel Kouba (Prague: Panorama, 1992), 13–14.
174. See note 94.
175. Zdeněk V. David, "Hegelova srážka s katolickým osvícenstvím v Čechách a zrod novodobého národního uvědomění," *Filosofický časopis* 54 (2006): 809–33.
176. See, for instance, Karl D. Bracher, *Die deutsche Diktatur: Entstehung, Struktur, Folgen des Nationalsozialismus*, 6th rev. ed. (Frankfurt/M: Ullstein, 1979), 24, 28, 52.
177. The recollection of the Utraquist spirit of tolerance, free discussion, and ecumenism harmonized with, and was strengthened by, the reform or liberal Catholicism of the Josephist era; see David, chapter 4 in this volume, 486–510.

Chapter 7

1. For a German commentary on the Bohemians' attachment to realism in contrast to the prevailing adherence to idealist philosophy in Russia and Poland, see "Anmerkung der Redaktion," *Zeitschrift für exacte Philosophie im Sinne des neuen philosophischen Realismus* (Leipzig) 11 (1875): 324.
2. On Seibt, see Mikuláš Teich, "Bohemia: From Darkness into Light," in *The Enlightenment in National Context,* ed. Roy Porter and Mikuláš Teich (New York: Cambridge University Press, 1981), 156. Pavel Křivský, "Dopisy Václava Stacha Josefu Dobrovskému," *Časopis Vlastivědné společnosti muzejní v Olomouci* 60 (1970): 159, 166; Pavel Křivský, "Korespondence Antonína Jaroslava Puchmajera s Josefem Dobrovským," *Literární archiv: Sborník Památníku národního písemnictví* 8 (1974): 200.
3. Richard E. Rubinstein, *Aristotle's Children: How Christians, Muslims, and Jews Rediscovered Ancient Wisdom and Illuminated the Dark Ages* (Orlando, Fla.: Harcourt, 2003), 192.
4. Sebastian Merkle, *Die katholische Beurteilung des Aufklärungszeitalters* (Berlin: K. Curtius, 1909), 7–8. On the distinction between the two scholasticisms, see also Otto Schaffner, *Eusebius Amort, 1692–1775, als Moraltheologe* (Pederborn: F. Schöningh, 1963), 166.
5. Bernhard Jansen, "Philosophen katholischen Bekenntnisses in ihrer Stellung zur Philosophie der Aufklärung," *Scholastik: Vierteljahresschrift für Theologie und Philosophie* (Freiburg i. B.), 11 (1936), 10–11.
6. On the modification of Aquinas's ontology of existence and essence, see Étienne Gilson, *Being and Some Philosophers,* 2nd ed. (Toronto: Pontifical Institute of Medieval Studies, 1952), 76–3 (Avicenna), 84–95 (Duns Scotus); Frederick Copleston, *History of Philosophy* (London: Burns and Oates, 1947–66), 3:379.
7. Schaffner, *Eusebius Amort,* 24–25. On Aquinas's distinction between essence and existence, see also John F. Wippel, *Metaphysical Themes in Thomas Aquinas* (Washington, D.C.: Catholic University of America Press, 1984), 107–32.
8. Gilson, *Being and Some Philosophers*, 105. The replacement of Thomism by the orientation fostered by Suárez is also illustrated by Jansen, "Philosophen katholischen Bekenntnisses," 16.
9. Suárez's denial of the Thomistic distinction between existence [*esse*] and

essence [*essentia*] in being [*ens*] appears in Disputation 31 of his *Disputationes metaphysicae* (Salamanca, 1597); see John P. Doyle, "Suárez, Francisco," *Routledge Encyclopedia of Philosophy*, ed. Edward Craig (London: Routledge, 1998), 9:191. Most recent edition: Francisco Suárez, *Disputationes metaphysicae* in his *Opera omnia* (Paris: Louis Vivès, 1856–6), vols. 25–26; Disputation 31, "De Essentia Entis Finiti Ut Tale Est, Et De Illius Esse, Eorumque Distinctione," appears in 26:224–312. Disputation 31 is also published in English translation as Francisco Suárez, *On the Essence of Finite Being as Such, On the Existence of That Essence and Their Distinction*, trans. and intro. Norman J. Wells (Milwaukee, Wisc.: Marquette University Press, 1983).

10. According to Merkle, the corrupt scholasticism that emerged in the wake of the Council of Trent "celebrated its orgies in the eighteenth century." See Merkle, *Die katholische Beurteilung*, 10–11. See also ibid., 77–78, and Merkle, *Die kirchliche Aufklärung im katholischen Deutschland* (Berlin: Reichel, 1910), 5, 78–80, 88; Jansen, "Philosophen katholischen Bekenntnisses," 1–51.

11. Copleston, *A History of Philosophy*, 3:379. See also Gilson, *Being and Some Philosophers*, 96–120, 170–76; Laurence K. Shook, *Etienne Gilson* (Toronto: Pontifical Institute of Medieval Studies, 1984), 244, 245, 263–64, 269, 288.

12. Gilson, *Being and Some Philosophers*, 97, referring to Francisco Suárez, *Disputationes metaphysicae*, Disputatio II, Sectio IV, 3–5, 8, 14; see Suárez, *Opera Omnia*, vol. 25: 87–92.

13. Gilson, *Being and Some Philosophers*, 100–101. Suárez does not reject outright the concept of "existence," but rather reduces it to virtually nothing. Gilson refers to Suárez's statement that existence was not a formal cause strictly and properly said, but merely an intrinsic and formal constituent of what it constituted. Gilson, *Being and Some Philosophers*, 101, referring to Francisco Suárez, *Disputationes metaphysicae*, Disputatio XXXI, Sectio V, 1; see Suárez, *Opera Omnia*, 26: 237. Ultimately, Suárez asserted that there was no real distinction between the actualized essence and its existence but a mere distinction of reason; Gilson, *Being and Some Philosophers*, 102, referring to Francisco Suárez, *Disputationes metaphysicae*, Disputatio XXXI, Sectio I, 13; see Suárez, *Opera Omnia*, 26: 228.

14. Gilson, *Being and Some Philosophers*, 118. See also John P. Donnelly, "Francisco Suárez," *Encyclopedia of the Renaissance*, ed. Paul F. Grendler (New York: Charles Scribner's Sons, 1999), 6:100: "[Suárez] rejected the cornerstone of Thomistic metaphysics, the real distinction between essence and existence."

15. Wells, "Introduction," to Suárez, *On the Essence of Finite Being as Such*, 20–21.

16. Josef de Vries, "Zur Geschichte und Problematik der Barockscholastik in Deutschland," *Theologie und Philosophie* 57 (1982): 3.

17. Stanislav Sousedík, *Filosofie v českých zemích mezi středověkem a osvícenstvím* (Prague: Vyšehrad, 1997), 245–46.

18. Ernst Lewalter, *Spanisch-jesuitische und deutsch-lutherische Metaphysik des 17. Jahrhunderts: Ein Beitrag zur Geschichte der iberisch-deutschen Kulturbeziehungen und zur Vorgeschichte des deutschen Idealismus* (Darmstadt: Wissenschaftliche Buchgesellschaft, 1967), 7–11, 58–59, 76; *Cambridge History of Renaissance Philosophy*, ed. Charles B. Schmitt and others (Cambridge: Cambridge University Press, 1988), 621, 629. Karl Eschweiler, "Die Philosophie der spanischen Spätscholastik an den deutschen Universitäten des 17. Jahrhunderts," *Spanische Forschungen der*

Görresgesellschaft, 1 (1928): 289–302. The reason for the Protestant preference for baroque over medieval scholasticism has been seen in part in the appeal of the former's systematic presentation of metaphysics, moreover couched in an impeccable humanistic Latin. The Iberians' Latin surpassed the "barbaric" Latin of the High Middle Ages; and Suárez "had the most excellent systematic presentation of metaphysics, available anywhere, while in Thomas [Aquinas] a systematic overall presentation is missing." De Vries, "Zur Geschichte und Problematik," 1–2.

19. See, for instance, Christian Wolff, *Philosophia prima, sive ontologia, methodo scientifica pertractata, qua omnis cognitionis humanæ principia continentur*. Ed. nova priori emendatior. (Francofurti & Lipsiæ, prostat in Officina libraria Rengeriana, 1736), in Christian Wolff, *Gesammelte Werke*, II. Abteilung, Band 3, ed. Joannes Ecole (Hildesheim: Georg Olms, 1962), pt. I, sec. 2, cap. 3, art. 169, pp.136–40; Georg W. F. Hegel, *Encyclopädie der philosophischen Wissenschaften im Grundrisse*, Erster Teil, Werke 8 (Frankfurt/M: Suhrkamp, 1970), art. 27, p. 93.

20. Copleston, *A History of Philosophy*, 3:379. Wolff occupied a rather ambiguous role in the relationship between baroque scholasticism and the Catholic Enlightenment. In contrast to viewing him as a figure linked with late scholasticism, and thus on the wrong side of the fence, Sousedík presents him as an influential figure in the Catholic Enlightenment, at least in Bohemia; Sousedík, *Filosofie v českých zemích*, 262–67. For Wolff's dependence on Suárez, see Gilson, *Being and Some Philosophers*, 113.

21. Gilson, *Being and Some Philosophers*, 141. For Hegel's diminished view of existence, see Hegel, *Encyclopädie der philosophischen Wissenschaften*, Erster Teil, art.123–24, 253–55.

22. Gilson, *Being and Some Philosophers*, 118.

23. Eschweiler, "Die Philosophie der spanischen Spätscholastik," 251–325.

24. Gilson, *Being and Some Philosophers*, 120; de Vries, "Zur Geschichte und Problematik," 5; Lewalter, *Spanisch-jesuistische und deutsch-lutherische Metaphysik*, 14. See also Ulrich G. Leinsle, "Protestantská školská metafysika a její význam pro německý idealismus," *Filosofický časopis* 42 (1984): 50–56. Paradoxically, considering Pietism's input into German idealism, Wolff lost his professorship at the University of Halle in 1723 at the insistence of the Pietists. He was accused of denying the freedom of will, holding that "every volition is determined by a sufficient reason." See Georg W. F. Hegel, *Elements of the Philosophy of Right*, trans. H. B. Nisbet (New York: Cambridge University Press, 1991), 399.

25. He compared Wolffianism favorably with the critical idealism of Kant:

> Taken in its most completely determined and most recent form, that manner of philosophizing was the metaphysics of the past [i.e., Wolff], such as it had become established before Kantian philosophy in our country. Nevertheless, that metaphysics is of the past for history of philosophy only, for, indeed, taken in itself, it remains something wholly present, namely, the simple consideration by understanding of the objects of reason.

See Hegel, *Encyclopädie der philosophischen Wissenschaften*, Erster Teil, art. 27, p. 93. See also Gilson, *Being and Some Philosophers*, 133. Hegel also agreed with Wolff in taking a dim view of Locke's empirical starting point in epistemology, considering it capricious (*willkürlich*); see Georg W. F. Hegel, *Vorlesungen über die Geschichte der Philosophie* 3, Werke 20 (Frankfurt/M: Suhrkamp, 1971), 222. On

Hegel's dependence on Wolff's teaching about psychology, see Franz S. Exner, *Die Psychologie der Hegelschen Schule* (Leipzig: F. Fleischer, 1842), 39, 43.

26. Jansen, "Philosophen katholischen Bekenntnisses," 12, 16, 28, 40–41, 50.

27. Ignác Frantz, *Annus primus philosophiae Pragensis ad gustum hodierni seculi metodo Recentiorum pertractatus continens cum philosophiae prolegomenis logicam atque metaphysicam* (Prague: Typ. Academicis, 1752); for references to Wolff, see 2:10, 51–54, 84, 140–49; to his treatise on teleology, *Vernünftigen Gedanken von den Absichten der natürlichen Dingen* (Frankfurt, 1724), see 136. Stepling contrasted Wolff with philosophers such as Hobbes, Spinoza, and Locke who were suspected of deism, if not atheism; Marie Pavlíková, *Bolzanovo působení na pražské univerzitě* (Prague: Univerzita Karlova, 1985), 16; Eduard Winter, *Der Josefinismus: die Geschichte des österreichischen Reformkatholizismus, 1740–1848* (Berlin: Rütten & Loening, 1962), 63–65.

28. Eugen Lemberg, *Grundlagen des nationalen Erwachens in Böhmen: Geistesgeschichtliche Studie, am Lebensgang Josef Georg Meinerts, 1773–1844* (Liberec: Verlag Gebrüder Stiepel, 1932), 74. Later, Nietzsche called attention to this kinship in his *Will to Power*, claiming that in a certain respect, "German philosophy [was] a piece of Counter Reformation"; see Walter Kaufmann, *Nietzsche: Philosopher, Psychologist, Antichrist*, 4th ed. (Princeton, N.J.: Princeton University Press, 1974), 353.

29. Standard literature on Josephism and Catholic Enlightenment in Austria has little, if anything, to say about this renaissance of the original anti-idealist Thomism. This literature includes Bedřich Slavík, *Od Dobnera k Dobrovskému* (Prague: Vyšehrad, 1975); Winter, *Der Josefinismus: die Geschichte des österreichischen Reformkatholizismus*, and his *Der Josefinismus und seine Geschichte: Beiträge zur Geistesgeschichte Österreichs, 1740–1848* (Brno: Rohrer, 1943); Fritz Valjavec, *Der Josephinismus: Zur geistigen Entwicklung Österreichs im 18. und 19. Jahrhundert* (Brno: Rohrer, 1944). Josef Král, *Československá filosofie: Nástin vývoje podle disciplin* (Prague: Melantrich, 1937), 19, states indiscriminately that in the eighteenth century the Jesuits presented at the University of Prague "Aristotelian philosophy in the version of Thomas Aquinas and the neo-scholastic Suárez."

30. On the realism and empiricism in thirteenth-century scholasticism, as well as intellectual links to the Age of Reason, see Edward Grant, *God and Reason in the Middle Ages* (New York: Cambridge University Press, 2001), especially, 283–93.

31. See, for instance, Karel Floss, "Tereziánská vysokoškolská reforma a olomoucký J. K. Reidinger," *Studia Comeniana et historica* 8/9 (1974): 127.

32. See, for instance, Josef Haubelt, *České osvícenství*, 2nd rev. ed. (Prague: Rodiče, 2004), 266; Arnošt Kraus, *Husitství v literatuře zejména německé* (Prague: Česká akademie, 1917–24), 2:192. For an early comment, see Kašpar Royko, *Synopsis historiae religionis et ecclesiae christianae: methodo systematica adumbratae* (Prague: Ioann Mangoldt, 1785), 135.

33. Winter, *Der Josefinismus: die Geschichte des österreichischen Reformkatholizismus*, 46–47; Floss, "Tereziánská vysokoškolská reforma," 126; Josef Tvrdý, "Vztahy Dobrovského k filosofii," *Bratislava* 4 (1930): 279.

34. John Locke, *Two Treatises of Government*, ed. Peter Laslett, 2nd ed. (Cambridge: Cambridge University Press, 1970), 56–57, 344, 444. On Locke and Aquinas, see Michael P. Zukert, *Launching Liberalism: On Lockean Political Philosophy* (Lawrence, Kansas: University Press of Kansas, 2002), 141; but he also cautions

on differences between Aquinas and Locke, especially on the issue of natural rights, ibid., 175–87. For the praise of Aristotle: "Aristotle, whom I look on as one of the greatest men among the ancients; whose large views, acuteness, and penetration of thought and judgment, few have equaled," see John Locke, *An Essay Concerning Human Understanding*, ed. Peter H. Nidditch (Oxford: Clarendon Press, 1979), 671 (bk. 4, chap. 17, para. 4).

35. Reference to "judicious Hooker" appears in Locke, *Two Treatises of Government*, 295. On Locke and Hooker, see Hans Aarsleff, "The State of Nature and the Nature of Man," in *John Locke: Problems and Perspectives*, ed. John Yolton (Cambridge: Cambridge University Press, 1969), 99–101. On Hooker and Aquinas, see Richard Hooker, *Folger Library Edition of the Works*, ed. William Speed Hill (Cambridge, Mass.: Harvard University Press; 1977–90), 6:92, 147, 265–66; Hooker's reference to Aquinas as "the greatest among the Schoole divines" appears in 1:236; see also Robert K. Faulkner, *Richard Hooker and the Politics of a Christian England* (Berkeley, Calif.: University of California Press, 1981), 50. Locke's influence, in turn, has been considered fundamental to the formation of the individualistic liberalism of the American political system; see Michael P. Zukert, *Natural Rights and the New Republicanism* (Princeton, N.J.: Princeton University Press, 1994), 18–25, 152–53.

36. Václav Nešpor, *Dějiny university olomoucké* (Olomouc: Národní výbor, 1947), 60–61.

37. Winter, *Der Josefinismus: die Geschichte des österreichischen Reformkatholizismus*, 51; Derek E. Beales, *Joseph II: In the Shadow of Maria Theresa, 1741–1780* (New York : Cambridge University Press, 1987), 441.

38. Adam Seigfried, "Die Dogmatik im 18. Jahrhundert unter dem Einfluss von Jansenismus und Aufklärung," in *Katholische Aufklärung und Josephinismus*, ed. Elisabeth Kovács (Vienna: Verlag für Geschichte und Politik, 1979), 258, 261. See also Winter, *Der Josefinismus: die Geschichte des österreichischen Reformkatholizismus*, 57–58.

39. Pietro Maria Gazzaniga, *Praelectiones theologicae*, secundis curis emendatae et auctae (Vienna: Typis Joannis Thomae de Trattnern, 1770–71), 3: f.) (2r–v. See also František Faustin Procházka, *De saecularibus liberalium artium in Bohemia et Moravia satis commentarius* (Prague: Litteris Scholae normalis, Schmadl factore, 1782), 411–12.

40. Gazzaniga, *Praelectiones theologicae*, 1:126; 3:219; 4:4, 48, 152. Gazzaniga stayed in Vienna until 1782.

41. Heribert Lebeda, *Medium cognitionis divinae, seu disputatio de decretis divinis ex se efficacibus* (Hradec Králové: Typis Joannis Clementis Tybelli, 1751), f. C2r. Haná, the region surrounding Olomouc, was known for its agricultural prosperity and solid cuisine.

42. Lebeda was arguing mainly against the theory of predestination approached through the scientia media, a concept originating with Pedro Fonseca (1528–99) and developed by Luis de Molina (1535–1600) in his *De Concordia liberi arbitrii cum Gratia Divina* (Lisbon, 1588). Known as Molinism, it was also endorsed by Suárez; Lebeda, *Medium cognitionis divinae*, f. A1v. It was resolutely opposed by the Thomists, particularly the Dominicans, as a blatant example of the Jesuit downgrading of Aquinas's teaching; see Hippolyte Gayraud, *Thomisme et Molinisme* (Toulouse: Édouard Privat, 1889), especially, 21–38.

43. Nešpor, *Dějiny university olomoucké*, 60–61. Oddly, this government-sponsored Thomistic revival is not noted in Sousedík's thorough *Filosofie v českých zemích mezi středověkem a osvícenstvím*.

44. The linking of Thomists with the Augustinians, in the theological reforms of the Austrian Enlightenment, was largely accidental, based on their common opposition to the Jesuits' philosophy; see Floss, "Tereziánská vysokoškolská reforma," 127; Winter, *Der Josefinismus: die Geschichte des österreichischen Reformkatholizismus*, 50.

45. Winter, *Der Josefinismus: die Geschichte des österreichischen Reformkatholizismus*, 50; Floss, "Tereziánská vysokoškolská reforma," 128–29; Pavel Bělina, Jiří Kaše, and Jan P. Kučera, *Velké dějiny zemí Koruny české*, vol. 10, 1740–92 (Prague: Paseka, 2001), 225.

46. Looking far ahead, this publication foreshadowed the official restoration of Thomism's authority later in the nineteenth century by Pope Leo XIII's encyclical "Aeterni Patris" of 1879; Floss, "Tereziánská vysokoškolská reforma," 129.

47. Ibid., 133.

48. Rudolf Zuber, *Osudy moravské církve v 18. století* (Olomouc: Matice cyrilometodějská, 1987–2003), 2:41, 44, 73.

49. See praise of Reidinger in František M. Pelcl and Mikuláš Adaukt Voigt, *Abbildungen Böhmischer und Mährischer Gelehrten und Künstler* (Prague: Wolfgang Gerle [vols. 1–2]; Johann K. Hraba [vol. 3]; Normalschulbuchdruckerei [vol. 4], 1773–82), 4:173–76. The highlight of the account is Reidinger's victory over a Jesuit opponent in justifying the Dominican Daniele Concina's (1687–1756) critique of the Jesuit Tommaso Tamburini (1591–1675) on the issue of probabilism; ibid., 174–75. See also Josef Táborský, *Reformní katolík Josef Dobrovský* (Brno: L. Marek, 2007), 53.

50. Pelcl and Voigt, *Abbildungen Böhmischer und Mährischer Gelehrten*, 4:174.

51. Leopold Johann Scherschnik, "Über den Ursprung und die Aufnahme der Bibliothek am Clementinischen Collegium zu Prag," *Abhandlungen einer Privatgesellschaft in Böhmen zur Aufnahme der Mathematik, der vaterländischen Geschichte und der Naturgeschichte* 2 (1776): 272, 277.

52. Franz Stephan Rautenstrauch, *Anleitung und Grundriss zur Systematischen Dogmatischen Theologie* (Vienna: Johann Thomas Edlen von Trattnern, 1776), 5–6; Rautenstrauch, *Entwurf zur Einrichtung der theologischen Schulen in den k. k. Erblanden,* 2nd ed. (Vienna: Sonnleithner and Hörling, 1784), 83.

53. Zuber, *Osudy moravské církve* 2:74.

54. Winter, *Der Josefinismus: die Geschichte des österreichischen Reformkatholizismus*, 58.

55. Thomas Aquinas appears to be the one scholastic philosopher whom he cites by name in his scholarly works. See Bernard Bolzano, *Wissenschaftslehre*, in Bernard Bolzano, *Gesamtausgabe*, ed. Eduard Winter, Jan Berg, Friedrich Kambartel, Jaromír Loužil, and Bob van Rootselaar (Stuttgart-Bad Cannstatt: Frommann Holzboog, 1979), Reihe I, Schriften, Band 11, 1:143. In a letter to Exner of December 15, 1844, Bolzano called Aquinas "the most learned among the scholastic theologians." See Bernard Bolzano, *Der Briefwechsel B. Bolzanos mit F. Exner*, ed. Eduard Winter (Prague: Königliche böhmische Gesellschaft der Wissenschaften, 1935), 120.

56. Bolzano, *Der Briefwechsel B. Bolzanos mit F. Exner*, 122, 135.

57. Bolzano, *Lehrbuch der Religionswissenschaft*, in Bolzano, *Gesamtausgabe*, Reihe I, Schriften: Band 6, part 1, 62–63.

58. Zdeněk V. David, "Central Europe's Gentle Voice of Reason: Bílejovský and the Ecclesiology of Utraquism," *Austrian History Yearbook* 28 (1997): 55; David, "Utraquism's Curious Welcome to Luther and the Candlemas Day Articles of 1524," *Slavonic and East European Review* 79 (2001): 66–67.

59. František Šmahel, "Paris und Prag um 1450: Johannes Versor und seine böhmischen Schüller," *Studia źródłoznawcze, Commentationes* (Warsaw and Poznań), 25 (1980): 67–68. Notable works used in Prague included Versor's *Logica vetus et nova, Quaestiones super librum 'De esse et essentia' Thomae de Aquino*, and *Quaestiones super decem libros 'Ethicorum' Aristotelis*; ibid., 70–71. Versor's writings circulated in Prague among both Utraquist theologians and theologians *sub una*; ibid., 71, n. 43. On Versor, see also Sousedík, *Filosofie v českých zemích*, 23–25; and Lewalter, *Spanisch-jesuistische und deutsch-lutherische Metaphysik*, 29–31.

60. Josef Petráň, *Nástin dějin filozofické fakulty univerzity Karlovy* (Prague: Univerzita Karlova, 1984), 38. The devotion to Aristotelian realism, firmly entrenched at the University of Prague by the mid-fifteenth century, contrasted with the brief fascination—under Wyclif's influence—with the Platonic ideas (confusingly, also called "realism") in the period 1380–1415, when its devotees included Matěj of Janov, Jan Hus, and Jerome of Prague; Vilém Herold, "Die Philosophie des Hussitismus: Zur Rolle der Ideenlehre Platons," in *Verdrängter Humanismus, Verzörgerte Aufklärung*, v. l: *Vom Konstanzer Konzil zum Auftreten Luthers*, ed. Michael Benedict (Vienna: Editura Triade, 1997), 103–18; Vilém Herold, "Platonic Ideas and 'Hussite' Philosophy," *The Bohemian Reformation and Religious Practice* 1 (1996): 13–17; Vilém Herold, "Philosophische Grundlagen der Eschatologie im Hussitismus," in *Ende und Vollendung: Eschatologische Perspektiven im Mittelalter*, Miscellanea Mediaevalis, Veröffentlichungen des Thomas-Instituts der Universität Köln, Band 29 (Berlin and New York: Walter de Gruyter, 2002), 742–43.

61. Martin Luther, *Tractatus de Libertate Christiana*, in his *Werke: Kritische Gesammtausgabe* (Weimar: Böhlau, 1897), 7:49, 51.

62. Martin Luther, *Ad librum eximii Magistri Nostri Magistri Ambrosii Catharini, defensoris Silvestri Prieratis accerimi, responsio. Cum exposita Visione Danielis viii. De Antichristo. 1521*, in his *Werke: Kritische Gesammtausgabe*, 7: 737; see also 738. On the limits of Thomas's respect for Aristotle, see Mark D. Jordan, *The Alleged Aristotelianism of Thomas Aquinas*, Etienne Gilson Series 15 (Toronto: Pontifical Institute of Mediaeval Studies, 1992), especially, 38–40. According to Luther, the scholastics in the Aristotelian tradition were also largely responsible for the Roman Church's misplaced emphasis on good deeds. As he maintained: "Hence Christ, the sun of truth and justice, was obscured, when moral virtues were stressed instead of faith, and innumerable hypotheses instead of the truth." Luther, *Ad librum eximii Magistri Nostri Magistri Ambrosii Catharini*, in his *Werke: Kritische Gesammtausgabe*, 7: 737. On Luther's rejection of Aquinas, see also Heiko A. Oberman, *The Two Reformations: The Journey from the Last Days to the New World*, ed. Donald Weinstein (New Haven: Yale University Press, 2003), 23, 30.

63. Heiko A. Oberman, "Luther and the Via Moderna: The Philosophical Backdrop of the Reformation Breakthrough," *Journal of Ecclesiastical History* 54 (2003): 641, 649–50; see also Heiko A. Oberman, *The Two Reformations*, 40, 46. A rejection of Aristotelian realism would later become a hallmark of metaphysical idealism all

the way to Heidegger; Richard Wolin, *Heidegger's Children: Hannah Arendt, Karl Löwith, Hans Jonas, and Herbert Marcuse* (Princeton, N.J.: Princeton University Press, 2001), 215, 223.

64. Ernst Troeltsch, *Protestantism and Progress: A Historical Study of the Relation of Protestantism to the Modern World*, trans. W. Montgomery (Eugene, Ore.: Wipf and Stock Publishers, 1999), 163–64. See also Leinsle, "Protestantská školská metafysika a její význam pro německý idealismus," 50–56. On the Lutheran background of Fichte's thought, see Anthony J. LaVopa, *Fichte: The Self and the Calling of Philosophy, 1762–1799* (New York: Cambridge University Press, 2001), 438–39. See also Mary Anne Perkins, *Nation and Word, 1770–1850: Religious and Metaphysical Language in European National Consciousness* (Aldershot, Hants, U.K.; Brookfield, Vt.: Ashgate, c1999), 32–33; "From Luther to Hitler" in Oberman, *The Two Reformations*.

65. Tomáš G. Masaryk, *Světová revoluce za války a ve válce, 1914–1918* (Prague: Čin, 1933), 589–90; Kaufmann, *Nietzsche*, 353.

66. Cited by Cyril O'Regan, *The Heterodox Hegel* (Albany, N.Y.: State University Press of New York, 1994), 16. For another personal affirmation of his Lutheranism, see James Yerkes, *The Christology of Hegel* (Missoula, Montana: Scholars Press, 1978), 1, 7 n. 3. See also Emil L. Fackenheim, *The Religious Dimension in Hegel's Thought*, 2nd ed. (Chicago: University of Chicago Press, 1982), 128–29, 181; Ulrich Asendorf, *Luther und Hegel: Untersuchungen zur Grundlegung einer neuen systematischen Theologie* (Wiesbaden: Steiner, 1982), xvi–xviii; and on the relationship of Kant and Fichte to Luther, ibid., 176–80, 203. On the influence of Luther on Fichte, see also Anthony J. La Vopa, *Fichte*, 66, 110, 146, 342. On Hegel's "uncritical admiration for Lutheran Protestantism," see also George H. Sabine, "Hegel's Political Philosophy," *Philosophical Review* 41 (1932): 281.

67. Georg W. F. Hegel, *Briefe von und an Hegel*, ed. J. Hoffmeister, 3rd ed. (Hamburg: Meiner, 1969–81), 2:89, cited by John E. Toews, *Hegelianism: Path toward Dialectical Humanism, 1805–1841* (Cambridge: Cambridge University Press, 1980), 66. Elsewhere, Hegel stated: "Thus philosophy is theology, and concern with it, or rather in it, is in itself worship," cited by George L. Kline, "Hegel and the Marxist-Leninist Critique of Religion," in *Hegel and the Philosophy of Religion*, ed. Darrel E. Christensen, Wofford Symposium, 1968 (The Hague: M. Nijhoff, 1970), 188. On Hegel's view of philosophy as secularized religion, see also Quentin Lauer, "Hegel on the Identity of Content in Religion and Philosophy," in *Hegel and the Philosophy of Religion*, 261–78, especially 274–75;, and Fackenheim, *The Religious Dimension in Hegel's Thought*.

68. Cited by John E. Smith, "Hegel's Reinterpretation of the Doctrine of Spirit and Religious Community," in *Hegel and the Philosophy of Religion*, 173.

69. James E. Bradley and Dale K. Van Kley, eds., *Religion and Politics in Enlightenment Europe* (Notre Dame, Ind.: University of Notre Dame Press, 2001), 9, citing Heinrich von Treitschke, *Deutsche Geschichte im neunzehnten Jahrhundert*, vol. 1, 6th ed. (Leipzig: S. Hirzel, 1897), 51, 90, 93.

70. See chapter 6 in this volume.

71. On Pietism among Lutheran Slovaks, see R. J. W. Evans, "Über die Ursprünge der Aufklärung in den habsburgischen Ländern," in *Das achtzehnte Jahrhundert und Österreich*, Jahrbuch der Österreichischen Gesellschaft zur Erforschung des achtzehnten Jahrhunderts, 2 (Vienna: Böhlaus, 1985), 10. Concerning

study by Slovak students and publication of Slovak books in Halle, see Ján, Ďurovič, "Slovenský pietizmus," *Historica Slovaca* 3–4 (1945–46): 170–71.

72. See the meticulous analysis of Cyril O'Regan, *The Heterodox Hegel* (Albany, N.Y.: State University Press of New York, 1994), 279–84. Hegel himself referred to Boehme as "the first German philosopher" who was unjustly neglected during the Enlightenment; Georg W. Hegel, *Vorlesungen über die Geschichte der Philosophie* 3, Werke 20, ed. Eva Moldenhauer and Karl M. Michel (Frankfurt/M: Suhrkamp, 1971), 91. On the relationship between Pietism and the thought of Boehme, see Johannes Wallmann, *Philipp Jakob Spener un die Anfänge des Pietismus* (Tübingen: J. C. B. Mohr, 1970), 322–24.

73. James Collins, *A History of Modern European Philosophy* (Milwaukee, Wisc.: Bruce, 1954), 657. Concerning Boehme's influence on Schelling, see ibid., 572, 584. See also O'Regan, *The Heterodox Hegel*, 118–19.

74. Copleston, *History of Philosophy*, 3:273.On the heterodox understanding of "immanent trinity" in Boehme and Hegel, see also O'Regan, *The Heterodox Hegel*, 109, 131. In July 1811, Hegel received an edition of Boehme's works in twelve volumes (published in 1715) that he proudly showed to visitors in his house; see Georg W. Hegel, *Briefe von und an Hegel*, 4/1:186, 353.

75. Robert Schneider, *Schellings und Hegels schwäbische Geistesahnen* (Würzburg: K. Triltsch, 1938), 24. At the same time, Schneider seeks to minimize Herder's influence on Schelling and Hegel; ibid., 20. On Oetinger as a mediator, see also Kurt Leese, *Von Jacob Boehme zu Schelling: Eine Untersuchung zur Metaphysik des Gottesproblems* (Erfurt: Kurt Stenger, 1927), 22–38; Leese points to the cabala as in turn another source of Oetinger's mystical lore, 30–32. In Schelling's case, there may have been an alternative route to Boehme's theosophy through Franz Baader (1765–1841), who himself had been influenced by Louis C. Saint-Martin (1743–1803), a translator of Boehme's *Aurora* into French; see Copleston, *History of Philosophy*, 3:273.

76. O'Regan, *The Heterodox Hegel*, 285. Hegel's philosophy, in fact, created problems for traditionalist Lutherans. In particular, the prominent Lutheran layman, Baron Hans E. Kottwitz, objected to Hegel's "pantheism and self-divinization [*Selbstvergötterung*]." In 1831, he urgently lobbied the Prussian minister of education, Karl Altenstein, and King Frederick William III against replacing Hegel in the professorship at the University of Berlin by a like-minded follower; see Ivo Tretera, *J. F. Herbart a jeho stoupenci na pražské univerzitě* (Prague: Univerzita Karlova, 1989), 59; *Allgemeine Deutsche Biographie* 2nd ed. (Berlin: Duncker und Humblot, 1968), 16:771.

77. Hegel divided German history into three periods: "the period up to Charlemagne, which [he] calls the kingdom of the Father; the period from Charlemagne to the Reformation, the Kingdom of the Son; and finally the Kingdom of the Holy Spirit, up to and including the Prussian Monarchy." See Anthony Kenny, *An Illustrated Brief History of Western Philosophy*, 2nd ed. (Oxford: Blackwell, 2006), 302. Fichte and Schelling were also affected by "Joachitic speculation"; see Eric Voegelin, *New Science of Politics: An Introduction* (Chicago: University of Chicago Press, 1952), 112–13.

78. Kaufmann, *Nietzsche*, xiii, 197–98, 343, 349–54.

79. Cited in Andreas-Urs Sommer, *Friedrich Nietzsches 'Der Antichrist': ein philosophisch-historischer Kommentar* (Basel: Schwabe, 2000), 138.

80. Sidney Hook, "A Personal Impression of Contemporary German Philosophy," *Journal of Philosophy* 27 (1930): 156.

81. Marie Bayerová, "Rakouské filozofické myšlení konce 19. století v českém kulturním životě," in *Povědomí tradice v novodobé české kultuře: Doba Bedřicha Smetany* (Prague, Národní galerie, 1988), 132.

82. Wolin, *Heidegger's Children*, 215, citing Hugo Ott, "Zu den katholischen Wurzeln im Denken Martin Heidegger's. Der theologische Philosoph," in *Akten der römischen Heidegger Symposions* (1992), 82; see also, ibid., 224.

83. Otto Neurath, *Gesammelte philosophische und methodologische Schriften*, ed. Rudolf Haller and Heiner Rutte (Vienna: Hölder, Pichler, Tempsky, 1981), 2:597, n. 3.

84. Bernard Bolzano, *Wissenschaft und Religion in Vormärz: Der Briefwechsel Bernard Bolzanos mit Michael Josef Fesl, 1822–1848*, ed. Eduard Winter and W. Zeil (Berlin: Akademie-Verlag, 1965), 21; Jan Patočka, "Bolzanovo místo v dějinách filosofie," in *Filosofie v dějinách českého národa* (Prague: Nakladatelství ČSAV, 1958), 111–12.

85. Herder felt certain about the eventual demise of such great monarchies of Europe; Frederick M. Barnard, *Herder on Nationality, Humanity, and History* (Montreal: McGill-Queen's University Press, 2003), 179; see also Johann G. Herder, *Sämmtliche Werke,* ed. Bernhard Suphan (Berlin: Weidmann, 1877–13), 18:314. It is, therefore, not surpring that Herder's works were not easy to find in the libraries of the Habsburg monarchy, especially during the restoration or *Vormärz* period; see János Rathmann, "Herder and the Hungarian Enlightenment," *7th International Congress on the Enlightenment,* 1987, *Budapest: Transactions*, Studies on Voltaire and the Eighteenth Century, 263–65 (Oxford: Voltaire Foundation, 1989), 1:498.

86. Fichte and Hegel, in particular, maintained that a nation became self-conscious of itself as a nation—and thus ready to perform its world-historical mission—only in a state of its own; see Anthony Kenny, *An Illustrated Brief History of Western Philosophy*, 2nd ed. (Oxford: Blackwell, 2006), 302.

87. *Allgemeine Deutsche Biographie*, 33:613; *Dějiny Univerzity Karlovy, 1348–1990*, ed., František Kavka and Josef Petráň (Prague: Karolinum, 1995–1998), 2: 125–27, 133.

88. As noted, they included Dobrovský, Bolzano, and Jungmann. Eugen Lemberg, *Grundlagen des nationalen Erwachens in Böhmen: Geistesgeschichtliche Studie, am Lebensgang Josef Georg Meinerts, 1773–1844* (Liberec: Verlag Gebrüder Stiepel, 1932), 64; Marta Vlasáková, "Životaběh B. Bolzana," in *Osamělý myslitel, Bernard Bolzano,* ed. Kateřina Trlifajová (Prague: Filosofia, 2006), 11–12. See also Eduard Winter, *Bernard Bolzano: Ein Lebensbild*, in *Bolzano, Gesamtausgabe, Einleitungsband*, First Part: *Biographie*, 12–15. On Seibt's key role see Josef Durdík, "O významu nauky Herbartovy," *Časopis českého musea* 50 (1876): 319.

89. František X. Němeček, "Züge aus der Geschichte der Wissenschaften und des Geschmackes in Böhmen; geschrieben im Jahre 1794," *Libussa*, eine vaterländische Vierteljahrschrift, ed. J. G. Meinert, vol. 2, 1804 (Prague: Calve), 57–58. See also Král, *Československá filosofie*, 20.

90. Winter, *Bernard Bolzano*, 15; Wilhelm Zeil, *Bolzano und die Sorben: ein Beitrag zur Geschichte des "Wendischen Seminars" in Prag zur Zeit der josefinischen Aufklärung und der Romantik* (Bautzen: Domowina, 1967), 30.

91. Wolf included Seibt in the company of "Jan Hodějovský of Hodějov, Simon Broxenius, Nikolaus Walter, Edmundus Campianus, Georg Schwertfer, Johann Widmann, Melchior Gutwirt, und heut zu Tage Karl Heinrich Seibt"; Johann Heinrich Wolf, *Geschichte des Königreichs Böheim zum Gebrauche der Studierenden Jugend in der K.K. Staaten* (Vienna: Johann Thomas von Trattner, 1783), 241. František Faustin Procházka, *De saecularibus liberalium artium in Bohemia et Moravia satis commentarius* (Prague: Litteris Scholae normalis, Schmadl factore, 1782), 415. Accordingly, the noted historian Václav Tomek later maintained that Seibt had opened a new era in the intellectual life of Bohemia; see Zeil, *Bolzano und die Sorben*, 31.

92. Král, *Československá filosofie*, 20; Günter Ulbricht, *Johann Bernard Basedow* (Berlin: Volk und Wissen, 1963); Dieter Kormann, *Der Anschauungsbegriff bei Comenius, Basedow und Hartwig: im Blick auf die anschauungsbezogenen methodischen Anforderungen im heutigen Fach Kunst* (Frankfurt am Main: P. Lang, 1992). Walter Schamschula's *Die Anwalterfänge der tschechischen Erneuerung und das deutsche Geistesleben, 1740–1800* (Munich: Fink, 1973), 205, avoids mentioning the English and French Enlightenment ingredients in Seibt's university teaching, discussing only his presentation of German sources like Kant and Gottsched.

93. On Herder's bitterness toward Basedow and their philosophical differences, see Wiltraut Finzel-Niederstadt, *Lernen und Lehren bei Herder und Basedow* (Frankfurt am Main: P. Lang, 1986), 29–33, 334–39.

94. Ibid., 69–71. Interestingly, Hegel also disapproved of Basedow's "play theory" of education; Hegel, *Elements of the Philosophy of Right*, 440.

95. Karl H. Seibt, *Von dem Einflusse der Erziehung auf die Glückseligkeit des Staates* (Prague: Mangoldische Buchhandlung, 1771), 28. For Bolzano's reference to Basedow, see Bolzano, *Lehrbuch der Religionswissenschaft*, in *Gesamtausgabe*, Reihe I, Schriften: Band 6, pt. 1, 60; pt. 2, 20; and he noted Johann B. Basedow's *Versuch für die Wahrheit des Christenthums als der Besten Religion* (Berlin and Altona, 1766); see Bolzano, *Philosophische Tagebücher* in *Gesamtausgabe*, Reihe II, Nachlass, B. Wissenschaftliche Tagebücher; Band 16/1, *1811–1817* (v.1–), 1:41, 209.

96. Seibt, *Von dem Einflusse der Erziehung*, 13, 35.

97. Ibid., 25–26.

98. Referring to Montesquieu's *Considérations sur les causes de la grandeur des Romains*; see Seibt, *Von dem Einflusse der Erziehung*, 24.

99. On *Klugheitslehre* as a part of *Sittenlehre*, see Bernard Bolzano, *Vermischte philosophische und physikalische Schriften, 1832–1848*, in *Gesamtausgabe*, Reihe II, Nachlass A, Band 12, pt. 3: 27.

100. Karl H. Seibt, *Klugheitslehre, praktisch abgehandelt, in akademischen Vorlesungen* (Prague: Elsenwanger, 1799), 1: intro., 5.

101. Jiří Černý, "K některým problémům osvícenského filosofického myšlení v Čechách," in *Filosofie v dějinách českého národa*, 99.

102. I was not able to locate this title. Evidently it is a paraphrase, possibly identical with Samuel Richardson's *A Collection of the Moral and Instructive Sentiments, Maxims, Cautions, and Reflexions, Contained in the Histories of Pamela, Clarissa, and Sir Charles Grandison* (London, 1755).

103. Seibt, *Klugheitslehre, praktisch abgehandelt*, 2:198–99.

104. Ibid., 2:231, 235, 239, 266, 356, 357.

105. "Shakespeare mit unreichbarer Vorzüglichkeit sich ausgezeichnet"; see Seibt, *Klugheitslehre, praktisch abgehandelt*, 2:201. He singled out for praise the characters of Falstaff (2:74), and Hamlet (2:357).

106. Particularly on the subject of friendship, see Seibt, *Klugheitslehre, praktisch abgehandelt*, 2:263–64; see also 2:51–52. The author's full name was Philip Dormer Stanhope, fourth earl of Chesterfield.

107. Seibt, *Klugheitslehre, praktisch abgehandelt*, 1:56; 2:288, 342.

108. Johann Georg Feder, *Lehrbuch der Logik und Metaphysik* (Göttingen: 1769); 8th ed. appeared in 1794; Johann Georg Feder, *Institutiones Logicae et Metaphysicae* (Göttingen: 1777); fourth edition appeared in 1797. See *Allgemeine Deutsche Biographie*, 6:596; *Dějiny Univerzity Karlovy*, 2:127.

109. Kant responded to Feder's challenge in the *Prolegomena zu jeder künftigen Metaphysik*, while Feder retorted by his *Ueber Raum und Causalität: Zur Prüfung der Kantischen Philosophie* (Göttingen: 1787), and by launching in 1788 a four-volume book series, *Philosophische Bibliotkek*, against Kant and his teaching; *Allgemeine Deutsche Biographie*, 6:596.

110. *Dějiny univerzity Karlovy*, 2:127.

111. In 1763, in applying for the teaching position in Prague, Seibt stressed that, as a Catholic, he preferred to teach in Bohemia to the Lutheran Saxony, where he was born and studied; *Dějiny univerzity Karlovy*, 2:126.

112. Winter, *Bernard Bolzano*, 14, 27.

113. Franz Stephan Rautenstrauch, *Diarium privatum*, Státní ústřední archív, Prague, MS Benediktini Břevnov, ŘBB 88, August 9, 1779, f. 100 v; see also f. 99v. Josef Hanzal dates the intervention to August 6; see his "F. Š. Rautenstrauch ve světle svých deníků," *Český časopis historický* 93 (1995): 88–89; J. Müller, "Zu den theologischen Grundlagen der Studienreform Rautenstrauchs," *Theologische Quartalschrift* 146 (1966): 71–72, cited by Rudolf Zuber, *Osudy moravské církve v 18. Století*, vol. 2 (Olomouc: Matice cyrilometodějská, 2003), 75.

114. Karl H. Seibt, *Katholisches Lehr- und Gebetbuch* (Prague, 1779): 2nd ed.: *Neues katholisches Gebetbuch* (Prague: 1783); a Czech translation by František J. Tomsa appeared as Karl H. Seibt, *Kniha katolická, obsahující v sobě naučení a modlitby* (Prague: Cís. král. normální škola, 1780).

115. Seibt, *Kniha katolická, obsahující v sobě naučení a modlitby*, 88–91, 119–20, 330–31.

116. Ibid., 99–100.

117. "Seibt," *Biographisches Lexikon des Kaiserthums Oesterreich*, ed. Constant von Wurzbach, 60 vols. (Vienna: Hof- und Staatsdruckerei, 1856–91), 33:326–29.

118. See chapter 6 in this volume.

119. Seibt received an official reprimand, and the work, considered offensive to the Habsburg dynasty, was proscribed. It could not be reprinted or translated into Czech until the mid-nineteenth century; see Josef Johanides, *František Martin Pelcl* (Prague: Melantrich, 1981), 137–46; Jaroslav Prokeš, "Aféra Seibtova roku 1779," in *Českou minulostí*, ed. Otakar Odložík, Jaroslav Prokeš, and Rudolf Urbánek (Prague: Laichter, 1929), 317–30.

120. Anna Drabek, "Die Frage der Unterrichtssprache im Königreich Böhmen im Zeitalter der Aufklärung," in *Österreichische Osthefte* 38 (1996): 339. The only concession was permitting continued temporary use of Czech in four gymnasia for three years; ibid., 340; Jan Šafránek, *Školy české; obraz jejich vývoje a osudů* (Prague:

Matice česká, 1913–18), 1:148. In this regard, Seibt's student, Ferdinand Kindermann (1740–1801), represented a parallel case. Entrusted with the reform of Bohemian elementary education in 1775, he did not wish to suppress the use of Czech language although he preferred German as the language of school instructions; Alexandr S. Myl'nikov, *Vznik národně osvícenské ideologie v českých zemích: Prameny národního obrození* (Prague: Univerzita Karlova, 1974), 204; Josef Hanzal, "Jazyková otázka ve vývoji obrozenského školství," *Československý časopis historický* (1966): 322; Josef Hanzal, "Vzdělanost a lidová osvěta," *Sborník historický* 18 (1971): 40–43.

121. Tomáš G. Masaryk, *Česká otázka. Naše nynější krize. Jan Hus*, Spisy 6 (Prague: Masarykův ústav, 2000), 30; Jan Novotný, *Matěj Václav Kramerius* (Prague: Melantrich, 1973), 17; Bernard Bolzano, *Vlastní životopis*, trans. and ed. Marie Pavlíková (Prague: Odeon, 1981), 28; Schamschula, *Die Anfänge der tschechischen Erneuerung*, 272, 281, 285.

122. On Seibt's relation to Dobrovský, see František Palacký, "Josefa Dobrovského život a vědecké působení," *Česká včela* 4 (1837): 262–63, 269. Concerning Seibt's influence on his appointment as professor of Hebrew in the Sorbian Seminary in 1777, see Zeil, *Bolzano und die Sorben*, 59. See also Táborský, *Reformní katolík Josef Dobrovský*, 33, 37.

123. Letters to Helfert of February 27, 1783, June 9, 1783, and September 23, 1784; see Josef Dobrovský, *Dopisy Josefa Dobrovského s Augustinem Helfertem*, ed. Josef Wolf and F. M. Bartoš, Spisy a projevy (Prague: Melantrich, 1941), 22:61, 70–72, 117–18.

124. See also Slavík, *Od Dobnera k Dobrovskému*, 114–15, 208–9, 282; Zdeněk David, "Národní obrození jako převtělení Zlatého věku," *Český časopis historický* 99 (2001): 486–518.

125. Slavík, *Od Dobnera k Dobrovskému*, 199, 209; Lemberg, *Grundlagen des nationalen Erwachens in Böhmen*, 74; Král, *Československá filosofie*, 20.

126. Lemberg, *Grundlagen des nationalen Erwachens in Böhmen*, 29, 74. The turn of the post-Kantian idealists against the rationalism of the Enlightenment is pointed out by Max Wundt: "Seine [Kant's] Nachfolger wollten von ihr [den bürgerlichen Welt] nichts mehr wissen. Ihnen war die Philosophie wie die Kunst Sache des Genies—für die Aufklärung ein grauenhafter Gedanke!—, und mit den Genies, den Dichtern und Künstlern, wollten sie in enger Geistesverbundenheit leben." [His (Kant's) followers did not wish to hear any more (about the civil society). For them philosophy, like art, was a matter of the genius—(they considered) the Enlightenment a ghastly idea—and they wished to live in a close intellectual communion with poets and artists.] See Max Wundt, "Die Philosophie in der Zeit des Biedermeiers." *Deutsche Vierteljahrschrift für Literatur* 13 (1935): 125.

127. Rautenstrauch, *Entwurf zur Einrichtung der theologischen Schulen*, 86–87.

128. Josef Dobrovský, *Korrespondence*, Díl 2: *Vzájemné dopisy Josefa Dobrovského a Jiřího Samuela Bandtkeho z let 1810–1827*, Sbírka pramenů ku poznání literárního života v Čechách, na Moravě a ve Slezsku, Skupina 2, Číslo 8, ed. A. V. Francev (Prague: Česká akademie pro vědy, slovesnost a umění, 1906), 48. Černý, "K některým problémům osvícenského filosofického myšlení v Čechách," 104–5. Dobrovský's alleged admiration for Kant is not supported by evidence; see, for instance, Josef Dobrovský, *Přednášky o praktické stránce v křesťanském náboženství*, ed. Josef Volf, Miloš B. Volf, and Josef Vraštil, Spisy a projevy, vol. 16 (Prague: Melantrich, 1948), 15.

129. Referring to his alleged desire to teach in the Viennese Theresianum: "Hier zu Prag glaubte man, ich hätte gesucht dabey angestellt zu werden, um die kantische Philosophie daselbst zu lehren. Man traut mir also noch keinen gesunden Verstand zu." See Josef Dobrovský, *Dopisy s B. A. Veršauserem a V. Krčmou. Z rodinný dopisů*, Spisy a projevy, vol. 21, ed. Josef Volf and Josef Páta (Prague: Melantrich, 1937), 93. In his younger years, Dobrovský to a degree sympathized with Kant's theory of practical reason, as a basis of religious belief, but he adamantly rejected the metaphysical constructs of Kant's pure reason; see Tvrdý, "Vztahy Dobrovského k filosofii," 277, 289.

130. Dobrovský, *Přednášky o praktické stránce v křesťanském náboženství*, 23, 53–54, 61, 64, 73; Tvrdý, "Vztahy Dobrovského k filosofii," 289. On Adelung's high esteem for Locke, see Siegfried Wollgast, "Johann Christoph Adelung als Philosophiehistoriker," in *Sprache und Kulturentwicklung in Blickfeld der deutschen Spätaufklärung: Der Beitrag Johann Christoph Adelungs*, ed, Werner Bahner (Berlin: Akademie Verlag, 1984), 61, 71. See also Táborský, *Reformní katolík Josef Dobrovský*, 35, n. 79. On Dobrovský's knowledge of English, see V. F. Francev, ed., *Dopisy neznámé české šlechtičny Josefu Dobrovskému z r. 1796* (Prague: Spolek českých bibliofilů, 1929), 8, 24,25.

131. Křivský, "Dopisy Václava Stacha Josefu Dobrovskému," 160.

132. Král, *Československá filosofie*, 304.

133. Vincenc Zahradník, *Filosofické spisy*, ed. František Čáda (Prague: Česká akademie pro vědy slovesnost a umění, 1907–8), 1:92. He cited Christian Garve, *Versuche über verschiedene Gegenstände aus der Moral, Literatur und dem gesellschaftlichen Leben* (Wrocław [Breslau]: W. G. Korn, 1792–1802); see *Slovník českých filozofů*, ed. Jiří Gabriel (Brno: Masarykova Univerzita, 1998), 644. Garve's favorite was the Scottish philosopher Adam Ferguson (1723–1816), who was in turn a disciple of Hume, Adam Smith, and Thomas Reid; see *The Encyclopedia of Philosophy*, 2nd ed., Donald M. Borchert (New York: Macmillan, 2006), 3:604–5; 4:24.

134. Jan Jakubec, *Děiiny literatury české*, 2nd ed. (Prague: Jan Laichter, 1929–34), 2:924.

135. Antonín Marek, *Základy filosofie: Logika. Metafysika*, Novočeská biblioteka (Prague: Řivnáč, 1844), viii. As noted, Bolzano in fact referred to Krug's *System der theoretischen Philosophie* in both the Königsberg 1806 and Vienna 1818 editions; see Bernard Bolzano, *Wissenschaftslehre, Gesamtausgabe*, Reihe I, Schriften, Band 11, 1:59, 239. Curiously, Jungmann feared that the reliance on Krug might lead to problems with imperial censorship; František Čáda, *Hynovo Dušesloví*, Rozpravy České akademie pro vědy, slovesnost a umění, ročník 10, třída 1, číslo 2 (Prague: Česká akademie, 1902), 9.

136. Marek formulates and characterizes Fichte's approach thus: "Názory nejsou než snové, a myšlení jest pramen všeho bytu i věcnosti, kterauž si osnuji, pramen mého bytí, mé moci, mého účelu, pravý sen o snu. Z toho patrno znáti, jaké nicotenství ze všeho vykvětá." [Perceptions are nothing else than dreams, and thinking is the source of all being and materiality, which I imagine; (it is) the source of my being, of my power, of my purpose—a genuine dream about a dream. Thus, it is evident what nihilism blossoms out of all this.]" See Marek, *Základy filosofie*, 14–15.

137. Wilhelm Traugott Krug, *Handbuch der Philosophie und der philosophischen Literatur*, Mit einen Vorwort und einer Einleitung von Lutz Geldsetzer und einem

Sachregister von Ute Geldsetzer. Düsseldorf, Stern-Verlag Janssen [c1969] 2 v. in 1. (Reprint of the 3rd rev. and enl. ed. published in Leipzig, 1828.), vii.

138. Marek, *Základy filosofie*, 262–63.

139. *Routledge Encyclopedia of Philosophy*, ed. Edward Craig (New York: Routledge, 1998), 3:798. In 1801, he published a critique of the metaphysics of Fichte and Schelling; see *Allgemeine Deutsche Biographie* 2nd ed. (Berlin: Duncker und Humblot, 1968), 8:75. He continued his critique in Jakob Friedrich Fries, *Fichtes und Schellings neueste Lehren von Gott und der Welt* (Heidelberg: Mohr and Zimmer, 1807).

140. Fries had a particularly low opinion of Fichte, criticizing him early in 1798 in an article: "Über das Verhältniss der empirischen Psychologie zur Metaphysik." Cited in *The Encyclopedia of Philosophy*, ed. Paul Edwards (New York: Macmillan, 1967), 3:253. In early twentieth-century Germany, Fries's epistemological concepts were used against Neo-Kantianism by Leonard Nelson and Rudolf Otto, until the Nazis put a stop to the anti-idealist line of thought in 1937. About the same time, Fries attracted the attention of analytical Anglophone philosophers. His "self-reliance on reason" harmonized with G. E. Moore's appeal to common sense, the logical positivists' appeal to a level of incorrigible knowledge, and Wittgenstein's notion that "the propositions of our ordinary knowledge are in perfect order." Cited in ibid., 3:255.

141. Bernard Bolzano, *Vermischte philosophische und physikalische Schriften, 1832–1848*, in *Gesamtausgabe*, Reihe II, Nachlass A, Band 12, part 2, 95, 98.

142. František Palacký, *An Historical Survey of the Science of Beauty and the Literature on the Subject*, ed. Tomáš Hlobil, trans. Derek and Marzia Paton (Olomouc: Palacký University, 2002), 54–55, 86.

143. Bernard Bolzano, *Der böhmische Vormärz in Briefen B. Bolzanos an F. Přihonský, 1824–1848: Beiträge zur deutsch-slawischen Wechselseitigkeit*, ed. Eduard Winter, Deutsche Akademie der Wissenschaften zu Berlin. Institut für Slawistik. Veröffentlichungen, nr. 11 (Berlin: Akademie-Verlag, 1956), 237. This work apparently was not published; see ibid., 241. See also Josef Emler, ed., "Listy Josefa Jungmanna k Antonínu Markovi," *Časopis českého musea* 56 (1882): 464–66.

144. Ferdinand Hyna, *Duševloví zkušebné*, Malá encyklopedie nauk, vol. 4 (Prague: Kronberg and Řivnáč, 1844).

145. Čáda, *Hynovo Duševloví*, 29, 71–72. For references to Lichtenfels, see Hyna, *Duševloví zkušebné*, 21, 129, 335. On Herbart, see *Routledge Encyclopedia of Philosophy*, 4:369.

146. Čáda, *Hynovo Duševloví*, 34–35, 39.

147. Ibid., 42, 43. Hyna rarely acknowledged his sources and referred to Schulze only once; see Hyna, *Duševloví zkušebné*, 130.

148. In *Kritischen Journal der Philosophie*, Bd. 1, Stück 2 (1802), 1–74, cited by *Allgemeine Deutsche Biographie*, 32:778.

149. In "Aphorismen über das Absolute als das alleinige Princip der wahren Philosophie," in *Neues Museum der Philosophie und Litteratur*, ed. Fr. Bouterwek, Leipzig, Band 3, Heft 2 (1803), cited in *Allgemeine Deutsche Biographie*, 32:779. Čáda suggests that Hyna, among other opponents of metaphysical idealism, used *Allgemeine praktische Philosophie* by Christoph Bardili (Stuttgart, 1795), which would seem likely in view of the link between Bardili and Reinhold's logical realism; Čáda, *Hynovo Duševloví*, 53.

150. Hyna, *Dušesloví zkušebné*, 21. Apparently, he used Wilhelm Traugott Krug, *System der theoretischen Philosophie* (Vienna, 1818), which was Marek's main source; see Čáda, *Hynovo Dušesloví*, 47.

151. Hyna, *Dušesloví zkušebné*, 271; presumably he referred to Karl F. Burdach's *Ueber Psychologie als Naturwissenschaft* (Berlin, 1828), Hyna, 171; and to Johann M. Sailer's *Handbuch der christlichen Moral*, 3 vols. (Vienna: Wimmer, 1818), vol. 2, 117–18; Hyna, 168. Čáda suggests that Hyna used Fries's *Handbuch des psychischen Anthropologie oder der Lehre von der Natur des menschlichen Geist* (Jena: Croker, 1820), but Fries's contributions were difficult to disentangle from Schulze's, on whom Fries heavily depended; see Čáda, *Hynovo Dušesloví*, 56, 70.

152. Václav B. Nebeský, "Několik slov o filosofii," *Časopis českého musea* 20 (1846): 235.

153. Ibid., 236–37.

154. Karel Štorch, "Hlas o německé literatuře," *Květy* 14, no. 67 (1847): 267–68.

155. Karel Štorch, "Filosofie a naše literatura: Několik myšlenek snad včas," *Časopis českého musea* 22, pt. 1 (1848): 66.

156. "V pomyslu jáství"; see František Čupr, "Počátkové filosofování řeckého," *Časopis českého musea* 21, pt. 1 (1847): 30.

157. Jiří Kořalka, *František Palacký, 1798–1876: Životopis* (Prague: Argo, 1998), 40.

158. The Anglo-Magyar cultural symbiosis, which turned Kollár against the British, evidently appealed to Palacký; see Robert B. Pynsent, *Questions of Identity: Czech and Slovak Ideas of Nationality and Personality* (Budapest: Central European University Press, 1994), 93.

159. See chapter 6 in this volume.

160. Bolzano studied Dugald Stewart; see Bolzano, *Philosophische Tagebücher*, in Bolzano, *Gesamtausgabe*, Reihe II, Nachlass, B. Wissenschaftliche Tagebücher; Band 17, *1817–1827*, 148.

161. Milan Machovec, "František Palacký," in *Slovník českých filozofů*, 432.

162. Anne L. Staël-Holstein, *De l'Allemagne* (Paris: Garnier frères, 1800), 457–64; František Kutnar, Oldřich Králík, and Jaromír Bělič, *Tři studie o Palackém* (Olomouc: Palackého universita, 1949), 98–99. De Staël's thinking was rooted in the Enlightenment, although she showed an interest in representatives of theosophy, romanticism, and idealism; see Auguste Viatte, *Les sources occultes du romantisme*, 2nd ed. (Paris: Honoré Champion, 1965), 2:131.

163. Cited in Kutnar, Králík, and Bělič, *Tři studie o Palackém*, 146.

164. Jiří Morava, *Palacký: Čech, Rakušan, Evropan*, 2nd ed. (Prague: Vyšehrad, 1998), 30. On the scarcity of references to Kant in Palacký's early notebooks, see Ottakar Hostinský, "Františka Palackého estetické studie," *Památník na oslavu stých narozenin Františka Palackého* (Prague: Matice česká, 1898), 378,

165. Milena Jetmarová, "Filosofie Palackého," in *Filosofie v dějinách českého národa*, 137. To the extent that Palacký credited Kant with profound influence it was not in the realm of philosophy but that of theology, helping him pass from orthodox Christianity to Enlightenment Deism; ibid., 138.

166. On dissatisfaction with Kant's aesthetics, see Josef Kalousek, "O vůdčích myšlénkách v historickém díle Palackého," *Památník na oslavu stých narozenin*, 181; on the issue of Kant's influence, see also ibid., 184; and Palacký, *An Historical Survey of the Science of Beauty*, 54–55, 86.

167. Simeon Potter, "Palacký a anglické písemnictví," *Časopis Matice Moravské* 53 (1929): 109.
168. Jetmarová, "Filosofie Palackého," 140.
169. See chapter 9 in this volume. Karel Mácha, *Glaube und Vernunft: Die Böhmische Philosophie in geschichtlicher Übersicht* (Munich: Sauer, 1987), 2:62.

Chapter 8

1. Karel Havlíček, "Podobizna Bolzanova," *Česká včela* 13 (1846): n. 51, 204; Josef Král, *Československá filosofie: Nástin vývoje podle disciplin* (Prague: Melantrich, 1937), 27, citing from *Národní noviny,* December 22, 1848; Antonín Měšťan, *Geschichte der tschechischen Literatur im 19. und 20. Jahrhundert* (Colgne: Böhlau, 1984), 100. Havlíček's high regard for the philosopher was summed up in a special tribute in Bolzano's obituary, *Národní noviny*, February 8, 1849, cited by Tomáš G. Masaryk, *Karel Havlíček: Snahy a tužby politického probuzení*, Spisy 7 (Prague: Masarykův ústav AV ČR, 1996), 194.
2. Eugen Lemberg, *Grundlagen des nationalen Erwachens in Böhmen: Geistesgeschichtliche Studie, am Lebensgang Josef Georg Meinerts, 1773–1844* (Liberec: Verlag Gebrüder Stiepel, 1932), 74; Král, *Československá filosofie*, 27; Arne Novák, *Stručné dějiny literatury české*, ed. Rudolf Havel and Antonín Grund (Olomouc: Promberger, 1946), 202.
3. Bernard Bolzano, *Wissenschaft und Religion in Vormärz: Der Briefwechsel Bernard Bolzanos mit Michael Josef Fesl, 1822–1848*, ed. Eduard Winter and Wilhelm Zeil (Berlin: Akademie-Verlag, 1965), 21; Karel Berka, "Předmluva," in Bernard Bolzano, *Vědosloví: výbor*, ed. Karel Berka, trans. Marie Bayerová and Jaromír Loužil. (Prague: Academia, 1981), 13; Jan Patočka, "Bolzanovo místo v dějinách filosofie," in *Filosofie v dějinách českého národa*, Protokol celostátní konference o dějinách české filosofie v Liblicích ve dnech 14.–17. dubna 1958 (Prague: Nakladatelství ČSAV, 1958), 115.
4. Helena Lorenzová, "Bolzanův proces," in *Bůh a bohové: Církve, náboženství a spiritualita v českém 19 století*, Sborník příspěvků z 22. ročníku sympozia k problematice 19. století, Plzeň, 7.–9 března 2002, ed. Zdeněk Hojda and Roman Prahl (Prague: KLP, 2003), 22–23; Eduard Winter, *Bernard Bolzano: Ein Lebensbild*, in Bernard Bolzano, *Gesamtausgabe*, ed. Eduard Winter, Jan Berg, Friedrich Kambartel, Jaromír Loužil, and Bob van Rootselaar (Stuttgart-Bad Cannstatt: Frommann Holzboog, 1969–in progress), *Einleitungsband*, First Part: *Biographie*, 31; Zeithammer, *Biographie Bolzanos* in Bolzano, *Gesamtausgabe*, Reihe IV, Band 2, 25–26.
5. Although Bolzano rarely cited Aristotle or Thomas Aquinas in his philosophical works, his ontological and epistemological realism was distinctly grounded in the Aristotelian teaching of medieval scholasticism, which culminated in the philosophy of Aquinas. Marie Pavlíková, *Bolzanovo působení na pražské univerzitě* (Prague: Univerzita Karlova, 1985), 36; Winter, *Bernard Bolzano*, 31–32; Zeithammer, *Biographie Bolzanos,* in Bolzano, *Gesamtausgabe*, Reihe IV, Band 2, 53–54; Marta Vlasáková, "Životabĕh B. Bolzana," in *Osamělý myslitel, Bernard Bolzano,* ed. Kateřina Trlifajová (Prague: Filosofia, 2006), 13–14.
6. Bolzano, *Lehrbuch der Religionswissenschaft*, in *Gesamtausgabe*, Reihe I, Schriften: Band 6, pt. 1, 62–63; Winter, *Bernard Bolzano*, 105.

7. See, for instance, Bolzano, *Lehrbuch der Religionswissenschaft*, in *Gesamtausgabe*, Reihe I, Schriften: Band 6, pt. 2, 25.

8. Hana Šmahelová, "Bernard Bolzano a české národní obrození," *Český časopis historický* 100 (2002): 74–115; Josef Durdík, *O filosofii a činnosti Bernarda Bolzana* (Prague: Akademický čtenářský spolek, 1881), 11; Karl H. Seibt, *Klugheitslehre, praktisch abgehandelt, in akademischen Vorlesungen* (Prague: Elsenwanger, 1799), 1: intro., 2–3; Johann Heinrich Wolf, *Geschichte des Königreichs Böheim zum Gebrauche der Studierenden Jugend in der K.K. Staaten* (Vienna: Johann Thomas von Trattner, 1783), 241. See also Wilhelm Zeil, *Bolzano und die Sorben: ein Beitrag zur Geschichte des "Wendischen Seminars" in Prag zur Zeit der josefinischen Aufklärung und der Romantik* (Bautzen: Domowina, 1967), 91.

9. Marie Červinková-Riegrová, *Bernard Bolzano; životopisný nástin* (Prague: F. Šimáček, 1881); Karolina Světlá, *Z literárního soukromí a drobné práce*, 2nd ed. (Prague: L. Mazáč, 1941), 205; Karel Mácha, *Glaube und Vernunft: Die Böhmische Philosophie in geschichtlicher Übersicht* (Munich: Sauer, 1987), 2:50–51; Durdík, *O filosofii a činnosti Bernarda Bolzana*, 10, 12.

10. Marie Pavlíková, *Bolzanovo působení na pražské univerzitě* (Prague: Univerzita Karlova, 1985), 68; Bernard Bolzano, *24 Erbauungsreden, 1808–1820*, ed. Kurt F. Strasser (Vienna: Böhlau, 2001); Jaromír Loužil, "Bernard Bolzano—učitel a vychovatel," in *Vzdělání a osvěta v české kultuře 19. století*, Sborník příspěvků z 24. ročníku sympozia k problematice 19. století, Plzeň 4.–6 března 2004, ed. Kateřina Bláhová and Václav Petrbok (Prague: Ústav pro českou literaturu Akademie věd ČR, 2004), 22–29; Zeil, *Bolzano und die Sorben*, 91–92.

11. Marie Pavlíková, "Bolzanův odkaz," in Bernard Bolzano, *Vlastní životopis*, trans. and ed. Marie Pavlíková (Prague: Odeon, 1981), 162; Helena Lorenzová, "Bolzano a jeho žáci (zejména Robert Zimmermann)," in *Vzdělání a osvěta v české kultuře 19. století*, ed. Bláhová and Petrbok, 32–38; Loužil, "Bernard Bolzano—učitel a vychovatel," 30.

12. Pavlíková, *Bolzanovo působení na pražské univerzitě*, 104. Her number is questioned as exaggerated by Jiří Kořalka, "František Palacký a čeští bolzanisté," in *Modernismus: studie nebo výzva? Studie ke genezi českého katolického modernismu*, Pontes Pragenses 24, ed. Zdeněk Kučera and Jan B. Lášek (Brno: L. Marek, 2002), 24.

13. Kořalka, "František Palacký a čeští bolzanisté," 24; also Kořalka, "František Palacký und die böhmischen Bolzanisten," in Helmut Rumpler, ed., *Bernard Bolzano und die Politik: Staat, Nation und Religion als Herausforderung für die Philosophie im Kontext von Spätaufklärung, Frühnationalismus und Restauration*. Studien zu Politik und Verwaltung, Band 61 (Vienna: Böhlau, 2000), 203–4.

14. See the list in Pavlíková, *Bolzanovo působení na pražské univerzitě*, 107–19.

15. Jan Jakubec, *Dějiny literatury české*, 2nd ed. (Prague: Jan Laichter, 1929–34), 2:537–38.

16. Jan Jakubec, ed., *Literatura česká devatenáctého století*, with Josef Hanuš, Jan Máchal, and Jaroslav Vlček, 2nd ed. (Prague: Jan Laichter, 1911–17), 1:786; Miloslav Kaňák, *Josef Franta Šumavský* (Prague: Melantrich, 1975), 24–25, 35.

17. Letter to Kamarýt, February 10, 1820; see František Ladislav Čelakovský, *Korespondence a zápisky*, Sbírka pramenů ku poznání literárního života v Čechách, na Moravě a ve Slezsku, Skupina 2, Číslo 10, 14, 21, ed. František Bílý (Prague: Česká akademie pro vědy, slovesnost a umění, 1909, 1910, 1914), 1:39.

18. On his article concerning the persecution of the two in 1819, see Josef Polišenský and Ella Illingová, *Jan Jeník z Bratřic* (Prague: Melantrich, 1989), 68.

19. Bolzano, *Wissenschaft und Religion in Vormärz*, 11; Novák, *Stručné dějiny literatury české*, 202; on Štulc, see *Ottův slovník naučný* (Prague: Otto, 1888–1908), 24:813.

20. Červinková-Riegrová, *Bernard Bolzano; životopisný nástin* (Prague: F. Šimáček, 1881), in *Ruch* 1882; see Karolina Světlá, *Z literárního soukromí a drobné práce*, 2nd ed. (Prague: L. Mazáč, 1941), 227–33.

21. See, for instance, Bolzano, *Vlastní životopis*, 160–62; Bolzano, *24 Erbauungsreden, 1808–1820*, 7.

22. Franz Stefan Rautenstrauch, *Entwurf zur Eirichtung der Genaralseminarien in den k. k. Erblanden* (Vienna, 1784), 12.

23. Eduard Winter, *Die sozial- und ethnoethik Bernard Bolzanos: Humanistischer Patriotismus oder romantischer Nationalismus im vormärzlichen Österreich: Bernard Bolzano contra Friedrich Schlegel* (Vienna: Verlag der Österreichischen Akademie der Wissenschaften, 1977).

24. Bolzano, *Philosophische Tagebücher, Gesamtausgabe*, Reihe II, Nachlass, B. Wissenschaftliche Tagebücher; Band 17, *1817–1827*, 13, 54.

25. Winter, *Die sozial- und ethnoethik Bernard Bolzanos*, especially 23ff.

26. Emerich Franzis, "Bernard Bolzano und die nationale Idee," *Historisches Jahrbuch* 51 (1931): 441.

27. František Kutnar, *Obrozenské vlastenectví a nacionalismus, Příspěvek k národnímu společenskému obsahu češství doby obrozenské* (Prague: Karolinum, 2003), 242. He argued for equality among human beings and for equal voting rights and also eligibility for women. He was opposed to any form of war, unless it was clearly defensive. Dagfinn Føllesdal, "Bolzano's Legacy," in *Bolzano and Analytic Philosophy*, ed. Wolfgang Künne and others, *Grazer Philosophische Studien, International Zeitschrift für analytische Philosophie* 53 (1997), 4, citing from Bolzano's *Vom besten Staate*, finished in 1837, but not published until 1932 in Prague. In the spring of 1848, Bolzano was encouraged that liberal political principles, which he had advocated in his treatise *Vom besten Staate*, were becoming realized in Europe, as well as in the United States; Bolzano, *Wissenschaft und Religion in Vormärz*, 417.

28. Jan Patočka, *Náš národní program*, ed. Jan Vít and Miroslav Petříček (Prague: Evropský kulturní klub, 1990), 52–53. Aleksandr S. Myl'nikov, *Kul'tura cheshskogo vozrozhdeniia* (Leningrad: Nauka, 1982), 4, even appropriates Bolzano for the Czech nation, calling him "an original Czech thinker."

29. Bernard Bolzano, *Der böhmische Vormärz in Briefen B. Bolzanos an F. Příhonský, 1824–1848: Beiträge zur deutsch-slawischen Wechselseitigkeit*, ed. Eduard Winter, Deutsche Akademie der Wissenschaften zu Berlin. Institut für Slawistik Veröffentlichungen, nr. 11 (Berlin: Akademie-Verlag, 1956), 57; Bernard Bolzano, *Mathematisch-Physikalische und Philosophische Schriften, 1842–1843*, in *Gesamtausgabe*, Reihe I, Schriften, Band 18, 63.

30. "Übrigens bin ich nicht Kenner der böhmischen Sprache genung, um ein Urteil über das Büchlein fällen zu können, gelesen aber habe ich es allerdings und es schien mir sehr zweckmässig eingerichtet zu sein. Besonders gefielen mir die versae memoriales für jeden Buchstaben und die Sprüchlein [Although I am not an expert on the Czech language to pass a judgment about the booklet, I have still read it and it appears to me very functionally arranged. Especially, I like the verses to im-

plant each letter in memory and the ditties.]"; see Bolzano, *Der böhmische Vormärz in Briefen B. Bolzanos*, 215. The textbook in question was K. A. Vinařický, *Obrázková abeceda česká* (Prague: Pospíšil, 1839). In the same period, Bolzano also provided editorial advice for the Czech-language journal *Časopis katolického duchovenstva* [Journal of the Catholic Clergy], managed by another representative of Reform Catholicism, Vinařický; Bolzano, *Der böhmische Vormärz in Briefen B. Bolzanos*, 133.

31. Bolzano, *Philosophische Tagebücher, 1817–1827*, in *Gesamtausgabe*, Reihe II, B, Band 17, 11–12.

32. Yehoshua Bar-Hillel, "Bolzano," *The Encyclopedia of Philosophy*, 2nd ed., ed. Donald M. Borchert (New York: Macmillan, 2006), 1:646

33. In 1835, Fesl recommended that he read Bentham's *Deontology;* Bolzano, *Wissenschaft und Religion in Vormärz*, 133, 135, 137. Fesl referred to Jeremy Bentham, *Deontologie*, ed. John Bowring (Leipzig, 1834–35).

34. He produced a lengthy analysis of Priestley's writings in his diary; see Franz Stephan Rautenstrauch, *Diarium eruditum*, Státní ústřední archív, Prague, MS Benediktini Břevnov, ŘBB 89, f. 162r–169v.

35. Bolzano, *Philosophische Tagebücher*, in *Gesamtausgabe*, Reihe II, Nachlass, B. Wissenschaftliche Tagebücher; Band 16/1, *1811–1817* (v.1–), 1:15, 70–73. On Bolzano's preference for utilitarian ethics à la Bentham over Kant's categorical imperative, see also Giuseppe Rutto, *Bernard Bolzano: Reformkatholizismus e utopia nella Praga della Restaurazione* (Turin: Giappichelli, 1984), 130–31.

36. He defined Kant's supreme moral law as "act according to those maxims of your will, about which you know that you can will them to become the law of a general legal system." (Handle nach derjenigen Maxime deines Willens, von der du wollen kannst, dass sie Gesetz einer allgemeinen Gesetzgebung [auch wohl Naturgesetz] würde.) See Bolzano, *Lehrbuch der Religionswissenschaft*, in *Gesamtausgabe*, Reihe I, Schriften: Band 6, part 2, 35. See also the explication of Bolzano's view in František Příhonský, *Neuer Anti-Kant: oder,Prüfung der Kritik der reinen Vernunft nach den in Bolzano's Wissenschaftslehre niedergelegten Begriffen* (Bautzen: A. Weller, 1850), 200–202.

37. In connection with his critique of Jacob T. Werner, *Die Rechtslehre von der Verbindlichkeit des erzwungenen Willens* (Frankfurt a. M., 1817), see Bolzano, *Philosophische Tagebücher*, Reihe II, Nachlass, B. Wissenschaftliche Tagebücher; Band 17, *1817–1827*, 58.

38. Bolzano, *Philosophische Tagebücher*, *Gesamtausgabe*, Reihe II, Nachlass, B. Wissenschaftliche Tagebücher; Band 16/1, *1811–1817* (v.1–), 1:156. Thus, at least by implication, he was also opposed to what would later become known as Hegelian communitarianism. Hegel argued against the liberals for "an ethical community based on shared substantive values," a principle that also passed on to socialism and other social theories "prioritizing the bonds of *fraternité*." *Dictionary of Social Sciences*, ed. Craig Calhoun (Oxford: Oxford University Press, 2002), 82.

39. On Bolzano's religious views, see Rutto, *Bernard Bolzano*; Hermann Schrödter, *Philosophie und Religion; Die Religionswissenschaft B. Bolzanos* (Meisenheim am Glan: A. Hain, 1972); Jaromír Loužil, "Bernard Bolzano—učitel a vychovatel," in *Vzdělání a osvěta v české kultuře 19. století*, 25.

40. Bolzano, *Lehrbuch der Religionswissenschaft*, *Gesamtausgabe*, Reihe I, Schriften: Band 6, pt. 1, 78–85; see also Føllesdal, "Bolzano's Legacy," 3; Eduard Winter,

"Religion und Offenbarung in der Religionsphilosophie B. Bolzanos," *Breslauer Studien zur historischen Theologie*, Band 20 (1932); Jaromír Loužil, "Bemerkungen zu Bolzanos Religiosität," *Mezi časy; kultura a umění v českých zemích kolem roku 1800*, ed. Zdeněk Hojda and Roman Prahl (Prague: KLP, 2000), 106–13.
   41. Føllesdal, "Bolzano's Legacy," 3. Thus, he expressed approval of the toleration of Quakers in the United States, even though they rejected military service; Bolzano, *Vermischte philosophische und physikalische Schriften, 1832–1848*, *Gesamtausgabe*, Reihe II, Nachlass A, Band 12, pt. 1, 56.
   42. Bernard Bolzano, *Perfektabilität des Katholicismus*, *Gesamtausgabe*, Reihe I, Schriften, Band 19, Teil 1–2, 365, 369.
   43. Ibid., 104, 143, 389; Bolzano, *Wissenschaft und Religion in Vormärz*, 139–40.
   44. Jaromír Loužil, *Bernard Bolzano* (Prague: Melantrich, 1978), 289; Král, *Československá filosofie*, 24. Concerning his possible inspiration from the Bohemian Reformation, it must be noted, however, that, unlike many of his predecessors, he did not argue for Hus as an orthodox Catholic. See Bolzano, *Perfektabilität des Katholicismus*, *Gesamtausgabe*, Reihe I, Schriften, Band 19, Teil 1–2, 256.
   45. Loužil, *Bernard Bolzano*, 149.
   46. Winter, *Bernard Bolzano*, 27. Bolzano's liberalizing views were criticized from the viewpoint of tridentine Catholicism by the prior of the Strahov Monastery in Prague, Antonio Stoppani, in their correspondence of 1832–33, published under the title, *The Perfectibility of Catholicism*, in 1845; see Bolzano, *Perfektabilität des Katholicismus*, *Gesamtausgabe*, Reihe I, Schriften, Band 19, Teil 1–2, for instance, 167–69, 191–200, 206–7, 233–34.
   47. Margaret Friedrich, "Bolzano's Project der Aufklärung," in *Bernard Bolzano und die Politik,* 29–30.
   48. He hoped, however, that Ronge would not depart from Christian orthodoxy: "mit dem Bade nicht auch das Kindlein auschütten wird." See Bolzano, *Der böhmische Vormärz in Briefen B. Bolzanos*, 250.
   49. Ibid., 252–53.
   50. Bolzano, *Lehrbuch der Religionswissenschaft*, *Gesamtausgabe*, Reihe I, Schriften: Band 6, pt. 2, 52–53, 55–65.
   51. Bolzano, *Lehrbuch der Religionswissenschaft*, in *Gesamtausgabe*, Reihe I, Schriften: Band 7, pt. 1, 29–30, 36–37, 46, 154; pt. 2, 11–12, 36, 127–28.
   52. Bolzano, *Vermischte philosophische und physikalische Schriften, 1832–1848*, *Gesamtausgabe*, Reihe II, Nachlass A, Band 12, pt. 1, 46–47. See also Bolzano, *Lehrbuch der Religionswissenschaft*, *Gesamtausgabe*, Reihe I, Schriften: Band 6, pt. 1, 240–41; Bolzano, *Wissenschaft und Religion in Vormärz*, 147.
   53. Bolzano, *Lehrbuch der Religionswissenschaft*, *Gesamtausgabe*, Reihe I, Schriften: Band 6, pt. 2, 82–83.
   54. See, for instance, Bolzano, *Wissenschaft und Religion in Vormärz*, 284, 312.
   55. Ján Pavlík, "Bernard Bolzano a německá klasická filosofie," *Filosofický časopis* 42 (1994): 1018–19. Patočka points out that Bolzano opposed Kant's subjective justification of objective truth; see Patočka, "Bolzanovo místo v dějinách filosofie," 116. At one point, Bolzano considered writing a critique of Kant, and of the philosophers inspired by Kant, for the French audience; see his letter to Fesl of August 7, 1837, in Bolzano, *Wissenschaft und Religion in Vormärz*, 199, 257. On Bolzano's critique of Kant, see also Frederick Copleston, *History of Philosophy*

(London: Burns and Oates, 1947–66), 7:256–59; and Mácha, *Glaube und Vernunft*, 2:51–52.

56. In his philosophical diary for 1811–17, Bolzano discusses no fewer than fourteen works of Kant, published between 1755 and 1799; for Kant's lesser works, he relied heavily on *Immanuel Kant's vermischte Schriften: Aechte und volständige Ausgabe*, ed. J. H. Tieftrunk (Halle, 1799); see Bolzano, *Philosophische Tagebücher, Gesamtausgabe*, Reihe II, Nachlass, B. Wissenschaftliche Tagebücher; Band 16/1, *1811–1817* (v.1–), 1:215–16. In the same period, he cited eight works of Fichte, published between 1792 and 1799, ibid., 1:212–13; and twenty works of Schelling, published between 1795 and 1813, ibid., 1:218–19. Altogether, the philosophical diaries of 1811–44 refer to eighteen works of Kant, fourteen of Fichte, and twenty-two of Schelling; see also *Wissenschaftliche Tagebücher*, Band 17, 141, 145–46; *Wissenschaftliche Tagebücher*, Band 18/2, 126–27, 129.

57. Pavlíková, *Bolzanovo působení na pražské univerzitě*, 51.

58. Jane Regenfelder, "Der sogennante 'Bolzano-Prozess' und das Wartburgfest," in *Bernard Bolzano und die Politik*, 155–56.

59. Bolzano, *Philosophische Tagebücher, 1817–1827, Gesamtausgabe*, Reihe II, Nachlass B. Wissenschaftliche Tagebücher, Band 17, 8. See also Patočka, "Bolzanovo místo v dějinách filosofie," 113.

60. Bolzano, *Vermischte philosophische und physikalische Schriften, 1832–1848, Gesamtausgabe*, Reihe II, Nachlass A, Band 12, pt. 1, 67–68; Alexander G. Baumgarten, *Metaphysik* (Halle: Hemmerdesche Buchhandlung, 1783).

61. Bolzano, *Lehrbuch der Religionswissenschaft, Gesamtausgabe*, Reihe I, Schriften: Band 6, pt. 1, 182.

62. J. Alberto Coffa, *The Semantic Tradition from Kant to Carnap: To the Vienna Station*, ed. Linda Wessels (New York: Cambridge University Press, 1991), 21.

63. "Was man heutiges Tages speculative Philosophie nennt, ist grösstentheils das unsauberste, unkritischste Ding von der Welt." See Bolzano, *Philosophische Tagebücher, 1827–1844, Gesamtausgabe*, Reihe II, Nachlass, B. Wissenschaftliche Tagebücher; Band 18/2, 2:61. Bolzano referred to Ludwig Feuerbach, *Pierre Bayle, nach seinen für die Geschichte der Philosophie und der Menschheit interessantesten Momenten, dargestellt und gewürdigt* (Ansbach: C. Brügel, 1838), 241.

64. Bolzano, *Vermischte philosophische und physikalische Schriften, 1832–1848, Gesamtausgabe*, Reihe II, Nachlass A, Band 12, pt. 2, 171, referring to Joseph Schram, *Beitrag zur Geschichte der Philosophie: Mit Bezug auf Geschichte unserer Zeit* (Bonn, 1836).

65. Rudolf Haller, "Bolzano and Austrian Philosophy," in *Bolzano's Wissenschaftslehre, 1837–1987*, International Workshop, Florence, Italy, September 16–19, 1987 (Florence: Olschki, 1992), 193.

66. Bolzano, *Mathematische und Philosophische Schriften, 1810–1816, Gesamtausgabe*, Reihe II, Nachlass A, Band 5, 22–23.

67. Bolzano, *Philosophische Tagebücher, 1811–1817, Gesamtausgabe*, Reihe II, Nachlass, B. Wissenschaftliche Tagebücher; Band 16/1, 15, 33, 57; Bolzano challenged Kant's view that concepts should be considered simply products of human imagination; see Bernard Bolzano, *Wissenschaftslehre, Gesamtausgabe*, Reihe I, Schriften: Band 11, 1:127.

68. "Kant nach seinem trancendentalen Idealismus behaupte, es gebe gar keine Dinge, und doch im Anfang gleich von Eindrücken, die sie auf uns machen (uns

afficiren) spreche." Bolzano, *Philosophische Tagebücher, 1827–1844, Gesamtausgabe*, Reihe II, Nachlass, B. Wissenschaftliche Tagebücher; Band 18/2, 2:56.

69. Bolzano, *Vermischte philosophische und physikalische Schriften, 1832–1848, Gesamtausgabe*, Reihe II, Nachlass A, Band 12, pt. 1, 21, referring to Kant's, *Critik der reinen Vernunft*, 2nd ed. (Riga: Hartknocht, 1787), 566 ff., and Schelling's *Philosophische Untersuchungen über das Wesen der menschlichen Freyheit*, vol. 1 of Schelling, *Philosophische Schriften* (Landshut: P. Krüll, 1809), 421, 465.

70. Bolzano, *Lehrbuch der Religionswissenschaft, Gesamtausgabe*, Reihe I, Schriften: Band 6, pt. 1, 188–94. See also Bernard Bolzano, *Výbor z filozofických spisů*, ed. Jiří Černý and Jaromír Loužil, trans. J. Loužil (Prague: Svoboda, 1981), 153–54. Against Kant's assertion that mathematical concepts were constructed from *a priori* intuitive viewpoint [*Anschauung*], Bolzano claimed such basic concepts were objective and formed eternal "truths in themselves." Arnošt Kolman, "Matematickologická stránka Bolzanovy filosofie," *Filosofie v dějinách českého národa*, 126.

71. Bolzano, *Lehrbuch der Religionswissenschaft, Gesamtausgabe*, Reihe I, Schriften: Band 6, pt. 1, 192–93.

72. Bolzano, *Wissenschaftslehre, Gesamtausgabe*, Reihe I, Schriften, Band 11–14.

73. Bolzano, *Philosophische Tagebücher, 1817–1827, Gesamtausgabe*, Reihe II, Nachlass, B. Wissenschaftliche Tagebücher; Band 17, 8.

74. Bolzano, *Wissenschaftslehre, Gesamtausgabe*, Reihe I, Schriften, Band 11, 1:184. He referred to Immanuel Kant, *Logik, ein Handbuch zu Vorlesungen* (Königsberg [Kaliningrad]: F. Nicolovius, 1800), 156.

75. Bolzano, *Wissenschaftslehre, Gesamtausgabe*, Reihe I, Schriften, Band 11, 1:13–15.

76. Ibid., 1:215–16.

77. Bolzano, *Vermischte philosophische und physikalische Schriften, 1832–1848, Gesamtausgabe*, Reihe II, Nachlass A, Band 12, pt. 2, 77–78.

78. Ibid., 174–75.

79. Bolzano, *Wissenschaftslehre, Gesamtausgabe*, Reihe I, Schriften, Band 11, 2:100–101; 3:161; Bolzano, *Lehrbuch der Religionswissenschaft, Gesamtausgabe*, Reihe I, Schriften: Band 6, pt. 1, 189–90.

80. Bolzano, *Wissenschaftslehre, Gesamtausgabe*, Reihe I, Schriften, Band 11, 2:150–51, referring to Immanuel Kant, *Logik*, 139–40.

81. Bolzano, *Vermischte philosophische und physikalische Schriften, 1832–1848, Gesamtausgabe*, Reihe II, Nachlass A, Band 12, pt. 2, 116–17.

82. Bolzano, *Wissenschaftslehre, Gesamtausgabe*, Reihe I, Schriften, Band 11, 2:170–71. He refers particularly to Kant's statement: "Also ist die ursprüngliche Vorstellung von Raume Anschauung a priori und nicht Begriff. [Thus the original idea of space is an *a priori* perception, not a concept.]" Kant, *Critik der reinen Vernunft*, 39–40. See also Bolzano, *Vermischte philosophische und physikalische Schriften, 1832–1848, Gesamtausgabe*, Reihe II, Nachlass A, Band 12, pt. 3, 120.

83. "Die Alten unter dem Stoff das Allgemeine, und unter der Form das Besondere, Kant aber umgekehrt unter der Form das Allgemeine (die allen Objecten einer Erkenntnissart gemeischaftliche Bedingung) und unter dem Stoffe das Besondere in einem Objecte verstanden habe. [The ancients understood under matter the general, and under form the particular; Kant, the other way around, under form understood the general—the condition for cognition common to all objects—and under matter the particular in an object.]" Bolzano, *Wissenschaftslehre, Gesamtausgabe*,

Reihe I, Schriften, Band 11, 2:196, citing from Salomon Maimon, *Versuch einer neuen Logik oder Theorie des Denkens* (Berlin: Felisch, 1794), 283–85.

84. Bolzano, *Wissenschaftslehre, Gesamtausgabe*, Reihe I, Schriften, Band 11, 3:150–54, citing Kant, *Critik der reinen Vernunft*, 128. See also Bolzano, *Lehrbuch der Religionswissenschaft, Gesamtausgabe*, Reihe I, Schriften: Band 6, pt. 1, 185.

85. The truth (*Wahrheit*) of the concept sentence could be viewed as independent of experience (*Erfahrung*); the truth of the perception sentence as not independent of experience. See Bernard Bolzano, *Wissenschaftslehre, Gesamtausgabe*, Reihe I, Schriften, Band 12, 1:97–99, referring to Kant, *Critik der reinen Vernunft*, 1–4.

86. Bolzano, *Vermischte philosophische und physikalische Schriften, 1832–1848, Gesamtausgabe*, Reihe II, Nachlass A, Band 12, pt. 2, 70.

87. Bolzano, *Wissenschaftslehre, Gesamtausgabe*, Reihe I, Schriften, Band 13, 1:141–42, 146, referring to Kant, *Critik der reinen Vernunft*, 432–595.

88. Bolzano, *Wissenschaftslehre, Gesamtausgabe*, Reihe I, Schriften, Band 13, 1:184–93, referring to Kant, *Critik der reinen Vernunft*, 10–12, 18–24, 34–35, 176–97, 740–66.

89. Bolzano, *Wissenschaftslehre, Gesamtausgabe*, Reihe I, Schriften, Band 12, 3:196–97.

90. Bolzano, *Wissenschaftslehre, Gesamtausgabe*, Reihe I, Schriften, Band 13, 2:50, referring to Kant, *Critik der reinen Vernunft*, 350–51.

91. Bolzano, *Philosophische Tagebücher, 1817–1827, Gesamtausgabe*, Reihe II, Nachlass, B. Wissenschaftliche Tagebücher; Band 17, 87.

92. In this connection Bolzano cited "Kant's assertion that the immediate pleasure from the beautiful refers regrettably to the expedient form of the imagination without any concept of purpose or any interest in the content."[Kants Erklärung das unmittelbare Wohlgefallen am Schönen beziehe sich lediglich auf eine zweckmässige Form der Vorstellungsart ohne Zweckbegriff und Interesse am Inhalt]. See Bolzano, *Philosophische Tagebücher, Gesamtausgabe*, Reihe II, Nachlass, B. Wissenschaftliche Tagebücher; Band 18/2, *1827–1844*, 16. Bolzano refers to Immanuel Kant, *Critik der Urtheilskraft* (Berlin and Libau: Lagarde und Friederich, 1790), 75.

93. Bolzano, *Mathematisch-Physikalische und Philosophische Schriften, 1842–1843, Gesamtausgabe*, Reihe I, Schriften, Band 18, 161.

94. Ibid., 178.

95. Bolzano, *Wissenschaftslehre, Gesamtausgabe*, Reihe I, Schriften, Band 11, 3:56–57, citing Kant, *Critik der reinen Vernunft*, 346.

96. "Dass zwischen zwei Nebenarten noch Zwischenarten möglich wären." See Bolzano, *Wissenschaftslehre, Gesamtausgabe*, Reihe I, Schriften, Band 11, 3:99, referring to Kant, *Critik der reinen Vernunft*, 685.

97. Bolzano, *Wissenschaftslehre, Gesamtausgabe*, Reihe I, Schriften, Band 12, 3:162.

98. Bolzano, *Vermischte philosophische und physikalische Schriften, 1832–1848, Gesamtausgabe*, Reihe II, Nachlass A, Band 12, pt. 2, 176.

99. Příhonský, *Neuer Anti-Kant: oder, Prüfung der Kritik der reinen Vernunft nach den in Bolzano's niedergelegten Begriffen*; see also Bolzano, *Wissenschaft und Religion in Vormärz*, 398.

100. Cited in Bolzano, *Výbor z filozofických spisů*, 156–57.

101. "Die Grundidee des Schellingschen System ist ganz die des Fichteschen. Beyde setzen die Vernunft, das Absolute, an die Spitze. Beyden ist das Absolute die absolute Identität des Idealen und Realen, des Subjektiven und Objektiven, der Geschichte (dem Geisterreiche) und der Natur." Bolzano, *Philosophische Tagebücher, 1811–1817, Gesamtausgabe*, Reihe II, Nachlass, B. Wissenschaftliche Tagebücher; Band 16/1, 194.

102. In a letter of Bolzano to Zimmermann of March 11, 1846, cited by Eduard Winter, *Der Josefinismus: die Geschichte des österreichischen Reformkatholizismus, 1740–1848* (Berlin: Rütten & Loening, 1962), 266.

103. "Wie kann etwas Ursache von sich selbst seyn! Diesen wichtigen Irrthum der Fichteschen und Schellingschen Philosophie scheint die Redensart des Katechismus (Gott ist das von sich selbst bestehende Wesen) vorbereitet zu haben!"[How can something be the cause of its own self? This important error of Fichte's and Schelling's philosophy seems to have been inspired by the statement of the catechism (God is a being derived from himself)!] Bolzano, *Philosophische Tagebücher, 1811–1817, Gesamtausgabe,* Reihe II, Nachlass, B. Wissenschaftliche Tagebücher; Band 16/1, 96.

104. "Mystische Philosophie." He comments on the book, *Betrachtungen über den gegenwärtigen Zustand der Philosophie in Teutschland überhaupt und über die Schellingische philosophie in Besondern* (Nuernberg: Schrag, 1813); see Bolzano, *Philosophische Tagebücher, 1811–1817, Gesamtausgabe*, Reihe II, Nachlass, B. Wissenschaftliche Tagebücher; Band 16/1, 126–27.

105. Bolzano, *Philosophische Tagebücher, 1817–1827, Gesamtausgabe*, Reihe II, Nachlass, B. Wissenschaftliche Tagebücher; Band 17, 36. Bolzano referred to Andreas Metz, *Handbuch der Logik zum Gebrauch akademischer Vorlesungen* (Bamberg and Würzburg, 1816).

106. Bolzano, *Wissenschaftslehre, Gesamtausgabe*, Reihe I, Schriften, Band 11, 1:30.

107. Ibid., 1:62–63

108. "Philosophie müsse mit der Voraussetzung beginnen, dass nur Eines sey, und ausser diesem Einem nichts." See Bolzano, *Philosophische Tagebücher, 1827–1844, Gesamtausgabe*, Reihe II, Nachlass, B. Wissenschaftliche Tagebücher; Band 18, pt. 2, 55.

109. Bolzano, *Wissenschaftslehre, Gesamtausgabe*, Reihe I, Schriften, Band 13, 1:125.

110. Bolzano, *Lehrbuch der Religionswissenschaft*, in *Gesamtausgabe*, Reihe I, Schriften: Band 6, pt. 2, 37–38.

111. Bolzano, *Vermischte philosophische und physikalische Schriften, 1832–1848, Gesamtausgabe*, Reihe II, Nachlass A, Band 12, pt. 2, 175.

112. Ibid., 132.

113. Ibid., 144, referring to Johann G. Fichte, *Die Thatsachen des Bewusstseins* (Stuttgart and Tübingen, 1817), 24ff, and also 6, 12, 18, 23.

114. "Von Fichte, zu welchem Ruhme er sich auch als Philosoph erhoben . . . , möchte ich doch geradezu behaupten, dass ihm die Gabe, sich seiner Gedanken deutlich bewusst zu sein, in hohem Grade gemangelt." See Bolzano, *Mathematisch-Physikalische und Philosophische Schriften, 1842–1843, Gesamtausgabe*, Reihe I, Schriften, Band 18, 185.

115. Bolzano, *Mathematische und Philosophische Schriften, 1810–1816, Gesamt-*

ausgabe, Reihe II, Nachlass A, Band 5, 179, referring to Friedrich W. Schelling, *System des transscendentalen Idealismus* (Tübingen: Cotta, 1800), 1.

116. Bolzano, *Philosophische Tagebücher, 1817–1827, Gesamtausgabe*, Reihe II, Nachlass, B. Wissenschaftliche Tagebücher; Band 17, 28. He referred to *Höchstwichtige Beyträge zur Geschichte der neuesten Literatur in Deutschland*, ed. Antibarbaro Labienus, St. Galen, 4 (1815).

117. "Das Leben an sich is das Unbedingte, ewig sich selbst Bildende und Bestimmende. Als Bestimmendes ist es frey, als Bestimmtes nothwendig; folglich frey und nothwendig zugleich." Bolzano, *Philosophische Tagebücher, 1817–1827, Gesamtausgabe*, Reihe II, Nachlass, B. Wissenschaftliche Tagebücher; Band 17, 53. Bolzano refers to *Jahrbücher der Literatur*, Vienna, 1 (1818).

118. Bolzano, *Vermischte philosophische und physikalische Schriften, 1832–1848, Gesamtausgabe*, Reihe II, Nachlass A, Band 12, pt. 2, 172.

119. Ibid., 180–81.

120. Ibid., 177–78, referring to Schelling, *Philosophische Untersuchungen über das Wesen der menschlichen Freyheit*, in his *Philosophische Schriften*, vol. 1 (Landshut: P. Krüll, 1809).

121. Bolzano, *Vermischte philosophische und physikalische Schriften, 1832–1848, Gesamtausgabe*, Reihe II, Nachlass A, Band 12, pt. 3, 111, 121.

122. Bolzano, *Wissenschaftslehre, Gesamtausgabe*, Reihe I, Schriften, Band 11, 1:218, referring to Friedrich W. Schelling, *System des transscendentalen Idealismus* (Tübingen: Cotta, 1800), 43.

123. Bolzano, *Vermischte philosophische und physikalische Schriften, 1832–1848, Gesamtausgabe*, Reihe II, Nachlass A, Band 12, pt. 2, 73–74, referring to Friedrich W. Schelling, *Philosophie und Religion* (Tübingen: Cotta, 1804).

124. Bernard Bolzano, *Wissenschaftslehre, Gesamtausgabe*, Reihe I, Schriften, Band 11, 1:229, citing from Friedrich W. Schelling, *Vorlesungen über die Methode des academischen Studium* (Tübingen: Cotta, 1803), 128. See also Bolzano, *Vermischte philosophische und physikalische Schriften, 1832–1848, Gesamtausgabe*, Reihe II, Nachlass A, Band 12, pt. 2, 73.

125. Ibid., 74, referring to Friedrich W. Schelling, *Philosophie und Religion* (Tübingen: Cotta, 1804).

126. "Da Schelling seine Begriffe so oft schon und so bedeutend umgeändert, so können wir nich beurtheilen, in welcher Weise er sich vielleicht auch über die Natur des Schönen aussprechen werde." See Bolzano, *Mathematisch-Physikalische und Philosophische Schriften, 1842–1843, Gesamtausgabe*, Reihe I, Schriften, Band 18, 185.

127. Bolzano, *Vermischte philosophische und physikalische Schriften, 1832–1848, Gesamtausgabe*, Reihe II, Nachlass A, Band 12, pt. 2, 173.

128. See, for instance, Bolzano, *Philosophische Tagebücher, 1817–1827, Gesamtausgabe*, Reihe II, Nachlass, B. Wissenschaftliche Tagebücher; Band 17, 92–98.

129. "Der Verfasser [Schopenhauer] . . . ist aber sichtbar wahnsinnig geworden." See ibid., 70.

130. Bolzano, *Philosophische Tagebücher, 1817–1827, Gesamtausgabe*, Reihe II, Nachlass, B. Wissenschaftliche Tagebücher; Band 17, 114, commenting on Schopenhauer's *Die Welt als Wille und Vorstellung* (Leipzig: Brokhaus, 1819).

131. Bolzano, *Der böhmische Vormärz in Briefen B. Bolzanos*, 197.

132. Bolzano, *Mathematische und Philosophische Schriften, 1810–1816*, *Gesamtausgabe*, Reihe II, Nachlass A, Band 5, 172.

133. Zeithammer, *Biographie Bolzanos* in Bolzano, *Gesamtausgabe*, Reihe IV, Band 2, 54–55.

134. *The Encyclopedia of Philosophy*, 2nd ed., 1:543–44; Friedrich Eduard Beneke, *Ungedruckte Briefe*, ed. Renato Pettoello and Nikola Barelmann (Aalen, Germany: Scientia, 1994), 100 [cf. 323], 189 [cf. 329], 195, 230.

135. Fesl's letter to Bolzano of December 22, 1838, in Bolzano, *Wissenschaft und Religion in Vormärz*, 233. See also chapter 11 in this volume.

136. *Routledge Encyclopedia of Philosophy*, ed. Edward Craig (New York: Routledge, 1998), 8:187; *Neue Deutsche Biographie* (Berlin: Duncker & Humblot, 1953–in progress), 21:369. Among Reinhold's works in the philosophy of language are *Grundlegung einer Synonymik für den allgemeinen Sprachgebrauch in den philosophischen Wissenschaften* (Kiel, 1812) and *Das menschliche Erkenntnisvermögen* (Kiel, 1816).

137. Bernard Bolzano, *Wissenschaftslehre*, *Gesamtausgabe*, Reihe I, Schriften, Band 11, 1:144–45, referring to Karl L. Reinhold, *Die alte Frage: Was ist die Wahrheit?* (Altona, 1820), 101.

138. He gave as an example of such truth (*Wahrheit*) the statement that "there is no quantity the square of which is –1." Bernard Bolzano, *Wissenschaftslehre*, *Gesamtausgabe*, Reihe I, Schriften, Band 11, 1:150, referring to Reinhold, *Die alte Frage*, 101.

139. Bolzano, *Wissenschaftslehre*, *Gesamtausgabe*, Reihe I, Schriften, Band 12, 2:60–66, citing from Reinhold, *Grundlegung einer Synonymik*, 109. Bolzano also followed the work of Karl Reinhold's less famous son, the philosopher Ernst C. Reinhold (1793–1855), whom he praised in a letter to Fesl of November 1, 1839, as "a resolute opponent of Schelling and Hegel." Falsely held as a "speculative dreamer," he was more—according to Bolzano—"the driest Naturalist or Rationalist" [*der trockenste Naturalist oder Rationalist*]; see Bolzano, *Wissenschaft und Religion in Vormärz*, 271.

140. See Christoph G. Bardili, *Grundriss der ersten Logik, gereiniget von den Irrthümmern bisheriger Logiken überhaupt, der Kantischen insbesondere: keine Kritik sondern eine medicina mentis, brauchbar hauptsächlich für Deutschlands kritische Philosophie* (Stuttgart: Franz C. Löflund, 1800); *Neue Deutsche Biographie*, 1:586.

141. *Allgemeine Deutsche Biographie*, 28:83–84. On Reinhold's attachment to Bardili's logic, see in Georg W. Hegel, *Differenz des Fichte'schen und Schelling'schen Systems der Philosophie in Beziehung auf Reinhold's Beiträge zur leichtern Übersicht der Philosophie zu Anfang des neunzehnten Jahrhunderts* (Jena: Akademische Buchhandlung, 1801) in Georg W. Hegel, *Jenaer Schriften, 1801–1807*, Werke 2, Eva Moldenhauer and Karl M. Michel (Frankfurt/M: Suhrkamp, 1970), 121, 135. Hegel also charges Reinhold with intention to conduct an intellectual revolution through reduction of philosophy to logic; ibid., 9. For his correspondence with Bardili, see Christoph G. Bardili, *Briefwechsel über das Wesen der Philosophie und das Unwesen der Spekulation* (Munich: [C. L. Reinhold], 1804).

142. Bolzano, *Wissenschaftslehre, Gesamtausgabe*, Reihe I, Schriften, Band 11, 1:130.

143. Wilhelm Traugott Krug, *Briefe über die Wissenschaftslehre. Nebst einer Abhandlung über die von derselben versuchte Bestimmung des religiösen Glaubens*. (Leipzig: Roch, 1800), 117–27.

144. Wilhelm Traugott Krug, *Briefe über den neuesten Idealism* (Leipzig: H. Müller, 1801), 1–6. Krug's main target against Friedrich W. Schelling was the treatise, *System des transzendentalen Idealismus* (Tübingen: Cotta, 1800); see Krug, *Briefe über den neuesten Idealism*, 5. His summary judgment over Schelling's system was that (1) it did not deliver what it promised; and (2) it contained contradictory assertions; ibid., 12.

145. Krug, *Briefe über den neuesten Idealism*, 98–99; Wilhelm Traugott Krug, *Handbuch der Philosophie und der philosophischen Literatur*. Mit einen Vorwort und einer Einleitung von Lutz Geldsetzer und einem Sachregister von Ute Geldsetzer. Düsseldorf, Stern-Verlag Janssen [c1969] 2 v. in 1. (Reprint of the 3rd rev. and enl. ed., published in Leipzig, 1828), 53.

146. "Allein ich war nie Kantianer im eigentlichen Sinne"; see Krug, *Handbuch der Philosophie*, xii. He took pride in the independence of his philosophical teaching as early outlined in Wilhelm Traugott Krug, *Entwurf eines neuen Organon's der Philosophie: oder Versuch über die Prinzipien der philosophischen Erkenntnis* (Meissen: Erbstein, 1801); see Krug, *Handbuch der Philosophie*, xiii.

147. Krug, *Handbuch der Philosophie*, 13, 21, 118, 123, 261 (on Herbart); 29, 179 (on Hobbes); 30, 102, 332 (on Hume); 29 (on Locke); 30 (on Thomas Reid); 124 (on Dugald Stewart).

148. "Denn was in der Welt kann uns berechtigen . . . die logische Identität zwischen dem Begriff und seinen Merkmalen in eine transcendentale (oder vielmehr transcendente) Identität des Objektiven und Subjektiven überhaupt zu verwandeln?" Wilhelm T. Krug, *System der theoretischen Philosophie*. Erster Teil. Denklehre oder Logik (Königsberg [Kaliningrad], 1806), 52; cited by Bolzano, *Wissenschaftslehre, Gesamtausgabe*, Reihe I, Schriften, Band 11, 1:218.

149. Bernard Bolzano, *Wissenschaftslehre, Gesamtausgabe*, Reihe I, Schriften, Band 11, 1:59, referring to Krug, *System der theoretischen Philosophie*. Erster Teil, 22.

150. Bolzano, *Wissenschaftslehre, Gesamtausgabe*, Reihe I, Schriften, Band 11, 1:163, referring to Krug, *System der theoretischen Philosophie*. Erster Teil, 82.

151. Bolzano, *Wissenschaftslehre, Gesamtausgabe*, Reihe I, Schriften, Band 11, 2:36–37, referring to Krug, *System der theoretischen Philosophie*. Erster Theil, 147. For Bolzano's corresponding view, see Bolzano, *Wissenschaftslehre, Gesamtausgabe*, Reihe I, Schriften, Band 11, 2:11.Bolzano also approved Krug's tendency to limit the concept of similarity (*Aenlichkeit*) among mental images (*Vorstellungen*). Some logicians had made the concept of "similarity" virtually useless by claiming that all "mental images" had some marks in common. Bolzano, *Wissenschaftslehre, Gesamtausgabe*, Reihe I, Schriften, Band 11, 3:26, referring to Krug, *System der theoretischen Philosophie*. Erster Teil, 150.

152. Bernard Bolzano, *Wissenschaftslehre, Gesamtausgabe*, Reihe I, Schriften, Band 11, 3:83–84, referring to Krug, *System der theoretischen Philosophie*. Erster Teil, 173–76.

153. Bernard Bolzano, *Wissenschaftslehre, Gesamtausgabe*, Reihe I, Schriften, Band 11, 3:151, referring to Wilhelm T. Krug, *System der theoretischen Philosophie, Zweyter Theil. Erkenntnisslehre oder Metaphysik* (Vienna, 1818), 93–94.

154. Bernard Bolzano, *Wissenschaftslehre, Gesamtausgabe*, Reihe I, Schriften, Band 12, 3:176–77, referring to Krug, *System der theoretischen Philosophie*. Erster Teil, 365–433.

155. Bolzano, *Vermischte philosophische und physikalische Schriften, 1832–1848*, *Gesamtausgabe*, Reihe II, Nachlass A, Band 12, pt. 1, 11, 170; Wilhelm T. Krug, *Antidoton: Ein Pendant zum Henotikon* (Leipzig: C. E. Kollmann, 1836). See also Bolzano, *Wissenschaft und Religion in Vormärz*, 175–76, 180, 185.

156. *Krug und Bolzano oder Schreiben an den Herrn Professor Krug in Leipzig und Prüfung seines gegen Prof. Bolzano's Lehrbuch der Religionswissenschaft gerichteten Antidoton*, herausgegeben von den "Aufgeforderten" (Sulzbach: Seidel, 1837), presumably by Johann A. Zimmermann. See Bolzano, *Wissenschaft und Religion in Vormärz*, 188.

157. He read John Locke's *An Essay Concerning Human Understanding* in a German translation as *Versuch über den menschlichen Verstand*, trans. Wilhelm G. Tennemann (Jena, 1795–97); see Bolzano, *Philosophische Tagebücher*, *Gesamtausgabe*, Reihe II, Nachlass, B. Wissenschaftliche Tagebücher; Band 17, *1817–1827*, 116, 142.

158. Ibid., 89–91.

159. "Knowledge then seems to me to be nothing but the perception of the connexion and agreement, or disagreement and repugnancy of any of our ideas." John Locke, *An Essay Concerning Human Understanding* (London, 1690), bk. 4, chap. 1, par. 2, cited by Bernard Bolzano, *Wissenschaftslehre*, *Gesamtausgabe*, Reihe I, Schriften, Band 11, 1:121.

160. "Er erklärte die Metaphysische Wahrheit als die reale Existenz der Dinge, sofern sie mit unseren Vorstellungen übereinstimmt." [He defined metaphysical truth as the real existence of a thing, as long as it coincided with our idea (of it).] Citing from Locke, *An Essay Concerning . . .* , (1690), bk. 4, chap. 5, par. 11, see Bolzano, *Wissenschaftslehre, Gesamtausgabe*, Reihe I, Schriften, Band 11, 1:166.

161. Locke, *An Essay Concerning . . . .* (1690), bk. 4, chap. 5, par. 2, cited by Bolzano, *Wissenschaftslehre, Gesamtausgabe*, Reihe I, Schriften, Band 11, 1:145.

162. Bolzano, *Wissenschaftslehre, Gesamtausgabe,* Reihe I, Schriften, Band 13, 1:49, referring to Locke's statement: "As a clear idea is that, where of the mind has such a full and evident perception, as it does receive from an outward object, operating duly on a well disposed organ." Cited from John Locke, *An Essay Concerning Human Understanding* (London, 1700), bk. 2, chap. 29, par. 4.

163. Bolzano, *Wissenschaftslehre, Gesamtausgabe*, Reihe I, Schriften, Band 12, 1:96, referring to John Locke, *An Essay Concerning Human Understanding* (London, 1775), bk. 4, chap. 3, par. 31; chap. 4, par. 6, 16.

164. Bolzano, *Wissenschaftslehre, Gesamtausgabe*, Reihe I, Schriften, Band 12, 1:144, referring to Locke, *An Essay Concerning . . . .* (1775), bk. 4, chap. 8, par. 4.

165. Bolzano, *Wissenschaftslehre, Gesamtausgabe*, Reihe I, Schriften, Band 13, 1:114, referring to Locke, *An Essay Concerning . . .* (1700), bk. 1, chap. 3. Bolzano also discussed Locke's theory on the grounds of the possibility of error, "dass wohl die meisten unserer Irrthümer blosse *Gedächtnissfehler* wären." See Bernard Bolzano, *Wissenschaftslehre, Gesamtausgabe*, Reihe I, Schriften, Band 13, 2:48, referring to Locke, *An Essay Concerning . . . .* (1700), bk. 4, chap. 2, par. 7; chap. 20, par. 1.

166. Dugald Stewart, *Elements of the Philosophy of the Human Mind* (Edinburgh: W. Creech, 1792–1827); see Bolzano, *Philosophische Tagebücher, Gesamtausgabe*, Reihe II, Nachlass, B. Wissenschaftliche Tagebücher; Band 17, *1817–1827*, 89–91, 148.

167. Bolzano, *Wissenschaftslehre, Gesamtausgabe*, Reihe I, Schriften, Band 13,

1:174, referring to James Beattie, *Versuch über die Natur und Unveränderlichkeit der Wahrheit im Gegensatze der Klügeley und der Zweifelsucht.* trans. H. W. von Gerstenberg (Copenhagen and Leipzig: Heineck and Faber, 1772), 55–71; Thomas Reid, *Essays on the Active Powers of Man* (Edinburgh: J. Bell, 1788), 113–17; and Locke, *An Essay Concerning Human Understanding,* 4th ed. (London: 1700), bk. 4, chap. 14.

168. Bolzano, *Wissenschaftslehre, Gesamtausgabe,* Reihe I, Schriften, Band 11, 1:59–60, 69, 76, referring to Antoine L. Destutt de Tracy, *Élémens d'idéologie.* Troisième partie. *Logique* (Paris: Courcier, 1805), 1, 143, 363–64.

169. Bolzano, *Wissenschaftslehre, Gesamtausgabe,* Reihe I, Schriften, Band 11, 1:185–86; referring to Destutt de Tracy, *Élémens d'idéologie.* Troisième partie, 155.

170. Bolzano, *Wissenschaftslehre, Gesamtausgabe,* Reihe I, Schriften, Band 11, 1:131, 185–86; referring to Antoine L. Destutt de Tracy, *Projet d'élémens d'idéologie* (Paris: Didot, 1801), 56.

171. Concerning the uniqueness of Bolzano's contribution to the field of logic, see Rolf George, "Psychologism in Logic: Bacon to Bolzano," *P&R: Philosophy and Rhetoric* 30 (1997): 213–42. For a competent summary, see Jan Berg, *Onthology without Filters and Possible Worlds: An Examination of Bolzano's Onthology* (Sankt Augustin: Academia Verlag, 1992).

172. Winter, *Bernard Bolzano,* 84. There is, in fact, no evidence of Bolzano's use of the concept of the monads or other metaphysical constructs of Leibniz. See also Bolzano, *Wissenschaft und Religion in Vormärz,* 241, 278; and comments on the relationship in Franz C. Brentano, *Psychologie vom empirischen Standpunkt,* ed. Oskar Kraus, 2nd ed. (Leipzig: Meiner, 1924–28), 2:265.

173. "Einen aus der Leibnizisch-Wolffischen Schule hervorgegangen usw. Eklektizismus"; see his letter to Fesl of August 28, 1840, in Bolzano, *Wissenschaft und Religion in Vormärz,* 290.

174. He made the deprecatory remark: "Leibnizens Philosophie stehet bei unsrer Regierung in gutem Rufe" [Leibniz's philosophy (has) a good reputation with the (Austrian Imperial government)], in letter to Fesl of January 31, 1848, in ibid., 408.

175. See his letter to Zimmermann of March 11, 1846, cited by Winter, *Der Josefinismus,* 266. Despite Bolzano's disclaimer, Leibniz and Wolff have been often cited in his philosophical pedigree; see, for instance, *Oxford Companion to Philosophy,* ed. Ted Honderich (New York: Oxford University Press, 1995), 98; *Slovník českých filozofů* (Brno: Masarykova univerzita, 1998), 43, claims that Leibniz's crucial influence reached him through Wolff, whom he had studied under Seibt; *Filosofický slovník* (Olomouc: Nakladatelství Olomouc, 2002), 57; William M. Johnston, *The Austrian Mind: An Intellectual and Social History, 1848–1938* (Berkeley: University of California Press, 1972), 274, and Helena Lorenzová, "Bernard Bolzano—estetik," in *Osamělý myslitel, Bernard Bolzano,* 149 n. 25, 171, characterize Bolzano as Leibniz's follower. Helmut Rumpler, "Bolzano als Grenzgänger zwischen Freiheit und Ordnung," in *Bernard Bolzano und die Politik,* 13, however, sees Bolzano constructing his philosophical position in opposition to both Kant and Leibniz.

176. Bolzano, *Wissenschaft und Religion in Vormärz,* 324.

177. On Seibt's philosophical orientation, see chapter 7 in this volume.

Chapter 9

1. Cited by Anthony Kenny, *An Illustrated Brief History of Western Philosophy*, 2nd ed. (Oxford: Blackwell, 2006), 302.
2. Ibid.
3. A. James Gregor, *Mussolini's Intellectuals: Fascist Political and Social Thought* (Princeton, N. J.: Princeton University Press, 2005), 152–53, 74–75, 88, 148, 151, 162; Paul Franco, "Hegel and Liberalism," *Review of Politics* 59 (1997): 860; Jaroslava Pešková, *Role vědomí v dějinách* (Prague: Lidové noviny, 1997), 81; George H. Sabine, *A History of Political Theory*, 4th ed., rev. Thomas L. Thorson (Fort Worth, Tex.: Holt, Rinehart, and Winston, 1973), 604.
4. Donald M. Borchert, ed., *The Encyclopedia of Philosophy*, 2nd ed. (New York: Macmillan, 2006), 1:543; ADB, 2:327–28. The book in question was Friedrich Eduard Beneke, *Grundlegung zur Physik der Sitten, ein Gegenstück zu Kants Grundlegung zur Metaphysik der Sitten* (Berlin und Posen: In commission bei E. S. Mittler, 1822). Altenstein's full name was Karl vom Stein zum Altenstein; *Neue Deutsche Biographie* (Berlin: Duncker & Humblot, 1953–), 1:216.
5. "Altenstein hat der Hegelschen Philosophie die Tore der preussischen Hochschulen weit geöffnet, und nicht zu Unrecht konnte man unter der Ära Altenstein-Schulze die Hegelsche Lehre als offizielle preussische Philosophie bezeichnen." *Neue Deutsche Biographie*, 1: 216–17.
6. He wrote to William Whewell: "Bei uns in Deutschland . . . Die eigentlichen Philosophen dünken sich auf ihren eigebildeten speculativen Thronen viel zu vornehm, als dass ich in der nächsten Zukunft auf Mitarbeiter hoffen könnte. Vielleicht wären in dem praktischen England solche zu gewinnen." Friedrich Eduard Beneke, *Ungedruckte Briefe*, ed.Renato Pettoello and Nikola Barelmann (Aalen, Germany: Scientia, 1994), 228. See also his letter to John F. Herschel, ibid., 222.
7. *Allgemeine Deutsche Biographie*, 2nd ed. (Berlin: Duncker und Humblot, 1968), 51:532.
8. Friedrich A. Lange's *Geschichte des Materialismus und Kritik seiner Bedeutung in der Gegenwart*, ed. Alfred Schmidt (Frankfurt a. M.: Suhrkamp, 1974), 2:512–13.
9. Sidney Hook, "A Personal Impression of Contemporary German Philosophy," *Journal of Philosophy* 27 (1930): 145.
10. Ibid., 144–46. See also Barry Smith, *Austrian Philosophy: The Legacy of Brentano* (Chicago: Open Court, 1994), 13.
11. Philipp Frank, *Modern Science and Its Philosophy* (Cambridge: Harvard University, 1949), 47–48.
12. See, for instance, Hubert Schleichert, ed., *Logischer Empirismus: der Wiener Kreis* (Munich: Fink, 1975), 7.
13. Max Wundt, "Die Philosophie in der Zeit des Biedermeiers," *Deutsche Vierteljahrsschrift für Literatur* 13 (1935): 128.
14. Pešková, *Role vědomí v dějinách*, 6–7, 80, 100.
15. On the relationship between Marx and Hegel, see, for instance, Richard Rorty, "The End of Leninism, Havel, and Social Hope," in his *Truth and Progress, Philosophical Papers* 3 (New York: Cambridge University Press, 1998), 232–36; Allen Wood, "Hegel and Marxism," in *Cambridge Companion to Hegel*, ed. Frederick C.

Beiser (New York: Cambridge University Press, 1993), 414–44; Richard Wolin, *Heidegger's Children: Hannah Arendt, Karl Löwith, Hans Jonas, and Herbert Marcuse* (Princeton, N.J.: Princeton University Press, 2001), 140–41, 154–56. Concerning the Marxist-Leninist view of Hegel, see also Milan Znoj, "Bělohradského zúčtování s Hegelem," in *Hegel v Čechách, na Moravě a v Americe*, Sborník k životnímu jubileu Milana Sobotky, profesora Karlovy univerzity (Prague: Katedra filosofie FFUK, 1993), 17.

16. Cited by Masaryk, *Otázka sociální. Základy marxismu filosofické a sociologické*. Spisy 9–10 (Prague: Masarykův ústav AV ČR, 2000), 1:38. Engels sincerely meant his panegyric on Hegel that appeared in his book on Feuerbach, which ended with a statement: "The German working class movement is the heir to German classical philosophy." Friedrich Engels, "Ludwig Feuerbach and the End of German Classical Philosophy," in Karl Marx and Frederick Engels, *Collected Works* (New York: International Publishers, 1990), 26: 398, also 358–65; Masaryk, *Otázka sociální. Základy marxismu filosofické a sociologické*, 1:53.

17. Particularly, in his *Filosofskie tetradi* (Philosophical Notebooks), written in 1914–16, Lenin replaced the contrast between materialism and idealism with one between dialectical and nondialectical thinking; see, for instance, *Oxford Companion to Philosophy*, ed. Ted Honderich (New York: Oxford University Press, 1995), 480; *The Encyclopedia of Philosophy*, 5:280; Lenin's *Filosofskie tetradi* are published in V. I. Lenin, *Polnoe sobranie sochinenii*, 5th ed. (Moscow: Izdatel'stvo politicheskoi literatury, 1967–70), vol. 29; on Hegel and dialectic, see especially 316–22, including the characterization of Hegel's view as ingenious (*kak genial'no zametil Gegel'*), 318; otherwise extensive notes on *Science of Logic*, 77–218, and *History of Philosophy*, 219–90. Lenin relied on Georg W. F. Hegel, *Werke*, Vollständige Ausgabe (Berlin: Duncker and Humblot, 1832–45).

18. Zdeněk Nejedlý, "Slovo o české filosofii," *Var* no. 1 (1950): 5; Zdeněk Nejedlý, *T. G. Masaryk* (Prague: Melantrich, 1930–37); 2nd ed., vols. 1–2, Sebrané spisy, 31–32 (Prague: Orbis, 1949–950), 3:313. See also Irena Michňáková, "Z filosofického odkazu Augustina Smetany," in *Filosofie v dějinách českého národa* (Prague: Nakladatelství ČSAV, 1958), 158.

19. Milan Machovec, "Problematika dějin české filosofie," in *Filosofie v dějinách českého národa*, 28.

20. Josef Král, *Československá filosofie: Nástin vývoje podle disciplin* (Prague: Melantrich, 1937), 29.

21. Josef Zumr, "Některé otázky českého herbartismu," in *Filosofie v dějinách českého národa*,172; *Antologie z dějin českého a slovenského myšlení, do roku 1848*, ed. Ústav pro filozofii a sociologii ČSAV and Ústav pro filozofii a sociologii SAV (Prague: Svoboda, 1981), 513.

22. "I have been myself studying Hegel a lot, and I admire him greatly." Letter of Nov. 17 and Dec. 25, 1949, in Jan Patočka, *Dopisy Václavu Richterovi*, Sebrané spisy, 20, ed. Ivan Chvatík and Jiří Michálek (Prague: Oikoymenh, 2001), 22. Later Patočka published a translation of Hegel's *Esthetics* (Prague, 1966) and worked on a translation of Hegel's *Logic;* ibid., 114, n. 7. He also signaled an agreement with Hegel's quasi-deification of the state as an earthly absolute; see Jan Patočka, *Komeniologické studie*, vol. 2, Sebrané spisy, 10, ed. Věra Schifferová (Prague: Oikoymenh, 1998), 349. See also Pešková, *Role vědomí v dějinách*, 90.

23. Pešková, *Role vědomí v dějinách*, 79, 100. More specifically, Nejedlý erro-

neously attributed a rejection of all philosophy to one of the leading anti-Hegelians of the 1840s, Karel Havlíček; see Nejedlý, "Slovo o české filosofii," 2.

24. Tomáš G. Masaryk, *Česká otázka. Naše nynější krize.* Jan Hus, Spisy 6 (Prague: Masarykův ústav, 2000), 103.

25. Pešková, *Role vědomí v dějinách*, 90, 100; Jitka Lněničková, *České země v době předbřeznové, 1792–1848* (Prague: Libri, 1999), 394.

26. Karel Mácha, *Glaube und Vernunft: Die Böhmische Philosophie in geschichtlicher Übersicht* (Munich: Sauer, 1987), 2:54.

27. She makes an exception for the writings of Augustin Smetana; see Lněničková, *České země v době předbřeznové*, 394.

28. Marie Pavlíková, *Bolzanovo působení na pražské univerzitě* (Prague: Univerzita Karlova, 1985), 36; concerning Hegel's alleged influence on Mácha, see František Fajfr, "Hegel bei den Čechen," in Dmytro Chyzhevskyi, ed., *Hegel bei den Slaven* (Reichenberg: Stiepel, 1934), 437. On Palacký as a Hegelian and idealist philosopher, see Stanislav Souček, "Příspěvek k poznání Erbena básníka," *Časopis matice moravské* 39 (1916): 258, n. 1. Ivan Pfaff, *Česká přináležitost k Západu, 1815–1878* (Brno: Doplněk, 1996), 20.

29. On the "reactionary" character of Czech philosophy, see, for instance, Nejedlý, "Slovo o české filosofii," 9–10.

30. Marie Bayerová, "Rakouské filozofické myšlení konce 19. století v českém kulturním životě," in *Povědomí tradice v novodobé české kultuře: Doba Bedřicha Smetany* (Prague: Národní galerie, 1988), 129.

31. This was the view of Oskar Kraus, "Besonderheit und Aufgabe der deutschen Philosophie in Böhmen," *Actes du huitième Congrès de Philosophie à Prague, 2–7 Septembre 1934* (Prague, 1936), 766–71, cited by Bayerová, "Rakouské filozofické myšlení konce 19. století v českém kulturním životě," 129, 136.

32. Nejedlý, "Slovo o české filosofii," 14.

33. Ibid., 14.

34. Jiří Černý, "Předmluva: K filozofickým názorům Bernarda Bolzana," in Bernard Bolzano, *Výbor z filozofických spisů*, ed. Jiří Černý and Jaromír Loužil, trans. J. Loužil (Prague: Svoboda, 1981), 10.

35. Zumr, "Některé otázky českého herbartismu," 168.

36. Applying Hegel's dialectic to the Enlightenment as a negation of the Counter-Reformation; see Josef Haubelt, *České osvícenství*, 2nd rev. ed. (Prague: Rodiče, 2004), 176.

37. The conflict was viewed as merely between "two different versions of Catholic doctrine"; see Arnošt Kolman, "Matematicko-logická stránka Bolzanovy filosofie," *Filosofie v dějinách českého národa*, 134.

38. Jaromír Loužil, *Bernard Bolzano* (Prague: Melantrich, 1978), 175.

39. Karel Berka, "Předmluva," in Bernard Bolzano, *Vědosloví: výbor*, ed. Karel Berka, trans. Marie Bayerová and Jaromír Loužil (Prague: Academia, 1981), 12; Černý, "Předmluva: K filozofickým názorům Bernarda Bolzana," in Bolzano, *Výbor z filozofických spisů*, 10.

40. On the charge of reactionary Herbartism, sponsored by the Austrian government, see, for instance, Nejedlý, "Slovo o české filosofii," 5. For a positive view of Herbart's influence, see Josef Zumr, *Máme-li kulturu je naší vlastí Evropa: Herbartismus a česká filosofie* (Prague: Filosofia, 1998).

41. Irena Šnebergová, "Franz Serafin Exner a Praha: Vzestup a pád kariéry

univerzitního profesora; z exnerovské korespondence," in *Rozjímání vpřed i vzad: Karlu Kosíkovi k pětasedmdesátinám*, ed. Irena Šnebergová, Václav Tomek, and Josef Zumr (Prague: Filosofia, 2001), 259–60.

42. Ivo Tretera, *J. F. Herbart a jeho stoupenci na pražské univerzitě* (Prague: Univerzita Karlova, 1989), 151.

43. Eduard Winter, *Bernard Bolzano und sein Kreis* (Leipzig: Hegner, 1933), 257.

44. On the issue of Catholic Enlightenment, see evidence in chapter 4, note 111. On the place of religion in the Enlightenment, see also Jonathan Sheehan, "Enlightenment, Religion, and the Enigma of Secularization: A Review Essay," *American Historical Review* 108 (2003): 1061–80; Dale K. Van Kley, "Christianity as Casualty and Chrysalis of Modernity: The Problem of Dechristianization in the French Revolution," *American Historical Review* 108 (2003): 1081–1106; Robert Sullivan, "Rethinking Christianity in Enlightened Europe," *Eighteenth-Century Studies* 34 (2001): 299.

45. Bohdan Chudoba, *Jindy a nyní: dějiny českého národa* (Prague: Vyšehrad, 1946), 261.

46. See his characterization of Václav Stach; Bedřich Slavík, *Od Dobnera k Dobrovskému* (Prague: Vyšehrad, 1975), 178–79. For an unenthusiastic survey of Joseph II's religious reforms, see also Pavel Bělina, Jiří Kaše, and Jan P. Kučera, *Velké dějiny zemí Koruny české*, vol. 10, 1740–92 (Prague: Paseka, 2001), 102–9.

47. For instance, Bernhard Jansen, "Philosophen katholischen Bekenntnisses in ihrer Stellung zur Philosophie der Aufklärung," *Scholastik: Vierteljahresschrift für Theologie und Philosophie* (Freiburg i. B.), 11 (1936), 1–4.

48. Rudolf Zuber, *Osudy moravské církve v 18. Století* (Olomouc: Matice cyrilometodějská, 2003), 2:82, 152.

49. Haubelt, *České osvícenství*. 176–77.

50. Arnošt Kraus, *Husitství v literatuře zejména německé* (Prague: Česká akademie, 1917–24), 2:158–59.

51. Ibid., 2:182, 195.

52. Král, *Československá filosofie*, 25.

53. Bernard Bolzano, *Lehrbuch der Religionswissenschaft, Gesamtausgabe*, ed. Eduard Winter, Jan Berg, Friedrich Kambartel, Jaromír Loužil, and Bob van Rootselaar (Stuttgart-Bad Cannstatt: Frommann Holzboog, 1994–97), Reihe I, Schriften: Band 6, pt. 2, 118–19. See also Bernard Bolzano, *Wissenschaft und Religion in Vormärz: Der Briefwechsel Bernard Bolzanos mit Michael Josef Fesl, 1822–1848*, ed. Eduard Winter and W. Zeil (Berlin: Akademie-Verlag, 1965), 12–14.

54. He felt that this reluctance was evident particularly in Bavaria; see Bolzano, *Lehrbuch der Religionswissenschaft, Gesamtausgabe*, Reihe I, Schriften: Band 7, pt. 1, 51–52.

55. He notes especially Eduard Winter, *Der Josefinismus und seine Geschichte: Beiträge zur Geistesgeschichte Österreichs, 1740–1848* (Brno: Rohrer, 1943), and the Czech version, Eduard Winter, *Josefinismus a jeho dějiny. Příspěvky k duchovním dějinám Čech a Moravy, 1740–1848* (Prague, 1945); see Jiří Rak, "Doslov," in František Kutnar, *Obrozenské vlastenectví a nacionalismus* (Prague: Karolinum, 2003), 351.

56. See, for instance, Haubelt, *České osvícenství*. 266–67. The connection between second scholasticism and German idealism is discussed in chapter 7 of this volume.

57. Zdeněk V. David, *Finding the Middle Way: The Utraquists' Liberal Challenge to Rome and Luther* (Washington, D.C.: Woodrow Wilson Center Press; Baltimore: Johns Hopkins University Press, 2003), xvii, 3–4, 380.

58. Elena Várossová, "Hegelovské inšpirácie u Štúra a Hurbana," in Várossová, *Filozofia vo svete: svet filozofie u nás* (Bratislava: Veda, 2005), 161–80; Rudolf Dupkala, *Štúrovci a Hegel: k problematike slovenského hegelianizmu a antihegelianizmu*, 2nd ed. (Prešov: Manacon, 2000), 19–23, 39–45; Robert B. Pynsent, "Slávy Herder," in Robert B. Pynsent, *Dáblové, ženy a národ: Výbor z úvah o české literatuře* (Prague: Karolinum, 2008), 91–104.

59. Jan Jakubec, ed., *Literatura česká devatenáctého století*, with Josef Hanuš, Jan Máchal, and Jaroslav Vlček, 2nd ed. (Prague: Jan Laichter, 1911–17), 2:24–25.

60. Arne Novák, *Josef Dobrovský* (Prague: Mánes, 1928), 9; Mácha, *Glaube und Vernunft*, 1:119; Král, *Československá filosofie*, 22.

61. Fajfr, "Hegel bei den Čechen," 452–53. František M. Klácel published two articles in *Časopis českého musea* 17 (1843): "O citu a rozumu," 53–92, and "O smrti," 329–47.

62. In a letter of January 21, 1843, in Josef Emler, ed., "Listy Josefa Jungmanna k Antonínu Markovi," *Časopis českého musea* 58 (1884): 416. See also František Fajfr, "Měl Hegel vliv na českou literaturu?" *Česká mysl* 28 (1932): 97.

63. Josef Jungmann, *Zápisky*, ed. Radek Lunga (Prague: Budka, 1998), 47; Václav Zelený, *Život Josefa Jungmanna* (Prague: Matice Česká, 1873), 43.

64. Antonín Marek, *Základy filosofie: Logika. Metafysika* (Prague: Řivnáč, 1844), vii–viii. Jungmann specifically recommended Jäger's *Metaphysics* as a source to Marek; see letter of November 13, 1841; Emler, ed., "Listy Josefa Jungmanna k Antonínu Markovi," 410. He shared an early interest in Kiesewetter with Marek; see letter of August 28, 1816, Josef Emler, ed., "Listy Antonína Marka k Josefu Jungmannovi," *Časopis českého musea* 62 (1888): 157. He also advised on the structure of Marek's textbook; see ibid., 66 (1892): 460.

65. Fajfr, "Měl Hegel vliv na českou literaturu?" 9. Despite the scrupulous avoidance of German idealism, the Austrian censor treated Marek's textbook with suspicion; see Josef Emler, ed., "Ještě několik listů Josefa Jungmanna k Antonínu Markovi," *Časopis českého musea* 60 (1886): 444.

66. "Jak dalece jeho zatmnělým sadám vyrozuměti lze"; see Marek, *Základy filosofie*, 263.

67. Ibid., viii.

68. See Georg W. Hegel, "Wie der gemeine Menschenverstand die Philosophie nehme, dargestellt an den Werken des Herrn Krugs," *Kritisches Journal der Philosophie* (Jena) 1, no. 1 (1802); reprinted in Georg W. Hegel, *Jenaer Schriften (1801–1807)*, Werke 2, ed. Eva Moldenh auer and Karl M. Michel (Frankfurt/M: Suhrkamp, 1970), 188–207. In his article, Hegel criticized Krug's *Entwurf eines neuen Organon's der Philosophie: oder Versuch über die Prinzipien der philosophischen Erkenntniss* (Meissen: Erbstein, 1801), and accused Krug of naive realism and philosophical dilettantism; ibid. 205–7. Krug's response was entitled *Wie der ungemeine Menschenverstand die Philosophie nehme* (Buxtehude, 1802). See *Allgemeine Deutsche Biographie*, 2nd ed. (Berlin: Duncker und Humblot, 1968), 17:221.

69. Wilhelm Traugott Krug, *Der Widerstreit der Vernunft mit sich selbst in der Versöhnungslehre dargestellt und aufgelöst. Nebst einem kurzen Entwurf zu einer philosophischen Theorie des Glaubens* (Züllichau: Darnmann, 1802).

70. See *Deutsche allgemeine Biographie*, 17:221. As late as 1835, Krug still attacked Hegel in two pamphlets, *Schelling und Hegel; oder, Die neueste Philosophie im Vernichtungs Kriege mit sich selbst Begriffen; ein Beitrag zur Geschichte der Philosophie des 19. Jahrhunderts* (Leipzig, 1835); and *Über das Verhältnis der Philosophie zum gesunden Menschenverstande, zur öffentlichen Meinung und zum Leben selbst, mit besonderer Hinsicht auf Hegel. Noch ein Beitrag zur Geschichte der Philosophie des 19. Jahrhunderts* (Leipzig, 1835).

71. *The Encyclopedia of Philosophy*, ed. Paul Edwards (New York: Macmillan, 1967), 3:253.

72. See Georg W. Hegel, *Differenz des Fichte'schen und Schelling'schen Systems der Philosophie in Beziehung auf Reinhold's Beiträge zur leichtern Übersicht der Philosophie zu Anfang des neunzehnten Jahrhunderts* (Jena: Akademische Buchhandlung, 1801), which is reprinted in Georg W. Hegel, *Jenaer Schriften, 1801–1807*, Werke 2, ed. Eva Moldenhauer and Karl M. Michel (Frankfurt/M: Suhrkamp, 1970), 9, 121, 132–36; and Christoph G. Bardili, *Grundriss der ersten Logik, gereiniget von den Irrthümmern bisheriger Logiken überhaupt, der Kantischen insbesondere: keine Kritik sondern eine medicina mentis, brauchbar hauptsächlich für Deutschlands kritische Philosophie* (Stuttgart: Franz C. Löflund, 1800).

73. Fajfr, "Hegel bei den Čechen," 452.

74. Vincenc Zahradník, *Filosofické spisy*, ed. František Čáda (Prague: Česká akademie pro vědy slovesnost a umění, 1907–8), 1:71–72.

75. Ibid., 1:92.

76. Ibid., 1: 7–15, 89, 181.

77. Fajfr, "Měl Hegel vliv na českou literaturu?" 10.

78. Zahradník, *Filosofické spisy*, 2:142–43. On his relationship to Bolzano, see ibid., 1:79–82. In the area of moral philosophy, he also found attractive the skeptic Michel de Montaigne appreciating his good sense, wittiness, and richness of thought; ibid., 2:180–81. On the debate, see also František Kryštůfek, *Dějiny církve katolické ve státech rakousko-uherských se zláštním zřetelem k zemím koruny české*, vol. 1: 1740–1848 (Prague: Kotrba, 1898), 356–79.

79. *Slovník českých filozofů*, ed. Jiří Gabriel (Brno: Masarykova Univerzita, 1998), 644.

80. Karel Alois [Vinařický], *Korespondence a spisy [pamětní]*, Sbírka prameny ku poznání literárního života v Čechách, na Moravě a ve Slezsku], Skupina 2, číslo 6, 13, 19, 24, ed. Václav Otakar Slavík (Prague: Česká akademie pro vědy, slovesnost a umění, 1903, 1909, 1914, 1925), 2:493–95. On Klácel's Hegelian articles, see ibid., 487 n.1.

81. Ibid., 2:487.

82. Ibid., 2:501. In a lighter vein, Tyl poked fun at Hegel in an article of 1845. He has his hero say, "I breathed in the Hegelian climate in Berlin; in Munich I drank goat beer." Josef K. Tyl, *Národní zábavník: Publicistika,1833–1845*, Spisy 11 (Prague: Odeon, 1981), 568.

83. Hana Šmahelová, "Bernard Bolzano a české národní obrození," *Český časopis historický*, 100 (2002): 74–115; Bernard Bolzano, *24 Erbauungsreden, 1808–1820*, ed. Kurt F. Strasser (Vienna: Böhlau, 2001). On Bolzano's critique of Kant, see Marie Bayerová, *Bernard Bolzano. Evropský rozměr jeho filosofického myšlení* (Prague: Filosofia, 1994), 23–45.

84. Loužil, *Bernard Bolzano*, 12.

85. Eduard Winter, *Der Josefinismus: die Geschichte des österreichischen Reformkatholizismus, 1740–1848* (Berlin: Rütten & Loening, 1962), 266.
86. Kenny, *An Illustrated Brief History of Western Philosophy*, 302.
87. Helmut Rumpler, ed., *Bernard Bolzano und die Politik: Staat, Nation und Religion als Herausforderung für die Philosophie im Kontext von Spätaufklärung, Frühnationalismus und Restauration.* Studien zu Politik und Verwaltung, Band 61 (Vienna: Böhlau, 2000), 59.
88. Isaiah Berlin, *Freedom and Its Betrayal: Six Enemies of Human Liberty*, ed. Henry Hardy (Princeton: Princeton University Press, 2002), 94.
89. Georg W. F. Hegel, *Wissenschaft der Logik*; vol. 1, pt. 1: *Die objektive Logik: Das Sein*; pt. 2: *Die Lehre vom Wesen*; vol. 2: *Die subjektive Logik oder Lehre vom Begriff* (Nurenberg, 1812–16); see Bernard Bolzano, *Philosophische Tagebücher, Gesamtausgabe*, Reihe II, Nachlass, B. Wissenschaftliche Tagebücher; Band 16, pt. 1, 1811–17, 195, 214. Georg W. F. Hegel, *Encyklopädie der philosophischen Wissenschaften im Grundrisse* (Heidelberg, 1817); see Bolzano, *Philosophische Tagebücher, 1817–1827, Gesamtausgabe*, Reihe II, Nachlass, B. Wissenschaftliche Tagebücher; Band 17, 140.
90. "Nicht immer die der Gleichheit, Gesteht auch, dass überall Verwirrung und Inconsequenz herrsche." Bolzano, *Philosophische Tagebücher, 1817–1827, Gesamtausgabe*, Reihe II, Nachlass, B. Wissenschaftliche Tagebücher; Band 17, 34.
91. Ibid., 88–89, 111. The reference is to Rixner's *Aphorismen der gesammten Philosophie* (Sulzbach, 1818), 1:4.
92. Bolzano, *Philosophische Tagebücher, 1827–1844, Gesamtausgabe*, Reihe II, Nachlass, B. Wissenschaftliche Tagebücher; Band 18, pt. 2, 47.
93. Ibid., 49–50. Later he noted the assertion of Karl Rosenkranz that Hegel himself privately and good-humoredly stated that his system did not mean the end of philosophy, ibid., 2:59, referring to Heinrich M. Chalybäus, "Natur- und Geistesphilosophie," *Zeitschrift für Philosophie und spekulative Theologie*, 3 (Bonn, 1839), 165.
94. ". . . lese ich oft viele Blätter, ohne im mindesten erraten zu können, was er mit all dem sagen, was er hier loben oder tadeln wolle und wie dies alles nur zu der Überschrift komme." Bolzano, *Wissenschaft und Religion in Vormärz*, 72, referring to Georg W. Hegel, *Phänomenologie des Geistes*, ed. J. Schulze (Berlin, 1832).
95. "Was werden Sie dazu sagen, wenn ich gestehe, dass ich seit mehr als 6 Wochen beinahe nichts anderes tue als lesen, Hegelschen und andern Unsinn lesen?" Bolzano, *Wissenschaft und Religion in Vormärz*, 205.
96. "Mit welchem Gedanken wir uns trösten wollen." See Bolzano, *Philosophische Tagebücher, 1827–1844, Gesamtausgabe*, Reihe II, Nachlass, B. Wissenschaftliche Tagebücher; Band 18, pt. 2, 55.
97. "Ist es nicht eine *Contradictio in adjecto*, noch etwas mehr von einer Sache kennen lernen zu wollen, als—welche Beschaffenheiten sie habe? Was heisst denn sonst sie kennen lernen? Ihr Wesen sagst du? Aber was ist das Wesen einer Sache, als der Inbegriff gewisser Beschaffenheiten derselben." See Bolzano, *Philosophische Tagebücher, 1827–1844, Gesamtausgabe*, Reihe II, Nachlass, B. Wissenschaftliche Tagebücher; Band 18, pt. 2, 55.
98. "Diese Stelle ist das offenste Geständnis, das man wünschen kann." See Bernard Bolzano, *Philosophische Tagebücher, 1827–1844, Gesamtausgabe*, Reihe II, Nachlass, B. Wissenschaftliche Tagebücher; Band 18, pt. 2, 59. Bolzano referred

to Heinrich M. Chalybäus, "Natur- und Geistesphilosophie," *Zeitschrift für Philosophie und spekulative Theologie*, 3 (Bonn, 1839): 189. Chalybäus was also the author of *Historische Entwickelung der spekulativen Philosophie von Kant bis Hegel* (Dresden: C. F. Grimmer, 1837).

99. For an analysis, see also Jindřich Zelený, "O kritice Hegelovy logiky v Bolzánově vědosloví," *Filozofický časopis* 29 (1981): 845–55.

100. "Denn auch hier ist ja noch der Gedanke von meinem Gedanken nicht eben derselbe, sondern ein anderer Gedanke." Bernard Bolzano, *Wissenschaftslehre, Gesamtausgabe*, ed. Eduard Winter, Jan Berg, Friedrich Kambartel, Jaromír Loužil, and Bob van Rootselaar (Stuttgart-Bad Cannstatt: Frommann Holzboog, 1979); Reihe I, Schriften: Band 11, 1:60–61, referring to Georg W. Hegel, *Wissenschaft der Logik*, Erster Band. Die objektive Logik (Nurnberg, 1812), xii.

101. Bolzano, *Wissenschaftslehre, Gesamtausgabe*, Reihe I, Schriften: Band 11, 1:132, referring to Georg W. Hegel, *Enzyklopädie der philosophischen Wissenschaften im Grundrisse* (Heidelberg, 1817), 83.

102. Bolzano, *Wissenschaftslehre, Gesamtausgabe*, Reihe I, Schriften: Band 11, 1:194, referring to Hegel's statement: "Zweifelt der Zweifler am Zweifel selbst, so verschwindet der Zweifel." Cited from Georg W. Hegel, *Vorlesungen über die Philosophie der Religion*, 1: 71, in Georg W. Hegel, *Werke*, ed. D. Ph. Marheineke (Berlin, 1832–42). See also Bernard Bolzano, *Vermischte philosophische und physikalische Schriften, 1832–1848, Gesamtausgabe*, Reihe II, Nachlass A, Band 12, pt. 2, 106.

103. Bolzano, *Wissenschaftslehre, Gesamtausgabe*, Reihe I, Schriften: Band 11, 1:229–30, referring to Hegel's statement: "Es ist eines der *Grundvorurtheile* des bisherigen Logik und des gewöhnlichen Vorstellens, als ob der *Widerspruch* nicht eine eben so wesentliche und immanente Bestimmung sey, als die Identität; ja wenn von Rangordnung die Rede wäre, so wäre der Widerspruch für das *Tiefere* und *Wesenhaftere* zu nehmen." Cited from Georg W. Hegel, *Wissenschaft der Logik*. Erster Band. Die objektive Logik. Zweites Buch. Die Lehre vom Wesen (Nurnberg, 1813), 77–79. On the falsity of Hegel's concept of contradictions, see also Bolzano, *Vermischte philosophische und physikalische Schriften, 1832–1848, Gesamtausgabe*, Reihe II, Nachlass A, Band 12, 1:105.

104. Bolzano, *Vermischte philosophische und physikalische Schriften, 1832–1848, Gesamtausgabe*, Reihe II, Nachlass A, Band 12, 2:56–57.

105. Bolzano, *Wissenschaftslehre, Gesamtausgabe*, Reihe I, Schriften: Band 11, 2:90–91, referring to Georg W. Hegel, *Wissenschaft der Logik*. Zweiter Band. Die subjective Logik oder Lehre vom Begriff (Nurnberg, 1816), 58.

106. Bernard Bolzano, *Mathematisch-Physikalische und Philosophische Schriften, 1842–1843, Gesamtausgabe*, Reihe I, Schriften, Band 18, 101; see also 200.

107. Bolzano, *Wissenschaftslehre, Gesamtausgabe*, Reihe I, Schriften: Band 11, 2:225–26, referring to Georg W. Hegel, *Wissenschaft der Logik*. Erster Band. Die objektive Logik. (Nuremberg, 1812), 37.

108. Bolzano, *Vermischte philosophische und physikalische Schriften, 1832–1848, Gesamtausgabe*, Reihe II, Nachlass A, Band 12, 1:117, referring to Georg W. Hegel, *Wissenschaft der Logik* (Nuremberg, 1812–16).

109. Bolzano, *Vermischte philosophische und physikalische Schriften, 1832–1848, Gesamtausgabe*, Reihe II, Nachlass A, Band 12, 1:105.

110. Ibid., 1:118–19.

111. Bolzano, *Wissenschaftslehre, Gesamtausgabe*, Reihe I, Schriften, Band 13,

Notes to Pages 187–189   351

1:27, referring to Georg W. Hegel, *Wissenschaft der Logik. Zweiter Band. Die subjective Logik oder Lehre vom Begriff* (Nuremberg, 1816), 36–70.

112. Bolzano, *Wissenschaftslehre, Gesamtausgabe*, Reihe I, Schriften, Band 13, 1:55, referring to Georg W. Hegel, *Wissenschaft der Logik. Zweiter Band. Die subjective Logik oder Lehre vom Begriff* (Nuremberg, 1816), 56.

113. Bolzano, *Vermischte philosophische und physikalische Schriften, 1832–1848, Gesamtausgabe*, Reihe II, Nachlass A, Band 12, 1:144.

114. "Uebrigens sehen wir (aus Hegels Werken . . . .) dass er den Nutzen der Logik gar nicht verkannt habe." Bolzano, *Wissenschaftslehre, Gesamtausgabe*, Reihe I, Schriften, Band 11, 2:68–69.

115. These notes appear under the title "Verbesserungen und Zusätze zur Logik" in Bolzano, *Vermischte philosophische und physikalische Schriften, 1832–1848, Gesamtausgabe*, Reihe II, Nachlass A, Band 12, 2:53–184.

116. Bolzano, *Vermischte philosophische und physikalische Schriften, 1832–1848, Gesamtausgabe*, Reihe II, Nachlass A, Band 12, 2:84, referring to Georg W. F. Hegel, *Naturrecht und Staatswissenschaft im Grundrisse . . . Grundlinien der Philosophie des Rechts* (Berlin, 1821).

117. Bolzano, *Vermischte philosophische und physikalische Schriften, 1832–1848, Gesamtausgabe*, Reihe II, Nachlass A, Band 12, 2:85–86.

118. Ibid., 2:136.

119. He challenged Hegel's assertion "Der Widerspruch ist der Wurzel aller Bewegung and Lebendigkeit." Bolzano, *Vermischte philosophische und physikalische Schriften, 1832–1848, Gesamtausgabe*, Reihe II, Nachlass A, Band 12, 2:86, referring to Georg W. Hegel, *Wissenschaft der Logik*, Erster Band. Die objektive Logik, 2. Die Lehre vom Wesen (Nuremberg, 1813), 77–79. See also ibid., 153.

120. The quotation from Socrates was "What I understand about it is excellent, and so I presume that what I do not understand might be excellent as well." ["Was ich davon verstehe, ist vortrefflich, und so vermuthe ich, es möge auch das vortrefflich sein, was ich nicht verstehe."] See Bolzano, *Vermischte philosophische und physikalische Schriften, 1832–1848, Gesamtausgabe*, Reihe II, Nachlass A, Band 12, 2:128.

121. Bolzano, *Mathematisch-Physikalische und Philosophische Schriften, 1842–1843, Gesamtausgabe*, Reihe I, Schriften, Band 18, 121.

122. Ibid., 184, referring to Georg W. F. Hegel, *Werke,* vol. 10/1: *Vorlesungen über die Ästhetik* (Berlin, 1835), 34.

123. Bolzano, *Mathematisch-Physikalische und Philosophische Schriften, 1842–1843, Gesamtausgabe*, Reihe I, Schriften, Band 18, 196.

124. Ibid., 200.

125. See, for instance, Bolzano, *Vermischte philosophische und physikalische Schriften, 1832–1848, Gesamtausgabe*, Reihe II, Nachlass A, Band 12, 3:39, 63, 77.

126. "Idee überhaupt ist nichts Anderes als der *Begriff*, die *Realtät* des Begriffes und die *Einheit* beider." See Bernard Bolzano, *Mathematisch-Physikalische und Philosophische Schriften, 1842–1843, Gesamtausgabe*, Reihe I, Schriften, Band 18, 201, citing Georg W. F. Hegel, *Werke,* vol. 10/1: *Vorlesungen über die Ästhetik* (Berlin, 1835), 137.

127. "Dass der Begriff als ideelle Einheit und Allgemeinheit *sich selbst negire,* und, was diese in sich schloss, *zu realer selbständiger Objectivität entlasse.*" Bolzano, *Mathematisch-Physikalische und Philosophische Schriften, 1842–1843, Gesamtaus-*

gabe, Reihe I, Schriften, Band 18, 202–3, citing Georg W. F. Hegel, *Werke*, vol. 10/1: *Vorlesungen über die Ästhetik* (Berlin, 1835), 142.

128. Bolzano, *Mathematisch-Physikalische und Philosophische Schriften, 1842–1843, Gesamtausgabe*, Reihe I, Schriften, Band 18, 206–7. See also Helena Lorenzová, "Bernard Bolzano—estetik," in *Osamělý myslitel, Bernard Bolzano*, ed. Kateřina Trlifajová (Prague: Filosofia, 2006), 148.

129. "Seine Lehre hält Hegel, wie man sieht, für das absolute Evangelium." See Bolzano, *Vermischte philosophische und physikalische Schriften, 1832–1848, Gesamtausgabe*, Reihe II, Nachlass A, Band 12, 2:184, referring to Joseph Willm, *Essai sur la philosophie de Hegel. Seconde partie*, in *Revue germanique* (Paris) 3rd series, 9 (1837), 32–33. The first part appeared in Strasbourg (F.G. Levrault, 1836).

130. "Hegel, der mit dem Glauben starb, dass er durch seine Philosophie den lieben Gott erst zu einem vollendeten Selbstbewusstsein gebracht hat." See Bolzano, *Vermischte philosophische und physikalische Schriften, 1832–1848, Gesamtausgabe*, Reihe II, Nachlass A, Band 12, 3:14.

131. Bernard Bolzano, *Drei philosophische Abhandlungen welche auch von Nichtphilosophen sehr wohl verstanden werden können*, ed. František Příhonský (Leipzig: Reclam,1851), included in Bolzano, *Vermischte philosophische und physikalische Schriften, 1832–1848, Gesamtausgabe*, Reihe II, Nachlass A, Band 12, 3:43–104. See also Bernard Bolzano, *Der böhmische Vormärz in Briefen B. Bolzanos an F. Příhonský, 1824–1848: Beiträge zur deutsch-slawischen Wechselseitigkeit*, ed. Eduard Winter, Deutsche Akademie der Wissenschaften zu Berlin. Institut für Slawistik. Veröffentlichungen, nr. 11 (Berlin: Akademie-Verlag, 1956), 215; Bolzano, *Wissenschaft und Religion in Vormärz*, 228.

132. Georg W. Hegel, *Grundlinien der Philosophie des Rechts oder Naturrecht und Staatswissenschaft im Grundrisse*, ed. E Gans (Berlin, 1838); see Bolzano, *Wissenschaft und Religion in Vormärz*, 228.

133. Bolzano, *Vermischte philosophische und physikalische Schriften, 1832–1848, Gesamtausgabe*, Reihe II, Nachlass A, Band 12, 3:45.

134. "Was Gott thut, das ist wohl gethan." See Bolzano, *Vermischte philosophische und physikalische Schriften, 1832–1848, Gesamtausgabe*, Reihe II, Nachlass A, Band 12, 3:49.

135. Bolzano, *Vermischte philosophische und physikalische Schriften, 1832–1848, Gesamtausgabe*, Reihe II, Nachlass A, Band 12, 3:60.

136. "Über Hegels und seiner Anhänger Begriff von der Geschichte überhaupt und in besondere von der Geschichte der Philosophie," in Bolzano, *Vermischte philosophische und physikalische Schriften, 1832–1848, Gesamtausgabe*, Reihe II, Nachlass A, Band 12, 3:61–82.

137. Ibid., 3:61–62.

138. Ibid., 3:63.

139. Ibid., 3:80–81.

140. Ibid., 3:65–66.

141. Bolzano, *Vermischte philosophische und physikalische Schriften, 1832–1848, Gesamtausgabe*, Reihe II, Nachlass A, Band 12, 3:67. On Hegel's pantheism, see also Bolzano, *Lehrbuch der Religionswissenschaft*, *Gesamtausgabe*, Reihe I, Schriften: Band 6, pt. 2, 86.

142. Bolzano, *Vermischte philosophische und physikalische Schriften, 1832–1848, Gesamtausgabe*, Reihe II, Nachlass A, Band 12, 3:62.

143. The statement about Hegel: "die Sache gern auf die Spitze gestellt hat." See Bernard Bolzano, *Vermischte philosophische und physikalische Schriften, 1832–1848, Gesamtausgabe,* Reihe II, Nachlass A, Band 12, 3:77.
144. Ibid., 3:70.
145. Ibid., 3:71.
146. Ibid., 3:75–76.
147. Bolzano, *Vermischte philosophische und physikalische Schriften, 1832–1848, Gesamtausgabe,* Reihe II, Nachlass A, Band 12, 3:79–80, referring to August Cieszkowski, *Prolegomena zur Historiosophie* (Berlin: Veit, 1838), 105, 133; and Heinrich M. Chalybäus. "Natur und Geistesphilosophie," *Zeitschrift für Philosophie und speculative Theologie* 3 (Bonn, 1839): 192–93.
148. Otto Weiss, "Bolzanisten und Güntherianer in Wien 1848–1851," in Rumpler, ed., *Bernard Bolzano und die Politik,* 265 ff.
149. Letter to František Příhonský, September 17, 1832, in Eduard Winter, *Leben und geistige Entwicklung des Sozialethikers und Mathematikers, Bernard Bolzano* (Halle: Niemeyer, 1949), 35, 38; cited by Weiss, "Bolzanisten und Güntherianer in Wien 1848–1851," 266.
150. "Jetzt erscheint er mir als der schwachsinnige Nachbeter der immer die neuesten Ansichten für die wahrsten gehalten und nicht betrogen, sondern selbst getäuscht wurde." In a letter to Michael Fesl of August 1, 1845, cited by Winter, *Bernard Bolzano und sein Kreis,* 222. He was reacting to Karl Rosenkranz, *Georg Wilhelm Friedrich Hegels Leben* (Berlin: Duncker und Humblot, 1844). Curiously, this letter is not included in Bolzano, *Wissenschaft und Religion in Vormärz,* although there is a mention of the biography in Fesl's letter of July 26, 1844, to Bolzano, 340–41.

Chapter 10

1. František Fajfr, "Měl Hegel vliv na českou literaturu?" *Česká mysl,* 28 (1932): 93, is of the opinion that especially Klácel's excessive enthusiasm provoked the reaction against Hegel.
2. Karel Havlíček, "Literatura: *Časopis českého musea.* 1845. 4tý svazek," *Česká včela* 12 (1845): 378.
3. "We must note that among other nations, of a higher standing than the Germans, namely the English and the French, there is no great respect for German philosophy; and it is our wish, in general, that our fellow citizens would cherish more those two literatures (French and English)." Karel Havlíček, "Školácká filosofie," *Česká včela* 26 (1847): 142–43.
4. For an overview of this encounter, see Karel Mácha, *Glaube und Vernunft: Die Böhmische Philosophie in geschichtlicher Übersicht* (Munich: Sauer, 1987), 2:62–67; *Antologie z dějin českého a slovenského myšlení, do roku 1848,* ed. Ústav pro filozofii a sociologii ČSAV and Ústav pro filozofii a sociologii SAV (Prague: Svoboda, 1981), 511–13; Josef Král, *Československá filosofie: Nástin vývoje podle disciplin* (Prague: Melantrich, 1937), 28–29; Dmytro Chyzhevs'kyi, ed., *Hegel bei den Slaven* (Liberec [Reichenberg]: Stiepel, 1934), 452–56; Jan Khéres, "Literární spor o filosofii v letech 1844–48; příspěvek k dějinám české filosofie," *České vyšší gymnasium*

v Uherském Hradišti, Výroční zpráva, 1913-14, 3-29; Josef Pešek and František Čáda, "Karel Boleslav Štorch jako filosof," *Česká mysl* 14 (1913): 11-12; Ferdinand Pelikán, *Boj za svobodu české filosofie* (Prague: Janda, 1927).

5. Vilém Gabler, "Něco o filosofii," *Časopis českého musea* 21/1 (1847): 269-91. Gabler was a student of Exner; see Fajfr, "Měl Hegel vliv na českou literaturu?" 99, n. 44.

6. Karel Havlíček, "Školácká filosofie," *Česká včela* 26 (1847): 142. See also, Karel Havlíček, "Literatura," *Česká včela* 12 (1845): 378. Even a friendly critic of Hegel stresses the difficulty of his style: "His writings are difficult, even infuriating —laden with impenetrable and pretentious jargon from which his meaning can be separated only with skilled and careful surgery, even then usually not without risk of mortal injury." See Allen W. Wood, editor's introduction to *Elements of the Philosophy of Right,* by Georg W. F. Hegel, trans. H. B. Nisbet (New York: Cambridge University Press, 1991), xxvii.

7. See Augustin Smetana, "Wie einige čechische Literaten die deutsche Philosophie nehmen," *Ost und West* 11 (1847): 193-95, 197-99, 201-4, 205-8; Josef Jiří Kolár, "Offenes Sendschreiben an den Redakteur der böhmischen Zeitschrift *Včela,*" *Ost und West* 11 (1847): 237-38, 241-43, 245-46; reprinted in František Čupr, *Sein oder Nichtsein der deutschen Philosophie in Böhmen* (Prague: G. Haase Söhne, 1847), 87-100.

8. Karel Havlíček, "Odporné, ale zdravé," *Česká včela* 14, no. 43 (1847): 171-72.

9. Vilém Gabler, "Erwiderung auf Herrn Dr. Smetana's Aufsatz," in *Sein oder Nichtsein der deutschen Philosophie in Böhmen,* ed. František Čupr (Prague: G. Haase Söhne, 1847), 119.

10. Karel Havlíček, "Med a vosk," *Česká včela* 14, no. 58 (1847): 232. See also Karel Havlíček, "Seiendes," *Česká včela* 14, no. 41 (1847): 164; Karel Havlíček, "Žihadlo," *Česká včela* 14, no. 46 (1847):184.

11. Václav B. Nebeský, "Několik slov o filosofii," *Časopis českého musea* 20 (1846): 235.

12. Ibid., 234.

13. Ibid., 238.

14. Karel Štorch, "Hlas o německé literatuře," *Květy* 14, no. 67 (1847): 267.

15. Review of G. Mohnike, *Lessingiana* (Leipzig, 1844) in *Edinburgh Review* 82 (July-October 1845): 453.

16. Karel Štorch, "Filosofie a naše literatura: Několik myšlenek snad včas," pt. 1, *Časopis českého musea* 22 (1848): 65.

17. František Kutnar, Oldřich Králík, and Jaromír Bělič, *Tři studie o Palackém* (Olomouc: Palackého universita, 1949), 145-46; Jiří Kořalka, *František Palacký, 1798-1876: Životopis* (Prague: Argo, 1998), 518, citing Palacký's letter of November 4, 1872, deposited in Památník národního písemnictví, Prague.

18. Zdeněk V. David, "British Liberalism in the Czech National Awakening." *Kosmas* 22, no. 2 (2009): 5-7; Jiří Morava, *Palacký: Čech, Rakušan, Evropan,* 2nd ed. (Prague: Vyšehrad, 1998), 31-32; 35; Simeon Potter, "Palacký a anglické písemnictví," *Časopis Matice Moravské* 53 (1929): 93-94, 96-97; František Palacký, *Korrespondence a zápisky.* Sbírka pramenů ku poznání literárního života v Čechách, na Moravě a ve Slezsku, Skupina 2, Číslo 4-5, 16 (Prague: Česká akademie pro vědy, slovesnost a umění, 1898-1911), 1:20, 25.

19. See Jan Heidler, "O vlivu hegelismu na filosofii dějin a na politický program

Frant. Palackého," *Český časopis historický* 17 (1911): 1–12, 152–66; Jaroslava Pešková, *Role vědomí v dějinách* (Prague: Lidové noviny, 1997), 82, 85, 89; Kutnar, Králík, and Bělič, *Tři studie o Palackém*, 145–46; Fajfr, "Měl Hegel vliv na českou literaturu?" 11–13.

20. Fajfr, "Hegel bei den Čechen," in Chyzhevs'kyi, *Hegel bei den Slaven*, 436.

21. Josef V. Frič, *Paměti*, ed. Karel Cvejn (Prague: Státní nakladatelství krásné literatury, hudby a umění, 1957–63), 2:516.

22. Stanislav Souček, "Příspěvek k poznání Erbena básníka," *Časopis matice moravské*, 39 (1916): 258, n. 1.

23. A. J. Vrťátko, "Dopisy Františka Palackého Janu Kollárovi," *Časopis českého musea* (1879): 480, cited by Josef Fischer, *Myšlenka a dílo Františka Palackého* (Prague: Čin, 1926–27), 2:50–51. See also Zdenka Sojková, *Na rozhraní dvou věků: K politické publicistice Ľudovíta Štúra z let 1847–55* (Prague: Slovensko-český klub, 2007), 20.

24. Characteristically, Hegel himself considered the epistemological approach of the Scottish philosophy distinctly inferior to that of Kant. He took the Scottish philosophers to task for relying on external impressions as the source of knowledge rather than "on thought or reason as such" (*Denken, Vernunft als solche*). Georg W. F. Hegel, *Vorlesungen über die Geschichte der Philosophie* 3, Werke 20 (Frankfurt/M: Suhrkamp, 1971), 281–82.

25. For their assessment, see Josef Durdík, "O významu nauky Herbartovy," *Časopis českého musea* 50 (1876): 320.

26. *Slovník českých filozofů*, ed., Jiří Gabriel (Brno: Masarykova Univerzita, 1998), 158, 517.

27. Ibid., 158. Hanuš then published his main Hegelian work, *Die Wissenschaft des slawischen Mythus* (1842), ibid.

28. Pešková, *Role vědomí v dějinách*, 88; see also Fajfr, "Měl Hegel vliv na českou literaturu?" 93–96.

29. *Slovník českých filozofů*, 518; Fajfr, "Hegel bei den Čechen," in Chyzhevs'kyi, *Hegel bei den Slaven*, 437. For a discussion of Smetana's Hegelianism, see also Fajfr, "Měl Hegel vliv na českou literaturu?" 204–11. He tentatively adds the poet Václav B. Nebeský among Czech Hegelians during the 1840s; ibid., 13–16.

30. See Zdeněk V. David, "Anti-Romanticism in the National Awakening: The Case of Karel Hynek Mácha," *Moravia from World Perspective*, ed. Tomáš Motlíček and Miloslav Rechcígl (Ostrava: Repronis, 2006), 1:211–22.

31. Fajfr, "Hegel bei den Čechen," in Chyzhevs'kyi, *Hegel bei den Slaven*, 431, 476; Fajfr, "Měl Hegel vliv na českou literaturu?" 8–9.

32. For a recognition of this denouement as obstructing the emergence of a Marxist philosophical tradition in Bohemia through Hegelianism, see Fajfr, "Měl Hegel vliv na českou literaturu?" 13; *Antologie z dějin českého a slovenského filozofického myšlení*, 513.

33. Fajfr, "Měl Hegel vliv na českou literaturu?," 100, points out that Václav V. Tomek and Karel B. Štorch had early abandoned their youthful interest in Hegel.

34. Elena Várossová, "Hegelovské inšpirácie u Štúra a Hurbana," in Várossová, *Filozofia vo svete: svet filozofie u nás* (Bratislava: Veda, 2005), 162. See also chapter 6.

35. For instance, Štúr wrote in his letter of March 13, 1841: "Naše zásada jest od oné Reformátů rozdílná; naše jest pokroku, Reformati naproti tomu od století v

lenivosti a stojitosti vězí." See Ľudovít Štúr, *Listy*, ed. Jozef Ambruš and Vladimír Matula (Bratislava: Vydavateľstvo Slovenskej akadémie vied, 1954–99), 1:215.

36. Jan Jakubec, ed., *Literatura česká devatenáctého století*, with Josef Hanuš, Jan Máchal, and Jaroslav Vlček, 2nd ed. (Prague: Jan Laichter, 1911–17), 2:24–25.

37. On the transition from Herder to Hegel in Slovak thought, see Vladimír Macura, *Znamení zrodu: České národní obrození jako kulturní typ*, rev. ed. (Prague: H & H, 1995), 176.

38. "Tato škaredá potvora Hegelovské Vámi a vašinci zbožňované filosofie nejen Vaší hlavě, ale ani Vašemu srdci čest nedělá." See Kollár's letter of February 1846 in Štúr, *Listy*, Ambruš and Matula, eds., 4:100. He also cited a derisive comment about Hurban's "deep, high, and broad Hegelian philosophizing." See ibid., 4:115. Concerning Šafárik's attitude, see Jan Novotný, *Pavel Josef Šafařík* (Prague: Melantrich, 1971), 146.

39. Tomáš G. Masaryk, *Česká otázka. Naše nynější krize. Jan Hus*, Spisy 6 (Prague: Masarykův ústav, 2000), 329, 341, 343, 417–18.

40. Šafárik actually criticized Štúr's theories about the mission of the Slovak nation as based on Hegel's philosophy of history, which he viewed as overspeculative and abstract. See Novotný, *Pavel Josef Šafařík*, 146.

41. Chyzhevs'kyi, *Hegel bei den Slaven*, 397; Král, *Československá filosofie*, 32.

42. Samuel Št. Osuský, *Štúrova filozofia*, vol. 1 of *Filozofia Štúrovcov* (Myjava: Daniel Pažický, 1926), 22–24. As late as 1873, Franz Brentano could not find any English philosophical literature in the university library at Leipzig; see Oskar Kraus, *Franz Brentano: Zur Kenntnis seines Lebens und seiner Lehre*, with contributions from Carl Stumpf and Edmund Husserl (Munich: Beck, 1919), 130.

43. Osuský, *Štúrova filozofia*, 22–24.

44. Franz S. Exner, *Die Psychologie der Hegelschen Schule* (Leipzig: F. Fleischer, 1842), 2–3. See also chapter 11 in this volume.

45. Chyzhevs'kyi, *Hegel bei den Slaven*, 400.

46. Osuský, *Štúrova filozofia*, 27–28.

47. "Die höchste Errungenschaft des menschlichen Geistes." Cited by Chyzhevs'kyi, *Hegel bei den Slaven*, 397. The universities of Halle and Berlin were considered particularly attractive as flourishing centers of Hegel's philosophy. Berlin, however, was too expensive for Štúr; see Ján Bystrík, "K štúdiu Ľudovíta Štúra v Nemecku," *Historický sborník* 5 (1947): 217–18. In a letter of September 19, 1842, Štúr asked the brothers Hroboň to send him Hegel's *Vorlesungen über die Aesthetik*, ed. H. G. Holtho (Berlin: Drucker and Humblot, 1842–43); see Štúr, *Listy*, Ambruš and Matula, eds., 1:323, 583, n. 9. See also Josette A. Baer, *National Emancipation, Not the Making of Slovakia: Ľudovít Štúr's Conception of the Slovak Nation*, St. Francis Xavier University, Center for Post-Communist Studies, Studies in Post-Communism, Occasional Paper 2 (2003), 24–28; and Rudolf Dupkala, *Štúrovci a Hegel: k problematike slovenského hegelianizmu a antihegelianizmu*, 2nd ed. (Prešov: Manacon, 2000), 19–23.

48. See Štúr, *Listy*, Ambruš and Matula, eds., 1:323, 483, n. 11; (Blaškovič) 2:414, n.13; 3:157, n. 9.

49. See Štúr, *Listy*, Ambruš and Matula, eds., 1:599, n. 15; 604, n. 29, 370, 617, n. 9, (Gal) 2:377, n. 6; (Šulek) 2:405, n.15; (Hrenčík), 3:180, n. 6; (Lanštják), 3:218.

50. Elena Várossová, "Štefan Launer: apokryfný typ slovenského hegelovca," in Várossová, *Filozofia vo svete: svet filozofie u nás*, 185. For continuity between the

manifestation of the world spirit in physical nature and then in human reason, Launer appealed to Schelling; see Štefan Launer, *Povaha Slovanstva se zvláštním ohledem na spisovní řeč Čechů, Moravanů a Slováků* (Leipzig, Slovanské kněhkupectví, 1847), 30.

51. Launer, *Povaha Slovanstva*, 5–6. See also Várossová, "Štefan Launer: apokryfný typ slovenského hegelovca," 183.

52. Launer, *Povaha Slovanstva*, v, 31–32. See also Várossová, "Štefan Launer: apokryfný typ slovenského hegelovca," 184.

53. Várossová, "Štefan Launer: apokryfný typ slovenského hegelovca," 183, 187; citing also Štefan Launer, *Slovo k národu svému* (Banská Štiavnica, 1847).

54. Launer, *Povaha Slovanstva*, 83.

55. Ibid., 122.

56. Ibid., 112–13.

57. Josef Jirásek, "Úvod," in L'udovít Štúr, *Das Slawenthum und die Welt der Zukunft*, ed. Josef Jirásek (Bratislava: Učená společnost Šafaříkova, 1931), 8–9; Albert Pražák, *České obrození* (Prague: E. Beaufort, 1948), 321; Osuský, *Štúrova filozofia*, 50.

58. *Dejiny Slovenska*, ed. Samuel Cambel (Bratislava: Veda, 1986–88), 2:791.

59. Samuel Št. Osuský, *Filozofia Štúrovcov* (Myjava: Daniel Pažický, 1926–32), 1:132–35; Várossová, "Hegelovské inšpirácie u Štúra a Hurbana," 168.

60. L'udovít Štúr, "Přednášení historická," ed. J. Ambruš, *Otázky marxistickej filozofie* 20 (1965): 498.

61. Ibid., 20 (1965): 491–92, 494.

62. Várossová, "Hegelovské inšpirácie u Štúra a Hurbana," 179–80.

63. L'udovít Štúr, "Život domáci a pospolitý," in Štúr, *Hlas k rodákom* (Bratislava: Tatran, 1971), 174–75, 188–90.

64. Chyzhevs'kyi, *Hegel bei den Slaven*, 398, 401. According to Štúr, the Germans were not able to fulfill the universal historical purpose, as outlined by Hegel: it was to be accomplished by the Slavs. See his letter of November 8, 1842, in Štúr, *Listy*, Ambruš and Matula, eds., 1:334–36, 590, n. 5.

65. L'udovít Štúr, "Přednášení historická," in *Antologie z dějin českého a slovenského myšlení*, 549. These lectures were first published from manuscript as L'udovít Štúr, "Přednášení historická," in *Otázky marxistickej filozofi*, 20, ed. J. Ambruš (1965): 491–501. Osuský, *Štúrova filozofia*, 54–59.

66. "We will rework [Hegel's philosophy], but first we have to firmly appropriate it." Letter to Samo B. Hroboň of November 8, 1842, Štúr, *Listy*, Ambruš and Matula, eds., 1:336, 590, n. 3; 4:82, 223.

67. Frič, *Paměti*, 1:201.

68. Král, *Československá filosofie*, 32; Chyzhevs'kyi, *Hegel bei den Slaven*, 402–3. In contrast, Kollár took a negative view of Hegel in particular, as well as Kant and Schelling. For him, German idealism represented a one-sided outlook that would be overcome in the Slavic intellectual synthesis of the future, envisioned according to the principles of Herder; see Jan Kollár, *Rozpravy o slovanské vzájemnosti*, ed. Miloš Weingart (Prague: Slovanský ústav, 1929), 105–7. See also *Jan Kollár, 1793–1852. Sborník statí o životě, působení a literární činnosti pěvce 'Slávy dcery,'* ed. František Pastrnka (Vienna: Český akademický spolek, 1893), 209.

69. L'udovít Štúr, *Slavianstvo i mir budushchego* (Moscow: Obshchestvo istorii i drevnostei rossiiskikh, 1867); 2nd ed. (St. Petersburg: Obshchestvo revnitelei

russkogo istoricheskogo prosveshcheniia, 1909). The original German version has appeared as L'udovít Štúr, *Das Slawenthum und die Welt der Zukunft*, ed. Josef Jirásek (Bratislava: Učená společnost Šafaříkova, 1931).

70. Chyzhevs'kyi, *Hegel bei den Slaven*, 410–15; Štúr, *Das Slawenthum und die Welt der Zukunft*, 8–9, 30, 43–44, 47–59, 62–67, 98, 105–8, 209, 226. Jirásek located Štúr's borrowings in Georg W. F. Hegel, *Vorlesungen über die Philosophie der Geschichte*, Sämtliche Werke, 11 (Stuttgart: Frommanns Verlag, 1928); and Georg W. F. Hegel, *Grundlinien der Philosophie des Rechts oder Naturrecht und Staatswissenschaft im Grundrisse*, Sämtliche Werke, 7 (Stuttgart: Frommanns Verlag, 1928).

71. "Die ganze Geschichte steht im Dienste des Geistes." See Štúr, *Das Slawenthum und die Welt der Zukunft*, 51.

72. Osuský, *Štúrova filozofia*, 157–58; Štúr, *Das Slawenthum und die Welt der Zukunft*, 30.

73. Štúr, *Das Slawenthum und die Welt der Zukunft*, 8–11.

74. Štúr exhorted him to study in Germany in 1840 when he completed his schooling in Bratislava, but Hurban lacked the financial means; Samuel Št. Osuský, *Hurbanova filozofia*, vol. 2 of *Filozofia Štúrovcov* (Myjava: Daniel Pažický, 1928), 2–13.

75. Osuský, *Hurbanova filozofia*, 130–31.

76. Osuský, *Štúrova filozofia*, 28–31; *Antologie z dějin českého a slovenského filozofického myšlení*, 495, 538–40.

77. Chyzhevs'kyi, *Hegel bei den Slaven*, 399; Osuský, *Hurbanova filozofia*, 132–33.

78. Jozef M. Hurban, *Cesta Slováka k bratrům slovanským na Moravě a v Čechách* (Pest, 1841), 122, cited by Várossová, "Hegelovské inšpirácie u Štúra a Hurbana," 166. See also Chyzhevs'kyi, *Hegel bei den Slaven*, 404.

79. Jozef M. Hurban, "Slovansko a jeho život literárni," *Slovenskje pohladi na vedi, umeňja a literatúru*, 1 (1846), svazok 1, 16. See also Milan Pišút, "Jozef Miloslav Hurban," in *Jozef Miloslav Hurban; sborník pri príležitosti 150. v ýročia jeho smrti*, comp. Štefan Kopčan (Bratislava: Osvetový ústav, 1967), 8.

80. Jozef M. Hurban, "Předmluva k Červenánkovu Zrcadlu Slovenska," in Benjamín Pravoslav Červenák, *Zrcadlo Slovenska* (Pešt: Trattner-Károlyi, 1844), iii; also in *Antologie z dějin českého a slovenského myšlení*, 498.

81. Osuský, *Hurbanova filozofia*, 147.

82. Várossová, "Hegelovské inšpirácie u Štúra a Hurbana," 174.

83. Osuský, *Hurbanova filozofia*, 142.

84. Jozef M. Hurban, "Slovansko a jeho život literárni," *Slovenskje pohladi na vedi, umeňja a literatúru*, 1 (1846): svazok 1, 16–17.

85. Osuský, *Hurbanova filozofia*, 166–68.

86. Ibid., 170–71.

87. Eugen Gerometta, "Slovanou náklonnosť ku sloboďe," *Slovenskje pohladi na vedi, umeňja a literatúru* 1 (1847): svazok 2, 32. See also Osuský, *Hurbanova filozofia*, 132.

88. P. Z. H., "Prvoťini vedi slovanskej," *Slovenskje pohladi na vedi, umeňja a literatúru* 2 (1851):123.

89. Ibid., 122–23.

90. "Povedali sme na začjatku, že človek slovanskí je ostatní sin v povesťi ludstva, a že veda slovanská je amen všetkej vedi ludskej." See P. Z. H., "Prvoťini vedi slovanskej," 164, also 125, 165.

91. Jan Kalinčiak, "Boj o Slovenčinu. III. Slovo p. Lichardovi od J. Kalinčiaka," *Slovenskje pohladi na vedi, umeňja a literatúru* 2 (1851): 203–4, 208–9.
92. Ibid., 205–6.
93. Ibid., 210.
94. Samuel Št. Osuský, *Hodžova filozofia*, vol. 3 of *Filozofia Štúrovcov* (Myjava: Daniel Pažický, 1932), 166–67.
95. Ibid., 311–12, 334.
96. Ibid., 279–80.
97. Ibid., 303, 311–12, 305.
98. Várossová, "Hegelovské inšpirácie u Štúra a Hurbana," 173.
99. Jozef M. Hurban, *Unia, čili spojení luteránů s kalvíny v Uhrách* (Budín: J. Gyurián a M. Bagó, 1846), 168–69; Štúr, *Listy*, Ambruš and Matula, eds., 3:31.
100. Hurban, *Unia, čili spojení luteránů s kalvíny*, 116–17, 195.
101. Ibid., 127–28; Hurban, "Předmluva k Červenánkovu Zrcadlu Slovenska," in Červenák, *Zrcadlo Slovenska*, vii.
102. Hurban, *Unia, čili spojení luteránů s kalvíny*, 119, 121.
103. Hurban in his comments on the article by Gerometta, "Slovanou náklonnosť ku slobod'e," 32.
104. Vrťatko, "Dopisy Františka Palackého k Janu Kollárovi," 480. Štúr, in fact, maintained that, according to Hegel, the world spirit reached its objectification only through specific ethnic groups and their languages; Chyzhevs'kyi, *Hegel bei den Slaven*, 405. See also Pražák, *České obrození*, 288, 376. Hurban likewise appealed to Hegel's teaching to justify the national separation of the Slovaks from the Czechs; see Chyzhevs'kyi, *Hegel bei den Slaven*, 407.
105. Vendelín Grünwald, "Z Vídně," *Květy* 12 (1845): n. 111, 443.
106. Jozef M. Hurban, "Odpověd' na článek z Vídně," *Květy* 12 (1845): n. 139, 557–58. See also Fajfr, "Měl Hegel vliv na českou literaturu?" 98.
107. Hurban, "Odpověd' na článek z Vídně," 557–58.
108. Nebeský, "Několik slov o filosofii," 240–41.
109. Hurban, "Odpověd' na článek z Vídně," 559.
110. Ibid., 560.
111. Letters to Klácel of February and March 1848, in Štúr, *Listy*, Ambruš and Matula, eds. 2:185–88, also 2:448–49.
112. Hurban, "Odpověd' na článek z Vídně," 560.
113. Štúr, *Listy*, Ambruš and Matula, eds., 2:517.
114. On the broad and deep influence of Hegelianism in Poland—in contrast to its limited role in Western Europe—see Andrzej Walicki, *Philosophy and Romantic Nationalism: The Case of Poland* (Oxford: Clarendon Press, 1982), 6. Naturally, there were exceptions. There were Polish opponents of romanticism and metaphysical idealism like Jan Śniadecki, ibid., 100–101, as there were Czech devotees of Hegel, like Klácel; see Chyzhevs'kyi, *Hegel bei den Slaven*, 445–50, 456–67.
115. Josef Dobrovský, *Korrespondence*, Díl 2: *Vzájemné dopisy Josefa Dobrovského a Jiřího Samuela Bandtkeho z let 1810–1827*, Sbírka pramenů ku poznání literárního života v Čechách, na Moravě a ve Slezsku, Skupina 2, Číslo 8, ed. A. V. Francev (Prague: Česká akademie pro vědy, slovesnost a umění, 1906), 40. This elicited Dobrovský's famous characterization of the German idealist systems as "foolish fancy" (*Hirngespinst*); ibid., 48.
116. Walicki, *Philosophy and Romantic Nationalism*, 121.

117. James H. Billington, *Russia in Search of Itself* (Washington, D.C.: Woodrow Wilson Center Press; Baltimore: Johns Hopkins University Press, 2004), 10–15; James H. Billington, *The Icon and the Axe: An Interpretive History of Russian Culture* (New York: Random House, 1970), 324–28; Andrzej Walicki, *A History of Russian Thought from Enlightenment to Marxism* (Stanford, Calif.: Stanford University Press, 1979), 115–34; Nikolai Berdiaev, *The Russian Idea* (New York: Macmillan Company, 1948), 72–76.

118. A phenomenon described as "Catholic Enlightenment in Poland" lacked the pronounced antitridentine tenor, the tendency toward papal minimalism, and the antimonasticism in general and anti-Jesuitism in particular that were characteristic of Josephist Reform Catholicism. The "Catholic Enlightenment" Polish-style seemed to involve a social rather than an ecclesiastical reform; see Jerzy Kloczowski, *A History of Polish Christianity* (New York: Cambridge University Press, 2000), 173–90. See also Maciej Janowski, *Polish Liberal Thought up to 1918*, trans. Danuta Przekop (Budapest: Central European University Press, c2002).

119. Sebastian Merkle, *Die katholische Beurteilung des Aufklärungszeitalters* (Berlin: K. Curtius, 1909), 7–8.

120. Wojciech Tylkowski was considered prototypical of the Jesuit scholasticism in Poland; see *Z dziejów plskiej myśli filozoficznej i społecznej*, ed. Nina Assorodobraj (Warsaw: Ksiazka i wiedza, 1956–57), 1:39–40. Władyslaw Tatarkiewicz, *Historia filozofii*, 8th ed. (Warsaw: Państwowe wydawnictwo naukowe, 1978), 2:88.

121. Władyslaw Tatarkiewicz, *Zarys dziejów filozofii v Polsce* (Cracow: Polska akademia umiejętności, 1948), 11–12; Władyslaw Tatarkiewicz, *Historia filozofii*, 2:186. Frederick Copleston, *History of Philosophy* (London: Burns and Oates, 1947–66), 3:379; Kloczowski, *A History of Polish Christianity*, 179, 182–83.

122. George Krzywicki-Herburt, "Polish Philosophy," *The Encyclopedia of Philosophy*, ed. Paul Edwards (New York: Macmillan, 1967), 6:365; *Z dziejów polskiej myśli filozoficznej i społecznej*, ed. Assorodobraj, 2:20.

123. Janowski, *Polish Liberal Thought up to 1918*, 73.

124. Tatarkiewicz, *Historia filozofii*, 2:188. As noted earlier (note 114), an opposition to speculative metaphysics was voiced in Poland by Jan Śniadecki (1757–1830), who conceived of philosophy in the manner of British empiricism, particularly Reid, and anticipated the themes of later positivism; Krzywicki-Herburt, "Polish Philosophy," 6:365.

125. On Mochnacki, see *Z dziejów polskiej myśli filozoficznej i społecznej*, ed. Assorodobraj, 3:93–96, 102–18; on Gołuchowski, see Tatarkiewicz, *Historia filozofii*, 2:231–32. The famous poet Adam Mickiewicz remained a devotee of Schelling; see Pešek and Čáda, "Karel Boleslav Štorch jako filosof," 9.

126. Krzywicki-Herburt, "Polish Philosophy," 6:366; Tatarkiewicz, *Historia filozofii*, 2:232–35. A special place in Polish idealist philosophy is occupied by Józef Maria Hoene-Wroński (1778–1853), who spent most of his life in France as an exile. Independently of Hegel, but in a similar way, he attempted to create a system of "absolute philosophy," using Kantian metaphysics as a point of departure; ibid., 2:229–31.

127. Kremer had the distinction of having actually studied under Hegel in Berlin. In his *Wykład systematyczny filozofii* (Cracow, 1849–52), he tried to identify Hegel's absolute with the personal God of theistic Christianity and "replaced Hegelian 'panlogism' with a conception of parallelism between thought and Being;"

see Walicki, *Philosophy and Romantic Nationalism*, 123 ; Tatarkiewicz, *Historia filozofii*, 2:233.

128. August Cieszkowski, *Prolegomena zur Historiosophie* (Berlin: Veit, 1838).

129. Bernard Bolzano, *Vermischte philosophische und physikalische Schriften, 1832–1848*, in *Gesamtausgabe*, ed. Eduard Winter, Jan Berg, Friedrich Kambartel, Jaromír Loužil, and Bob van Rootselaar (Stuttgart-Bad Cannstatt: Frommann Holzboog, 1977–78), Reihe II, Nachlass A, Band 12, 3:62.

130. Ibid., 3:70.

131. Andrzej Walicki, *Philosophy and Romantic Nationalism*, 142–45, 173–76.

132. Dmytro Chyzhevs'kyi, *Gegel' v Rossii* (Paris: Dom knigi, [1939]), especially 12–31, 210–26, 260–65; Tomáš G. Masaryk, *The Spirit of Russia: Studies in History, Literature, and Philosophy*, trans. Eden and Cedar Paul, and W. R. and Z. Lee, 2nd ed. (London: Allen & Unwin, 1961–67), 1: 149–50, 217, 222; Boris V. Jakovenko, *Ein Beitrag zur Geschichte des Hegelianismus in Russland* (Prague: Bartl, 1934).

133. Nikolai A. Berdiaev, *The Origin of Russian Communism* (Ann Arbor: University of Michigan Press, 1960), 9, 20–21; see also Chyzhevs'kyi, *Gegel' v Rossii*, 10–11; Tomáš G Masaryk, *Slovanské studie a texty z let 1889–1891*, Spisy 20 (Prague: Masarykův ústav AV ČR, 2007), 96.

134. Zdeněk V. David, "The Influence of Jacob Boehme on Russian Religious Thought," *Slavic Review* 21 (1962): 43–64; Chyzhevs'kyi, *Gegel' v Rossii*, 7–10; Martin Žemla, "Svět Jakuba Boehma," in Jacob Boehme, *Cesta ke Kristu*, ed. Martin Žemla (Prague: Vyšehrad, 2003), 87.

135. On Boehme's influence on German idealism, see Andrew Weeks, *Boehme: An Intellectual Biography of the Seventeenth-Century Mystic* (Albany: State University of New York Press, 1991), 2–3, 90, 129, 207. See also Andrew Weeks, *German Mysticism from Hildegard of Bingen to Ludwig Wittgenstein: A Literary and Intellectual History* (Albany: State University of New York Press, 1993), 229; Chyzhevs'kyi, *Gegel' v Rossii*, especially, 12–31.

136. Masaryk, *The Spirit of Russia*, 1:122–23; cited by Jakovenko, *Ein Beitrag zur Geschichte des Hegelianismus in Russland*, 24.

137. Walicki, *Philosophy and Romantic Nationalism*, 296. On the attachment of the Poles and the Russians to the speculative philosophy of Hegel in contrast to the vogue of Herbart's realism in Bohemia, see also Josef Durdík, "Über die Verbreitung der Herbat'schen Philosophie in Böhmen," *Zeitschrift für exacte Philosophie im Sinne des neuen philosophischen Realismus* 11 (1875): 324.

138. Peter Simons, *Philosophy and Logic in Central Europe from Bolzano to Tarski* (Dordrecht: Kluwer, 1992), 7–8, 14–15, 157; Barry Smith, *Austrian Philosophy: The Legacy of Brentano* (Chicago: Court, 1994), 8; Lubomír Valenta, *Problémy analytické filozofie* (Olomouc: Nakladatelství Olomouc, 2003), 185–88. See also Marie Pavlíková, "Bolzanův odkaz," in Bernard Bolzano, *Vlastní životopis*, trans. and ed. Marie Pavlíková (Prague: Odeon, 1981), 158. On Twardowski and the Polish school of logic, later known as the L'viv-Warsaw School, see the epilogue to this book.

139. *Slovník českých filozofů*, ed. Gabriel, 158.

140. For instance, Král, *Československá filosofie*, 29; *Oxford Companion to Philosophy*, ed. Ted Honderich (New York: Oxford University Press, 1995), 174.

141. As, for instance, Ayer, "Demonstration of the Impossibility of Metaphysics," 339.

142. In Wales, Bishop Thirlwall expressed the following opinions in 1849:

My own examination of certain portions of Hegel's works, which I had occasion to study attentively, has impressed me with the deepest conviction that he is, to say the least, one of the most impudent of all literary quacks.... I do not believe that any genuine philosopher ever wrote a volume, or even a page, of what a well-informed contemporary could consider as arrant nonsense. Whether Hegel's volumes, after the subtraction of their commonplace, contain anything else, is more than I am, or probably ever shall be, able to say. I have so much faith in the force of truth as to believe that sooner or later Hegel's name will only be redeemed from universal condemnation by the recollection of the immense mischief he has done.

See Connop Thirlwall, *Letters, Literary and Theological*, ed. John J. Perowne and Louis Stokes (London: R. Bentley, 1881), 195, cited by John C. Thirlwall, *Connop Thirlwall: Historian and Theologian* (London: Society for Promoting Christian Knowledge, [1936]), 48. Thirlwall had held a membership in the *Matice česká* since 1847; Josef Hanuš, *Národní museum a naše obrození: k stoletému jubileu založení Musea* (Prague: Národní museum, 1921–23), 2:424; Karel Tieftrunk, *Dějiny Matice české* (Prague: Řivnáč, 1881), 133.

143. This was noted, for instance, by Mácha, *Glaube und Vernunft*, 3:66.

144. Exner, *Die Psychologie der Hegelschen Schule*, 26.

145. Friedrich Eduard Beneke, *Grundlegung zur Physik der Sitten, ein Gegenstück zu Kants Grundlegung zur Metaphysik der Sitten* (Berlin und Posen, In commission bei E. S. Mittler, 1822), ix. An advocate of empirical and realist epistemology, Beneke later encountered severe obstacles to replacing Hegel at the University of Berlin; Donald M. Borchert, ed., *The Encyclopedia of Philosophy*, 2nd ed. (New York: Macmillan, 2006), 1:543. In the area of ethics, Beneke stressed the superiority of Adam Smith's approach to Kant's categorical imperative; Beneke, *Grundlegung zur Physik der Sitten*, 253–65. Categorical imperatives were to him ineffectual "phantoms" (*Schattenbilder*), ibid., 343. He also questioned Kant's concept of reason (*Vernunft*), ibid., 306–7; and the idealist epistemology of Jacobi, Kant, Fichte, and Schelling, ibid., 344–54, especially 352.

146. "Wurm und Engel, Birke und Krystalldrüse und—Gott (?!)—," Beneke, *Grundlegung zur Physik der Sitten*, 297. In an 1844 letter to John F. W. Herschel, he expressed a fervent hope that Schelling's and Hegel's philosophies would soon be on the way to oblivion; Friedrich Eduard Beneke, *Ungedruckte Briefe*, ed. Renato Pettoello and Nikola Barelmann (Aalen, Germany: Scientia, 1994), 230.

147. Beneke, *Ungedruckte Briefe*, 11, 223, 226, 234, 238; see also "Whewell," *Dictionary of National Biography* (Oxford: Oxford University Press, 1921–22), 20:1365, 1367. Another English correspondent was the philosopher of science John F. W. Herschel, an adherent in epistemology to the Scottish common sense school; Beneke, *Ungedruckte Briefe*, 221, 229, 233, 237, 243, 273, 279; see also *The Encyclopedia of Philosophy*, 2nd ed., 4:339.

148. Václav B. Nebeský, "W. Shakespeare," *Časopis českého musea* 25 (1851): 125. He cites as examples the views of Karl Eduard Vehse, *Shakespeare als Protestant, Politiker, Psycholog und Dichter* (Hamburg, 1851), and Georg Gottfried Gervinus, *Shakespeare* (Leipzig, 1849–850).

149. Jungmann even referred to metaphysics as "the learning of all learning"

(*věda všech věd*); see Antonín Marek, *Základy filosofie: Logika. Metafysika*, Novočeská biblioteka, 4 (Prague: Řivnáč, 1844), vii. On his negative view of philosophical idealism, see Josef J. Jungmann, *Zápisky*, ed. Radek Lunga (Prague: Budka, 1998), 47.

150. *Slovník českých filozofů*, ed., Gabriel, 157.

151. Karel Havlíček, "Leibniz a jeho idea," *Česká včela* 13 (1846): n. 55, 219; Karel Havlíček, "Podobizna Bolzanova," *Česká včela* 13 (1846): n. 51, 204.

152. J. Fidrmuc, "Je-li potřebí filosofie literatuře české," *Časopis českého musea* 18 (1844): 240, 242.

153. Nebeský, "Několik slov o filosofii," 244, 247–48.

154. Gabler, "Něco o filosofii," 291.

155. In recent writing on Central European philosophy, the "Austrian tradition" has been distinguished as the empirical complex, while the other—the metaphysical—complex has been designated as the "German tradition." See Smith, *Austrian Philosophy*, 1. On the distinctive Austrian philosophy, see also Rudolf Haller, "Bolzano and Austrian Philosophy," in *Bolzano's Wissenschaftslehre, 1837–1987*, International Workshop, Firenze, September 16–17, 1987 (Florence: Olschki, 1992), 191–206; Rudolf Haller, *Studien zur österreichischen Philosophie: Variationen über ein Thema* (Amsterdam: Rodopi, 1979), especially 5–22. Even in the 1930s, the Austrian and the German traditions were distinguished by Otto Neurath, "Die Entwicklung des Wiener Kreises und die Zukunft des logischen Empirismus," and "Der Logische Empirismus und der Wiener Kreis," in Otto Neurath, *Gesammelte philosophische und methodologische Schriften*, ed. Rudolf Haller and Heiner Rutte (Vienna: Hölder-Pichler-Tempsky, 1981), 2:676, 742; on the Austrian School, see Marie Bayerová, "Rakouské filozofické myšlení konce 19. století v českém kulturním životě," in *Povědomí tradice v novodobé české kultuře: Doba Bedřicha Smetany* (Prague, Národní galerie, 1988), 128–36. An analogous differentiation between a German and an Austrian School has also emerged in the field of economic theory; see, for instance, Marek Loužek, *Spor o metodu mezi rakouskou školou a německou historickou školou* (Prague: Karolinum, 2001), 9–14.

156. Gabler, "Erwiderung auf Herrn Dr. Smetana's Aufsatz," 119; Nebeský, "Několik slov o filosofii," 233; Štorch, "Hlas o německé literatuře," 267–68.

157. Durdík, "O významu nauky Herbartovy," 322–23.

158. Concerning the line of development of Bolzano-Brentano-Husserl-Meiong, see Marie Bayerová, *Bernard Bolzano. Evropský rozměr jeho filosofického myšlení* (Prague: Filosofia, 1994), 23–45. Ironically, Bolzano himself considered north Germans to be more gifted philosophers than south Germans; see Bernard Bolzano, *Der böhmische Vormärz in Briefen B. Bolzanos an F. Příhonský, 1824–1848: Beiträge zur deutsch-slawischen Wechselseitigkeit*, ed. Eduard Winter, Deutsche Akademie der Wissenschaften zu Berlin. Institut für Slawistik. Veröffentlichungen, nr. 11 (Berlin: Akademie-Verlag, 1956), 207.

Chapter 11

1. Pavel Křivský, "Korespondence Jana Leopolda Haye, Josefa Františka Hurdálka a Augustina Zippa s Josefem Dobrovským," *Literární archiv: Sborník Památníku národního písemnictví* 5 (1970): 143–44.

2. "Danni della infernal legge di Giuseppe," cited by Eduard Winter, *Der Josefinismus: die Geschichte des österreichischen Reformkatholizismus, 1740–1848* (Berlin: Rütten & Loening, 1962), 213.

3. Severoli complained to Rome in January 1804: "che l'adorato sistema di Giuseppe von sostra cambiamenti, onde debba la Chiesa continuare a gemere nella sua Babilonica Schiavità," cited in ibid., 215.

4. Derek E. Beales, *Enlightenment and Reform in Eighteenth-Century Europe* (New York: I. B. Tauris, 2005), 291. Eduard Winter drew a distinction between the Austrian Catholic Restoration, fostered by the imperial government, and the Roman Catholic Restoration, working in the interest of the papacy; see Winter, *Bernard Bolzano: Ein Lebensbild*, in *Gesamtausgabe*, ed. Eduard Winter, Jan Berg, Friedrich Kambartel, Jaromír Loužil, and Bob van Rootselaar (Stuttgart-Bad Cannstatt: Frommann Holzboog, 1969–), Einleitungsband, First Part: *Biographie*, 34–35.

5. For a time, the works of both Kant and Hegel were on the papal index of prohibited books, as was the theology of Georg Hermes (1775–1831), who attempted to employ concepts of Kant and Fichte in the teaching of the Roman Church; see Barry Smith, "Austrian Origins of Logical Positivism," in *Logical Positivism in Perspective: Essays on Language, Truth, and Logic,* ed. Barry Gower (Totowa, N.J.: Barnes & Noble Books, c1987), 41. Pope Gregory XVI condemned Hermes's *Einleitung in die christkatholische Theologie* (1819–29) in September 1835; *New Catholic Encyclopedia,* Prepared by the editorial staff at the Catholic University of America, Washington, D.C. (New York: McGraw-Hill, 1967–79), 6:1075–76. The teaching of Kant's philosophy in the universities was temporarily prohibited in 1804, and Hegel's philosophy came under official suspicion in the 1850s; see Jan Šebestík, "Bolzano, Exner, and the Origins of Analytical Philosophy," *Grazer Philosophische Studien*, International Zeitschrift für analytische Philosophie 53 (1997): 37. See also, however, the note of caution in Josef Durdík, "O významu nauky Herbartovy," *Časopis českého musea* 50 (1876): 294.

6. Vincenc Zahradník, *Filosofické spisy*, ed. František Čáda (Prague: Česká akademie pro vědy slovesnost a umění, 1907–8), 1:12–17, 105–18.

7. Jane Regenfelder, "Der sogennante 'Bolzano-Prozess' und das Wartburgfest," in *Bernard Bolzano und die Politik: Staat, Nation und Religion als Herausforderung für die Philosophie im Kontext von Spätaufklärung, Frühnationalismus und Restauration*. Studien zu Politik und Verwaltung, Band 61, ed. Helmut Rumpler (Vienna: Böhlau, 2000), 149.

8. Zahradník, *Filosofické spisy*, 1:12–15; Bernard Bolzano, *Der böhmische Vormärz in Briefen B. Bolzanos an F. Příhonský, 1824–1848: Beiträge zur deutschslawischen Wechselseitigkeit*, ed. Eduard Winter, Deutsche Akademie der Wissenschaften zu Berlin. Institut für Slawistik. Veröffentlichungen, nr. 11 (Berlin: Akademie-Verlag, 1956), 4.

9. Helena Lorenzová, "Bolzanův proces," in *Bůh a bohové: církve, náboženství a spiritualita v českém 19 století,* ed. Zdeněk Hojda and Roman Prahl (Prague: KLP, 2003), 28, 32; Beales, *Enlightenment and Reform in Eighteenth-Century Europe*, 291.

10. Ibid., 25.

11. Josef Haubelt, *České osvícenství,* 2nd rev. ed. (Prague: Rodiče, 2004) 560; reference is to the second edition. Among others, Arnošt K. Růžička, the bishop of České Budějovice (1813–45), like his predecessor Jan P. Schaaffgotsche (1784–1813)

was a convinced Josephist Reform Catholic and believed that "his episcopal office ... [came] directly from God independently of the Apostolic See." Rudolf Svoboda, "Pastores boni?" *Osvícenství a katolická církev,* ed. Rudolf Svoboda and others (České Budějovice: Jihočeská univerzita, Teologická fakulta, 2005), 28–31.

12. He lived in Prague until 1830, when he moved to the estate of Anna Hoffmann in Těchobuz, and he returned to reside in Prague in 1841. See Gregor Zeithammer, *Biographie Bolzanos,* in Bolzano, *Gesamtausgabe,* ed. Winter and others (1997), Reihe IV, Band 2, 248.

13. See the witness of Robert Zimmermann, "Palacký," *Památník na oslavu stých narozenin Františka Palackého* (Prague: Matice česká, 1898), 43. Marie Pavlíková, "Bolzanův odkaz," in Bernard Bolzano, *Vlastní životopis,* trans. and ed. Marie Pavlíková (Prague: Odeon, 1981), 154–55.

14. See Bernard Bolzano, *Wissenschaft und Religion in Vormärz: Der Briefwechsel Bernard Bolzanos mit Michael Josef Fesl, 1822–1848,* ed. Eduard Winter and Wilhelm Zeil (Berlin: Akademie-Verlag, 1965); Bolzano, *Der böhmische Vormärz in Briefen B. Bolzanos an F. Příhonský*; Winter, *Bernard Bolzano: Ein Lebensbild,* in *Gesamtausgabe,* Einleitungsband, First Part: *Biographie,* 103.

15. Reflected in his biography of Jesus, František Schneider, *Geschichte unseres Herrn und Heilands Jesu Christi nach den vierfachen Berichten der heiligen Evangelien* (Prague, 1835; 2nd ed.,Prague, 1848), cited by Jiří Kořalka, "František Palacký und die böhmischen Bolzanisten," in Rumpler, ed., *Bernard Bolzano und die Politik,* 207.

16. Fiebrich, originally assigned to watch over Fesl in Vienna and Graz, acted as a secret member of Bolzano's circle; Bolzano, *Wissenschaft und Religion in Vormärz: Der Briefwechsel Bernard Bolzanos mit Michael Josef Fesl,* 8–9. Fiebrich also encouraged Bolzano through Fesl to write a special critique of Schelling's and Hegel's philosophy; Bolzano considered a provisional title, *Beleuchtung einiger philosophischer Vorurteile der Jeztzeit*; see Bolzano's letter to Fesl of April 17, 1840, in ibid., 281. Bolzano was eager to learn Fiebrich's view on an international prize that his publisher proposed in 1838–39 for the assessment of Bolzano's *Wissenschaftslehre*; see ibid., 239–40, 244–45. One may wonder whether Fiebrich did not in fact carry out the official policy of the imperial government to bolster philosophy emanating from Catholic (albeit liberal) sources that opposed German philosophy, the roots of which were Protestant.

17. Šebestík, "Bolzano, Exner, and the Origins of Analytical Philosophy," 39.

18. František Příhonský, *Neuer Anti-Kant: oder, Prüfung der Kritik der reinen Vernunft nach den in Bolzano's Wissenschaftslehre niedergelegten Begriffen* (Bautzen: A. Weller, 1850).

19. Otto Weiss, "Bolzanisten und Güntherianer in Wien 1848–1851," 259–60, in Rumpler, ed., *Bernard Bolzano und die Politik* ; see also Wilhelm Zeil, *Bolzano und die Sorben: ein Beitrag zur Geschichte des "Wendischen Seminars" in Prag zur Zeit der josefinischen Aufklärung und der Romantik* (Bautzen: Domowina, 1967).

20. Bolzano, *Der Briefwechsel B. Bolzanos mit F. Exner,* x–xi. For a survey of Herbart's critique of Kant and hence subsequent German idealism, see Frederick Copleston, *History of Philosophy* (London: Burns and Oates, 1947–66), 7:249–55. As noted earlier, between Příhonský and Exner, philosophy was taught at the University of Prague mainly by Johann Peithner von Lichtenfels (1826–31), a disciple of Rembold and an opponent of speculative idealism, especially of Fichte; see Král, *Československá filosofie,* 28.

21. František Kavka and Josef Petráň, eds., *Dějiny Univerzity Karlovy, 1348–1990* (Prague: Karolinum, 1995–98), 3:74; Šebestík, "Bolzano, Exner, and the Origins of Analytical Philosophy," 38.

22. Exner thereby prevented German idealism from flourishing in the monarchy, and this inhibition extended even to Neo-Kantianism, which would gain prominence in Germany after 1878. Michael Heidelberger, *Nature from Within: Gustav Theodor Fechner and His Psychophysical Worldview*, trans. Cynthia Klohr (Pittsburgh, Pa.: University of Pittsburgh Press, 2004), 64. See also Berta Karlik and Erich Schmid, *Franz Serafim Exner und sein Kreis: Ein Beitrag zur Geschichte der Physik in Österreich* (Vienna: Verlag der Österreichischen Akademie der Wissenschaften, 1982); and Rudolf Koschnitzke, *Herbart und Herbartschule* (Aalen: Scientia, 1988). On Herbart's philosophy as a barrier to German idealism in Bohemia and Austria, see also Tomáš G. Masaryk, *Světová revoluce za války a ve válce, 1914–1918,* Spisy 15 (Prague: Masarykův ústav AV ČR, 2005), 424.

23. Ivo Tretera, *J. F. Herbart a jeho stoupenci na pražské univerzitě* (Prague: Univerzita Karlova, 1989), 156–57; see also Jiří Gabriel, ed. *Slovník českých filozofů* (Brno: Masarykova Univerzita, 1998), 118.

24. Bernard Bolzano, *Der böhmische Vormärz in Briefen B. Bolzanos an F. Příhonský*, 57; *Antologie z dějin českého a slovenského filozofického myšlení* (Prague: Svoboda, 1981), 525; Pavlíková, *Bolzanovo působení na pražské univerzitě*, 106.

25. Václav V. Nebeský, "Několik slov o filosofii," *Časopis českého musea* 20 (1846): 233, 238–39; František Čupr, "Počátkové filosofování řeckého," *Časopis českého musea* 21, pt. 1 (1847): 29, 36, n. 3.

26. *Slovník českých filozofů*, ed. Gabriel, 118; Tretera, *J. F. Herbart*, 155.

27. Král, *Československá filosofie*, 248. Josef Wilhelm Nahlowsky (1812–85), who subsequently taught philosophy in Olomouc, Pest, and Graz, is to be distinguished from the Bolzanist, František Náhlovský (1807–53), and his brother Vincenc Náhlovský (1817–91), a professor of theology at the University of Prague (1846–87). Privately, Bolzano wished to see Exner replaced by Gregor Zeithammer in the philosophy chair at Prague University in 1848; see Bolzano, *Der böhmische Vormärz in Briefen B. Bolzanos an F. Příhonský*, 289.

28. The anti-Hegelian orientation continued to prevail in academic philosophy in Bohemia, even among its German-language practitioners. See Král, *Československá filosofie*, 249. Aristotle was considered the father of formal logic and juxtaposed to Hegel's logic equating thought with being; see Max Wundt, "Die Philosophie in der Zeit des Biedermeiers," *Deutsche Vierteljahrschrift für Literatur* 13 (1935): 131–32.

29. On the continuities between Bolzano and Herbart, see Eva Schmidt-Hartmann, *Tomáš G. Masaryk's Realism: Origins of a Czech Political Concept*, Veröffentlichungen des Collegium Carolinum, 52 (Munich: Oldenbourg, 1984), 60–61. Herbart became extremely critical not only of Fichte's philosophy but also of his political theory; see Tretera, *J. F. Herbart*, 22–26, 55–56.

30. Tomáš G. Masaryk, *Moderní člověk a náboženství*, Spisy, 8 (Prague: Masarykův ústav AV ČR, 2000), 95. Against Hegel, as the consummate representative of idealism; see Wundt, "Die Philosophie in der Zeit des Biedermeiers," 123, 131, 134.

31. Josef Zumr, "Některé otázky českého herbartismu," in *Filosofie v dějinách českého národa* (Prague: Nakladatelství ČSAV, 1958), 166, 168.

32. This impressed particularly the later Czech followers of Herbart; see Josef Durdík, "O významu nauky Herbartovy," *Časopis českého musea* 50 (1876): 315–17.

33. Herbart was considered an opponent of metaphysical speculation. Thus, during the great anti-Hegelian debate, Vilém Gábler, responding to Augustin Smetana's charge, denied that he was denouncing the philosophy of Herbart; rather, his critique was directed against the school of German idealism; see Vilém Gábler, "Erwiderung auf Herrn Dr. Smetana's Aufsatz," in *Sein oder Nichtsein der deutschen Philosophie in Böhmen*, ed. František Čupr (Prague: G. Haase Söhne, 1847), 119. See also chapter 10 in this volume.

34. Franz S. Exner, *Die Stellung der Studierenden auf der Universität*: eine Rede gehalten an der k. k. Universität zu Prag, vor der Immatrikulation, den 20. Dezember 1834 (Prague: Gottlieb Haase Söhne, 1837), 5–11.

35. Ibid., 14.

36. Ibid., 11–12, 14–16.

37. Ibid., 15.

38. Franz S. Exner, *Die Psychologie der Hegelschen Schule* (Leipzig: F. Fleischer, 1842), 2–3. See also Georg W. F. Hegel, *Enzyklopädie der philosophischen Wissenschaften im Grundrisse*, 1–3, Werke 8–10, ed. Eva Moldenhauer and Karl M. Michel (Frankfurt/M: Suhrkamp, 1970).

39. Johann K. Rosenkranz, *Psychologie, oder die Wissenschaft des subjektiven Geistes* (Königsberg, 1831); Karl Ludwig Michelet, *Anthropologie und Psychologie, oder die Philosophie des subjektiven Geistes* (Berlin: Sander, 1840); and Johann E. Erdmann, *Grundriss der Psychologie für Vorlesungen* (Leipzig: F. C. W. Vogel, 1840).

40. Exner, *Die Psychologie der Hegelschen Schule*, 3, 5.

41. Ibid., 8.

42. Ibid., 44.

43. Ibid., 11–12.

44. Ibid., 28.

45. Ibid., 32–33.

46. Ibid., 54.

47. Ibid., 80–81.

48. "Gewiss, wer in irgend einer anderen Wissenschaft Solches wagte, der würde für immer mit dem Mahle geistiger Unfähigkeit und schamloser Anmassung gebrandmarkt sein." See Exner, *Die Psychologie der Hegelschen Schule*, 105–6, also 112.

49. Bolzano, *Wissenschaft und Religion in Vormärz: Der Briefwechsel Bernard Bolzanos mit Michael Josef Fesl*, 315–16; Pavel Křivský, *Augustin Smetana* (Prague: Karolinum, 1990), 128–29; Gabriel, ed., *Slovník českých filozofů*, 118.

50. Concerning Exner's respect for Herbart's philosophy, see Exner, *Die Psychologie der Hegelschen Schule*, 110–12. See also Kavka and Petráň, *Dějiny Univerzity Karlovy, 1348–1990*, 3:74.

51. Šebestík, "Bolzano, Exner, and the Origins of Analytical Philosophy," 37, 57. Robert Zimmermann, *Philosophische Propädeutik für Obergymnasien* (Vienna: W. Braumüller, 1853; 2nd ed., 1860; 3rd ed., 1867). For a positive assessment of Herbart's role in Czech philosophy, see Josef Zumr, *Máme-li kulturu je naší vlastí Evropa: Herbartismus a česká filosofie* (Prague: Filosofia, 1998).

52. See Král, *Československá filosofie*, 249.

53. Bolzano, *Der Briefwechsel B. Bolzanos mit F. Exner*, x–xi. See also Bernard

Bolzano, *On the Mathematical Method and Correspondence with Exner* (Amsterdam and New York: Rodopi, 2004).

54. Gabriel, ed., *Slovník českých filozofů,* 118. On the close relationship between Bolzano and Herbart, and later between them and Franz Brentano, see also Rudolf Haller, *Studien zur österreichischen Philosophie: Variationen über ein Thema* (Amsterdam: Rodopi, 1979), 6, 167.

55. Bolzano, *Wissenschaft und Religion in Vormärz: Der Briefwechsel Bernard Bolzanos mit Michael Josef Fesl,* 15.

56. Weiss, "Bolzanisten und Güntherianer in Wien 1848–1851," in Rumpler, ed., *Bernard Bolzano und die Politik,* 267; Bolzano considered Günther a visionary (*Phantast*), leading a retrograde movement; see Bolzano, *Der böhmische Vormärz in Briefen B. Bolzanos an F. Příhonský,* 146. See also Bolzano, *Der Briefwechsel B. Bolzanos mit F. Exner,* ix–x.

57. Bolzano, *Der böhmische Vormärz in Briefen B. Bolzanos an F. Příhonský,* 201 n. 4. Writing to Fesl in January 1848, Bolzano indicated his satisfaction with Exner's oral assurances of agreement with, and support of, his ideas; Bolzano, *Wissenschaft und Religion in Vormärz: Der Briefwechsel Bernard Bolzanos mit Michael Josef Fesl,* 408.

58. Bolzano, *Der Briefwechsel B. Bolzanos mit F. Exner,* xi.

59. For a helpful outline of the disputed issues, see Šebestík, "Bolzano, Exner, and the Origins of Analytical Philosophy," 39–53. The question of "objectless ideas" subsequently became an issue debated within the Austrian school by members, including Brentano, Kazimierz Twardowski, Meinong, Husserl and Frege; ibid., 49. On differences between Bolzano and Exner, see also Brigitte Mazohl-Wallnig, "Bolzanisten und österreichische Universitätsreform der Jahre 1848/49," in Rumpler, ed., *Bernard Bolzano und die Politik,* 232.

60. Bolzano, *Der Briefwechsel B. Bolzanos mit F. Exner,* xiv.

61. Ibid., x.

62. Ibid., xix.

63. Bolzano, *Der Briefwechsel B. Bolzanos mit F. Exner,* 37–38. Concerning Exner's skepticism also toward Kant's psychology, see Exner, *Die Psychologie der Hegelschen Schule,* 110.

64. "Exner ist nicht so arg, als Sie sich vorstellen mögen." See also Bolzano, *Wissenschaft und Religion in Vormärz: Der Briefwechsel Bernard Bolzanos mit Michael Josef Fesl,* 257.

65. Bolzano, *Der Briefwechsel B. Bolzanos mit F. Exner,* 122, 135. On Gazzaniga, see chapter 7 in this volume.

66. Exner, *Die Psychologie der Hegelschen Schule,* 80–81.

67. Bolzano, *Wissenschaft und Religion in Vormärz: Der Briefwechsel Bernard Bolzanos mit Michael Josef Fesl,* 257, 316, 326, 408.

68. Bolzano, *Der Briefwechsel B. Bolzanos mit F. Exner,* xviii.

69. Bernard Bolzano, *Mathematisch-Physikalische und Philosophische Schriften, 1842–1843,* in *Gesamtausgabe,* Reihe I, Schriften, Band 18, 67.

70. Bolzano, *Der Briefwechsel B. Bolzanos mit F. Exner,* xvi–xvii. Yet, Bolzano confided to Příhonský in a letter of July 21, 1838, that in his opinion Exner did not possess a first-rate philosophical mind; see Bolzano, *Der böhmische Vormärz in Briefen B. Bolzanos an F. Příhonský,* 207.

71. He then prepared an outline of Herbart's *Lehrbuch zur Einleitung in die*

Philosophie (Kaliningrad [Königsberg]: Unser, 1813); see Bolzano, *Philosophische Tagebücher*, in *Gesamtausgabe*, Reihe II, Nachlass, B. Wissenschaftliche Tagebücher; Band 16/1, *1811–1817*, 1:106–9. In 1816, he noted Johann Friedrich Herbart, *Lehrbuch zur Psychologie* (Kaliningrad [Königsberg] and Leipzig, 1816); ibid., 1:137.

72. Johann F. Herbart, *Psychologie als Wissenschaft, neu gegründet auf Erfahrung, Metaphysik und Mathematik*, Erster Theil (Kaliningrad [Königsberg]: A. W. Unser, 1824).

73. Based on Johann F. Herbart, *Lehrbuch zur Einleitung in die Philosophie*, 2nd ed. (Kaliningrad [Königsberg]: Unser, 1821); see Bolzano, *Philosophische Tagebücher*, in *Gesamtausgabe*, Reihe II, Nachlass, B. Wissenschaftliche Tagebücher; Band 18/2, *1827–1844*, 2:16.

74. For both, according to Bolzano, imagination (*Vorstellung*) resulted from "collision between the forces of the soul and the forces of an external object" ("als Resultate des Zusammenstossens der eigenen Kraft der Seele mit den Kräften der äusseren Dinge"). See Bolzano, *Philosophische Tagebücher*, in *Gesamtausgabe*, Reihe II, Nachlass, B. Wissenschaftliche Tagebücher; Band 18/2, *1827–1844*, 2:26.

75. "Mir däucht, dass der Unterschied zwischen seiner und meiner Lehre in diesem Stücke beynahe auf blossen Worten beruhet." See Bolzano, *Philosophische Tagebücher*, in *Gesamtausgabe*, Reihe II, Nachlass, B. Wissenschaftliche Tagebücher; Band 18/2, *1827–1844*, 2:26.

76. Bolzano, *Der Briefwechsel B. Bolzanos mit F. Exner*, 8

77. Miloš Havelka, "Byl Herbart filosofem biedermeieru? Herbartův pokus o realistickou akceptaci rozdvojenosti člověka a světa," *Biedermeier v českých zemích*, Sborník příspěvků z 23. ročníku sympozia k problematice 19. Století, Plzeň, 6.–8 března 2003, ed. Helena Lorenzová and Taťána Petrasová (Prague: KLP, 2004), 28–37, discusses the anti-Kantian epistemology of Herbart without, however, noting the parallel with Bolzano.

78. Bolzano, *Wissenschaftslehre*, in *Gesamtausgabe*, Reihe I, Schriften, Band 11, 1:63

79. Ibid., Reihe I, Schriften, Band 11, 1:60, 2:44.

80. Bolzano, *Vermischte philosophische und physikalische Schriften, 1832–1848*, in *Gesamtausgabe*, Reihe II, Nachlass A, Band 12, part 1, 79.

81. Bolzano, *Wissenschaftslehre*, in *Gesamtausgabe*, Reihe I, Schriften, Band 11, 1:110.

82. Ibid., Band 11, 2:38–39, citing Herbart, *Lehrbuch zur Einleitung in die Philosophie* (1813), 21–23, 125–26.

83. Bolzano, *Wissenschaftslehre*, in *Gesamtausgabe*, Reihe I, Schriften, Band 11, 2:86

84. The issue concerned the question whether one object could have more than one true quality (*wahre Qualität*), which were independent of each other; see ibid., Band 11, 2:89–90.

85. Ibid., Band 11, 3:142, referring to Herbart, *Lehrbuch zur Einleitung in die Philosophie* (1813), 26.

86. Bolzano, *Wissenschaftslehre*, in *Gesamtausgabe*, Reihe I, Schriften, Band 13, 1:27.

87. Ibid., Band 13, 1:112, referring to Herbart, *Lehrbuch zur Psychologie*, 101–2. For his disagreement with Herbart on this topic, see Bolzano, *Wissenschaftslehre*, 1:116–19.

88. Bolzano, *Wissenschaftslehre*, in *Gesamtausgabe*, Reihe I, Schriften, Band 13, 1:184, referring to Herbart, *Lehrbuch zur Psychologie*, 167–78.

89. Bolzano claimed that Herbart's definition was not specific enough; it could also cover history. See Bolzano, *Vermischte philosophische und physikalische Schriften, 1832–1848*, in *Gesamtausgabe*, Reihe II, Nachlass A, Band 12, pt. 2, p. 175.

90. Among the secondary works, he cited Moritz W. Drobisch, *Beiträge zur Orientierung ueber Herbarts System der Philosophie* (Leipzig, 1834); and Ludwig Strümpell, *Erläuterungen zur Herbarts Philosophie* (Göttingen, 1834). See Bolzano, *Der böhmische Vormärz in Briefen B. Bolzanos an F. Příhonský*, 199; Bolzano, *Vermischte philosophische und physikalische Schriften, 1832–1848*, in *Gesamtausgabe*, Reihe II, Nachlass A, Band 12, pt. 2, 113–14. In the 1830s, he also started writing an exposition, "Herbarts System," based on Herbart's *Lehrbuch zur Einleitung in die Philosophie* (1813); see Bolzano, *Vermischte philosophische und physikalische Schriften, 1832–1848*, in *Gesamtausgabe*, Reihe II, Nachlass A, Band 12, pt. 1, 71–72.

91. Tretera, *J. F. Herbart*, 151–52; Bolzano, *Wissenschaft und Religion in Vormärz: Der Briefwechsel Bernard Bolzanos mit Michael Josef Fesl*, 18, 237–38, 240, 242–45, 250–52. See also Robert Zimmermann, "Die literarische Preisaufgabe des Prof. B. Bolzano im Jahre 1839," *Wiener Zeitung*, Beilage, October 30 and November 1, 1849; cited in ibid., 233, n. 1.

92. Fesl's letter to Bolzano of December 22, 1838, in Bolzano, *Wissenschaft und Religion in Vormärz: Der Briefwechsel Bernard Bolzanos mit Michael Josef Fesl*, 233.

93. See ibid., 238.

94. Ibid., 260–62, 287.

95. Bolzano, *Der böhmische Vormärz in Briefen B. Bolzanos an F. Příhonský*, 228.

96. Bernard Bolzano, *Mathematisch-Physikalische und Philosophische Schriften, 1842–1843,* in *Gesamtausgabe*, Reihe I, Schriften, Band 18, 93, citing Robert Zimmermann, *Aesthetik. Erster Theil: Geschichte der Aesthetik als philosophischer Wissenschaft* (Vienna, 1858), 800–803.

97. Zumr, "Některé otázky českého herbartismu," 174, 185. See also "Czech philosophy," *Oxford Companion to Philosophy*, ed. Ted Honderich (New York: Oxford University Press, 1995), 174.

98. Barry Smith, "Austrian Origins of Logical Positivism," in *Logical Positivism in Perspective,* ed. Gower, 40–41.

99. For instance, this was the view of Oskar Kraus, "Besonderheit und Aufgabe der deutschen Philosophie in Böhmen," *Actes du huitième Congrès de Philosophie à Prague, 2–7 Septembre 1934* (Prague, 1936), 766–71, cited by Marie Bayerová, "Rakouské filozofické myšlení konce 19. století v českém kulturním životě," in *Povědomí tradice v novodobé české kultuře: Doba Bedřicha Smetany* (Prague, Národní galerie, 1988), 129, 136.

100. Zumr, "Některé otázky českého herbartismu," 171–72. He also cites Josef Durdík, "O významu nauky Herbartovy," *Časopis českého musea* 50 (1876): 294.

101. Král, *Československá filosofie*, 28; Kavka and Petráň, eds., *Dějiny University Karlovy*, 3:73.

102. See, for instance, Tretera, *J. F. Herbart*, 157.

103. Šebestík, "Bolzano, Exner, and the Origins of Analytical Philosophy," especially 54. See also their cordial correspondence in Bolzano, *Der Briefwechsel B. Bolzanos mit F. Exner.*

104. Pavlíková, "Bolzanův odkaz," in Bolzano, *Vlastní životopis*, 158. Robert

Zimmermann was son of one of Bolzano's early students, Johann A. Zimmermann; see Tretera, *J. F. Herbart*, 161–62. Robert was a favorite student of Bolzano, who highly praised his philosophical acumen in a letter to Fesl of September 1843; see Bolzano, *Wissenschaft und Religion in Vormärz: Der Briefwechsel Bernard Bolzanos mit Michael Josef Fesl*, 316, 331–32.

105. Robin D. Rollinger, *Husserl's Position in the School of Brentano* (Dordrecht: Kluwer Academic, 1999), 70.

106. "Was erwarten wir von der Philosophie," (1852), cited by Král, *Československá filosofie*, 27.

107. Petr Urban, "Bolzano a raný Husserl," in *Osamělý myslitel, Bernard Bolzano*, ed. Kateřina Trlifajová (Prague: Filosofia, 2006), 174; Robert Zimmermann, *Philosophische Propädeutik für Obergymnasien* (Vienna: W. Braumüller, 1853; 2nd ed., 1860; 3rd ed., 1867).

108. "Bolzano underlined the inadequacy of the Kantian philosophy of mathematics, above all its dependence on 'forms of intuition' and its inability to treat infinite objects." Šebestík, "Bolzano, Exner, and the Origins of Analytical Philosophy," 37.

109. Ibid., 36–38.

110. Rudolf Haller, "Bolzano and Austrian Philosophy," in *Bolzano's Wissenschaftslehre, 1837–1987* (Florence: Olschki, 1992), 201; Barry Smith, *Austrian Philosophy: The Legacy of Brentano* (Chicago: Open Court, 1994), 185–91.

111. "Die Bolzano, Herbart, Brentano vertraten eine logisierende Tradition, die sich immer wieder dem Kantianismus und der deutschen idealistischen Philosophie entgegenstemmte." Otto Neurath, "Einheitswissenschaft und Psychologie," in Otto Neurath, *Gesammelte philosophische und methodologische Schriften*, ed. Rudolf Haller and Heiner Rutte (Vienna: Hölder, Pichler, Tempsky, 1981), 2:597, n. 3.

112. See the epilogue to this volume.

113. On the opposition to the Enlightenment, especially on the part of Jiljí Chládek and Josef M. Král, calling for a completion of the Counter-Reformation, see Viktor Viktora, *K pramenům národní literatury* (Plzeň: Fraus, 2003), 198.

114. Bolzano, *Der böhmische Vormärz in Briefen B. Bolzanos an F. Příhonský*, 268, 279.

115. Bolzano, *Wissenschaft und Religion in Vormärz: Der Briefwechsel Bernard Bolzanos mit Michael Josef Fesl*, 386.

116. Martin C. Putna, *Česká katolická literatura, 1848–1918* (Prague: Torst, 1998), 145.

117. Král, *Československá filosofie*, 25.

118. Concerning Havlíček's liberal Catholicism, see his program in *Národní noviny*, June 7, 1848, cited by Masaryk, *Karel Havlíček: Snahy a tužby politického probuzení*, 193; Putna, *Česká katolická literatura, 1848–1918*, 149–51; Josef Kaizl, *České myšlenky*, 2nd ed. (Prague: Edvard Beaufort, 1896), 53–54.

119. Bolzano, *Der böhmische Vormärz in Briefen B. Bolzanos an F. Příhonský*, 103–4; František Kryštůfek, *Dějiny církve katolické ve státech rakousko-uherských se zláštním zřetelem k zemím koruny české*, vol. 1: 1740–1848 (Prague: Kotrba, 1898), 509–17; Putna, *Česká katolická literatura, 1848–1918*, 145–52; Jaroslav Kadlec, *Přehled českých církevních dějin* (Prague: Zvon, 1991), 2: 195–98.

120. Bolzano, *Der böhmische Vormärz in Briefen B. Bolzanos an F. Příhonský*, 103–4.

121. In an article by its editor, Sebastian Brunner; ibid., 288. Fesl pleaded against the Güntherianers for a reconciliation between the German Austrians and "the wonderful nation of the Slavs" (*herrlichen Nation de Slawen*); see Weiss, "Bolzanisten und Güntherianer in Wien 1848–1851," in Rumpler, ed., *Bernard Bolzano und die Politik*, 259.

122. Ibid., 262–64.

123. Bolzano's letter of October 8, 1848, written shortly before his death; see Bolzano, *Der böhmische Vormärz in Briefen B. Bolzanos an F. Příhonský*, 104, 290; Putna, *Česká katolická literatura, 1848–1918*, 148.

124. See "The Austrian Concordat," in Owen Chadwick, *A History of the Popes* (Oxford: Clarendon Press, 1998), 105–8.

125. Putna, *Česká katolická literatura, 1848–1918*, 149–50.

126. Jan Neruda, *Národní Listy*, February 18, 1877, cited by Jan Jakubec, *Antonín Marek: Jeho život a působení i význam v literatuře české* (Prague: Bačkovský, 1896), 241.

127. Hence, the lack of religiosity in the civilization revived by the awakening did not negate the link with the Bohemian Reformation, in particular with the tolerance, universalism, and populism of the Utraquist sixteenth century; Kaizl, *České myšlenky*, 14.

128. This development is discussed in chapters 9 and 10 in this volume.

129. See chapter 4 in this volume.

130. The process of the retridentization of the Roman Church in the Habsburg monarchy was eventually enshrined in the concordat with the Holy See in 1855; see Peter Leisching, "Die römisch-katholische Kirche in Cisleithanien," in *Die Konfessionen*, vol. 4 of *Die Habsburgmonarchie, 1848–1918*, ed. Adam Wandruszka and Peter Urbanitsch (Vienna: Verlag der Österreichischen Akademie der Wissenschaften, 1973–93), 25–34.

131. Tomáš G. Masaryk, *Česká otázka. Naše nynější krize. Jan Hus*, Spisy 6 (Prague: [Masarykův ústav], 2000), 329, 347.

132. Ibid., 178, 330, 347–48; Stanislav Polák, *T.G. Masaryk* (Prague: [Masarykův ústav] AV ČR, 2000–2009), 3:13.

Epilogue

1. Rudolf Haller, "Bolzano and Austrian Philosophy," in *Bolzano's Wissenschaftslehre, 1837–1987* (Florence: Olschki, 1992), 192–93. As the starting point, as Otto Neurath, one of the founders of the Vienna Circle, put it: "Austria spared itself the interlude with Kant." See Otto Neurath, "Die Entwicklung des Wiener Kreises und die Zukunft des logischen Empirismus," in Otto Neurath, *Gesammelte philosophische und methodologische Schriften*, ed. Rudolf Haller and Heiner Rutte (Vienna: Hölder, Pichler, Tempsky, 1981), 2:676. See also ibid., 2:677–79.

2. "The Austrian tradition that begins with Bernard Bolzano and continues with Franz Brentano and then leads to Wittgenstein is one of the most productive in the history of philosophy." R. M. Chisholm, "Opening Address," *Philosophy of Mind, Philosophy of Psychology*, ed. R. M. Chisholm, J. C. Marek, J. T. Blackmore, A. Hübner (Vienna: Hölder, Pichler, Tempsky, 1985), cited by Rudolf Haller, "Bolzano and Austrian Philosophy," 194. On Bolzano and Exner as precursors of

analytical philosophy, see Jan Šebestík, "Bolzano, Exner, and the Origins of Analytical Philosophy," *Grazer Philosophische Studien*, International Zeitschrift für analytische Philosophie 53 (1997): 33–59. See also Peter Simons, *Philosophy and Logic in Central Europe from Bolzano to Tarski* (Dordrecht: Kluwer, 1992), 143–58.

3. See chapter 9 in this volume.

4. Tomáš G. Masaryk, *Otázka sociální. Základy marxismu filosofické a sociologické*. Spisy 9–10 (Prague: Masarykův ústav AV ČR, 2000), 2:52, characterized the relationship in the following way: "Marx's philosophical basis, I would say, his philosophical skeleton, is found in Hegel's philosophy. Hegel formulated the spirit of Marx." Further, ibid., 53: "Hegel affected Marx from the very start and constantly; and affected him not only by the richness and depth of his ideas, but also by the totality (albeit artificial) of his spectacular system and particularly by his method."

5. Barry Smith, "Austrian Origins of Logical Positivism," in *Logical Positivism in Perspective: Essays on Language, Truth, and Logic*, ed. Barry Gower (Totowa, N.J.: Barnes & Noble Books, c1987), 35. On Lenin's *Materialism and Empirio-Criticism* (1909), see Donald M. Borchert, ed., *The Encyclopedia of Philosophy*, 2nd ed. (New York: Macmillan, 2006), 5:28; Zdeněk Nejedlý, "Slovo o české filosofii," *Var*, 1950, no. 1: 4–5.

6. On Bolzano as progenitor of analytic philosophy, see *Bolzano and Analytic Philosophy*, ed. Wolfgang Künne, Mark Siebel, and Mark Textor (Amsterdam: Rodopi, 1997); *Bolzano's Wissenschaftslehre, 1837–1987* (Florence: Olschki, 1992), especially 191–206.

7. Barry Smith, "The Production of Ideas: Notes on Austrian Intellectual History from Bolzano to Wittgenstein," in *Structure and gestalt: Philosophy and Literature in Austria-Hungary and Her Successor States,* ed. Barry Smith (Philadelphia: Benjamins, 1981), 221; Eva Schmidt-Hartmann, *Tomáš G. Masaryk's Realism: Origins of a Czech Political Concept*, Veröffentlichungen des Collegium Carolinum, 52 (Munich: Oldenbourg, 1984), 61–62; Jan Patočka, "Bolzanovo místo v dějinách filosofie," in *Filosofie v dějinách českého národa* (Prague: Nakladatelství ČSAV, 1958), 116.

8. Petr Urban, "Bolzano a raný Husserl," in *Osamělý myslitel, Bernard Bolzano,* ed. Kateřina Trlifajová (Prague: Filosofia, 2006), 173. See also Robin D. Rollinger, *Husserl's Position in the School of Brentano* (Dordrecht: Kluwer Academic, 1999), 69–82.

9. Smith, "Austrian Origins of Logical Positivism," 58–59; Stanislav Polák, *T. G. Masaryk* (Prague: Masarykův ústav Av ČR, 2000–2009), 1:177.

10. Franz Clemens Brentano, *Über die Zukunft der Philosophie; nebst den Vorträgen: Über die Gründe der Entmutigung auf philosophischem Gebiet, Über Schellings System, sowie den 25 Habilitationsthesen,* 2nd rev. ed. (Hamburg, F. Meiner [1968]), 8, 11, 20. On the relationship between Bolzano and Brentano, see Hugo Bergmann, *Das philosophische Werk B. Bolzanos* (Halle: Niemeyer, 1909). See also Polák, *T. G. Masaryk,* 1:180.

11. Barry Smith, "Austrian Origins of Logical Positivism," in *Logical Positivism in Perspective,* ed. Gower, 46. Brentano, *Über die Zukunft der Philosophie; nebst den Vorträgen* .

12. Brentano's own attitude toward Bolzano was rather ambiguous. On the one hand, he claimed credit for having brought Bolzano's work to the forefront of the

philosophical scene in Austria. On the other hand, he denied any indebtedness to Bolzano for his own philosophical thinking. See Haller, "Bolzano and Austrian Philosophy," 201; and Franz C. Brentano, *Psychologie vom empirischen Standpunkt,* 2nd ed., ed. Oskar Kraus (Leipzig: 1924–28), 2:10, 265–66.

13. Haller, "Bolzano and Austrian Philosophy," 195; Simons, *Philosophy and Logic in Central Europe,* 7–8, 14–15; Anton Marty, "Was Ist Philosophie?" in Anton Marty, *Gesammelte Schriften* (Halle: Niemeyer, 1916), vol. 1, pt. 1, 91. On Bolzano in Brentano's teaching, see also Oskar Kraus, *Franz Brentano: Zur Kenntnis seines Lebens und seiner Lehre,* with contributions from Carl Stumpf and Edmund Husserl (Munich: Beck, 1919), 157.

14. Urban, "Bolzano a raný Husserl," 174; Robert Zimmermann, *Philosophische Propädeutik für Obergymnasien* (Vienna: W. Braumüller, 1853; 2nd ed., 1860; 3rd ed., 1867).

15. See Marie Pavlíková, "Bolzanův odkaz," in Bernard Bolzano, *Vlastní životopis,* trans. and ed. Marie Pavlíková (Prague: Odeon, 1981), 158; Smith, "Austrian Origins of Logical Positivism," 49–50; Liliana Albertazzi, "Brentano, Twardowski, and Polish Scientific Philosophy," in *Polish Scientific Philosophy: The Lvov-Warsaw School,* ed. Francesco Coniglione and others (Amsterdam: Rodopi, 1993), 11–29, especially 28.

16. Smith, "Austrian Origins of Logical Positivism," 55–57; Rollinger, *Husserl's Position in the School of Brentano,* 69–73; Urban, "Bolzano a raný Husserl," 173–86.

17. Edmund Husserl, *Logical Investigations,* trans. John N. Findlay (London: Routledge, 2001), 142.

18. Ibid., 143.

19. Alfred J. Ayer, *The Meaning of Life* (New York: Scribner's, 1990), 3–6; Alfred J. Ayer, ed., *Logical Positivism* (Glencoe, Illinois: Free Press, 1959), 9–10; Ben Rogers, *A. J. Ayer: A Life* (New York: Grove Press, 1999), 220; Simons, *Philosophy and Logic in Central Europe,* 147–55. European logical positivism was "a reflection of the interplay of the intellectual and institutional influence of Brentano and his school with developments in logic and in the philosophy of physics inspired by Russell and Wittgenstein and by Mach and his successors in Vienna and Prague." See Smith, "Austrian Origins of Logical Positivism," 57. There was also a revival of interest in Locke's epistemological realism; *Oxford Dictionary of National Biography* (New York: Oxford University Press, 2004), 34:228.

20. *Oxford Companion to Philosophy,* ed. Ted Honderich (New York: Oxford University Press, 1995), 28. Carnap, however, became interested in *Principia Mathematica* of Russell and Alfred N. Whitehead in 1919 under the influence of Gottlob Frege (1845–1925), with whom he had studied at the University of Jena in 1910–14; see Rudolf Carnap, "Intellectual Autobiography," in *The Philosophy of Rudolf Carnap,* Library of Living Philosophers 11, ed. Paul A. Schilpp (La Salle, Ill.: Open Court, 1963), 5–6, 11.

21. Sibyl A. Schwarzbach, "Rawls, Hegel, and Communitarianism," *Political Theory* 19 (1991): 539, citing Peter Hylton, *Russell, Idealism and the Emergence of Analytic Philosophy* (Oxford: Clarendon Press, 1990), 44ff.

22. Hubert Schleichert, ed., *Logischer Empirismus: der Wiener Kreis* (Munich: Fink, 1975), 7–11; Alfred J. Ayer, "Editor's introduction" to *Logical Positivism,* ed. A. J. Ayer, 3–28; Neurath, "Die Entwicklung des Wiener Kreises und die Zukunft des logischen Empirismus," 695–99; Viktor Kraft, *The Vienna Circle: The Origin of*

Neo-Positivism, a Chapter in the History of Recent Philosophy (New York: Greenwood Press, 1969).

23. As noted earlier, Twardowski's students included Tadeusz Kotarbiński (1886–1981), Stanisław Leśniewski (1886–1939), and Jan Łukasiewicz (1878–1956); see Jan Woleński, "Tarski as a Philosopher," in *Polish Scientific Philosophy*, ed. Coniglione and others, 323; and he influenced Polish phenomenologists, such as Roman W. Ingarden (1893–1970), see ibid., 41–58; and Robin D. Rollinger, *Husserl's Position in the School of Brentano*, 139. On the appreciation of the Polish school by the Vienna Circle, see Carnap, "Intellectual Autobiography," 30–31. Quine likewise had an opportunity in 1933 to meet members of the Polish school of logic, in particular Leśniewski, Łukasiewicz, and Tarski; see Willard Van Orman Quine, *The Time of My Life: An Autobiography* (Cambridge, Mass.: MIT Press, 1985), 102–4.

24. Roberto Poli, "At the Origins of Analytic Philosophy," *Aletheia* 6 (1993–94): 222; Smith, "Austrian Origins of Logical Positivism," 37.

25. Otto Neurath, "Erster Internationaler Kongress für Einheit der Wissenschaft in Paris 1935," in Neurath, *Gesammelte philosophische und methodologische Schriften*, ed. Haller and Rutte, 2:654.

26. In a letter from Vienna, dated February 26, 1933, to Isaiah Berlin in Oxford; cited by Ben Rogers, *A. J. Ayer* (New York: Grove Press, 1999), 94.

27. Quine, *The Time of My Life*, 92–95. Through the Vienna Circle, Quine also met Reichenbach; ibid., 96.

28. Alfred J. Ayer, "Reflections on Language, Truth and Logic," in *Logical Positivism in Perspective,* ed. Gower, 24–25.

29. Rogers, *A. J. Ayer*, 99.

30. Albert E. Blumberg and Herbert Feigl, "Logical Positivism, a New Movement in European Philosophy," *Journal of Philosophy* 28 (1931): 281–82. Metaphysics was defined as the science of being in itself, of the absolute, and of the empirically unattainable foundations of experiential knowledge. Rudolf Carnap characterized the theories of metaphysicians as consisting of meaningless series of words, which in principle did not differ from such statements as "Berlin Pferd blau" or even "bu ba bi." See Rudolf Carnap, *Scheinprobleme in der Philosophie. Das Fremdpsychische und der Realismusstreit* (Frankfurt a. M.: Suhrkamp, 1966), 49, 90–91. On logical positivism and metaphysics, see also Ayer, ed., *Logical Positivism*, 10–17; Rudolf Carnap, "The Old and the New Logic," in ibid., 145.

31. Rudolf Carnap, "The Elimination of Metaphysics through Logical Analysis of Language," in Ayer, ed., *Logical Positivism*, 80.

32. Ibid., 73, 75; the former statement was also ridiculed by Oskar Kraus, "Die Grundzüge der Welt- und Lebensanschauung T. G. Masaryks," in *La pensée de T. G. Masaryk*, Internationale Bibliothek für Philosophie 3 (1937), nos. 3–5: 106.

33. Carnap, "The Old and the New Logic," in Ayer, ed., *Logical Positivism*, 134. Originally published as Rudolf Carnap, "Die alte und die neue Logik," *Erkenntnis* 1 (1930–31): 12–26.

34. Alfred J. Ayer, "Demonstration of the Impossibility of Metaphysics," *Mind*, 43 no. 171 (1934): 339. See also Rogers, *A. J. Ayer*, 98.

35. His object was "zu zeigen, dass es jenseits des zentraleuropäischen Obskurantismus—Hegel-Marx'scher Provenienz—einen weltweiten Versuch gibt, mit Hilfe logischer und sprachkritischer Methoden der Philosophie einen Bereich wissenschaftlich beartbeitbarer Aufgaben zu stellen und damit Unklarheiten und

Verwirrungen zu beseitigen, die dieser ältesten Wissenschaft, vielleicht eben auf Grund ihres mythischen Alters, noch immer anhaften." Rudolf Haller, "Der 'Wiener Kreis' und die analytische Philosophie," in Rudolf Haller, *Studien zur österreichischen Philosophie: Variationen über ein Thema* (Amsterdam: Rodopi, 1979), 98.

36. See, for instance, Alfred J. Ayer, "The Claims of Theology," in Alfred J. Ayer, *Central Questions of Philosophy* (New York: Morrow, 1975), 211–35.

37. Charles Ernest Vouillemin, *La logique de la science et l'École de Vienne* (Paris: Hermann, 1935); Charles Ernest Vouillemin, *Science et philosophie: unité de la connaissance* (Paris: Michel, 1945). Late in life, Ayers moved to a position that propositions that were "meaningless" were not necessarily "wrong." See Alfred J. Ayer, *Freedom and Morality and Other Essays* (New York: Oxford University Press, 1984), 49–50. On the other hand, Ayers disagreed with Wittgenstein's attempt to claim that magical and religious beliefs were not necessarily "irrational" by treating them as symbolic or self-validated through internal coherence; see Alfred J. Ayer, *Wittgenstein* (Chicago: University of Chicago Press, 1986), 92. See also Rogers, *A. J. Ayer*, 329–30.

38. Vouillemin, *Science et philosophie: unité de la connaissance*, 182. The metaphysical agnosticism of positivism was in a way more compatible with Catholic theology than the "pantheism" of metaphysical idealism, which subsumed everything earthly within the divinity; see Georg Moenius, *Paris, Frankreichs Herz* (Munich: Limes Verlag, 1928), 113.

39. "Cette attitude a l'égard de Notion et Etre est absolument celle de l'Empirisme logique; elle est fondamentale dans le réalisme chrétien, qui s'élève à Dieu 'par le moyen de ses oeuvres, qui rendent apparentes à intelligence ses perfections invisibles.'" Vouillemin, *Science et philosophie: unité de la connaissance*, 183–84.

40. Philipp Frank, *Modern Science and Its Philosophy* (Cambridge: Harvard University, 1949), 175.

41. Ibid., 25, 49.

42. Poli, "At the Origins of Analytic Philosophy," 222.

43. " It is the Catholics with their rigid set of dogmas, which stands only at the start of their reasoning, who can subsequently devote themselves to logical and systematic analysis without being [further] burdened by metaphysical particulars; their [dogmatic] premises are, of course, open to criticism, but the conclusions are often of great clarity and consistency, while the Lutherans and the philosophers, who are their descendants, make their starting premises more plausible [rationally] and in consequence saturate everything with metaphysics. Who among the Catholics begins to doubt a single dogma, he very easily frees himself from the totality of dogmas and then still has at his disposal, as a legacy, a very effective instrument of logic. It is otherwise among the Lutherans, where the rigidity of dogmas has been loosened, and the ecclesiastical power weakened. There, if one has evaded the belief in an explicit set of dogmas, a half- or quarter-hearted metaphysical bend of mind persists in many philosophers and savants of all disciplines, as a legacy of the imperfectly suppressed theology." ["Gerade Katholiken mit ihrer kompakten Dogmatik, die am Anfang ihrer Reflexion steht, können zuweilen besonders unbeschwert von metaphysischen Einzelheiten sich logisch-systematischer Analyse widmen, Ihre *Voraussetzungen* sind vor allem angreifbar, aber die Konklusionen oft von grosser Klarheit and Konsequenz, während die lutheraner und die von ihnen abstammenden Philosophen die Voraussetzungen plausibler machen und daher alles mit Metaphysik

durchtränken; wer im Bereich des Katholizismus überhaupt an einem Dogma zu zweifeln beginnt, befreit sich besonders leicht von der Gesamtheit der Dogmen und verfügt dann über ein sehr wirksames logisches Instrument als Restbestand! Anders im Bereich des Luthertums, wo die starre Dogmatik aufgelockert, die Kirchenmacht geschwächt wurde. Dort hat man, vielfach ein Bekenntnis zu einer klaren Dogmatik vermeidend, halbmetaphysische, viertelmetaphysische Wendungen als Restbestand unvollkommen verdrängter Theologie bei vielen Philosophen und Gelehrten aller Disziplin bewahrt."] Otto Neurath, "Einheitswissenschaft und Psychologie," in Neurath, *Gesammelte philosophische und methodologische Schriften*, ed. Haller and Rutte, 2:597, n. 3.

44. Otto Neurath, "Drei Diskussionsbeiträge," in Neurath, *Gesammelte philosophische und methodologische Schriften*, ed. Haller and Rutte, 2:765.

45. Otto Neurath, "Der Logische Empirismus und der Wiener Kreis," in Neurath, *Gesammelte philosophische und methodologische Schriften*, ed. Haller and Rutte, 2: 742; and Neurath, "Die Entwicklung des Wiener Kreises und die Zukunft des logischen Empirismus," *Gesammelte philosophische und methodologische Schriften*, 2:688–89. In addition to the tradition of empiricism stemming from the Enlightenment, Neurath also called attention to "utilitarianism and free trade movement of England"; see Smith, "Austrian Origins of Logical Positivism," 43.

46. He never considered becoming a Protestant and detested Prussia and its politics, especially Bismarck, whom he considered Germany's evil spirit. See Carl Stumpf's reminiscences in Kraus, *Franz Brentano*, 113–14; also testimony of Husserl, ibid., 156.

47. Ibid., 98–99, 104.

48. *The Encyclopedia of Philosophy*, ed. Borchert, 9:280.

49. Sidney Hook, "A Personal Impression of Contemporary German Philosophy," *Journal of Philosophy* 27 (1930): 153. In another context, Ayer maintained a long-standing friendship with the Jesuit philosopher Frederick Copleston; see Rogers, *A. J. Ayer*, 357. The relationship dated at least to their radio debate in 1949; see Alfred J. Ayer, "Logical Positivism: A Debate," in *The Meaning of Life*, 18; a comment on the debate by Wittgenstein in Ray Monk, *Ludwig Wittgenstein: The Duty of Genius* (New York: Free Press, 1990), 543. See also Rogers, *A. J. Ayer*, 224–25.

50. Smith, "Austrian Origins of Logical Positivism," 47.

51. "The Bolzanos, Brentanos, and Herbarts represent a tradition of logic which always posited a barrier against Kantianism and German idealism." ["Die Bolzano, Herbart, Brentano vertraten eine logisierende Tradition, die sich immer wieder dem Kantianismus und der deutschen idealistischen Philosophie entgegenstemmte."] Otto Neurath, "Einheitswissenschaft und Psychologie," in Neurath, *Gesammelte philosophische und methodologische Schriften*, ed. Haller and Rutte, 2:597, n. 3.

52. Smith, "Austrian Origins of Logical Positivism," 50–53. On the cultural interaction between Prague and Vienna, see also ibid., 35–36.

53. *Slovník českých filozofů*, ed. Jiří Gabriel (Brno: Masarykova Univerzita, 1998), 639.

54. Durdík viewed Hegel's philosophy as a system that, despite a certain brilliance, represented a blind alley in contrast to the sobriety but lasting value of Herbart's thought. See Josef Durdík, "O významu nauky Herbartovy," *Časopis českého musea* 50 (1876): 295. Karel Mácha, *Glaube und Vernunft: Die Böhmische Philosophie in geschichtlicher Übersicht* (Munich: Sauer, 1987), 2:94–96.

55. It is opposed to any form of idealism, monism, or mysticism; Durdík, "O významu nauky Herbartovy," 309–10.

56. Ibid., 313.

57. This exclusivity explained why Hegel's philosophy attracted so little attention among other nations and appeared old-fashioned even in Germany. Durdík, "O významu nauky Herbartovy," 314.

58. His ideas in natural science were full of anachronisms, especially in physics and astronomy, citing the references to Goethe and Newton; Durdík, "O významu nauky Herbartovy," 314.

59. Ibid., 314–15.

60. The national onesidedness of Hegelianism and kindred philosophical trends became manifest in explosive outbursts of contempt, even hatred against the Slavs; Durdík, "O významu nauky Herbartovy," 315.

61. Ibid., 324.

62. Ibid., 317–18.

63. Ibid., 322. While Durdík considered it worthwhile to explore British and French philosophy, particularly the teaching of Auguste Comte and John S. Mill, he felt that Herbart's philosophy was more advanced in some respects, especially in ethics, psychology, and pedagogy; see Durdík, "O významu nauky Herbartovy," 322–23. In part, he might have been dismayed by the flourishing of British Hegelianism in the latter part of the nineteenth century; for overviews, see "British Philosophy," in *The Encyclopedia of Philosophy*, ed. Edwards, 1:379.

64. Durdík, "O významu nauky Herbartovy," 324–25. See also Josef Durdík, "Über die Verbreitung der Herbat'schen Philosophie in Böhmen," *Zeitschrift für exacte Philosophie im Sinne des neuen philosophischen Realismus* 11 (1875): 317–26.

65. Josef Zumr, "Některé otázky českého herbartismu," in *Filosofie v dějinách českého národa* (Prague: Nakladatelství ČSAV, 1958), 174; František Fajfr, "Měl Hegel vliv na českou literaturu?" *Česká mysl* 28 (1932): 211. See also Josef Dastich, "O poměru zkoumání empirického k bádání filosofickému," *Časopis českého musea* 35: (1861), especially 60–63, with his contrast between the "fantastic" ideas of Kant, Fichte, Schelling, and Hegel, which led to the decay of philosophy, and the major advances in natural sciences; Josef Durdík, "O domnělém úpadku filosofie," *Osvěta*, 1872: 161; Gustav A. Lindner, "O úpadku filosofie," *Časopis českého musea* 56 (1882): 490–92, viewed the idealistic philosophers, such as Schelling, Hegel, and Schopenhauer, as philosophical poets, whose subjectivism was opposed to philosophy proper. Among the latter, he highlighted Herbart and J. S. Mill, seeing them on the same wavelength as Darwin in biology, as well as Dain, Wundt, and Helmholtz in psychology; ibid, 494.

66. Durdík, "O domnělém úpadku filosofie," 346–47; Josef Král, *Československá filosofie: Nástin vývoje podle disciplin* (Prague, Melantrich, 1937), 37.

67. Durdík, "O významu nauky Herbartovy," 319, 328. Fajfr, "Měl Hegel vliv na českou literaturu?" 211–12, surveying the anti-Hegelian front in Bohemia in the second half of the nineteenth century, added Czech positivists to the followers of Herbart and Brentano: Masaryk, František Čáda (1855–1918), František Drtina (1861–1925), Otakar Kádner (1870–1936), and František Krejčí (1858–1934).

68. Zdeněk Nejedlý, *T. G. Masaryk* (Prague: Melantrich, 1930–37); 2nd ed., vols. 1–2, Sebrané spisy, 31–32 (Prague: Orbis, 1949–50), 1: 461. Brentano became

personally acquainted with Fechner during a visit to Leipzig in November 1873; Carl Stumpf, "Reminiscences of Franz Bolzano," in *The Philosophy of Brentano,* ed. Linda L. McAlister (Atlantic Highlands, N.J.: Humanities Press, 1977), 34.

69. Gustav A. Lindner, *Lehrbuch der empirischen Psychologie als induktiver Wissenschaft,* 2nd ed. (Vienna: Gerold, 1868), iv, 6, 9, 26f, 40, 52, 61, 73, 75. See also Josef Zumr, "Die theoretischen und methodologischen Voraussetzungen der Herbartschen Metaphysik," *Wiener Jahrbuch für Philosophie* 1 (1968): 185–99.

70. Vlastimil Hála, "Oskar Kraus: pražský představitel brentanovské školy," *Filosofický časopis* 51 (2003): 19–37. The archive was transferred to Manchester, U.K., in 1938, and the society was proscribed by the Czechoslovak Communist government in 1958; see *Slovník českých filozofů,* ed. Gabriel and others, 306.

71. Kraus, "Die Grundzüge der Welt- und Lebensanschauung T. G. Masaryks," 105–6. On Bergmann, see also Smith, "Austrian Origins of Logical Positivism," 51.

72. Rudolf Haller, "Brentanos Spuren im Werk Masaryks," in *T. G. Masaryk und die Brentano-Schule,* ed. Josef Zumr and Thomas Binder (Prague: Filosofický ústav Československé akademie věd, 1992), 10 ff. See also Zdeněk V. David, "Masaryk and the Austrian Philosophical Tradition: Bolzano and Brentano," in *Czech and Slovak Culture in International and Global Context,* ed. Miloslav Rechcigl and others (České Budějovice: University of South Bohemia, 2008), 191–200.

73. Josef Zumr, "Masaryk a němečtí filozofové jeho doby," in *T. G. Masaryk a situace v Čechách a na Moravě od konce XIX. století do německé okupace Československa,* ed. Eva Broklová (Prague: Ústav T. G. Masaryka, 1998), 22–23. Ehrenfels also attempted to establish cooperation between the followers of Brentano and Meinong; see Felix Weltsch, "Christian Ehrenfels," *Česká mysl* 28 (1932): 266.

74. František Weyr, *Paměti* (Prague: Atlantis, 1999), 1:244.

75. José G. Merquior, *From Prague to Paris: A Critique of Structuralist and Post-Structuralist Thought* (London: Verso, 1986), 25.

76. Rudolf Carnap, "Überwindung der Metaphysik durch logische Analyse der Sprache," *Erkenntnis* 2 (1931–32): 219–41; reprinted in Schleichert, ed., *Logischer Empirismus: der Wiener Kreis,* 149–71; English trans. in Ayer, ed., *Logical Positivism,* 60–81. See also Carnap, *Scheinprobleme in der Philosophie. Das Fremdpsychische und der Realismusstreit,* 53, 73, 113. Carnap had been in contact with Reichenbach since the 1920s; see Carnap, "Intellectual Autobiography," 14.

77. Král, *Československá filosofie,* 250–52. Quine characterized his meeting with Carnap in Prague in 1932 as "[the] most notable experience of being intellectually fired by a living teacher"; see Quine, *The Time of My Life,* 98. Ayer also visited Prague, as well as Budapest, during his study in Vienna in 1933 but apparently as a tourist only; see Rogers, *A. J. Ayer,* 95.

78. Quine, *The Time of My Life,* 94.

79. See, for instance, Blumberg and Feigl, "Logical Positivism, a New Movement in European Philosophy," 281–96.

80. Neurath, "Die Entwicklung des Wiener Kreises und die Zukunft des logischen Empirismus," 2:698.

81. He would die there a year later in 1937; see *Neue Deutsche Biographie* (Berlin: Duncker & Humblot, 1953–), 4:145.

82. Hans Reichenbach was dismissed from his post at the University of Berlin in 1933; see *The Encyclopedia of Philosophy,* ed. Borchert, 8:318. Moritz Schlick,

the founder of the Vienna Circle, was murdered at the University of Vienna in 1936; see Schleichert, ed., *Logischer Empirismus: der Wiener Kreis*, 8. Simons, *Philosophy and Logic in Central Europe*, 9.

83. Schlick's assassin was released from jail after the German annexation of Austria; Frank, *Modern Science and Its Philosophy*, 49–50.

84. After an interlude at the University of Istanbul in Turkey (1933–38), he taught at the University of California in Los Angeles until his death in 1953; see *The Encyclopedia of Philosophy*, Borchert, 8:318.

85. Rudolf Carnap,, "Intellectual Autobiography," in *The Philosophy of Rudolf Carnap*, Library of Living Philosophers, 11, ed. Paul A. Schilpp (La Salle, Ill.: Open Court, 1963), 40.

86. Ayer, ed., *Logical Positivism*, 6–10. On the connection of the Vienna Circle with analytic philosophy, see Haller, "Der 'Wiener Kreis' und die analytische Philosophie," in Haller, *Studien zur österreichischen Philosophie: Variationen über ein Thema*, 79–98; David S. Clarke, *Philosophy's Second Revolution: Early and Recent Analytic Philosophy* (Chicago: Open Court, 1997); William W. Tait, ed., *Early Analytic Philosophy: Frege, Russell, Wittgenstein: Essays in Honor of Leonard Linsky* (Chicago: Open Court, 1997).

87. The salient features of analytical philosophy have been described as "employment of mathematical logic as a tool, or method, of philosophy; its emphasis on language and meaning; its generally atomistic and empiricist assumptions; and the fact that many of its practitioners have viewed science, especially physics, as a paradigm of human knowledge." Hylton, *Russell, Idealism and the Emergence of Analytic Philosophy*, 14.

88. Ibid., 14. See also Edward Craig, ed., *Routledge Encyclopedia of Philosophy* (New York: Routledge, 1998), 1:226–27.

89. *Kodansha Encyclopedia of Japan* (Tokyo: Kodansha, 1983), 5:232; *Encyclopedia of Asian Philosophy*, ed. Oliver Leaman (London: Routledge, 2001), 279, 328. See also L. A. Bobrova, *Poisk putei k istine: opyt analiticheskoi filosofii* (Moscow: Rossiiskaia akademiia nauk, 1995); Yi Jiang, "Analytic Philosophy in China," *Social Sciences in China* 23, no. 2 (2002): 65–74; G. C. Nayak, "The Analytic Philosophy of Nagarjuna and Candrakirti: Some Implications," *Journal of Indian Council of Philosophical Research* 2, no. 2 (1985): 51–60; Jorge J. E. Gracia, "The Impact of Philosophical Analysis in Latin America," *Philosophical Forum* 20 (1989): 129–40; Barry Hallen, *African Philosophy: The Analytic Approach* (Trenton, N.J.: Africa World Press, 2005).

90. On Nebeský, Štorch, and Tomek, see Fajfr, "Měl Hegel vliv na českou literaturu?" 16, 100. On Vincenc Zahradník, *Filosofické spisy*, ed. František Čáda, 2 vols. (Prague: Česká akademie pro vědy slovesnost a umění, 1907–8), 1:92; on Bolzano, see also Karel Janský, ed., *Karel Hynek Mácha ve vzpomínkách současníků* (Prague: Svobodné slovo, 1958), 186–87, 199–200.

91. The reference is to Šmahel's characterizations of the Bohemian religious wars of the early fifteenth century as "a revolution before revolutions" or "a reformation before reformations." See František Šmahel, *Husitská revoluce*, 2nd ed. (Prague: Univerzita Karlova, 1996), 4:168.

92. *Deutsche Biographische Enzyklopaedie* (Munich: K. G. Sauer, 1995–2000), 2:14.

93. See chapter 2 in this volume.
94. See chapter 5 in this volume.

Appendix

1. The first set of dates refers to the years of appointment; the second set to the life span.

2. The Czech University of Prague was closed down by the Nazis from 1939 to 1945.

Chronology of Events from the Bohemian Reformation and the National Awakening

The Bohemian Reformation

1415, July 6: Jan Hus was executed at the Council of Constance.

1420–1431: Bohemian religious wars.

1420s: Utraquism defined its tenets as a liberal Catholicism in contest against Protestant-like radicals, mainly the Taborites in the 1420s, establishing an ecclesiastical organization under a consistory by 1431.

1436: The *Compactata* of the Council of Basel recognized the Utraquists as a part of the Roman Catholic Church as "communicants in two kinds" or the *sub utraque*, and equal to other Roman Catholics ("the communicants in one kind" or the *sub una*).

1452: The Taborites were suppressed.

1457: Their Protestant-like religiosity was revived by the Unity of Brethren.

1462: The *Compactata* was revoked by Pope Pius II.

1485: The Peace of Kutná Hora reaffirmed religious freedom for the Utraquists and the *sub una* for all classes of population, including the subject peasantry.

1517: The Protestant Reformation began.

Mid-sixteenth century: Utraquist theologians Bohuslav Bílejovský (c. 1480–1555) and Pavel Bydžovský (1496–1559) defined their liberal Catholicism vis-à-vis Protestant Lutheranism.

1545–63: The Council of Trent took place, and a line of Roman archbishops of Prague restarted in 1561, both events largely disregarded by the Utraquists.

1575, September: Lutherans (adherents to the Bohemian Confession, virtually identical to the Augsburg Confession) and the Unity of Brethren received an oral grant of religious freedom from the Bohemian King and Holy Roman Emperor, Maximilian II.

1609, July: The Letter of Majesty, issued by Bohemian King and Holy Roman Emperor Rudolf II, confirmed the grant of religious freedom in writing. The Utraquist Consistory henceforth turned into an administrative body for the Lutherans and the Brethren, as well as for the Utraquists, with each denomination preserving its distinctive theology, liturgy, and clergy.

1618, May: The uprising of the Bohemian estates began out of fear that the Habsburg kings, who favored the Counter-Reformation, would curtail religious freedom.

1620, November 8: The Battle of the White Mountain, near Prague, ended the uprising and ushered in the Counter-Reformation under King and Emperor Ferdinand II, with the Jesuit Order given primary control over the religious, intellectual, and cultural life of the country.

1621: The Utraquist Consistory was abolished and the Lutheran and Brethren clergy expelled; the Utraquist clergy were forced to integrate with the Roman Church under the discipline of the decrees of the Council of Trent.

1627, May: The Renewed Land Ordinance, issued by Ferdinand II, proclaimed tridentine Catholicism the only permissible religion; deviation from it equated with treason against the state.

The National Awakening

1740–80: Empress and Queen Maria Theresa, an advocate of moderate Enlightenment, with the assistance of reform-minded advisers, among whom Bishop Ambrose S. Stock was particularly prominent, initiated educational reforms to limit the influence of the Jesuits, beginning in 1752.

1759: The Dominicans were entrusted with the teaching of theology and philosophy at the universities of Prague and Olomouc. The realism of Thomas Aquinas replaced the essentialism of Francisco Suárez, favored by the Jesuits.

1763–1801: Karl Heinich Seibt (1735–1806) held a key position in teaching philosophy and humanities at the University of Prague.

1773, September: The Jesuit Order was suppressed in the Habsburg monarchy, including Bohemia.

1780–90: Emperor Joseph II introduced in the Habsburg monarchy, including Bohemia, a pervasive cultural Enlightenment, known after him as Josephist.

1781, November: The Toleration Patent granted religious freedom to Protestants. This measure, together with the introduction of the freedom of the press, signified the complete end of the Counter-Reformation.

1782, František Faustin Procházka rehabilitated and presented as a model the scholarship and culture of the Utraquist sixteenth century in his *De saecularibus liberalium artium in Bohemia et Moravia satis commentarius*.

1783, March: The General Seminaries were established to educate clergy in the spirit of liberal Reform Catholicism. Their pedagogical and theological guidance was outlined by Abbot Franz S. Rautenstrauch, particularly in his *Entwurf zur Einrichtung der theologischen Schulen in den k. k. Erblanden* (1782).

1784: Johann Heinrich Wolf declared, in his *Leben, Lehre, Wandel und Tod des im J. 1415 lebendig verbrannten Johann Hus,* that Hus and the

Utraquists were unjustly characterized as Protestant by both the Jesuits and the Lutherans.

1785: Otto Steinbach of Kranichstein celebrated the state of religious toleration in sixteenth-century Bohemia in his treatise, "Versuch einer Geschichte der alten und neuen Toleranz im Königreich Böhmen und Markgraftum Mähren."

1786: František Faustin Procházka launched his project of systematic and comprehensive republication of the classics of the Golden Age in several series.

1791: Josef Dobrovský eulogized the intellectual freedom and the high cultural standard of the Golden Age in his *Geschichte der böhmischen Sprache und Literatur*.

1804–20: Bernard Bolzano (1781–1848) taught at the Prague University in the Department of Religion.

1805: František J. Tomsa published a *Chrestomathie* (Anthology), containing a selection of texts from the Utraquist classics for the use of students and public, and thus initiating a diffusion of the Reformation ideas through the school books.

1817–20: František Palacký became steeped in the literature of the Scottish Enlightenment during his studies in Bratislava.

1825: Josef Jungmann completed the search for Czech publications of the Utraquist period in his *Historie literatury české*.

1827–30: John Bowring was in touch with František L. Čelakovský, Josef Jungmann, and Josef Dobrovský to collect materials for his *Cheskian Anthology: Being a History of the Poetical Literature of Bohemia* (1832), highlighting the influence of British liberalism.

1831–48: Franz Exner (1802–53) taught philosophy at the University of Prague.

1837: Bolzano published his magnum opus *Wissenschaftslehre*, with the dominant idea of discrediting Kant's philosophy.

1837: Jan Kollár published his *O literaturnéj vzájemnosti mezi kmeny a nářečími slávskými*, a treatise according to Herder's essentialist and linguistic view of nationality.

1842: Franz Exner published his critical *Die Psychologie der Hegelschen Schule*.

1844: Antonín Marek and Ferdinand Hyna defended logical realism against German idealism in the first modern Czech-language textbooks of philosophy and psychology, respectively, in *Základy filosofie: Logika. Metafysika* and in *Dušesloví zkušebné*.

1845: A dispute about Hegel between Vendelín Grünwald and Josef M. Hurban in the journal *Včela* highlighted the contrast between Czech realism and Slovak idealism.

1846–48: Josef M. Hurban propagated Hegelianism as editor of the journal *Slovenskje pohladi na vedi, umeňja a literatúru*.

1847: The great debate about German idealism was led by Vilém Gabler and Karel Havlíček.

1848: The March Revolution led to the temporary introduction of a constitutional regime in the Austrian Empire, from April 1848 until March 1849.

1848, May 18–22: František Náhlovský, Bolzano's disciple in philosophy and theology, organized a convocation of priests in the Sorbian Seminary. The meeting celebrated Bolzano, Fesl, and Hurdálek as heroes. Proposals for liberalization paralleled Utraquist ecclesiological principles.

1855: The Austrian Concordat with the Holy See led to a retridentization of the Roman Church in the empire, spelling the end of hopes for reviving Utraquism under the guise of Reform Catholicism of the Josephist Enlightenment.

Glossary

Bohemian Confession: virtually identical with the Augsburg Confession, was submitted to Bohemian King and Holy Roman Emperor Maximilian II by Czech Lutherans in 1575 with a petition to receive a legal status in Bohemia comparable to that of the *sub utraque* (the Utraquists) and *the sub una.* Maximilian granted them informal toleration.

Catholic Enlightenment: in the Habsburg Monarchy drew much inspiration from Febronianism in ecclesiology and from Jansenism in its stress on the central role of moral theology; with cautious beginnings in the reign of Maria Theresa (1740–80), it developed fully under Joseph II (1780–90), especially in Austria and Bohemia.

Compactata: an agreement concluded between the Council of Basel and Bohemian reformers in 1436 that recognized the Utraquists or the "communicants in two kinds" (*sub utraque*) as a part of the Roman Catholic Church.

Febronianism: An approach to ecclesiastical reform advocating submission of Catholic churches to state authority and limiting papal jurisdiction over bishops. A German counterpart to French Gallicanism.

Jansenism: a Catholic reform movement originating in seventeenth-century France and also influential in the first half of the eighteenth in Central Europe; its stress on moral teaching rather than on religious dogma and elaborate liturgy subsequently influenced the Catholic Enlightenment.

Josephist Enlightenment: the culminating stage of the Catholic Enlightenment in Austria and Bohemia in the reign of Emperor Joseph II (1780–90).

Judge of Cheb: an agreement between representatives of the Council of Basel and the Bohemian reformers in 1432 that religious issues between the council and the Bohemians would be decided not according to papal or conciliar edicts but according to the Scripture and the recognized church fathers and doctors, as long as the latter did not contradict the biblical text.

Hereditary Lands: describe the Austrian and Bohemian lands under Habsburg rule. The designation was used mostly between 1526 and 1849.

Letter of Majesty: issued by Bohemian King and Holy Roman Emperor Rudolf II in July 1609, formally granted religious freedom to the Lutherans and the Unity of Brethren, who thus came to enjoy the same degree of toleration as the Utraquists and the *sub una*.

Reform Catholicism: developed as a part of the Josephist Enlightenment and opposed religiously inspired asceticism (including priestly celibacy, monasticism, and mystical devotions), as well as ultramontanism in ecclesiology. It favored moral and legal tolerance of other religious believers.

Renewed Land Ordinance: issued by Ferdinand II in May 1627, proclaimed tridentine Catholicism the only permissible religion in Bohemia.

Revolutions of 1848: spread from France to much of Central Europe, including the Austrian Empire, where the March Revolution led to the temporary establishment of a constitutional regime from April 1848 to March 1849.

***Sola fide*:** Lutheran principle that salvation is secured by faith alone, not by good works.

***Sola scriptura*:** Lutheran principle that the word of God in Scripture is sufficient for salvation, without an input from church fathers and doctors, or the extrabiblical ecclesiastical tradition.

Sub una: *communicantes sub una specie* (communicants in one kind), Catholics in Bohemia from the fifteenth through the seventeenth century, who remained under papal jurisdiction and received communion in the form of bread only.

Sub utraque: *communicantes sub utraque specie* (communicants in both kinds, the Utraquists) were the Catholics in Bohemia, who from ca 1417 rejected papal jurisdiction and received communion in the form of bread and wine.

Taborites: a radical wing in the Bohemian Reformation since 1416–18; under the probable influence of the medieval sects of the Waldensian and the Pickards, they rejected the apostolic, sacramental, and liturgical principles of traditional Western Christianity and embraced fierce militarism, inspired by apocalyptic visions. Defeated militarily in 1436, the Taborites were suppressed in 1452.

Ultramontanism: a strong emphasis on papal authority and on centralization of the Roman Catholic Church; the opposite of Febronianism and Gallicanism.

Unity of Brethren: established in 1457, a small, but devout, sect that resumed within the Bohemian Reformation the Taborite opposition to the beliefs and practices of medieval Christianity, but replaced the Taborite militarism with uncompromising pacifism and moral puritanism.

Vormärz: the period in the Austrian Empire from 1815 until the March Revolution of 1848.

White Mountain, Battle of: on November 8, 1620, ended the uprising of the Bohemian estates against King and Emperor Ferdinand II and ushered in the Counter-Reformation with the expulsion of the Lutheran and Brethren clergy from the country and the forcible integration of Utraquist priests into the posttridentine Roman Church. The Jesuit Order assumed primary control over the religious, intellectual, and cultural life of the country.

Bibliography

Archival Sources

Jeník z Bratřic, Jan. *Bohemica I (Bohemica Buriana)*. Nar. Muz. Prague, MS IV G 13.
Rautenstrauch, Franz Stephan. *Diarium privatum*, Státní ústřední archív. Prague, MS Benediktini Břevnov, ŘBB 88.
———. *Diarium eruditum*. Státní ústřední archív, Prague, MS Benediktini Břevnov, ŘBB 89.

Primary Sources

Rare Czech titles are accompanied by references to entry numbers in *Knihopis českých a slovenských tisků*. Vol. 2, in 9 pts., *Tisky z let 1501–1800*. Prague: Nakladatelství Československé akademie věd, 1939–67; *Dodatky*, 1994–, cited as *Knihopis*. Rare Latin titles are accompanied by references to page number in Josef Hejnic and Jan Martínek, eds. *Rukověť' humanistického básnictví v Čechách a na Moravě od konce 15. do začátku 17. století*. 5 vols. Prague: Academia, 1966–82, cited as *Rukověť'*.
Abbildungen Böhmischer und Mährischer Gelehrten und Künstler, ed. František M. Pelcl and Mikuláš Adaukt Voigt. 4 vols. Vol. 1–2, Prague: Wolfgang Gerle, 1773–75; vol. 3, Prague: Johann Karl Hraba, 1777; vol. 4, Prague: Normalschulbuchdruckerei, 1782. *Knihopis* 6963.
Abhandlungen einer Privatgesellschaft in Böhmen zur Aufnahme der Mathematik, der vaterländischen Geschichte und der Naturgeschichte. 6 vols. Prague: 1775–84.
Abhandlungen der böhmischen Gesellschaft der Wissenschaften zu Prag. 4 vols. Prague: 1785–88.
Neuere Abhandlungen der k. böhmischen Gesellschaft der Wissenschaften, 3 vols. Prague: 1790–98. [1(1790): Franz Jeřábek; 2(1795): Calve; 3(1798): Franz Jeřábek].
Abhandlungen der königlichen böhmischen Gesellschaft der Wissenschaften vom Jahre . . ., 8 vols. Prague: 1804–24.

Adam z Veleslavína, Daniel. *Kalendář historický: Krátké a summovní poznamenání všechněch dnů jednohokaždého měsíce přes celý rok.* Prague: Daniel Adam z Veleslavína, 1590. *Knihopis* 59.

———. *Kalendář historický: To jest krátké poznamenání všech dnuov jednokaždého měsíce přes celý rok.* Prague: Daniel Adam z Veleslavína, 1578. *Knihopis* 58.

———. *Sylva quadrilinguis vocabulorum et phrasium Bohemicae, Latinae, Graecae et Germanicae linguae.* Prague: Daniel Adam z Veleslavína, 1598. *Rukověť* 1:41.

Antologie z dějin českého a slovenského filozofického myšlení. Prague: Svoboda, 1981. 1st ed., *Antologie z dějin československé filosofie.* Prague: Nakladatelství Československé akademie věd, 1963.

Archiv český. See Palacký, František.

Ayer, Alfred J. *Central Questions of Philosophy.* New York: Morrow, 1975.

———. "Editor's Introduction." In *Logical Positivism*, edited by Alfred J. Ayer, 3–28. Glencoe, Ill.: Free Press, 1959.

———. *Freedom and Morality and Other Essays.* Oxford: Clarendon Press, 1984.

———, ed. *Logical Positivism.* Glencoe, Illinois: Free Press, 1959.

———. "Logical Positivism: A Debate." In *The Meaning of Life,* 18ff. New York: Scribner's, 1990.

———. "Reflections on *Language, Truth and Logic.*" In *Logical Positivism in Perspective: Essays on Language, Truth, and Logic,* edited by Barry Gower, 23–34. Totowa, N.J.: Barnes & Noble Books, c1987.

———. *Wittgenstein.* Chicago: University of Chicago Press, 1986.

Bacon, Francis. *Vypsání nového světa.* Translated by Bohumír Jan Dlabač. Prague: Kramerius, 1798. *Knihopis* 919. Translation of Bacon's *New Atlantis*, originally published in 1628.

Bardili, Christoph G. *Briefwechsel über das Wesen der Philosophie und das Unwesen der Spekulation.* Munich: [C. L. Reinhold], 1804.

———. *Grundriss der ersten Logik, gereiniget von den Irrthümmern bisheriger Logiken überhaupt, der Kantischen insbesondere: keine Kritik sondern eine medicina mentis, brauchbar hauptsächlich für Deutschlands kritische Philosophie.* Stuttgart: Franz C. Löflund, 1800. Reprint series, Aetas Kantiana, 13. Brussels: Culture et civilisation, 1970.

Barnes, Robert. *Kronyky. A životů sepsání nejvrchnějších Biskupů Římských jináč Papežů.* Translated by Ennius Glatouinus. Nuremberg: Woldřich Nejber and Jan Montán, 1565. *Knihopis* 958.

Bartoš Písař. *Kronika pražská.* In *Fontes rerum Bohemicarum,* edited by Josef V. Šimák, 6: 1–297. Prague: Nadání Františka Palackého, 1907.

Beneke, Friedrich Eduard. *Grundlegung zur Physik der Sitten, ein Gegenstück zu Kants Grundlegung zur Metaphysik der Sitten.* Berlin und Posen: In commission bei E. S. Mittler, 1822.

Beneš, Edvard. *Projevy, články, rozhovory, 1935–1938.* Prague: Masarykův ústav, 2006.

Bergmann, Hugo. *Das philosophische Werk B. Bolzanos.* Halle: Niemeyer, 1909.

Bílejovský, Bohuslav. *Kronyka cýrkevní.* Edited by Josef Skalický. Prague: Fetterl z Vilden, 1816.

Blair, Hugh. *Lectures on Rhetoric and Belles Lettres.* 3 vols. New York: Garland, 1970. [Reprint of 2nd ed., 1785.]

Bolingbroke, Henry St. John. *Historical Writings.* Edited by Isaac Kramnick. Chicago: University of Chicago Press, 1972.

———. *Letters on the Study and Use of History.* 2 vols. New York: Garland, 1970. [Reprint of 1752 ed.]

Bolzano, Bernard, see also Zeithammer, Gregor.

Bolzano, Bernard. *Der böhmische Vormärz in Briefen B. Bolzanos an F. Příhonský, 1824–1848: Beiträge zur deutsch-slawischen Wechselseitigkeit.* Edited by Eduard Winter, Deutsche Akademie der Wissenschaften zu Berlin. Institut für Slawistik. Veröffentlichungen, nr. 11. Berlin: Akademie-Verlag, 1956.

———. *Der Briefwechsel B. Bolzanos mit F. Exner.* Edited by Eduard Winter. Prague: Königliche böhmische Gesellschaft der Wissenschaften, 1935.

———. *Drei philosophische Abhandlungen welche auch von Nichtphilosophen sehr wohl verstanden werden können.* Leipzig: Reclam, 1851.

———. *Gesamtausgabe.* Edited by Eduard Winter, Jan Berg, Friedrich Kambartel, Jaromír Loužil, and Bob van Rootselaar. 40 vols. in 57 parts. Series: Einleitug; I. Schriften; II. Nachlass; III. Briefwechsel; IV. Dokumente. Stuttgart-Bad Cannstatt: Frommann Holzboog, 1969–.

———. *Lehrbuch der Religionswissenschaft*, in *Gesamtausgabe.* Reihe I, Schriften: Band 6, Erster Teil (2 vols.); Band 7, Zweiter Teil (2 vols.); Band 8, Dritter Teil (2 vols.).

———. *Mathematisch-Physikalische und Philosophische Schriften, 1842–1843*, in *Gesamtausgabe.* Reihe I, Schriften, Band 18.

———. *Mathematische und Philosophische Schriften, 1810–1816, Gesamtausgabe.* Reihe II, Nachlass A, Band 5.

———. *On the Mathematical Method and Correspondence with Exner.* Translated by Paul Rusnock and Rolf George. Amsterdam and New York: Rodopi, 2004.

———. "O poměru obou národností v Čechách." In *Obrození národa: svědectví a dokumenty*, edited by Jan Novotný, 163–79. Prague: Melantrich, 1979.

———. *Perfektabilität des Katholicismus*, in *Gesamtausgabe.* Reihe I, Schriften, Band 19, Teil 1–2.

———. *Philosophische Tagebücher, Gesamtausgabe.* Reihe II, Nachlass, B. Wissenschaftliche Tagebücher; Band 16, *1811–1827* (vol.1–); Band 17, *1817–1827*; Band 18, *1827–1844* (vol. 2).

———. *Řeči vzdělávací akademické mládeži.* 4 vols. Prague: Urbánek, 1884.

———. *Theory of Science: Attempt at a Detailed and in the Main Novel Exposition of Logic with Constant Attention to Earlier Authors.* Edited and translated by Rolf George. Berkeley: University of California Press, 1972. Partial translation of *Wissenschaftslehre* [see below].

———. *Über das Verhältniss der beiden Volkstämme in Böhmen.* Vienna: Wilhelm Braumüller, 1849.

———. *Vědosloví: výbor.* Edited by Karel Berka. Translated by Marie Bayerová and Jaromír Loužil. Prague: Academia, 1981. Partial translation of *Wissenschaftslehre,* see below: *Wissenschaftslehre*, in *Gesamtausgabe.*

———. *Vermischte philosophische und physikalische Schriften, 1832–1848*, in *Gesamtausgabe.* Reihe II, Nachlass A, Band 12, Teil 1–3.

———. *24 Erbauungsreden, 1808–1820.* Edited by Kurt F. Strasser. Vienna: Böhlau, 2001.

———. *Vlastní životopis.* Edited and translated by Marie Pavlíková. Prague: Odeon, 1981.

———. *Výbor z filozofických spisů*. Edited by Jiří Černý and Jaromír Loužil. Translated by Jaromír Loužil. Prague: Svoboda, 1981.

———. *Wissenschaftslehre*, in *Gesamtausgabe*. Reihe I, Schriften: Band 11, Teil 1–3; Band 12, Teil 1–3; Band 13, Teil 1–3; Band 14, Teil 1–3.

———. *Wissenschaft und Religion in Vormärz: Der Briefwechsel Bernard Bolzanos mit Michael Josef Fesl, 1822–1848*. Edited by Eduard Winter and W. Zeil. Berlin: Akademie-Verlag, 1965.

Borový, Klement. *Jednání a dopisy konsistoře katolické a utrakvistické*. 2 vols. Prague: I. L. Kober, 1868.

Bossuet, Jacques Bénigne. *Učení katolického v těch věcech, o kterých rozepře jsou, vyložení*. Prague: C. k. školní knihtiskárna, 1778. *Knihopis* 1234.

[Bowring, John]. "Appréciation de l'état politique et militaire de la Monarchie Autrichienne." *Revue britannique* 4 (1831): 49–65.

———. *Cheskian Anthology: Being a History of the Poetical Literature of Bohemia*. London: Rowland Hunter, 1832.

———. "Historie literatury české . . . prací Josefa Jungmanna [Bohemian Literature]." *Foreign Quarterly Review* 2 (1828): 145–74.

[———]. "Joseph Dobrowsky." *Foreign Quarterly Review* 4 (1829): 335–36. [Concerning the authorship, see Otakar Odložilík, "Dobrovský a anglický slavista John Bowring." In *Josef Dobrovský, 1753–1829: sborník statí k stému výročí smrti Josefa Dobrovského*, edited by Jiří Horák, Matyáš Murko, and Miloš Weingart, 256. Prague: Výbor I. Sjezdu slovanských filologů, 1929.]

———. "Kralodworsky Rukopis [Ancient Bohemian Ballads]." *Westminster Review* 12 (1830): 304–21.

———. "Littérature et la poésie de la Bohême." *Revue britannique* 17 (1828): 225–50.

Brentano, Franz Clemens. *Über die Zukunft der Philosophie; nebst den Vorträgen: Über die Gründe der Entmutigung auf philosophischem Gebiet, Über Schellings System, sowie den 25 Habilitationsthesen*. 2nd rev. ed. Hamburg: Meiner [1968].

———. *Die vier Phasen der Philosophie und ihr augenblicklicher Stand. Nebst Abhandlungen über Plotinus, Thomas von Aquin, Kant, Schopenhauer und Auguste Comte*. Edited by Oskar Kraus, with new introduction by Franziska Mayer-Hillebrand. 2nd ed. Hamburg: Meiner, 1968.

Brykcí z Licska. *Regule, To jest řeholy obecné z latinských učitelův práv vybrané . . . .* Prague: Bartoloměj Netolický, 1541. *Knihopis* 1349.

Bydžovský, Pavel. *Děťátka a neviňátka hned po přijetí křtu sv. Tělo a Krev Boží, že přijímati mají*. Prague: Bartoloměj Netolický, 1541. *Knihopis, Dodatky*, 1388.

———. *Historiae aliquot Anglorum martyrum, quibus Deus suam ecclesiam exornare sicut syderibus coelum dignatus est*. Prague: J. Cantor, 1554.

———. *Knížky o přijímání Těla a Krve Pána našeho Ježíše Krysta . . . .* Prague, 1539. *Knihopis* 1393.

———. *Odvolání jednoho Bratra z Roty Pikhartské*. 2nd ed. Prague: Jan Jičínský, 1588. *Knihopis, Dodatky* 1395.

———. *Tato Knížka toto try ukazuje . . . .* N.p., 1542. *Knihopis* 1391.

———. *Tento spis ukazuje, že Biskupové Biskupa a Biskup kněží, a kněží od řádných Biskupů svěcení, Těla a Krve Boží posvěcovati mají*. N.p., 1543. *Knihopis* 1396.

Carnap, Rudolf. "Die alte und die neue Logik." *Erkenntnis* 1 (1930–31): 12–26.

―――. "The Elimination of Metaphysics through Logical Analysis of Language." In *Logical Positivism,* edited by Alfred J. Ayer, 60–81. Glencoe, Ill.: Free Press, 1959. English translation with a 1957 addition, 80–81, of the German original of Carnap's "Überwindung der Metaphysik durch logische Analyse der Sprache." *Erkenntnis* 2 (1931–32): 219–41.

―――. *Intellectual Autobiography.* Edited by P. I. Schipp, Library of Living Philosophers 9. La Salle, Ill.: Open Court, 1963.

―――. "Intellectual Autobiography." In *The Philosophy of Rudolf Carnap*, edited by Paul A. Schilpp, Library of Living Philosophers 9. La Salle, Ill.: Open Court, 1963, 1–84.

―――. "The Old and the New Logic." In *Logical Positivism,* edited by Alfred J. Ayer, 133–46. Glencoe, Ill.: Free Press, 1959.

―――. *Scheinprobleme in der Philosophie. Das Fremdpsychische und der Realismusstreit.* Frankfurt a. M.: Suhrkamp, 1966.

Cassiodorus, Flavius Magnus. *Historie cýrkevní.* Translated by Jan Kocín z Kocinétu. Prague: Daniel Adam z Veleslavína, 1594. *Knihopis* 1470.

Čechura, Jaroslav, and Jana Čechurová, eds. *Korespondence Josefa Pekaře a Kamila Krofty.* Prague: Karolinum, 1999.

Čelakovský, František Ladislav. *Korespondence a zápisky.* 3 vols. Sbírka pramenů ku poznání literárního života v Čechách, na Moravě a ve Slezsku, Skupina 2, Číslo 10, 14, 21. Edited by František Bílý. Prague: Česká akademie pro vědy, slovesnost a umění, 1909–14.

―――. "Obrana." *Česká včela* 2 (1835): 287–88.

―――. "Slovo o Slávy Dceři p. Jana Kollára." *Časopis českého musea* 5 (1831): 39–54.

Čenský, Ferdinand, ed. *Z dob našeho probuzení: Sbírka přátelských dopisů.* Prague: Urbánek, 1875.

Červenák, Benjamín Pravoslav. *Zrcadlo Slovenska.* Pešt: Trattner-Károlyi, 1844.

Chmelenský, Josef K. "Literatura r. 1836." *Časopis českého musea* 10 (1836): 207–19.

Comenius, Johann Amos, see Komenský, Jan.

Cornova, Ignác. *Briefe an einen kleinen Liebhaber der vaterländischen Geschichte.* 3 vols. Prague: Calve, 1796–97. See also Stránský, Pavel.

―――. "Hat Schirach König Georgen von Böhmen nicht nur katholische Rechtgläubigkeit, sondern auch Religion überhaupt mit Grund abgesprochen?" *Neuere Abhandlungen der königlichen Böhmischen Gesellschaft der Wissenschaften* 3 (1798): 161–72.

Čupr, František. "Článek o vlastenectví. *Česká včela* 13 (1846): 283–84, 289–90, 292–94.

―――. "Ferdinanda Hýny dušesloví zkušebné." *Časopis českého musea* 20 (1846): 516–27, 657–61.

―――. "Ohlas strany německé literatury." *Květy* 14 (1847): 287–88.

―――. "O národovědě." *Časopis českého musea* 22 (1848): pt. 2, 113–42.

―――. "Počátkové filosofování řeckého." *Časopis českého musea* 21, pt. 1 (1847): 22–37.

―――. "Schreiben an Herrn Dr. A. Smetana betreffend die Recension des Gablerschen Artikels." *Ost und West* 11 (1847): 233–35, 238.

———. *Sein oder Nichtsein der deutschen Philosophie in Böhmen.* Prague: G. Haase Söhne, 1847.
Cykáda, Jan V. *Hody křesťanské na které Bůh Otec skrze Syna svého zve.* Prague: Impressí Šumanská, 1607. *Knihopis* 1707.
Dastich, Josef. "O poměru zkoumání empirického k bádání filosofickému." *Časopis českého musea* 35 (1861): 54–71.
Dobner, Gelasius, see Hájek, Václav of Libočany.
Dobrovský, Josef. *Die Bildsamkeit der Slawischen Sprache an der Bildung der Substantive und Adjective in der Böhmischen Sprache dargestellt.* Prague: Herrl'schen-Buchhandlung, 1799. *Knihopis* 1974.
———. *Böhmische Litteratur auf das Jahr 1779.* Prague: Mangoldische Buchhandlung, 1779. *Knihopis* 1983.
———. *Böhmische und Mährische Litteratur auf das Jahr 1780–81.* Prague: Mangoldische Buchhandlung, 1780–84. *Knihopis* 1983.
———. *Briefwechsel zwischen Dobrovský und Kopitar, 1808–1828.* Edited by Vatroslav Jagić. Berlin: Weidmann'sche Buchhandlung, 1885.
———. *Dějiny české řeči a literatury v redakcích z roku 1791, 1792 a 1818* Critical edition in German of *Geschichte der böhmischen Sprache und Literatur.* 1791, 1792, 1818. Edited by Benjamin Jedlička. Prague: Melantrich, 1936.
———. *Deutsch-böhmisches Wörterbuch.* 2 vols. Prague: Herrlische Buchhandlung, 1802–21. Vol. 1, 2nd rev. ed., 1821. *Knihopis* 1994.
———. *Dopisy Josefa Dobrovského s Augustinem Helfertem.* Spisy a projevy. Vol. 22. Edited by Josef Volf and F. M. Bartoš. Prague: Melantrich, 1941.
———. *Dopisy s B. A. Veršauserem a V. Krčmou. Z rodinný dopisů.* Spisy a projevy. Vol. 21. Edited by Josef Volf and Josef Páta. Prague: Melantrich, 1937.
———. "Dopisy Václava Stacha Josefu Dobrovskému." Edited by Pavel Křivský. *Časopis Vlastivědné společnosti muzejní v Olomouci* 60 (1970): 159–71; (1971): 95–105.
———. *Korespondence*, Díl 1: *Vzájemné dopisy Josefa Dobrovského a Fortunata Duricha z let 1778–1800*, Sbírka pramenů ku poznání literárního života v Čechách, na Moravě a ve Slezsku, Skupina 2, Číslo 2. Edited by Adolf Patera. Prague: Česká akademie pro vědy, slovesnost a umění, 1895.
———. *Korespondence*, Díl 2: *Vzájemné dopisy Josefa Dobrovského a Jiřího Samuela Bandtkeho z let 1810–1827*, Sbírka pramenů ku poznání literárního života v Čechách, na Moravě a ve Slezsku, Skupina 2, Číslo 8. Edited by A. V. Francev. Prague: Česká akademie pro vědy, slovesnost a umění, 1906.
———. *Korespondence*, Díl 3: *Vzájemné dopisy Josefa Dobrovského a Josefa Valentina Zlobického z let 1781–1807*, Sbírka pramenů ku poznání literárního života v Čechách, na Moravě a ve Slezsku, Skupina 2, Číslo 9. Edited by Adolf Patera. Prague: Česká akademie pro vědy, slovesnost a umění, 1908.
———. *Korespondence*, Díl 4: *Vzájemné listy Josefa Dobrovského a J. Rybaye z let 1783–1810*, Sbírka pramenů ku poznání literárního života v Čechách, na Moravě a ve Slezsku, Skupina 2, Číslo 18. Edited by Adolf Patera Prague: Česká akademie pro vědy, slovesnost a umění, 1913.
———. "Korespondence Antonína Jaroslava Puchmajera s Josefem Dobrovským." Edited by Pavel Křivský. *Literární archiv: Sborník Památníku národního písemnictví* 8 (1974): 199–258.
———. "Korespondence Jana Leopolda Haye, Josefa Františka Hurdálka a Au-

gustina Zippa s Josefem Dobrovským." Edited by Pavel Křivský. *Literární archiv: Sborník Památníku národního písemnictví* 5 (1970): 133–68.

———. *Litterarisches Magazin von Böhmen und Mähren*. Prague: Schönfeld, Stück 1 (1786), Stück 2 (1786), Stück 3 (1787). *Knihopis* 1984.

———. *O zavedení a rozšíření knihtisku v Čechách*. Critical edition in German of *Über Einführung und Verbreitung der Buchdruckerkunst in Böhmen*, 1782. Prague: Nakladatelství Československé akademie věd, 1954.

———. *Přednášky o praktické stránce v křesťanském náboženství*. Edited by Josef Volf, Miloš B. Volf, and Josef Vraštil, Spisy a projevy. Vol. 16. Prague: Melantrich, 1948.

[———]. *Zur richtigen Verurtheilung des Thamischen deutsch-böhmischen National-Lexikons*. 3 pts. Prague: Herrlischer Buchhandlung, [1798]. *Knihopis* 1993, 1993a, 1993b.

Doucha, František. "Česká literatura v Anglicku." *Česká včela* 12 (1845): 198.

Dubravius, Jan. *Ad collegium Pragense de ecclesiae oeconomia epistola* printed in *Ioanis, Dei gratia episcopi Olomucensis, In psalmum ordine quintum ecclesiae deprecantis typum gerentem, cuius initium est: Verba mea auribus percipe, Domine, enarratio.* . . . Prostějov: Ioannes Guntherus, 1549. *Rukověť* 2:81.

Durdík, Josef. *Dějiny filosofie nejnovější*. Prague: Otto, 1887.

———. "O domnělém úpadku filosofie." *Osvěta* 2, pt. 2 (1872): 161–70, 251–62, 336–55.

———. *O filosofii a činnosti Bernarda Bolzana*. Prague: Akademický čtenářský spolek, 1881.

———. *O módní filosofii naší doby*. Prague: Otto, 1883.

———. "O významu nauky Herbartovy." *Časopis českého musea* 50 (1876): 294–328.

———. "Über die Verbreitung der Herbat'schen Philosophie in Böhmen." *Zeitschrift für exacte Philosophie im Sinne des neuen philosophischen Realismus* 11 (1875): 317–26.

Durych, Václav Fortunatus. *Bibliotheca Slavica antiquissimae dialecti communis et ecclesiasticae universae Slavorum gentis*. Vol. 1. Vienna: S. Novakovitsch, 1795. *Knihopis* 2145.

———. *De Slavo-Bohemica sacri codicis versione dissertatio*. Prague: Litteris Joannae Pruchianae, 1777. *Knihopis* 2146.

Dvorský, Bartoloměj (Curius). *Proti Alchoranu*. Prague: Severyn, 1542. *Knihopis* 2154.

Dvorský, František, ed. *Dopisy kněží Šimona z Habru a Jana faráře Německo-Brodského o rozdílech ve víře, 1528–1529*. In *Archiv český* 14 (1895): 324–67.

Dvorský, Mikuláš, see Weller, Hieronymus.

Emler, Josef, ed. "Ještě několik listů Josefa Jungmanna k Antonínu Markovi." *Časopis českého musea* 60 (1886): 433–44.

———, ed. "Listy Antonína Marka k Josefu Jungmannovi." *Časopis českého musea* 62 (1888): 151–69, 385–405; 63 (1889): 264–74; 66 (1892): 292–304, 457–82.

———, ed. "Listy Josefa Jungmanna k Antonínu Markovi." *Časopis českého musea* 55 (1881): 499–530; 56 (1882): 26–44, 161–84, 445–76; 57 (1883): 45–59, 330–53, 496–512; 58 (1884): 54–70, 285–97, 406–25.

Erasmus, Desiderius. *The Correspondence*. 11 vols. Toronto: University of Toronto Press, 1974–92.

———. *Ratio seu methodus compendio perveniendi ad veram theologiam.* Prague: Joann Mangoldt, 1786.
Eusebius of Caesarea (Pamphilus). *Historie církevní.* Translated by Jan Kocín z Kocinétu. Prague: Daniel Adam z Veleslavína, 1594. *Knihopis* 2390.
Exner, Franz S. *Die Psychologie der Hegelschen Schule.* Leipzig: F. Fleischer, 1842.
———. *Die Stellung der Studierenden auf der Universität: eine Rede gehalten an der k. k. Universität zu Prag, vor der Immatrikulation, den 20. Dezember 1834.* Prague: Gottlieb Haase Söhne, 1837.
Fidrmuc, J. "Je-li potřebí filosofie literatuře české." *Časopis českého musea* 18 (1844): 236–45.
Filosofie v dějinách českého národa, Protokol celostátní konference o dějinách české filosofie v Liblicích ve dnech 14.–17. dubna 1958. Prague: Nakladatelství ČSAV, 1958.
Francev, V. F., ed. *Dopisy neznámé české šlechtičny Josefu Dobrovskému z r. 1796.* Prague: Spolek českých bibliofilů, 1929.
Franklin, Benjamin. "Hry v šachy," and "Chudý starý Richard aneb prostředek bohatým býti." Translated by Josef Jungmann. *Hlasatel* II/3 (1807): 494–504.
Frantz, Ignác. *Annus primus philosophiae Pragensis ad gustum hodierni seculi metodo Recentiorum pertractatus continens cum philosophiae prolegomenis logicam atque metaphysicam,* 2 vols. Prague: Typ. Academicis, 1752.
Fries, Jakob Friedrich. *Fichtes und Schellings neueste Lehren von Gott und der Welt.* Heidelberg: Mohr und Zimmer, 1807.
Gabler, Vilém. "Erwiderung auf Herrn Dr. Smetana's Aufsatz." In *Sein oder Nichtsein der deutschen Philosophie in Böhmen,* edited by František Čupr, 108–33. Prague: G. Haase Söhne, 1847, 108–33.
———. "Něco o filosofii." *Časopis českého musea* 21, pt. 1 (1847): 269–91.
Gazzaniga, Pietro Maria. *Praelectiones theologicae,* secundis curis emendatae et auctae. 4 vols. Vol. 1, title differs: *Praelectiones de deo, ejusque proprietatibus,* secundis curis emendatae et auctae, 1770; vol. 2, subtitle: Tom. II, *De Trinitate, de Actibus Humanis, et de Beatitudine,* 1770; vol. 3, subtitle: Tom. III, *De Gratia Actuali, & Habituali,* 1771; vol. 4, subtitle: Tom. IV, *De Vertutibus Theologicis: Fide, Spe, et Caritate,* 1771. Vienna: Typis Joannis Thomae de Trattnern, 1770–71.
———. *Theologia dogmatica in systema redacta.* Vienna, 1776.
Gerometta, Eugen. "Boj o Slovenčinu. II. Pán Eugen Gerometta pánu Danielovi Lichardovi." *Slovenskje pohladi na vedi, umeňja a literatúru* 2 (1851): 198–203.
———. "Slovanou náklonnosť ku slobod'e." *Slovenskje pohladi na vedi, umeňja a literatúru* 1 (1847): svazok 2, 29–44.
Gervinus, Georg Gottfried. *Shakespeare.* 4 vols. Leipzig: Wilhelm Engelmann, 1849–50.
Gilson, Etienne. *Being and Some Philosophers.* 2nd ed. Toronto: Pontifical Institute of Medieval Studies, 1952.
Gindely, Anton. *Quellen zur Geschichte der böhmischen Brüder.* Vienna: Hof und Staatsdruckerei, 1859.
Grillparzer, Franz. *Selbstbiographie.* Edited by Arno Dusini. Salzburg: Residenz Verlag, 1994.
Grünwald, Vendelín. "Z Vídně." *Květy* 12 (1845): 443–44.

Hájek of Libočany, Václav, *Annales Bohemorum e Bohemica editione Latine redditi*, ed. Gelasius Dobner, 6 vols. Prague, Litteris viduae Kirchneri, 1761–82. *Knihopis* 1962.

Havlíček, Karel. *Korespondence*. Edited by Ladislav Quis. Prague, 1903.

———. "Leibniz a jeho idea." *Česká včela* 13 (1846): 218–19.

———. "Literatura: *Časopis českého musea*. 1845. 4tý svazek." *Česká včela* 12 (1845): 378, 382.

———. "Literatura: *Poslední Čech*. Novela Jos. Kajetana Tyla." *Česká včela* 12 (1845): 211–12, 215–16.

———. "Med a vosk." *Česká včela* 14 (1847): 232.

———. "Odporné, ale zdravé." *Česká včela* 14 (1847): 170–72.

———. "Podobizna Bolzanova." *Česká včela* 13 (1846): 204.

———. *Politické spisy*. Edited by Zdeněk V. Tobolka. 3 vols. in 5 pts. Prague: Laichter, 1900–1902.

———. "Seiendes." *Česká včela* 14, no. 41 (1847): 164.

———. "Školácká filosofie." *Česká včela* 14 (1847): 26, 142–43.

———. "Žihadlo." *Česká včela* 14 (1847): 184.

Hegel, Georg W. *Briefe von und an Hegel*. Edited by Johannes Hoffmeister. 3rd ed., 4 vols in 5 parts. Hamburg: Meiner, 1969–81.

———. *Differenz des Fichte'schen und Schelling'schen Systems der Philosophie in Beziehung auf Reinhold's Beiträge zur leichtern Übersicht der Philosophie zu Anfang des neunzehnten Jahrhunderts*. Jena: Akademische Buchhandlung, 1801. In *Jenaer Schriften, 1801–1807*, Werke 2, edited by Eva Moldenhauer and Karl M. Michel, 9–138. Frankfurt/M: Suhrkamp, 1970.

———. *Elements of the Philosophy of Right*. Translated by H. B. Nisbet. New York: Cambridge University Press, 1991.

———. *Enzyklopädie der philosophischen Wissenschaften im Grundrisse*, 1–3, Werke 8–10. Edited by Eva Moldenhauer and Karl M. Michel. Frankfurt/M: Suhrkamp, 1970.

———. *Grundlinien der Philosophie des Rechts oder Naturrecht und Staatswissenschaft im Grundrisse*, Werke 7. Edited by Eva Moldenhauer and Karl M. Michel. Frankfurt/M: Suhrkamp, 1969. Also Sämtliche Werke, 7. Stuttgart: Frommanns Verlag, 1928.

———. *Hegel's Political Writings*. Translated by T. M. Knox. Introduction by Z. A. Pelczynski. Oxford: Clarendon Press, 1964.

———. *Vorlesungen über die Geschichte der Philosophie* 1–3, Werke 18–20. Edited by Eva Moldenhauer and Karl M. Michel. Frankfurt/M: Suhrkamp, 1971.

———. *Vorlesungen über die Philosophie der Geschichte*. Sämtliche Werke, 11. Stuttgart: Frommanns Verlag, 1928.

———. "Wie der gemeine Menschenverstand die Philosophie nehme, dargestellt an den Werken des Herrn Krugs." *Kritisches Journal der Philosophie* (Jena) 1, no. 1 (1802); in *Jenaer Schriften (1801–1807)*, Werke 2, edited by Eva Moldenhauer and Karl M. Michel, 188–207. Frankfurt/M: Suhrkamp, 1970.

Hek, František V. "Přivítání strašlivé, radostné ale propuštění." *Květy* (1834): 422–24.

Herder, Johann G. *Listové z dávnověkosti*. Translated by František L. Čelakovský. Prague: Josefa Fetterlová, 1823.

———. *Outlines of a Philosophy of the History of Man.* Translated by T. Churchill. 2 vols., 2nd ed. New York: Bergman Publishers, [1966].
———. *Sämmtliche Werke.* Edited by Bernhard Suphan. 33 vols. Berlin: Weidmann, 1877–1913.
———. "Slavische Völker." In *Ideen zur Philosophie der Geschichte der Menshheit, in Sämmtliche Werke,* edited by Bernhard Suphan. 14: 277–80. 33 vols. Berlin: Weidmann, 1877–1913.
Hooker, Richard. *Folger Library Edition of the Works.* 7 vols. Cambridge, Mass.: Harvard University Press, 1977–98.
Hurban, Jozef Miloslav. *Cesta Slováka k slovanským bratom na Moravě a v Čechách, 1839.* Edited and translated by Jozef Ambruš. Bratislava: Slovenské vydavatelstvo krásnej literatúry, 1960.
———. "Odpověd' na článek z Vídně." *Květy* 12 (1845): n. 139, 557–60.
———. "Předmluva" and "Životopis Bejamína Pravoslawa Červenáka." In *Zrcadlo Slovenska,* by Benjamín Pravoslav Červenák, iii–xix and 127–41. Pešt: Trattner-Károlyi, 1844. Also in "Předmluva k Červenánkovu 'Zrcadlu Slovenska,'" by Hurban. In *Antologie z dějin českého a slovenského myšlení: do roku 1848,* ed. Ústav pro filozofii a sociologii ČSAV and Ústav pro filozofii a sociologii SAV, 489–508. Prague: Svoboda, 1981.
———. "Slovansko a jeho život literárni." *Slovenskje pohladi na vedi, umeňja a literatúru* 1 (1846): svazok 1, 14–35.
———. *Unia, čili spojení luteránů s kalvíny v Uhrách.* Budín: J. Gyurián a M. Bagó, 1846.
Hus, Jan. *Vermischte Schriften des M. J. Hus von Hussinecz. Aus dem Lateinischen.* [Edited and translated by Augustin Zitte]. Leipzig and Prague: Wolfgang Gerle, 1784.
———. *Výklady,* Magistri Iohannis Hus Opera Omnia, 1. Prague: Academia, 1975.
Husserl, Edmund. *Logical Investigations.* Translated by John N. Findlay. 2 vols. London: Routledge, 2001.
Hyna, Ferdinand. *Duchosloví zkušebné.* Malá encyklopedie nauk, 4. Prague: Kronberg and Řivnáč, 1844.
Jaitner, Klaus, ed. *Die Hauptinstruktionen Clemens' VIII. für die Nuntien und Legaten an den europäischen Fürstenhöfen, 1592–1605.* Tübingen: Max Niemayer, 1984.
Jeník z Bratřic, Jan. *Z mých pamětí.* Edited by Josef Polišenský. Prague: ELK, 1947.
Jirsík, Jan Valerián. *Populäre Dogmatik, oder Glaubenslehre der katholischen Kirche.* 4th ed. Vienna: L. Mayer's Verlag, 1865.
Josephus, Flavius. *Historia židovská. Na knihy čtyry rozdělená.* Translated, with introduction, by Václav Plácel z Elbingu. Prague: Daniel Adam z Veleslavína, 1592. *Knihopis* 3628.
Jungmann, Josef. "Dopisy Josefa Jungmann k Janu Kollárovi." Edited by Antonín J. Vrťátko. *Časopis Českého Musea* 54 (1880): 38–59, 196–218.
———. *Historie literatury české.* Prague: Antonín Straširypka, 1825. 2nd ed. Prague: Řivnáč, 1849.
———. "O jazyku českém rozmlouvání druhé." *Hlasatel český* 1, no. 3 (1806): 321–53.
———. "O jazyku českém rozmlouvání první." *Hlasatel český* 1, no. 1 (1806): 43–49.
———. *Slovesnost.* 3rd ed. Prague: Kronberger and Řivnáč, 1846.

———. *Zápisky.* Edited by Radek Lunga. Prague: Budka, 1998.
Kaizl, Josef. *České myšlenky.* 2nd ed. Prague: Edvard Beaufort, 1896.
Kalinčiak, Jan. "Boj o Slovenčinu. III. Slovo p. Lichardovi od J. Kalinčiaka." *Slovenskje pohladi na vedi, umeňja a literatúru* 2 (1851): 203–12.
Kampelík, František Cyril. *Pokladnice Franklinova.* Banská Bystrica: Filip Machold, 1838.
Klácel, Matouš F. "O citu a rozumu." *Časopis českého musea* 17 (1843): 53–92.
———. "O smrti." *Časopis českého musea* 17 (1843): 329–47.
———. "Shakespeare, Goethe, Schiller." *Časopis českého musea* 21, pt. 1 (1847): 250–69. [See under Čupr]
Kniha Jozefova. Sepsaná od jistého spatřujícího osmnácté století. Dílem již stalé věci a dílem proroctví. Na způsob Biblí. Prague: Kramerius, 1784. Translation of anonymous *Das Buch Joseph* (Prague: Wolgang Gerle, 1783). *Knihopis* 4044, 4045.
Kocín z Kocinétu, Jan. *Ioannis Bodini Nova distributio iuris universi... explicata a Ioanne Cocino.* Prague: J. Negrin, 1581. *Rukověť*, 3:53.
Kolár, Josef Jiří. "Offenes Sendschreiben an den Redakteur der böhmischen Zeitschrift *Včela.*" *Ost und West* 11 (1847): 237–38, 241–43, 245–46; also in *Sein oder Nichtsein der deutschen Philosophie in Böhmen,* by František Čupr, 87–100. Prague: G. Haase Söhne, 1847.
Kollár, Jan. *Básně.* Edited by Mojmír Otruba. Prague: Československý spisovatel, 1981.
———. *Prózy.* Vybrané spisy, 2. Edited by F. R. Tichý. Prague: Státní nakladatelství kràsné literatury, hudby a umění, 1956.
———. *Rozpravy o slovanské vzájemnosti.* Edited by Miloš Weingart. Prague: Slovanský ústav, 1929.
Komenský, Jan [Johann Amos Comenius]. *De rerum humanarum emendatione consultatio catholica.* 2 vols. Prague: Academia, 1966.
Koranda, Václav Jr. *Manualník.* Edited by Josef Truhlář. Prague: Nákl. České společnosti nauk, 1888.
———. *Traktát o velebné a božské svátosti oltářní.* Prague: Tiskař Korandy, 1493. *Knihopis* vol. 1, no. 11.
Koubek, Jan Pravoslav. "Doctorovi [sic] Bowringovi." Reported by Čeněk Zíbrt. *Časopis českého musea* 81 (1907): 310.
Kraus, Oskar. "Besonderheit und Aufgabe der deutschen Philosophie in Böhmen." *Actes du huitième Congrès de Philosophie à Prague, 2–7. Septembre 1934,* 766–71. Prague: Orbis, 1936.
———. *Franz Brentano.* Munich: Beck, 1919.
Krause, Karl Christian Friedrich. *Die drei ältesten Kunsturkunden der Freimauerbrüderschaft.* 3rd ed., 2 vols. Leipzig: Arnoldische Buchhandlung, 1849.
Křivský, Pavel, see Dobrovský, Josef.
Krug, Wilhelm Traugott. *Briefe über den neuen Idealism.* Leipzig: H. Müller, 1801.
———. *Briefe über die Wissenschaftslehre.* Nebst einer Abhandlung über die von derselben versuchte Bestimmung des religiösen Glaubens. Leipzig: Roch, 1800.
———. *Entwurf eines neuen Organon's der Philosophie: oder Versuch über die Prinzipien der philosophischen Erkenntniss.* Meissen: Erbstein, 1801.
———. *Handbuch der Philosophie und der philosophischen Literatur.* Mit einen Vorwort und einer Einleitung von Lutz Geldsetzer und einem Sachregister von Ute

Geldsetzer. 2 vols. Düsseldorf: Stern-Verlag Janssen [c1969]. [Reprint of the 3rd rev. and enlarged ed., Leipzig, 1828.]

———. *Henotikon, oder, Entwurf eines neuen Religionsgesetzes für christliche Staaten: nebst einer Petizion an die Königlich-Sächsische Ständeversammlung.* Leipzig: C. E. Kollmann, 1836.

———. *Schelling und Hegel; oder, Die neueste Philosophie im Vernichtungs Kriege mit sich selbst Begriffen; ein Beitrag zur Geschichte der Philosophie des 19. Jahrhunderts.* Leipzig, 1835.

———. *System der theoretischen Philosophie.* 3 vols. in 5 parts. Vol. 1 in 2 pts., Denklehre, oder Logik; vol. 2, Erkenntnisslehre, oder Metaphysik; vol. 3 in 2 pts., Geschmackslehre, oder Aesthetik. Vienna: F. Härter, 1818.

———. *Über das Verhältnis der Philosophie zum gesunden Menschenverstande, zur öffentlichen Meinung und zum Leben selbst, mit besonderer Hinsicht auf Hegel. Noch ein Beitrag zur Geschichte der Philosophie des 19. Jahrhunderts.* Leipzig, 1835.

———. *Der Widerstreit der Vernunft mit sich selbst in der Versöhnungslehre dargestellt und aufgelöst.* Nebst einem kurzen Entwurf zu einer philosophischen Theorie des Glaubens. Züllichau: Darnmann, 1802.

———. *Wie der ungemeine Menschenverstand die Philosophie nehme.* Buxtehude, 1802.

Krug und Bolzano oder Schreiben an den Herrn Professor Krug in Leipzig und Prüfung seines gegen Prof. Bolzano's Lehrbuch der Religionswissenschaft gerichteten Antidoton, herausgegeben von den Aufgeforderten. Sulzbach: Seidel, 1837.

Launer, Štefan. *Povaha Slovanstva se zvláštním ohledem na spisovní řeč Čechů, Moravanů a Slováků.* Leipzig: Slovanské kněhkupectví, 1847.

Lauterbeck, Georg. *Politica historica: O vrchnostech a správcích světských knihy patery.* Translated by Daniel Adam z Veleslavína. Prague: Daniel Adam z Veleslavína, 1584. *Knihopis* 4735. 2nd ed., Prague: Dědici Daniele Adama z Veleslavína, 1606. *Knihopis* 4736. Originally published as *Regentenbuch . . . allen Regenten und Oberkeiten zu Anrichtung und Besserung erbarer und guter Policey.* (Leipzig: J. Berwald, 1556).

Lebeda, Heribert. *Medium cognitionis divinae, seu disputatio de decretis divinis ex se efficacibus.* Hradec Králové: Typis Joannis Clementis Tybelli, 1751.

"*Lessingiana* von Dr. Gottlieb Mohnike. Leipsig: 1844." *Edinburgh Review* 82 (July 1845–October 1845): 451–70.

Lindner, Gustav A. "O úpadku filosofie." *Časopis českého musea* 56 (1882): 489–95.

Locke, John. *An Essay concerning Human Understanding.* Edited by Peter H. Nidditch. Oxford: Clarendon Press, 1979.

———. *A Paraphrase and Notes on the Epistles of St. Paul to the Galatians, 1 and 2 Corinthians, Romans, Ephesians.* Edited by Arthur W. Wainwright. 2 vols. Oxford: Clarendon Press, 1987.

———. *Two Treatises of Government.* Edited by Peter Laslett. 2nd ed. Cambridge: Cambridge University Press, 1970.

Luther, Martin. *Ad librum eximii Magistri Nostri Magistri Ambrosii Catharini, defensoris Silvestri Prieratis accerimi, responsio. Cum exposita Visione Danielis viii. De Antichristo. 1521,* in his *Werke: Kritische Gesammtausgabe,* 7:698–778. Weimar: Böhlau, 1897.

———. *Katechysmus Doktora Martina Lutera, s obšírným katechetyckým výkladem vysoce osvíceného Doktora Jana Gottfrýda Herdera, bývalého generálního Superintendenta Církví ev. A. V. v knížectví Waymarském, k prospěchu škol evangelických*. Edited by Jiří Palkovič. Translated by Jan Grýša. 4th ed. Prešpork [Bratislava]: Karel K. Snížek, 1825.

———. *Tractatus de Libertate Christiana*, in his *Werke: Kritische Gesammtausgabe*, 7:49–73. Weimar: Böhlau, 1897.

Marek, Antonín, see also Shakespeare, William.

Marek, Antonín. *Logika nebo umnice*. Prague: Fetterlová, 1820.

———. *Základy filosofie: Logika. Metafysika*. Novočeská biblioteka, 4. Prague: Řivnáč, 1844.

Marty, Anton. *Gesammelte Schriften*. Edited by Josef Eisenmeier, Alfred Kastil, and Oskar Kraus. 2 vols. Halle: Niemeyer, 1916–20.

Masaryk, Tomáš G. *Česká otázka. Naše nynější krize. Jan Hus*, Spisy 6. Prague: Masarykův ústav AV ČR, 2000.

———. *Karel Havlíček: Snahy a tužby politického probuzení*, Spisy 7. Prague: Masarykův ústav AV ČR, 1996.

———. *The Making of a State: Memories and Observations, 1914–1918*. Edited by Henry W. Steed. New York: George Allen and Unwin, 1927. The original fuller Czech version was published as *Světová revoluce za války a ve válce, 1914–1918* (Prague: Čin and Orbis, 1925).

———. "Masarykovy zápisky z let 1880–1881." Edited by Josef Zumr. *Filosofický časopis* 48 (2000): 300–314.

———. *Moderní člověk a náboženství*, Spisy, 8. Prague: Masarykův ústav AV ČR, 2000.

———. *Národnostní filosofie doby novější*. 2nd ed. Prague: Melantrich, 1919.

———. *Otázka sociální. Základy marxismu filosofické a sociologické*. 2 vols. Spisy 9–10. Prague: Masarykův ústav AV ČR, 2000.

———. *The Spirit of Russia: Studies in History, Literature, and Philosophy*. Translated by Eden and Cedar Paul and W. R. and Z. Lee. 2nd ed., 3 vols. London: Allen & Unwin, 1961–67.

Mohnike, G., see *Lessingiana*.

Montagu, Richard. *A Gagg for the New Gospell? No, a New Gagg for an Old Goose*. London: T. Snodham, 1624.

More, Thomas. *Complete Works*. 21 vols. New Haven: Yale University Press, 1963–97.

Muratori, Lodovico Antonio. *O pravé křesťanské pobožnosti*. Prague: Pravidelní školská knihtiskárna, 1778. *Knihopis* 5974.

Nebeský, Václav B. "Několik slov o filosofii." *Časopis českého musea* 20 (1846): 231–48.

———. "W. Shakespeare." *Časopis českého musea* 25 (1851): 122–41; 26 (1852): 152–68.

Nejedlý, Zdeněk. *Jan Kollár: Tři projevy*. Prague: Československý spisovatel, 1952.

———. *Korespondence s českými historiky*. Edited by Josef Hanzal and Blanka Svadbová. Prague: Academia, 1978.

———. *O smyslu českých dějin*, Spisy 16. Prague: Svoboda, 1952. Later ed., Prague: Státní nakladatelství politické literatury, 1953.

———. "Slovo o české filosofii." *Var*, no. 1 (1950).

Němeček, František X. "Züge aus der Geschichte der Wissenschaften und des

Geschmackes in Böhmen; geschrieben im Jahre 1794." *Libussa*, eine vaterländische Vierteljahrschrift, edited by J. G. Meinert, 2:18–58. Prague: Calve, 1804.

Neurath, Otto. *Gesammelte philosophische und methodologische Schriften.* Edited by Rudolf Haller and Heiner Rutte. 2 vols. Vienna: Hölder-Pichler-Tempsky, 1981.

Nietzsche, Friedrich. *Die Geburt der Tragödie, oder Griechentum und Pessimismus.* In *Werke in drei Bänden,* edited by Karl Schlechta, 1:7–134. 2nd ed., 3 vols. Munich: Carl Hanser Verlag, 1960.

"Nové knihy české." *Časopis českého musea* 12 (1838): 129–30.

Novotný, Jan, ed. *Obrození národa: svědectví a dokumenty.* Prague: Melantrich, 1979.

Nožička z Votína, Blažej. *Knížka proti bludům některým před tisíci lety odsouzeným.* Prague: Jan Kantor, 1566. *Knihopis* 6491.

Nuntiaturberichte aus Deutschland nebst ergänzenden Aktenstücken. Erste Abteilung 1533–59. 1. Band, Nuntiaturen des Vergerio, 1533–36, edited by W. Friedensburg. Gotha: F. A. Perthes, 1892; Zweite Abteilung, 1560–72. 8. Band, Nuntius G. Delfino und Kardinallegat G.F. Commendone, 1571–72, edited by Johann Rainer. Graz: Boehlaus, 1967; Dritte Abteilung, 1572–85, 6. Band: Nuntiatur Giovanni Delfinos, 1572–73, edited by Helmut Goetz. Tübingen: Max Niemayer, 1982; 7. Band: Nuntiatur Giovanni Dolfins, 1573–74, edited by Almut Bues. Tübingen: Max Niemayer, 1990; 8. Band: Nuntiatur Giovanni Dolfins, 1575–76, edited by Daniela Neri. Tübingen: Max Niemayer, 1997.

Pačuda, Matauš. *Spis v němž se obsahuje které věci (z stran lidského pokolení) předešly příchod a narození mesiaše pravého Krista.* Prague: Matěj Pardubický, 1616. *Knihopis* 6691.

Palacký, František. *Dílo.* Edited by Jaroslav Charvát. 4 vols. Prague: Mazáč, 1941.

———. "Dopisy Františka Palackého k Janu Kollárovi." Edited by Antonín J. Vrťátko. *Časopis Českého Musea* 53 (1879): 379–481.

———. *Gedenkblätter.* Prague: F. Tempsky, 1874.

———. *Geschichte von Böhmen.* 5 vols. in 10 parts. Osnabrück: Zeller, 1968.

———. *An Historical Survey of the Science of Beauty and the Literature on the Subject.* Edited, with an introduction, by Tomáš Hlobil. Translated by Derek and Marzia Paton. (Přehled dějin krásovědy a její literatury. English.) Olomouc: Palacký University, 2002.

———. "Josefa Dobrovského život a vědecké působení." *Česká včela* 4 (1837): 261–63, 268–70, 276–78, 284–85, 294–95, 299–301, 308–10.

———. *Korespondence a zápisky.* 3 vols. Sbírka pramenů ku poznání literárního života v Čechách, na Moravě a ve Slezsku, Skupina 2, Číslo 4, 5, 16. Prague: Česká akademie pro vědy, slovesnost a umění, 1898–1911.

———. "Literní zprávy: Z Prahy." *Časopis českého musea* 2 (1828), pt. 2, 131–35; pt. 3, 132–36. [see under Čupr]

———. *Obrana husitství.* Edited and translated by František M. Bartoš. Prague: Blahoslav, 1926.

———. "Předmluva k vlasteneckému čtenářstvu." *Časopis českého musea* 11(1837): 3–8.

———. *Radhost: sbírka spisů drobných z oboru řeči a literatury české, krásovědy, historie a politiky.* 3 vols. Prague: Tempsky, 1871–73.

[———]. Review of Edward Robinson, *Historical View of the Slavic Language in*

Its Various Dialects. The Biblical Repository. Andover, Mass.: Flagg, Gould, and Newman, 1834. In *Časopis českého musea* 8 (1834): 456–59.
———. *Spisy drobné.* Edited by Bohuš Rieger. 3 vols. Prague: Bursík a Kohout, [1898–1902].
———. *Würdigung der alten böhmischen Geschichtschreiber*, Neue Ausgabe. Prague: Tempsky, 1869.
———. *Zur böhmischen Geschichtschreibung: actenmässige Aufschlüsse und Worte der Abwehr.* Prague: F. Tempsky, 1871.
Palacký, František, Josef Kalousek, and Gustav Friedrich, eds. *Archiv český* čili staré písemné památky české a moravské. Vols. 1–33, 35–37. Prague, 1840–1904.
Pařízek, Aleš V. *Versuch einer Geschichte Böhmens für den Bürger.* Prague: Verlag der kais. königl. Normalschule, 1781. 2nd ed. 1782. *Knihopis* 6909, 6910.
Patočka, Jan. *Co jsou Češi? Malý přehled fakt a pokus o vysvětlení.* Edited by Ivan Chvatík and Pavel Kouba. Prague: Panorama, 1992.
———. *Dopisy Václavu Richterovi*, Sebrané spisy, 20. Edited by Ivan Chvatík and Jiří Michálek. Prague: Oikoymenh, 2001.
———. *Dvojí rozum a příroda v německém osvícenství: Herderovská studie.* Prague: Václav Petr, 1942.
———. "J. G. Herder a jeho filosofie humanity," [Introductory study] in *Vývoj lidskosti,* by Johann G. Herder. Translated by Jan Patočka. Prague: Jan Laichter, 1941, 451–63.
———. "Komenského všeobecná porada." In *Komeniologické studie*, by Jan Patočka. 3 vols. Edited by Věra Schifferová. Prague: Oikúmené, 1997–2003, 2:149–211.
———. *Náš národní program.* Edited by Jan Vít and Miroslav Petříček. Prague: Evropský kulturní klub, 1990.
Patrčka, Silorad. "Země česká." *Květy české* 1 (1834): 351.
Pavlíková, Marie. "Vztah Josefa Jungmanna k Bernardu Bolzanovi a jeho žákům." *Literární archiv*: Sborník Památníku národního písemnictví, 8–9 (1974): 79–100.
Pažout, Julius. *Jednání a dopisy konsistoře pod obojí způsobou přijímajících, 1562–1570.* Prague: Historický spolek, 1906.
Pekař, Josef. "Bílá Hora: její příčiny a následky." In *Postavy a problémy českých dějin,* edited by František Kutnar, 131–231. Prague: Vyšehrad, 1990.
———. "O periodizaci českých dějin." *Český časopis historický* 38 (1932): 1–11.
———. *Postavy a problémy českých dějin.* Edited by František Kutnar. Prague: Vyšehrad, 1990.
———. "Tři kapitoly z boje o sv Jana Nepomuckého." In *Postavy a problémy českých dějin,* edited by František Kutnar, 232–64. Prague: Vyšehrad, 1990.
———. *Žižka a jeho doba.* 4 vols. Prague: Vesmír, 1927–33.
Pelcl, František Martin. "Abhandlung über den Samo." *Abhandlungen einer Privatgesellschaft in Böhmen zur Aufnahme der Mathematik, der vaterländischen Geschichte und der Naturgeschichte.* 6 vols. Prague, 1775–84: 1 (1775): 222–42.
———. *Boehmische, Maehrische und Schlesische Gelehrte und Schriftsteller aus dem Ordern der Jesuiten von Anfang der Gesellschaft bis auf gegenwärtige Zeit.* Prague: Im Verlag des Verfassers, 1786. *Knihopis* 6965.
———. *Geschichte der Böhmen von den ältesten bis auf die neuesten Zeiten.* 3rd ed., 2 pts. in 1 vol. Prague: Schönfeld, 1782. *Knihopis* 6968.
———. *Grundsätze der böhmischen Grammatik.* Prague: Jeřábek, 1795. *Knihopis* 6969.

———. *Grundsätze der böhmischen Grammatik.* 2nd ed. Prague: Jeřábek, 1798. *Knihopis* 6970.

———. *Kurzgefasste Geschichte der Böhmen, von den ältesten bis auf itzigen Zeiten.* 2 pts. in 1 vol. Prague: Adam Hagen, 1774. *Knihopis* 6966.

———. *Kurzgefasste Geschichte der Böhmen, von den ältesten bis auf itzigen Zeiten.* 2nd ed. Prague: Adam Hagen, 1779. *Knihopis* 6967.

[———]. *Neue Kronik von Böhmen.* 2 vols. Prague: Schönfeld, 1780–81. *Knihopis* 6975.

———. *Nová kronika česká.* 3 vols. Prague: Impressí normální školy [1–2], František Jeřábek [3], 1791–93. *Knihopis* 6976.

———. *Paměti.* Translated by Jan Pán. Prague: Státní nakladatelství krásné literatury, hudby a umění, 1956.

Pelcl, František M., and Mikuláš Adaukt Voigt, eds. *Abbildungen Böhmischer und Mährischer Gelehrten und Künstler.* 4 vols. Vols. 1–2, Prague: Wolfgang Gerle, 1773–75; vol. 3, Prague: Johann Karl Hraba, 1777; vol. 4, Prague: Normalschulbuchdruckerei, 1782. *Knihopis* 6963.

Petrarca, Francesco. *Knihy dvoje o lékařství proti štěstí a neštěstí.* Prague: Jan Severýn z Kapí Hory, 1501. *Knihopis* 7049.

Piccolomini, Aeneas Sylvius (Pope Pius II). *Historia Bohemica.* Rome: Johannes N. Hanheymer and Johannes Schurener, 1475. New ed., Basel: [Michael Furter?], ca. 1489.

Plch, Jaromír. *Antologie z české literatury národního obrození.* Prague: Státní pedagogické nakladatelství, 1978.

Polon, Valentin. *Pomni na mne: Knižka obahující v sobě kratičká spasidedlná Naučení a sebrání . . .* Staré Město Pražské: Buryan Valda, 1589. *Knihopis* 14.153.

Popp, Ignaz. *Ecclesiae sanctae epitome historica.* Olomouc: Melchior Windhauer, 1755.

———. *Romani imperii ab urbe condita, tum ab sua origine rerum Austriae, Bohemiae, Moraviae, Epitome Historica.* Olomouc: Melchior Windhauer, 1753.

Priestley, Joseph. "Letters to a Philosophical Unbeliever. Part I." In *The Theological and Miscellaneous Works,* edited by John Towill Rutt. 25 vols. in 26 parts, 4:317–411. London: G. Smallfield, 1817–32.

Příhonský, František. *Neuer Anti-Kant: oder, Prüfung der Kritik der reinen Vernunft nach den in Bolzano's Wissenschaftslehre niedergelegten Begriffen.* Bautzen: A. Weller, 1850.

Procházka, František Faustin . "Critische Nachricht von den bisherigen Producten der Pressfreiheit in Böhmen." *Miscellaneen der Böhmischen und Mährischen Litteratur,* Band 1, Theil 2 (1785): 234–60.

———. *De saecularibus liberalium artium in Bohemia et Moravia satis commentarius.* Prague: Litteris Scholae normalis, Schmadl factore, 1782. *Knihopis* 14.386.

———. *Miscellaneen der Böhmischen und Mährischen Litteratur, seltener Werke, und verschiedenen Handschriften.* Vol. 1, 3 pts. Prague: Caspar Widtmann, 1784–85. *Knihopis* 14.389.

Pubička, František. *Chronologische Geschichte Böhmens.* 6 vols. in 10 parts. Leipzig: F. A. Höchenberg, 1770–1801. *Knihopis* 14.687.

Puchmajer, Antonín. *Die Lehrgebäude der russischen Sprache.* Prague: J. G. Calve, 1820.

———. *Pravopis rusko-český*. Prague: Bohumil Hás, 1805. *Knihopis* 14.695.

P. Z. H. "Prvot'ini vedi slovanskej." *Slovenskje pohladi na vedi, umeňja a literatúru* 2 (1851): 121–26, 161–65, 196–98.

[Rautenstrauch, Franz Stephan]. *Anleitung und Grundriss zur Systematischen Dogmatischen Theologie*. Vienna: Johann Thomas Edel von Trattnern, 1776.

———. Franz Stephan. *Entwurf zur Einrichtung der theologischen Schulen in den k. k. Erblanden*. 2nd ed. Vienna: Sonnleithner and Hörling, 1784. 1st ed., 1782.

———. *Entwurf zur Einrichtung der Genaralseminarien in den k. k. Erblanden*. Vienna: Sonnleithner and Hörling, 1784.

———. *Positiones Ex Universo Systemate Theologico*. Prague: Franciscus Guzabok, 1784.

———. *Warum kömmt Pius der VI. nach Wien? Eine patriotische Betrachtung*. Pressburg: Landerer, 1782.

Reinhold, Karl L. *Beiträge zur leichtern Übersicht der Philosophie zu Anfang des neuzehten Jahrhunderts*. 6 vols. in 3 parts. Hamburg: Perthes, 1801–3.

Říčan, Rudolf, ed. *Čtyři vyznání*. Prague: Komenského evangelická bohoslovecká fakulta, 1951.

Rieger, František L. *Řeči*. Edited by Josef Kalousek. 4 vols. Prague: J. Otto, 1883–88.

Robertson, William. *History of America*. 2 vols. London: W. Strahan, 1777.

———. *History of America*. Books 9 and 10, containing the history of Virginia to 1688 [and New England to 1652]. London: A. Strahan, 1796.

———. *History of Scotland during the Reigns of Queen Mary and King James VI till His Accession to the Crown of England*. 2 vols. London: A. Millar, 1759.

———. *History of the Reign of the Emperor Charles V*. 3 vols. London: W. Strahan, 1769.

Rorty, Richard. *Philosophical Papers*. Vol. 1, *Objectivity, Relativism, and Truth*; vol. 2, *Essays on Heidegger and Others;* vol. 3, *Truth and Progress*. New York: Cambridge University Press, 1991–98.

Rosenkranz, Karl. *Georg Wilhelm Friedrich Hegels Leben*. Berlin: Duncker und Humblot, 1844.

———. *Psychologie, oder die Wissenschaft des subjektiven Geistes*. Kaliningrad [Königsberg]: Gebrüder Bornträger, 1843.

Rotteck, Karl W., and Karl T. Welcker. *Das Staats-Lexikon. Encyklopädie der sämmtlichen Staatswissenschaften für alle Stände*. 12 vols. Altona: J. F. Hammerich, 1845–48.

Royko, Kašpar. *Einleitung in die christliche Religions- und Kirchengeschichte*. Prague: Joh. Jos. Diesbach, 1788. 2nd ed., Prague: Windtmannsche Buchhandlung, 1790.

———. *Geschichte der grossen allgemeinen Kirchenversammlung zu Kostniz*. 4 vols. Vols. 1–2, 2nd rev. ed., Vienna and Graz: In Commission der Weingand, 1782; vol. 3, Prague gedruckt: In Commission der Ferstlischen Buchhandlung zu Graz, 1784; vol. 4, Prague: im Verlage des Verfassers, 1785.

———. *Historie velikého sněmu kostnického*. Translated by Václav Petryn [Václav Stach]. 2 vols. Prague: Diesbach, 1785. *Knihopis* 14.903.

———. *Synopsis historiae religionis et ecclesiae christianae: methodo systematica adumbratae*. Prague: Ioann Mangoldt, 1785.

Rvačovský of Rvačov, Vavřinec Leander. *Klevetník*. Hradec Králové, early 19th century. Knihopis 15.125.

———. *Masopust*. Prague: Melantrich, 1580. *Knihopis* 15.127.

———. *Všetýčka*. N. p., end of 18th or beginning of 19th century. *Knihopis* 15.128.

Sabina, Karel. "Procházky v oboru mystiky, romantiky a bájení." *Časopis českého musea* 21, pt. 1 (1847): 311–24, 347–65, 478–97, 569–83. [See under Čupr]

Šafárik, Jozef P. "Dopisy Pavla Josefa Šafaříka Janu Kollárovi." Edited by Antonín J. Vrťátko. *Časopis českého musea* 47 (1873): 119–47, 382–407; 48 (1874): 54–90, 278–99, 414–26; 49 (1875): 134–52.

Šafárik, Pavol J. *Geschichte der Slawischen Sprache und Literatur nach allen Mundarten*. Budapest: Universitäts-Schriften, 1826.

———. *Korespondence Pavla Josefa Šafaříka s Františkem Palackým*. Edited by Věnceslava Bechyňová and Zoe Hauptová. Prague: Nakladatelství Československé akademie věd, 1961.

Scherschnik, Leopold Johann. "Über den Ursprung und die Aufnahme der Bibliothek am Clementinischen Collegium zu Prag." *Abhandlungen einer Privatgesellschaft in Böhmen zur Aufnahme der Mathematik, der vaterländischen Geschichte und der Naturgeschichte* 2 (1776): 258–86.

Seibt, Karl H. *Akademische Vorübungen, aus den von Karl H. Seibt . . . gehaltenen Vorlesungen über die deutsche Schreibart*. Prague: Elsenwanger, 1769.

———. *Katholisches Lehr- und Gebetbuch*. Prague, 1779. 2nd ed., *Neues katholisches Gebetbuch*. Prague, 1783.

———. *Klugheitslehre, praktisch abgehandelt, in akademischen Vorlesungen*. 2 vols. Prague: Elsenwanger, 1799.

———. *Kniha katolická, obsahující v sobě naučení a modlitby*. Prague: Cís. král. normální škola, 1780. *Knihopis* 15.277.

———. *Von dem Einflusse der Erziehung auf die Glückseligkeit des Staates*. Prague: Mangoldische Buchhandlung, 1771.

Šembera, Alois V. *Dějiny řeči a literatury československé*. 2 vols. Vienna: By author, 1858–61.

Shakespeare, William. *Kupec z Venedyku. Nebo láska a přátelství*. Jindřichův Hradec: Hilgartner, 1782. *Knihopis* 15.330.

———. *Makbet, truchlohra v pěti jednáních*. Translated by Karel Ignác Thám. Prague: Schönfeld, 1786. *Knihopis* 15.332.

———. *Makbet, vůdce skotského vojska*. Jindřichův Hradec: Hilgartner, 1782. *Knihopis* 15.331.

———. *Omylové, dle Shakespeara vzdělaná veselohra*. Translated by Bolemír Izvolský [pseud. Antonín Marek]. Prague: Fetterlová, 1823.

Simko, Immanuel Wylem (Šimko, Emanuel V.). *Památka smrti D. Martina Lutera*. Bratislava: Ludwik Weber, 1846.

Slavata, Vilém. *Paměti nejvyššího kancléře království českého*. Edited by Josef Jireček. 2 vols. Prague: Kober, 1866–68.

Slavík, František. "Vzájemné dopis Václava Hanky a Jana Kollára." *Časopis českého musea* 71 (1897): 227–45.

"Die slawischen Völker und ihr Verhältniss zu den Deutschen." *Deutsche Vierteljahrschrift* 4, no. 12 (1840): 81–107. [Published in Stuttgart and Tubingen]. Part reprint: Daniel Rapant, *Slovenský prestolný prosbopis*, 2: 90–96. Liptovský svatý Mikuláš: Tranoscius, 1943.

Smetana, Augustin, *Sebrané spisy*. 2 vols. Prague: Nakladatelství Československé akademie věd, 1960–62.

———. "Wie einige čechische Literaten die deutsche Philosophie nehmen." *Ost und West* 11 (1847): 193–95, 197–99, 201–4, 205–8.
Sněmy české od léta 1526 až po naši dobu. Vols. 1–11, 15. Prague: Zemský výbor, 1877–1941.
Spor o smysl českých dějin, 1895–1938. Edited by Miloš Havelka. Prague: Torst, 1995.
Stach, Václav, see Royko, Kašpar.
Staël-Holstein, Anne L. *De l'Allemagne.* Paris: Garnier frères, 1800.
Štelcar Želetavský z Želetavy, Jan, *Kázání dvoje.* Prague: [Jiří Dačický?], 1586. *Knihopis* 15.982.
Steinbach of Kranichstein, Otto. "Versuch einer Geschichte der alten und neuen Toleranz im Königreich Böhmen und Markgraftum Mähren." *Abhandlungen der Böhmischen Gesellschaft der Wissenschaften zu Prag auf das Jahr 1785*, Zweite Abteilung (1786): 200–233.
Štorch, Karel. "Filosofie a naše literatura: Několik myšlenek snad včas." *Časopis českého musea* 22, pt.1 (1848): 53–73. [See under Čupr]
———. "Historie a vzdělanost." *Časopis českého musea* 30 (1856): 91–111.
———. "Hlas o německé literatuře." *Květy* 14 (1847): 266–68.
———. "K Ohlasu v č. 72." *Květy* 14 (1847): 296.
———. "Komenského snahy pansofické." *Časopis českého musea* 25, no. 3 (1851): 85–113; no. 4, 3–26.
Stránský, Pavel. *Staat von Böhmen.* Translated, revised, and supplemented by Ignác Cornova. 7 vols. Prague: J. G. Calve, 1792–1803. [Last 3 vols. are Cornova's own history of Bohemia since the mid-17th century.] *Knihopis* 15.742.
Štúr, L'udovít. *Hlas k rodákom.* Bratislava: Tatran, 1971.
———. *Listy.* Edited by Jozef Ambruš and Vladimír Matula. 4 vols. Bratislava: Vydavatelstvo Slovenskej akadémie vied, 1954–99.
———. "Přednášení historická." Edited by J. Ambruš. *Otázky marxistickej filozofie* 20 (1965): č. 5, 491–501. Abbreviated version: Štúr, "Přednášení historická." In *Antologie z dějin českého a slovenského myšlení: do roku 1848*, edited by Ústav pro filozofii a sociologii ČSAV and Ústav pro filozofii a sociologii SAV, 542–549. Prague: Svoboda, 1981.
———. *Das Slawenthum und die Welt der Zukunft.* Edited by Josef Jirásek. Bratislava: Učená společnost Šafaříkova, 1931.
———. "Život domáci a pospolitý." In *Hlas k rodákom,* 173–90. Bratislava: Tatran, 1971.
Suárez, Francisco. *Disputationes metaphysicae* vols. 25–26 of his *Opera omnia.* 28 vols. in 30 parts. Paris: Louis Vivès, 1856–66.
———. *On the Essence of Finite Being as Such, On the Existence of That Essence and Their Distinction* (De Essentia Entis Finiti Ut Tale Est, Et De Illius Esse, Eorumque Distinctione). Translated, with an introduction, by Norman J. Wells. Milwaukee, Wisc.: Marquette University Press, 1983.
Svátek, Josef. *Majestát Rudolfa II: Román ze století XVI. a XVII.* 3rd ed. Prague: Topič, 1927.
Světlá, Karolina. *Z literárního soukromí a drobné práce.* 2nd ed. Prague: L. Mazáč, 1941.
Thám, Karel Ignác. *Antikritik oder Rechtfertigung.* 3 pts. Prague, 1798. *Knihopis* 16.139.
———. *Böhmische Grammatik zum Gebrauche der Deutschen.* Prague: Diesbach,

1798. *Knihopis* 16.144 [Considered 2nd ed.; 3rd ed. evidently never existed. See *Knihopis* 16.145.]

———. *Böhmische Grammatik zum Gebrauche der Deutschen* Vierte Auflage. Prague: Diesbach, 1801. *Knihopis* 16.146; Fünfte Auflage, Prague: Diesbach, 1804; *Knihopis* 16.147.

———. *Deutsch-böhmisches Nationallexikon.* Prague: Schönfeld, 1788. *Knihopis* 16.155.

———. *Kurzgefasste böhmische Sprachlehre.* Prague: Schönfeld, 1785. [Considered 1st ed. of *Böhmische Grammatik zum Gebrauche der Deutschen.*] *Knihopis* 16,165.

———. *Neuestes ausführliches und vollständiges deutsch-böhmisches synonymisch-phraseologisches Nationallexikon oder Wörterbuch.* 2 pts. Prague: Neureutter, 1799–1800. [Considered 2nd ed.] *Knihopis* 16.156.

[———]. *Neuestes ausführliches und vollständiges deutsch-böhmisches synonymisch-phraseologisches Nationallexikon oder Wörterbuch.* 2 pts., 2nd pt.: bearbeitet von Franz Tomsa (P-Ž). Prague: Neureutter, 1805–7. *Knihopis* 16.157.

———. *Neuestes ausführliches und vollständiges deutsch-böhmisches synonymisch-phraseologisches Nationallexikon oder Wörterbuch.* 2 pts. Prague: M. Neureutter, 1814. [Considered 3rd ed.] Knihopis 16.158.

———. *Obrana jazyka českého proti zlobivým jeho utrhačům.* Prague: Schönfeld, 1783. *Knihopis* 16.160.

———. *Über den Karakter der Slawen, dann über den Ursprung, die Schicksale, Volkommenheiten, die Nützlichkeit und Wichtigkeit der bömischen Sprache.* Prague: Johann Diesbach'schen Buchhandlung, 1803. *Knihopis* 16.148.

Thám, Václav A. *Básně v řeči vázané,* První sebrání. Prague: U Rosenmüllerských dědiců, 1785; Sebrání druhé. Prague: Schönfeld, 1785. *Knihopis* 16.172.

Thirlwall, Connop. *Letters, Literary and Theological.* Edited by John J. Perowne and Louis Stokes. London: R. Bentley, 1881.

———. *Letters to a Friend.* Edited by Arthur P. Stanley. Boston: Roberts Brothers, 1883.

Tomek, Václav V. *Paměti z mého života,* Spisy muzejní 169. 2 vols. Prague: F. Řivnáč, 1904–5.

Tomíček, Jan Slavomír. *Děje anglické země.* Prague: F. Řivnáč, 1849.

———. "Máj, báseň od Karla Hynka Máchy." In *Dílo,* by Karel Hynek Mácha. Vol. 1, *Básně, dramatické zlomky,* edited by Karel Janský. Prague: Fr. Borový, 1948, 426–29.

———. "Počátek a vznik severo-amerikánského soustátí." *Česká včela* 2 (1835): 205–6, 211–13, 222–23, 228–30, 241–43, 252–55, 260–63, 267–69, 275–77.

Tomsa, František Jan. *Über die Veränderungen der čechischen Sprache, nebst einer čechischen Chrestomathie.* Prague: Tomsa, 1805. *Knihopis* 16.257.

———. *Vollständiges Wörterbuch der böhmisch-deutsch-lateinischen Sprache.* Prague: in der von Schönfeld-Meissnerischen Handlung, 1791. *Knihopis* 16.261.

Treitschke, Heinrich von. *Deutsche Geschichte im neunzehnten Jahrhundert.* 5 vols. Leipzig: S. Hirzel, 1879–94.

Tyl, Josef K. "Jan Hus." In *Historická dramata,* Spisy 20, 97–211, 298–371. Prague: Státní nakladatelství kràsné literatury, hudby a umění, 1954.

---. "Žižka z Trocnova." In *Historická dramata*, Spisy 20, 298–371. Prague: Státní nakladatelství kràsné literatury, hudby a umění, 1954.

---. "Von dem Zustande der Schulen und der Lateinischen Literatur in Böhmen vor Errichtung der hohen Schule zu Prague." *Abhandlungen einer Privatgesellschaft in Böhmen zur Aufnahme der Mathematik, der vaterländischen Geschichte und der Naturgeschichte*, 6 (1784):127–217.

---. "Žižka's militärische Briefe und Verordnungen." *Neuere Abhandlungen der königlichen Böhmischen Gesellschaft der Wissenschaften*, 1 (1790): 371–89.

Vavřinec z Březové. *Husitská kronika*. Edited by Marie Bláhová. Prague: Svoboda, 1979.

Vehse, Karl Eduard. *Shakespeare als Protestant, Politiker, Psycholog und Dichter*. 2 vols. Hamburg: Hoffmann und Campe, 1851.

Vinařický, Karel Alois. *Korespondence a spisy pamětní*. 4 vols. Sbírka pramenů ku poznání literárního života v Čechách, na Moravě a ve Slezsku, Skupina 2, Číslo 6, 13, 19, 24. Edited by Václav Otakar Slavík. Prague: Česká akademie pro vědy, slovesnost a umění, 1903, 1909, 1914, 1925.

Voigt, Mikuláš Adaukt. *Acta litteraria Bohemiae et Moraviae*. 2 vols. Prague: Wolfgang Gerle, 1774–84. Knihopis 16.599, 16.600.

---. *Effigies virorum eruditorum atque artificum Bohemiae et Moraviae*. 2 vols. Prague: Gerle, 1773–75. Knihopis 16.602.

---. *Über den Geist der böhmischen Gesetze in den verschiedenen Zeitaltern*. Dresden: Waltherische Hofbuchhandlung, 1788. Knihopis 16.603.

---. "Über den Kalendar der Slaven, besonders der Böhmen." *Abhandlungen einer Privatgesellschaft in Böhmen zur Aufnahme der Mathematik, der vaterländischen Geschichte und der Naturgeschichte*, 3 (1777): 99–130.

---. "Untersuchung über die Einführung, den Gebrauch, und Abänderung der Buchstaben und des Schreibens in Böhmen." *Abhandlungen einer Privatgesellschaft in Böhmen zur Aufnahme der Mathematik, der vaterländischen Geschichte und der Naturgeschichte*. 1 (1775): 164–99.

Vouillemin, Charles Ernest. *La logique de la science et l'École de Vienne*. Paris: Hermann, 1935.

---. *Science et philosophie: unité de la connaissance*. Paris: Michel, 1945.

Vrťátko, Antonín J., see Jungmann, Josef; Palacký, František; and Šafařík, Pavel J. *Výbor z literatury české*. 2 vols. Vol. 1, *Od nejstarších časů až do počátku XV. století*, edited by Josef J. Jungmann with František Palacký and others; vol. 2, *Od počátku XV až do konce XVI. století*, edited by Karel J. Erben. Prague: Kronberger and Řivnáč, 1845–68.

Weller, Hieronymus. *De officio ecclesiastico, politico, et oeconomico, libellus pius et eruditus*. Nuremberg: Montanus and Neuborus, 1552.

---. *Jeronýma Wellera kniha o povinnostech všech úřadův duchovních i světských*. Translated by Mikuláš Dvorský. N.p., 1591. Knihopis 16.960.

Weyr, František. *Paměti*. 3 vols. Prague: Atlantis, 1999.

Winter, Eduard. *Bernard Bolzano: Ein Lebensbild*. In *Bernard Bolzano, Gesamtausgabe*, edited by Eduard Winter, Jan Berg, Friedrich Kambartel, Jaromír Loužil, and Bob van Rootselaar. 40 vols. in 57 parts. Stuttgart-Bad Cannstatt: Frommann Holzboog, 1969–in progress, *Einleitungsband*. 1st pt.: *Biographie*.

Winter, Eduard, and Maria Winter, eds. *Der Bolzanokreis, 1824–1833: In Briefen von Anna Hoffmann, Michael Josef Fesl, Franz Schneider und Franz Prihonsky.* Vienna: Böhlau, 1970. See also Bolzano, Bernard.

Wolf, Johann Heinrich. *Dějiny království českého k užívání studující mládeže v c. k. státech.* Translated by Jan Putna. Vienna: C. k. školní knihosklad, 1819. New ed., Knihovnička Času, no. 64. Introduction by Jan Herben. Prague: 1912.

———. *Geschichte des Königreichs Böheim zum Gebrauche der Studierenden Jugend in der K.K. Staaten.* Vienna: Johann Thomas von Trattner, 1783.

———. *Die grossen Heldenthaten des böhmischen König Georg aus dem Hause Poděbrad.* Prague, 1792.

[———]. *Leben, Lehre, Wandel und Tod des im J. 1415 lebendig verbrannten Johann Hus.* Rome, [Prague: Schönfeld], 1784.

[———]. *Leben des Königs Georg von Böhmen, aus dem Hause Podiebrad.* Prague: Wolfgang Gerle, 1785.

Wolff, Christian. *Philosophia prima, sive ontologia, methodo scientifica pertractata, qua omnis cognitionis humanæ principia continentur.* Ed. nova priori emendatior. Francofurti & Lipsiæ, prostat in Officina libraria Rengeriana, 1736. In *Gesammelte Werke*, by Christian Wolff. Abteilung, II, Band 3, edited by Joannes Ecole. Hildesheim: Georg Olms, 1962.

Wolff, Franz. *Commentarium in Sacram scripturam.* 4 pts. Olomouc: Typis J. Hirnlianae, 1765–68.

Wratislaw, Albert H., ed. *Lyra Czecho-Slovanská: Bohemian Poems Ancient and Modern.* London: J. W. Parker, 1849.

———, trans. *Manuscript of the Queen's Court: A Collection of Old Bohemian Songs, with Other Ancient Bohemian Poems.* Edited by Václav Hanka, 3–10. Prague: Printed by Haase's sons, 1852.

Zahradník, Vincenc. *Filosofické spisy.* Edited by František Čáda. 2 vols. Prague: Česká akademie pro vědy slovesnost a umění, 1907–8.

Zeithammer, Gregor. *Biographie Bolzanos.* In Bolzano, *Gesamtausgabe*, edited by Eduard Winter, Jan Berg, Friedrich Kambartel, Jaromír Loužil, and Bob van Rootselaar. 40 vols. in 57 parts. Stuttgart-Bad Cannstatt: Frommann Holzboog, 1969–, Reihe IV, Band 2.

Zimmermann, Robert, *Philosophische Propädeutik für Obergymnasien.* Vienna: W. Braumüller, 1853; 2nd ed., 1860; 3rd ed., 1867.

Zippe [Zyppe], Augustin. *Sechs Predigten, gehalten, auf Veranlassung der in Böhmischkamnitz errichteten Armenversorgungsanstalt.* Prague: Anton Elsenwanger, 1782.

———. *Von der moralischen Bildung angehender Geistlichen in dem Generalseminario in Prag.* Prague: Wenzel Peskaček, 1784.

Zitte, Augustin, see also Hus, Jan.

Zitte, Augustin. *Lebensbeschreibung der drei ausgezeichnetsten Vorläufer M. Joh. Huss von Hussinec, bekanntlich: des Konrad Stiekna, Johann Milicz und Mathias von Janow, nebst einer Übersicht der böhmischen Religionsgeschichte bis auf seine Zeit.* Prague: Wolfgang Gerle, 1786.

———. *Lebensbeschreibung des Englischen Reformators Johannes Wiklef.* Prague: Wolfgang Gerle, 1786.

―――. *Lebensbeschreibung des Magisters Johannes Huss von Hussinecz.* 2 vols. Prague: W. Gerle, 1789–90. Later published in Czech translation as *Obšírný životopis mistra Jana Husi z Husince,* trans. by J. V. Sommer (Prague: Jan Spurný, 1850).

―――. *Neun neue Exhorten, oder Ermahnungen bei Gelegenheit einer alten Noven.* gehalten bei St. Salvator, an erzbischöflichen Priesterhause in der Altstadt Prag, von 23.–31. Juli, im Jahre 1781. Prague: Mangoldt, 1783.

Zumr, Josef, see Masaryk, Tomáš G.

Secondary Sources

Agnew, Hugh L. *Origins of the Czech National Renascence.* Pittsburgh, Pa.: University of Pittsburgh Press, 1993.

"AHR Forum: How Revolutionary Was the Print Revolution?" *American Historical Review* 107 (2002): 84–128.

Albertazzi, Liliana. "Brentano, Twardowski, and Polish Scientific Philosophy." In *Polish Scientific Philosophy: The Lvov-Warsaw School,* edited by Francesco Coniglione and others, 11–40. Amsterdam: Rodopi, 1993.

Almond, Gabriel A., and Sidney Verba. *The Civic Culture: Political Attitudes and Democracy in Five Nations.* New ed., Newbury Park, Calif.: Sage Publications, 1989.

Anderson, Benedict R. *Imagined Communities: Reflections on the Origin and Spread of Nationalism.* Rev. ed. London: Verso, 1991.

Asendorf, Ulrich. *Luther und Hegel: Untersuchungen zur Grundlegung einer neuen systematischen Theologie.* Wiesbaden: Steiner, 1982.

Asomura, Tomoko. "The Ephemeral Dream of the Bohemian Nation, 1770–1848." In *Češi a svět; sborník k pětasedmdesátinám Ivan Pfaffa,* edited by Josef Polišenský, 71–78. Prague: Euroslavica, 2000.

Assorodobraj, Nina, ed. *Z dziejów plskiej myśli filozoficznej i społecznej.* 3 vols. Warsaw: Ksiazka i wiedza, 1956–57.

Atkinson, James. "Die römisch-katholische Kirche und die Reformation in anglikanischer Sicht." In *Vierhundertfünfzig Jahre lutherische Reformation 1517–1967: Festschrift für Franz Lau zum 60. Geburtstag,* edited by Helmar Junghans and others, 9–16. Göttingen: Vanderhoeck and Ruprecht, 1967.

Auer, Stefan. *Liberal Nationalism in Central Europe.* New York: RoutledgeCurzon, 2004.

Augustijn, Cornelis. "Verba valent usu: was ist Erasmianismus?" In *Erasmianism: Idea and Reality,* edited by M.E.H.N. Mout, H. Smolinsky, and J. Trapman, 5–14. North-Holland: Amsterdam: Koninklijke Nederlandse Akademie van Wetenschappen, 1997.

Backus, Irena. "Erasmus and the Spirituality of the Early Church." In *Erasmus' Vision of the Church,* edited by Hilmar M. Pabel, 95–114. Kirksville, Mo.: Sixteenth Century Journal Publishers, 1995.

Baer, Josette A. "National Emancipation, Not the Making of Slovakia: L'udovít Štúr's Conception of the Slovak Nation." Occasional Paper 2. St. Francis Xavier University, Center for Post-Communist Studies, Studies in Post-Communism. 2003.

Bahner, Werner, ed. *Sprache und Kulturentwicklung in Blickfeld der deutschen Spätaufklärung: Der Beitrag Johann Christoph Adelungs.* Berlin: Akademie Verlag, 1984.

Barnard, Frederick M. *Herder on Nationality, Humanity, and History.* Montreal: McGill-Queen's University Press, 2003.

———. *Herder's Social and Political Thought: From Enlightenment to Nationalism.* Oxford: Clarendon Press, 1965.

Bartoš, František M. "Dobrovského pojetí husitství a reformace." *Slavia* 23 (1954): 198–200.

———. *Husitská revoluce.* 2 vols. České dějiny, vol. 2, pts. 7–8. Prague: Československá akademie věd, 1965–66.

———. *The Hussite Revolution, 1424–1437.* Edited by John M. Klassen. Boulder, Colo.: East European Monographs, 1986.

Bayerová, Marie. *Bernard Bolzano. Evropský rozměr jeho filosofického myšlení.* Prague: Filosofia, 1994.

———. "Česká filosofie předbřeznová." In *Sebrané spisy,* by Augustin Smetana. Edited by Marie Bayerová, 2:5–55. 2 vols. Prague: Nakladatelství Československé akademie věd, 1960–62.

———. "Rakouské filozofické myšlení konce 19. století v českém kulturním životě." In *Povědomí tradice v novodobé české kultuře: Doba Bedřicha Smetany.* Sborník sympozia v Plzni 7.–11. března 1984, 128–36. Prague: Národní galerie, 1988.

Beales, Derek E. *Enlightenment and Reform in Eighteenth-Century Europe.* New York: I. B. Tauris, 2005.

———. *Joseph II: In the Shadow of Maria Theresa, 1741–1780.* New York: Cambridge University Press, 1987.

Bednář, Miloslav. *České myšlení.* Prague: Philosophia, 1996.

Bělič, Jaromír. "František Martin Pelcl a český jazyk." *Slavia Pragensia* 21 (1978): 115–32.

Bělina, Pavel, ed. *Od nejstarší doby do sloučení pražských měst, 1784,* vol. 1 of *Dějiny Prahy.* Prague: Paseka, 1997.

Bělina, Pavel, Jiří Kaše, and Jan P. Kučera. *Velké dějiny zemí Koruny české.* Vol. 10, 1740–92. Prague: Paseka, 2001.

Benetka, Bořivoj. *P. Stanislav Vydra, učitel, kněz a vlastenec.* Olomouc: Vítězové, 1938.

Benoist, Jocelyn. *Représentations sans objet: aux origines de la phénoménologie et de la philosophie analytique.* Paris: Presses universitaires de France, 2001.

———. "Sur l'état présent de la phénoménologie." In *Après le post-modernisme, quelle philosophie,* edited by Petr Horák, Josef Korb, and François Rivenc, 36–57. Brno: Masarykova univerzita, 2003.

Berdyaev, Nicolai. *The Origin of Russian Communism.* Ann Arbor: University of Michigan Press, 1960.

———. *The Russian Idea.* New York: Macmillan Company, 1948.

Berend, Ivan T. *Decades of Crisis: Central and Eastern Europe before World War II.* Berkeley: University of California Press, 1998.

Berg, Jan. *Ontology without Filters and Possible Worlds: An Examination of Bolzano's Ontology.* Sankt Augustin: Academia Verlag, 1992.

Berka, Karel. "Bolzanovo *Vlastní vědosloví.*" *Filosofický časopis* 46 (1998): 931–47.
———. "Předmluva." In *Vědosloví: výbor*, by Bernard Bolzano. Edited by Karel Berka and translated by Marie Bayerová and Jaromír Loužil, 5–50. Prague: Academia, 1981.
Berkes, Tamás. "České obrození jako literární kánon." In *Česká literatura na konci tisíciletí*, Příspěvky z 2. kongresu světové literárněvědné bohemistiky, Prague 3.–8. července 2000, 1:117–27. 2 vols. Prague: Ústav pro českou literaturu AV ČR, 2001.
Berlin, Isaiah. "Kant as an Unfamiliar Source of Nationalism." In his *The Sense of Reality: Studies in Ideas and Their History.* Edited by Henry Hardy, 232–48. New York: Farrar, Straus and Giroux, 1996.
———. *Three Critics of the Enlightenment: Vico, Hamann, Herder*. Princeton, N.J.: Princeton University Press, 2000.
Bernard, George W. *The King's Reformation: Henry VIII and the Remaking of the English Church.* New Haven: Yale University Press, 2005.
Billington, James H. *The Icon and the Axe: An Interpretive History of Russian Culture*. New York: Random House, 1970.
———. *Russia in Search of Itself.* Washington, D.C.: Woodrow Wilson Center Press; Baltimore: Johns Hopkins University Press, 2004.
Bílý, Jiří. *Jezuita Antonín Koniáš: Osobnost a doba.* Prague: Vyšehrad, 1996.
Bireley, Robert. *The Refashioning of Catholicism, 1450–1700: A Reassessment of the Counter Reformation.* Washington, D.C.: Catholic University of America Press, 1999.
"Bishop Thirlwall." *Church Quarterly Review* 16 (1883): 95–129.
Bittner, Konrad. *Deutsche und Tschechen: Zur Geistesgeschichte des böhmischen Raumes.* Brno: R. M. Rohrer, 1936.
———. *Herders Geschichtsphilosophie und die Slaven.* Veröffentlichungen der Slavistischen Arbeitsgemeinschaft and der Deutschen Universität in Prag, Heft 6, Reichenberg [Liberec]: Gebrüder Stiepel, 1929.
Bláhová, Kateřina. "Česká historiografie přelomu století v dialogu s Evropou: prolegomena k tématu." In *Komunikace a izolace v české kultuře 19. století*, Sborník příspěvků z 21. plzeňského sympozia, edited by Kateřina Bláhová, 186–96. Praha: KLP, 2002.
Blanke, Richard. *Polish-Speaking Germans? Language and National Identity among the Masurians since 1871.* Cologne: Böhlau, 2001.
Blumberg, Albert E., and Herbert Feigl. "Logical Positivism, a New Movement in European Philosophy." *Journal of Philosophy* 28 (1931): 281–96.
Bohatcová, Mirjam. "Erasmus Roterdamský v českých tištěných překladech 16.–17. Století." *Časopis národního muzea*, Řada historická 155 (1986): 37–58.
Bohatcová, Mirjam, and Josef Hejnic. "O vydavatelské činnosti Veleslavínské tiskárny." *Folia Historica Bohemica* 9 (1985): 291–388.
Bobrova, L. A. *Poisk putei k istine: opyt analiticheskoi filosofii.* Moscow: Rossiiskaia akademiia nauk, 1995.
Bobrownicka, Maria. *Narkotyk mitu: Szkice o świadomości narodowej i kulturowej Słowian zachodnich i południowych.* Cracow: Universitas, 1995.
Bollacher, Eberhard. *Das Hultschiner Ländchen im Versailler Friedensvertrag.* Stuttgart: Ausland und Heimat Verlagsaktiengesellschaft, 1930.

Borový, Klement. *Antonín Brus z Mohelnice, arcibiskup pražský; Historicko-kritický životopis.* Prague: Dědictví sv. Prokopa, 1873.
Bradley, James E., and Dale K. Van Kley, eds. *Religion and Politics in Enlightenment Europe.* Notre Dame, Ind.: University of Notre Dame Press, 2001.
Bradshaw, Brendan. "The Controversial Sir Thomas More." *Journal of Ecclesiastical History* 36 (1985): 535–69.
Brandl, Manfred. *Der Kanonist Joseph Valentin Eybel, 1741–1805: sein Beitrag zur Aufklärung in Österreich.* Steyr: Ennsthaler, 1976.
Brandl, Vincenc. *Život Josefa Dobrovského.* Brno: Matice moravská, 1883. New ed., Prague: Neklan, 2003.
Brock, Peter. *The Political and Social Doctrines of the Unity of Czech Brethren in the Fifteenth and Sixteenth Centuries.* The Hague: Mouton, 1957.
Broklová, Eva. "K politické kultuře německých aktivistických politických stran, 1918–1938." In *T. G. Masaryk a situace v Čechách a na Moravě od konce XIX. století do německé okupace Československa,* edited by Eva Broklová, 91–101. Prague: Ústav T. G. Masaryka, 1998.
———. *Politická kultura německých aktivistických stran v Československu, 1918–1938.* Prague: Karolinum, 1999. See review by Jan Rataj in *Český časopis historický* 100 (2002): 143–44.
Brown, Stewart J., ed. *William Robertson and the Expansion of the Empire.* New York: Cambridge University Press, 1997.
Brtáň, Rudo. *Barokový slavizmus.* Lipt. Sv. Mikuláš: Tranoscius, 1939.
Buchan, James. *Crowded with Genius, the Scottish Enlightenment: Edinburgh's Moment of the Mind.* New York: HarperCollins, 2003.
Budín, Stanislav. *Karel Havlíček Borovský.* Prague: Státní nakladatelství politické literatury, 1954.
Budovec of Budov, Václav. *Antialkorán.* Edited by Noemi Rejchrtová. Prague: Odeon, 1989.
Burger, Heinz. *Die Gedankenwelt der grossen Schwaben: Von der Klosterkultur am Bodensee bis Hegel.* Stuttgart: Steinkopf, 1978.
Burian, Tomáš. "Český jazyk v Novém městě za Vídní." *Časopis českého musea* 12 (1843): 515–33.
Burns, Tony, and Ian Fraser, eds. *Hegel-Marx Connection.* New York: St. Martin's Press, 2000.
Bůžek, Václav. "Literární mecenát nižší šlechty v předbělohorských Čechách." In *Husitství, Reformace, Renesance: Sborník k 60. narozeninám Františka Šmahela,* edited by Jaroslav Pánek and others, 3:831–43. 3 vols. Prague: Historický ústav, 1994.
Bystrík, Ján. "K štúdiu Ľudovíta Štúra v Nemecku." *Historický sborník* 5 (1947): 216–20.
———. "Príspevok k štúdiu Slovákov vo Viedni." *Historický sborník* 5 (1947): 480–98.
Čáda, František. *Hynovo Dušesloví,* Rozpravy České akademie pro vědy, slovesnost a umění, ročník 10, třída 1, číslo 2. Prague: Česká akademie, 1902.
Cameron, Euan. "The Possibilities and Limits of Conciliation." In *Conciliation and Confession: The Struggle for Unity in the Age of Reform, 1415–1648,* edited

by Howard P. Louthan and Randall Zachman, 73–88. Notre Dame, Ind.: University of Notre Dame Press, 2004.
Čapek, Jan B. *Duch české literatury předbřeznové a předmájové: Ideové proudy a osobnosti 1825–1858.* Prague: Knihovna Svazu národního obrození, 1938.
Cartwright, Nancy, and others. *Otto Neurath: Philosophy between Science and Politics.* New York: Cambridge University Press, 1996.
Čechura, Jaroslav. *České země v letech 1378–1437: Lucemburkové na českém trůně.* 2 vols. Prague: Libri, 1999–2000.
Černý, Jiří. "K některým problémům osvícenského filosofického myšlení v Čechách." In *Filosofie v dějinách českého národa,* Protokol celostátní konference o dějinách české filosofie v Liblicích ve dnech 14.–17. dubna 1958, 90–110. Prague: Nakladatelství ČSAV, 1958.
———. "Předmluva: K filozofickým názorům Bernarda Bolzana." In *Výbor z filozofických spisů,* by Bernard Bolzano. Edited by Jiří Černý and Jaromír Loužil and translated by J. Loužil, 8–42. Prague: Svoboda, 1981.
Červinková-Riegrová, Marie. *Bernard Bolzano; životopisný nástin.* Prague: F. Šimáček, 1881.
Chaloupecký, Václav. *František Palacký.* Prague: Zlatoroh, 1912.
Chirot, Daniel. "Herder's Multicultural Theory of Nationalism and Its Consequences." *EEPS: East European Politics and Societies* 10 (1996): 1–15.
Christensen, Darrel E., ed. *Hegel and the Philosophy of Religion.* Wofford Symposium, 1968. The Hague: M. Nijhoff, 1970.
Christian, Curt, ed. *Bernard Bolzano, Leben und Wirkung.* Vienna: Verlag der Österreichischen Akademie der Wissenschaften, 1981.
Chudoba, Bohdan. *Jindy a nyní: dějiny českého národa.* Prague: Vyšehrad, 1946.
Chyzhevskyi, Dmytro. *Gegel' v Rossii.* Paris: Dom knigi, [1939].
———. *Hegel bei den Slaven.* Reichenberg: Stiepel, 1934.
———. *Štúrova filozofia života.* Bratislava: Slovenská učená spoločnost, 1941.
Clark, Robert T. *Herder: His Life and Thought.* Berkeley: University of California Press, 1955.
Clarke, David S. *Philosophy's Second Revolution: Early and Recent Analytic Philosophy.* Chicago: Open Court, 1997.
Coakley, John. "Mobilizing the Past: Nationalist Images of History." *Nationalism and Ethnic Politics* 10 (2004): 531–60.
Coen, Deborah R. *Vienna in the Age of Uncertainty: Science, Liberalism, and Private Life.* Chicago: University of Chicago Press, 2007.
Coffa, J. Alberto. *The Semantic Tradition from Kant to Carnap: To the Vienna Station.* Edited by Linda Wessels. New York: Cambridge University Press, 1991.
Collingwood, Robin G. *The Idea of History.* New ed. Oxford: Clarendon Press, 1993.
Čornej, Petr. *Rozhled, názory a postoje husitské inteligence v zrcadle dějepisectví 15. století.* Prague: Univerzita Karlova, 1986.
Čornej, Petr. "Vztah Zdeňka Nejedlého ke kulturním tradicím 19. Století." In *Povědomí tradice v novodobé české kultuře: Doba Bedřicha Smetany.* Sborník sympozia v Plzni 7.–11. března 1984, 261–73. Prague: Národní galerie, 1988.
Cvejn, K., Z. Pešat, and M. Jankovič. *Česká literatura a náboženství: Havlíček, Machar, Hašek.* Prague: Československá společnost pro šíření politických a vědeckých znalostí, 1961.

David, Zdeněk V. "A Brief Honeymoon in 1564–1566: The Utraquist Consistory and the Archbishop of Prague." *Bohemia* 39 (1998): 265–84.

———. "British Liberalism in the Czech National Awakening." *Kosmas: Czechoslovak and Central European Journal* 22, no. 2 (Spring 2009): 1–28.

———. *Finding the Middle Way: The Utraquists' Liberal Challenge to Rome and Luther.* Washington, D.C.: Woodrow Wilson Center Press; Baltimore: Johns Hopkins University Press, 2003.

———. "Frič, Herzen, and Bakunin: The Clash of Two Political Cultures." *EEPS: East European Politics and Societies* 12 (1998): 1–30.

———. "The Influence of Jacob Boehme on Russian Religious Thought." *Slavic Review* 21(1962): 43–64.

———. "The Integrity of the Bohemian Reformation: The Problem of Neo-Utraquism." *Bohemian Reformation and Religious Practice* 5, pt. 2 (2005): 329–51.

———. "John Bowring and British Liberalism in the Czech National Awakening." *Slavonic and East European Review* 86 (2008): 634–64.

———. "Masaryk and the Austrian Philosophical Tradition: Bolzano and Brentano." In *Czech and Slovak Culture in International and Global Context*, edited by Miloslav Rechcigl and others. České Budějovice: University of South Bohemia, 2008, 191–200.

———. "Národní obrození jako převtělení Zlatého věku." *Český časopis historický* 99 (2001): 486–518.

———. "Pavel Bydžovský and Czech Utraquism's Encounter with Luther." *Communio Viatorum* 38 (1996): 36–63.

———. "The Plebeianization of Utraquism: The Controversy over the Bohemian Confession of 1575." *The Bohemian Reformation and Religious Practice* 2 (1998): 127–58.

———. "The Strange Fate of Czech Utraquism: The Second Century, 1517–1621." *Journal of Ecclesiastical History* 46 (1995): 641–68.

———. "Utraquists, Lutherans, and the Bohemian Confession of 1575." *Church History* 68 (1999): 294–336.

Demetz, Peter. *Prague in Black and Gold: Scenes from the Life of a European City.* New York: Hill and Wang, 1997.

Denis, Ernest. *Fin de l'indépendance bohême.* 2nd ed., 2 vols. Paris: Librairie Leroux, 1930.

Deym, Franz X. *Friedrich Graf Deym und die österreichische Frage in der Paulskirche.* Leipzig: Breitkopf and Härtel, 1891.

Dobner, Gelasius. "Autobiografie." *Český časopis historický* 23 (1917): 129–38.

D'Oro, Giuseppina. "Collingwood on the Re-Enactment and the Identity of Thought." *Journal of the History of Philosophy* 38 (2000): 87–101.

Douglas, Richard M. *Jacopo Sadoleto, 1477–1547: Humanist and Reformer.* Cambridge, Mass.: Harvard University Press, 1959.

Dowling, Maria. *Fisher of Men: A Life of John Fisher, 1469–1535.* New York: St. Martin's Press, 1999.

Drabek, Anna. "Die Frage der Unterrichtssprache im Königreich Böhmen im Zeitalter der Aufklärung." *Österreichische Osthefte* 38 (1996): 329–55.

Dufour, Alain. "Humanisme et Reformation." In *Histoire politique et psychologie historique,* 37–62. Geneva: Librairie Droz, 1966.

Dummert, Michael A. *Ursprünge der analytischen Philosophie.* Frankfurt: Suhrkamp, 1988. Enlarged revised ed., London: Duckworth, 1993.

Dupkala, Rudolf. *Štúrovci a Hegel: k problematike slovenského hegelianizmu a antihegelianizmu.* 2nd ed. Prešov:: Manacon, 2000.

Ďurovič, Ján. "Slovenský pietizmus." *Historica Slovaca* 3–4 (1945–46): 165–201.

Dussen, W. J. van der. *History as a Science: The Philosophy of R. G. Collingwood.* The Hague: Martinus Nijhoff, 1981.

Dvořák, Jaromír, František Valouch, and Miloslav Pospíchal, eds. *Pocta Františku Palackému: Václavkova Olomouc 1976.* Olomouc: Univerzita Palackého, 1979.

Dvořáková, Zdeňka. *F. M. Klácel.* Prague: Melantrich, 1976.

Dvorský, František. "František Palacký a náš nepřítel." In *Památník na oslavu stých narozenin Františka Palackého,* 443–72. Prague: Matice česká, 1898.

Eberhard, Winfried. *Konfessionsbildung und Stände in Böhmen.* Munich: Oldenbourg, 1981.

———. "Zur reformatorischen Qualität und Konfessionalisierung des nachrevolutionären Hussitismus." In *Häresie und vorzeitige Reformation im Spätmittelalter,* Schriften des Historischen Kollegs Kolloquien 39, edited by František Šmahel, 213–38. Munich: Oldenbourg, 1998.

———. "Zur Religionsproblematik in der bömischen Landesverfassung der Reformationsepoche." In *Vladislavské zřízení zemské a počátky ústavního zřízení v Českých zemích, 1500–1619.* Sborník příspěvků z mezinárodní konference konané ve dnech 7–8 prosince 2000 v Praze, edited by Karel Malý and Jaroslav Pánek, 249–66. Prague: Historický ústav Akademie věd České Republiky; Ústav právních dějin Právnické fakulty Univerzity Karlovy, 2001.

Eggel, Dominic, Andre Liebich and Deborah Mancini-Griffoli. "Was Herder a Nationalist?" *Review of Politics* 69 (2007): 48–78.

Ergang, Robert R. *Herder and the Foundations of German Nationalism.* New York: Columbia University, 1931.

Eschweiler, Karl. "Die Philosophie der spanischen Spätscholastik an den deutschen Universitäten des 17. Jahrhunderts." *Spanische Forschungen der Görresgesellschaft* 1 (1928): 251–325.

Evans, Robert J. W. *Austria, Hungary, and the Habsburgs: Essays on Central Europe, c.1683–1867.* New York: Oxford University Press, 2006.

———. "Hungarica in the Bodleian: A Historical Sketch." *Bodleian Library Record* 9 (1978): 333–45.

———. "Introduction." *Czechoslovakia in a Nationalist and Fascist Europe, 1918–1948,* edited by Mark Cornwall and R. J. W. Evans, 1–11. New York: Oxford University Press, 2007.

———. "Moravia and the Culture of Enlightenment in the Habsburg Monarchy." In *Staatskanzler Wenzel Anton von Kaunitz-Rietberg, 1711–1794,* edited by Grete Klingenstein and Franz A. Szabo, 383–99. Graz: Andreas Schneider, 1996.

———. *Rudolf II and his World: A Study in Intellectual History, 1576–1612.* Oxford : Clarendon Press, 1984.

———. "Über die Ursprünge der Aufklärung in den habsburgischen Ländern." In *Das achtzehnte Jahrhundert und Österreich,* Jahrbuch der Österreichischen Gesellschaft zur Erforschung des achtzehnten Jahrhunderts. 2:9–31. Vienna: Böhlaus, 1985.

Fackenheim, Emil L. *The Religious Dimension in Hegel's Thought*. 2nd ed. Chicago: University of Chicago Press, 1982.
Fajfr, František. "Měl Hegel vliv na českou literaturu?" *Česká mysl* 28 (1932): 8–20, 92–101, 204–16.
Faulkner, Robert K. *Richard Hooker and the Politics of a Christian England*. Berkeley: University of California Press, 1981.
Fawn, Rick. *The Czech Republic: A Nation of Velvet*. Amsterdam: Harwood Academic, 2000.
Fenlon, Dermot. *Heresy and Obedience in Tridentine Italy: Cardinal Pole and the Counter Reformation*. Cambridge: Cambridge University Press, 1972.
Fiala, Jiří. *Chronologický přehled dějin české literatury národního obrození*. Olomouc: Univerzita Palackého, Filozofická fakulta, 1992.
Filosofie v dějinách českého národa. Protokol celostátní konference o dějinách české filosofie v Liblicích ve dnech 14.–17. dubna 1958. Prague: Nakladatelství ČSAV, 1958.
Finzel-Niederstadt, Wiltraut. *Lernen und Lehren bei Herder und Basedow*. Frankfurt am Main: P. Lang, 1986.
Fischer, Josef. *Myšlenka a dílo Františka Palackého*. 3 vols. Prague: Čin, 1926–27.
Fleischacker, Samuel. "The Impact on America: Scottish Philosophy and the American Founding." In *The Cambridge Companion to the Scottish Enlightenment*, edited by Alexander Broadie, 316–37. New York: Cambridge University Press, 2003.
Floss, Karel. "Tereziánská vysokoškolská reforma a olomoucký J. K. Reidinger." *Studia Comeniana et historica* 8–9 (1974): 125–38.
Fox, Russell A. "J. G. Herder on Language and the Metaphysics on National Community." *Review of Politics* 65 (2003): 237–62.
Fraenkel, Peter. "Utraquism or Co-Existence: Some Notes on the Earliest Negotiations before the Pacification of Nuernberg, 1531–1532." *Studia theologica* 18, no. 2 (1964): 119–58.
Franco, Paul. "Hegel and Liberalism." *Review of Politics* 59 (1997): 831–60.
Franzen, August. *Bischof und Reformation: Erzbischof Hermann von Wied in Köln vor der Erscheidung zwischen Reform und Reformation*. Munster: Aschendorff, 1971.
Franzis, Emerich. "Bernard Bolzano und die nationale Idee: Ein Beitrag zur Geschichte des Nationalismus." *Historisches Jahrbuch* 51 (1932): 433–44.
Friedrich, Johann. *Beiträge zur Kirchengeschichte des 18. Jahrhunderts*, Aus dem handschriftlichen Nachlass des regul. Chorherrn Eusebius Amort zusammengestellt. Munich: Verlag der K. Akademie, in commission bei G. Franz, 1876.
Friedrich, Margaret. "Bolzano's Project der Aufklärung." In *Bernard Bolzano und die Politik: Staat, Nation und Religion als Herausforderung für die Philosophie im Kontext von Spätaufklärung, Frühnationalismus und Restauration*. Studien zu Politik und Verwaltung, Band 61., edited by Helmut Rumpler, 23–48. Vienna: Böhlau, 2000.
Freimanová, Milena, ed. *Povědomí tradice v novodobé české kultuře: Doba Bedřicha Smetany*. Sborník sympozia v Plzni 7.–11. března 1984. Prague: Národní galerie, 1988.
Fudge, Thomas A. *The Magnificent Ride: The First Reformation in Hussite Bo-*

hemia. St. Andrew's Studies in Reformation History. Brookfield, Vt.: Ashgate, 1998.

———. "The Problem of Religious Liberty in Early Modern Bohemia." *Communio Viatorum* 38 (1996): 64–87.

Gayraud, Hippolyte. *Thomisme et Molinisme.* Part 1: *Préliminaires historiques et Critique du Molinisme.* Toulouse: Édouard Privat, 1889.

Gellner, Ernest. *Encounters with Nationalism.* New York: Blackwell, 1995.

———. *Nations and Nationalism.* Ithaca, N.Y.: Cornell University Press, 1983.

George, Rolf. "Psychologism in Logic: Bacon to Bolzano." *P & R: Philosophy and Rhetoric* 30 (1997): 213–42.

Gervinus, Georg Gottfried. *Shakespeare.* 4 vols. Leipzig, 1849–50.

Gillies, Alexander. *Herder.* Oxford: Blackwell, 1945.

Gilson, Étienne. *Being and Some Philosophers.* 2nd ed. Toronto: Pontifical Institute of Medieval Studies, 1952.

Gindely, Anton. *Geschichte der Ertheilung des böhmischen Majestätsbriefes von 1609.* Prague: Carl Bellmann's Verlag, 1858.

Ginzel, J. A. *Bischof Hurdalek: Ein Charakterbild aus der Geschichte der bömischen Kirche.* Prague: Bohemia, 1873.

Giusti, Wolfgango. *Mazzini e gli Slavi.* Milan: Istituto per gli studi di politica internazionale, 1940.

Gleason, Elisabeth G. *Gasparo Contarini: Venice, Rome, and Reform.* Berkeley: University of California Press, 1993.

Gleig, George R. *Germany, Bohemia, and Hungary, Visited in 1837.* 3 vols. London: J. W. Parker, 1839.

Glücklich, Julius. "Koncept Majestátu a vznik Porovnání." *Český časopis historický* 23 (1917): 110–28.

Gower, Barry, ed. *Logical Positivism in Perspective: Essays on Language, Truth, and Logic.* Totowa, N.J. : Barnes & Noble Books, c1987.

Gracia, Jorge J. E. "The Impact of Philosophical Analysis in Latin America." *Philosophical Forum* 20 (1989): 129–40.

Greenfeld, Liah. *Nationalism: Five Roads to Modernity.* Cambridge, Mass.: Harvard University Press, 1992.

Gregor, A. James. *The Faces of Janus: Marxism and Fascism in the Twentieth Century.* New Haven, Conn.: Yale University Press, 2000.

Gui, Francesco. *L'attesa del concilio: Vittoria Colonna e Reginald Pole nel movimento degli "spirituali."* Rome: Editoria Università Elettronica, 1997.

Guy, John. *Thomas More.* London: Arnold, 2000.

Hacohen, Malachi H. "Karl Popper, the Vienna Circle, and Red Vienna." *Journal of the History of Ideas* 59 (1998): 711–34.

Haerpfer, Christian W. *Democracy and Enlargement in Post-Communist Europe: The Democratisation of the General Public in Fifteen Central and Eastern European Countries, 1991–1998.* New York: Routledge, 2002.

Hafner, Stanislaus. "Aus B. Kopitars römischen Briefen an Josef Fesl." In *Studia Slovenica Monacensia: In honorem Antonii Slodnjak septuagenarii,* edited by Hans-Joachim Kissling, 29–42. Munich: Trofenik, 1969.

Hála, Vlastimil. "Bolzano jako představitel 'rakouské filosofie?'" *Filosofický časopis* 46 (1998): 915–30.

———. "Oskar Kraus: pražský představitel brentanovské školy." *Filosofický časopis* 51 (2003): 19–37.
Hallen, Barry. *African Philosophy: The Analytic Approach.* Trenton, N.J.: Africa World Press, 2005.
Haller, Rudolf. "Bolzano and Austrian Philosophy." In *Bolzano's Wissenschaftslehre, 1837–1987*, International Workshop, Firenze, 16–19 September 1987, 191–206. Florence: Olschki, 1992.
———. "Österreichische Philosophie." In his *Studien zur österreichischen Philosophie: Variationen über ein Thema,* 6–22. Amsterdam: Rodopi, 1979.
———. *Studien zur österreichischen Philosophie: Variationen über ein Thema.* Amsterdam: Rodopi, 1979.
———. "Der 'Wiener Kreis' und die analytische Philosophie." In his *Studien zur österreichischen Philosophie: Variationen über ein Thema,* 79–98. Amsterdam: Rodopi, 1979.
Haman, Aleš. *Nástin dějin české literární kritiky.* Jinočany: H & H, 2000.
Hanlon, Gregory. "The Decline of a Provincial Military Aristocracy: Siena 1560–1740." *Past and Present* 155 (1997): 64–108.
Hanuš, J. "Dobrovského časopisy." *Bratislava* 3 (1929): 373–467.
———. "Josefa Dobrovského *Geschichte der böhmischen Sprache* (1791), *Geschichte der böhmischen Sprache und Literatur* (1792), *Geschichte der böhmischen Sprache und ältern Literatur* (1818)." *Bratislava* 3 (1929): 494–574.
———. *Národní museum a naše obrození: k stoletému jubileu založení Musea.* 2 vols. Prague: Národní museum, 1921–23.
———. *O pobělohorské protireformaci: Úvodem k českému obrození,* Universita Komenského. Bratislava, Filosofická fakulta, Sborník 4, no. 39 (1926). Bratislava, 1926.
———. *Pavel Josef Šafařík v životě a spisích.* Prague: E. Grégr, 1895.
———. "Počátky kritického dějezpytu v Čechách." *Český časopis historický* 15 (1909): 277–302, 425–63.
———. *Život a spisy Václava Bolemíra Nebeského.* Prague: Česká akademie pro vědy, slovesnost a umění, 1896.
Hanzal, Josef. "F. Š. Rautenstrauch ve světle svých deníků." *Český časopis historický* 93 (1995): 86–97.
———. "Jazyková otázka ve vývoji obrozenského školství." *Československý časopis historický* 16 (1968): 317–40.
———. *Josef Pekař: život a dílo.* Prague: Karolinum, 2002.
———. "Martin Bacháček z Nauměřic a městské školy ve středních Čechách před Bílou Horou." *Středočeský sborník historický* 10 (1975): 137–50.
———. *Od baroka k romantismu: Ke zrození novodobé české kultury.* Prague: Academia, 1987.
———. "Vzdělanost a lidová osvěta." *Sborník historický* 18 (1971): 39–69.
Haubelt, Josef. *České osvícenství.* 2nd rev. ed. Prague: Rodiče, 2004. 1st ed. Prague: Svoboda, 1986.
Hayes, Carlton J. "Contributions of Herder to the Doctrine of Nationalism." *American Historical Review* 32 (1927): 719–36.
Hechter, Michael. *Containing Nationalism.* Oxford: Oxford University Press, 2000.

Hegel v Čechách, na Moravě a v Americe, Sborník k životnímu jubileu Milana Sobotky, profesora Karlovy univerzity. Prague: Katedra filosofie FFUK, 1993.

Heidler, Jan. "O vlivu hegelismu na filosofii dějin a na politický program Frant. Palackého." *Český časopis historický* 17 (1911): 1–12, 152–66.

Hejnic, Josef. "Daniel Adam of Veleslavín: Zu den gegenseitigen Beziehungen zwischen der tschechischen und lateinischen Literatur im letzten Viertel des 16. Jahrhunderts." In *Studien zum Humanismus in den böhmischen Ländern.* Schriften des Komitees der Bundesrepublic Deutschland zur Förderung der Slawischen Studien, 11, edited by Hans-Bernd Harder and Hans Rothe, 261–73. Cologne: Böhlau, 1988.

Henze, Barbara. *Aus Liebe zur Kirche Reform: die Bemühungen Georg Witzels (1501–1573) um die Kircheneinheit.* Münster: Aschendorff, 1995.

Herold, Vilém. *Pražská univerzita a Wyclif: Wyclifovo učení o ideách a geneze husitského revolučního myšlení.* Prague: Univerzita Karlova, 1985.

Hersche, Peter, ed. *Der aufgeklärte Reformkatholizismus in Oesterreich.* Bern: Herbert Lang, 1976.

Heymann, Frederick G. "The Crusades against the Hussites." In *A History of the Crusades*, edited by Kenneth M. Setton, 3:586–646. 6 vols. Madison, Wisc.: University of Wisconsin Press, 1969–89.

———. *George of Poděbrady: King of Heretics.* Princeton, N.J.: Princeton University Press, 1965.

———. "The Hussite Movement in the Geography of the Czech Awakening." In *The Czech Renaissance of the Nineteenth Century,* edited by Peter Brock and H. Gordon Skilling, 224–38. Toronto: University of Toronto Press, 1970.

———. "John Rokycana: Church Reformer between Hus and Luther." *Church History* 28 (1959): 240–80.

———. *John Žižka and the Hussite Revolution.* Princeton, N.J.: Princeton University Press, 1955.

———. "The Role of the Bohemian Cities during and after the Hussite Revolution." *Tolerance and Movements of Religious Dissent in Eastern Europe*, edited by Bela K. Kiraly, 27–41. New York: Columbia University Press, 1975.

Hilsch, Peter. *Johannes Hus (um 1370–1415): Prediger Gottes und Ketzer.* Regensburg: Pustet, 1999.

Himmelfarb, Gertrude. *The Roads to Modernity: The British, French, and American Enlightenments.* New York: Alfred A. Knopf, 2004.

Hobsbawm, Eric J. *Nations and Nationalism since 1780.* 2nd ed. New York: Cambridge University Press, 1992.

Hobsbawm, Eric J., and Terence Ranger, eds. *The Invention of Tradition.* New York: 1983.

Holeton, David R. "Church or Sect: The *Jednota bratrská* and the Growth of Dissent from Mainline Utraquism." *Communio Viatorum* 38 (1996): 5–35.

———. *La communion des tout-petits enfants: Étude du mouvement eucharistique en Bohême vers la fin du Moyen-Âge.* Rome: Edizioni Liturgiche, 1989.

———. "The Communion of Infants: The Basel Years." *Communio Viatorum* 29 (1986): 35–36.

———. "The Communion of Infants and Hussitism." *Communio Viatorum* 27 (1984): 217–19.

———. "The Evolution of Utraquist Eucharistic Liturgy: A Textual Study." *The Bohemian Reformation and Religious Practice* 2 (1998): 97–126.

———. "The Role of Jakoubek of Stříbro in the Creation of Czech Liturgy: Some Further Reflections." In *Jakoubek ze Stříbra: Texty a jejich působení*, edited by Ota Halama and Pavel Soukup, 49–86. Prague: Filosofia, 2006.

———. "Sacramental and Liturgical Reform in Late Medieval Bohemia." *Studia Liturgica* 28, no. 1 (1987): 87–96.

Holinka, Rudolf. "K Dobrovského koncepci českých dějin." *Slavia* 23 (1954): 201–4.

Holý, Ladislav. *The Little Czech and the Great Czech Nation: National Identity and the Post-Communist Social Transformation.* New York: Cambridge University Press, 1996.

Holzknecht, Georgine. *Ursprung und Herkunft der Reformideen Kaiser Josef II. auf kirchlichem Gebiet.* Innsbruck, Wagner, 1914.

Hook, Sidney. "A Personal Impression of Contemporary German Philosophy." *Journal of Philosophy* 27 (1930): 141–60.

Horák, Jiří, Matyáš Murko, and Miloš Weingart, eds. *Josef Dobrovský, 1753–1829: sborník statí k stému výročí smrti Josefa Dobrovského.* Prague: Výbor I. Sjezdu slovanských filologů, 1929.

Horák, Petr. *Svět Blaise Pascala.* Prague: Vyšehrad, 1985.

Horálek, Karel. *Studie o populární literatuře českého obrození.* Prague: Československý spisovatel, 1990.

Hostinský, Ottakar. "Františka Palackého estetické studie." *Památník na oslavu stých narozenin Františka Palackého,* 367–90. Prague: Matice česká, 1898.

Hrbata, Zdeněk. *Romantismus a Čechy: Témata a symboly v literárních a kulturních souvislostech.* Prague: H &H, 1999.

Hrejsa, Ferdinand. *Česká konfesse: Její vznik, podstata a dějiny.* Prague: Česká akademie pro vědy, slovesnost a umění, 1912.

———. *Dějiny křest'anství v Československu.* 6 vols. Prague: Husova Československá evangelická fakulta bohoslovecká, 1946–50.

Hroch, Miroslav. *Evropská národní hnutí v 19. století: společenské předpoklady vzniku novodobých národů.* Prague: Svoboda, 1986.

———. *Social Preconditions on National Revival in Europe: A Comparative Analysis of the Social Composition of Patriotic Groups among the Smaller European Nations.* Translated by Ben Fowkes. New York: Columbia University Press, 2000.

———. *V národním zájmu: požadavky a cíle evropských národních hnutí devatenáctého století ve srovnávací perspektivě.* Prague: Lidové noviny, 1999.

Hrubý, František. "Nové příspěvky k historii bitvy na Bílé hoře." *Časopis českého musea* 27 (1922): 277–88.

Hudson, Anne. "*Poor Preachers, Poor Men*: Views of Poverty in Wyclif and His Followers." In *Häresie und vorzeitige Reformation*, Schriften des Historischen Kollegs Kolloquien 39, edited by František Šmahel, 41–54. Munich: Oldenbourg, 1998.

Hughes, Michael. *Nationalism and Society: Germany 1800–1945.* London: E. Arnold, 1988.

Humboldt, Wilhelm. *On Language: The Diversity of Human Language-Structure *and Its Influence on the Mental Development of Mankind.* Translated by Peter Heath. Introduction by Hans Aarsleff. New York: Cambridge University Press, 1988.

———. *Über die Verschiedenheit des menschlichen Sprachbaues und ihren Einfluss auf die geistige Entwicklung des Menchengeschlechts.* N.p., 1836. [Reprint, Bonn: F. Dümmler, 1968.]

Hylton, Peter. *Russell, Idealism, and the Emergence of Analytic Philosophy.* Oxford: Clarendon Press, 1990.

Israel, Jonathan. *The Dutch Republic: Its Rise, Greatness, and Fall, 1477–1806.* Oxford: Clarendon Press, 1995.

———. "Enlightenment! Which Enlightenment?" *Journal of the History of Ideas* 67 (2006): 523–45.

———. *Radical Enlightenment: Philosophy and the Making of Modernity.* Oxford: Clarendon Press, 2001.

Jacob, Margaret, and Wijnand W. Mijnhardt, eds. *The Dutch Republic in the Eighteenth Century: Decline, Enlightenment, and Revolution.* Itaca, N.Y.: Cornell University Press, 1992.

Jagić, Vatroslav. *Istoriia slavianskoi filologii*, Entsiklopediia slavianskoi filologii, Vyp. 1. St. Petersburg: Akademiia nauk, 1910.

Jakovenko, Boris V. *Ein Beitrag zur Geschichte des Hegelianismus in Russland.* Prague: Bartl, 1934.

Jakubec, Jan. *Antonín Marek: Jeho život a působení i význam v literatuře české.* Prague: Bačkovský, 1896.

———. "Dobrovský spolupracovníkem Hromádkových *Vídeňských novin.*" In *Sborník prací věnovaných Janu Máchalovi k sedmdesátým narozeninám*, edited by Jiří Horák and Miloslav Hýsek, 38–43. Prague: Klub moderních filologů, 1925.

———. *O životě a působení Jana Kollára.* Prague: Slavia, 1893.

Janáček, Josef. "Královská města česká na zemském sněmu r. 1609–1610." *Sborník historický* 5 (1956): 226–51.

———. "České stavovské povstání, 1618–1620: Otázky a problem." *Folia Historica Bohemica* 8 (1985): 7–41.

Jančárek, Petr. *Vincenc Zahradník.* Ústí nad Labem: Okresní vlastivědné muzeum, 1991.

Janek, František. *Upevňovanie vzťahov Čechov a Slovákov pri vučovaní dejepisu.* Bratislava: Slovenské pedagogické nakladateľstvo, 1961.

Janowski, Maciej. *Polish Liberal Thought up to 1918.* Translated by Danuta Przekop. Budapest: Central European University Press, 2004.

Jansen, Bernhard. "Philosophen katholischen Bekenntnisses in ihrer Stellung zur Philosophie der Aufklärung." *Scholastik: Vierteljahresschrift für Theologie und Philosophie* (Freiburg i. B.) 11 (1936): 1–51.

Jedlička, Alois, ed. *Slovanské spisovné jazyky v době obrození: sborník k 200. výročí narození Josefa Jungmanna.* Prague: Univerzita Karlova, 1974.

Jedlička, Benjamin. *Dobrovského 'Geschichte' ve vývoji české literární historie,* Archiv pro bádání o životě a díle Josefa Dobrovského, sv. 1. Prague: Komise pro vydávání spisů Josefa Dobrovského při Královské české společnosti nauk, 1934.

Jeřábek, Dušan. *Václav Vladivoj Tomek a Karel Havlíček v letech Bachovské reakce.* Filozofická fakulta, Spisy, 223. Brno: Univerzita J. E. Purkyně, 1979.

Jetmarová, Milena. "Filosofie Palackého." In *Filosofie v dějinách českého národa*, Protokol celostátní konference o dějinách české filosofie v Liblicích ve dnech 14.–17. dubna 1958,135–149. Prague: Nakladatelství ČSAV, 1958.

———. *František Palacký*. Praha: Svobodné slovo, 1961.

Jiang, Yi. "Analytic Philosophy in China." *Social Sciences in China* 23, no. 2 (2002): 65–74.

Jirát, Vojtěch. "O klasicismu, zvláště pak o klasicismu českém." In *Portréty a studie*, 11–23. Prague: Odeon, 1978.

———. "Úloha 'biedermeieru' v českém národním obrození." In *Portréty a studie*, 548–51. Prague: Odeon, 1978. Originally published as "Le rôle du 'Biedermeier' dans le réveil national tchéque." *Europe central*, 12 Année, no. 1 (1937): 10–12.

Johanides, Josef. *František Martin Pelcl*. Prague: Melantrich, 1981.

Johnston, William M. *The Austrian Mind: An Intellectual and Social History, 1848–1938*. Berkeley: University of California Press, 1972.

Jordan, Mark D. *The Alleged Aristotelianism of Thomas Aquinas*. Etienne Gilson Series 15. Toronto: Pontifical Institute of Medieval Studies, 1992.

Josek, Otakar. *Život a dílo Josefa Kalouska*. Prague: Historický spolek, 1922.

Kadlec, Jaroslav. *Jan Valerián Jirsík*. České Budějovice: Sdružení sv. Jana Neumanna, 1993.

Kalista, Zdeněk. *Josef Pekař*. Prague: Torst, 1994.

Kalivoda, Robert. *Husitská epocha a J. A. Komenský*. Prague: Odeon, 1992.

———. *Husitské myšlení*. Prague: Filosofia, 1997.

Kalousek, Josef. "O vůdčích myšlénkách v historickém díle Palackého." In *Památník na oslavu stých narozenin Františka Palackého*, 177–232. Prague: Matice česká, 1898.

Kameníček, František. "Pod obojí (utrakvisté)." In *Zemské sněmy a sjezdy moravské, 1526–1628*. 3:404–22. 3 vols. Brno: Zemský výbor Markrabství moravského, 1900–1905.

Kaminsky, Howard. *A History of the Hussite Revolution*. Berkeley: University of California Press, 1967.

———. "The University of Prague in the Hussite Revolution: The Role of the Masters." In *Universities in Politics: Case Studies from the Late Middle Ages and Early Modern Period*, edited by John W. Baldwin and Richard A. Goldthwaite, 79–105. Baltimore: Johns Hopkins Press, 1972.

Kaňák, Miloslav. *John Viklef: Život a dílo anglického Husova předchůdce*. Prague: Blahoslav, 1973.

———. *Josef Franta Šumavský*. Prague: Melantrich, 1975.

Kann, Robert A., and Zdeněk V. David. *The Peoples of the Eastern Habsburg Lands, 1526–1918*. Vol. 6, *A History of East Central Europe*. Seattle and London: University of Washington Press, 1984.

Karlik, Berta, and Erich Schmid. *Franz Serafim Exner und sein Kreis: Ein Beitrag zur Geschichte der Physik in Österreich*. Vienna: Verlag der Österreichischen Akademie der Wissenschaften, 1982.

Káša, Peter. "Český 'romantizmus' očami J. M. Hurbana a L'. Štúra." In *Česká literatura na konci tisíciletí*, Příspěvky z 2. kongresu světové literárněvědné bohemistiky, Prague 3.–8. července 2000. 2 vols. Prague: Ústav pro českou literaturu AV ČR, 2001, 1:153–165.

Kaufmann, Walter, ed. *Hegel's Political Philosophy*. New York: Atherton, 1970.

———. *Nietzsche: Philosopher, Psychologist, Antichrist.* 4th ed. Princeton, N.J.: Princeton University Press, 1974.
Kazbunda, Karel. "Pobyt Dra Fr. Lad. Riegra v cizině, r. 1849–1850." *Zahraniční politika* 8 (1929): 749–62, 913–34, 1016–36.
Keen, Ralph. *Divine and Human Authority in Reformation Thought: German Theologians on Political Order, 1520–1555.* Nieuwkoop: De Graaf, 1997.
Keenan, Edward L. *Josef Dobrovský and the Origins of the Igor's Tale.* Cambridge, Mass.: Harvard Ukrainian Research Center, 2003.
———. "Was Iaroslav of Halych Really Shooting Sultans in 1185?" *Harvard Ukrainian Studies* 22 (1998): 313–27.
Kejř, Jiří. *Kvodlibetní disputace na pražské universitě.* Prague: Univerzita Karlova, 1971.
———. "Trest smrti v husitské revoluci." *Bohemian Reformation and Religious Practice* 6 (2007): 143–63.
Kenny, Anthony. *An Illustrated Brief History of Western Philosophy.* 2nd ed. Oxford: Blackwell, 2006.
Khéres, Jan. "Literární spor o filosofii v letech 1844–1848: příspěvek k dějinám české filisofie." *Výroční zpráva reálného gymnasia v Uherském Hradišti* (1913–14): 3–29.
Kieniewicz, Stefan, and Witold Kula, eds. *Historia Polski, 1831–1864.* Vol. 2, pt. 3, of *Historia Polski,* edited by Tadeusz Manteuffel. Warsaw: Państwowe wydawnictwo naukowe, 1959.
Klabouch, Jiří. *Osvícenské právní nauky v českých zemích.* Prague: Nakladatelství Československé akademie věd, 1958.
Kline, George L. "Hegel and the Marxist-Leninist Critique of Religion." In *Hegel and the Philosophy of Religion,* edited by Darrel E. Christensen, 187–215. The Hague: M. Nijhoff, 1970.
Klueting, Harm. "Kaunitz, die Kirche und der Josephinismus. Protestantisches landesherrliches Kirchenregiment, rationaler Territorialismus und theresianisch-josephinisches Staatskirchentum." In *Staatskanzler Wenzel Anton von Kaunitz-Rietberg, 1711–1794,* edited by Grete Klingenstein and Franz A. Szabo, 169–96. Graz: Andreas Schneider, 1996.
Kneidl, Pravoslav. "Městský stav v Čechách v době předbělohorské." PhD diss., Univerzita Karlova, Prague,1951.
Knoll, Samson B. "Herder's Concept of *Huminität.*" In *Johann Gottfried Herder, Innovator through the Ages,* edited by Wulf Koepke and Samson B. Knoll, 9–19. Bonn: Bouvier, 1982.
Kočí, Josef. *České národní obrození.* Prague: Svoboda, 1978.
Koepke, Wulf, ed. *Johann Gottfried Herder: Language, History, and Enlightenment.* Columbia, S.C.: Camden House, 1990.
———. "Das Wort 'Volk' im Sprachgebrauch Johann Gottfried Herders." *Lessing Yearbook* 19 (1987): 209–21.
Koepke, Wulf, and Samson B. Knoll, eds. *Johann Gottfried Herder, Innovator through the Ages.* Bonn: Bouvier, 1982.
Kohn, Hans. *Pan-Slavism, Its History and Ideology.* Notre Dame, Ind.: University of Notre Dame Press, 1953.
———. *Prelude to Nation States: The French and German Experience, 1789–1815.* Princeton, N.J.: Van Nostrand, 1967.

Kolár, Jaroslav. *Česká zábavná próza 16. století a t. zv. knížky lidového čtení*. Prague: Nakladatelství Československé akademie věd, 1960.

———. *Návraty bez konce: Studie k starší české literatuře*. Edited by Lenka Jiroušková. Brno: Atlantis, 1999.

Koldínská, Marie. *Každodennost renesančního aristokrata*. Prague: Paseka, 2001.

Kolman, Arnošt. "Matematicko-logická stránka Bolzanovy filosofie." In *Filosofie v dějinách českého národa*, Protokol celostátní konference o dějinách české filosofie v Liblicích ve dnech 14.–17. dubna 1958,124–34. Prague: Nakladatelství ČSAV, 1958.

Kopčan, Štefan, comp. *Jozef Miloslav Hurban; sborník pri príležitosti 150. výročia jeho smrti*. Bratislava: Osvetový ústav, 1967.

Kopecký, Milan. *Daniel Adam z Veleslavína*. Prague: Svobodné slovo, 1962.

———. "Poznámky k vývoji české historické beletrie předobrozenské." *Sborník prací Filozofické Fakulty Brněnské Univerzity* D 14 (1967): 49–66.

———. "Tradice a její žánrová modifikace." In *Speculum medii aevi: Zrcadlo středověku*, edited by Lenka Jiroušková, 150–62. Prague: Koniasch Latin Press, 1998.

Kopičková, Božena. *Jan Želivský*. Prague: Melantrich, 1990.

Kořalka, Jiří. *František Palacký, 1798–1876: Životopis*. Prague: Argo, 1998.

———. "František Palacký a čeští bolzanisté." In *Modernismus: studie nebo výzva? Studie ke genezi českého katolického modernismu*, Pontes Pragenses 24, edited byZdeněk Kučera and Jan B. Lášek, 23–47. Brno: L. Marek, 2002.

———. *Tschechen im Habsburger Reich und in Europa, 1815–1914*. Munich: Oldenbourg, 1991.

Kormann, Dieter. *Der Anschauungsbegriff bei Comenius, Basedow und Hartwig: im Blick auf die anschauungsbezogenen methodischen Anforderungen im heutigen Fach Kunst*. Frankfurt am Main: P. Lang, 1992.

Koschnitzke, Rudolf. *Herbart und Herbartschule*. Aalen: Scientia, 1988.

Kovács, Elisabeth, ed. *Katholische Aufklärung und Josephinismus*. Vienna: Verlag für Geschichte und Politik, 1979.

Kovařík, Jiří. "Proměny feudální třídy v Čechách v předbělohorském období." In *Proměny feudální třídy v Čechách v pozdním feudalismu*, edited by Josef Petráň. Acta Universitatis Carolinae, Philosophica et historica 1 (1976), Studia historica, 14. Prague: Univerzita Karlova, 1976, 137–64.

Kraft, Viktor. *The Vienna Circle: The Origin of Neo-Positivism, a Chapter in the History of Recent Philosophy*. New York: Greenwood Press, 1969.

Kraus, Arnošt. *Husitství v literatuře zejména německé*. 3 vols. Prague: Česká akademie, 1917–24.

Krejčí, František V. *František Palacký, jeho význam v českém probuzení*. Prague: Svěcený, 1912.

Kreuz, Petr. "Edice zemských zřízení a ústavně historických pramenů k dějinám českých zemí v raném novověku, 1500–1619." In *Vladislavské zřízení zemské a počátky ústavního zřízení v Českých zemích, 1500–1619*. Sborník příspěvků z mezinárodní konference konané ve dnech 7–8 prosince 2000 v Praze, edited by Karel Malý and Jaroslav Pánek, 267–90. Prague: Historický ústav Akademie věd České Republiky; Ústav právních dějin Právnické fakulty Univerzity Karlovy, 2001.

Křišťan, Alois. *Počátky pastorální teologie v českých zemích*. Prague: Triton, 2004.

Křivský, Pavel. *Augustin Smetana*. Prague: Karolinum, 1990.

Krofta, Kamil. "Boj o konsistoř podobojí v l. 1562–1575 a jeho historický základ." *Český časopis historický* 17 (1911): 28–57, 178–99, 283–303, 383–420.
———. *Dějiny selského stavu*, his Dílo sv. 3. Edited by Emanuel Janoušek. Prague: Laichter, 1949.
———. "František Pubička předchůdce Palackého v zemském dějepisectví českém." *Časopis společnosti přátel starožitností* 51–53 (1943–45): 1–24.
———. *K pramenům českých dějin*. Prague: Sfinx-Janda, 1948.
———. *Listy z náboženských dějin*. Prague: Historický klub, 1936.
———. *Majestát Rudolfa II.* Prague: Historický klub, 1909.
———. *Nesmrtelný národ: Od Bílé Hory k Palackému*. Prague: Laichter, 1940.
———. "Nový názor na český vývoj náboženský v době předbělohorské." In *Listy z náboženských dějin českých*, 373–90. Prague: Historický klub, 1936.
———. "O některých spisech M. Jana z Příbramě." *Časopis Českého muzea* 73 (1899): 209–20.
———. "Slovo o knězi Bohuslavu Bílejovském. " In *Listy z náboženských dějin českých*, 288–301. Prague: Historický klub, 1936.
———. "Václav Koranda mladší z Nové Plzně a jeho názory náboženské." In *Listy z náboženských dějin českých*, 241–87. Prague: Historický klub, 1936.
Kroiher, František. J. "Nevlastenectví českých stavů nekatolických v době předbělohorské." *Sborník historického kroužku* Sešit 3 (1894): 55–73.
Kryštůfek, František. *Dějiny církve katolické ve státech rakousko-uherských se zláštním zřetelem k zemím koruny české.* Vol. 1, 1740–1848. Prague: Kotrba, 1898.
Krzyźanowski, Julian. *Od średniowiecza do baroku. Studia naukowo-literackie.* Warsaw: Roj, 1938.
Kubka, František. " Dobrovského 'rusofilství.'" In *Sborník prací věnovaných Janu Máchalovi k sedmdesátým narozeninám*, edited by Jiří Horák and Miloslav Hýsek, 44–49. Prague: Klub moderních filologů, 1925.
Kučera, Jan P., and Jiří Rak. *Bohuslav Balbín a jeho místo v české kultuře*. Prague: Vyšehrad, 1983.
Kudělka, Milan. "Gelasius Dobner." *Československá akademie věd, Věstník* 78 (1969): 205–22.
———. *Spor Gelasia Dobnera o Hájkovu kroniku*. Prague, 1964. (Československá akademie věd, Rozpravy. Řada společenských věd. Roč. 74, seš. 11.)
Künne, Wolfgang, Mark Siebel, and Mark Textor, eds. *Bolzano and Analytic Philosophy*. Grazer Philosophische Studien 53. Amsterdam: Rodopi, 1997.
Kutnar, František. "Česká obrozenská společnost na prahu velké buržoasní revoluce francouzské." *Sborník vysoké školy pedagogické v Olomouci, Historia* 2 (1955): 7–43.
———. *Obrozenské vlastenectví a nacionalismus, Příspěvek k národnímu společenskému obsahu češství doby obrozenské*. Prague: Karolinum, 2003.
Kutnar, František, Oldřich Králík, and Jaromír Bělič. *Tři studie o Palackém*. Olomouc: Palackého univiversita, 1949.
Lahey, Stephen. "Toleration in the Theology and Social Thought of John Wyclif." In *Difference and Dissent: Theories of Tolerance in Medieval and Early Modern Europe,* edited by Cary J. Nederman and John C. Laursen, 53–58. Lanham, Md.: Rowman and Littlefield, 1996.
Lake, Peter. *Anglicans and Puritans? Presbyterianism and English Conformist Thought from Whitgift to Hooker*. London: Unwin Hyman, 1988.

Lambert, Sheila. "Richard Montagu, Arminianism and Censorship." *Past and Present* 124 (1989): 36–68.
Lášek, Jan B. "František Náhlovský und das Reformprogramm vom Jahre 1848 zur Erneuerung der Kirche in Böhmen (Nachdruck des Textes)." In *Modernismus: studie nebo výzva? Studie ke genezi českého katolického modernismu*, Pontes Pragenses 24, edited by Zdeněk Kučera and Jan B. Lášek, 98–134. Brno: L. Marek, 2002.

———. "Johann Anton Theiner: ein radikaler Reformgeistlicher aus Schlesien und Bolzanos Polemik gegen ihn." In *Živý odkaz modernismu*, Sborník příspěvků z mezinárodní konference pořádané Husitskou teologickou fakultou Karlovy univerzity . . . dne 29. listopadu 2002, Pontes Pragenses 30, edited by Zdeněk Kučera, Jiří Kořalka, and Jan B. Lášek, 36–43. Brno: L. Marek, 2003.

———. "Priest Ambrož and East-Bohemian Utraquism: Hradec and Oreb." *Bohemian Reformation and Religious Practice* 3 (2000): 105–18.

La Vopa, Anthony J. *Fichte: The Self and the Calling of Philosophy, 1762–1799*. New York: Cambridge University Press, 2001.

Ledvinka, Václav. "Feudální velkostatek a poddanská města v předbělohorských Čechách." In *Česká města v 16.–18. století: Sborník příspěvků z konference v Pardubicích 14. a 15. listopadu 1990*, edited by Jaroslav Pánek, 95–120. Prague: Historický ústav, 1991.

Leeb, Rudolf, Maximilian Liebmann, Georg Scheibelreiter, and Peter G. Tropper. *Geschichte des Christentums in Österreich: Von der Spätantike bis zur Gegenwart.* Vienna: Ueberreuter, 2003.

Leese, Kurt. *Von Jacob Boehme zu Schelling: Eine Untersuchung zur Metaphysik des Gottesproblems.* Erfurt: Kurt Stenger, 1927.

Leinsle, U. G. "Protestantská školská metafysika a její význam pro německý idealismus." *Filosofický časopis* 42 (1984): 39–57.

Leisching, Peter, "Die römisch-katholische Kirche in Cisleithanien," in *Die Konfessionen*, vol. 4 of *Die Habsburgmonarchie, 1848–1918*, edited by Adam Wandruszka and Peter Urbanitsch. Vienna: Verlag der Österreichischen Akademie der Wissenschaften, 1973–93, 25–34.

Lemberg, Eugen. *Grundlagen des nationalen Erwachens in Böhmen: Geistesgeschichtliche Studie, am Lebensgang Josef Georg Meinerts, 1773–1844.* Liberec: Verlag Gebrüder Stiepel, 1932.

———. *Nationalismus.* 2 vols. Reinbek bei Hamburg: Rowohlt, 1964.

Lewalter, Ernst. *Spanisch-jesuistische und deutsch-lutherische Metaphysik des 17. Jahrhunderts: Ein Beitrag zur Geschichte der iberisch-deutschen Kulturbeziehungen und zur Vorgeschichte des deutschen Idealismus.* Hamburg: Ibero-amerikanisches Institut, 1935. 2nd ed., Darmstadt: Wissenschaftliche Buchgesellschaft, 1967.

Linker, Damon. "The Reluctant Pluralism of J. G. Herder." *Review of Politics* 62 (2000): 267–94.

Lněničková, Jitka. *České země v době předbřeznové, 1792–1848.* Prague: Libri, 1999.

Lorenz, Franz. "Karl Heinrich Seibt." In *Sudentendeutsche Lebensbilder*, Bd. 3, edited by Erich Gierath, 243–50. Liberec: Strepel, 1934.

Lorenzová, Helena. "Bernard Bolzano—estetik." In *Osamělý myslitel, Bernard Bolzano*, edited by Kateřina Trlifajová, 137–72. Prague: Filosofia, 2006.

———. "Bolzano a jeho žáci (zejména Robert Zimmermann)." In *Vzdělání a osvěta v české kultuře 19. století*, Sborník příspěvků z 24. ročníku sympozia k problematice 19. století, Plzeň 4.–6 března 2004, edited by Kateřina Bláhová and Václav Petrbok, 32–38. Prague: Ústav pro českou literaturu Akademie věd ČR, 2004.

Lorman, Jaroslav, and Daniela Tinková, eds. *Post tenebras spero lucem: Duchovní tvář českého a moravského osvícenství*. Prague: Casablanca, 2009.

Loukotka, Jiří. *Humanismus v naší filosofické tradici a dnešek: Na okraj minulých i přítomných zápasů naší filosofie o člověka*. Praha: Svoboda, 1974.

Loužek, Marek. *Spor o metodu mezi rakouskou školou a německou školou*. Prague: Karolinum, 2001.

Loužil, Jaromír. *Bernard Bolzano*. Prague: Melantrich, 1978.

———. "Bernard Bolzano—apologet nebo kacíř?" *Filosofický časopis* 46 (1998): 895–914.

———. "Bernard Bolzano, Josef Jungmann und die Anfänge der tschechischen Nationalbewegung." In *Bernard Bolzano und die Politik: Staat, Nation und Religion als Herausforderung für die Philosophie im Kontext von Spätaufklärung, Frühnationalismus und Restauration*. Studien zu Politik und Verwaltung, Band 61, edited by Helmut Rumpler, 181–200. Vienna: Böhlau, 2000.

———. "Filozofie v českém národním obrození." In *Národní obrození severovýchodních a východních Čech*, 45–59. Hradec Králové: Krajské muzeum, 1971 (Fontes musei reginahradensis, 8).

———. *Ignác Jan Hanuš*. Prague: Melantrich, 1971.

Ludvíkovský, Jaroslav. "Dobrovský a Komenský." *Archiv pro bádání o životě a spisech J. A. Komenského* 15 (1940): 16–28.

———. "Platonsko-stoický prvek v Palackého idei božnosti." *Listy filologické* 68 (1941): 232–41.

Maass, Ferdinand, ed. *Der Josephinismus: Quellen zur seinen Geschichte in Österreich, 1760–1790*. 5 vols. Fontes Rerum Austriacarum II/71–75. Vienna, 1951–61.

MacCulloch, Diarmaid. *The Later Reformation in England, 1547–1603*. New York: St. Martin's Press, 1990.

———. *Thomas Cranmer: A Life*. New Haven, Conn.: Yale University Press, 1996.

Macek, Josef. "Osudy basilejských kompaktát v jagelonském věku." In *Jihlava a Basilejská Kompaktáta: Sborník příspěvků z mezinárodního sympozia k 555. výročí přijetí Basilejských kompaktát, 26–28. červen 1991*, by František Šmahel, Zdeněk Jaroš, and Dana Nováková, 193–202. Jihlava: Muzeum Vysočiny, 1992.

———. *Víra a zbožnost jagellonského věku*. Prague: Argo, 2001.

Macháčková, Veronika. "Církevní správa v době jagellonské na základě administrátorských akt." *Folia Historica Bohemica* 9 (1985): 235–90.

Macháčková, Veronika, and Antonín Mařík. "Praha v činnosti administrátorů pod jednou v letech 1450–1550." *Documenta Pragensia* 9, pt. 2 (1991): 407–15.

Machovec, Milan. *František Palacký a česká filosofie*. Československé akademie věd, *Rozpravy*, Ročník 71 [1961], Sešit 2. Prague, 1961.

———. *Husovo učení a význam v tradici českého národa*. Prague: Nakl. Československé akademie věd, 1953.

———. *Josef Dobrovský*. Prague: Svobodné slovo, 1964.

———. "Problematika dějin české filosofie." In *Filosofie v dějinách českého národa*, Protokol celostátní konference o dějinách české filosofie v Liblicích ve dnech 14.–17. dubna 1958, 25–39. Prague: Nakladatelství ČSAV, 1958.

Macura, Vladimír. "Paradox obrozenského divadla." In *Divadlo v české kultuře 19.*

století, Sborník sympozia v Plzni 10.–12 března 1983, 36–43. Prague: Národní galerie, 1985.

———. *Znamení zrodu: České národní obrození jako kulturní typ*. Rev. ed. Prague: H & H, 1995. 1st ed., Prague: Československý spisovatel, 1983.

Macůrek, Josef. "Dobrovského pojetí českých dějin a stanovisko k našemu historickému vývoji." *Slavia* 23 (1954): 164–90.

———. "Husitství v rumuských zemích." *Časopis Matice moravské* 51 (1927): 1–98.

Malcolm, Noel. *De Dominis (1560–1624): Venetian, Anglican, Ecumenist and Relapsed Heretic*. London: Strickland and Scott Academic Publications, 1984.

Maleczyńska, Ewa. *Ruch husycki w Czechach i w Polsce*. Warsaw: Ksiazka i Wiedza, 1959.

Malý, Karel. "Právní kultura v českém stavovském státě." In *Vladislavské zřízení zemské a počátky ústavního zřízení v Českých zemích, 1500–1619*. Sborník příspěvků z mezinárodní konference konané ve dnech 7–8 prosince 2000 v Praze, edited by Karel Malý and Jaroslav Pánek, 55–66. Prague: Historický ústav Akademie věd České Republiky; Ústav právních dějin Právnické fakulty Univerzity Karlovy, 2001.

Malý, Karel, and Jaroslav Pánek, eds. *Vladislavské zřízení zemské a počátky ústavního zřízení v Českých zemích, 1500–1619*. Sborník příspěvků z mezinárodní konference konané ve dnech 7–8 prosince 2000 v Praze. Prague: Historický ústav Akademie věd České Republiky; Ústav právních dějin Právnické fakulty Univerzity Karlovy, 2001.

Manninem, Juha. *Valistus ja kansallinen identiteeti: Aatehistoriallinen tutkimus 1700-luvun Pohjalasta* [The Enlightenment and National Identity]. Helsinki: Suomalaisen Kirjallisuuden Seura, 2000. See review by A. F. Upton in *English Historical Review* 117 (2002): 198–99.

Mansfield, Bruce. *Erasmus in the Twentieth Century, c. 1920–2000*. Toronto: University of Toronto Press, 2003.

Marfany, Joan-Lluís. "'Minority' Languages and Literary Revivals." *Past and Present* 184 (August 2004): 137–67.

Martin, Rex. *Historical Explanation: Reenactment and Practical Inference*. Ithaca, N.Y.: Cornell University Press, 1977.

Marx, Anthony W. *Faith in Nation: Exclusionary Origins of Nationalism*. New York: Oxford University Press, 2003.

Matheson, Peter. *Rhetoric of the Reformation*. Edinburgh: T&T Clark, 1998.

Matoušek, Josef., "Kurie a boj o konsistoř pod obojí za administrátora Rezka." *Český časopis historický* 37 (1931): 16–41, 252–92.

Matthíasdóttir, Sigríður. "The Renovation of Native Pasts: A Comparison between Aspects of Icelandic and Czech Nationalist Ideology." *Slavonic and East European Review* 78 (2000): 688–709.

Mattušová, Milada. "Guiseppe Mazzini o Češích a české kultuře." *Časopis pro moderní filologii* 38 (1956): 91–102.

Maurer, Wilhelm. "Erasmus und das Kanonische Recht." In *Vierhundertfünfzig Jahre lutherische Reformation, 1517–1967: Festschrift für Franz Lau zum 60. Geburtstag*, edited by Helmar Junghans and others, 222–32. Göttingen: Vanderhoeck and Ruprecht, 1967.

Mayer, Thomas F. "'Heretics be not in all things heretics': Cardinal Pole, His Circle, and the Potential for Toleration." In *Beyond the Persecuting Society: Toleration*

before the Enlightenment, edited by John C. Laursen and Cary J. Nederman, 107–24. Philadelphia: University of Pennsylvania Press, 1998.
Mazohl-Wallnig, Brigitte. "Bolzanisten und österreichische Universitätsreform der Jahre 1848/49." In *Bernard Bolzano und die Politik: Staat, Nation und Religion als Herausforderung für die Philosophie im Kontext von Spätaufklärung, Frühnationalismus und Restauration.* Studien zu Politik und Verwaltung, Band 61, edited by Helmut Rumpler, 221–46. Vienna: Böhlau, 2000.
[Mazzini, Guiseppe]. "The Slavonian National Movement." *Lowe's Edinburgh Magazine,* Sept. 1847, 540–46.
McConica, James Kelsey. "The English Reception of Erasmus." In *Erasmianism: Idea and Reality,* edited by M. E. H. N. Mout, H. Smolinsky, and J. Trapman, 37–46. North-Holland, Amsterdam: Koninklijke Nederlandse Akademie van Wetenschappen, 1997.
Menzel, Beda Franz. *Abt Franz Stephan Rautenstrauch von Břevnov-Braunau: Herkunft, Umwelt und Wirkungskreis.* Königstein/Ts: Königsteiner Institut für Kirchen- und Geistesgeschichte der Sudentenländer, 1969.
Merkle, Sebastian. "Johann Michael Sailer." In *Religiöse Erzieher der katholischen Kirche aus den letzten vier Jahrhunderten,* edited by Sebastian Merkle and Bernhard Bess, 183–212. Leipzig: Quelle und Meyer, [1922].
———. *Die katholische Beurteilung des Aufklärungszeitalters.* Berlin: K. Curtius, 1909.
———. *Die kirchliche Aufklärung im katholischen Deutschland.* Berlin: Reichel, 1910.
Merkle, Sebastian, and Bernhard Bess, eds. *Religiöse Erzieher der katholischen Kirche aus den letzten vier Jahrhunderten.* Leipzig: Quelle und Meyer, [1922].
Merquior, José G. *From Prague to Paris: A Critique of Structuralist and Post-Structuralist Thought.* London: Verso, 1986.
Mersereau, John, Jr., and David Lapeza. "Russian Romanticism." In *Romanticism in National Context,* edited by Roy Porter and Mikuláš Teich, 284–316. New York: Cambridge University Press, 1988.
Měšťan, Antonín. *Geschichte der tschechischen Literatur im 19. und 20. Jahrhundert.* Colgne: Böhlau, 1984.
———. "Scott und das historische Bewusstsein der Tschechen und Deutschen in Böhmen." In *Grossbritannien, die USA und die böhmischen Länder 1848–1938* [*Great Britain, the United States, and the Bohemian Lands, 1848–1938*], Vorträge der Tagung des Collegium Carolinum, 2–6 November 1988, edited by Eva Schmidt-Hartmann and Stanley B. Winters, 229–37. Munich: Oldenbourg, 1991.
Michňáková, Irena. *Augustin Smetana.* Praha: Svobodné slovo, 1963.
———. "Z filosofického odkazu Augustina Smetany." In *Filosofie v dějinách českého národa,* Protokol celostátní konference o dějinách české filosofie v Liblicích ve dnech 14.–17. dubna 1958, 150–65. Prague: Nakladatelství ČSAV, 1958.
———. "Zum ideellen Profil des tschechischen Hegelianismus des 19. Jahrhunderts." In *Der Streit um Hegel bei den Slawen,* edited by Jan Garewicz and Irena Michňáková, 57–75. Prague: Academia, 1967.
Míka, Alois. "Národnostní poměry v Čechách před třicetiletou válkou." *Československý časopis historický* 20 (1972): 207–33.
Milton, Anthony. *Catholic and Reformed: The Roman and Protestant Churches in English Protestant Thought, 1600–1640.* New York: Cambridge University Press, 1995.

Moenius, Georg. *Paris, Frankreichs Herz.* Munich: Limes Verlag, 1928.
Molnár, Amedeo. "Martin Lupáč: Modus disputandi pro fide." *Folia Historica Bohemica* 4 (1982): 161–77.
Molnár, Amedeo, and others. *Soudce smluvený v Chebu*, Sborník příspěvků přednesených na symposiu k 550. výročí. Cheb, 1982.
Monk, Ray. *Ludwig Wittgenstein: The Duty of Genius.* New York: Free Press, 1990.
Morava, Jiří. *Palacký: Čech, Rakušan, Evropan.* 2nd ed. Prague: Vyšehrad, 1998.
Mukařovský, Jan, ed. *Torso a tajemství Máchova díla*, Sborník pojednání Pražského linguistického kroužku. Prague: Borový, 1938.
Müller, Josef. *Das pastoraltheologisch-didaktische Ansatz in Franz Stephan Rautenstrauchs "Entwurf einer besseren Einrichtung theologischen Schulen,"* Wiener Beiträge zur Theologie, 25. Vienna: Herder, 1969.
Murko, Matija. *Deutsche Einflüsse auf die Anfänge der böhmischen Romantik.* Graz: Styria, 1897.
Mutula, Vladimir, ed. *Ľudovít Štúr: Život a dielo, 1815–1856.* Bratislava: Vydavateľstvo Slovenskej akadémie vied, 1956.
Myľnikov, Aleksandr S. *Epokha Prosveshcheniia v cheshskikh zemliakh: Ideologiia natsional'noe samosoznanie, kul'tura.* Moscow: Nauka, 1977.
———. *Kul'tura cheshskogo vozrozhdeniia.* Leningrad: Nauka, 1982.
———. *Vznik národně osvícenské ideologie v českých zemích: Prameny národního obrození.* Prague: Univerzita Karlova, 1974.
Myška, Milan, ed. *Památník Palackého, 1798–1968.* Ostrava: Profil, 1968.
Nairn, Tom. *Faces of Nationalism: Janus Revisited.* London: Verso, 1997.
Navrátil, Bohumil. *Biskupství olomoucké 1576–1579 a volba Stanislava Pavlovského.* Prague: Česká společnost nauk, 1909.
Nayak, G. C. "The Analytic Philosophy of Nagarjuna and Candrakirti: Some Implications." *Journal of Indian Council of Philosophical Research* 2, no. 2 (1985): 51–60.
Nejtek, Vilém. *Novinář Karel Havlíček Borovský.* Prague: Novinář, 1979.
Nešpor, Václav. *Dějiny university olomoucké.* Olomouc: Národní výbor, 1947.
Neurath, Otto. "Drei Diskussionsbeiträge." In *Gesammelte philosophische und methodologische Schriften*, edited by Rudolf Haller and Heiner Rutte, 2:588–610. 2 vols. Vienna: Hölder, Pichler, Tempsky, 1981.
———. "Die Entwicklung des Wiener Kreises und die Zukunft des Logischen Empirismus." In *Gesammelte philosophische und methodologische Schriften*, edited by Rudolf Haller and Heiner Rutte, 2:673–702. 2 vols. Vienna: Hölder, Pichler, Tempsky, 1981.
———. "Erster Internationaler Kongress für Einheit der Wissenschaft in Paris 1935." In *Gesammelte philosophische und methodologische Schriften*, edited by Rudolf Haller and Heiner Rutte, 2:649–71. 2 vols. Vienna: Hölder, Pichler, Tempsky, 1981.
———. *Gesammelte philosophische und methodologische Schriften.* Edited by Rudolf Haller and Heiner Rutte. 2 vols. Vienna: Hölder, Pichler, Tempsky, 1981.
———. "Der Logische Empirismus und der Wiener Kreis." In *Gesammelte philosophische und methodologische Schriften*, edited by Rudolf Haller and Heiner Rutte, 2:739–47. 2 vols. Vienna: Hölder, Pichler, Tempsky, 1981.
Nisbet, H. Barry. "Herder's Conception of Nationhood and Its Influence in East-

ern Europe." In *The German Lands and Eastern Europe: Essays on the History of Their Social, Cultural and Political Relations,* edited by Roger Bartlett and Karen Schönwälder, 115–35. New York: St. Martin's Press, 1999.

Novák, Arne. *Josef Dobrovský*. Prague: Mánes, 1928.

———. "Josef Dobrovský a jeho předchůdcové v českém literárním dějepise." In *Josef Dobrovský, 1753–1829: sborník statí k stému výročí smrti Josefa Dobrovského,* edited by Jiří Horák, Matyáš Murko, and Miloš Weingart, 241–51. Prague: Výbor I. Sjezdu slovanských filologů, 1929.

Novák, Jan V. "Spor Bratří s p. Vojtěchem z Pernštejna a na Prostějově r. 1557 a 1558." *Časopis českého musea* 65 (1891): 43–56, 197–208.

Novotný, Jan. *František Cyril Kampelík*. Prague: Melantrich, 1975.

———. *Matěj Václav Kramerius*. Prague: Melantrich, 1973.

———. *Pavel Josef Šafařík*. Prague: Melantrich, 1971.

Novotný, Václav. *Jan Hus: Život a učení,* I. *Život a dílo.* 2 vols. Prague: Laichter, 1919–21.

Nyíri, János Kristóf, ed. *From Bolzano to Wittgenstein.* Vienna: Hölder, Pichler, Tempsky, 1986.

Oberman, Heiko Augustinus. *The Two Reformations: The Journey from the Last Days to the New World.* Edited by Donald Weinstein. New Haven, Conn.: Yale University Press, c2003.

Odložilík, Otakar. *The Hussite King: Bohemia in European Affairs, 1440–1471.* New Brunswick, N.J.: Rutgers University Press, 1965.

Okey, Robin. *The Habsburg Monarchy: From Enlightenment to Eclipse.* New York: St. Martin's Press, 2001.

Olivová, Věra. *Manipulace s dějinami první republiky.* Prague: Společnost Edvarda Beneše, 2001.

Olšáková, Doubravka. "Český překlad Denisova díla v kontextu sporu o smysl českých dějin." *Dějiny a součastnost* 23/5 (2001): 28–32.

O'Regan, Cyril. *The Heterodox Hegel.* Albany: State University Press of New York, 1994.

Osuský, Samuel Št. *Filozofia Štúrovcov.* 3 vols. Vol. 1: *Štúrova filozofia,* 1926; vol. 2: *Hurbanova filozofia,* 1928; vol. 3: *Hodžova filozofia.* 1932. Myjava: Daniel Pažický, 1926–32.

Otáhal, Milan. "Spor české filozofie a českého nacionalismu jako spor o předpoklady tolerance." In *Problém tolerance v dějinách a perpektivě,* edited by Milan Machovec, 139–56. Prague: Academia, 1995.

Pabel, Hilmar M. "The Peaceful People of Christ: The Irenic Ecclesiology of Erasmus of Rotterdam." In *Erasmus' Vision of the Church,* Sixteenth Century Essays and Studies, 33, edited by Hilmar M. Pabel, 57–93. Kirksville, Mo.: Sixteenth Century Journal Publishers, 1995.

Palti, Elías José. "The Nation as a Problem: Historians and the 'National Question.'" *History and Theory* 40 (2001): 324–46.

Pánek, Jaroslav, ed. *Česká města v 16.–18. století: Sborník příspěvků z konference v Pardubicích 14. a 15. listopadu 1990.* Prague: Historický ústav, 1991.

———. "Český stát a stavovská společnost na prahu novověku ve světle zemských zřízení." In *Vladislavské zřízení zemské a počátky ústavního zřízení v Českých zemích, 1500–1619.* Sborník příspěvků z mezinárodní konference konané ve dnech 7–8 prosince 2000 v Praze, edited by Karel Malý and Jaroslav Pánek,13–54. Prague: Historický ústav Akademie věd České Republiky; Ústav právních dějin Právnické fakulty Univerzity Karlovy, 2001.

———. "Republikánské tendence ve stavovských programech doby předbělohorské." *Folia Historica Bohemica* 8 (1985): 43–62.

———. *Stavovská opozice a její zápas s Habsburky, 1547–1577*. Prague: Academia, 1982.

———. "Stavovství v předbělohorské době." *Folia Historica Bohemica* 6 (1984): 163–219.

Pastrnka, Fratišek, ed. *Jan Kollár, 1793–1852. Sborník statí o životě, působení a literární činnosti pěvce 'Slávy dcery'*. Vienna: Český akademický spolek, 1893.

Patočka, Jan. "Bolzanovo filosofické působení." In *Osamělý myslitel, Bernard Bolzano*, edited by Kateřina Trlifajová, 203–13. Prague: Filosofia, 2006.

———. "Bolzanovo místo v dějinách filosofie." In *Filosofie v dějinách českého národa*, Protokol celostátní konference o dějinách české filosofie v Liblicích ve dnech 14.–17. dubna 1958, 111–23. Prague: Nakladatelství ČSAV, 1958.

———. "Husserl a Bolzano." In *Osamělý myslitel, Bernard Bolzano*, edited by Kateřina Trlifajová, 187–201. Prague: Filosofia, 2006.

Patterson, William B. "Hooker on Ecumenical Relations: Conciliarism in the English Reformation." In *Richard Hooker and the Construction of Christian Community*, edited by Arthur S. McGrade, 283–303. Tempe, Ariz.: Medieval and Renaissance Texts and Studies, 1997.

Pauza, Miroslav. "Bernard Bolzano jako objekt zkoumání českých teoretiků." *Filosofický časopis* 50 (2002): 933–41.

———. "Brentanova koncepce 'racionálního teismu.'" In *Živý odkaz modernismu*, Sborník příspěvků z mezinárodní konference pořádané Husitskou teologickou fakultou Karlovy univerzity . . . dne 29. listopadu 2002, Pontes Pragenses 30, edited by Zdeněk Kučera, Jiří Kořalka, and Jan B. Lášek, 175–82. Brno: L. Marek, 2003.

Pavlík, Ján. "Bernard Bolzano a německá klasická filosofie." *Filosofický časopis* 42 (1994): 1013–30.

Pavlíková, Marie. *Bolzanovo působení na pražské univerzitě*. Prague: Univerzita Karlova, 1985.

———. "Bolzanův odkaz." In *Bernard Bolzano, Vlastní životopis*, edited and translated by Marie Pavlíková, 137–67. Prague: Odeon, 1981.

———. "Vztah Josefa Jungmanna k Bernardu Bolzanovi a jeho žákům." *Literární archív*, Sborník Památníku národního písemnictví 8–9 (1974): 79–100.

Pelczynski, Zbigniew A. "An Introductory Essay." In *Hegel's Political Writings*, by Georg W. F. Hegel, 5–137. Translated by T. M. Knox. Oxford: Clarendon Press, 1964.

Pelikán, Ferdinand. *Boj za svobodu české filosofie*. Prague: Janda, 1927.

———. *Boj za svobodu české filosofie a historické hodnocení*. Prague: Srdce, 1929.

Perkins, Mary Anne. *Nation and Word, 1770–1850: Religious and Metaphysical Language in European National Consciousness*. Brookfield, Vt.: Ashgate, c1999.

Pešek, Jiří. "Kultura českých předbělohorských měst, 1547–1620." *Česká města v 16.–18. stoletíí*: Sborník příspěvků z konference v Pardubicích 14. a 15. listopadu 1990, edited by Jaroslav Pánek, 203–13. Prague: Historický ústav, 1991.

———. "Měšťanská kultura a vzdělanost v rudolfínské Praze." *Folia Historica Bohemica* 5 (1983): 173–87.
———. *Měšťanská vzdělanost a kultura v předbělohorských Čechách, 1547–1620.* Prague: Karolinum, 1993.
Pešek, Josef, and František Čáda. "Karel Boleslav Štorch jako filosof." *Česká mysl* 14 (1913): 1–16; 129–259, 365–81.
———. "Soustavný nákres filosofie Štorchovy." *Česká mysl* 15 (1914): 29–56.
Pešková, Jaroslava. "Místo filosofie v procesu formování novodobé české společnosti." In *Role vědomí v dějinách,* 77–92. Prague: Lidové noviny, 1997.
———. "Problém tradice a jejího vlivu na národní character." In *Povědomí tradice v novodobé české kultuře: Doba Bedřicha Smetany.* Sborník sympozia v Plzni 7.–11. března 1984, 112–18. Prague: Národní galerie, 1988.
Petráň, Josef. "Ke genezi novodobé koncepce českých národních dějin." *Acta Universitatis Carolinae, Philosophica et Historica 5, Studia Historica* 26 (1982): 67–89.
Petráň, Josef, and others. *Počátky českého národního obrození: Společnost a kultura v 70. až 90. letech 18. století.* Prague: Academia, 1990.
Petrů, Eduard. *Vzdálené hlasy: studie o starší české literatuře.* Olomouc: Votobia, 1996.
Pfaff, Ivan. *Česká přináležitost k Západu v letech 1815–1878.* Brno: Doplněk, 1996.
Phillipson, Nicholas. "The Scottish Enlightenment." In *The Enlightenment in National Context,* edited by Roy Porter and Mikuláš Teich, 19–40. New York: Cambridge University Press, 1981.
Pirie, Donald. "The Agony in the Garden: Polish Romanticism." In *Romanticism in National Context,* edited by Roy Porter and Mikuláš Teich, 317–44. New York: Cambridge University Press, 1988.
Pišút, Milan. "Jozef Miloslav Hurban." In *Jozef Miloslav Hurban; sborník pri príležitosti 150. výročia jeho smrti,* compiled by Štefan Kopčan, 3–30. Bratislava: Osvetový ústav, 1967.
Plch, Jaromír. *Antonín Marek.* Prague: Melantrich, 1974.
Pocock, J. G. A. *Barbarism and Religion: The Enlightenments of Edward Gibbon, 1737–1764.* Cambridge: Cambridge University Press, 1999.
Podlaha, Antonín. "Úpadek strany podobojí na sklonku XVI. století." *Sborník historického kroužku* 5 (1904): 29–36, 65–69, 161–64, 219–27.
Pokorná, Magdaléna. *Milován a sledován: Český spisovatel Prokop Chocholoušek, 1819–1864.* Prague: Práh, 2001.
Polák, Stanislav. *T. G. Masaryk.* 5 vols. Prague: Masarykův ústav AV ČR, 2000–2009.
Poli, Roberto. "At the Origins of Analytic Philosophy." *Aletheia* 6 (1993–94): 218–31.
Polišenský, Josef, and Ella Illingová. *Jan Jeník z Bratřic.* Prague: Melantrich, 1989.
Potter, Simeon. "Palacký a anglické písemnictví." *Časopis Matice Moravské* 53 (1929): 87–141.
Pražák, Albert. *České obrození.* Prague: E. Beaufort, 1948.
———. "Herder a Češi." In, *Vývoj lidskosti,* by Johann G. Herder, v–xxxiii. Translated by Jan Patočka. Prague: Laichter, 1941.
———. "J. W. Goethe a Slováci." *Goethův sborník.* Památce 100. výročí básníkovy smrti vydali čeští germanisté, 139–81. Prague: Státní nakladatelství, 1932.
———. *Obrozenské tradice.* Prague: Svaz národního osvobození, 1928.

Pražák, Richard. "Zu den Beziehungen zwischen den Böhmischen Ländern und Ungarn zu Zeiten Matthias Corvinus." In *Matthias Corvinus and the Humanism in Central Europe*, edited by Tibor Klaniczay and József Jankovics, 193–202. Budapest: Balassi Kiadó, 1994.

Procházka, Václav. *Karel Havlíček Borovský*. Prague: Svobodné slovo, 1961.

Prokeš, J. "Aféra Seibtova roku 1779." In *Českou minulostí*, edited by Otakar Odložík, Jaroslav Prokeš, and Rudolf Urbánek, 317–30. Prague: Laichter, 1929.

———. "Osudy prvního vydání Balbínovy 'Obrany jazyka českého.'" *Časopis českého muzea* (1925): 245–59.

Prokeš, Jaroslav. *Počátky České společnosti nauk do konce XVIII století*. Vol. 1, *1774–1789*. Prague: Česká společnost nauk, 1938.

Putna, Martin C. *Česká katolická literatura, 1848–1918*. Prague: Torst, 1998.

Pynsent, Robert B. "The Baroque Continuum of Czech Literature." *Slavonic and East European Review* 62 (1984): 321–43.

———. *Ďáblové, ženy a národ: Výbor z úvah o české literatuře*. Prague: Karolinum, 2008.

———. "Doslov." In *Ďáblové, ženy a národ: Výbor z úvah o české literatuře*, 555–617. Prague: Karolinum, 2008.

———, ed. *The Literature of Nationalism: Essays on East European Identity*. Basingstoke, United Kingdom: Macmillan, 1996.

———. *Questions of Identity: Czech and Slovak Ideas of Nationality and Personality*. Budapest: Central European University Press, 1994.

———. "Slávy Herder." In *Ďáblové, ženy a národ: Výbor z úvah o české literatuře*, 91–104.

———. "Západno-východné zovretie—dve východiská: L'udevít Štúr a Štěpan Launer." In *Ďáblové, ženy a národ: Výbor z úvah o české literatuře*, 129–44.

Rak, Jiří. "Dělníci na vinici Páně nebo na roli národní?" In *Bůh a bohové: Církve, náboženství a spiritualita v českém 19 století*, Sborník příspěvků z 22. ročníku sympozia k problematice 19. století, Plzeň, 7.–9 března 2002, edited by Zdeněk Hojda and Roman Prahl, 128–38. Prague: KLP, 2003.

———. "Doslov." In František Kutnar, *Obrozenské vlastenectví a nacionalismus, Příspěvek k národnímu společenskému obsahu češství doby obrozenské*, 345–54. Prague: Karolinum, 2003.

Rammelt, Johannes. *J. B. Basedow, der Philantropinismus und das Dessauer Philantropin*. Dessau: Schwalbe, 1929.

Rathmann, János. "Herder and the Hungarian Enlightenment." *Transactions of the Seventh International Congress on the Enlightenment, 1987, Budapest.* 3 vols. Studies on Voltaire and the Eighteenth Century, 263–65. Vol. 1: 497–500. Oxford: Voltaire Foundation, 1989.

Raupach, Hans. *Der tschechische Frühnationalismus: Ein Beitrag zur Gesellschafts- und Ideengeschichte des Vormärz in Böhmen*. Essen: Essener Verlagsanstalt, 1939. Reprint, Darmstadt: Wissenschaftliche Buchgesellschaft, 1969.

Regenfelder, Jane. "Der sogennante 'Bolzano-Prozess' und das Wartburgfest." In *Bernard Bolzano und die Politik: Staat, Nation und Religion als Herausforderung für die Philosophie im Kontext von Spätaufklärung, Frühnationalismus und Restauration*. Studien zu Politik und Verwaltung, Band 61, edited by Helmut Rumpler, 149–78. Vienna: Böhlau, 2000.

Reimann, Paul. *Von Herder bis Kisch: Studien zur Geschichte der deutsch-österreichisch-tschechischen Literaturbeziehungen.* Berlin: Dietz Verlag, 1961.
Rejchrtová, Noemi. "Jan Bechyňka: Kněz a literát." In *Praga Mystica: Z dějin české reformace,* vol. 3 of *Acta reformationem bohemicam illustrantia,* edited by Amedeo Molnár, 3:8–34. Prague: Kalich, 1984.
———. "Listy osamělého politika." In *Z korespondence,* by Karel starší ze Žerotína, 7–38. Edited by Noemi Rejchrtová. Prague: Odeon, 1982.
———. "Obrazoborecké tendence utrakvistické mentality jagellonského období a jejich dosah." *Husitský Tábor* 8 (1985): 59–68.
———. "Role utrakvizmu v českých dějinách." In *Traditio et Cultus,* Miscellanea historica bohemica Miloslao Vlk, archiepiscopo Pragensi, ab eius collegis amicisque ad annum sexagesimum dedicata, edited by Zdeňka Hledíková, 73–77. Prague: Univerzita Karlova, 1993.
Rejzek, Antonín. *Blahoslavený Edmund Kampián, kněz Tovaryšstva Ježíšova, pro sv. víru mučeník ve vlasti své.* Brno: K. Winiker, 1889.
Řepa, Milan. "'Ját' jsem jej příkladem Robertsona Škotského poráželi hladal.' Dílo skotského osvícenského historika jako možný vzor Palackého Dějin." In *Historik v proměnách doby a prostředí 19. století,* edited by Jiří Hanuš a Radomír Vlček, 49–55. Brno: Matice moravská, 2007.
Reynolds, Ernest E. *Thomas More and Erasmus.* New York: Fordham University Press, 1965.
Říčan, Rudolf. *The History of the Unity of Brethren: A Protestant Hussite Church in Bohemia and Moravia.* Translated by C. Daniel Crews. Bethlehem, Pa.: Moravian Church in America, 1992.
Riss, Josef. "Život a literné působení Sixta z Ottersdorfu." *Časopis českého musea* 35, pt. 1 (1861): 72–84, 159–70, 361–65.
Robek, Antonín. *Lidové zdroje národního obrození,* Acta Universitatis Carolinae, Philosophica et historica, Monographia, 48. Prague: Univerzita Karlova, 1974.
———. *Městské lidové zdroje národního obrození,* Acta Universitatis Carolinae, Philosophica et historica, Monographia, 69. Prague: Univerzita Karlova, 1977.
Rogers, Ben. *A. J. Ayer: A Life.* New York: Grove Press, 1999.
Rollinger, Robin D. *Husserl's Position in the School of Brentano.* Dordrecht: Kluwer Academic, 1999.
Rosenbaum, Karol. "Die Funktion der Herderschen Humanitätsidee in der slowakischen nationalen Wiedergeburt." In *Herder-Kolloquium, 1978,* edited by Walter Dietze and others, 334–38. Weimar: Böhlau, 1980.
Rotrekl, Zdeněk. *Barokní fenomén v součastnosti.* Prague: Trost, 1995.
Rumpler, Helmut, ed. *Bernard Bolzano und die Politik: Staat, Nation und Religion als Herausforderung für die Philosophie im Kontext von Spätaufklärung, Frühnationalismus und Restauration.* Studien zu Politik und Verwaltung, Band 61. Vienna: Böhlau, 2000.
Rutto, Giuseppe. *Bernard Bolzano: Reformkatholizismus e utopia nella Praga della Restaurazione.* Turin: Giappichelli, 1984.
Ryba, Bohumil. "Václav Písecký, Eneáš Sylvius a Lukianos." *Listy filologické* 57 (1930): 138–46.

Rybička, Antonín. "Josef M. Rautenkranc." *Časopis českého musea* 41 (1867): 278–80.
———. "Rvačovský Vavřinec Leander." *Časopis českého musea* 45 (1871): 326.
———. "Vzpomínka na Vincence Zahradníka." *Časopis českého musea* 45 (1871): 28–38.
Rýdl, Karel. "Jan Amos Komenský ve vývoji evropského pedagogického a filozofického myšlení v 18. století." In *Pocta Univerzity Karlovy J. A. Komenskému,* edited by Jaroslava Pešková, Josef Cach, and Michal Svatoš, 184–92. Prague: Karolinum, 1991.
Saari, Heikki. *Re-enactment: A Study in R. G. Collingwood's Philosophy of History.* Acta Academiae Aboensis, Ser. A, Humaniora, vol. 63, no. 2. Abo: Abo akademi, 1984.
Sabine, George H. "Hegel's Political Philosophy." *Philosophical Review* 41 (1932): 261–82.
Sak, Robert. *Josef Jungmann: Život obrozence.* Prague: Vyšehrad, 2007.
———. *Rieger: Konzervativec nebo liberál?* Prague: Academia, 2003.
Šalda, František Xaver. *Listy F. X. Šaldy a Zdeňka Nejedlého z let 1910–1932.* Edited by Václav Pekárek. Prague: Československý spisovatel, 1974.
———. "O krásné próze Máchově." In *Torso a tajemství Máchova díla,* Sborník pojednání Pražského linguistického kroužku, edited by Jan Mukařovský, 181–200. Prague: Borový, 1938.
Šamalík, František. *Úvahy o dějinách české politiky: Od reformace k osvícenství.* 2nd ed. Prague: Victoria Publishing, 1996.
Santoli, S. "Wirtschaftliche Grundlagen des Josefinismus." *Österreichisches Archiv für Kirchenrecht* 13 (1962): 213–32.
Sauder, Gerhard, ed. *Johann Gottfried Herder, 1744–1803.* Studien zum achtzehnten Jahrhundert, 9. Hamburg: Felix Meiner Verlag, 1987.
Sayer, Derek. *The Coasts of Bohemia: A Czech History.* Princeton, N.J.: Princeton University Press, 1998.
———. "The Language of Nationality and the Nationality of Language: Prague, 1780–1920." *Past and Present* 153 (1996): 164–210.
Schaffner, Otto. *Eusebius Amort, 1692–1775, als Moraltheologe.* Pederborn: F. Schöningh, 1963.
Schamschula, Walter. *Die Anfänge der tschechischen Erneuerung und das deutsche Geistesleben, 1740–1800.* Munich: Fink, 1973.
———. "Dobrovskýs und Pelzels Beiträge zu den 'Lieferungen für Böhmen von Böhmen.'" In *Aus der Geisteswelt der Slaven. Dankesgabe an Erwin Koschmieder,* edited by Alois Schmaus and Ilse Kunert, 144–61. Munich: Sagner, 1967.
———. *Geschichte der tschechischen Literatur.* 2 vols. Cologne: Böhlau, 1990–96.
———. "Der slovenische Kirchenhistoriker Kaspar Royko und die tschechische Erneuerung." In *Studia Slovenica Monacensia: In honorem Antonii Slodnjak septuagenarii,* edited by Hans-Joachim Kissling, 104–11. Munich: Trofenik, 1969.
———. "V. F. Durich in München. Zur Geschichte der tschechischen Slavistik im 18. Jahrhundert." *Die Welt der Slaven* 10 (1965): 188–202.
Schilpp, Paul A., ed. *The Philosophy of Rudolf Carnap,* Library of Living Philosophers, 11. La Salle, Ill.: Open Court, 1963.
Schmidt, Ingeborg. "Zur pantheistischen Weltsicht in Herders ästhetischer Theo-

rie." In *Herder-Kolloquium, 1978,* edited by Walter Dietze and others, 345–50. Weimar: Böhlau, 1980.
Schmidt-Hartmann, Eva. *Tomáš G. Masaryk's Realism: Origins of a Czech Political Concept*, Veröffentlichungen des Collegium Carolinum, 52. Munich: Oldenbourg, 1984.
Schneemann, Gerhard. *Die Entstehung der thomistisch-molinistichen Controverse.* Freiburg im Breisgau: Herder'sche Verlagshandlung, 1879.
Schneider, Robert. *Schellings und Hegels schwäbische Geistesahnen.* Würzburg: K. Triltsch, 1938.
Schoeck, R. J. "From Erasmus to Hooker." In *Richard Hooker and the Construction of Christian Community,* edited by Arthur S. McGrade, 66–73. Tempe, Ariz.: Medieval and Renaissance Texts and Studies, 1997.
Schrödter, Hermann. *Philosophie und Religion: Die Religionswissenschaft B. Bolzanos.* Meisenheim am Glan: A. Hain, 1972.
Schuhmann, Karl. "Husserl and Twardowski." In *Polish Scientific Philosophy: The Lvov-Warsaw School,* edited by Francesco Coniglione and others, 41–58. Amsterdam: Rodopi, 1993.
Schullerus, Dieter. "Die Herder-Rezeption in Rumänien." In *Herder-Kolloquium, 1978,* edited by Walter Dietze and others, 327–33. Weimar: Böhlau, 1980.
Schwarzbach, Sibyl A. "Rawls, Hegel, and Communitarianism." *Political Theory* 19 (1991): 539–71.
Schwinges, Rainer C. *Deutsche Universitätsbesucher im 14. und 15. Jahrhundert: Studien zur Sozialgeschichte des Alten Reiches.* Stuttgart: Franz Steiner, 1986.
Screenivasan, Govind. "The Social Origins of the Peasants' War of 1525 in Upper Swabia." *Past and Present* 171 (May 2001): 40–55.
Šebestík, Jan. "Bolzano, Exner, and the Origins of Analytical Philosophy." *Grazer Philosophische Studien*, International Zeitschrift für analytische Philosophie 53 (1997), 33–59. Translated as "Bolzano, Exner a počátky analytické filosofie." In *Analytická filosofie; Druhá čítanka*, edited by Jiří Fiala, 1–32. Plzeň: OPS, 2000.
———. "Bolzanova pře s Kantem." *Filosofický časopis* 46 (1998): 949–58.
Seibt, Ferdinand. "'Hussiten' als historischer Begriff." In *Hussitica: Zur Struktur einer Revolution,* 10–15. Cologne: Böhlau, 1965.
Seigfried, Adam. "Die Dogmatik im 18. Jahrhundert unter dem Einfluss von Jansenismus und Aufklärung." In *Katholische Aufklärung und Josephinismus,* edited by Elisabeth Kovács, 241–65. Vienna: Verlag für Geschichte und Politik, 1979.
Seton-Watson, Hugh. *Nations and States: An Enquiry into the Origins of Nations and the Politics of Nationalism.* London: Methuen, 1977.
Shirokova, A. G., and G. P. Neshchimenko. "Vozrozhdenie cheshskogo literaturnogo iazyka kak neobkhodimyi komponent formirovaniia cheshskoi natsii." In *Slavianskie kul'tury v epokhu formirovaniia i razvitiia slavianskikh natsii 18.–19. Vekov,* edited by Dmitrii F. Markov, 128–33. Moscow: Akademiia nauk SSSR, Institut slavianovedeniia i balkanistiki, 1978.
Siljak, Ana. "Between East and West: Hegel and the Origins of Russian Dilemma." *Journal of the History of Ideas* 62 (2001): 335–58.
Šimák, Josef V. "Bohuslava Bílejovského Kronika česká." *Český časopis historický* 38 (1932): 92–102.
Šimek, František. "Příspěvky k Antonínu Markovi." *Listy filologické* 73 (1949): 198–200, 263–68.

Simons, Peter. *Philosophy and Logic in Central Europe from Bolzano to Tarski.* Dordrecht: Kluwer, 1992.

Skýbová, Anna. "Cesta po Čechách v roce 1561." *Český lid* 63 (1975): 98–101.

———. "Le ordinazioni dei sacerdoti utraquisti a Venezia nella prima metà del XVI secolo." In *Italia e Boemia nella cornice del rinascimento europeo*, edited by Sante Graciotti, 51–65. Florence: Leo S. Olschki, 1999.

Slavík, Bedřich. *Od Dobnera k Dobrovskému.* Prague: Vyšehrad, 1975.

Šmahel, František. *Husitská revoluce.* 2nd ed., 4 vols. Prague: Univerzita Karlova, 1995–96.

Šmahel, František, Zdeněk Jaroš, and Dana Nováková. "Husitské artikuly a jihlavská kompaktáta." In *Jihlava a Basilejská Kompaktáta: Sborník příspěvků z mezinárodního sympozia k 555. výročí přijetí Basilejských kompaktát, 26–28. červen 1991*, 11–28. Jihlava: Muzeum Vysočiny, 1992.

———. "The Medieval 'Rebirth' of the Czech Nation." *Acta Universitatis Carolinae, Philosophica et Historica 3, Studia Historica* 44 (1996): 33–39.

———. "Nástin proměn stavovské skladby Českého království od konce 14. do počátku 16. Století." *Vladislavské zřízení zemské a počátky ústavního zřízení v Českých zemích: 1500–1619. Sborník příspěvků z mezinárodní konference konané ve dnech 7–8 prosince 2000 v Praze*, edited by Karel Malý and Jaroslav Pánek, 71–80. Prague: Historický ústav Akademie věd České Republiky; Ústav právních dějin Právnické fakulty Univerzity Karlovy, 2001.

———. "Paris und Prag um 1450: Johannes Versor und seine böhmischen Schüler." *Studia źródłoznawcze, Commentationes* (Warsaw and Poznań) 25 (1980): 65–76.

Šmahel, František, and Eva Doležalová. *František Palacký, 1798–1998, dějiny a dnešek: Sborník z jubilejní konference.* Prague: Historický ústav Akademie v ěd ČR, 1999.

Šmahel, František, and others. *Jihlava a Basilejská Kompaktáta: Sborník příspěvků z mezinárodního sympozia k 555. výročí přijetí Basilejských kompaktát, 26–28. červen 1991.* Jihlava: Muzeum Vysočiny, 1992.

Šmahelová, Hana. "Bernard Bolzano a české národní obrození." *Český časopis historický* 100 (2002): 74–115.

———. "Kollárova vize slovanské vzájemnosti." *Česká literatura* 50 (2002): 125–48.

Smith, Anthony D. *Chosen Peoples: Sacred Sources of National Identity.* New York: Oxford University Press, 2003.

———. *The Nation in History: Historiographical Debates about Ethnicity and Nationalism.* Hanover, N.H.: University Press of New England, 2000.

Smith, Barry. "Austrian Origins of Logical Positivism." In *Logical Positivism in Perspective: Essays on Language, Truth, and Logic,* edited by Barry Gower, 35–68. Totowa, N.J.: Barnes & Noble Books, c1987.

———. *Austrian Philosophy: The Legacy of Brentano.* Chicago: Open Court, 1994.

———. "The Production of Ideas: Notes on Austrian Intellectual History from Bolzano to Wittgenstein." In *Structure and Gestalt: Philosophy and Literature in Austria-Hungary and Her Successor States,* edited by Barry Smith, 211–33. Amsterdam: Benjamins, 1981.

———, ed. *Structure and Gestalt: Philosophy and Literature in Austria-Hungary and Her Successor States.* Amsterdam: Benjamins, 1981.

Smith, John E. "Hegel's Reinterpretation of the Doctrine of Spirit and Religious

Community." In *Hegel and the Philosophy of Religion*, Wofford Symposium, 1968, edited by Darrel E. Christensen, 157–85. The Hague: M. Nijhoff, 1970.
Smith, Steven B. *Hegel's Critique of Liberalism: Rights in Context.* Chicago: University of Chicago Press, 1989.
Šnebergová, Irena. "Franz Serafin Exner a Praha: Vzestup a pád kariéry univerzitního profesora; z exnerovské korespondence." In *Rozjímání vpřed i vzad: Karlu Kosíkovi k pětasedmdesátinám,* edited by Irena Šnebergová, Václav Tomek, and Josef Zumr, 257–80. Prague: Filosofia, 2001.
Snyder, Louis. *The Meaning of Nationalism.* Preface by Hans Kohn. New Brunswick, N.J.: 1954.
Sobotka, Milan. "J. A. Komenský a filosofie jeho doby." In *Pocta Univerzity Karlovy J. A. Komenskému,* edited by Jaroslava Pešková, Josef Cach, and Michal Svatoš, 117–26. Prague: Karolinum, 1991.
Sojková, Zdenka. *Na rozhraní dvou věků: K politické publicistice L'udovíta Štúra z let 1847–55.* Prague: Slovensko-český klub, 2007.
Šolle, Zdeněk. *Století české politiky: Počátky moderní české politiky od Palackého a Havlíčka až po realisty Kaizla, Kramáře a Masaryka.* Prague: Mladá fronta, 1998.
Sorkin, David. "Reclaiming Theology for the Enlightenment: The Case of Siegmund Jacob Baumgarten, 1706–1757." *Central European History* 36 (2003): 503–30.
———. "Reform Catholicism and Religious Enlightenment." *Austrian History Yearbook* 30 (1999): 187–219. See also "Comments," by T. C. W. Blanning and R. J. W. Evans, 221–35.
Souček, Stanislav, "Příspěvek k poznání Erbena básníka." *Časopis matice moravské,* 39 (1916), 195–260.
Soukup, Ladislav. "Poddaní a jejich právní postavení v zemských zřízeních doby předbělohorské v Čechách." In *Vladislavské zřízení zemské a počátky ústavního zřízení v Českých zemích: 1500–1619.* Sborník příspěvků z mezinárodní konference konané ve dnech 7–8 prosince 2000 v Praze, edited by Karel Malý and Jaroslav Pánek, 239–48. Prague: Historický ústav Akademie věd České Republiky; Ústav právních dějin Právnické fakulty Univerzity Karlovy, 2001.
Sousedík, Stanislav. *Filosofie v českých zemích mezi středověkem a osvícenstvím.* Prague: Vyšehrad, 1997.
Spencer, Vicki. "In Defense of Herder on Cultural Diversity and Interaction." *Review of Politics* 69 (2007): 79–105.
Spiess, Bedřich. "Jan Kocín z Kocinétu co historik církevní." *Časopis českého musea* 46 (1872): 60–72.
Spinka, Matthew. *John Hus: A Biography.* Princeton, N.J.: Princeton University Press, 1968.
Spurr, John. *English Puritanism, 1603–1689.* New York: St. Martin's Press, 1998.
Štaif, Jiří. *Historici, dějiny a společnost: Historiografie v českých zemích od Palackého a jeho předchůdců po Gollovu školu.* 2 vols. Prague: Filozofická fakulta Univerzity Karlovy, 1997.
Štaif, Jiří. *Obezřetná elita: Česká společnost mezi tradicí a revolucí.* Prague: Dokořán, 2005.
Štefek, Karel. "Palacký a Hegel." In *František Palacký, 1798–1998, dějiny a dnešek: Sborník z jubilejní konference,* edited by František Šmahel and Eva Doležalová, 43–51. Prague: Historický ústav Akademie věd ČR, 1999.

Steinberg, Michael P. "'Fin-de-siècle Vienna' Ten Years Later: 'Viel Traum, Wenig Wirklichkeit.'" *Austrian History Yearbook* 22 (1991): 151–62.
Štěpánek, Vladimír. *K historickému výkladu obrozenské literatury.* Acta Universitatis Carolinae. Philologica. Monographia, 60. Prague: Univerzita Karlova, 1976.
Stellner, František. "Slovanství v české a ruské společnosti v první polovině 19. století." *Historický obzor* 15 (2004): 207–8.
Stern, J. P. "Language Consciousness and Nationalism in the Age of Bernard Bolzano." *Journal of European Studies* 19 (1989): 169–89.
Stewart, M. A., ed. *Studies in the Philosophy of the Scottish Enlightenment.* Oxford: Oxford University Press, 1990.
Stich, Alexandr. *Od Karla Havlíčka k Františku Halasovi: Lingvoliterární studie.* Praha: Torst, 1996.
Stloukal, Karel. "Počátky nunciatury v Praze: Bonhomi v Čechách, 1581–84." *Český časopis historický* 34 (1928): 1–24, 237–79.
Strasser, Kurt F., ed. *Die Bedeutung Bernard Bolzanos für die Gegenwart.* Prague: Filosofia, 2003.
Sullivan, Robert. "Rethinking Christianity in Enlightened Europe; Review Essay." *Eighteenth-Century Studies* 34 (2001): 298–309.
Šusta, Josef. *Král cizinec.* České dějiny. Vol. 2, pt. 2. Prague: Laichter, 1939.
Svatoš, Michal. "Humanismus an der Universität Prag im 15. und 16. Jahrhundert." In *Studien zum Humanismus in den böhmischen Ländern.* Schriften des Komitees der Bundesrepublic Deutschland zur Förderung der Slawischen Studien, 11, edited by Hans-Bernd Harder and Hans Rothe, 195–206. Cologne: Böhlau, 1988.
Svoboda, Rudolf. "Pastores boni?" *Osvícenství a katolická církev*, edited by Rudolf Svoboda and others, 22–43. České Budějovice: Jihočeská univerzita, Teologická fakulta, 2005.
Svoboda, Rudolf, and others, eds. *Osvícenství a katolická církev.* České Budějovice: Jihočeská univerzita, Teologická fakulta, 2005.
Szabo, Franz A. J. *Kaunitz and Enlightened Absolutism, 1753–1780.* New York: Cambridge University Press, 1994.
Táborský, Josef. *Reformní katolík Josef Dobrovský.* Pontes pragenses, 48. Brno: L. Marek, 2007.
Tait, William W., ed. *Early Analytic Philosophy: Frege, Russell, Witgenstein: Essays in Honor of Leonard Linsky.* Chicago: Open Court, 1997.
Tatarkiewicz, Władyslaw. *Historia filozofii.* 8th ed., 3 vols. Warsaw: Państwowe wydawnictwo naukowe, 1978.
———. *Zarys dziejów filozofii v Polsce.* Cracow: Polska akademia umiejętności, 1948.
Teich, Mikuláš. "Bohemia: From Darkness into Light." In *The Enlightenment in National Context,* edited by Roy Porter and Mikuláš Teich, 141–63. New York: Cambridge University Press, 1981.
———. *Bohemia in History.* New York: Cambridge University Press, 1998.
Thirlwall, John C. *Connop Thirlwall: Historian and Theologian.* London: Society for Promoting Christian Knowledge, [1936].
Tichá, Zdeňka. *Cesta starší české literatury.* Prague: Panorama, 1984.
Tieftrunk, Karel. *Dějiny Matice české.* Prague: Řivnáč, 1881.
Tierney, Brian. *The Idea of Natural Rights: Studies on Natural Rights, Natural Law and Church Law, 1150–1625.* Atlanta, Ga.: Scholars Press for Emory University, 1997.

Toegel, Miroslav. "Politické snahy J. A. Komenského a jejich výraz v jeho spisech." *Československý časopis historický* 14 (1966): 15–35. Comments on Toegel's article by Bedřich Šindelář, "Komenský němečtí protestanté a Vestfálský mír." *Československý časopis historický* 14 (1966): 862–66.

Toews, John E. *Hegelianism: Path toward Dialectical Humanism, 1805–1841.* Cambridge: Cambridge University Press, 1980.

Trlifajová, Kateřina, ed. *Osamělý myslitel, Bernard Bolzano.* Prague: Filosofia, 2006.

Truhlář, Antonín. "Z redaktorských příhod Palackého." In *Památník na oslavu stých narozenin Františka Palackého,* 290–98. Prague: Matice česká, 1898.

Trusen, Winfried. *Um die Reform und Einheit der Kirche: Zum Leben und Werk Georg Witzels.* Vereinsschriften der Gesellschaft zur Herausgabe des Corpus Catholicorum, 14. Münster: Aschendorffsche Verlagsbuchhandlung, 1957.

Tvrdý, Josef. "Vztahy Dobrovského k filosofii." *Bratislava* 4 (1930): 276–95.

Ulbricht, Günter. *Johann Bernard Basedow.* Berlin: Volk und Wissen, 1963.

Urban, Petr. "Bolzano a raný Husserl." In *Osamělý myslitel, Bernard Bolzano,* edited by Kateřina Trlifajová, 173–86. Prague: Filosofia, 2006.

Urbánek, Rudolf. "Český mesianismus ve své době hrdinské." *Od pravěku k dnešku: Sborník k 60. narozeninám J. Pekaře.* 1:262–84. 2 vols. Prague: Historický klub, 1930.

Urfus, Valentin. "Stát v představách české národní společnosti smetanovského období." In *Povědomí tradice v novodobé české kultuře: Doba Bedřicha Smetany.* Sborník sympozia v Plzni 7.–11. března 1984, 22–28. Prague: Národní galerie, 1988.

Urválková, Zuzana. "František Martin Pelcl o Jezuitech." In *Bůh a bohové: Církve, náboženství a spiritualita v českém 19 století,* Sborník příspěvků z 22. ročníku sympozia k problematice 19. století, Plzeň, 7.–9 března 2002, edited by Zdeněk Hojda and Roman Prahl, 123–26. Prague: KLP, 2003.

Valjavec, Fritz. *Der Josephinismus: Zur geistigen Entwicklung Österreichs im 18. und 19. Jahrhundert.* Brno: Rudolf M. Rohrer, 1944.

Válka, Josef. "František Palacký: Historik." In *Památník Palackého, 1798–1968,* edited byMilan Myška, 31–59. Ostrava: Profil, 1968.

———. "Palacký a francouzští liberální historikové II." In *František Palacký, 1798–1998, dějiny a dnešek: Sborník z jubilejní konference,* edited by František Šmahel and Eva Doležalová, 93–100. Prague: Historický ústav Akademie věd ČR, 1999.

Van Kley, Dale K. "Christianity as Casualty and Chrysalis of Modernity: The Problem of Dechristianization in the French Revolution." *American Historical Review* 108 (2003): 1081–1106.

———. "Piety and Politics in the Century of Lights." In *Cambridge History of Eighteenth-Century Political Thought,* edited by Mark Goldie and Robert Wokler, 110–43. New York: Cambridge University Press, 2006.

Várossová, Elena. *Filozofia vo svete: svet filozofie u nás.* Bratislava: Veda, 2005.

———. "Hegelovské inšpirácie u Štúra a Hurbana." In *Filozofia vo svete: svet filozofie u nás,* 161–80. Bratislava: Veda, 2005.

———. "Kultúrny nacionalizmus Jána Kollára." In *Filozofia vo svete: svet filozofie u nás,* 146–160. Bratislava: Veda, 2005.

———. "Štefan Launer: apokryfný typ slovenského hegelovca." In *Filozofia vo svete: svet filozofie u nás,* 181–94. Bratislava: Veda, 2005.

Vávra, Jaroslav. "Dobrovský v politických zápasech své doby." *Slavia* 23 (1954): 191–97.
Viatte, Auguste. *Les sources occultes du romantisme.* 2nd ed., 2 vols. Paris: Honoré Champion, 1965.
Viktora, Viktor. *K pramenům národní literatury.* Plzeň: Fraus, 2003.
Vintr, Josef, and Jana Pleskalová, eds. *Vídeňský podíl na počátcích českého národního obrození. J. V. Zlobický (1743–1810) a současníci: život, dílo, korespondence.* Prague: Academia, 2004.
Vlasáková, Marta. "Životaběh B. Bolzana." In *Osamělý myslitel, Bernard Bolzano,* edited by Kateřina Trlifajová, 11–26. Prague: Filosofia, 2006.
Vočadlo, Otakar. "V zajetí babylonském: cizí vlivy na českou kulturu." *Nové Čechy* 7 (1924): 114–25.
Vorel, Petr. "Města jako sídla feudálních vrchností." *Česká města v 16.–18. století: Sborník příspěvků z konference v Pardubicích 14. a 15. listopadu 1990,* edited by Jaroslav Pánek, 121–35. Prague: Historický ústav, 1991.
Vries, Josef de. "Zur Geschichte und Problematik der Barockscholastik in Deutschland." *Theologie und Philosophie* 57 (1982): 1–20.
Vydra, Bohumil. "Ohlasy polských událostí z konce XVIII. století v českém obrozeneckém tisku." In *Z dějin východní Evropy a Slovanstva: Sborník věnovaný Jaroslavu Bidlovi k šedesátým narozeninám,* edited by Miloš Weingart and others, 315–23. Prague: A. Bečková, 1928.
Wagner, Murray L. *Petr Chelčický: A Radical Separatist in Hussite Bohemia.* Scottdale, Pa.: Herald Press, 1983.
Waldron, Jeremy. *God, Locke, and Equality: Christian Foundations of Locke's Political Thought.* New York: Cambridge University Press, 2002.
Walicki, Andrzej. *The Enlightenment and the Birth of Modern Nationhood: Polish Political Thought from Noble Republicanism to Tadeusz Kościuszko.* Notre Dame, Ind.: University of Notre Dame Press, 1989.
———. "Ernst Gellner and the Constructionist Theory of Nation." *Harvard Ukrainian Studies* 22 (1998): 611–19.
———. *A History of Russian Thought from Enlightenment to Marxism.* Stanford, Calif.: Stanford University Press, 1979.
———. *Philosophy and Romantic Nationalism: The Case of Poland.* Oxford: Clarendon Press, 1982.
Wallmann, Johannes. *Philipp Jakob Spener un die Anfänge des Pietismus.* Tübingen: J. C. B. Mohr, 1970.
Wandruszka, Adam. "Der Reformkatholizismus des 18. Jahrhunderts in Italien und in Österreich." In *Festschrift Hermann Wiesflecker zum sechzigsten Geburtstag,* edited by Alexander Novotny and Othmar Pickl, 231–40. Graz: Selbstverlag des Historischen Instituts der Universität Graz, 1973.
Wanegffelen, Thierry. *Une difficile fidelité: Catholiques malgré concile en France, XVIe–XVII-e siècles.* Paris: Presses Universitaires de France, 1999.
Weeks, Andrew. *Boehme: An Intellectual Biography of the Seventeenth-Century Mystic.* Albany: State University of New York Press, 1991.
———. *German Mysticism from Hildegard of Bingen to Ludwig Wittgenstein: A Literary and Intellectual History.* Albany: State University of New York Press, 1993.
Wehler, Hans-Ulrich. *Nationalismus: Geschichte, Formen, Folgen.* Munich: Beck, 2001.

Weiss, Otto. "Bolzanisten und Güntherianer in Wien 1848–1851." In *Bernard Bolzano und die Politik: Staat, Nation und Religion als Herausforderung für die Philosophie im Kontext von Spätaufklärung, Frühnationalismus und Restauration.* Studien zu Politik und Verwaltung, Band 61, edited by Helmut Rumpler, 247–80. Vienna: Böhlau, 2000.

Wellek, René. *Essays on Czech Literature.* Introduction by Peter Demetz. The Hague: Mouton, 1963.

Weltsch, Felix. "Christian Ehrenfels." *Česká mysl* 28 (1932): 265–73.

Werner, Ernst. *Jan Hus: Welt und Umwelt eines Prager Frühreformators,* Forschungen zur mittelalterlichen Geschichte, 34. Weimar: Böhlau, 1991.

Williams, Howard. "The End of History in Hegel and Marx." In *Hegel-Marx Connection,* edited by Tony Burns and Ian Fraser, 198–216. New York: St. Martin's Press, 2000.

Winter, Eduard. *Bernard Bolzano: Ein Denker und Erzieher im österreichischen Vormärz.* Graz: Böhlaus, 1967.

———. *Bernard Bolzano: Ein Lebensbild.* Stuttgart-Bad Cannstatt: Frommann Holzboog, 1969. (Bernard Bolzano, *Gesamtausgabe,* Einleitungsband, vol. 1).

———. *Bernard Bolzano und sein Kreis.* Leipzig: Hegner, 1933.

———. *Der Bolzanoprozess: Dokumente zur Geschichte der Prager Karlsuniversität im Vormärz.* Brno: Rudolf M. Rohrer, 1944.

———. *Der Josefinismus: die Geschichte des österreichischen Reformkatholizismus, 1740–1848.* Berlin: Rütten & Loening, 1962.

———. *Josefinismus und Gegenwart.* Schriftreihe der Nordwestdeutschen Universitätsgesellschaft, Heft 32. [Wilhelmshaven]: Nordwestdeutsche Universitätsgesellschaft, [1962].

———. *Der Josefinismus und seine Geschichte: Beiträge zur Geistesgeschichte Österreichs, 1740–1848.* Brno: Rohrer, 1943.

———. *Leben und geistige Entwicklung des Sozialethikers und Mathematikers, Bernard Bolzano, 1781–1848.* Halle: Niemeyer, 1949.

———. *Die sozial- und ethnoethik Bernard Bolzanos: Humanistischer Patriotismus oder romantischer Nationalismus im vormärzlichen Österreich: Bernard Bolzano contra Friedrich Schlegel.* Vienna: Verlag der Österreichischen Akademie der Wissenschaften, 1977.

———. *Tausend Jahre Geisteskampf im Sudetenraum: das religiöse Ringen zweier Völker.* Salzburg and Leipzig: Otto Müller, 1938.

———. *Über die Perfektibilität des Katholizismus: Grundsätzliche Erwägungen in Briefen von Pascal, Bolzano, Brentano und Knoll.* Berlin: Akademie, 1971.

Winter, Zikmund. *Děje vysokých škol pražských od secessí cizích národů po dobu bitvy bělohorské, 1409–1622.* Prague: Česká akademie pro vědy, slovesnost a umění, 1895.

———. *Kulturní obraz českých měst: život veřejný v XV. a XVI. věku.* 2 vols. Prague: Matice česká, 1890–92.

———. *Život a učení na partikulárních školách v Čechách v XV. a XVI. století.* Prague: Česká akademie pro vědy, slovesnost a umění, 1901.

———. *Život církevní v Čechách: Kulturně-historický obraz v XV. a XVI. století.* 2 vols. Prague: Česká akademie pro vědy, slovesnost a umění, 1895.

———. *Zlatá doba měst českých.* Prague: Odeon, 1991.

Wippel, John F. "'First Philosophy' according to Thomas Aquinas." In *Metaphys-*

ical Themes in Thomas Aquinas, 55–68. Washington, D.C.: Catholic University of America Press, 1984.

Wolchik, Sharon L. "Czechoslovakia." In *Eastern Europe: Politics, Culture, and Society since 1939,* edited by Sabrina P. Ramet, 35–70. Bloomington: Indiana University Press, 1998.

———. "Reflections of the Czechoslovak Republic in the Post-Communist Period." In *Birth of Czechoslovakia,* Seminar on the Founding of Independent Czechoslovakia, Library of Congress, October 8, 1998, edited by Sharon L. Wolchik and Ivan Dubovický. Prague: Set Out Roman Míšek, [1999].

Wollgast, Siegfried. "Johann Christoph Adelung als Philosophiehistoriker." In *Sprache und Kulturentwicklung in Blickfeld der deutschen Spätaufklärung: Der Beitrag Johann Christoph Adelungs,* edited by Werner Bahner, 55–71. Berlin: Akademie Verlag, 1984.

Wood, Allen. "Hegel and Marxism." In *Cambridge Companion to Hegel,* edited by Frederick C. Beiser, 414–44. New York: Cambridge University Press, 1993.

Wotke, Karl. "Karl Heinrich Seibt, der erste Universtätprofessor der deutschen Sprache in Prag, ein Schüler Gellerts und Gottscheds. Ein Beitrag zur Geschichte des Deutschunterrichts in Österreich." *Beiträge zur österreichischen Erziehungs- und Schulgeschichte,* 9, 1–174. Vienna: Carl Fromme, 1907.

Yerkes, James. *The Christology of Hegel.* Missoula, Montana: Scholars Press, 1978. Reprint, Albany, N.Y.: SUNY Press, 1983.

Zába, Gustav. "Filosofie." In *Památník na oslavu padesátiletého panovnického jubilea Františka Josefa I: vědecký a umělecký rozvoj v národě českém,* 1–33. Prague: Česká akademie pro vědy, slovesnost a umění, 1898.

Žalud, Augustin. *Karel Havlíček: život působení a význam.* 2nd ed., Prague: Beaufort, [1906].

Zammito, John H. *Kant, Herder, and the Birth of Anthropology.* Chicago: University of Chicago Press, c2002.

Závodský, Artur. *František Ladislav Čelakovský.* Prague: Melantrich, 1982.

Zeil, Wilhelm. *Bolzano und die Sorben: ein Beitrag zur Geschichte des "Wendischen Seminars" in Prag zur Zeit der josefinischen Aufklärung und der Romantik.* Bautzen: Domowina, 1967.

Zelený, Jindřich. "O kritice Hegelovy logiky v Bolzánově vědosloví." *Filozofický časopis* 29 (1981): 845–55.

Zelený, Václav. *Život Josefa Jungmanna.* Prague: Matice česká, 1873.

Zeman, Herbert, ed. *Die Österreichische Literatur: ihr Profil im 19. Jahrhundert, 1830–1880.* Graz: Akademische Druck- und Verlagsanstalt, 1982.

Žemla, Martin. "Svět Jakuba Boehma." In *Cesta ke Kristu,* by Jacob Boehme, 1–87. Prague: Vyšehrad, 2003.

Zimmermann, Robert von. "Palacký." In *Památník na oslavu stých narozenin Františka Palackého,* 41–44. Prague: Matice česká, 1898.

Zöllner, Erich. "Bemerkungen zum Problem der Beziehungen zwischen Aufklärung und Josephinismus." In *Österreich und Europa: Festgabe für Hugo Hantsch zum 70. Geburtstag,* 203–19. Graz, Styria, 1965.

Zouhar, Jan, Helena Pavlincová, and Jiří Gabriel. *Demokracie je diskuze . . . : Česká filosofie, 1918–1938.* Olomouc: Nakladatelství Olomouc, 2005.

Zuber, Rudolf. *Osudy moravské církve v 18. století.* 2 vols. Olomouc: Matice cyrilometodějská, 1987–2003.

Zuckert, Michael P. *Launching Liberalism: On Lockean Political Philosophy.* Lawrence, Kansas: University Press of Kansas, 2002.
———. *Natural Rights and the New Republicanism.* Princeton, N.J.: Princeton University Press, 1994.
Zumr, Josef. *Máme-li kulturu je naší vlastí Evropa: Herbartismus a česká filosofie.* Prague: Filosofia, 1998.
———. "Některé otázky českého herbartismu." In *Filosofie v dějinách českého národa,* Protokol celostátní konference o dějinách české filosofie v Liblicích ve dnech 14.–17. dubna 1958,166–85. Prague: Nakladatelství ČSAV, 1958.
———. "Die theoretischen und methodologischen Voraussetzungen der Herbartschen Metaphysik." *Wiener Jahrbuch für Philosophie* 1 (1968): 185–99.

Reference Books

Allgemeine Deutsche Biographie. 2nd ed. 56 vols. Berlin: Duncker und Humblot, 1968.
American National Biography. 24 vols. New York: Oxford University Press, 1999.
Antologie z dějin českého a slovenského filozofického myšlení. Prague: Svoboda, 1981.
Antologie z dějin československé filosofie. Prague: Nakladatelství Československé akademie věd, 1963.
Beiser, Frederick C., ed. *Cambridge Companion to Hegel.* New York: Cambridge University Press, 1993.
Biographisches Lexikon des Kaiserthums Oesterreich, ed. Constant von Wurzbach, 60 vols. Vienna: Hof- und Staatsdruckerei, 1856–91.
Borchert, Donald M. *The Encyclopedia of Philosophy.* 2nd ed. 10 vols. New York: Macmillan, 2006.
Broadie, Alexander, ed. *Cambridge Companion to the Scottish Enlightenment.* New York: Cambridge University Press, 2003.
Cambel, Samuel, ed. *Dejiny Slovenska.* 6 vols. Bratislava: Veda, 1986–88.
Chadwick, Owen. *A History of the Popes.* Oxford: Clarendon Press, 1998.
Copleston, Frederick. *History of Philosophy.* 8 vols. London: Burns and Oates, 1947–66.
Craig, Edward, ed. *Routledge Encyclopedia of Philosophy.* New York: Routledge, 1998.
Deutsche Biographische Enzyklopaedie. 12 vols. Munich: K. G. Sauer, 1995–2000.
Dictionary of National Biography. 22 vols. Oxford: Oxford University Press, 1921–22.
Edwards, Paul, ed. *The Encyclopedia of Philosophy.* 8 vols. New York: Macmillan, 1967.
Encyklopédia Slovenska. 6 vols. Bratislava: Veda, 1978–82.
Forst, Vladimír, Jiří Opelík, and Luboš Merhaut, eds. *Lexikon české literatury: Osobnosti, díla, instituce.* 4 vols. in 7 parts. Prague: Academia, 1985–2008.
Franzen, August. *Malé církevní dějiny.* Prague: Zvon, 1992.
Gabriel, Jiří, ed. *Slovník českých filozofů.* Brno: Masarykova Univerzita, 1998.
Grendler, Paul F., ed. *Encyclopedia of the Renaissance.* 6 vols. New York: Charles Scribner's Sons, 1999.
Hejnic, Josef, and Jan Martínek, eds. *Rukověť humanistického básnictví v Čechách a na Moravě od konce 15. do začátku 17. Století.* 5 vols. Prague: Academia, 1966–82.

Held, Joseph, ed. *Columbia History of Eastern Europe in the Twentieth Century.* New York: Columbia University Press, 1992.
Holmes, Urban T., III. *What Is Anglicanism.* Harrisburg, Pa.: Morehouse, 1982.
Honderich, Ted, ed. *Oxford Companion to Philosophy.* New York: Oxford University Press, 1995.
Horowitz, Maryanne, ed. *New Dictionary of the History of Ideas.* 6 vols. Farmington Hills, Mich.: Thomson Gale, 2005.
Horyna, Břetislav, and others, eds. *Filosofický slovník.* 2nd ed. Olomouc: Nakladatelství Olomouc, 2002.
Jakubec, Jan. *Dějiny literatury české.* 2nd ed., 2 vols. Prague: Jan Laichter, 1929–34.
Jakubec, Jan, ed., with Josef Hanuš, Jan Máchal, and Jaroslav Vlček. *Literatura česká devatenáctého století.* 2nd ed., 2 vols. Prague: Jan Laichter, 1911–17.
Jireček Josef. *Rukověť k dějinám literatury české.* 2 vols. Prague: Tempsky, 1875–76.
Kadlec, Jaroslav. *Přehled českých církevních dějin.* 2 vols. Prague: Zvon, 1991.
Kavka, František, and Josef Petráň, eds. *Dějiny Univerzity Karlovy, 1348–1990.* 4 vols. Prague: Karolinum, 1995–98.
Kodansha Encyclopedia of Japan. 9 vols. Tokyo: Kodansha, 1983.
Král, Josef. *Československá filosofie: Nástin vývoje podle disciplin.* Prague, Melantrich, 1937.
Lehár, Jan, Alexandr Stich, Jaroslava Janáčková, and Jiří Holý. *Česká literatura od počátků k dnešku.* Prague: Lidové noviny, 1998.
Lehár, Jan, and others. *Česká literatura od počátků k dnešku: kniha textů.* 4 vols. Prague: Lidové noviny, 2000–2001.
Luther, Martin. *Werke: Kritische Gesammtausgabe.* 113 vols., 4 series. Weimar: Böhlau, 1883–1996.
Mácha, Karel. *Glaube und Vernunft: Die Böhmische Philosophie in geschichtlicher Übersicht.* 3 vols. Munich: Sauer, 1987.
Martinich, Aloysius, and David Sosa, eds. *A Companion to Analytic Philosophy.* Malden, Mass.: Blackwell, 2001.
Malá československá encyklopedie. 6 vols. Prague: Academia, 1984–87.
Michala, Lubomir, and Eduard Petrů, eds. *Panorama české literatury: Literární dějiny od počátků do současnosti.* Olomouc: Rubico, 1994.
Motyl, Alexander, ed. *Encyclopedia of Nationalism.* 2 vols. San Diego, Calif.: Academic Press, 2001.
Mukařovský, Jan, ed. *Dějiny české literatury.* 4 vols. Prague: Nakladatelství Československé akademie věd, 1959–95.
Neue Deutsche Biographie. Berlin: Duncker & Humblot, 1953–.
New Catholic Encyclopedia. 17 vols. New York: McGraw-Hill, 1967–79.
Novák, Arne. *Dějiny českého písemnictví.* Edited by Antonín Grund. 2d ed. Prague: Sfinx, 1946; 3rd ed. Edited by Bohumil Svozil. Prague: Brána, 1994.
———. *Přehledné dějiny literatury české.* 4th ed., 2 vols. Olomouc: Promberger, 1936–39.
———. *Stručné dějiny literatury české.* Edited by Rudolf Havel and Antonín Grund. Olomouc: Promberger, 1946.
Novotný, Václav, ed. *M. Jana Husi korespondence a dokumenty.* Prague: Komise pro vydávání pamenů náboženského hnutí českého, 1920.
Ottův slovník naučný. 37 vols. Prague: Otto, 1888–1908.

Oxford Dictionary of National Biography. 61 vols. New York: Oxford University Press, 2004.
Rutherford, Donald, ed. *Cambridge Companion to Early Modern Philosophy*. New York: Cambridge University Press, 2006.
Schmitt, Charles B., and others. *Cambridge History of Renaissance Philosophy*. New York: Cambridge University Press, 1988.
Sněmy české od léta 1526 až po naši dobu. Vols. 1–11, 15. Prague: Zemský výbor, 1877–1941.
Snyder, Louis. *Encyclopedia of Nationalism*. New York: Paragon House, 1990.
Vlček, Jaroslav. *Dějiny české literatury.* 2 vols. Prague: Československý spisovatel, 1951.
Wandruszka, Adam, and Peter Urbanitsch, eds., *Die Habsburgmonarchie, 1848–1918,* 6 vol. in 8 parts. Vienna: Verlag der Österreichischen Akademie der Wissenschaften, 1973–93.

Index

Figures and notes are denoted by "f" and "n" following the page number.

Abbildungen Böhmischer und Mährischen Gelehrten und Künstler (Pelcl & Voigt), 140
Abeceda pobožné manželky a rozšafné hospodyně (Kocín), 92
Abhandlungen der Königlichen böhmischen Gesellschaft der Wissenschaften (Exner), 222
Abhandlung über den Ursprung der Sprache (Herder), 121, 124
Acta litteraria Bohemiae et Moraviae (Voigt), 4, 84, 91
Adams, John, 271n23
Addison, Joseph, 147
Adelung, Johann Christoph, 89, 149, 291n49
aesthetics, 42–44, 164, 168, 188–92, 336n92
Agnew, Hugh, 5, 10–12, 121, 281n47
Albertus Magnus, 141
Allgemeine böhmische Bibliothek (Ungar), 84
Alphabetum Bohemicum, 88
Altenstein, Karl vom Stein zum, 175, 321n76
Ammon, Christoph F., 225
analytical philosophy, 241

Die Anfänge der tschechischen Erneuerung und das deutsche Geistesleben (Schamschula), 5
Anglican Church, 21, 252n8, 257n51. *See also* Church of England
Anleitung und Grundriss zur Systematischen Dogmatischen Theologie (Rautenstrauch), 62
Antichrist (Nietzsche), 144
anti-Hegelianism, 194–214; demise of Hegelianism in Bohemia, 194–98, 354n6; and divisiveness of Hegel, 207–8; and German issue, 212–14; global legacy of, 231–43; and Hodža, 205–7; and Hurban, 203–5; and Launer, 200–201; in Lněničková's writing, 14; and Polish paradox, 208–12; and Slovak contrast, 198–207; Slovaks and German Lutheran universities, 198–200; and Štúr, 201–3. *See also* Hegel, Georg
Aquilinas, Pavel, 92
Aquinas. *See* Thomas Aquinas
aristocracy. *See* nobles and nobility
Aristotle, 142
Arkleb of Boskovice, 261n93
Arndt, Ernst, 130
Arriaga, Roderigo, 136–37

asceticism, 58–59, 60–61, 62
Augsburg Confession, 21. *See also* Lutheranism
Augustine, Saint, 67
Austrian philosophical tradition, 213–14, 231–37, 363n155
authoritarianism. *See* liberal thought and authoritarian Church
Avicenna, 136
Ayer, Alfred J., 231, 234, 235, 376n37

Bacháček, Martin, 44, 45
Bacon, Francis, 125, 147, 154
Bakunin, Mikhail, 211
Balbín, Bohuslav, 80, 113, 122, 148
Balthasar (Spanish general), 54, 273n44
Bandtke, Samuel, 209
Bardili, Christoph, 168, 169, 170, 182
Barnard, Frederick M., 108
Barnes, Robert, 35
baroque scholasticism. *See* second or Suárezian scholasticism
Bartolomeides, Ladislav, 92
Bartoš Písař, 92, 97
Basedow, Johann B., 145–46
Básně v řeči vázané (V. Thám), 52, 55, 66, 72, 81, 85–86
Battle of White Mountain. *See* White Mountain, Battle of
Baumgarten, Alexander, 161
Bavorovský, Tomáš, 91
Bayerová, Marie, 144
Beattie, James, 171, 172
Bechyňka, Jan, 42
Beiträge zu einer begründeteren Darstellung der Mathematik (Bolzano), 227
Beiträge zur Buchdruckerkunst in Böhmen (Voigt), 85
Beiträge zur leichteren Uebersicht des Zustandes der Philosophie (Bardili & K.L. Reinhold), 170
Bělina, Pavel, 12–13, 15–16
Belinskii, Vissarion G., 211
Benedikti, Ján, 118, 200

Benedikt z Nudožer, Vavřinec, 88
Beneke, Friedrich Eduard, 169, 175, 212, 225, 343n6, 362n145
Bentham, Jeremy, 159
Berdiaev, Nikolai, 211
Bergmann, Hugo, 239, 246
Berlin, Isaiah, 184
Bible. *See* scriptures and Bible
bibliographers and bibliographic record, 7, 12, 84–85, 90–98
Bílejovský, Bohuslav: bibliographical details, 259n70; on Czechs as true Roman Catholics, 260n82; erudition of, 45; and Luther, 23; and Taborite violence, 27, 283n72; and universalism, 32; and Utraquism, 29, 79; on vernacular language, 42
Bismarck, Otto von, 236, 377n46
Bláhová, Kateřina, 117
Blair, Hugh, 125
Blasphemy Act of 1650 (England), 22
Blätter der Vorzeit (Herder), 124
Boccacio, Giovanni, 44
Bock, Jan, 137
Boehme, Jakob, 109, 143, 210, 211
Bohemia: demise of Hegelianism in, 194–98, 354n6; Herder's influence in, 120–33; historical rights of Bohemian state, 101–4; political culture of, 242–43; religious void in, 229–30
Bohemia docta (Balbín), 85
Bohemian Chronicle (Bílejovský), 42, 45
Bohemian Confession, 21–22, 23, 27, 37, 253n17. *See also* Utraquist Church and Utraquism
Bohemian Diet. *See* Diet of Bohemia
Bohemian Learned Society, 51–52
Bohemian National Museum, 271n24
Bohemian Reformation. *See* Czech national awakening and Bohemian Reformation
Bohemian Royal Chancery, 19
Böhmische Grammatik zum Gebrauche der Deutschen (K.I. Thám), 89, 95
Böhmische Litteratur auf das Jahr (Dobrovský), 62

Bolzano, Bernard, 155–73, 245; and Aquinas, 156, 329n5; and Bardili, 170; and Catholic Enlightenment, 134; and Destutt, 172; and ecclesiology, 227–29; and empirical realists, 168–72; and Exner, 158, 217–18, 222–23, 232; and Fesl, 82, 156, 217, 223, 225; and Fichte, 156, 165–68; and Gazzaniga, 141, 156; and Hegel, 160, 183–94, 210, 212–13, 222, 231; and Herbart, 224–27, 229; and Herder, 124–25, 173; influence of, 17, 106, 155–58, 232–34, 243; and Kant, 159, 161–65, 173, 332n36, 334n56, 334n67, 336n92, 371n108; and Krug, 170–71, 340n151; language usage, 112, 113, 302n40; his *Lehrbuch der Religionswissenschaft*, 159, 160–61, 162, 166; liberal Catholicism of, 82, 115, 158–61, 215, 331n27; and Locke, 156, 171–72; and Macura, 7; and metaphysical idealists, 161–68, 180; and national awakening, 214; his *Perfektabilität des Katholicismus*, 228; persecution of, 216; and philosophy of common sense, 153; and Příhonský, 156, 165, 189, 217, 223; and progressivism, 179; and Reinhold (K.L.), 156, 168–69; and Schelling, 160–61, 165–68, 184, 334n56; and Seibt, 156, 173; and Thomism, 141; his *Über den Begriff des Schönen*, 187, 188–89, 225; utilitarianism of, 277n105; and Vienna Circle, 242
book burning. *See* burning of books
Bořita of Martinice, Jaroslav, 102
Born, Ignaz A., 140
Borovský, Karel Havlíček. *See* Havlíček Borovský, Karel
Bosanquet, Bernard, 233
Bossuet, Jacques, 50, 60, 61
Boudin, Jean, 41
Bowring, John, 124, 128
Bracciolini, Poggio, 96
Bradley, Francis H., 233

Bradshaw, Brendan, 34
Brahe, Tycho de, 44
Brandl, Vincenc, 104
Brennan, John W., 269n8
Brentano, Franz: and anti-Hegelianism, 212; and Austrian philosophical school, 232–33, 236–37; and Bolzano, 227, 373n12; influence of, 243; and Kraus, 239; and Masaryk, 239–40; and national awakening, 214; and Twardowski, 211
Brentano Archives, 239
Brentano Society, 239
Brethren. *See* Unity of Brethren
Březina, Otokar, 308n95
Briefe über den neuesten Idealismus (Krug), 170
Briefe über die Wissenschaftslehre (Krug), 170
Brikcí of Licko, 102, 104
British influences, literary, 127–28, 196; and Bowring, 124, 128; and Jungmann, 292n62; and Palacký, 125, 154, 196–97. *See also* Scott, Walter; Shakespeare, William
British influences, philosophical, 113, 135, 139, 170, 182–83, 232; and Bolzano, 171–72; and Exner, 212; and Havlíček, 128, 195; and Seibt, 121, 147–50, 173. *See also* Scottish Enlightenment
British influences, religious, 21, 25, 28, 38, 256n44. *See also* Wyclif, John
Das Buch Joseph (Zitte), 53, 61, 272n32
Burdach, Karl F., 152
burning of books, 56–57, 84, 273n50
Bydžovský, Pavel, 23, 27–28, 32, 35, 45

Caetano, Antonio, 266n145
Calvin, John, 28
Calvinism, 30, 206–7, 264n117
Campeggi, Lorenzo, 36
Candlemas Day Articles of 1524, 255n39
Carnap, Rudolf, 234–35, 240, 241, 246, 379n77

Časopis českého musea (journal): Anglophone Slavic studies in, 128; anti-Hegelianism in, 195, 196; and appreciation of literature, 98; and Herder, 125–26; idealist metaphysics in, 154; on Kant, 152; Klácel's articles in, 183; and language preservation, 71

Catholic Enlightenment, 64–82; and anti-idealism, 144–48; in Bělina's writing, 15–16; and Counter-Reformation, 47–63; and German idealism, 135; and Hegel, 174–93; and language preservation, 70–71; liberalism, free discussion, and tolerance, 68–69; in Lněničková's writing, 14; and plebeianism, 68, 71–73, 281*n*47; puzzle of, 179–81; realism of, 138–41; Reform Catholicism and Utraquism, 73–80; and religious question, 115; and religious symbiosis, 80–82; and secular aspects of Utraquist century, 65–73; and Seibt, 144–48. *See also* Counter-Reformation; Roman Catholicism

Catholicism. *See* Catholic Enlightenment; Counter-Reformation; liberal Catholicism; Roman Catholicism; Roman Curia; Tridentine Catholicism

Čelakovský, František K.: and Bolzano, 157; and Czech language, 94; and German nationalism, 127–28; and Herder, 124; and Hus, 82, 100–101; and Veleslavín, 67

celibacy, 58, 160, 275*n*71

censorship, 65, 100–101, 160

Červenák, Benjamín P., 199

Češka, Jan, 86

Česká včela (journal), 194–95

České literatura od počátků k dnešku (Lehár et al.), 250*n*61

České národní obrození (Kočí), 2

České osvícenství (Haubelt), 2, 3, 12, 13

České země v době předbřeznové (Lněničková), 12

Českých přísloví sbírka (Srnec), 93

Cesta a Prahy do Benátek (Prefát of Vlkanov), 93

Čest a nevina pohlaví ženského (Veleslavín), 92

Chaadaev, Petr I., 211

Chalybäus, Heinrich M., 186, 192

Charles IV, 42, 59

Charles V, 36

Charles University (Universitas Carolina), philosophy faculty at, 245–46. *See also* University of Prague

Chernyshevskii, Nikolai G., 211

Cheskian Anthology (Bowring), 124

Chesterfield, Lord, 147

Chládek, Jiljí Bartoloměj, 88

Chłędowski, Walenty, 209

Chlumčanský, Václav Leopold, 161, 216–17

Chotek, Karel, 129

Christ-katholische nützliche Hauspostille (Eybel), 57

Chronologische Geschichte Böhmens (Pubička), 76, 99

chronology of events, 383–87

Chrysostom, John, 91–92, 97

Chudoba, Bohdan, 179

Church of England, 24, 26, 27, 33. *See also* Anglican Church

Cieszkowski, August, 192, 203, 210

City of God (St. Augustine), 67

classics, reprinting of, 7, 90–94

Clement XIV, 49

clergy. *See* priests and clergy

Cochlaeus, Johannes, 76, 77

Collingwood, R.G., 48

Colloredo, Jerome, 58

Colonna, Vittoria, 35

Comenius, John A. *See* Komenský, Jan Amos

Commentarium in Sacram scripturam (Wolff), 75

communion, sacrament of, 19, 20, 32, 34. See also *sub una* communicants; *sub utraque* communicants

Compactata: and Bohemian Confession, 22; and Four Articles of Prague, 25; and Peace of Kutná Hora, 27; revocation of, 31–32, 34; and *sub una* communicants, 69; and universalism, 30; and Utraquist legitimacy, 20
Comte, Auguste, 234, 238, 378*n*63
Confederation of 1619, 101
confessionalization, 28, 30
consensus and freedom, 24–26, 68–69
Consistory, Utraquist,19, 20–22
constitutionalism, 101–2
Contarini, Gasparo, 35, 36, 262*n*98
Cornova, Ignác, 64, 100, 103, 149
"Correspondence about the Substance of Philosophy and the Nullity of Speculation" (Bardili and K.L. Reinhold), 170
cosmopolitanism, 71, 111–13, 149–50, 174, 217, 232, 243; and Bolzano, 113, 156, 158; and Durdík, 238; and Exner, 179, 219; and Palacký, 153; and Seibt, 145–46. *See also* cultural monism; cultural universalism
Council of Basel, 20, 25, 30, 31
Council of Constance, 24
Council of Trent, 3, 34, 36
Counter-Reformation, 47–63; in Bělina's writing, 15–16; and Catholic Enlightenment, 58–63; and cultural revolution, 49–53, 271*n*23; Jesuits' role in, 15–16; in Lněničková's writing, 14; negative perception of, 53–57; new, 216–17
Cranmer, Thomas, 260*n*85
Critique of Pure Reason. See Kant, Immanuel: his *Kritik der reinen Vernunft*
cultural monism, 174–75, 243
cultural revolution, 49–53, 271*n*23
cultural universalism, 59, 223, 282*n*64
Čupr, František, 152–53, 213, 215, 218, 245
Cykáda, Jan Václav, 38, 42, 263*n*115

Czech language: and Bolzano, 158–59, 331*n*30; books in, 66–67, 83; and Counter-Reformation, 54; in Hroch's writing, 9; and linguistic nationalism, 11–12, 15; as literary medium, 7, 11, 68; nobles' use of, 73; norms of, 6–7, 8, 11, 14, 87–90; as obligatory subject, 271*n*26; philosophical terminology in, 177; preservation of, 68, 70–71, 122; regard for, 6, 11, 111; revival of, 15, 17, 111–13; Slovak use of, 117, 181; vernacular language, 8, 41–42, 104
Czech national awakening and Bohemian Reformation, 1–17; and Agnew, 10–12; and Golden Age liberalism, 16–17, 230; in history and literature, 98–101; and legacy of anti-Hegelianism, 243; Marxist-Leninist interlude, 2–5; and religious question, 115; and Schamschula, Macura, and Hroch, 5–10; and twenty-first century, 12–16. *See also* Czech national awakening as Renaissance
Czech national awakening as Renaissance, 17, 83–105; and bibliographic record, 84–85; Bohemian Reformation in history and literature, 98–101; and historical rights of Bohemian state, 101–4; and infrastructure of Restoration, 83–90; Italian Renaissance compared, 48–49; and language norms, 87–90; and publication programs, 85–87; and reprinting classics, 90–94; and *Das schöne oder goldene Zeitalter*, 104–5; and textbooks, 94–98. *See also* Czech national awakening and Bohemian Reformation
The Czech Question (Masaryk), 109

Dačický, Václav, 39
Dalimil, 85, 86, 92
Daniel Adam of Veleslavín. *See* Veleslavín, Daniel Adam of

Darwin, Charles, 10
Dastich, Josef, 239, 245
De Dominis, Marco Antonio, 261n91
Dedukce o právní nepřetržitosti práv a svobod českých (Palacký), 102, 298n153
Dějiny národu českého v Čechách a na Moravě (Palacký), 100
Dějiny řeči a literatury československé (Šembera), 95
"Dekret kutnohorský" (Tyl), 101
De l'Allemagne (De Staël), 153
Della regolata divozione d'Cristiani (Muratori), 50
Demuth, Karel J., 104
Denis, Ernst, 29
De poëtica philosophandi ratione (Krug), 182
De saecularibus liberalium artium in Bohemia et Moravia (Procházka), 65, 76, 84, 145, 278n11
Desatery knihy Eusebiovy církevní historie (Eusebius), 93
Descartes, René, 135
Desideria (Bohemian Diet), 102
De Staël, Madame. *See* Staël-Holstein, Anne L.
De statu ecclesiae et legitima potestate Romani Pontificis (Hontheim), 50
Destutt de Tracy, Antoine L., 172
Deutsch-böhmisches Nationallexikon (K.I. Thám), 89
Deutsch-böhmisches Wöterbuch (Dobrovský), 90
Diesbach, Jan J., 91
Diet of Bohemia, 19, 25, 101–2, 103–4, 298n157
Diet of 1575, 21, 41
Dissertatio apologetica pro lingua Slavonica preacipue Bohemica (Balbín), 113, 122, 148
Dittrich, Josef, 81, 91, 228
Dlabač, Jan B., 86, 92, 100
Dobner, Gelasius, 99
Dobřenský, Václav, 93, 98

Dobrovský, Josef: in Bělina's writing, 16; and bibliographic record, 84, 85; and Bohemian Learned Society, 51–52; on Bohemian literature, 67, 100; and Bohemian National Museum, 271n24; and Bolzano, 216–17; and Counter-Reformation, 53–54; and Enlightenment ideals, 61, 64, 65, 110; and German idealism, 149; on Golden Age, 247n1; and Herder, 121; on Hus, 78; and language, 6, 70–71, 88–90, 112, 113; his *Lectures Concerning the Practical Side of the Christian Religion*, 61–62; and liberalism, 61–62, 68, 276n102; in Lněničková's writing, 14, 15; in Macura's writing, 8; on monastic librarians, 273n39; on Muratori, 270n15; and plebeianism, 72; and publication programs, 85; and Rautenstrauch, 62; and Reidinger, 140; and religious symbiosis, 82; and religious tolerance, 69, 180; and reprinting of classics, 93, 94; and Seibt, 113, 148–49; and Slavdom, 122; on Taborites, 74; at University of Prague, 50, 270n18; and Utraquist Reformation, 80; and Van Swieten, 62
Dominicans, 139–40
Doppler, J.C., 218
Dubislav, Walter, 241
Duguet, Jacques, 60
Duhem, Pierre M. M., 236
Dungersheim, Hieronymus, 76
Durdík, Josef, 155, 213–14, 226, 238–39, 246, 282n64, 377n54, 378n63
Durych, Václav Fortunát, 87,121, 276n98
Dušesloví zkušebné (Hyna), 151
Dutch national awakening, 111
Dvě kroniky o založení země České, 92
"Dvojí rozmlouvání o jazyku českém" (Jungmann), 90
Dvorský z Helfenberka, Jindřich, 44

Ecclesiastical History (Eusebius), 93, 98
ecclesiology, 18, 23, 24, 30, 32, 227–29
Eckhart, Friedrich, 81
Eckhart, Meister, 143
Edict of Nantes, 60
Edict of Religious Toleration (Joseph II), 69
Edinburgh Review, 196
Effigies (Voigt), 76
Ehrenfels, Christian, 240, 246
Einheitswissenschaft (Carnap), 240
"Einleitung zum Kritischen Journal" (Schelling), 170
Eisenmeyer, Josef, 246
Elements of the Philosophy of the Human Mind (Stewart), 172
Elimination of Metaphysics through Logical Analysis of Language (Carnap), 240
Elizabeth I, 60
empirical realism, 168–72
Emser, Hieronymus, 76
Enchridion (Erasmus), 86, 92
Encomion moriae (Erasmus), 70
Engels, Friedrich, 176, 344*n*16
Enlightenment, 106, 110–15. *See also* Catholic Enlightenment; Josephism and Josephist Enlightenment
Enzyklopädie der philosophischen Wissenschaften im Grundrisse (Hegel), 185, 220
epistemology, 188–92
Epokha Prosveshcheniia v cheshskikh zemliakh: Ideologiia, natsional'noe samosoznanie, kul'tura (Myl'nikov), 4
Erasmus, Desiderius: on Bohemian intellectual life, 44; and civil discourse, 256*n*49; and "critical Catholics," 35; Gazzaniga on, 139; and German language, 302*n*32; and Greek patristics, 260*n*89; and humanist Catholicism, 37; and "Hussite" solution, 36; influence of, 28; liberalism of, 34; translations of, 70

Erbauungsreden (Bolzano), 156–57, 161
Erben, Karel J., 72, 92, 95–96
Erdmann, Johann E., 199–200, 220
Erkenntnis (journal), 240
Essai sur la philosophie de Hegel (Willm), 189
"essentialism," 135–38, 163, 209
Eusebius of Caesarea, 42, 93
Exner, Franz, 245: anti-Hegelianism of, 179, 199, 212; and Bolzano, 158, 217–18, 222–24, 232; and German idealism, 134, 220–22; and Havlíček, 218; and Hegel, 220–22, 223; and Herbart, 218–19, 222; influence of, 17, 213; and liberal Catholicism, 215, 217–20; in Lněničková's writing, 14; and Palacký, 218; and Rembold, 151, 218
Eybel, Josef Valentin, 50, 57
Ezopovy básně (Kramerius), 93

Faber, Johann, 76
Facilis, Jan, 264*n*125
Febronianism, 4, 389
Febronius, Justus. *See* Hontheim, Johann N. von
Fechner, Gustav T., 239
Feder, Johann Georg, 147
Ferdinand I, 34, 36, 60, 68
Ferdinand II, 384
Ferjenčík, Samuel, 118
Ferus, Johann, 85
Fesl, Michael J., 14, 276*n*102: and Bolzano, 82, 156, 217, 223, 225; and ecclesiology, 228; influence of, 286*n*123; and language usage, 112, 113; persecution of, 216
Feuerbach, Ludwig, 161
Fiala, Jan, 13, 269*n*5
Fichte, Immanuel H., 225
Fichte, Johann: and Bolzano, 161, 165–68, 334*n*56; and German nationalism, 130, 203; and Herbart, 219; and Herder, 109; "ich/nicht ich" dichotomy of, 152; and idealism,

Fichte, Johann (*continued*) 149; and national self-consciousness, 322*n*86; and Palacký, 153; his *Reden an die deutsche Nation*, 109, 203; as romanticist, 114. *See also* German idealism
Fidrmuc, J., 213
Fiebrich, Vinzenz, 217, 365*n*16
Fisher, John, 34, 260*n*89
Flavia Jozefa o válce židovské knihy sedmery (Josephus), 92–93, 97
Fonseca, Pedro da, 136, 137, 317*n*42
Fortlage, Carl, 185
Four Articles of Prague of 1419, 24–25, 37
Fraenkel, Peter, 36
Frank, Philipp, 176, 236
Franke, August Hermann, 143
Frantz, Ignác, 137
Frederick William III, 321*n*76
freedom and consensus, 24–26, 68–69
Frege, Gottlob, 169
Frič, Josef V., 197, 202
Fries, Jakob F., 150, 152, 182, 327*n*140
Fuchs, Rudolf, 130

Gabler, Vilém, 154, 177, 195, 213, 367*n*33
Gaj, Ljudevit, 119
Garve, Christian, 150, 182
Gazzaniga, Pietro Maria, 138–39, 140, 141, 156, 223; and Bolzano, 141, 146; and Locke, 139
Gelenius, Sigismund, 89
Gellner, Ernest, 47
general seminaries, 60, 276*n*91
Genersich, Johann, 118
George of Poděbrady, 23, 38, 70, 74, 76, 100
Gerbert, Martin, 140
German idealism, 134–54; and Bolzano, 161–68; and Dobrovský, 149; "essentialism" of second or Suárezian scholasticism, 135–38; existence over essence, 135–41; and Exner, 134, 220–22; and Herbart, 226; and Hurban, 204; and Jungmann, 151; and Palacký, 153; prestige of, 175–77; and progressivism, 178–79; and realism of Catholic Enlightenment, 138–41; as secularized Lutheran eschatology, 141–44, 236n45; and Seibt, Catholic Enlightenment, and anti-idealism, 144–48; and Staël-Holstein, 153

Germans and Germany: and anti-Hegelianism, 212–14; German language, 111–13, 148, 302*n*32; German model, 106, 116–17; German spirit, 174; and Lutheran universities, 198–200; nationalism of, 107, 127–30; and Utraquism, 32, 259*n*75. *See also* German idealism
Gerometta, Eugen, 204
Geschichte der Böhmen (Pelcl), 79
Geschichte der böhmischen Sprache und Literatur (Dobrovský), 85, 100
Geschichte des Königreichs Böheim (J. H. Wolf), 54–55, 81, 99
Gillies, Alexander, 108
Gilson, Étienne, 136, 137, 314*n*13
Glaser, Rudolf, 129
glossary of terms, 389–91
Golden Age, 1, 7, 16–17, 68, 104–5, 247*n*1
Gołuchowski, Józef, 210
Göttinger gelehrten Anzeigen (journal), 147
Gottwald, Klement, 4, 248*n*18
Grammatica linguae Bohemicae (Pól), 87
"Greats of Vienna," 50, 58
Green, Thomas H., 233
Gregory of Valencia, 136
Grundlegung einer Synonymik (Reinhold), 169
Grundlehren der Religion (Sailer), 141
Grundriss der ersten Logik (Bardili), 182
Grundriss der Psychologie, als Einleitung in die Philosophie (Lichtenfels), 151

Grundriss der Psychologie für Vorlesungen (Erdmann), 199
Grundsätze der böhmischen Grammatik (Pelcl), 291*n*53
Grünwald, Vendelín, 207
Günther, Anton, 193, 222
Gutenberg, Johannes, 47
Gwagnin, Aleksander, 92, 98, 122

Hádání pravdy a lži (Tovačovský), 97
Hájek, Tadeáš, 44
Hájek of Libočany, Václav, 66, 76, 85, 88, 91, 92
Haliczanin (journal), 209
Haller, Rudolf, 235
Hamann, Johann G., 108
Handbuch der Philosophie und der philosophischen Literatur (Krug), 170
Hanka, Václav, 87
Hanuš, Ignác J., 197, 208, 212, 213, 245
Hartmann, Eduard von, 238
Hasištenjnský of Lobkovice, Bohuslav, 91
Haubelt, Josef, 2, 3, 12, 13, 178, 247*n*2, 272*n*32
Havlíček Borovský, Karel, 127; and anti-Hegelianism, 194–95; on Bolzano, 155, 218; and common sense, 177; and Czech national awakening, 110; and ecclesiology, 228, 229; and Exner, 218; and German nationalism, 127, 128; and Herder, 126; and Macura, 8, 15; and philosophy, 213; and plebeianism, 72–73; on respect for German philosophy, 353*n*353; and Slavdom, 122, 123
Hay, Jan Leopold, 50, 59, 62, 80, 88
Hayes, Carleton, 114–15
Hegel, Georg, 174–93; and Boehme, 143; and Bolzano, 160, 183–94, 210, 212–13, 222, 231; Carnap on, 235; and claim of progressivism, 177–79; and comments in notebooks, 184–86; and communitarianism, 332*n*38; and critique in Bolzano's *The Theory of Knowledge,* 186–88; early encounters with, 181–83; essays on aesthetics, epistemology, and history, 188–92; and Exner, 220–22, 223; final assessment of, 192–93; and German history, 321*n*77; on Index of Prohibited Books, 364*n*5; influence of, 175–81, 229; and Lutheranism, 142–43, 321*n*76; and metaphysical monism, 10, 14, 107; and national self-consciousness, 322*n*86; and ontic cultural pluralism, 30; and Poland, 208–10; and politics, 184; and prestige, 175–77; and puzzle of Catholic Enlightenment, 179–81; and Russia, 211; and second or Suárezian scholasticism, 136–37; and slavery, 221; and Slovak factor, 181; and Wolff, 137. *See also* anti-Hegelianism
Hegelianism. *See* anti-Hegelianism; Hegel, Georg
Heidegger, Martin, 144
Heinke, Franz J., 58
Hek, František V., 86, 90
Helfert, Augustin, 61, 121
Henning, Justus, 270*n*13
Henry IV (France), 60
Henry VIII (England), 34
Herbart, Johann: and anti-Hegelianism, 195, 367*n*33; anti-Kantian orientation of, 150, 151, 170; and Bolzano, 224–27, 229; and Exner, 218–19, 222; and Durdík, 238–39; and Hyna, 151; influence of, 243; in Prague, 237–39; and progressivism, 178–79; and Rembold, 218, 226
Herberstein, Johann Karl, 58
Herder, Johann Gottfried, 106–33; and Boehme, 109; and Bolzano, 124–25, 173; his *Briefe zur Beförderung der Humanität,* 121, 125, 130; and Enlightenment, 106, 110–15; and German model, 106, 116–17; and German nationalism, 107, 127–30, 173; idealism of, 145–46; his *Ideen zur Philosophie der Geschichte der Menschheit,* 118, 121, 123; influence

Herder, Johann Gottfried (*continued*) of, 109–17, 120–33; manipulative use of his ideas by the awakeners, 121, 129–30; metaphysical monism of, 14; ontic cultural pluralism of, 30; philosophy of history of, 10; proto-romanticism and idealism of, 107–9; reason vs. emotion, 130–33; and religious question, 115–16; and Slavs, 201, 202; and Slovak question, 109–10, 198; and Slovaks' romantic idealism, 106, 117–20; and *Vormärz* period, 322*n*85

Hermes, Georg, 364*n*5

Herzen, Alexander, 211

Heyrenbach, Joseph Benedikt, 121

Hieronymi ordinis Praedicatorum episcopi Aemoniensis de D. Thomae Aquinatis doctrina et scriptis libri duo (Dominicans of Olomouc), 139

Histoire de la naissance, progrès et décadence de l'herésie de ce siècle (Remond), 75

Historia Bohmenica (Piccolomini), 76, 97

Historia o jednom sedlském pacholk u a poběhlém židu (Mouřenín), 93–94

Historical View of the Slavic Language in Its Various Dialects (Robinson), 128

Historie církevní (Eusebius), 42

Historie o císaři Karlovi IV (Lupáč), 92, 98

Historijí dvanácte o bratru Janu Palečkovi, 93

Hlasatel český (newspaper), 11, 82, 90

Hobbes, Thomas, 154

Hobsbawm, Eric J., 47

Hodža, Michal M., 119, 199, 205–7; and German idealism, 206; and Herder, 119

Hody křesťanské (Cykáda), 38, 42, 263*n*115

Hoene-Wroński, Józef Maria, 360*n*126

Hohenwart, Sigismund Anton von, 216

Holeton, David R., 252n2, 254n29, 264n116, 266n144

Hontheim, Johann N. von, 50, 61. *See also* Febronianism

Hook, Sidney, 144, 175–76

Hooker, Richard, 28, 138, 256*n*44, 256*n*47, 259*n*79; as an Anglican Thomist, 138, 317n35

Hortensius Zahrádka, Jan, 44

Hosius, Matouš, 86, 92, 98, 122

Hostinský, Otakar, 239, 246

Hroboň, Samo B., 202

Hroch, Miroslav, 5–10, 15, 106, 249*n*42

Hromada (proposed literary society), 88

Hrubý of Jelení, Řehoř, 44

Hrubý of Jelení, Zikmund, 267*n*155

Huerda, Martin, 54, 273*n*44

Humboldt, Wilhelm, 108, 119, 300*n*11

Hume, David, 125, 145, 146, 151, 154

Hungarians. *See* Magyars

Hurban, Jozef M., 119, 131, 199, 207–8; and Hegel, 203–5; and Herder, 118

Hurdálek, Josef F., 62, 80, 82, 216, 275*n*71

Hus, Jan: in Bělina's writing, 15; and bibliographic record, 84; and Bohemian history, 99–100; and burning of heretics, 26; Bydžovský's translations of, 32; censorship of writing of, 101; and Enlightenment liberalism, 13; Herder on, 121, 130; and Hussite Church, 19–20; intellectual openness of, 24, 25; and Luther, 75–76; and Macura, 8; moderation of, 75; rehabilitation of, 5, 6, 77–82, 248*n*21; and religious tolerance, 69; and Utraquist Church, 18, 19, 22–23; veneration of, 31; and vernacular language, 42; in *Výbor z literatury české,* 96; and Zitte, 4, 15, 79–80, 101, 285*n*109

Husitského v Čechách kacířství počátku zrůstu, a pádu vejtah (Remond), 75

Husserl, Edmund, 233, 237
Hussite Church and Hussitism, as a misnomer, 19–20, 55, 252*n*6. *See* Utraquist Church and Utraquism
Hylton, Peter, 241
hymns, religious, 80, 286*n*112
Hyna, Ferdinand, 151–52, 215, 387; and Herbart, 151

idealism: anti-idealism, 144–48; and Herder, 107–9, 117–20; and Krug, 170–71; metaphysical, 10, 161–68; post-Kantian, 165–68. *See also* German idealism; metaphysics and metaphysical idealism
Ideen zu einer Philosophie der Natur (Schelling), 109
Index Bohemicorum Librorum Prohibitorum (Koniáš), 85
Index of Prohibited Books, 52, 54, 55, 64, 83, 86, 364*n*5
An Inquiry into the Principle and Causes of the Wealth of Nations (Smith), 147
Institutiones Logicae et Metaphysicae (Feder), 147

Jablonský, Boleslav, 157
Jacobi, Friedrich H., 124, 218
Jäger, Josef N., 182
Jakobson, Roman, 240
Jakoubek of Stříbro, 32, 254*n*29, 255*n*35
James, William, 176
Jana Mandyvilly, znamenitého rytíře cesty po světě (Kramerius), 93
Jan Hus (Tyl), 101
Jan of Německý Brod, 27
Jansenism, 4, 50, 115, 276*n*98
Jan the Elder of Valdštejn, 40
Jefferson, Thomas, 271*n*23
Jeník of Bratřice, Jan: and Bohemian history, 98, 100; and Bohemian literature, 67; and Bolzano, 157; on constitutionalism, 102; and Enlightenment, 64; and Herder, 124; on Hus, 297*n*143; on Jesuits, 57; and liberal Catholicism, 14, 51, 82; and plebeianism, 281*n*53; and publication programs, 86; and religious tolerance, 69
Jenisch, Bernhardt, 123
Jerome of Prague, 77, 84, 96
Jesuits: and Counter-Reformation, 14, 15–16, 54–55, 57; dissolution of, 49, 63; Enlightenment realism versus Jesuit essentialism, 138–40; intolerance of, 74; and nobles, 39; and purgatory, preaching on, 56; and Wolff, 137, 209. *See also* second or Suárezian scholasticism; Suárez, Francisco
Jewel, John, 256*n*44
Jewish War (Josephus), 92, 97
Jews, 59–60
Jirásek, Josef, 202
Joachim of Fiore, 143
Johann Žižka, chevalier von Trocznow (Steinsberg), 99
Joseph II: and cultural revolution, 50, 52–53; and Reform Catholicism, 49; reforms of, 15, 61, 77, 110, 228; and religious tolerance, 60, 68–69
Josephism and Josephist Enlightenment, 4, 10, 16, 49–50, 69, 149, 251*n*90. *See also* Catholic Enlightenment; Joseph II
Josephus, Flavius, 92, 97
Judge of Cheb, 24–25, 27
Jungmann, Josef: and bibliographic record, 84; and Bolzano, 151; and Counter-Reformation, 57; and cultural universalism, 71; and Czech national awakening, 110; and Enlightenment, 64, 113–14; and Hegel, 181–82, 213; and Herder, 123; his *Historie literatury české*, 85, 95; on Hus, 82; and language, 7, 11, 67, 71, 90, 111, 282*n*63, 292*n*62; in Lněničková's writing, 15; and Macura, 8; and plebeianism, 72; and textbooks, 95; and Western liberal tradition, 127

Kabátník, Martin, 122
Kafka, Franz, 239
Kaizl, Josef, 111
Kalendář historický (Veleslavín), 97–98
Kalinčiak, Jan, 205
Kalousek, Josef, 29, 95
Kamarýt, Josef V., 127
Kampelík, František Cyril, 98
Kant, Immanuel: and Bolzano, 159, 161–65, 173, 332*n*36, 334*n*56, 334*n*67, 336*n*92, 371*n*108; Brentano on, 232; "critical" philosophy of, 161–65; and German idealism, 137, 149–51, 315*n*25; and Herbart, 219; and Herder, 109, 173; on Index of Prohibited Books, 364*n*5; his *Kritik der reinen Vernunft*, 147, 161, 164; and Krug, 170, 171; and Lutheranism, 142; Palacký on, 153–54, 328*n*165; post-Kantian idealism, 165–68; his *Die Religion innerhalb der Grenzen der blossen Vernunft*, 161; and Seibt, 173
Karel the Elder of Žerotín, 40–41, 70, 265*n*130
Kaše, Jiří, 12–13
Katholisches Lehrund Gebetbuch (Seibt), 148
Kaufmann, Walter, 142
Kaukal, Josef, 75
Kaunitz, Wenzl A., 50, 58, 68
"Kdož jste Boží bojovníci" (Taborites' battle hymn), 74
Kellner-Hostinský, Petr Záboj, 199
Kennan, George, 123, 309*n*115
Kenny, Anthony, 174
Kepler, Johannes, 44, 45
Khomiakov, Aleksei S., 203
Kiesewetter, Johann G., 182
Kindermann, Ferdinand, 113, 325*n*120
Kireevskii, Ivan, 203, 211
Kisch, Egon Erwin, 130
Klácel, František M., 128, 181, 183, 194, 197, 208
Klar, Aloys, 149, 245
Klatovský, Šimon Ennius, 35

Klevetník (Rvačovský), 93
Klicpera, Václav V., 92, 94
Klueting, Harm, 270*n*13
Klugheitslehre, praktisch abgehandelt, in akademischen Vorlesungen (Seibt), 146–47
Kniha o napravení padlého (Chrysostom), 91–92, 97
Kniha Tovačovská (Tovačovský), 104
Knihy památné o nepokojných letech (Sixt), 97
Knoll, Josef Linhart, 129, 218
Kočí, Josef, 2–3
Kocín of Kocinét, Jan, 66, 88, 93, 98
Kohn, Hans, 10, 106, 249*n*43
Kolár, Jaroslav, 43–44
Koldín, Pavel Kristián, 97
Kollár, Jan: and Czech national awakening, 115; and German idealism, 357*n*68; and German nationalism, 127–28, 130–31; and Herder, 118–19, 130, 306*n*81; in Lněničková's writing, 15; and Macura, 7–8; Slavism of, 120, 123, 307*n*95; and Slovaks, 109–10, 125, 198–99; his *Ueber die literarische Wechselseitigkeit*, 119
Kolof, Wawrzyniec Mitzlof de, 209
Komenský, Jan Amos, 8, 66, 88, 305*n*63: and Herder, 120–21; his *Labyrint světa*, 85; his secularized eschatology, 116
Konáč of Hodiškov, Mikuláš, 97
Koniáš, Antonín, 56, 85, 273*n*50
Kopp, Johann, 86
Koppmann, Adolph, 161
Kořalka, Jiří, 153
Koranda the Younger, Václav, 32, 42, 96
Kornelius of Všehrdy, Viktorin, 91, 92, 97, 102, 103
Kottwitz, Hans E., 321*n*76
Kotzebue, August, 118
Koubek, Jan P., 94, 127, 150
Král, Josef, 177, 246
Královédvorský manuscript, 101
Krameriovy noviny (Kramerius), 67, 89

Kramerius, Václav Matěj: and Counter-Reformation, 14, 51, 57; and Enlightenment, 64; and language, 67, 89, 113; and publication programs, 86–87; and religious reform, 61; and reprinting of classics, 87, 92, 93; translations by, 88; view of Germans, 131; and Žižka biography, 81
Krátké naučení mladému hospodáři (Kramerius), 93
Kraus, Arnošt, 180
Kraus, Oskar, 239, 240, 241, 246
Krbec, J.E., 93
Krejčí, František V., 110, 246
Kremer, Józef, 210, 360*n*127
Kresl of Qualtenberg, Franz K., 51
Křišťan of Prachatice, 77
Kristián, Pavel, 41, 97
Kritik der theoretischen Philosophie (Schulze), 151
Krofta, Kamil, 29, 43, 257*n*56, 268*n*1
Krok (journal), 71
Kronika Česká (Bílejovský), 32, 79; renamed *Kronika Církevní* in 1816 ed., 91
Kronika Česká (Hájek), 76, 92
Kronika Česká (Pulkava), 92
Kronika Moskevská (Gwagnin), 92, 98, 122
Kronika o Žižkovi (Kuthen), 97
Kronika Pražská (Bartoš Písař), 92, 97
Kroniky dvě o založení země české (Veleslavín), 97
Krug, Willhelm T., 150–51, 154, 168, 170–71, 182, 326*n*135, 340*n*151
Kučera, Jan P., 12–13
Kurzgefasste böhmische böhmisches Nationallexikon (K.I. Thám), 52, 95
Kurzgefasste böhmische Sprachlehre (K.I. Thám), 52, 55, 70
Kurzgefasste Geschichte der Böhmen (Pelcl), 99
Kuthen, Martin, 92, 97
Kutná Hora. *See* Peace of Kutná Hora
Kutnar, František, 12–13

Kuzmany, Karol, 197
Květy (journal), 196, 207

Lagarde, Paul de, 175
Lamanskii, Vladimir I., 202
Lange, Friedrich A., 175
Langer, Josef Jaroslav, 124
language. *See* Czech language; Germans and Germany
late scholasticism. *See* second or Suárezian scholasticism
Launer, Štefan, 199, 200–201
Lauterbeck, Georg, 27, 41
Lebeda, Hilibert, 139, 317*n*42
Leben, Lehre, Wandel und Tod des im J. 1415 lebendig verbrannten Johann Hus (J. H. Wolf), 78
Lebensbeschreibung des Magisters Johannes Huss von Hussinecz (Zitte), 69
Lebensgeschichte des römischen und böhmischen Königs Wenzeslaus (Pelcl), 99
legal history, 101–4
Lehrbuch der Logik und Metaphysik (Feder), 147
Lehrbuch zur Einleitung in die Philosophie (Herbart), 224
Lehrbuch zur Psychologie (Herbart), 225
Leibniz, Gottfried Wilhelm, 59, 126, 165, 172
Lemberg, Eugen, 108, 155, 299*n*6
Lenin, Vladimir, 176, 232, 344*n*17
Leninism. *See* Marxism-Leninism
Leonhard of Aretin, 96
Lessing, Gotthold Ephraim, 152
Letopisové Trojanští (Kramerius), 67, 93, 131
Letter of Majesty of July 9, 1609, 22, 23, 27, 69
Letters to His Son (Chesterfield), 147
Lexicon symphonum (Gelenius), 89
liberal Catholicism, 235–36: and Bolzano, 158–61; and Dobrovský, 61–62; and Exner, 219–20; Havlíček,

liberal Catholicism (*continued*)
228; Nahlovský, 228–29; and Seibt, 147–48
liberalism: of Bohemian Reformation, 230; of Bolzano's Catholicism, 82, 115, 158–61, 331*n*27; and Catholic Enlightenment, 68–69, 106; and Dobrovský, 61–62, 68, 276*n*102; of Golden Age, 16–17; and Hus, 13; and tolerance, 23–30; of Utraquism, 13, 23–30, 68, 104, 229; in Western thought, 127, 133. *See also* liberal thought and authoritarian Church
liberal thought and authoritarian Church, 215–30; Bolzano and Exner, 222–23; Bolzano and Herbart, 224–27; Exner and German idealism, 220–22; Exner and liberal Catholicism, 217–20; liberal Catholicism's demise in ecclesiology, 227–29; new Counter-Reformation, 216–17; religious void in Bohemia, 229–30
Libsteinský of Kolovraty, Antonín, 281*n*49
Lichard, Daniel, 205
Lichtenfels, Johann Peithner von, 151; 213, 215, 245; and Herbart, 151
Lidové zdroje národního obrození (Robek), 2
Linda, Josef, 87, 157
Lindner, Gustav A., 239, 246
List proti Pikartóm (Rokycana), 96
Listy z dávnověkosti (Herder), 124
Lněničková, Jitka, 12, 13–15, 177, 250*nn*68–69
Locke, John, 135, 138, 139, 154, 156; and Aquinas, 316n34; and Bolzano, 171–72; and Dobrovský, 149; and Hooker, 317n35; and Palacký, 154
Logical Investigations (Husserl), 233
Logische Vorbegriffe (Bolzano), 167
Lomnický of Budeč, Šimon, 93
Louis XIV, 60
"Lučatínská Víla" (Kuzmany), 197

Die Lücken des Hegelschen Systems der Philosophie (Fortlage), 185
Ludwig, Johann Peter von, 121
Lupáč, Martin, 31
Lupáč of Hlaváčov, Prokop, 92, 98
Luther, Martin: anti-Aristotelian stance of, 107; Bydžovský on, 27–28; and ecclesiastical power, 40; and German idealism, 141–42; and Hus, 75–76; and observance of "the law of God," 29–30; opposition to teachings in Prague, 38; solafideism of, 29; and Utraquism, 23
Lutheranism: and Bohemian Confession, 22; and Bohemian nobles, 21; and Calvinism, 206–7; and confessionalization, 30; and German idealism, 141–44; and German universities, 198–200; and Hegel, 142–43, 321*n*76; population size of, 262*n*107; Slovak, 117, 120, 181, 198, 201; and Unity of Brethren, 16
Lvovský, Cyprian, 44

MacCullough, Diarmaid, 257*n*52
Macek, Josef, 259*n*78
Mach, Ernst, 232, 236, 237, 246
Mácha, Karel Hynek, 92, 177, 197, 307*n*95
Machovec, Milan, 176
Macura, Vladimír, 5–10, 11, 15
Madison, James, 271*n*23
Magyars, 130–31, 206–7
Mährischer Magazin (journal), 104
Maimon, Salomon, 164
Marek, Antonín, 150, 181–82, 215, 279*n*27, 326*n*136, 387; and Hegel, 182
Maria Theresa, 50, 68, 110, 138–39, 145, 148, 271*n*26
Maritain, Jacques, 236
Marivaux, Pierre Carlet de Chamblain de, 147
Martini, Karl Anton, 50
Martin of Mělník, 264*n*122

Martin V, 74
Marty, Anton, 233, 237, 240, 246
Marxism-Leninism: and baroque culture, 11; and Bělina, 16; and German idealism, 176; and Hegel, 178, 198, 231, 373n4; and Hroch, 9, 10; literature of period, 1–5; and Schamschula, 6
Masaryk, Tomáš G., 246: on Bohemian Reformation, 6, 17, 230, 258n60; and Brentano, 239–40; and "Czech positivism," 177; and "Czech question," 29; and Enlightenment, 114; and Herder, 108, 115, 116, 131, 304n60; on Kant, 142; and language, 302n40; and plebeianism, 73; on Russians in German universities, 211; and Slovak question, 109, 120
Masopust (Rvačovský), 38, 93, 98
Matěj of Janov, 31, 80
Matice česká (academic publisher), 14, 129, 151
Matouš of Chlumčany, 103
Maximilian II, 21–22, 27, 34, 39, 68–69, 264n122, 269n8
Mayr, Beda, 141, 156
megalomania, 35–37
Meinong, Alexius, 233, 240
Meissner, August G., 113, 127, 156, 245
Meistersänger, 65
Melanchton, Philipp, 28, 44
Mělnický, Martin, 257n56
Meluzína (Klicpera), 94
"The Merits of the Czech Language" (Písecký), 94
Merkle, Sebastian, 136, 314n10
Městské lidové zdroje národního obrození (Robek), 2
metaphysical monism, 174–75, 243
metaphysics and metaphysical idealism, 10, 14, 107, 161–68, 234–35, 375n30
Metaphysik (Baumgarten), 161
Michelet, Karl Ludwig, 220
Mickiewicz, Adam, 197, 206

Míka, Johann Marian, 156
Mikuláš of Pelhřimov, 77, 84
Milíč of Kroměříž, Jan, 31, 80
Mill, John S., 249n42, 378n63
Milton, John, 292n62
Mirabeau, Honoré de, 68
Miscellaneen der Böhmischen und Mährischen Litteratur (Procházka), 84, 91
Mochnacki, Maurycy, 210
Molina, Luis de, 317n42
monism, cultural, 174–75, 243. *See also* cultural universalism; tolerance, universalism, and plebeianism
Monluc, Jean de, 35
Monse, Joseph Vratislav E. von, 249n29
Montagu, Richard, 256n44
Montesquieu, Charles-Louis de, 145, 146
Moore, George E., 233–34, 327n140
More, Thomas, 34, 35, 37, 147, 260n89
Morris, Charles W., 240, 241
Moscow Chronicle (Hosius), 86
Mouřenín, Tobiáš, 93
Mukařovský, Jan, 240
Müller, Ignaz, 50
Muratori, Lodovico Antonio, 50, 60, 61, 156, 270n15
Myl'nikov, Aleksandr S., 3–5, 108

Nagel, Ernst, 241
Náhlovský, František, 160, 217–18, 228–29
Nahlowsky, Josef W., 219, 245
Národní noviny (newspaper), 228
Naše národní obrození (Kočí), 2
national awakening. *See* Czech national awakening and Bohemian Reformation; Czech national awakening as Renaissance
nationalism: ethnic, 17; German, 107, 127–30; Kohn's theories of, 10, 106; linguistic, 11–12, 15, 132; as nineteenth-century "invention," 47
Nausea, Friedrich, 35

Nazis, 129, 130, 241
Nebeský, Václav B.: and anti-Hegelianism, 195–96, 207–8, 212; and Exner, 218; and Herder, 126; and idealism, 152, 213; liberalism of, 215
"Něco o filosofii" (Gabler), 195
Nejedlý, Jan, 82, 90, 94
Nejedlý, Zdeněk, 3, 13, 176, 178
Nejstarší listiny české (collection of legal documents), 103
Nelson, Leonard, 327*n*140
Němeček, František X., 245; and bibliographic record, 84; on Bohemian culture, 65–66; and Counter-Reformation, 56–57; and German idealism, 137, 150; and Josephism, 149; and language preservation, 70; on Seibt, 145; on Taborite violence, 283*n*67; on Utraquists, 80
Neo-Thomists, French, 237; and the Vienna Circle, 235–36. See also Duhem, Pierre M. M.; Vouillemin, Charles Ernest
Neruda, Jan, 229
Neue Literatur (journal), 147
Neuestes ausführliches und vollständiges deutsch-böhmisches synonymisch-phraseologisches Nationallexikon oder Wörterbuch (K.I. Thám), 94
Neurath, Otto, 144, 227, 231, 236, 376*n*43
Nicol, Pierre, 60
Nietzsche, Friedrich: Apollonian and Dionysian spirit, 133; and Counter-Reformation, 316*n*28; and Lutheranism, 144
nobles and nobility, 39–40, 45–46, 72–73
Novák, Arne, 43, 155
Nožička, Blažej, 27

Obrana jazyka českého (K.I. Thám), 70, 72
Obrozenské vlastenectví a nacionalismus, Příspěvek k národnímu společenskému obsahu češství doby obrozenské (Kutnar), 12–13
Ockham, William of, 236
Od Dobnera k Dobrovskému (Slavík), 3, 180
"Ode on Jan Žižka of Trocnov" (Puchmajer), 81
Oetenger, Friedrich C., 143
Okey, Robin, 108
Ondřej of Dubá, 103
O právách, o soudech i o deskách země české knihy devatery (Kornelius), 91
O připravení k smrti (Erasmus), 86, 92
O'Regan, Cyril, 143
Origins of the Czech National Renascence (Agnew), 10, 281*n*47
Ormis, Samuel, 199
O sněmu kutnohorském po smrti krále Jiřího, 96
O spravedlnosti a právu (Koldín), 97
Ost und West (journal), 195
Otto, Rudolf, 327*n*140
Outline of the First Logic; Purged of the Errors of Logicians in General, and Kantian Ones in Particular (Bardili), 170

Pačuda, Matauš, 45
Palacký, František: and Blair, 125; and Bohemian history, 100; on Bohemian literature, 67; and Bolzano, 158, 217; and Counter-Reformation, 57; and cultural universalism, 71; and Exner, 218; and German idealism, 153–54, 328*n*158; and Hegelianism, 176, 196–97, 207; and Herder, 125–26; his *History of the Czech Nation*, 126; on Krug, 151; and language, 71, 90, 111; and liberalism, 127; and Macura, 8; and religious tolerance, 69; and Robertson, 125; and Scottish Enlightenment, 125; and textbooks, 95; view of Germans, 131
Palkovič, Jiří, 118

Pařízek, Alexius, 77
parliamentarianism, 102, 298*n*157
Pascal, Blaise, 149
Pastor Bonus (van Opastraet), 61
Patent of Religious Toleration for the Hereditary Lands of the Habsburg Monarchy, 60
Patočka, Jan, 246; and Enlightenment, 13, 114; and German model, 116–17; Hegelianism of, 177; and Herder, 108, 129, 131, 132
Pavlíková, Marie, 157
Payne, Peter, 76–77
Peace of Kutná Hora (1485), 26–27, 38, 69
Pekař, Josef, 10–11, 13, 17, 43, 258*n*60, 259*n*77, 268*n*1
Pelcl, František M.: and bibliographic record, 84; and Bohemian history and culture, 53, 65–66, 99, 100; and Counter-Reformation, 51, 56; and Czech literature, 83; and historical rights of Bohemian state, 102; and Josephism, 14, 149; and language, 6, 11, 70, 88, 89, 291*n*53; and Marxism, 16; as national awakener, 64; and publication programs, 86; and Reidinger, 140; and religious tolerance, 68; and secularized eschatology, 116; on Taborite radicalism, 74; and textbooks, 94; on Utraquism, 77, 79, 81, 285*n*106
Pereira, Benito, 136, 137
Petr of Chelčice, 96
Petráň, Josef, 2–3
Pflanzpastor, Benedikt A., 225
Phänomenologie des Geistes (Hegel), 185, 200
Philosophie der Geschichte (Hegel), 200, 202, 207
Philosophie des Geistes (Hegel), 202
Philosophie des Rechts (Hegel), 182, 188, 189
philosophy professors at Charles University (Universitas Carolina), 245–46

Philosophy of Right. See *Philosophie des Rechts* (Hegel)
Piccolomini, Aeneas Sylvius, 76, 97
Pietism, 117, 143, 144, 315*n*24
Písecký, Václav, 94, 259*n*69
Pišely, Antonín, 93
Pius II, 20, 31
Pius IV, 30
Pius V, 69
Pius VI, 69
Pius VII, 216
Pius IX, 227
Plato, 136, 163
plebeianism, 37–40, 45–46, 68, 71–73, 104, 281*n*47. See also tolerance, universalism, and plebeianism
Plekhanov, Georgii V., 211
Počátky českého národního obrození: Společnost a kultura v 70. až 90. letech 18. století (Petráň), 3
Pogodin, Mikhail P., 203
Pól, Jan V., 87–88
Poland, Hegelianism in, 208–12
Pole, Reginald, 35, 261*n*90
Polon, Valentin, 258*n*63
Popp, Iganz, 75–76, 77
Popper, Karl, 234
Poselstvie krále Jiřího do Říma k papeži (Koranda), 96
Praelectiones theologicae (Gazzaniga), 139, 141, 223
Prager Gelehrte Nachrichten, 53
Prague, legacy of anti-Hegelianism in, 237–42
Prague Linguistic Circle, 240
Práva a zřízení zemská královstí českého (law code of Bohemia), 104
Práva městská (Brikcí), 102, 104
Práva městská království českého (Koldín), 97
Právník (journal), 103
Pražák, Albert, 202, 304*n*61
predestination, 264*n*117, 317*n*42
Prefát of Vlkanov, Oldřich, 86, 93
"Pre-White Mountain Era," 105, 299*n*174

Příbram, Jan, 32, 76–77, 96, 255*n*35
Priestly, Joseph, 59, 159
priests and clergy, 19, 26, 29, 252*n*4
Příhody Václava Vratislava z Mitrovic (Pelcl), 83, 93
Příhonský, František, 245; and anti-Hegelianism, 213; and Bolzano, 156, 165, 189, 217, 223; and ecclesiology, 229; and liberal thought, 215
Příkladné řeči a užitečná naučení vybraná z knih hlubokých mudrců (Češka), 86
Procházka, František Faustin: and bibliographic record, 84, 85; on Bohemian scholars and writers, 65; and Counter-Reformation, 54; and language, 6, 87; and national awakening, 64; and publication programs, 86; and reprinting of classics, 91, 92; and secularized eschatology, 116; on Seibt, 145, 149; Slavík on, 4; on Taborites, 74, 76–77
progressivism, 177–79
prohibited books index. *See* Index of Prohibited Books
Prokop Holý, 100
Prokop of Plzeň, 96
Prolegomena zur Historiosophie (Cieszkowski), 210
Proxen of Sudety, Šimon, 44
"Prvot'ini vedi slovanskej" (P.Z.H.), 205
Psychische Anthropologie (Schulze), 151
Psychologie als Wissenschaft (Herbart), 224
Die Psychologie der Hegel'schen Schule (Exner), 199, 220
Pubička, František, 14, 51, 76, 77, 99
publication programs, 85–87
Puchmajer, Antonín J., 62, 74, 81, 90
Pulkava of Radenín, Příbík, 92
Puteo, Antonio, 266*n*145
Pynsent, Robert, 53, 118, 122

Quakers, 333*n*41
Quine, Willard V., 231, 234, 240, 241, 379*n*77

Rada všelikých zvířat, 93
Řád práva zemského (articles on court procedures), 103
Rak, Jiří, 180
Rautenstrauch, Franz S.: and asceticism, 60–61; and Bolzano, 158, 159; and cultural revolution, 50–51, 52; and Dobrovský, 62, 270*n*18; and general seminaries, 60; and German idealism, 149; and pastoral care, 59; and persecution of Bohemian dissidents, 77; and Seibt, 147; and theological education, 140–41; and Utraquist Reformation, 80
realism: and Aquinas, 141–42; of Catholic Enlightenment, 138–41; empirical, 168–72; Exner's teaching of, 219; and metaphysical idealism, 319*n*63; rational realism, 170
reenactment, theory of, 48
Reform Catholicism, 49, 69, 135, 156, 179–81, 230. *See also* liberal Catholicism
Reichenbach, Hans, 241, 379*n*82, 380*n*84
Reid, Thomas, 169, 171, 172
Reidinger, Qualbert (Jan), 139, 140; his *Hieronymi Vielmii*, 140
Reinhold, Ernst, 172, 339*n*139
Reinhold, Karl L., 150, 156, 168–69, 170, 182
Religionswissenschafterteidigung der natürlichen, christlichen und katholischen Religion nach dem Bedürfnisse unserer Zeit (Mayr), 141
Rembold, Leopold, 151, 218, 226
Remond, Florimond de, 75
Renaissance. *See* Czech national awakening as Renaissance
Renewed Land Ordinance of 1627, 102
Respublica Boiema (Stránský), 102, 103
Rieger, František L., 128
Riegger, Josef A., 50
Riegger, Paul J., 50
The Rise and Progress of Language (Blair), 125

Rixner, Thaddäus, 185
Robek, Antonín, 2–3
Robertson, William, 125
Robinson, Edward, 128
Rokycana, Jan, 8, 13, 23, 77, 96
Roman Catholicism: and Counter-Reformation, 216; and ecclesiology, 227–29; "Ultra-Catholicism," 63; Utraquists' ties to, 32–34, 259nn77–78. *See also* Catholic Enlightenment; liberal Catholicism; liberal thought and authoritarian Church; Reform Catholicism; Roman Curia; Tridentine Catholicism; Utraquism, viewed as Roman Catholicism
Roman Curia: and Peace of Kutná Hora, 26; resistance to, 23, 24, 31; and Utraquists, 29, 32–34, 259nn77–78. *See also* Roman Catholicism
romanticism: and Enlightenment, 114; and Herder, 107–9, 117–20; and idealism, 135; Slovak, 106, 117–20, 143, 207
Ronge, Johann, 160
Rosacius of Carlsperg, Adam, 91
Rosenkranz, Johann Karl, 220, 221, 225; as Hegel's biographer, 193, 349n93
Royal Bohemian Society of Sciences, 72, 217, 223–24
Royko, Kašpar: and Bohemian history, 100; and Catholic Enlightenment, 4, 5; and Counter-Reformation, 54; and cultural revolution, 53; on Erasmus, 86; his *Historie velkého sněmu kostnického*, 78; positions held by, 50, 81, 286n118; and Reform Catholicism, 180, 230; and rehabilitation of Hus, 6; and religious tolerance, 60, 69; and Taborites, 74, 75; and theological education reform, 61; on Utraquism, 77–78, 79, 81
Rudolf II, 11, 21, 22, 27, 69
Rusbrochius, Johann, 58

Russell, Bertrand, 233–34
Russia: Czech interest in, 122–23; and German idealism, 211; and Hegelianism, 211; and Palacký, 126; world historical role, 201
Rvačovský, Vavřinec Leander, 38, 93, 98, 263n114
Ryle, Gilbert, 234

Sadoleto, Jacopo, 36
Šafárik, Pavol J., 118, 119, 123, 198–99
Sailer, Johann M., 141, 152, 156
St. Clement's College, 84
Saint-Martin, Louis-Claude de, 210
St. Wenceslaus, 59
St. Wenceslaus' Day Contract, 103
Samotné rozmlouvání duše (Pseudo-Austustine), 86
Schaller, Julius S., 199
Schamschula, Walter, 5–10, 11, 12, 108, 112–13, 276n98, 299n6
Schelling, Friedrich: and Bolzano, 160–61, 165–68, 184, 334n56; and Hegel, 188; and Herder, 109; and idealism, 149, 170; Nebeský on, 152; and Palacký, 153; Polish interest in, 209, 210; and Schulze, 151
Scherschnik, Leopold Johann, 65, 84, 140
Schlegel, Friedrich von, 130, 158
Schleiermacher, Friedrich, 130
Schlick, Mortiz, 234, 237
Schlözer, August L., 123
Schmalkaldic War, 103
Schneider, František, 217, 218, 223, 228
scholasticism, 135–38, 144, 209, 237. *See also* second or Suárezian scholasticism
Das schöne oder goldene Zeitalter, 104–5
Schönfeld, Johann Ferdinand of, 87, 92
Schopenhauer, Arthur, 168, 238
Schram, Joseph, 162
Schrenk, Alois F., 217, 222, 228
Schulze, Gottlob E., 151

Scott, Walter, 119, 127
Scottish Enlightenment, 153, 197
Scotus, Duns, 136
scriptures and Bible, 25, 31–32, 55
second or Suárezian scholasticism: demise in Austria and Bohemia, 135, 138–40; its essentialism, 135–38, 209; and Hegel, 137; in Poland, 209; and Wolff, 137
Seibt, Karl H., 245; and Bolzano, 156, 158, 160, 173; and Catholic Enlightenment, 144–48; contemporaries and followers of, 148–54; criticism of, 114; and German idealism, 134; and German language, 112–13; and Herder and Kant, 173; influence of, 17, 106, 121, 243; in Lněničková's writing, 14; and national awakening, 214; and Utraquist Reformation, 80; and Western liberal tradition, 127
"*Seibtkreis*" (Seibt's circle), 113
Šembera, Alois V., 95
seminaries, general, 60, 276*n*91
Severoli, Antonio, 216
Shaftesbury, Anthony, 149
Shakespeare, William, 128, 147, 212; his *Romeo and Juliet*, 128
Shevyrev, Stepan P., 203
Sigismund, Emperor and King, 24, 25–26, 74, 99
Šimek, Maximilian, 87, 88
Šimon of Habry, 27
Sixt of Ottersdorf, 88, 95, 97
Slavata, Vilém, 102
Slavík, Bedřich, 3, 4, 5, 180
Slavs, destiny of, 205–6; and Balbín, 113, 122; and Havlíček, 110, 122; and Jungmann, 110, 123; and Kollár, 120, 123, 307*n*95; and Štúr, 119–20, 202–3
Slávy dcera (Kollár), 118–19, 127–28
Das Slawenthum und die Welt der Zukunft (Štúr), 202–3
Šlechta, Jan, 35
Slivka, Anton, 217

Slovaks and Slovakia: and anti-Hegelianism, 198–207; and German Lutheran universities, 198–200; and Hegel, 181; and Herder, 109–10, 117–20, 131, 198; Lutheranism of, 117, 120, 181, 198, 201; romanticism of, 106, 117–20, 143, 207. See also anti-Hegelianism
Slovenskje pohladi na vedi, umeňja a literatúru (journal): German idealism in, 204; and Slovak destiny, 205
Slovesnost (Jungmann), 95
Šmahel, František, 242, 380*n*91
Smetana, Augustin, 195, 197, 367*n*33; and demise of Hegelianism, 197
Smith, Adam, 147
Śniadecki, Jan, 360*n*124
Social Preconditions of National Revival in Europe: A Comparative Analysis of the Social Composition of Patriotic Groups among the Smaller European Nations (Hroch), 5, 8
Society for Empirical Philosophy (Berlin), 213, 234, 241
Society of Jesus. See Jesuits
Socrates, 163, 188, 351*n*120
sola fide principle, 20–21, 29, 390
sola scriptura principle, 21, 390
Sommer, J.V., 101
Sonnensfels, Josef, 50
Spectator (Addison), 147
Spener, Jakob, 143
Spinoza, Benedict de, 139
Spis v němž se obsahuje (Pačuda), 45
Srnec of Varvažov, Jakub, 93
Staat von Böhmen (Stránský), 103
Stach, Václav: and Catholic Enlightenment, 4, 5, 13, 14, 81; and Counter-Reformation, 51; and German idealism, 149–50; and liberal Catholicism, 230; translations by, 62, 78; and Utraquism, 81
Stadion, Christoph von, 36
Staël-Holstein, Anne L., 125, 153
Staré Město a Malá Strana (Tyl), 72

Steinbach of Kranichstein, Otto: and Catholic Enlightenment, 50, 54; on Hus, 15, 77; and religious tolerance, 59–60, 68–69; and religious violence, 74; and Utraquists, 80, 286n111
Steinsberg, Franz Guolfinger, 99
Steinský, František, 137, 149
Štěkna, Konrád, 80
Štěpán, Václav R., 93
Stepling, Joseph, 137, 245
Šternberk, František Josef, 281n49
Stewart, Dugald, 153, 169, 171
Šteyer, Matěj V., 56
Stich, Alexandr, 250n61
Stock, Ambros Simon, 50, 138–39
Štorch, Karel B., 126–27, 152, 195, 196, 215
Stoyko, Melchior, 284n93
Strakonický dudák (Tyl), 94
Stránský, Pavel, 102, 103
Štulc, Václav S., 95, 157, 183
Stumpf, Carl, 233, 237, 240, 246
Štúr, Ľudevít: and Hegelianism, 197, 198–99, 200, 201–3, 207, 208; on Magyars, 131; his "Přednášení historická," 201; and Russia, 202–3; and Slovak romantic idealism, 118, 119–20
Šturm, Václav, 112
Stypacius, Mikuláš, 93
Suárez, Francisco, 136–38, 314n13, 316n29; and *essentia realis*, 136
sub una communicants, 20, 21–22, 29, 31, 32, 69
sub utraque communicants, 19, 22, 31, 34, 36. See also Utraquist Church and Utraquism
Šumavský, Josef F., 95, 157
Světecký, Ignác, 139
Světlá, Karolina, 157–58
witkowski, Piotr, 209
Sylva quadrilinguis vocabulorum et phrasium Bohemicae, Latinae, Graecae et Germanicae linguae (Veleslavín), 89, 94

symbiosis, religious, 80–82
System der theoretischen Philosophie (Krug), 150, 182
Szaniawski, Józef K., 209–10

Tablic, Bohuslav, 118
Taborites: differences between Utraquists and, 76–77; radicalism of, 4, 20, 25, 68, 74–75, 248n18, 279n27; and Unity of Brethren, 22–23; violence and militarism of, 27, 283n67, 283n72
Tarski, Alfred, 234
Tauler, Johann, 58
Teich, Mikuláš, 302n35
Tetens, Johann N., 124
Textbook of Empirical Psychology (Lindner), 239
textbooks, 48, 62, 94–98
Thám, Karel Ignác: and bibliographic record, 84; on Bohemian writers, 66–67; and Counter-Reformation, 55; and Herder, 121; and language, 11, 52, 70, 87, 89–90, 272n27; as national awakener, 64; and plebeianism, 72; and reprinting of classics, 94; and secularized eschatology, 116; and textbooks, 95
Thám, Václav A.: on Bohemian writers, 66; and Counter-Reformation, 55, 81; and Joseph II, 52; and language, 113, 303n42; as national awakener, 64; and plebeianism, 72; and publication programs, 85–86
Theologia dogmatica in systema redacta (Gazzaniga), 139
Theologica Polemica (Gazzaniga), 141
The Theory of Knowledge. See *Wissenschaftslehre* (Bolzano)
"theory of reenactment," 48
Thirlwall, Connop, 212
Tholuck, Friedrich A., 142
Thomas Aquinas, 136, 138–42, 237, 316n29, 319n62, 329n5. See also Thomism

Thomasius, Christian, 270*n*13
Thomism, 136, 137, 138–41, 209, 318*n*44, 318*n*46. See also Neo-Thomists, French
Thun, Leo, 218
Tobolka zlatá (Tomsa), 93
tolerance, universalism, and plebeianism, 17, 18–46; and aesthetics, 42–44; and Catholic Enlightenment, 68–69; cultural universalism, 59, 282*n*64; and ethics question, 28–30; freedom and consensus, 24–26; and idiosyncrasy, 34–35; and liberalism, 23–30; and Maximilian II, 269*n*8; and megalomania, 35–37; and nobles' aversion to Utraquism, 39–40; and plebeianism, 37–40, 45–46; and provincialism, 44–45; and religious peace, 26–28, 255*n*40; and Steinbach, 59–60; and sycophancy, 32–34; towns' ascendancy in culture, 40–45; and Uniate solution, 31–32; universalism's legacy, 30–37; and Utraquism, 18–23, 37–40, 45–46, 104; and vernacular language, 41–42
Tomáš of Štítné, 96
Tomek, Václav, 29, 323*n*91
Tomsa, František Jan, 86–89, 90, 95
Tovačovský of Cimburk, Ctibor, 97, 104
Towiański, Andrzej, 210
towns, ascendancy in culture of, 40–45
transubstantiation, doctrine of, 76, 80
Trautson, Johann, 58
Treitschke, Heinrich von, 143
Trentowski, Bronisław F., 203, 210
Tribunal Polemicum adversus atheistas, theistas et omnes Christiani nominis hostes, sycretistarum Lutheranorum, Hussitarum errores (Kaukal), 75
Tridentine Catholicism, 49–50, 215, 230
Troeltsch, Ernst, 142
Twardowski, Kazimierz, 211, 233
Tyl, Josef Kajetán, 72, 94, 101, 348*n*82

Über den Geist der Böhmischen Gesetze (Voigt), 102
Über den Karakter der Slawen (K.I. Thám), 55, 70, 121
Über den Ursprung der Sprachen und der Schrift (Tetens), 124
Über die Lehre von der Einheit des Denkens und Seins (Exner), 222
Über die Veränderung der čechischen Sprache (Tomsa), 95
Über Einführung und Verbreitung der Buchdruckerkunst in Böhmen (Dobrovský), 85
"Über Hegel's berühmten Spruch: Alles wirkliche ist vernünftig und alles Vernünftige ist wirklich" (Bolzano), 189
Über Leibnizens Universal-Wissenschaft (Exner), 213
Über Nominalismus und Realismus (Exner), 222
ultramontanism, 50, 60–61. See also Günther, Anton
Ungar, Karel Raphael, 52, 64, 83, 84–85, 99–100
Uniate church, 31–32
Unity of Brethren: and Bohemian Reformation, 116; and doctrine of nonresistance to evil, 27; and Lutheranism, 16; and Maximilian, 22; population size of, 262*n*107; portrayal in historical sources of, 29, 257*n*56; radical dissent of, 20; and Taborites, 22–23
universalism. See cultural universalism; tolerance, universalism, and plebeianism
universities, German Lutheran, 198–200. See also second or Suárezian scholasticism; Slovaks and Slovakia
University of Halle, 199–200. See also Slovaks and Slovakia
University of Leipzig, 239. See also Herbart, Johann

University of L'viv (Lwów, Lemberg), 197, 233. *See also* Twardowski, Kazimierz

University of Prague: Dobrovský at, 50; Josephism at, 149; and legacy of anti-Hegelianism, 237–39, 240; philosophy faculty at, 245–46; scholars' reputation at, 66; urban intellectuals at, 41; and Utraquism, 45

Untersuchungen über den menschlichen Willen (Feder), 147

utilitarianism, 79, 173, 236n45; and Bolzano, 156, 159, 184; and Exner, 219; and Seibt, 146

Utraquism, viewed as Roman Catholicism, 4–5, 75–80, 229–30

Utraquist Church and Utraquism: and aesthetics, 42–44; ascendancy of, 18–23; and Catholic Enlightenment, 64–82; consensual administration of, 26, 255n39; differences between Taborites and, 76–77; and ethics question, 28–30; and Hus, 18, 19, 22–23; and idiosyncrasy, 34–35; intellectual outlook of, 2, 28; liberalism of, 13, 23–30, 68, 104, 229; and megalomania, 35–37; neo-Utraquism, 29; nobles' aversion to, 39–40; origin of term, 19; and plebeianism, 37–40, 45–46, 104; population size of, 262n107; and provincialism, 44–45; secular aspects of, 65–73; and sycophancy, 32–34; and theological aspects of reform Catholicism, 73–80; ties to Roman Curia, 32–33, 259nn77–78; tolerance of, 23–30; and universalism, 30–37, 104; and vernacular language, 41–42; as *via media*, 18–23, 49, 115, 132, 141, 181. *See also* Catholic Enlightenment; Utraquism, viewed as Roman Catholicism

Václavík, Pavel F., 140
Václav of Vrbno, 141

Vančura, Jaroslav, 268n1
van Opastraet, Johann, 61
Van Swieten, Gerhard, 50, 62, 270n18
Vater, Johann S., 123
Vávra, Jan, 94
Vavřinec of Březová, 37, 96
Velenský of Mnichov, Oldřich, 92
Veleslavín, Daniel Adam of: and Czech language, 11, 42, 70, 88, 90; as literary model, 66; publishing program of, 65; on religious warfare, 27; Slavism of, 122; in *Výbor z literatury české,* 97–98

Velké dějiny zemí Koruny české (Bělina, Kaše, and Kučera), 12–13, 15

Veřejné napomenutí Čechům i Moravanům (Prokop of Plzeň), 96

vernacular. *See* Czech language

Versor, Johannes, 141

Versuch einer Geschichte der alten und neuen Toleranz im Königreich Böhmen und Markgraftum Mähren (Steinbach of Kranichstein), 15, 68

Vienna Circle, 176, 213, 233–37, 242

Vinařický, Karel, 64, 124, 129, 157, 159, 183

Vitae Romanorum Pontificum (Barnes), 35

V národním zájmu: požadavky a cíle evropských národních hnutí devatenáctého století ve srovnávací perspektivě (Hroch), 9

Vodička, Felix, 6

Voigt, Mikuláš Adaukt: and bibliographic record, 84; and Bohemian history, 5, 99–100; and constitutionalism, 102; on Hus, 76, 77; as national awakener, 64; and Reidinger, 140; on religious wars, 74; and reprinting of classics, 91; and secularized eschatology, 116; and Seibt, 149

Vojtěch of Pernštejn, 40

Volkmann, Fridolin Wilhelm, 239, 245

Vollständiges Wörterbuch (Tomsa), 87, 88–89
Voltaire, François-Marie Arouet, 59, 114, 145
Von den böhmischen Landständen, Landtagen und Landesämtern (Stránský), 103
Vorlesungen über die Philosophie der Religion (Hegel), 142–43, 188
Vormärz period, 193, 322n85
"Ein Vorschlag zur Vermeidung vieler Missverständnisse in der Philosophie" (Bolzano), 224
Vorschule der spekulativen Theologie (Günther), 193
Vouillemin, Charles Ernest, 235–36
Vrtkavé štěstí (Dobřenský), 93, 98
Všetýčka (Rvačovský), 93
Výbor z literatury české (Jungmann), 95–98, 103, 104
Vydra, Stanislav, 14, 51, 149
Výklad na právo země české (Ondřej of Dubá), 103
Vznik národně osvícenské ideologie v českých zemích: Prameny národního obrození (Myl'nikov), 4

Wahre Andacht (Muratori), 156
Wallenstein, Albrecht, 102
Wellek, René, 43
Weller, Hieronymus, 41
Wenceslaus IV, 59–60, 79
Wendel, Johann Andreas, 183
Wenzig, Josef, 157
Werfel, Franz, 129–30
Weyr, František, 240
Whewell, William, 212, 343n6
White Mountain, Battle of, 46, 54, 101
Die Widerstreit der Vernunft mit sich selbst (Krug), 182
Wied, Hermann von, 260n85
Wiener Kirchenzeitung (newspaper) on church reform, 228
Willm, Joseph, 189
Willmann, Otto Philip, 237–38, 246
Will to Power (Nietzsche), 316n28

Windtmann, Caspar, 91
Winter, Eduard, 180, 276n98, 364n4
Wiśniewski, Antoni, 209
Wissenschaft der Logik (Hegel), 184–85
Wissenschaftslehre (Bolzano): and Beneke, 169; and Brentano, 233; critique of Hegel in, 186–88; and Destutt, 172; and Exner, 223; and Fichte, 166; and Herbart, 224; and Herder, 124; and Kant, 162–63, 164, 165; and Krug, 150–51; and Locke, 171; and *Outline of the First Logic*, 170; Příhonský on, 217; and prize for evaluation of Bolzano's views, 225; and Schelling, 167
Wissenschaftslehre (Fichte), 166
Wittgenstein, Ludwig J., 169, 233, 234, 237
Witzel, Georg, 34, 35, 37, 260n84
Wolf, Johann Heinrich: and Bohemian history, 99; and Counter-Reformation, 51, 54–55, 65; and freedom of press, 52; and liberal Catholicism, 230; as national awakener, 64; and rehabilitation of Hus, 4, 5, 13, 248n21; on Seibt, 145, 323n91; textbook by, 54–55, 81; and theological education reform, 61; on Utraquism, 77, 78–79, 81, 285n106
Wolff, Christian, 137, 139, 209, 315n24
Wolff, Franz, 75, 283n74
Wollaston, William, 183
The World as Will and Representation (Schopenhauer), 168
world spirit (Hegelian concept), 200–201, 202, 206
Wundt, Max, 325n126
Wyclif, John, 25, 38, 75–76, 79, 80, 254n31, 264n120
Wykład systematyczny filozofii (Kremer), 360n127

xenophobia, 106, 130, 212, 243

Young, Edward, 147

Zahradník, Vincenc: and Counter-Reformation, 64; and Dobrovský, 82; and Fesl, 286n123; and Garve, 182; and Hegel, 182–83; and Herder, 124; and language norms, 67, 90, 292n64; persecution of, 216; realism of, 150; and textbooks, 94
Základy filosofie: Logika, Metafysika (Marek), 150, 152, 182
Zalužanský of Zalužany, Adam, 91
Zdeněk of Lobkoviec, 39
Zelenohorský manuscript, 101
Želetavský, Jan Štelcar, 264n118
Zerdahely, Nina, 125
Zieger, F.A., 52–53
Zimmermann, Johann A., 217, 223
Zimmermann, Robert, 211, 222, 225, 226–27, 232–33, 245; and Bolzano, 226; and Brentano, 211, 233; and his *Philosophische Propädeutik*, 222, 227, 233
Zippe, Augustin, 51, 58–59, 61–62, 80, 81, 272n32

Zitte, Augustin: and asceticism, 59; and Bohemian Reformation, 13; and *Das Buch Joseph*, 52–53, 272n32; and Counter-Reformation, 54; and Hus, 4, 15, 79–80, 101, 285n109; and liberal Catholicism, 230; and religious tolerance, 69, 180; and Utraquism, 81
Život Eneáše Sylvia (Veleslavín), 97
Život kněží táborských (Příbram), 96
Žižka, Jan, 8, 74, 77, 81, 97, 100, 296n134
Žižka z Trocnova (Tyl), 101
Z kněh o právích země české (Kornelius), 103
Zlobický, Josef V., 83
Znamení zrodu: České národní obrození jako kulturní typ (Macura), 5, 7
Zřízení privilegií koruny a království (Matouš of Chlumčany), 103–4
Zumr, Josef, 226
Zütphen, Gerhard von, 58